Business Information Systems

Business Information Systems

Paul Beynon-Davies

Professor of Business Informatics, Cardiff Business School, Cardiff University

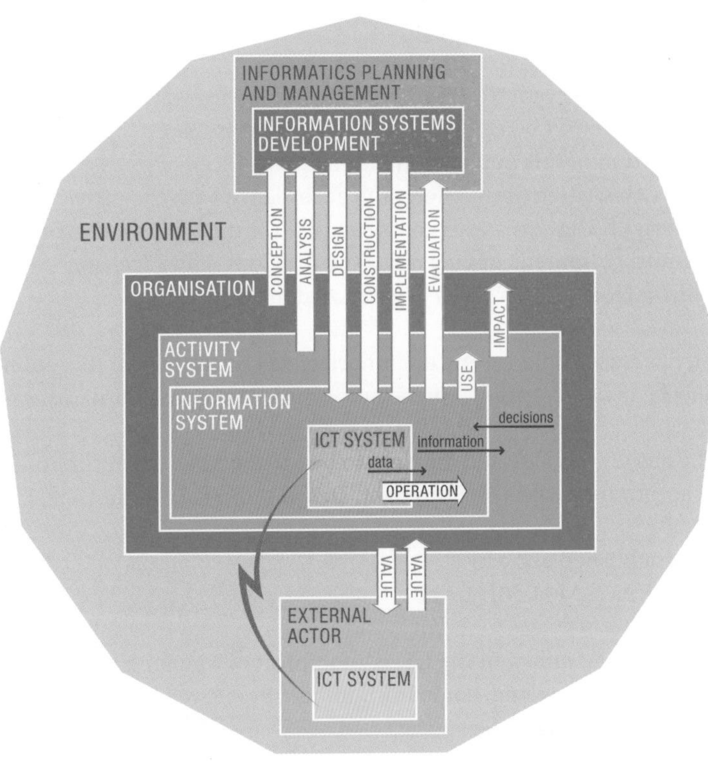

Consultants:
Bob Galliers
Provost and Vice-President for Academic Affairs
Bentley University, USA

Chris Sauer
Fellow in Information Management
Saïd Business School,
University of Oxford, UK

First published 2009 by
PALGRAVE MACMILLAN

Palgrave Macmillan in the UK is an imprint of Macmillan Publishers Limited, registered in England, company number 785998, of Houndmills, Basingstoke, Hampshire RG21 6XS.

Palgrave Macmillan in the US is a division of St Martin's Press LLC, 175 Fifth Avenue, New York, NY 10010.

Palgrave Macmillan is the global academic imprint of the above companies and has companies and representatives throughout the world.
Palgrave® and Macmillan® are registered trademarks in the United States, the United Kingdom, Europe and other countries

ISBN-13: 978-0-230-20368-6
ISBN-10: 0-230-20368-X

This book is printed on paper suitable for recycling and made from fully managed and sustained forest sources. Logging, pulping and manufacturing processes are expected to conform to the environmental regulations of the country of origin.

A catalogue record for this book is available from the British Library.

A catalog record for this book is available from the Library of Congress.

10 9 8 7 6 5 4 3 2 1
18 17 16 15 14 13 12 11 10 09

Printed and bound in China

Photos on pages 29, 131, 197, 291 courtesy of www.istockphoto.com

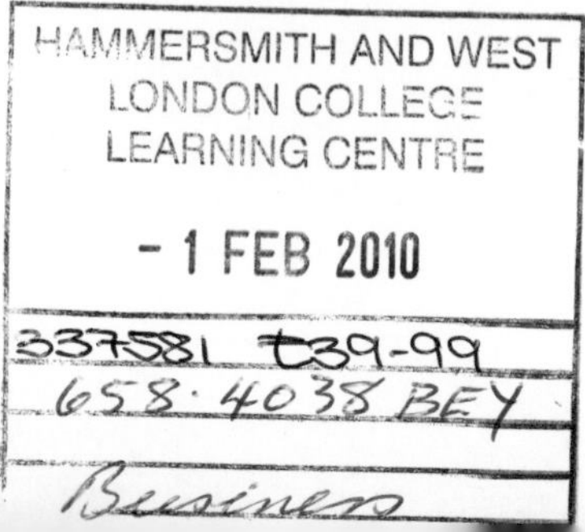

Short contents

Contents

Figures

Tables and case studies

Tables

Case studies

See page 402 for a more detailed list of case studies, including those published on the companion website only at:
www.palgrave.com/business/beynon-daviesbis

About the author

Paul Beynon-Davies is currently professor in business informatics at the Cardiff Business School, Cardiff University. He received his BSc in Economics and Social Science and PhD in Computing from University of Wales College, Cardiff. Before taking up an academic post he worked for several years in the informatics industry in the United Kingdom in both the public and private sectors. He still regularly acts as a consultant to the public and private sectors particularly in the area of information and communication technology (ICT) and its impact on organisational performance.

Professor Beynon-Davies has published widely in the field of information systems and ICT. He has written 11 books including *Information Systems, Information Systems Development* and *Database Systems.* He has also published over 50 academic papers on topics including the foundations of information systems, electronic business, electronic government, information systems planning, information systems development, database systems and artificial intelligence.

Paul Beynon-Davies has engaged in a number of government-funded projects related to the impact of information and communication technology on the economic, social and political spheres. He was involved in an evaluation of electronic local government in Wales and was seconded part-time to the National Assembly for Wales (NAfW) as an evaluator of its Cymru-ar-Lein/Information Age strategy for Wales. From 2006–08 he was director of the eCommerce Innovation Centre at Cardiff University which also included the Broadband Observatory for Wales.

Acknowledgements

My thanks to Professor Bob Galliers and Professor Chris Sauer for the valuable guidance on the content and structure of the book they provided. Thanks also to the reviewers who contributed comments on developing drafts of the book, including:

- Colin Ashurst, University of Durham, UK
- Vladlena Benson, Kingston University, UK
- Laura Campoy, University of the West of England, UK
- Julian Coleman, University of Bolton, UK
- Gordon Harris, University of Exeter, UK
- Ulf Höglind, Swedish Business School, at Örebro University, Sweden
- Ghulam Musa, London Metropolitan University, UK
- Martin Rich, Cass Business School, UK

Also, I wish to thank Ursula Gavin and in particular Catherine Travers at Palgrave Macmillan for their support in the production of this work.

The photo on page 436 is sourced from http://en.wikipedia.org/wiki/Image:Quipu.png. Photos on the part title pages are used with permission from www.istockphoto.com.

Message to students

Why it is important to read this book

This book introduces both current and aspiring business professionals to three topic areas that are critical to their working life.

First, **information** is so important to the modern world that some have even referred to it as the global information society. This book helps the reader unravel the ways in which information underpins business activity of many forms. It demonstrates that information underlies the work of not only managers but also shop-floor workers.

Second, organisations establish **information systems** in order to control their current activities and also as the basis for changing and improving their ways of doing things. The book describes a number of typical information systems in businesses which drive their operation. It also describes the ways in which information systems are now critically important for managing activities and relationships with customers and suppliers.

Third, **information and communication technology (ICT)** has been used to increase the efficiency and effectiveness of both information systems and business practice. Much of the way modern business works is embedded or encoded in its ICT. Without ICT systems many organisations would cease to function.

These topics are not isolated areas of concern for the modern business. For instance, the modern business organisation may have the aim of improving its performance through the collection and use of better information. But in order to do this the business must develop an efficient information system, which is likely to require the use of ICT. This book provides a guide to best practice in each area, as well as an understanding of the relationships between these areas.

This book is based on my experience of teaching various undergraduate, postgraduate and commercial courses in the area; it is has also been enhanced by my consulting and professional practice. Hence, the concepts and frameworks described in this textbook have been 'field-tested' not only in an educational context but also in practical work.

Why this book is different

My aim in writing this book has been to create a coherent path through the subject area which addresses some of the needs I have identified during over three decades of experience in the area.

The book covers essential core material in the area of business information, systems and technology. Care has been taken to ensure that only material that is critical for business students is included. Some material included in other texts in the area has been excluded to provide a more relevant exploration of the subject.

Many business information systems textbooks consist of a collection of interesting but disconnected topics. This book is different in that it considers the material as an integrated and seamless web of ICT application in organisations. It therefore makes it easier for you to make sense of the subject as a whole. It also makes it easier for you to see how different elements of the subject interrelate.

The book provides a balanced coverage of both theory and practice. The aim is to use precise definitions of a number of foundation concepts to provide an understanding of the xvi

place of information, information systems and ICT in business. This understanding then makes it possible to identify and explain a number of key skills that are important to business professionals of many forms.

So what you will get from this book is a rounded but grounded conception of this important area of business. The book will equip you with knowledge which will enable you to better perform as a business professional in the modern, complex organisational world.

For more details on the book's structure, learning features and companion website materials, please see the 'About the book' section on page xix.

Message to lecturers

Mission

My aim in writing this book has been to create a coherent path through the subject area which addresses some of the needs I have identified during over three decades of experience in the area. *Business Information Systems* includes the following distinctive characteristics:

- **Coverage of core material**. The book covers essential core material in the area of business information, systems and technology which will be useful for both academic and commercial courses. It has taken care to exclude material present in other texts in the area that is not critical for students of business, in order to provide a more precise and relevant exploration of the subject.
- **Use of clear terminology.** The book uses a more precise set of terms than competing texts for explaining the area. For instance, rather than using the conventional term *information systems* for the field of study it uses *organisational informatics* throughout as a convenient and less confusing label. It also makes great play of the distinction between an information and communication technology (ICT) system, an information system and an activity system.
- **Integrated account.** It is unfortunate that many textbooks in this area appear to consist of a collection of interesting but disconnected topics. This book presents a much more integrated and holistic account. I believe that organisational informatics is not a series of interesting but independent organisational and technological issues – rather, it is a seamless web of ICT application in organisations. This book enables students to make sense of this as a whole and to gain an appreciation of the interrelationship between elements of the subject.
- **Based in theory.** Over the last two decades, organisational informatics has achieved a greater degree of coherence as a discipline. However, most introductory and intermediate texts on the subject tend to de-emphasise the coverage of theory. Here, the aim is to provide a stronger theoretical foundation than competing texts. Foundation concepts discussed in earlier chapters are used throughout the text to provide coherence to the description of current practice. For example, the distinction made between an ICT system, an information system and an activity system is not simply a matter of convenience: it has practical implications in the sense that the design and use of an ICT system is affected very much by the context of communication (the information system) in which it is placed and the activity system it is meant to support.
- **Practical emphasis.** Having stronger theory does not mean less relevance to practice. In fact, I would argue the opposite; as the American sociologist Kurt Lewin once said, 'nothing is as practical as a good theory'. Theory hence guides good practice in organisational informatics. Throughout, the book highlights good practice of relevance to organisational practitioners who are aiming to improve the adoption of ICT, as well as those more generally who are attempting to improve organisational activity through better management of information and information systems.
- **Design emphasis.** Some see organisational informatics as very much a 'design science' in the sense that it is interested in the effective design and construction of organisational systems of various forms. This book provides coverage of a number of key design skills of importance. The emphasis is very much on modelling systems and using such models as the

basis not only for understanding current issues within organisations but also for describing possible futures for organisational life.

- **Field-tested.** As well as being based on my experience of teaching various undergraduate, postgraduate and commercial courses in the area, it is has also been enhanced by my consulting and professional practice. Hence, the concepts and frameworks described in this textbook have been 'field-tested' not only in an educational context but also in practical work.

Using the book as part of your course or module

The coverage in this book emphasises the interconnected nature of the subject and presents material in an deliberate sequence where later concepts are based upon concepts covered in earlier chapters. It is therefore ideally suited for an intensive undergraduate or postgraduate course or series of modules on business information systems.

Since the coverage is necessarily broad, there are also a number of ways in which this material might be used within educational courses or modules at different levels:

- The book deliberately attempts to demonstrate the importance of considering business information and information systems in isolation from ICT. Hence, it is possible to use the first three chapters of the book to build a coherent account of business information management.
- A module on electronic business or electronic commerce can be built around the content in the environment and eBusiness chapters. The two chapters on ICT infrastructure supporting contemporary business may also be used for this purpose.
- A module on information systems and ICT management would use the chapters on planning and management, service and operations and possibly use and impact.
- The chapter on information systems development acts as an introduction to this area and together with the two ICT infrastructure chapters could be used within a module on business ICT.

For more details on the book's structure, learning features and companion website materials, please see the 'About the book' section on page xix.

About the book

Structure

Chapter 1	Introduction: The domain of business information systems
Part I	KEY CONCEPTS
Chapter 2	Organisations and systems
3	Data, information and knowledge
4	Information systems
Part II	UNDERSTANDING ICT
Chapter 5	Communication infrastructure
6	ICT systems infrastructure
Part III	APPLYING INFORMATION SYSTEMS TO BUSINESS
Chapter 7	The business environment
8	Electronic business and electronic commerce
9	Assessing the use and impact of information systems
Part IV	MANAGING INFORMATION SYSTEMS IN BUSINESS
Chapter 10	Planning, strategy and management
11	Services, projects and operations
12	Development
Chapter 13	Successful informatics practice

Chapter 1 Introduction: The domain of business information systems

The material in the book is organised in 13 chapters. The opening chapter considers the importance of an understanding of information systems to the effective performance of organisations of various kinds. It then introduces a model of the domain, which is used to emphasise the necessarily multifaceted and interconnected nature of information systems in business. This model is useful in demonstrating that the successful adoption and application of information and communication technology (ICT) in organisations relies on the positive interaction between different elements. These diverse elements range from the effective planning and management of information to the successful development, implementation and use of information systems.

Each element of this domain model is then considered in a separate chapter. It is also used as a device in the final chapter to help structure and summarise good practice in information systems or organisational informatics. By the final chapter readers should therefore have a clear conception of good practices to utilise in their future careers.

Part I: Key concepts

Chapter 2 Organisations and systems

The purpose of ICT can only be considered in terms of human activity in organisations. This chapter examines what an organisation is, and uses this as a basis for considering the relevance of information, information systems and ICT to organisations. It uses the concept of system to relate to each other many of the issues seen as critical to the modern organisation, including strategy, management and performance. The chapter concludes with coverage of process modelling and design.

Chapter 3 Data, information and knowledge

The concept of information is much taken for granted. This chapter argues that an understanding of the multi-faceted nature of information is essential in this field. It uses the concept of a sign to help explain the crucial relationship between data, information, decision and action. It also considers the practical importance of modelling data, information and knowledge in organisations.

Chapter 4 Information systems

This chapter defines the concept of an information system as a communication system used to support a given activity system. It argues for its place as a sociotechnical system in that it covers both activities and ICT. The chapter concludes with an examination of a typical information systems infrastructure for the modern business.

Part II: Understanding ICT

Chapter 5 Communication infrastructure

The adoption of ICT is promoted in both the public and private sector as a means of improving the efficacy, efficiency and effectiveness of the delivery of services and goods to internal and external stakeholders. Modern organisations therefore rely on effective ICT infrastructure. This book considers infrastructure in two parts. Chapter 5 examines key elements making up the communication infrastructure. This includes access devices and channels, communication networks, the Internet and the World Wide Web. It also considers the importance of networks for carrying business transactions and the ongoing attempts to develop standards in this area.

Chapter 6 ICT systems infrastructure

This chapter begins by considering the component elements of an ICT system and how their processing is now distributed across communication networks. This leads to a discussion of front-end ICT systems and the important role of websites and web content in them. It then considers the place of the business tier and the concept of business rules. This is followed by a consideration of back-end ICT systems and the critical place of data management in modern ICT infrastructure. The chapter concludes with a discussion of the integration of front-end and back-end infrastructure and securing data, both within ICT systems and across the communication infrastructure.

Part III: Applying information systems to business

Chapter 7 The business environment

In this book an organisation is seen primarily as an activity system (or more accurately a collection of interacting activity systems) that is affected by forces in its environment. Organisations are not isolated entities, they are open systems. This means that the success of any organisation depends on how well it integrates with aspects of its environment. This chapter focuses on the economic environment of the organisation, and describes ways in which organisations can be considered as systems producing value that travels within and between them. Hence, activity systems provide supportive mechanisms for customer, supply and internal value chains. The chapter outlines the key elements of these value chains, and describes them as conduits within a wider value network which coordinates the flow of goods, services and transactions.

Chapter 8 Electronic business and electronic commerce

Much of the economic environment globally now relies on ICT infrastructure for effective operation, so many modern businesses are 'electronic' businesses to a greater or lesser extent. This chapter considers the use of ICT using the concept of the value network to help distinguish between various forms of electronic business. The term eBusiness as used here incorporates eCommerce. Intra-business eBusiness involves the use of ICT to support the internal value chain. Business to consumer (B2C) eCommerce is concerned with the place of ICT in the customer chain. Business to business (B2B) eCommerce particularly focuses on the place of ICT in the supply chain. Consumer to consumer (C2C) eCommerce covers the application of ICT in the community chain. Lastly, partner to partner (P2P) eBusiness concerns the use of ICT in support of collaboration networks.

Chapter 9 Assessing the use and impact of information systems

After an information system is introduced, it begins to have effects on the organisation. There are both first-order effects, which concern issues of use, and second-order effects, which concern the impact of the system on individuals, groups and the organisation as a whole. Both use and impact are critical to the assessment of the success or failure of an information system. This chapter considers the issues of use, impact and success, and concludes by considering ways in which the worth of information systems can be established.

Part IV: Managing information systems in business

Chapter 10 Planning, strategy and management

This chapter considers two of the critical processes that affect an organisation's informatics infrastructure , management and planning. It looks at the importance of informatics planning to the effective coupling of informatics strategy with general business strategy, then at the management activities associated with current and future informatics infrastructures.

Chapter 11 Service, projects and operations

This chapter considers the structure of the informatics industry and the informatics service, which might be either in-house or outsourced to a vendor organisation. It looks at two critical activities of an informatics service: the essentials of project management as a key skill, and the neglected topic of operating the ICT infrastructure, now often called ICT services management.

Chapter 12 Development

This chapter considers information systems development as a key organisational process. Since it is a process it can be considered as a system in itself. The key inputs into the process are ICT resources and developer resources, including a toolkit of methods, techniques and tools. The development process is normally organised in projects and managed using defined phases of activity. Each of these phases is discussed.

Chapter 13 Successful informatics practice

This final chapter synthesises the material from previous chapters using the domain model from Chapter 1. It then applies this model to a well-known case study, the London Ambulance Services Computer Aided Despatch (LASCAD) system. This summarises some of the key elements of the body of knowledge for the discipline and area of practice. The chapter also considers the likely future for informatics, in both organisations and the wider environment.

Pedagogical features

This book contains a range of carefully thought-out features designed to enhance learning, engage student interest and provide the lecturer with a variety of sources for discussion and case study analysis.

At the start of each chapter

A set of features is designed to orientate readers and prepare them for what follows:

- **Learning outcomes** set out what the student can expect to gain. Each is linked to a core principle which can be applied to business, so students can see how each piece of knowledge is relevant.
- **Chapter outlines** give an overview of the content of the chapter and highlight the key skills sections (see below) using the icon.
- A brief **introduction** sets the scene.

Throughout each chapter

Throughout the text, the following features appear:

Regular **recap** features appear at the end of each main section, to remind students of the key issues and how they relate to the previous and subsequent information.

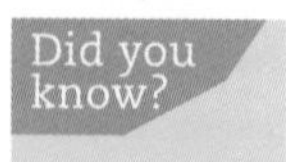

'Did you know?' features highlight interesting or intriguing facts related to the subject to inform and entertain readers.

Reflect comments and questions encourage students to consider how the subject relates to real-world issues.

Key skill sections provide students with an appreciation of crucial skills and how they apply to business (for example, modelling, evaluation and eMarketing).

Regular **case check** sections encourage students to relate the case studies (which appear at the end of the book and on the website) to a range of different issues discussed throughout the book. Case studies appearing on the website are identified with a W icon.

Brief **examples** highlight the concepts just discussed and an on-page **glossary** is provided for handy quick reference.

At the end of each chapter

The main points are highlighted in the chapter summary, followed by a **focus on value** feature demonstrating how the material in the chapter relates to the concept of value. This is followed by an extensive section of activities: a review test, a series of exercises and suggestions for student projects:

- The **review test** questions are designed to test understanding and the ability to recall appropriate answers. Answers can be obtained by re-reading the chapter.
- **Exercises** are opportunities for the reader to take what has been learned and extend knowledge, or apply it to some other situation. They are deliberately open-ended and may be used in tutorials or other learning opportunities to structure more extensive learning about a topic.
- **Student research projects** outline a larger piece of work (in both effort and duration) than a student exercise. Typically they involve:
  - independent investigation including formulating a project proposal
  - production of a plan of work
  - data collection
  - analysis and presentation of the results.

Ideally, a student research project should display elements of independent and critical thinking. It should be noted that what are provided here are the outlines of interesting research questions; they will demand much further work to develop into a working project proposal.

Each chapter concludes with a **further reading** section identifying key texts for further research, followed by full list of **references**.

At the end of the book

A series of specially written **case studies** provide more detail on the application of concepts discussed to real-world experience. Each describes an organisation, project or technology relevant to the topic. The case studies are deliberately written as independent but rich resources of educational content. This means they can be used as sources of consolidation and for discussion across a range of chapters and topic areas. They are referred to throughout the book and each is supported by a list of issues for discussion and a 'key terms' section. Further case studies are available online.

At the end of the book, a **glossary** and **index** make it easier to skim search for coverage of particular topics.

For information on how the material in this book can be used to support a range of information systems-related courses, please see the **Message to lecturers** on page xvii.

Website

Business Information and Systems is accompanied by extensive online materials, accessible to lecturers and students at **www.palgrave.com/business/beynon-daviesBIS.** This companion website is packed with valuable features to aid teaching and learning, including free access to selected articles from the *Journal of Information Technology.* These are supported by commentary, keywords and a list of issues to discuss in the 'case studies' section of the book itself.

In addition to the unique journals zone, the following password-protected online materials have been carefully designed to support lecturers in delivering their course:

- **PowerPoint lecture slides** for each chapter (including relevant diagrams, charts and figures; the slides can be customized by lecturers to suit module needs).
- **Lecturer manual** including:
  - lecture outlines and teaching tips
  - suggested answers and discussion guidelines for questions in the book
  - sample course outline giving suggested course structure for a range of courses
  - sample end-of-module exam paper and guideline answer.
- **Additional in-depth case studies** for classroom use, supported by:
  - questions, role-play and activities, and links to multimedia resources
  - teaching notes.

- **Selected additional content** from other textbooks by the author.
- **Testbank** to use as a resource for creating end-of-module assessments.
- **VLE-compatible cartridge** of the above materials, enabling them to be loaded direct into BlackBoard, WebCT or Moodle learning platforms.

Students will be able to check and expand their learning using the following features:

- **Multiple choice questions** for each chapter to self-test and check understanding
- **Searchable glossary** of key terms for quick reference
- **Annotated weblinks** to relevant sites and articles
- **Career and learning section** including student case studies and links to advice on study skills.

Guided tour of the book

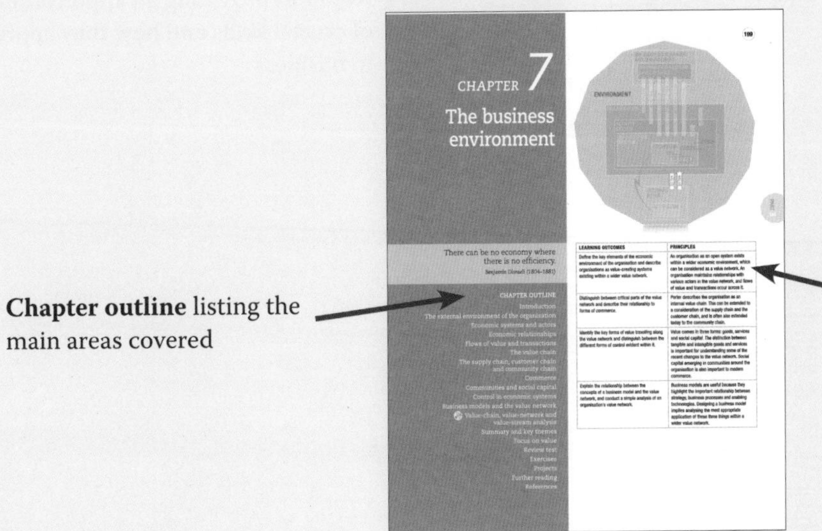

Chapter outline listing the main areas covered

Learning outcomes outlining what students will gain from the chapter and how it relates to core principles

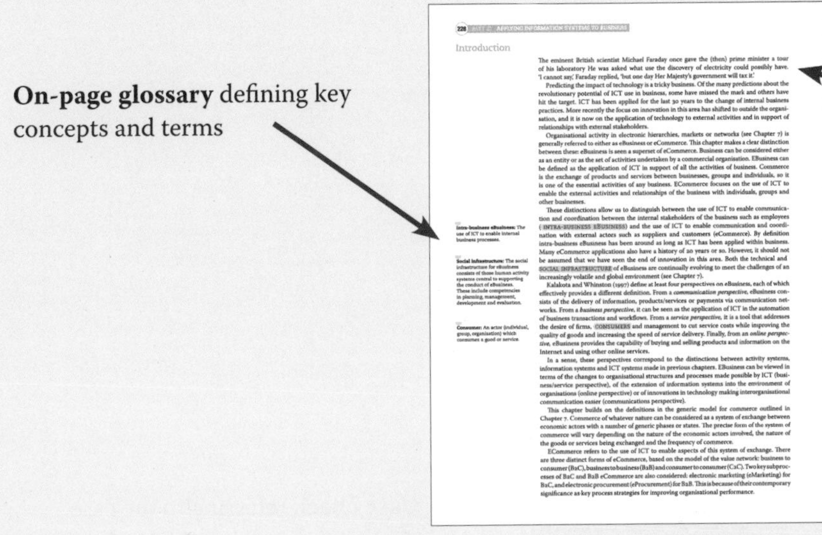

On-page glossary defining key concepts and terms

Introduction to set the scene

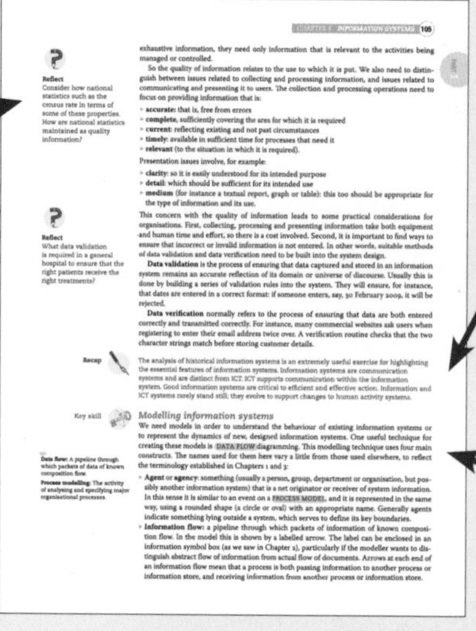

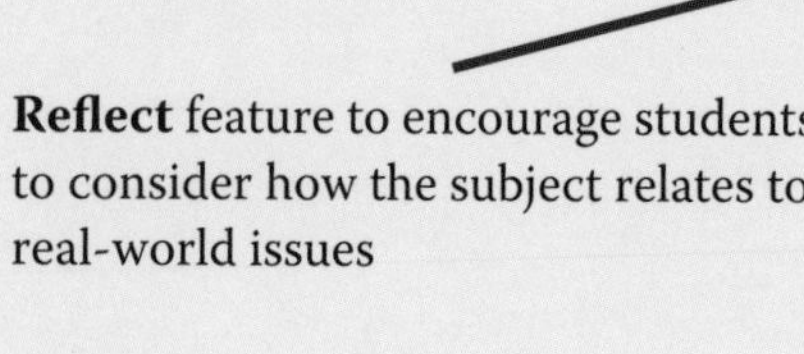

Reflect feature to encourage students to consider how the subject relates to real-world issues

Recap selections highlighting the main points in each section

Key skill providing an appreciation of crucial skills and how they apply to business

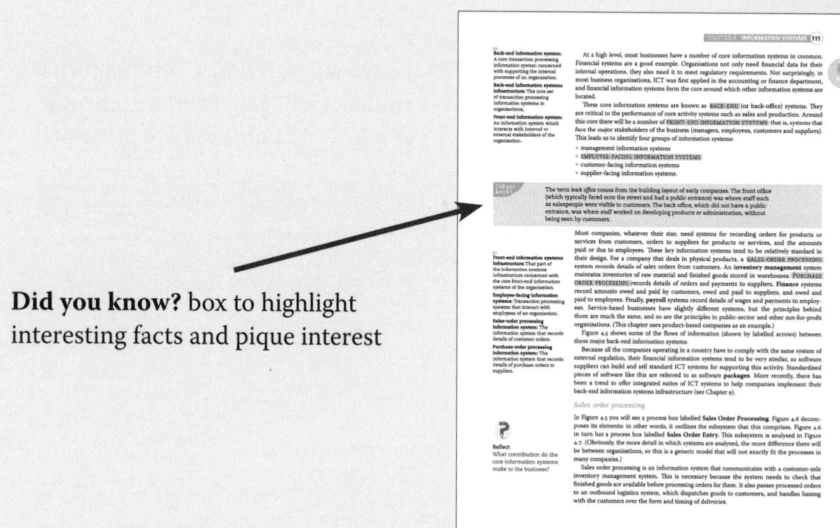

Did you know? box to highlight interesting facts and pique interest

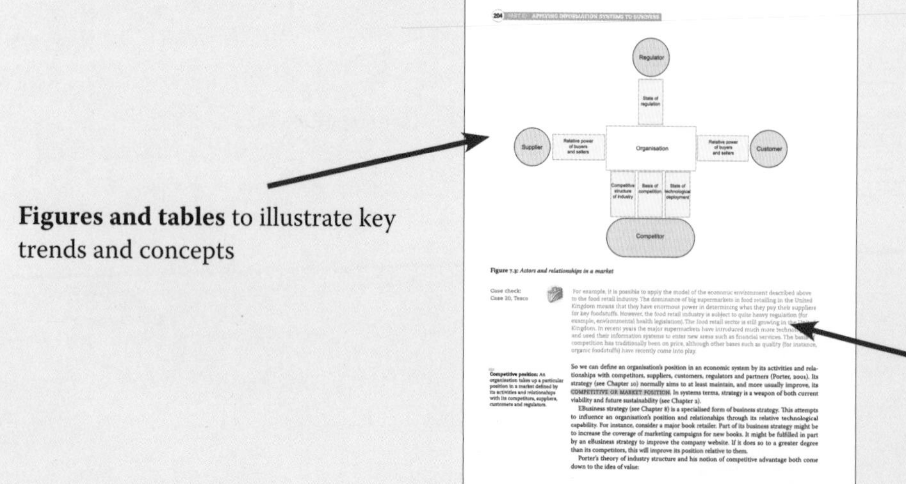

Figures and tables to illustrate key trends and concepts

Case check referring to the case studies at the end of the book

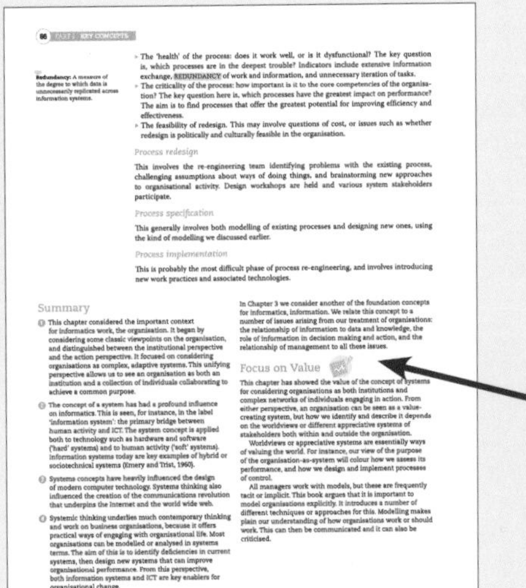

Conclusion showing how the main points in the chapter interrelate and focusing on the value informatics brings to business

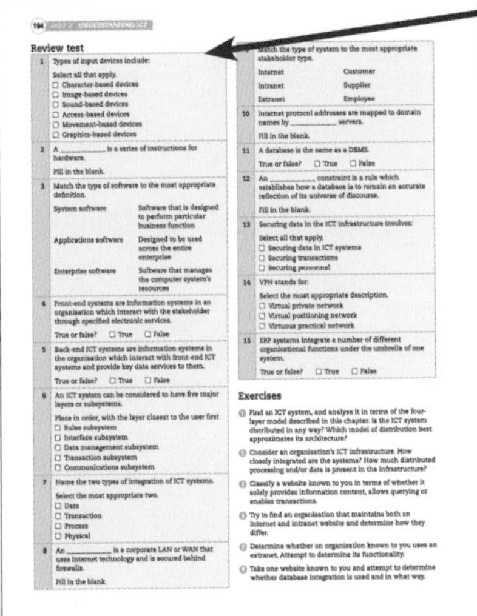

Review test to test understanding

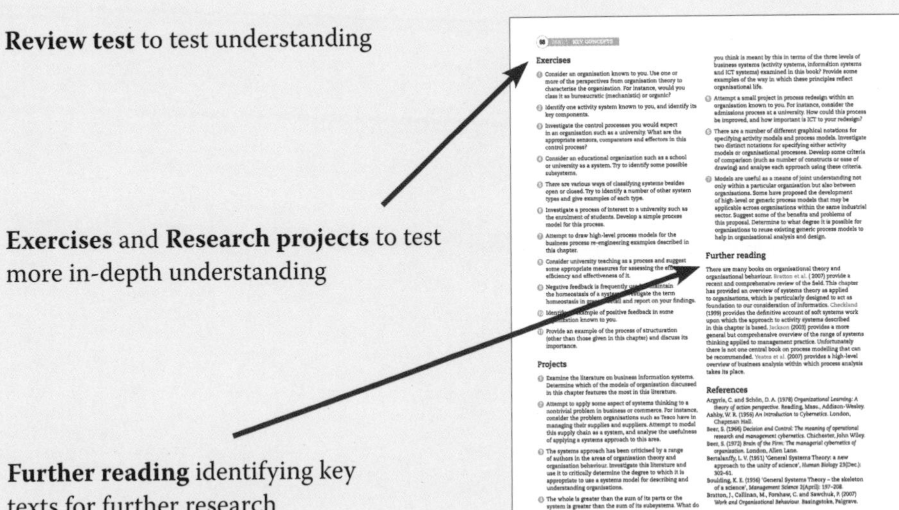

Exercises and **Research projects** to test more in-depth understanding

Further reading identifying key texts for further research

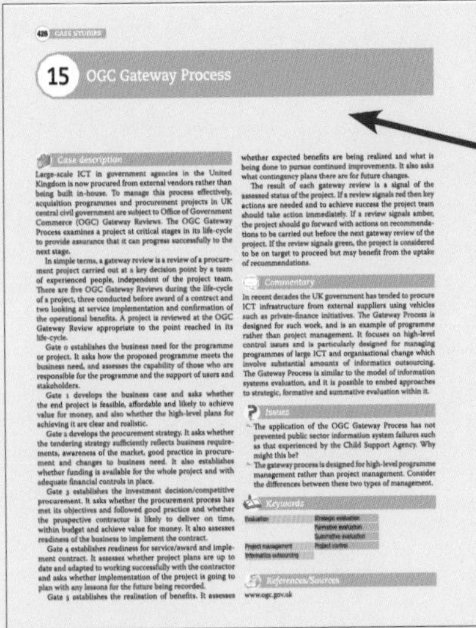

Case studies complete with discussion points to relate theory to practice

CHAPTER 1

Introduction: the domain of business information systems

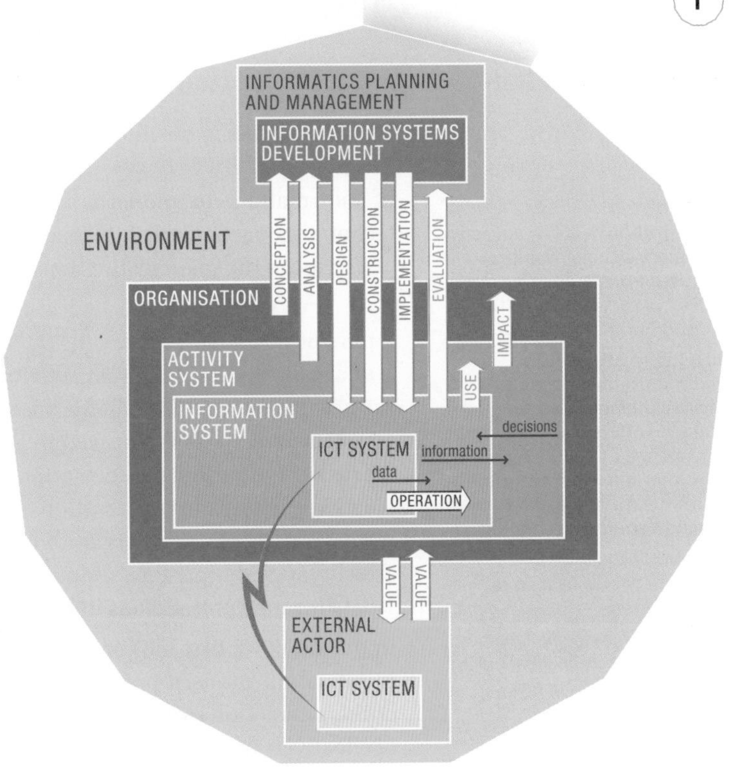

'When I use a word', Humpty Dumpty said in a rather scornful tone, 'it means just what I choose it to mean – neither more or less.'

Lewis Carroll (1832–1898), Through the Looking Glass (1871), Chapter 6.

CHAPTER OUTLINE

What are business, information and systems all about?

Organisation: A social collective in which formal procedures are used for coordinating the activities of members in the pursuit of joint objectives.

ICT: Information and communication technology, any technology used to support information gathering, processing, distribution and use. A term used to encapsulate hardware, software, data and communications technology.

Output: The elements that a system passes back to its environment.

Information system: A system of communication between people. A system involved in the gathering, processing, distribution and use of information.

This book looks at the intersection between business organisations, information and systems. Business ORGANISATIONS can be thought of as systems of activity which rely on systems of information. In modern businesses, information systems in turn rely on systems of technology, particularly information and communication technology (ICT).

These are the main distinctions between these three types of business system:

- An **activity system** is a logical collection of activities performed by a group of people in pursuit of a goal. The key OUTPUT of an organisational activity system is therefore activity or action. Synonyms for an activity system are an organisational or business process.
- An INFORMATION SYSTEM is a system of communication between people. Information systems are systems involved in gathering, processing, distributing and using information. The key output of an information system is of course information, which is used to support activity systems in organisations.
- An ICT SYSTEM is an organised collection of hardware, software, data and communication technology designed to support aspects of an information system. An ICT system outputs data for interpretation as information within an activity system.

In this book we first look in some detail at the make-up of each of these systems, and how it is critical for modern businesses to design them effectively. Second, we consider the effects of the interaction or intersection between these systems. Finally, we discuss the importance of effectively managing both business systems and their interaction, and the contribution this makes to modern business success.

Why study business information systems?

ICT system: A technical system, sometimes referred to as a 'hard' system. An organised collection of hardware, software and communications technology designed to support aspects of an information system.

System: A coherent set of interdependent components which exists for some purpose, has some stability, and can usefully be viewed as a whole.

Process: A transformation of input into output. In information systems a process is a transformation of incoming data flow(s) into outgoing data flow(s).

ICT underpins many aspects of daily life, but the SYSTEMS and PROCESSES that support it, and the ethics surrounding it, are often overlooked. Often we only notice that ICT is involved in something, and what it does, when there is a problem with either the technology or the way it is being used.

For example, consider mobile phones. Your personal unblocking key (PUK) code is critical to the successful operation of the system: you must have it to change network, or to unblock a phone that has been blocked by mistake. But the chances are you won't even know it exists until you need it. Or take a credit card theft insurance scheme: perhaps you use one of those too. It will be based on a database the company running the scheme sets up, into which it puts the credit card details of subscribers. If the scheme works correctly, you probably won't give a thought to this database. But if something goes wrong – perhaps it sends out your credit card details to the wrong postal address – you'll become very aware that it's an ICT system, and a fallible one with a design fault. You might ask yourself then, what is really the greater risk: having your details on this database, where they might get into the hands of the wrong people, or actually having your credit card stolen?

When things are running smoothly, the only people who take much notice of ICT systems are ICT professionals. But things only run smoothly if businesses are able to anticipate future needs, plan what they need to do to meet them, and put those plans into practice. To do this, they need managers who understand the needs of the market and the organisation, and the capabilities of ICT systems. and are able to reconcile them.

Information: Data interpreted in a meaningful context.

Power: The ability of a person or social group to control the behaviour of some other person or social group.

Transactional data: Data that records events taking place between individuals, groups and organisations.

Supplier: A key type of organisational stakeholder. Organisations that supply goods and services to an organisation.

Data: Sets of symbols.

Why information systems are important for business

It's often said that INFORMATION is POWER. In business there's certainly truth in that: all over the world, information is critical to the competitiveness of the private sector. The modern business organisation demands information about, for example, its customers, orders, sales, stock and inventory. It needs this information to be integrated, and it needs it to be accurate and up to date. As a result the management of information is critical to business success.

Companies collect significant amounts of TRANSACTIONAL DATA about their own activities, and about the behaviour of their SUPPLIERS and customers (Burnham, 1983). Transactional data are DATA that record events that take place between individuals, groups and organisations. They are essential to monitoring the performance of organisations in competitive MARKETS. For example, Tesco collects vast amounts of information about what people buy in its supermarkets. It uses this both to find out how well particular stores are performing, and to discover which product lines sell best to which types of customer.

Market: A medium for exchanges between buyers and sellers.

Today we often hear terms like eBusiness (electronic business), eCommerce (electronic commerce) and eGovernment (electronic government), which show how important ICT and information systems are to modern organisations. Although these are relatively new terms, ICT has been used to transform internal and external business processes for at least three decades. But it can be argued that the role it plays has become larger and more central over time, as technology has developed and led to new business TECHNIQUES, both internally and more recently externally. For instance, although Tesco has used ICT for many years, it is only relatively recently that it was able to offer customers the ability to order their groceries online.

Technique: A systematic activity within the development process.

As individuals we also need an increasing range of information, in order to live our lives effectively, at work, at home and in our leisure time. For example, we need an increasingly large range of identity information: passports, driving licences, credit cards, debit cards, library cards, employee identity cards and so on.

ICT has also caused changes to the way work is carried out. One significant change over time is in the degree to which individuals work from home or on the move. Now they can use ICT to keep in contact with an 'organisational hub' wherever they are. A European survey conducted in 2003 (SIBIS, 2003) showed that 2.5 per cent of UK employees were then working remotely from home using ICT on at least one day each week. A further 9 per cent in the United Kingdom did so occasionally or on a supplementary basis. Many people believe these percentages have doubled since 2003.

So we can say with confidence that information underpins modern society. In the 1970s Daniel Bell, a US sociologist, made a series of predictions about the state of Western societies in his influential book *The Coming of Post-Industrial Society* (1972). He claimed that they were becoming information societies, and it is now generally accepted that this has happened. The same is true in much of Asia. Bell's argument was that just as there was an industrial revolution in the nineteenth century, in the latter part of the twentieth century there was an information revolution. This has led some commentators to suggest that where in the twentieth century we lived in an industrial society, our twenty-first century society will be best described as an information society (Castells, 1996).

One key indicator of an INFORMATION SOCIETY is the way in which information is increasingly regarded as an important economic 'commodity'. For instance, it underpins news media, the music industry and the entertainment industry. These so-called 'content' industries are experiencing some of the most rapid growth in western economies. Many organisations in other sectors now also devote most of their time to information-related activities, so they can be described as information corporations. One of the clearest examples is Google, the market leader in the web search sector.

Information society: A term very loosely used to refer to the effect of ICT, information systems and information generally on modern society.

Many people expect this trend to continue. ICT forms the critical infrastructure for modern organisations; they are converging around common standards, and this is leading to increased integration and interoperability of electronic devices and systems.

However, the picture is not entirely rosy. Many people are worried that this type of CONVERGENCE could enable governments (or other groups) to take greater control over people, and about the dangers if information falls into the wrong hands. In many countries there is continuous debate and negotiation over what information the government or other bodies should be allowed to collect about individuals, what purposes this information can be used for, and how its integrity can be protected.

Digital convergence: The convergence around digital standards allowing interoperability of digital technologies on a global scale.

How business information systems relates to other academic disciplines

Not surprisingly, since information systems are essential in so many ways for modern organisations and individuals, this area is very interdisciplinary in nature. Business students will be familiar with some of the disciplines with which it overlaps, from other modules in their course.

To understand how business information systems relates to other disciplines, we can view it as being made up of a number of interdependent areas of interest. We look at all of them in this book, and they are also shown in Figure 1.1.

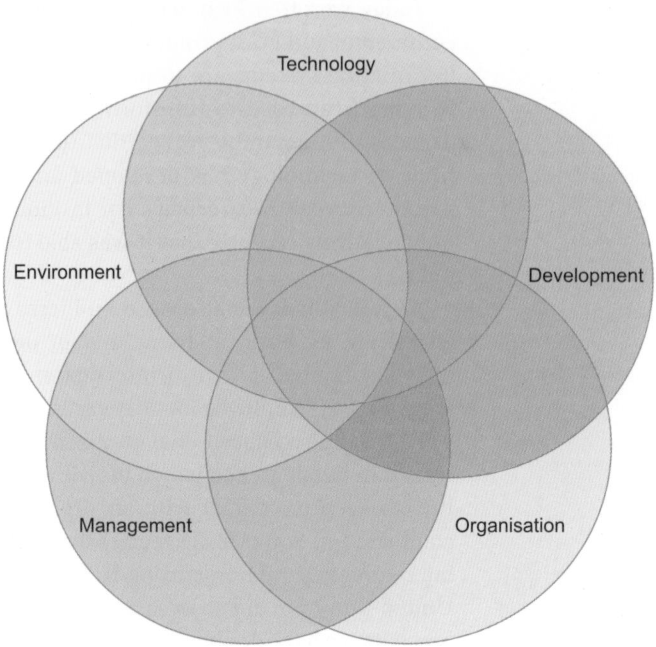

Figure 1.1: *Elements of the field*

Environment: Anything outside the organisation from which it receives inputs and to which it passes outputs.

Management: A key control process for organisations.

- **Environment**. To understand the value of information systems to organisations we need to understand the economic, social, political and physical environment within which the organisations using them operate.
- **Organisations.** One of the main focuses of the book is on how modern information systems contribute to organisational performance: supporting traditional organisational forms, and leading to new ones being introduced.
- **Management.** The promise of the technology is only achieved when managers find effective ways of managing information, information systems and ICT in their organisations.
- **Technology.** Of course, those studying this field need to know something about the technology involved. This includes both the use of the technology, and the principles that underlie it.
- **Development.** This concerns appropriate ways of constructing information systems that support human activity, particularly decision making.

This way of dividing the subject area enables us to consider more clearly how business information systems overlaps with five other established disciplines (Figure 1.2). These are known as **reference disciplines** (Keen, 1980), since they provide us with major frames of academic reference.

- **Economics**, **politics** and **sociology** overlap with the subject through its emphasis on context, particularly the social and economic effects of information systems and ICT.
- **Organisational theory** (and particularly **organisational behaviour**) overlaps with the subject through its emphasis on organisational issues.
- **Management science and operations management** overlap with the subject through its interest in appropriate management.
- **Computer science** overlaps with the subject because of the need for KNOWLEDGE about the workings of contemporary ICT.
- **Software engineering** overlaps with the subject through its interest in the process of developing information systems.

Knowledge: Knowledge is derived from information by integrating information with existing knowledge.

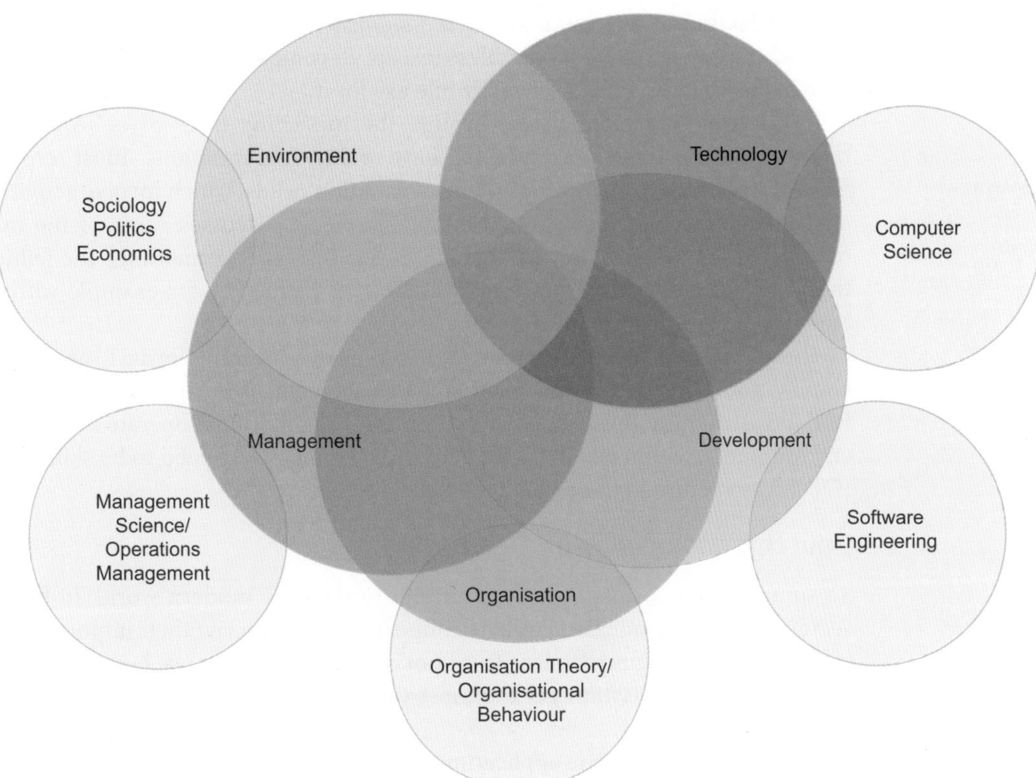

Figure 1.2: *Reference disciplines*

Concept: The idea of significance. The collection of properties that in some way characterise a phenomenon.

Within the area of **business and management** itself (see Chapters 4 and 5), the CONCEPTS of **information** and **system** are both integral and integrating. This means that information systems are critical to understanding contemporary operational practices in marketing, sales, customer relations, production, finance, human resources, procurement and distribution. An understanding of information, information systems and ICT is particularly important to management practice in these areas, so there is a strong argument for placing an understanding of this area at the heart of operating and managing the modern business.

Information systems and value

The idea of *value* is critical to the study of information systems. We can map some of the many shades of meaning of 'value' onto the different contexts we have just outlined:

- the concept of value as the essence of economic systems
- the organisation as a value-creating system embedded within a wider value network
- the human values embedded within information systems (meaning that the design of such systems is a value-laden activity).

Taking value and ICT together leads to questions such as:

- What is the value of ICT to business?
- How do we ensure the value of ICT to business?
- How do we improve the value of ICT to business?

In one sense, these questions are relatively easy to answer. If modern organisations switched off their ICT systems they would fail to operate effectively; many would fail to operate at all. In another sense, the questions are more difficult to answer. Chief executives in many global companies have continually asked questions about the value of ICT. Many billions of dollars has been invested globally in ICT, but companies still find it difficult to put an accurate monetary value on the return to the organisation from this investment.

Typically this is because of the way in which ICT is considered by both business managers and technologists. Both groups tend to focus more on the technology itself than on its application. But all the value lies *in the application*: the most advanced and brilliantly networked computer system is worthless (except to companies that make or sell the equipment) unless the organisation has a worthwhile use for it.

ICT infrastructure: The set of interrelated ICT systems used by an organisation.

ICT is translated into value through the mediating force of *information*. This means that to ensure that ICT systems have value, organisations must ensure that their ICT INFRASTRUCTURE matches their information needs, which involve activities both inside and outside the individual organisation. Chapter 9 discusses some of the many examples of information systems that have failed in organisations. Sometimes the failure was so bad that it brought down the entire organisation, as happened, for example with the UK Child Support Agency.

Throughout this book we argue that to improve the value of ICT, organisations need to employ good practice in the planning, management, development and operation of their ICT infrastructure. Businesses (and nonprofit organisations) operate in increasingly volatile environments, within which their needs often change; they need to be skilled in adapting the ICT infrastructure to these changing needs.

How this book will help

To summarise, information systems are critical to the modern world: in business, in other sectors, and to individuals as well. It's important to appreciate their importance and to understand their founding principles. This book shows you how to use best practice to ensure that you and your organisation get the most value out of your ICT investment, now and in the future.

The focus here is on the application of information systems *in organisations*, and because this is so intimately tied up with other aspects of organizational management, we look at some of those as well. We introduce a number of key skills that are important not only for information systems professionals, but for general business management. These are intended to provide an appreciation of important approaches, frameworks and techniques in the area.

Models are useful, to help us understand what is going on, and plan how to change it. A number of modelling techniques are used throughout the book. Together, they provide a good grounding in the applications of modelling, especially for the analysis and design of many kinds of business systems.

Overall, this book should enable you to develop an understanding and practical appreciation of information systems. It will serve you well, both in the study of related disciplines and in your working career.

Organisational informatics

Informatics: The study of information, information systems and information technology applied to various phenomena.

The term 'information systems' is used in a number of different ways, so let us expand on the brief definition we gave at the beginning of this chapter. It can refer to:

- **A product**: a system of communication between members of a group of people. (These days many communication systems involve technology, although there are ways of communicating without technology too, of course, and have been for thousands of years.) For example, an orders and sales processing system is an information system, used to communicate between members of the selling organisation, and between them and their customers. In modern settings such a system of communication is likely to use various elements of ICT. So a sales orders processing system within some organisation is an information system designed to handle and record sales orders from customers.
- **An academic field of study**. Over the last three decades the field of information systems has become established in many centres of higher education around the world, in both teaching and research.
- **An area of industrial practice.** Many organisations across the world work in planning, managing and developing information systems for other organisations. Many of the largest and best-known business consultancies do a lot of their work in this field. Some organisations in other fields, which originally developed their expertise in setting up their own systems, also sell their know-how to others.

Informatics field: The academic study of informatics issues and problems.

It can be confusing, though, to use the same term in each of these different contexts, so in this book we use a set of terms with distinctive meanings:

- Here, **information system** refers to a system of communication between people, within and between organisations.
- **ICT system** is the term we use for technology: hardware, software, data and communication technology designed to support an information system.
- **Informatics** is our term for the related academic discipline and area of professional activity.

Informatics is a particularly useful term. It covers a broader area of interest than simply information systems. It considers the place of information in communication and action, and the use of various artefacts or technologies as tools within this process: in short, it takes in information systems, ICT systems, the processes that concern them and the information that flows between them. It's also a term that is often used in relation to specific *applications*. For instance, health informatics, bio-informatics and chem-informatics are the terms for the application of information, information systems and ICT systems to processes within the health sector, biology and chemistry respectively.

The main focus of this book is on applications in organisations: by which we mean not just businesses, but a range of private sector, public sector and voluntary sector organisations. The study of applications in this context is known as **organisational informatics**. This is a wider term than the related **business informatics**. So from now on, 'informatics' is used as shorthand for organisational informatics, which is broadly used as a synonym for the discipline of information systems.

Informatics is very much a *systemic* discipline. It is interested not in ICT, information systems, information and organisations in isolation, but in their *interaction* and its effects. To make sense of systems of any kind it is useful to create models which illustrate the interactions of their components, interdependencies, and their effects. This book is structured around a core model (which we shall encounter shortly) which captures the key elements of informatics as well as the interaction between these elements. In essence, this model provides a map of the entire area, which we call here the **informatics domain**.

Our model is founded on the premise that the effects of an information system for an organisation emerge over time, as the result of interaction of the system and its organisational context. We need to understand these effects in order to design and run systems that provide benefits for the organization, and avoid the hazards that information systems are sometimes prone to (Silver, Markus and Beath, 1995).

The informatics domain model forms the basic structure for the book. Each of the component elements contained in the model is covered in much more detail in one chapter of the book. So you might not understand all the concepts introduced here right away, but you can explore them throughout the book, and follow links to further chapters at any time if you want to delve into one particular aspect. This chapter not only introduces the model, it acts as a summary and reference for it.

Introducing the informatics domain model

The model begins with the key context for the application of information systems: the organisation itself (see Figure 1.3). Any organisation is considered as a series of interdependent activity systems. When these are combined in action they produce value of some form (see Chapter 2). VALUE is the key flow between an organisation and actors in its environment (see Chapter 7). The value produced by a business organisation is typically the products or services it provides for its customers. (Of course, nonprofit organisations have value too, although there it takes different forms.) The organisation also receives value from other actors in its environment, such as its suppliers or partners. Hence, a business organisation is a value-creating system which interacts with a wider value network that makes up its environment.

Value: A general term used to describe the outputs from an organisation.

Any activity system relies on an information system. An information system (see Chapter 4) is a system of communication between a group of people, which is used by the group to coordinate its members' actions. On the basis of information supplied by the information system, people in the group decide what actions to take (see Figure 1.4). So information is essential to the effective control of organisational action.

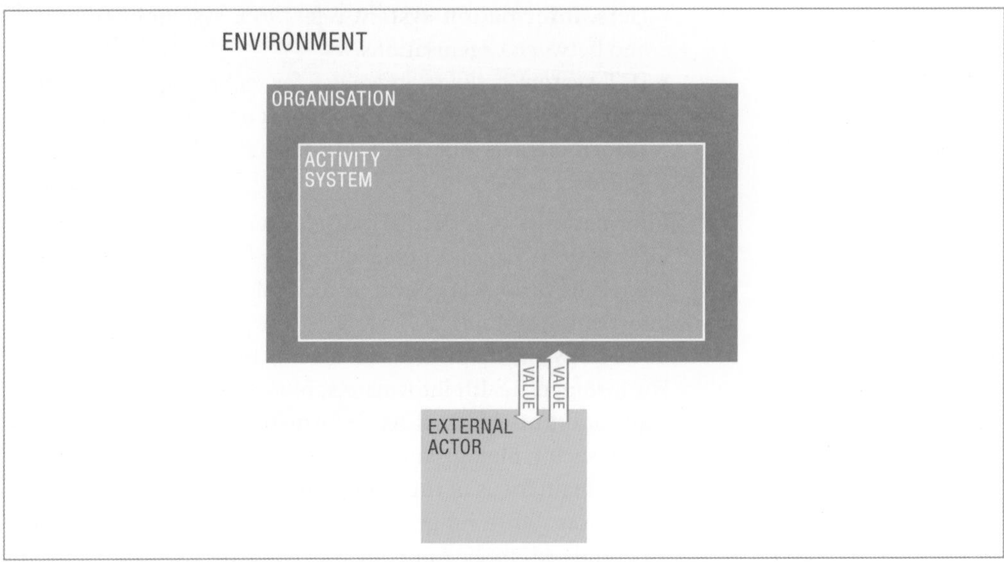

Figure 1.3: *Organisation, activity systems and environment*

Datum: A unit of data.

Information is data interpreted in some context (see Chapter 3). The context for business information is the wider activity system. A DATUM – that is, a unit of data – is one or more symbols used to represent something. Data is supplied to the information system by its ICT system (see Chapters 5 and 6). The ICT system processes business data, such as records of sales orders, and produces information, such as the total number of sales orders received in the last quarter, for the purpose of business decision making (see Figure 1.5).

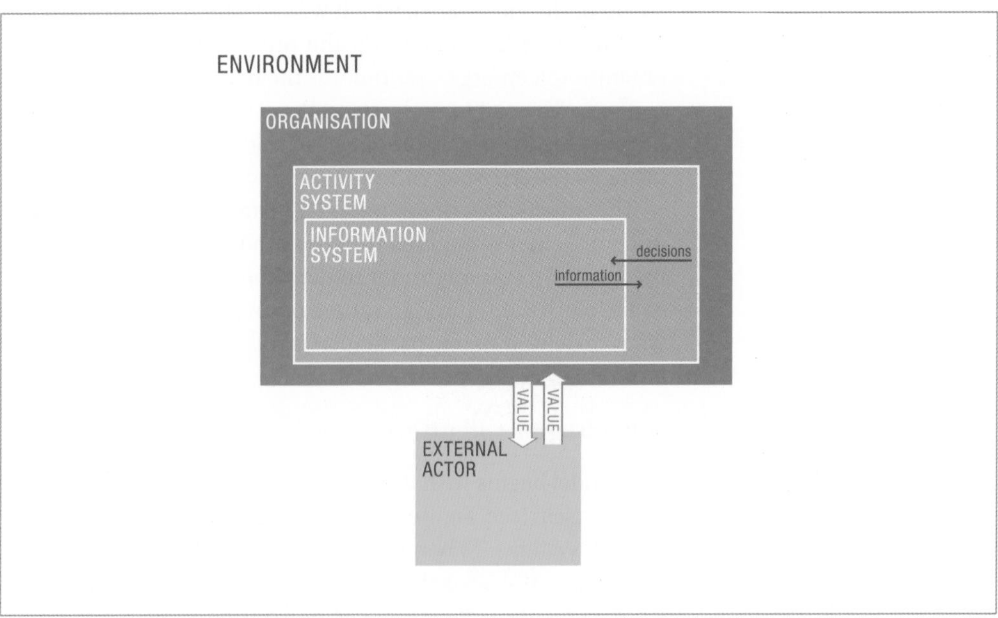

Figure 1.4: *Information systems*

eBusiness: Electronic business. The conduct of business using information and communication technology. A superset of eCommerce.

eCommerce: Electronic commerce. The conduct of business commerce using ICT such as that supporting the Internet.

ICT (see Chapters 5 and 6) consists of hardware, software, data and communication technology used in support of an information system. Traditionally, ICT has been used to improve the operation of internal activity systems in organisations. More recently, it has also been used to improve activity systems between the organisation and its wider value network. Central to this is EBUSINESS and ECOMMERCE (see Chapter 8). eCommerce refers to the use of ICT to enable activities within the wider value network. We use eBusiness as a term for the use of ICT to enable both internal and external activities (see Figure 1.6).

Business systems have to be developed. By this we mean that a clear case has to be made for their creation, the key requirements of the system have to be determined and represented, a design has to be produced for the system, and the system has to be built and implemented. Since the focus of this book is business information systems, we focus on these activities in a business context. All these activities (see Figure 1.7) are stages within what we refer to as the **information systems development process** (see Chapter 12).

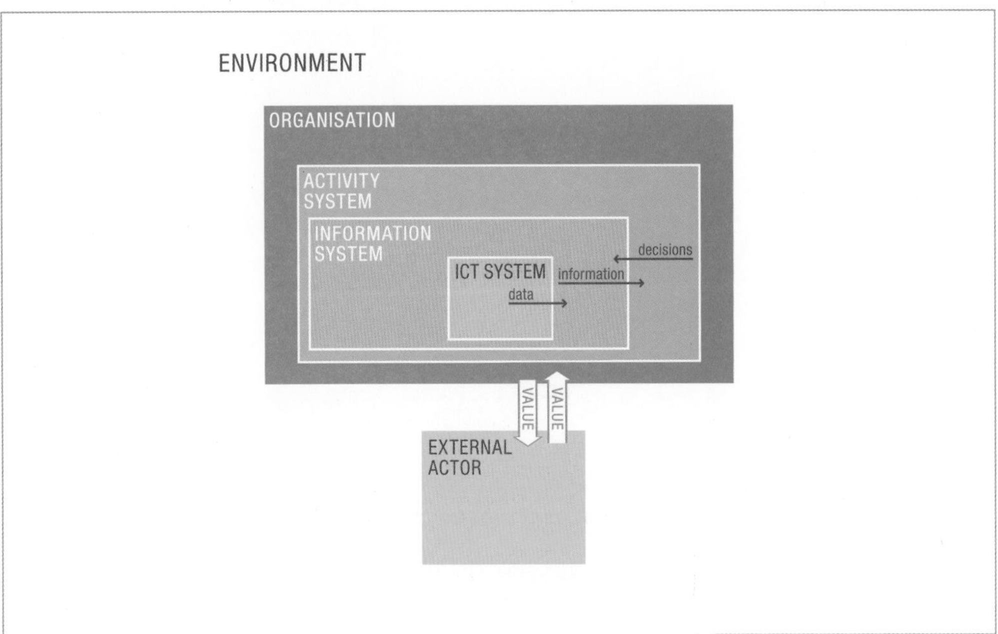

Figure 1.5: *Data and information*

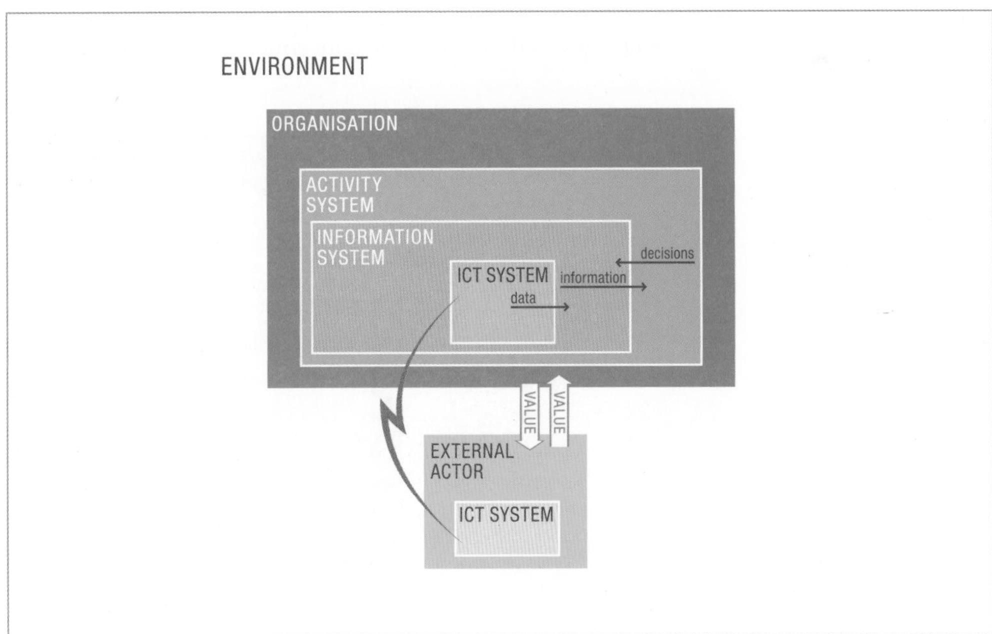

Figure 1.6: *ICT systems and infrastructure*

After an information system is introduced, it begins to have effects on the organisation (see Figure 1.8). We can divide these into **first-order effects**, which concern issues of use, and **second-order effects**, which concern the impact of the information system on the activities of individuals, groups and the organisation as a whole (see Chapter 9).

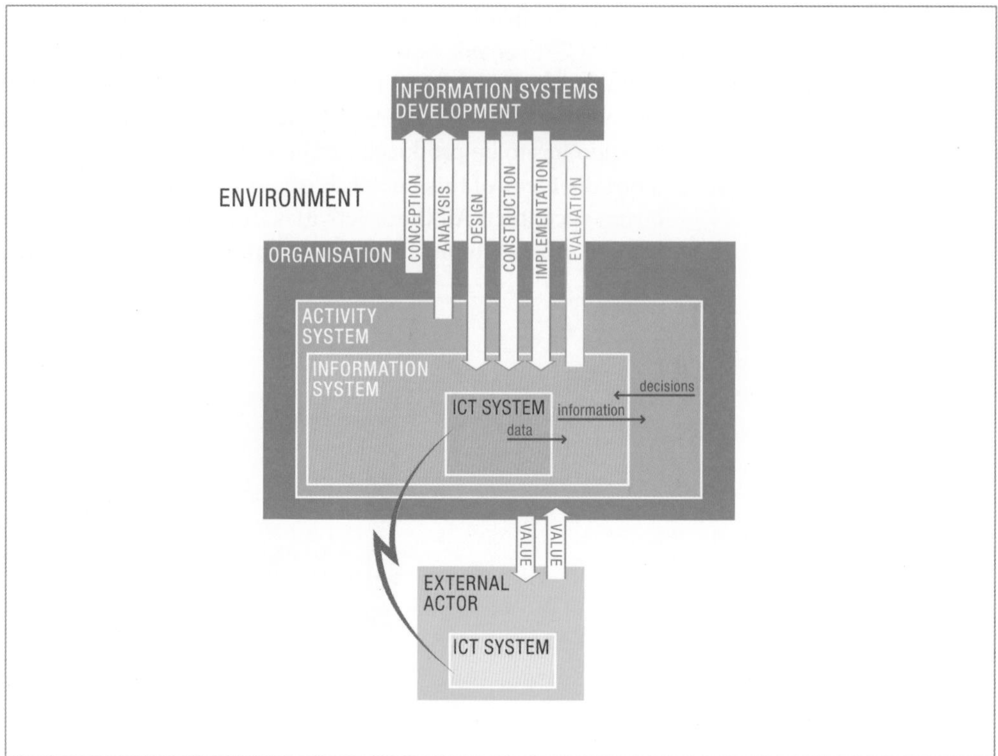

Figure 1.7: *Information systems development*

Peter Drucker's 'The theory of the business' (1994) attributes organisational success to three factors:

- businesses understanding their external environments
- businesses undertaking missions (developing strategies) consistent with their external environments
- businesses developing the core competencies needed to accomplish their missions.

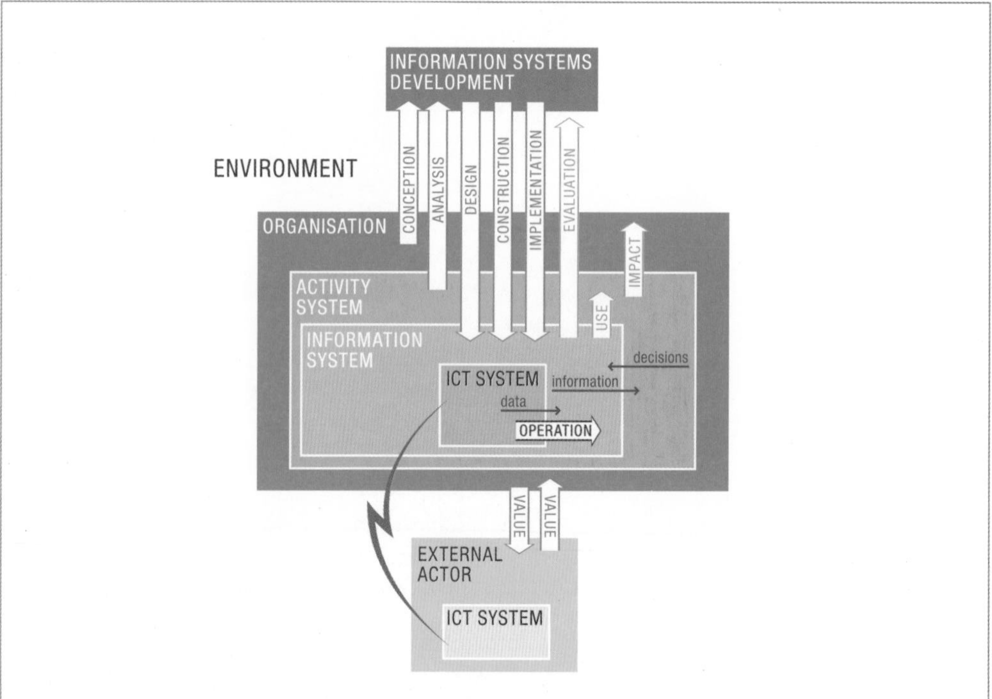

Figure 1.8: *Use and impact*

Since information is central to the modern organisation, organisational success depends not least on information systems success, and this calls for effective informatics planning and management. Planning and management (see Figure 1.9) are necessary to ensure that information systems are aligned with organisational strategy (see Chapter 10).

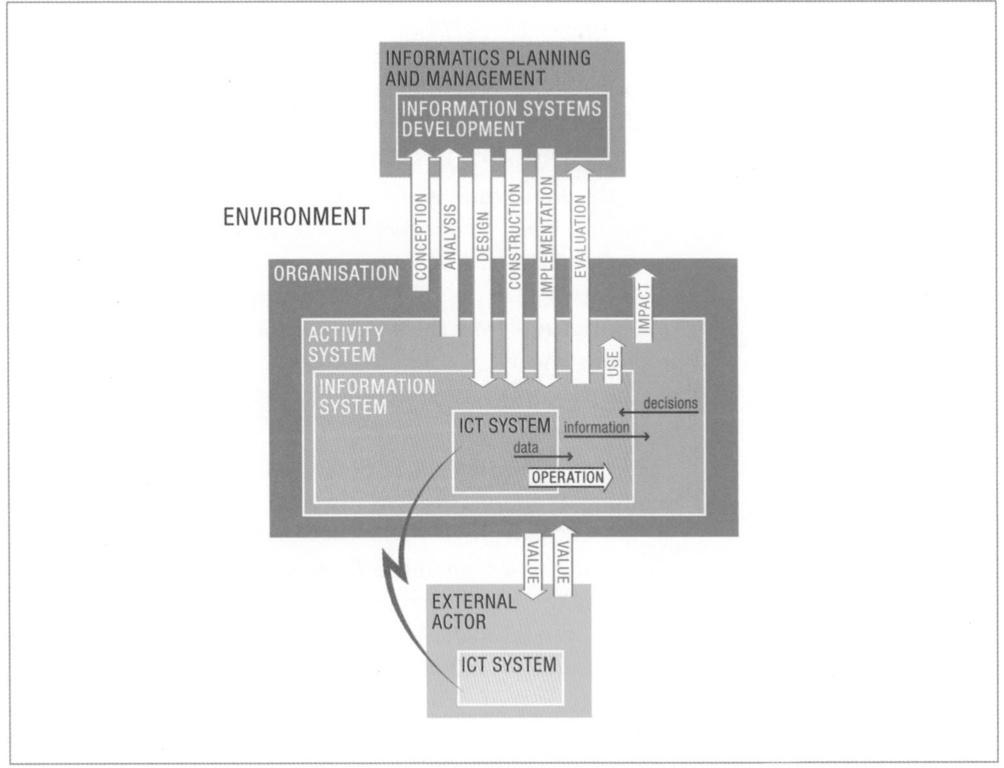

Figure 1.9: *Planning, management and operations*

Informatics infrastructure: The sum total of information, information systems and information technology resources available to the organisation at any one time.

The rest of this chapter introduces key elements from this model, and shows its relevance by applying it to a case study of a small company that is part of a multinational organisation. First we describe the position the organisation found itself in during the mid-1980s, with little use of ICT, then we consider how and why the organisation developed its first ICT system, and what form this took. It had some early success with the system, and this led to the gradual rollout and extension of an integrated INFORMATICS INFRASTRUCTURE throughout its parent organisation. But that was less easy, and there are still management problems with which it is grappling today.

Organisation and environment: an illustrative case

Production: The set of activities concerned with the creation of goods and services for human existence.

Goronwy Galvanising is a small company which specialises in treating steel products such as lintels (beams), crash barriers and palisades (fenceposts) produced by other manufacturers. (Although the name is fictionalised it is based on a real company.) It is a subsidiary of a large multinational, Rito Metals, whose primary business includes the extraction and processing of base metals such as zinc and the PRODUCTION of various metal alloys. Rito Metals has ten galvanising plants similar to Goronwy across Europe. The Rito Metals head office coordinates administrative activities such as finance and human resources, but each plant manages its own operational activities in areas such as sales and logistics.

Put simply, galvanising involves dipping steel products into baths of molten zinc to provide a rustproof coating. In the trade, untreated steel products are known as 'black' and treated ones as 'white'. The galvanising process causes a slight gain in weight.

As much as 80 per cent of Goronwy's business (in the mid-1980s, when this case study starts) was with one major regular customer, Blackwalls steel, with the rest coming from other customers on a more irregular basis.

Goronwy's staff comprise a plant manager, a production controller, an office clerk, three shift foremen and 50 shop-floor workers. The plant remains open 24 hours per day, seven days a week, so most of the production workers, including the foremen, work shift patterns.

We can think of Goronwy Galvanising as a system, as indeed we can any organisation. A system can be defined as a coherent set of interdependent components that exists for some purpose, has some stability, and can usefully be viewed as a whole. Systems of interest to informatics are generally referred to as OPEN SYSTEMS. These are systems that interact with their environment. So we can model them using an **input–process–output** model, of the organisation within its environment.

Open system: A system that interacts with its environment.

- By the **environment** of a system we mean anything outside the system that has an effect on the way the system operates. We usually identify a number of agents or actors with which the system interacts.
- The INPUTS to the system are the resources it acquires from agents in its environment.
- The **outputs** from the system are those things that it supplies back to agents or actors in its environment.
- The **process** of the system is that set of activities that transform system inputs into system outputs.

Input: The elements that a system takes from its environment.

Figure 1.10 illustrates at a high level the component, physical elements of Goronwy Galvanising as an open system. Its main inputs are black products and its main outputs white products. Both these PHYSICAL FLOWS are represented as broad arrows on the diagram. The process, or **transformation**, is the galvanisation. Along with the physical flow of steel products there is a corresponding information flow, consisting of documents which detail deliveries and dispatches of material. These are represented on the diagram as narrow arrows with document symbols.

Physical flow: This represents the flow of tangible or physical goods and services such as foodstuffs and automobiles.

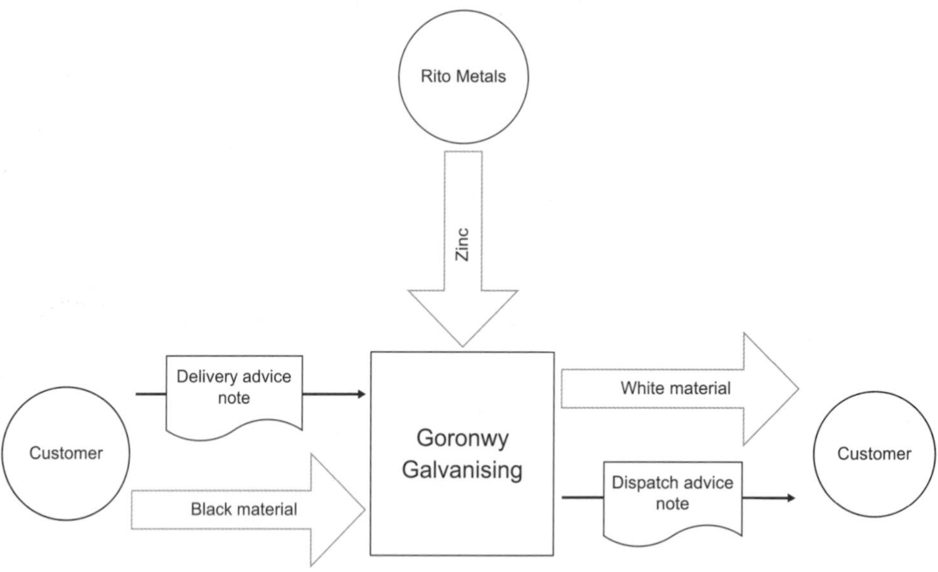

Figure 1.10: *Goronwy Galvanising as a system*

The main actors in Goronwy's environment are its suppliers and customers. There are two kinds of supplier, one of which is also its customer: the steel fabrication firms – Blackwalls and the smaller customers – that provide black goods to be galvanised. The second supplier is Rito Metals, which supplies zinc as raw material for the galvanising process.

From this perspective, we can see the overall purpose of the organisation as being to create value, through the process or transformation at its core. For commercial organisations that value becomes concrete when they sell their products or services and make a profit. We can also think of the organisation as part of a **value network**, in which there are flows of value between the organisation and the actors in its environment (its customers and suppliers). So as well as creating value itself, Goronwy adds value to the outputs of other actors in its value network. Steel producers, steel fabricators and zinc producers are all part of Goronwy's value network.

We shall encounter the concept of system in a number of different ways in this book. In a sense, it acts as a unifying theme. For example, we discuss and make distinctions between:

- a system of activity (an activity system)
- a system of communication (an information system)
- a system of technology (an ICT system).

In the sections that follow we investigate each of these in turn.

Activity systems

We can view an organisation as a number of interdependent human activity systems (or **activity systems** for short). An activity system is a social system, sometimes referred to as a 'soft' system. It consists of a logical collection of activities, processes or tasks performed by a group of people in pursuit of a goal. The precedence or order of activities is normally critical, as this determines the flow necessary for the coordination of work.

For Goronwy, the main activity systems consist of processes for:

- receiving unfinished products
- galvanising these products
- dispatching finished products back to customers.

The 'black' material – steel fabricated products of various forms – is delivered to Goronwy on large trailers in bundles referred to as batches. It is unpacked by an inbound logistics operative and checked for discrepancies or problems that would make it unsuitable for galvanising. If satisfactory, the products are then galvanised and left to dry. The white material is then checked again, and any unsatisfactory material is regalvanised. Satisfactory white material is bundled on trailers and dispatched back to the customer. The activity system is shown in Figure 1.11, with dotted lines indicating the precedence of each activity in the system. In other words, the dotted lines indicate the workflow through the activity system.

Control: The mechanism that implements regulation and adaptation in most systems.

Feedback: The way in which a control process adjusts the state of a system being monitored to keep it within specified limits.

In any activity system there will also be some form of embedded CONTROL. Control is the idea that any system (including social systems such as organisations) needs to be regulated in some way, and must also be able to adapt to changes in its environment. Regulatory control is typically implemented through a process known as FEEDBACK, in which information is collected from a monitored process and is compared against defined levels of performance for the system. This information then triggers actions designed to maintain the system's performance within given bounds.

Figure 1.11 includes two regulatory control processes. Each one consists of a sensing or monitoring activity, a decision-making activity (represented by a triangle) and an effecting activity. The first control process checks to see that black material is of a suitable form to be processed. If the material is satisfactory it is passed on to galvanisation. If it is not satisfactory, it is returned to the customer ungalvanised. The second control process checks to see that galvanisation has operated effectively on particular batches of steel products. Therefore, in both control processes, information and decisions will trigger appropriate action to ensure that the organisation performs effectively, such as returning damaged unfinished products to the customer or regalvanising steel products before dispatch.

Information systems

Information system: A system of communication between people. A system involved in the gathering, processing, distribution and use of information.

Every activity system relies on an associated INFORMATION SYSTEM: that is, a system of communication between people. Information systems are systems involved in the gathering, processing, distribution and use of information. In this way they support human activity.

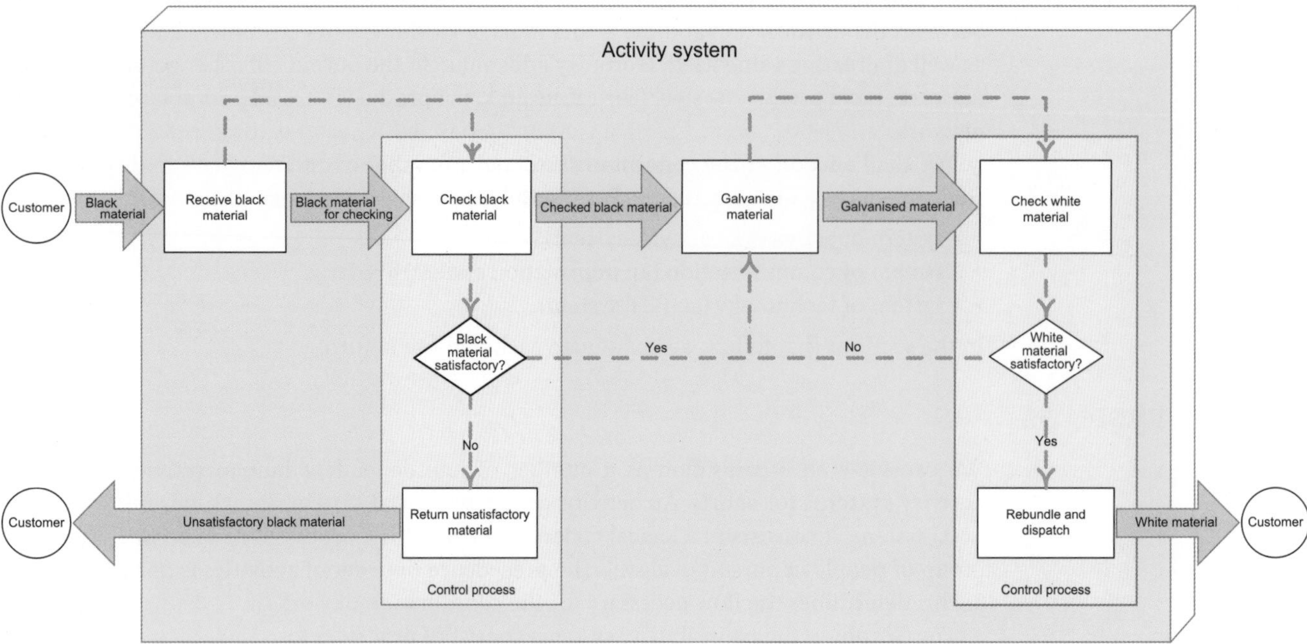

Figure 1.11: *The activity system at Goronwy*

By way of example, let's look first at the information system Goronwy Galvanising used in the 1980s, before mass computerisation. It was a manual information system in the sense that it relied on the flow of documents to inform the coordination of activity.

A trailer arriving from a customer might be loaded with a number of different types of steel product. These were divided into batches, and each batch was labelled with a unique order number. Each trailer was given a delivery advice note detailing all the associated batches on it.

Since Blackwalls was Goronwy's major customer, the delivery advice note system was designed to dovetail with Blackwalls' own internal system. Blackwalls itself generated the order numbers. Figure 1.12 shows a typical delivery advice note from Blackwalls detailing all the black material on a particular trailer. The information about each particular batch is referred to as an **order line**.

Blackwalls Steel Products		Delivery Advice			
Advice no.: A3137	Date: 20/01/1988	Customer Name: Goronwy Galvanising		Instructions: Galvanise and Return	
Order no.	Description	Product code	Item length	Delivery qty	Weight (tonnes)
13/1193G	Lintels	UL150	1500	20	145
44/2404G	Lintels	UL1500	15000	20	145
70/2517P	Lintels	UL135	1350	20	130
23/2474P	Lintels	UL120	1200	16	80
Haulier: International 5	Received in good order: ✓				

Figure 1.12: *Sample delivery advice note*

On arrival at the galvanising plant the black material was unpacked by an inbound logistics operative and checked for discrepancies with the information on the delivery advice note. There are two major types of discrepancy:

- A **count discrepancy**, between the number of items delivered and the number indicated on the delivery advice note.
- A **non-conforming black discrepancy** arises when some of the material is unsuitable for galvanising. For instance, a steel lintel might be bent or the material be of the wrong type.

The operative would note both kinds, by making a comment in the appropriate box on the delivery advice note.

When all the material had been checked, the delivery advice note was passed on to the production controller who, with the office clerk, copied by hand all the details on the delivery advice note, including any discrepancies, to a job sheet. A separate job sheet was filled in for each order line on the delivery advice note (a sample is shown in Figure 1.13).

Job Sheet		Job No.: 2046			
Order no.	Description	Product code	Item length	Order qty	Batch weight
13/1193G	Lintels	L150	1500	20	145
Count discrepancy	Non-conforming black	Non-conforming white	Non-conforming no change		
Galvanised	Despatch no.	Despatch date	Qty returned	Weight returned	
Y					

Figure 1.13: *Sample job sheet*

The job sheet was passed down to the shop floor of the factory, where the shift foreman used it to record details of processing. Most jobs passed through the galvanising process smoothly. The steel items were placed on racks, dipped in the zinc bath and left to cool. The site foreman then checked each job. If all items had been galvanised properly he put a Y for yes in the box on the job sheet, and passed it back to the production controller.

Occasionally, some of the items were not galvanised properly. They were classed as non-conforming white, and also noted on the job sheet (and typically scheduled for regalvanising).

When the shop floor had treated a series of jobs, the production controller issued a **dispatch advice note** and sent it to the outbound logistics section. Workers in this section used the information on it to stack the white material on trailers – one trailer to a dispatch advice note – ready to be returned to the manufacturer.

The discrepancies meant there was not a one-to-one correspondence between the delivery advice notes and the dispatch advice notes, so the production controller needed to record the separate dispatches associated with a delivery on the job sheet. You can see how this worked from the typical dispatch advice in Figure 1.14, where the final order, 23/2474P, had not yet been delivered in full.

Figure 1.15 is a diagram of the entire information flow through the system. This information or document flow parallels the flow of work or activity through the system, so it shows both physical transformation processes and information-handling activities. The open boxes represent information stores, places where records such as delivery notes were kept.

Information

After this first introduction to information systems, let's step back and take a look in more detail at the idea of information itself.

Delivery notes, dispatch notes and job sheets are all **information elements** within the information system: they flow through the system. Employees use the information on these documents to make decisions: in Goronwy's case, for example, what material to galvanise. They then act on the basis of their decisions. If the information is incorrect, the wrong decisions will be made, and the process will not perform effectively. Information – and more particularly, good-quality information – is therefore essential for the effective coordination of activity. Without the information recorded on delivery notes, dispatch notes and job sheets it would prove difficult to coordinate the work of inbound and outbound logistics staff with shop-floor staff galvanising material. The same is true of the relationship between information and systems on a more general level: all systems rely on the provision of accurate information in order to operate control processes effectively.

Goronwy Galvanising		Dispatch Advice					
Advice no.: 101	Date: 22/01/2003	Customer Name and Address: Blackwalls					
Order no.	Description	Product code	Item length	Order qty	Batch weight	Returned qty	Batch weight
13/1193G	Lintels	UL150	1500	20	145	20	150
44/2404G	Lintels	UL1500	15000	20	145	20	150
70/2517P	Lintels	UL135	1350	20	130	20	135
23/2474P	Lintels	UL120	1200	16	100	14	82
Driver:	Received by:						

Figure 1.14: *Sample dispatch advice note*

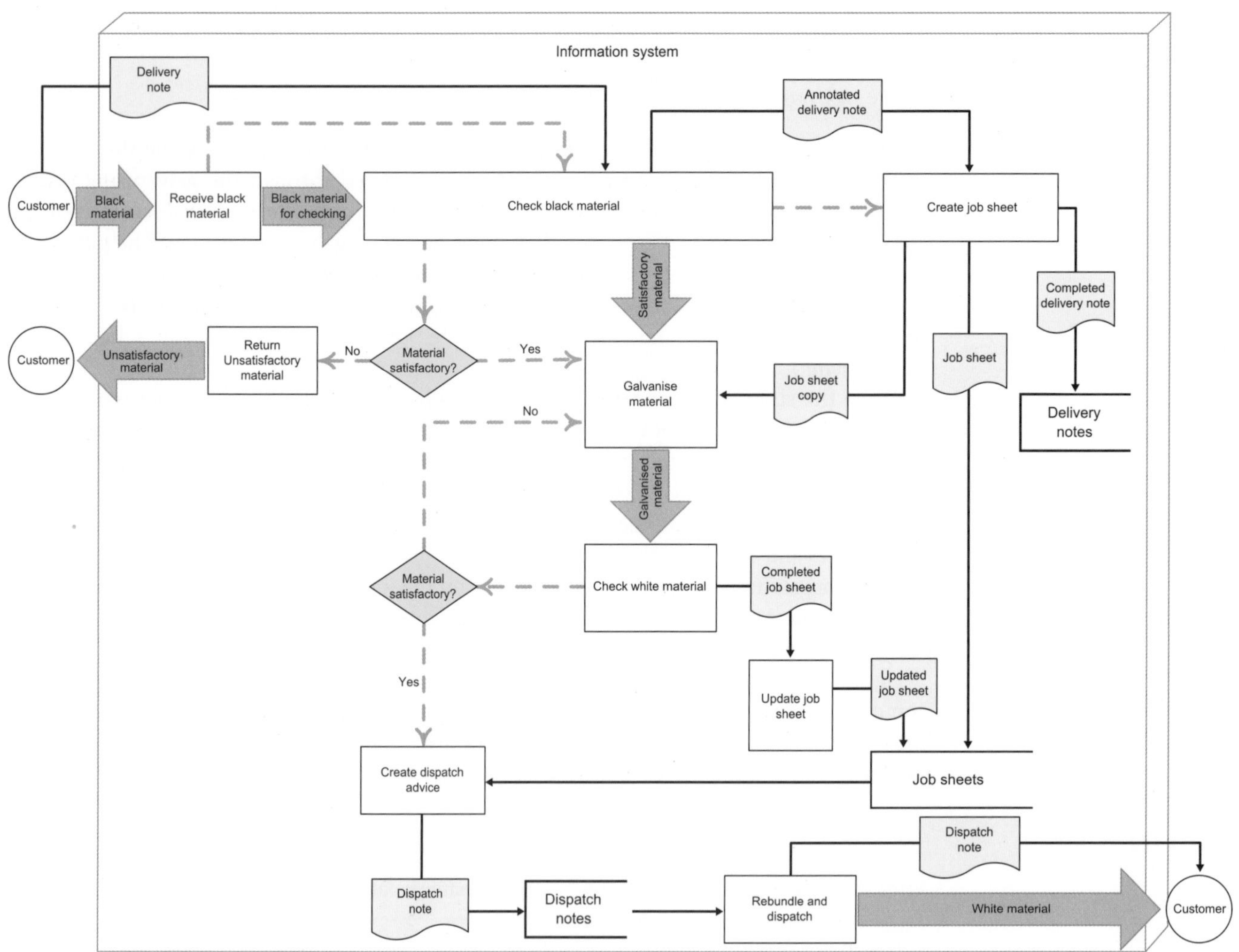

Figure 1.15: *The information system at Goronwy*

Information therefore supports human activity, in the sense that it enables decisions to be made about appropriate actions in particular circumstances. Decisions and decision making lie between information and action, and are a critical aspect of any activity system. In this sense, management can be seen as a control process in organisations. Management is an activity system that controls other operational activity systems. The primary activity of management is making decisions concerning organisational action.

Effective management decision making relies on three interrelated information-handling activities:

- Effective definitions of the performance of an activity system. This means turning the defined purpose or purposes of the activity system into a defined set of performance measures.
- The construction of effective performance management systems for managerial activity. This means establishing clear ways of establishing the performance of operational activity systems against performance measures.
- The collection and processing of information from operational activity systems. This means establishing effective information systems to capture and manipulate the information required for performance management.

To stay with the Goronwy example, one definition for the performance of this system might be to achieve efficient throughput of materials for the galvanising process. Goronwy could measure this efficiency in a number of different ways. For example, it might measure the amount or proportion of non-conforming black and white material identified over a particular period, such as one month. This would involve keeping track of the amount of non-conforming material, and the total amount of material processed, perhaps categorised by type using product codes, as well as the date of processing. So Goronwy needs an effective information system that captures and processes this type of information.

In defining an information system we not only need to represent the *flow* of information, we need to model the *structure* of information, particularly the information of relevance to decision making. For this purpose we need an **information model**. There is a sample information model for Goronwy Galvanising in Figure 1.16.

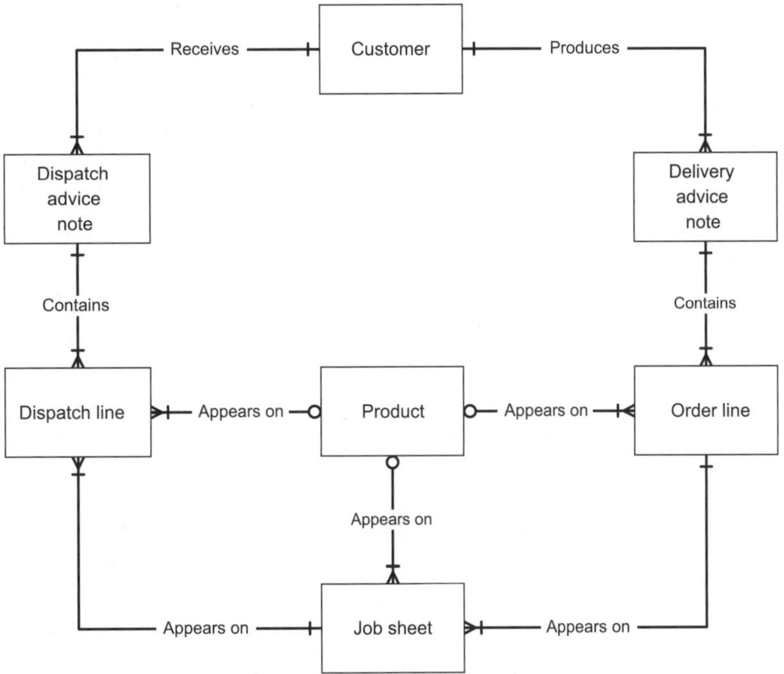

Figure 1.16: *Information model for Goronwy Galvanising*

The boxes on this diagram indicate individual elements of information, and are referred to as **information classes**. The connecting lines indicate an association between information classes. The symbols attached to each line represent a number of rules governing the behaviour of the association between classes: this is explored in more detail in Chapter 3.

For example, a fork or crowsfoot on the end of a line indicates a one-to-many relationship. So a delivery advice note (class) contains (association) many order lines (class). Each order line corresponds to a row or record of information on the delivery advice note in Figure 1.12. An order line represents information about one particular order, such as the product to be galvanised and the quantity of the product in the batch. Therefore, the order line directly corresponds to a batch on an inbound trailer. It also directly corresponds to a job sheet, which may also indicate the non-conforming black material that is returned because of identified discrepancies.

ICT systems

As the Goronwy example has shown, information systems do not need to use modern ICT. But modern ICT makes systems work better and faster, and in today's complex global world, most information systems use it to at least some degree. We can see why by looking at some of the problems with the system Goronwy used in the 1980s:

- Information needs to be shared among a number of people: for Goronwy, they include inbound logistics operatives, production controllers, shift foremen and outbound logistics operatives. So copies of it are needed, and making manual copies is slow and therefore expensive.
- A lot of time was taken transferring information from one type of form to another: for instance, from delivery advice notes to job sheets.
- Every transfer stage is an opportunity for human error to creep in, and this can lead directly to processing errors, which are costly and time-consuming to correct.
- It is difficult to analyse information held manually. Even if it works well for production purposes, it does not provide a good resource for managers who want to collate and analyse it to determine trends such as the throughput of the plant or the productivity of the workforce.

As a result, Goronwy and its parent company looked at moving to an ICT-based system for basic administrative functions. Let's consider what this means in practice.

Technology amounts to a set of artefacts for doing things. ICT is the term for any type of technology used to support data gathering, processing, distribution and use. ICT systems consist of hardware, software, data management technology and communication technology:

Hardware: The physical (hard) aspects of ICT consisting of processors, input devices and output devices.

Input device: A device concerned with the input of data.

Output device: A device that outputs data.

Software: The non-physical (soft) aspects of information technology. Software is essentially programs – sets of instructions for controlling computer hardware.

Programming language: A language for instructing a computer system.

Data management: The set of facilities needed to manage data.

- **Hardware** is the term for the physical aspects of ICT: processors, INPUT DEVICES such as keyboards and OUTPUT DEVICES such as monitors.
- **Software** is the term for the non-physical aspects of ICT. Essentially this means programs: sets of instructions for controlling computer hardware. Types of software include operating systems (such as Windows Vista), PROGRAMMING LANGUAGES (such as Java) and office productivity packages (such as Microsoft Word).
- **Data management technology** consists of artefacts for storing data on peripheral devices such as hard disks. Data are normally stored in databases managed by a database management system (such as Microsoft Access).
- **Data communication technology** consists of programs and devices used to manipulate and transmit data. Communication technology forms the interconnective tissue of ICT, and includes cabling, transmitters and routers. Communication networks between computing devices are essential elements of the modern ICT infrastructure of organisations (see Chapter 8).

ICT systems are technical systems. They are frequently referred to as 'hard' systems in the sense that they consist of an assembly of designed artefacts. But an ICT system is not just made up of hardware: it is an organised collection of hardware, software, data and communication technology designed to support aspects of an information system. It takes data as input, manipulates the data as a process, and outputs manipulated data for interpretation within a human activity system. The relationship between these three types of system is shown in Figure 1.17.

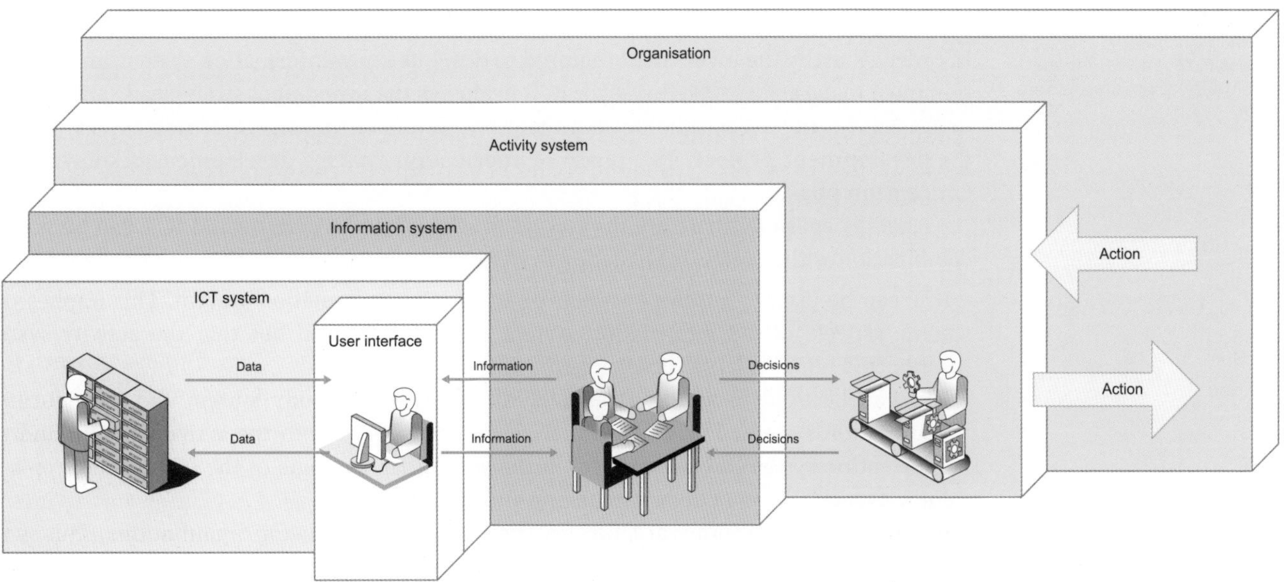

Figure 1.17: *An ICT system, information system and activity system*

Data, information and sociotechnical systems

A **datum** is, as we said earlier, a symbol (or group of symbols) that is used to represent something. (**Data** is its plural.) Since an ICT system deals with manipulating and transmitting data, it is therefore more accurately referred to as a **data processing system**.

Information is *interpreted* data: it consists of data placed within a meaningful context. The use of the term 'information' therefore implies a group of people doing interpretation (for more on this, see Chapter 3). Consider the string of symbols UL150. Taken together these symbols form a datum, but by themselves they are meaningless. To turn these symbols into information we have to supply a meaningful context. We have to interpret them. In the Goronwy Galvanising information system, this group of symbols is a product code identifying a type of steel lintel of a particular length.

Let's look at how Goronwy Galvanising might set up an ICT system. Staff would enter (or input) data that describe the properties of orders on delivery advice notes (such as product codes and quantities). This *data* is then manipulated, by linking it to other data collected (such as discrepancies identified at inbound logistics), to provide *information* on processed orders. This part of the ICT system then supports *human activities and actions* concerned with the effective quality control of raw material into the production process. For instance, the ICT system might identify that two pieces of data do not match. But it would take a human being to interpret this information, and come to the conclusion that a lintel has been lost from a particular order. And it's down to human beings to take *action*: perhaps to return a batch to the customer. So the organisation introducing an ICT system really needs two things; first, a good data and ICT system, and second, human beings who effectively and efficiently make use of the system to ensure that the organisation meets the needs of its customers.

Sociotechnical system:
A system of technology used within a system of activity.

The key lesson to be drawn from Figure 1.17 is therefore that many systems in organisations are examples of sociotechnical systems. A SOCIOTECHNICAL SYSTEM is a system of technology used within a system of activity. Information systems are primary examples of sociotechnical systems: they consist of ICT used within an activity system. They therefore span ICT and activity. Part of the human activity will involve the use of ICT systems, through an interface. The information provided by the information system will also drive decision making, leading to further action within the organisation.

The development process

Business case: The case made for the utility of an information system.

In order to justify the investment required to develop a new information system, an organisation must make a BUSINESS CASE for it. It evaluates the investment strategically and assesses its feasibility. The organisation also attempts to estimate the degree of **risk** associated with the **development project.** This phase of information systems development is known as the **conception phase.**

Generally speaking there are three ways in which human activity and ICT can be used in combination within a new information system:

- ICT can be used to **support** aspects of an existing information system. This implies that some aspects of the information system are computerised but that the activity system supported remains largely unchanged.
- ICT can be used to **supplant** aspects of an existing activity system and its associated information system. This implies that certain aspects of both the activity system and the information system are automated, in the sense that the logic of the ICT system replaces some aspect of human decision making and action.
- ICT can be used to **innovate**, creating new activity systems for organisations. This is the most radical use of technology.

Let's go back to Goronwy Galvanising. Its managers drew up a business case for a new ICT system which outlined many of the problems with the existing manual information system. They decided to keep the existing activity system much as it was, and to base the design of the associated ICT system closely on it. They chose this **support** option because there was a low risk of failure in the development effort.

Systems analysis: The part of the development process devoted to eliciting and representing the requirements for systems.

If the business case for a new information system is made successfully, then the development process progresses to the SYSTEMS ANALYSIS phase. This involves identifying and specifying requirements for the new information system. These typically describe the **functionality** of the information system: that is, they concentrate on what an information system should be able to *do*.

For instance, a core part of the functionality for Goronwy's system involved capturing, storing and manipulating data associated with the receipt of orders from customers. Another part was a function for reporting regularly on the number of orders from particular customers and the amount of non-conforming material returned.

Systems design: The part of the development process devoted to designing the functionality of systems.

Once the required functionality has been identified, the next development phase is SYSTEMS DESIGN. This is the process of planning the shape of the information system to meet the requirements established by the earlier analysis. If the aim is to use ICT to supplant an existing system or to innovate, then it is necessary to jointly design an ICT system and its associated activity system. In other words, the designer does not only need to consider the shape of software, hardware, data and communication, they also need to design new forms of work to be used with the new ICT. But when the aim is to use ICT to support existing ways of doing things, the focus of design is primarily on the shape of the ICT system alone. This is what we focus on in the rest of this section.

We can think of an ICT system as consisting of three interdependent subsystems or layers for which designs need to be formulated (see Figure 1.18):

- a data management layer
- a business layer
- an interface layer.

The data management layer

Database: An organised pool of logically related data.

Since ICT systems are essentially data processing systems, they rely on a core repository: somewhere to keep the data used in the system. This repository is normally referred to as a DATABASE, and is controlled by the **data management layer**. The design for the structure of the database at the heart of the ICT system is referred to as a **data model**. Essentially, this data model defines what data is stored within the system and in what form.

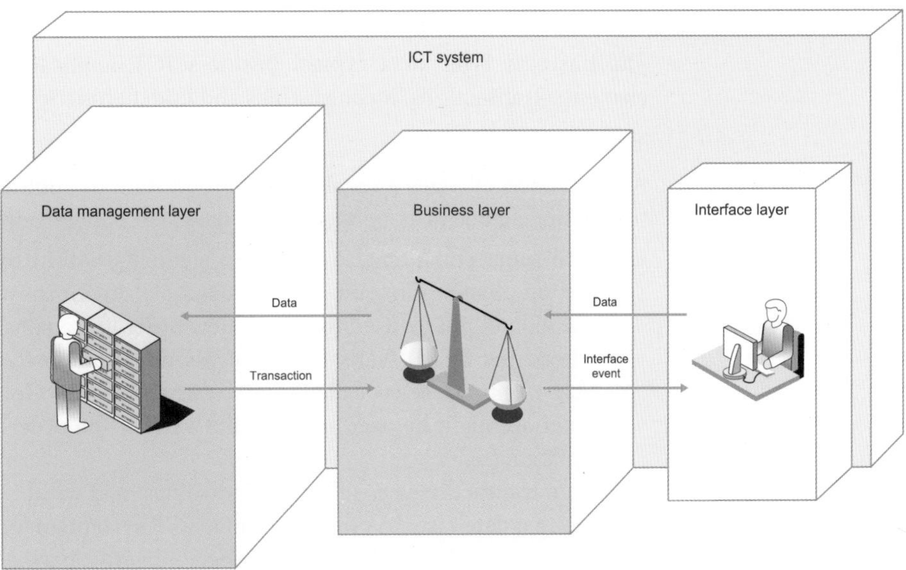

Figure 1.18: *Layers of an ICT system*

For Goronwy, the structure of data might be defined as:

Customers (Customer name, Customer address, Customer telephone no.)
DispatchAdvices (Dispatch no., Dispatch date, Customer name)
DeliveryAdvices (Delivery no., Delivery date, Customer name)
Job-sheets (Job no., Order no, Count discrepancy, Non conforming black, Non conforming white, Non conforming no change)
Products (Product code, Product description, Item length)
Order lines (Order no., Delivery no., Product code, Order qty, Order weight)
Dispatch lines (Order no., Dispatch no., Returned qty, Returned weight).

Table: The major data structure in the relational data model.

These definitions are derived directly from the information model represented in Figure 1.16. They act as a design shorthand for specifying data structures in this database, such as *Customers* and *Dispatches.* Each data structure is a collection of data elements, and each data element consists of a set of data items. A sample of the data that might be entered into 'Order lines' is shown in Figure 1.19. In this example, *OrderNo* and *DeliveryNo* are examples of data items. Each row of the TABLE represents a data element. Each data element is identified by a key data item: in this example, the key is the value associated with an *OrderNo,* and such keys are underlined in the data structure definitions above.

Data structure

Order-lines

Order No.	Delivery No.	Product Code	Order Qty	Order Weight
13/1193G	A3137	UL150	20	145
44/2404G	A3137	UL1500	20	145
70/2517P	A3137	UL135	20	130
23/2474P	A3137	UL120	20	180

Data element

Data item

Figure 1.19: *Order lines data structure*

The business layer

The business layer of a typical business ICT application consists of three interrelated elements: transactions, business rules and update functions.

Transactions

A transaction changes a database from one state to another. There are four major types of transaction activities associated with a database, collectively referred to as CRUD:

- **Create** transactions create new data elements within the data structures of a database (more on this in Chapter 6). For example, in Goronwy's new ICT system, a 'create' transaction might be used to enter a new order line against a particular delivery advice.
- **Retrieval** (or **Read**) transactions access data contained within the data structures of a database, and are often called query transactions. In Goronwy's new ICT system a 'read' transaction might be used to assemble a list of the order lines appropriate to a particular delivery advice.
- **Update** transactions cause changes to values held within particular data items of data elements in a database. In Goronwy's new ICT system an 'update' transaction might be used to change the value OrderWeight associated with a particular order line.
- **Delete** transactions erase particular data elements. In Goronwy's new ICT system, a delete transaction might be used to remove a particular order line from the database.

Business rules

A considerable amount of the functionality of an ICT system is taken up with **business rules**. These are found in both the business layer and the data management layer. They ensure that the data held in the data management layer remains an accurate reflection of the activity system it represents. In other words, the data held in an ICT system should display integrity; it should accurately reflect the state of its activity system. In the case of Goronwy, the data stored in the data structure *jobs* should accurately represent batches of material that either have been successfully processed by the company in the past or are in the process of undergoing galvanisation.

Update functions

Update functions represent units of functionality associated with a particular ICT system. They include both business rules and transaction types. Update functions are triggered by **events**, which are typically activated from the interface or from other update functions. When an update function is activated, transactions are fired at the data management layer of the ICT system and cause changes to the database.

For instance, the Goronwy ICT system might have an update function named *create order line*. When activated, this function would first check that a dispatch advice existed for the order line. Then it would check to see that the order line had not already been entered and that the data to be entered was in the correct format: for instance, that the order number is unique and a correct product code had been entered. If all these checks proved satisfactory, a new row would be entered in the order-lines table.

The interface layer

User interface: The part of an ICT system that allows the end-user to use the system.

The interface layer is responsible for managing interaction with the user, and is generally referred to as the USER INTERFACE, or sometimes as the **human-computer interface**. User interfaces are typically designed by creating mock-ups of menus and screens.

Menus enable the user to navigate between different elements of the interface.

Screens are normally concerned with data maintenance or data retrieval. Data maintenance screens allow the user to enter new data into the system or amend existing data, and trigger update functions which handle create, update or delete transactions as described above. Data retrieval screens allow the user to extract data from the system, and trigger update functions which handle retrieve transactions.

Figure 1.20 shows a proposed design for a menu and data entry screen associated with the Goronwy Galvanising system. The data entry screen permits the user either to enter a new Jobs record or amend an existing Jobs record.

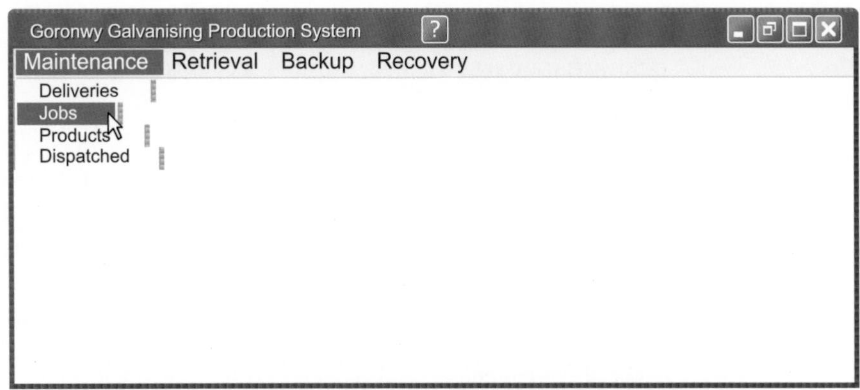

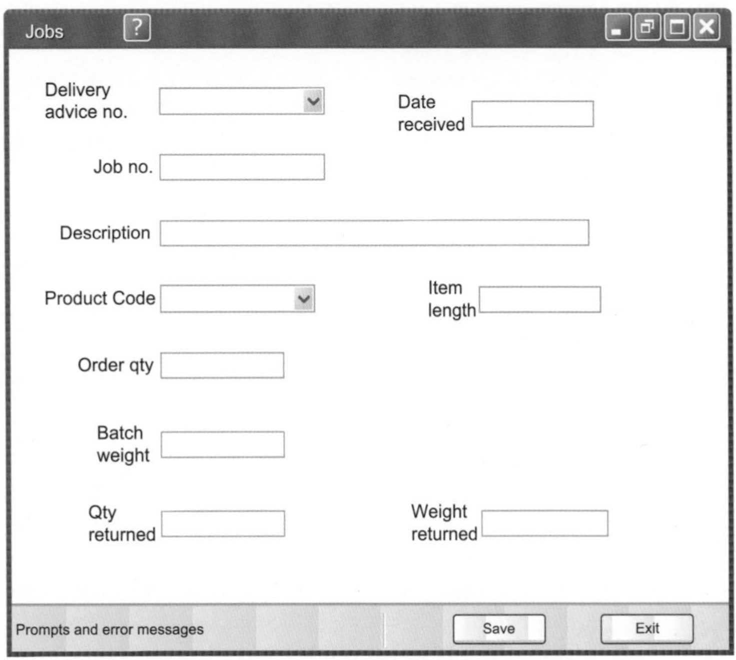

Figure 1.20: *Part of the proposed interface for the Goronwy ICT system*

Systems construction: The part of the development process devoted to constructing systems.

Outsourcing: The strategy in which the whole or part of the informatics service is handed over to an external vendor.

Systems implementation: The part of the development process devoted to delivering the system into its context of use.

The design or system specification acts as a blueprint for SYSTEMS CONSTRUCTION. Once the ICT system has been designed, the systems construction phase can begin. This involves building the three layers of the ICT system (data management, business and interface) using development tools such as programming languages and database management systems (which are discussed in Chapter 9).

Systems construction may be undertaken either by a team internal to the organisation or by an outside contractor (a form of construction known as OUTSOURCING). Many information systems are now also bought in as packages and tailored to organisational requirements. In the case of Goronwy there were no internal technical staff in the organisation and staff could find no external package covering all the desired functionality, so they outsourced construction to an external vendor.

The final phase in the development process is SYSTEMS IMPLEMENTATION. This involves the delivery of the system into its context of use. It can be done in a confident manner by immediately moving from the old to the new system. Alternatively, it can be approached in a cautious way in which the old and new systems are run in parallel for a period to ensure that there is a fallback position. Because Goronwy was new to innovations of this form, it decided to run the manual system in parallel with the new ICT system for two months. At the end of this period it had had no significant problems with the technology, so the plant moved over entirely onto the ICT system.

Operation, use, impact and evaluation

Once an information system is built and implemented it has to be operated and used. The information system will then impact upon its activity system.

Operation

The process of operation not only involves using the ICT system for data entry, retrieval and processing, it also involves enacting procedures to ensure that the system is continuously available as a safe service to use by workers. This means ensuring that security procedures and technologies are in place to protect against unauthorised ACCESS to data. It also means ensuring that both the availability and continuity of the system are assured. Hence, for example, suitable procedures have to be put in place for backing up data and recovering it in the event of system failure.

Access: A precondition for the electronic delivery of services and goods. Stakeholders must have access to remote access devices.

Use and impact

Obviously, once an information system is introduced into an organisation, it begins to be used and to have effects on that organisation. It is important to evaluate closely how it is used and what impact it has, in order to ensure that the objectives for introducing it in the first place are achieved.

Two questions need to be asked:

- **Is the system actually being used?** In reality many systems do not get used; they may be abandoned instead.
- **How is it being used**, and is this in line with what was intended in its original design? If not, is the unintended use positive or negative? For example:
  - A system supporting decision making might also be used as a tool for improving customer relations.
  - A system designed for use by management executives might be used to intimidate subordinates and stifle creativity and innovation.

In order to evaluate impact, we must consider the effect of the information system on individuals, groups and the organisation as a whole (this is examined in greater depth in Chapter 9). For example, it could lead to shifts in the power and influence of certain groups or individuals.

Goronwy tried to minimise the risk associated with the introduction of its new ICT system, but it still led to a number of changes, many of which were unintended. For example, inbound logistics and outbound logistics staff began to assume more responsibility for correct entry of data. The production controller gradually began to assume more of a supervisory role, especially in quality control, and the office clerk did much of the data entry associated with production.

Evaluation

On the surface at least, business organisations invest in information systems for one of three reasons: to do things more efficaciously, to be more efficient or to be more effective. Each type of gain can lead to improved profitability.

Efficacy: A measure of the extent to which a system achieves its intended transformation.

Efficiency: A measure of the extent to which a system achieves its intended transformation with the minimum use of resources.

Effectiveness: A measure of the extent to which the system contributes to the purposes of a higher-level system.

- EFFICACY relates to the core competencies of the organisation. For example, appropriate application of ICT can improve output from those activities that the organisation has to do well.
- EFFICIENCY relates to ways in which ICT can enable better utilisation of resources: for example, increased worker productivity. Efficiency measures relate the inputs to the activity system to its outputs. Hence, improvements in efficiency mean doing the same thing with less resource or doing more with similar resource.
- EFFECTIVENESS in organisational terms means improving the contribution an activity system makes to the organisation as a whole. This normally involves attempts to increase market share or competitiveness (Checkland, 1999).

In order to evaluate the performance of a new information system, a business should assess whether or not the efficiency, efficacy or effectiveness of the business has been enhanced as a result. If it has, the next question is whether this has led to a financial return greater than the initial investment in the system.

When Goronwy introduced its new system, it found staff were identifying much more non-conforming black and white material, because more quality checks could be made both at inbound logistics and after production. This initially caused problems with customers: they were getting more non-conforming material returned to them, and it took more time to return finished goods. However, after a few months customers began to comment favourably: they saw they were getting a better quality of service. Workers seemed to adapt to higher quality control standards, and over time production times started to decrease because there were fewer problems with both inbound and outbound material. Higher levels of customer satisfaction tend to lead to more orders, from the satisfied customers themselves or from their recommendations to others. So in *efficacy* terms, the ICT system seemed to have a good effect. Both satisfaction levels and order levels can be used to measure this effect.

In terms of *efficiency*, smoother throughput led to greater productivity. This enabled the plant to take on more business, and as a result it became the most profitable galvanising operation within the Rito Metals group for two years running. Hence, Goronwy proved itself to be the most *effective* galvanising plant in the group.

eBusiness and eCommerce

The application of informatics to organisational issues in the private sector is known as electronic business (eBusiness) or electronic commerce (eCommerce). The two are not the same.

eBusiness

An eBusiness is a business in which the use of ICT is critical to supporting both its internal value chain and its external value network. The internal **value chain** consists of the series of activity systems by which the organisation delivers a product or service to its customers. The external **value network** consists of the activities, relationships and flows of value between the organisation and actors in its external environment.

For Goronwy, it is possible to show how the introduction of the new ICT system led to the establishment of its parent company, Rito Metals, as an eBusiness. Goronwy's new ICT system continued in operation for a couple of years, then Rito Metals carried out an evaluation. It concluded that the system had improved the plant's performance in a number of ways, as we have seen. Executives at headquarters made a strategic decision to roll out the ICT system to all ten galvanising plants in the group. As well as wanting to improve the information handling at the plants, they wanted to see them using standard activity systems.

This rollout took a further two years to complete, as some plants found it difficult to adapt. When it was complete it became possible to create a management information system (MIS) at headquarters, fed with data from the individual plant ICT systems. To enable this, a dedicated wide-area communication network was created, linking each plant with headquarters.

Now Rito Metals could carry out more effective strategic management of its galvanising plants, because it was able to obtain an accurate and up-to-date picture of operations and problems at particular plants, making them easier to identify and rectify. In this sense, the MIS enabled more effective control of the separate business units.

In developing an integrated ICT and information systems infrastructure, Rito Metals moved in the direction of becoming an eBusiness, because the use of ICT became critical to supporting its internal value chain.

eCommerce

eCommerce means the use of ICT in value chains within the wider value network, such as supply and customer chains :

Supply chain: The chain of activities that an organisation performs in relation to its suppliers.

- The SUPPLY CHAIN consists of activity systems by which an organisation obtains goods and services from other organisations to enable it to conduct its business.

Customer chain: The chain of activities that an organisation performs in the service of its customers.

Access channel: An access device plus an associated communication channel.

Access device: A mechanism used to formulate, transmit, receive and display messages.

Communication channel: The medium along which messages travel.

Stakeholder: The group of people to whom an information system is relevant.

Front-end ICT system: An ICT system that supports a front-end information system.

- The CUSTOMER CHAIN consists of activity systems by which an organisation distributes value to its customers.

The objective of much eCommerce is the redesign of activity systems with ICT to support electronic delivery of products and services. Such joint organisational and technological change typically involves:

- Investigating and implementing various ACCESS CHANNELS for different organisational stakeholders (such as managers and employees concerned with the internal value chain and customers and suppliers in the wider value network). An access channel consists of an ACCESS DEVICE and COMMUNICATION CHANNEL.
- Constructing front-end ICT to manage interaction with STAKEHOLDERS (such as customers and suppliers working in supply and customer chains)
- Re-engineering or constructing back-end ICT.
- Ensuring front-end/back-end ICT systems integration.
- Ensuring secure stored data as well as secure transactions along communication channels.

Back-end systems are those that are used within the organisation, while FRONT-END SYSTEMS are those that it uses to interface with its stakeholders (its customers and suppliers).

Among the commonly used access channels are face-to-face contact and telephone conversations, but channels that use ICT are being introduced more and more in both the public and private sectors. Typical remote access devices are Internet-enabled personal computers (PCs) and a growing range of mobile devices such as personal digital assistants (PDAs). Front-end ICT systems include corporate websites. Using these brings a number of advantages to both the organisation and its external stakeholders: for example, customers can log on to the website to access an organisation's services 24 hours a day, 365 days a year.

Goronwy went down this route in the mid-1990s. It started by introducing hand-held devices for inbound and outbound logistics operatives, linked via a plant wireless communication network. The workers could use the devices to access data from the central system, and update it with information on receipt and dispatch.

Goronwy used the Internet and the web to upgrade its customer chain technology. These are often thought of as the same, but in fact they are distinct:

Internet: A set of interconnected computer networks distributed around the globe.

World Wide Web (WWW): A set of standards for hypermedia documentation. It has now become synonymous with the Internet.

- The INTERNET is a set of interconnected computer networks distributed around the globe.
- The WORLD WIDE WEB (WWW or Web) is an application which runs on top of the Internet. It is basically a set of standards for the representation and distribution of chunks of content (such as text, graphics and images) connected through associative links, known as hyperlinks.

One of the most critical examples of the use of the web in business is of course corporate websites, made up of logical collections of web documents normally stored on a computer system referred to as a web server.

Application: A term generally used as a synonym for an ICT system or another piece of software designed to perform a particular function.

Initially, corporate websites were created primarily as an additional promotional tool, to inform customers about the business and provide them with contact details, but many businesses have since invested to increase their levels of interactivity and therefore their APPLICATIONS. Many companies now provide fully transactional websites through which customers can choose and purchase items, track delivery progress, email queries and so on.

Goronwy initially invested in a limited corporate website which merely promoted its services and provided contact details. It then created a companion website specifically for repeat customers such as Blackwalls, so they could enter details of orders and track their progress from receipt through galvanisation to dispatch.

To enable fully transactional websites, organisations need to update the information dynamically from back-end databases, and to ensure that information entered by stakeholders updates the company information systems effectively. So when a customer inputs delivery details, this information needs to be available to all the other systems that need it. This demands integration and interoperability of front-end and back-end systems within the ICT infrastructure. For Goronwy, the back-end ICT infrastructure managed the data model we described above as well as the business rules, update functions and transactions critical to what we referred to as the business layer.

Database system: A term used to encapsulate the constructs of a data model, DBMS and database.

After ten years of operation, Goronwy decided to upgrade its ICT system onto a new hardware and software base, to make it easier to develop web interfaces and integrate them with a central corporate DATABASE SYSTEM. The system was redesigned and rewritten, and the company also invested to ensure the privacy of electronic data held in the system, and the security of transactions travelling both within Goronwy and between Goronwy and the central ICT systems at Rito Metals. This continual investment in the ICT infrastructure is evidence of its growing value to the performance of the business.

Planning and management

For Goronwy, information systems and ICT infrastructure are central not only for the operation of its individual galvanising plant, but also to the ongoing operation of the Rito Metals group. There is also increasing pressure from the competitive environment: Goronwy, like all organisations, needs to match what its competitors do, and to offer some things they do not, to gain a competitive edge. ICT is central to this.

Informatics planning: The process of defining the optimal informatics architecture for an organisation.

Informatics service: The organisational function devoted to the delivery of informatics services.

This creates a need for effective planning for and management of information, information systems and ICT. We call these collectively the **informatics infrastructure.** This is known as INFORMATICS PLANNING.

All this means, of course, that an organisation needs informatics professionals to provide an INFORMATICS SERVICE, which consists of planning, management, development and operation of information systems. It has the choice of employing people to carry out these functions, or outsourcing them.

Goronwy's choices are dictated in part by the fact that it is one organisation within a larger group. It initiates formal informatics planning and incorporates it into the ongoing development of general business strategy. Rito Metals runs a periodic review of its infrastructure in the light of technological developments. Most recently this process led to the rollout of radio frequency identification (RFID) tagging (see Chapter 8). This enables the company to better integrate its information across supply, internal and customer chains.

Initially, Rito Metals took the strategic decision to employ no informatics professionals. It outsourced all the development of its initial systems, but as it came to use more and more ICT and information systems, top-level management decided the group needed an internal workforce devoted to informatics processes. It still uses some outsourcing, however. Much informatics planning and management is tackled in-house by a group of from 10 to 20 individuals, but most development and operations work is conducted by external vendors. For instance, provision and operation of its communication network has been outsourced for a number of years.

Conclusion and key themes

This book is about the *interaction* of business systems with information and its wider context. Because our focus is on the application of informatics in organisations, there are a number of themes that run through the book. Each of them relates to the issue of value and ICT.

- An information system need not necessarily be computerised. The processes of gathering, processing, storing and distributing information have been undertaken in human societies for many thousands of years. Technologies based around the digital computer are only the latest form of information and communication technology (ICT).
- Organisational informatics is concerned with information in general, as well as information systems and ICT in particular. It is important to understand what information is, and how it is related to effective decision making and human action.
- We cannot properly understand information and an information system without understanding the context. This operates at several different levels: the organisation or part of an organisation that uses the systems; markets, societies and economies (for instance, with systems making up a national financial infrastructure); and more recently focus has shifted to the global scale, particularly for information systems such as the web.
- An information system must fit its context: the organisation, its strategy, its processes

and its environment. Information systems that do not fit are likely to be resisted, under-used, misused, sabotaged and unprofitable. They are likely to have negative effects on organisational performance.

- The 'value' of ICT in a given organisation relates to ICT's place within its information systems, and the way in which these information systems impact on the organisation, enabling it to remain viable and sustainable.

The next three chapters consider the fundamental bedrock of the issue of value. In Chapter 2 we consider the organisation as a value-creating system. This leads us to consider the place of information in support of value-creation and value-adding activity in Chapter 3. The concepts of system and information are then brought together in our consideration of the place of information systems in organisations, and the role of ICT in those systems, in Chapter 4.

Focus on Value

The concept of value is a common thread which ties together the range of topics considered in this book. The *Oxford English Dictionary* defines value as *the importance or usefulness of something*. Here we are concerned with the value of ICT to organisations. We can only understand it if we consider the layered contexts within which ICT is used and applied.

There is key value in organisational informatics as an academic field of study and an area of organisational practice. In an academic field of study, much new knowledge emerges at the boundaries between established disciplines. Organisational informatics is interdisciplinary in its interest in the interaction between organisational or business systems of many forms. Much current organisational experience relies on the interaction between these systems, so knowledge of organisational informatics is particularly important for the business practitioner in helping to understand and control their performance.

References

Bell, D. (1972) *The Coming of Post-Industrial Society*. Reading, Mass., Addison-Wesley.

Burnham, D. (1983) *The Rise of the Computer State*. New York, Random House.

Castells, M. (1996) *The Rise of the Network Society*. Mass., Blackwell.

Checkland, P. (1999) *Soft Systems Methodology: A thirty year retrospective*. Chichester, John Wiley.

Drucker, P. F. (1994) 'The theory of the business', *Harvard Business Review* **72**(5): 95–104.

Keen, P. G. W. (1980) 'Reference disciplines and a cumulative IS tradition.' International Conference on Information Systems.

Statistical Indicators Benchmarking the Information Society (SIBIS) (2003) Telecommunication and Access. SIBIS.

Silver, M. S., Markus, M. L. and Beath, C. M. (1995) 'The information technology interaction model: a foundation for the MBA core course', *MIS Quarterly* **19**(3): 361–90.

PART I

KEY CONCEPTS

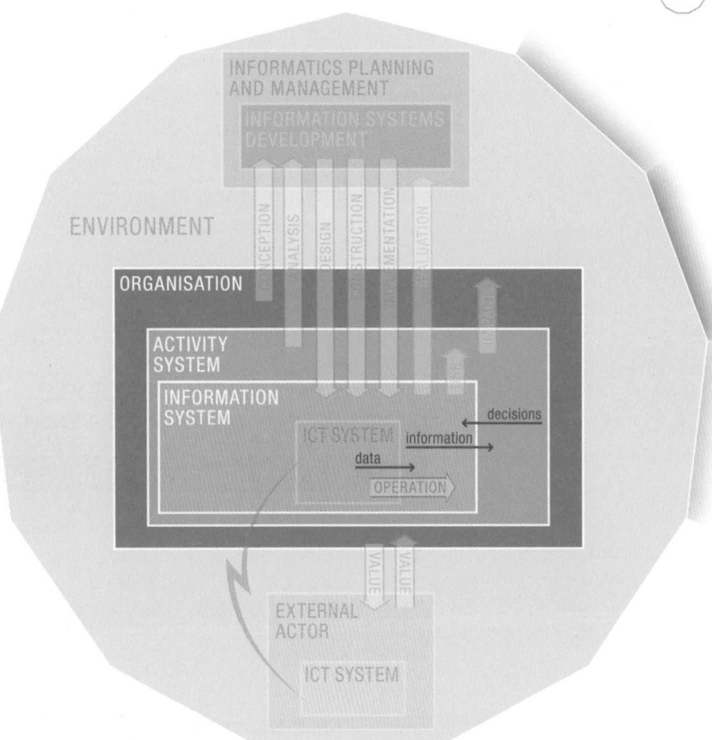

OVERVIEW

The chapters in this part cover the following key areas:

Information
Systems
Human activity systems
Information systems
Business information systems
Management and decision making
Modelling activity systems, information and information systems
Informatics infrastructure

This part examines some of the fundamental or foundation concepts of the discipline of information systems or organisational informatics.

Chapter 2 considers what organisations actually are. It looks first to organisation theory for a number of perspectives on organisations. It then uses elements of **systems thinking** to distinguish between three forms of system of interest to organisational informatics: human activity systems, information systems and ICT systems. The focus of this chapter is on human activity systems. It considers the importance of modelling them in various ways, and introduces the ideas of process modelling and process design as practical approaches of engaging with organisations. It also considers the influence of informatics on issues of organisational structure and culture.

Chapter 3 discusses **information**, a concept which is not well covered in other texts. It is covered in some depth, and considered from the perspective of semiotics, which helps to understand its multi-faceted nature. This approach makes it possible to make clear connections between information, data and knowledge, as well as decision making and action. The chapter also considers the importance of modelling data, information and knowledge, and examines some approaches in this area.

In **Chapter 4** the two concepts of information and system come together in discussing the concept of an **information system**. The chapter describes the critical importance of information systems to activity systems throughout history. This leads to a consideration of some generic information systems underlying business activity, which form what we refer to as the back-end information systems infrastructure of many modem commercial organisations. Around this core a number of front-end information systems interface with major internal and external stakeholders: managers, employees, customers and suppliers.

CHAPTER 2

Organisations and systems

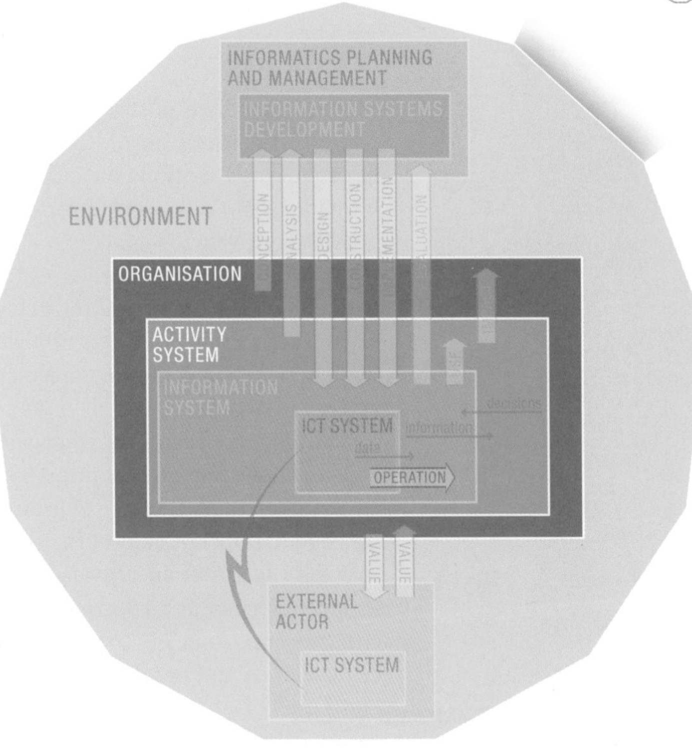

Observe how system into system runs,
What other planets circle other suns.

Alexander Pope (1688–1744),
An Essay on Man (1733), Epistle 1.

CHAPTER OUTLINE

LEARNING OUTCOMES	PRINCIPLES
Understand the fundamental elements of all systems.	The concept of system is fundamental to the three types of systems considered in this work: activity systems, information systems and ICT systems.
Explain the idea of the organisation as a value-creating system.	An organisation can be considered as an open system interacting with a wider value network that makes up its environment.
Discuss the place of control in the regulation and adaptation of systems.	Control is essential both to the internal regulation of systems such as organisations, and to the ways in which organisations adapt to changes in their external environment.
Explain the importance of modelling to informatics work and construct a simple rich picture, root definition, activity system model and process model.	Modelling is important to help managers understand their organisations while providing tools for intervening in organisations. Four types of model relevant to considering the organisation as a system are introduced.

Introduction

In the immediate post-war period William H. Whyte published an influential book, *The Organization Man* (1956). Its central theme was the rise of the modern organisation and the effects of organisations on individuals, particularly in the United States. It chronicled how individuals not only worked for organisations but in many ways *belonged* to organisations.

Although Whyte's analysis is still controversial today, it is undoubtedly true that organisations dominate the modern world. People worldwide spend a substantial proportion of their lives either working in or interacting with organisations. Much of modern-day life is therefore organisational life. This explains why, in organisational informatics, we are interested in the ways in which information and communication technology (ICT) is used to support human activity in organisations.

This chapter examines what we mean by an organisation. In the following chapters we consider how information, information systems and ICT are relevant to shaping organisations.

To understand the place of information, information systems and ICT in the modern world we need to look critically at the concept of organisation. For instance, it has become accepted that the success of an organisation is dependent on its information systems, since they can support efficient and effective human activity. The development of information systems also typically contributes in important ways to changes in human activity in organisations. Modern societies and economies therefore rely on information systems to perform effectively. For these reasons, understanding the nature of organisations is critical for understanding the nature of informatics.

The proper place to start is with the theory of organisations. Unfortunately, there is not just one theory; there is a series of useful viewpoints, each offering a partial insight. In this chapter, we consider these insights by contrasting two perspectives on the organisation: top-down and bottom-up. The top-down perspective emphasises how organisations are institutions that constrain human activity. The bottom-up perspective emphasises how organisations are built out of individuals who decide and act.

It is possible to integrate aspects of the top-down and bottom-up perspectives into a view of the organisation as a complex adaptive system. This leads us to define an organisation as a social arrangement which pursues collective goals, which controls its own performance, and which has a boundary separating it from its environment. This conception of both the unit and the process of organisation is important because it allows us to define clearly, and to relate, issues of activity, information and technology.

The major part of this chapter explains a number of the core concepts underlying **systems thinking**, or systemics. We show how these concepts allow us to relate to each other many of the issues critical to management in the modern organisation, including strategy, control, performance and change.

The word 'organisation' derives from the Greek word *organon*, meaning a tool. This is useful because it suggests the value of treating organisations as tools for action. A systems view of organisations is important because it suggests practical ways of analysing the dynamics of existing organisations, and of designing new organisational forms. So we consider throughout the chapter approaches for modelling aspects of organisations within the processes of both analysis and design.

Organisation theory

Institutional perspective: The perspective on organisations that treats them as wholes or units.

Action perspective: The perspective on organisations that focuses on the process of organising.

Generally speaking there are two major ways to consider an organisation. One looks at them from the top down, as institutions with their own particular characteristics and behaviour. This is known as the INSTITUTIONAL PERSPECTIVE on organisations. The other sees an organisation in a bottom-up fashion, as formed from the everyday engagement of people in the process of organising joint action. This is known as the ACTION PERSPECTIVE on organisations.

Each perspective acts as an umbrella for a series of metaphors for understanding organisations (Morgan, 1986). Each metaphor serves to highlight a particular feature of organisations and organisational life.

The institutional perspective

Organisations are social collectives, but not all social collectives are organisations. In organisations, formal procedures are used for coordinating the activities of members in pursuit of joint objectives.

The institutional perspective (Durkheim, 1936) views organisations as entities which exist independently of the humans belonging to them. Human actions are directed or constrained by these larger social structures. Institutions have a life over and above the life of their members. In this sense they are objective structures, and can be studied by looking at their representative patterns or features.

In essence, the institutional perspective focuses on the **unit** of organisation, and is interested in the features of organisations as wholes. Four main metaphors have been applied to organisations which fall broadly within the institutional perspective: structure, system, environment and information processor.

The most common metaphor sees organisations as **structures** which are divided into parts, or functional departments. Each department is characterised by a pattern of precisely defined roles. Roles are organised in a clear hierarchical fashion, with designated lines of authority from superior to subordinate. This hierarchical structure is so well formalised that it can be captured in an **organisational chart** or organogram. We consider the issue of organisation structure in more detail later.

Scientific management: An approach to management thinking created by Frederick Taylor.

This classic structural account of organisations is related to the SCIENTIFIC MANAGEMENT movement popularised by Frederick Taylor in the United States in the early years of the twentieth century (Taylor, 1911). Scientific management is founded on three principles:

- Managers should be given total responsibility for the organisation of work; workers should concentrate on manual tasks. A 'thinking' department of managers should be set up to be responsible for task planning and design.
- All work tasks should be examined and if necessary redesigned to improve efficiency. If we take a task and look at the approach adopted, the tools used and the fatigue it generates, we can draw up an optimum procedure for it.
- Workers should be selected, trained and monitored methodically, to ensure that their work is done efficiently.

Taylor was particularly interested in analysing the performance of manual tasks such as shifting coal from a railway truck to a factory coal store. He experimented with different numbers of men and different ways of doing the job, and this enabled him to work out what was the optimal system, in terms of labour used and time spent.

Underlying this approach is the assumption that people in organisations act in a rational way that can be closely defined and designed. This model of work is clearly associated with that type of organisation known as a **bureaucracy** (Weber, 1946). In a bureaucracy roles are precisely defined, tasks are explicitly documented and control of work is exercised in a strict hierarchical fashion.

Did you know?

The work of Frederick Taylor had a great influence on Henry Ford's design of mass assembly lines for manufacturing automobiles. It was caricatured in the film *Modern Times*, directed by Charlie Chaplin.

Chapter 1 introduced the concept of an organisation as an **open system**: a unit which takes resources from its environment and processes them to create products or services which it supplies back to its environment. The resources provided by the environment can be categorized into **capital** (which includes both money, and the equipment and so on that money can buy) and **labour**.

The concept of an open system implies that an organisation works within an environment, and that the interaction between an organisation and its environment is one of mutual influence. In other words, the organisation's activities can influence its environment, and the environment can influence the organisation, and particularly its form. Pioneering work by Burns and Stalker (1961) established a link between the stability of the external environment and the shape of an organisation. Generally speaking, they found that organisations whose environment was subject to rapid change were more likely to be what they called **organic organisations**. In contrast, when the external environment was relatively stable for extended periods, what they called **mechanistic** organisations were most likely to be found.

The mechanistic organisation has many similarities with the bureaucratic form of organisation discussed above. In organic forms of organisation, roles are less formally defined and the structure tends to be less hierarchical. In effect Burns and Stalker were putting forward an evolutionary model of organisational change, in which organisations adapt their form to meet changes in their environment. We consider the organisation and its environment in more depth in Chapter 7.

The metaphor of the organisation as an **information processor** arose primarily during and immediately after the Second World War, when the electronic computer was invented. In the late 1940s and the 1950s there was much talk of the computer as a kind of electronic brain. It was a short step from an analogy between a brain and a computer, to an analogy between an organisation and a computer.

Satisficing: The term used by Herbert Simon to describe the characteristics of human decision making that is adequate rather than idealised.

Herbert Simon's work is a notable example of the information-processing viewpoint. It looked particularly at decision making in organisations (Simon, 1976). Effective decision making by managers is clearly critical to organisational success. However, Simon argued that human decision making was not rational, it was SATISFICING. For a rational decision to be made two conditions must be satisfied: the decision maker needs to have all the information relevant to a problem, and needs to be able to process all of it. Simon argued that in most practical organisational situations these conditions cannot be satisfied. People do not have all the relevant information, and they probably could not consider it all if they did. A satisficing decision is one that considers enough information for the decision about a particular problem to be satisfactory. We consider the relationship between information and decision making in more detail in Chapter 3.

Case check:
Case 20, Tesco plc

Tesco plc is an international grocery and general merchandising retail organisation. From an institutional perspective, Tesco can be seen as a large multinational company, retailing goods, offering services and competing in a number of markets. Other aspects of interest are the strategy of the organisation and ways of designing its activities to improve its performance, in areas such as its supermarket operations. This would lead us to examine the place of information in support of activities such as deciding which products to stock, in which stores and at what times.

The action perspective

In contrast to the institutional perspective, the action perspective (Silverman, 1982) maintains that social institutions are fundamentally constructed by actions performed by human beings. In other words, they do not exist independently of the people who belong to them. So organisational reality is subjective: that is, it is different for each individual. The only valid way of studying organisational reality is through the interpretation of human action.

In a sense, the action perspective focuses on the **process** of organising rather than the **unit** of organisation. The critical interest is in how humans generate structures of coordination and cooperation in work. As such, this perspective is interested in how organisations are formed and recreated through the interaction of their component parts. Three main metaphors have been used under the umbrella of an action perspective on organisations: networks, productions and constructions.

Reflect
Consider an organisation known to you. In what way can it be considered an institution? Does an organogram (organisation chart) exist for it?
Would you regard it as a mechanistic or organic form of organisation?

During the 1930s in the United States, partly as a reaction to Taylorism, a number of social psychologists conducted experimental research at the Hawthorne Electric company, Their initial interest in what are now known as the Hawthorne experiments was in what later became known as ergonomics – the effect of work environment on worker performance. Not surprisingly, the experimenters found that when they changed such things as lighting conditions or decor in the factory, this had a positive effect on worker productivity (Mayo, 1933). When they looked in more detail, they found that informal **networks** of interaction between people in the workplace had an impact on the relationship between environmental changes and productivity increases. These were shown to be important in supplying support

Reflect
Think of an organisation you are a member of (not necessarily a work organisation), and reflect on how important social networks are to your experience of organisational life. To what degree is what you do dependent on tacit knowledge (in other words knowledge that is not written down anywhere, but which you have had to acquire informally in your time with the organisation)?

and context for people's work. We consider the issue of social networks and the value they generate for members more closely in Chapter 5.

This research led to a number of changes to managerial practice which are still evident today in many modern organisations. One of the most significant was the emphasis on team working in work situations such as those found in manufacturing plants. The work also influenced the movement in sociotechnical design – the idea that the design of technical systems should occur in parallel with the design of social systems. This philosophy is critical to our approach to information systems development discussed in Chapter 12.

During the 1970s studies of organisations shifted to the micro level. Researchers became interested in the question of how people in work produce organisational life. Some of the most significant research in this area was conducted by Erving Goffman (1990). His work particularly focused on the importance of work to an individual's identity. He also studied the importance of particular ideologies to the organisation of work. This focus on the process of organising emphasises the ways in which individuals in social situations account for their behaviour to others. So-called 'accounting' devices are essential in organisational work to enable organisational actors to effectively coordinate their activity. The concept of an information system (as discussed in Chapter 4) can be seen as a system supporting the communication of this 'accounting' between individuals in a system of activity.

Tacit knowledge: Knowledge accessible only with difficulty through elicitation techniques.

Garfinkel's work (1967) focuses on the related issue of the 'methods' individuals use in constructing their work, and the way they reason about it. His **ethnomethodology** is particularly useful as a way of emphasising the richness of organisational work and the importance of TACIT KNOWLEDGE to work. Tacit knowledge is the name given by Michael Polanyi (1962) to the ability of human beings to perform tasks without being able to describe how they do them. Garfinkel appeared to be thinking mainly of the way in which people orient their own work to that of the people working alongside them. It is important to understand the role of this type of tacit knowledge in order to design information systems effectively (see also Chapter 12).

Case check: Case 20, Tesco plc

Looking at Tesco from an action perspective, we would be interested in how its employees perform their work. How, for instance, do they operate checkouts, stock shelves and receive goods into the supermarket? We would look not only at any written instructions, but at what people do in practice, even though it is not formally spelled out to them: that is, their tacit knowledge. How do they acquire this knowledge, and how do they communicate it to others? And how do they account for their activity to others?

Structuration

For much of its history, organisation theory, like other social-science disciplines, acted as if the institutional and action perspectives were mutually exclusive. People took one position or the other, and used it to orient their research. In practice, of course, they are both legitimate and valid positions. We all act and interact with fellow human beings within organisations, and appreciate the fluidity of organisational life. We all also experience the monolithic nature of organisations, and the constraints imposed on our actions by these institutional structures.

Did you know?
The word *bureaucracy* stems from the word *bureau*, used from the early eighteenth century in Western Europe to refer not just to a writing desk, but to an office: that is, a workplace, where officials worked.

Structuration: The process by which human action both produces and reproduces social structure, and also how social structure both informs and constrains human action.

Structuration theory was created by the sociologist Anthony Giddens (Walsham and Han, 1991) as an attempt to reconcile the action and institutional perspectives. Structuration theory speaks of the 'duality of structure'. On the one hand, the structure of social institutions is created by human action and is only evident in human action. Through human interaction, social structures are reproduced but may also change. On the other hand, human action is constrained by the way in which humans utilise institutional structure as a resource in interpreting their own and other people's actions. This cyclical process Giddens calls the process of structuration.

Figure 2.1 illustrates this process. Social structure both informs and constrains human action. In turn, human action both produces and reproduces social structure.

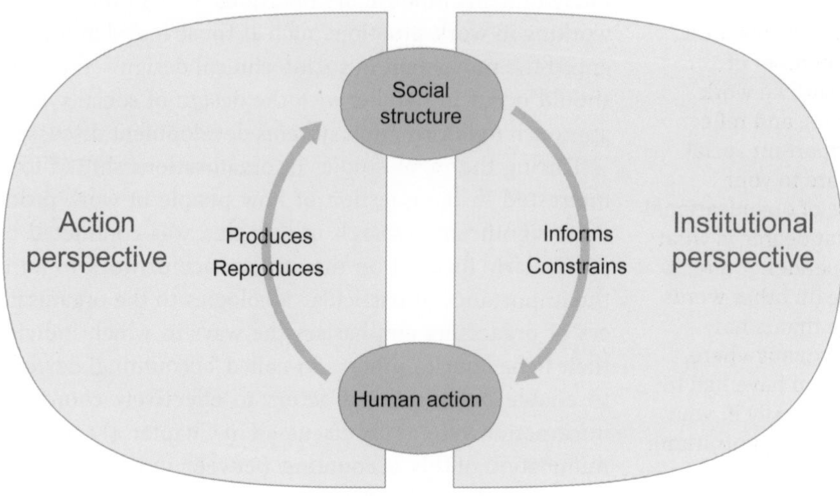

Figure 2.1: *The process of structuration*

The example of human natural languages illustrates the importance of this duality. There is an analogy between English. for example, and the features of organisations we have discussed. A necessary precondition for conversation (or speech acts) is that people have a common language. We can talk about the language without talking about specific conversations: for instance, discussing its vocabulary, grammar and syntax (see also Chapter 3). In this sense English has an existence independent of the people who speak or write it. However, spoken language is only really evident in actual speech acts. People use language as a resource for communication, they produce and re-produce it through speech acts. Over time speech acts change the structure of a language. New vocabulary, grammar and syntax evolve. For example, the English in Shakespearean plays is recognisably the same language, but many of the words Shakespeare used have fallen out of favour today, and many other words have different meanings in the modern context.

Reflect
Again, think about an organisation you have joined. Reflect on your experience of entering this new organisational setting. How long did it take you to understand how things were done there? How did you acquire this knowledge? In the time that you have been a member, have its practices and expectations changed? If so, how and why?

There is a similarity between the notion of structuration, and the technique of considering organisations as complex adaptive systems (Stacey, 2003). Although the system perspective used to be seen as a top-down, institutional perspective (looking at the organisation as a whole and the ways it regulates itself), more recently systems theorists have become interested in how organisation occurs through the complex interaction of multiple individuals. This bottom-up perspective offers useful insight into how organisations adapt and change.

A systemic conception of organisations is therefore useful in a number of ways (Jackson, 2003). First, it has clear ways of addressing some classic concerns of organisation theory discussed above, such as decision making, coordinated action and information processing. Second, the conceptual tools of systemics offer managers practical ways of engaging with or intervening in organisations for which they are responsible: not only so they can ensure operational effectiveness, but also to understand environmental uncertainty, plan strategy and manage change.

Recap 

There are two major perspectives on organisational life, the institutional perspective and the action perspective. The institutional perspective considers organisations as units which constrain or structure people's behaviour. It emphasises features such as relationships of control, systems of activity, processes of information flow, and interactions with the environment. The action perspective considers organisations as arising out of human interaction. It emphasises informal networks of organisational members producing behaviour and using established methods for accounting for this behaviour to others.

Systemics

We are surrounded by things we call systems. We see our bodies as made up of systems, such as a digestive system and a central nervous system. We live on a planet that is part of the solar system. We engage with people in groups which form social, political and economic systems. We are educated in the use of number systems. Organisations would collapse without information systems.

At first sight these varied systems appear to have little in common. However, on closer examination we can see that all these examples are collections of things that are interrelated through defined relationships. Systems theory, systems thinking, or as we prefer to call it, **systemics**, is the attempt to study the generic features of all systems.

The next section summarises the conceptual framework underlying the discipline of systemics. This is sometimes known as a **formal systems model** (Checkland, 1999; Wilson, 1990). Here, we refer to it as the fundamental 'language' of systemics, in the sense that it provides a set of terms denoting concepts that comprise the base elements of systems. Like any language, these core systemic concepts can be used to produce representations of 'reality', so they enable us to debate the nature of reality (Fortune and Peters, 2005).

Principles of systems thinking are evident in the work of the ancient Greek philosopher Aristotle and the German philosopher Hegel (Wright, 1989). They include:

- The whole is more than the sum of its parts.
- The whole determines the nature of the parts.
- The parts cannot be understood in isolation from the whole.
- The parts are dynamically interrelated and interdependent.

You should be able to see the parallels between this set of principles, and the ideas we have just discussed, of a social structure (the whole) informing and constraining human action (the parts), while human action in turn produces and reproduces social structure.

Holistic thinking: Thinking about the properties of whole systems rather than their parts.

Elementary systems thinking emerged in the work of the Gestalt psychologists, a collection of psychologists who emphasised the study of the mind as a whole unit, rather than as a collection of psychological aspects. This approach they described as HOLISTIC THINKING (Ellis, 1938). Their key argument was that living organisms do not perceive things in terms of isolated elements but in terms of meaningful, organised wholes, which exhibit qualities that are not present in the parts themselves.

General systems theory: An endeavour which attempted to study the properties and behaviour of all systems.

However, the idea of using the concept of a system to understand phenomena is normally attributed to work in the 1930s conducted by Ludwig von Bertalanffy, a German biologist. He gave the name GENERAL SYSTEMS THEORY to a discipline devoted to formulating principles that apply to all systems (Bertalanffy, 1951). Following Bertalanffy's pioneering work, systems thinking began to be applied to numerous fields, leading eventually to the creation of the Society for General Systems Research, a group including Bertalanffy, Rapaport, Boulding and Gerard. Systems theory also developed within the work of the cybernetics group which ran the Macy group of conferences between 1946 and 1953. Regular members of the group included the eminent scholars Bateson, Lazarsfeld, Lewin, McCulloch, Mead, von Neumann and Wiener. Invited members included Ashby and Shannon (Heims, 1991). Boulding's work (1956) in particular highlighted certain phenomena that were present in many disciplines, such as populations, individuals in environments, growth, information and communication. This established some of the fundamental principles of what became known as general systems theory.

Did you know? John von Neumann, a member of the cybernetics group, is seen as one of the founding fathers of computer science.

Systems ideas had a significant impact in the field of organisational and management science (Churchman, Ackoff and Arnoff, 1957; Emery and Trist, 1960; Katz and Kahn, 1966; Maurer, 1971). Much of the thrust for contemporary information systems derives from adaptation of the application of the systems idea to thinking about organisations.

The relevance of the concept of systems received a boost during the 1970s and 1980s, with the interest generated in the mathematical concepts of chaos and complexity (Gleick, 1997). **Complexity theory**, as it became known, is interested in the ways in which complex systems evolve and are organised. One of the most interesting applications of systems thinking is the concept of the earth as a complex dynamic system. This Gaia hypothesis (Lovelock, 2000) is now taken seriously in considerations of global issues such as climate change.

So the systems concept is widely used in a variety of contexts, but what actually underlies a systemic approach to things? Two key principles are significant, **holism** and **emergence**.

Aristotle first said that *the whole is more than the sum of its parts*, and this implies that it is important to investigate and understand complex phenomena holistically: that is, as a whole, not by reducing them to components. This latter is known as the **scientific method**, and early ideas in systemics can be seen as a reaction against the reductionism inherent in it. Capra (1996) argues that it is part of the ancient dichotomy between substance (matter, structure, quantity) and form (pattern, order, quality).

Reductionism is the conventional approach to scientific investigation. It involves dissecting a problem into its smallest parts, attempting to understand the workings of parts, and building up a conception of the whole from this understanding. It was extremely successful in developing natural scientific understanding. However, a major criticism is that a reductionist approach frequently fails to provide an adequate understanding of the whole from the interaction of parts. To use a cliché, reductionists tend not to see the forest for the trees.

In contrast, holism takes the whole as the primary focus of investigation. It is interested in studying how the complex interaction of parts creates and sustains the identity and behaviour of the whole. It is also interested in how the behaviour of the system emerges from the interactions among system parts (Johnson, 2002). A system is a complex entity which has properties that do not belong to any of its constituent parts, but emerge from the relationships or interaction of its constituent parts. Again, the whole is more than the sum of its parts.

Systems

Object: A real world thing which can be uniquely identified. A package of data and procedures.

The term **system** has a Greek origin. The word *systema* derives from *syn*, meaning together, and *histemi*, meaning to set. In very broad terms a system may be defined as a set of OBJECTS and a set of relations. This embodies the idea of a network in which objects relate to and potentially influence other objects (Capra, 1996).

For example, Figure 2.2 shows a set of six different things labelled A–F (Beer, 1966). As a set of dissimilar things they constitute a collection but not a system. Now suppose we represent each thing as a node in a network and indicate relations between these things with arrows as in Figure 2.2. In this figure, arrows are drawn in both directions between any two nodes to indicate that relation A → B is different from B → A. Suppose also that each relation is effectively a 'switch' that can be turned on or off, perhaps indicating the effect of one node in the network on another. Here we have a simple system, since the collection of things now interacts; it operates or behaves.

Reflect
Consider how often you use the term 'system' in everyday life to describe things. For instance, when people refer to a systemic failure in some aspect of life, what do they actually mean? Are they using the word appropriately?

Our very general definition of a system clearly encompasses a vast array of phenomena. For a certain interesting class of systems (open systems) on which we shall focus, a popular way is to specify certain types of objects and relations as of interest. Systems of this type are generally portrayed in terms of an input–process–output model, in which the system exists in a given environment.

In this view, systems can be seen as being composed of:

- one or more operational processes or mechanisms of transformation
- one or more sets of inputs and outputs from agents in the environment
- one or more control processes.

The relationship between these elements is illustrated in Figure 2.3. Next. we discuss the meaning and application of these elements.

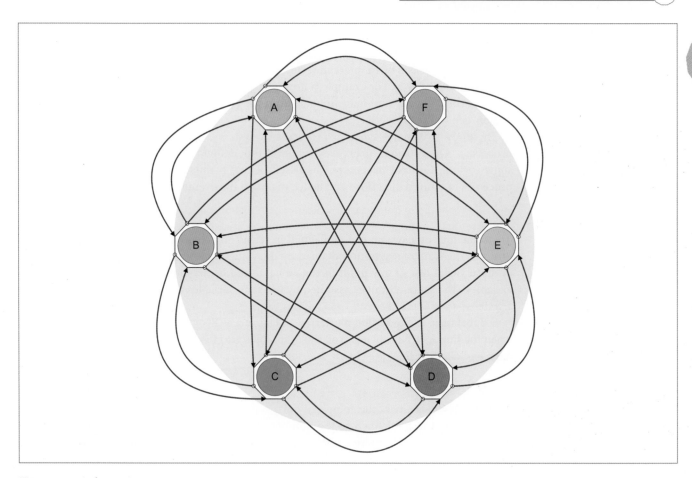

Figure 2.2: *A dynamic system*
Source: after Beer (1966).

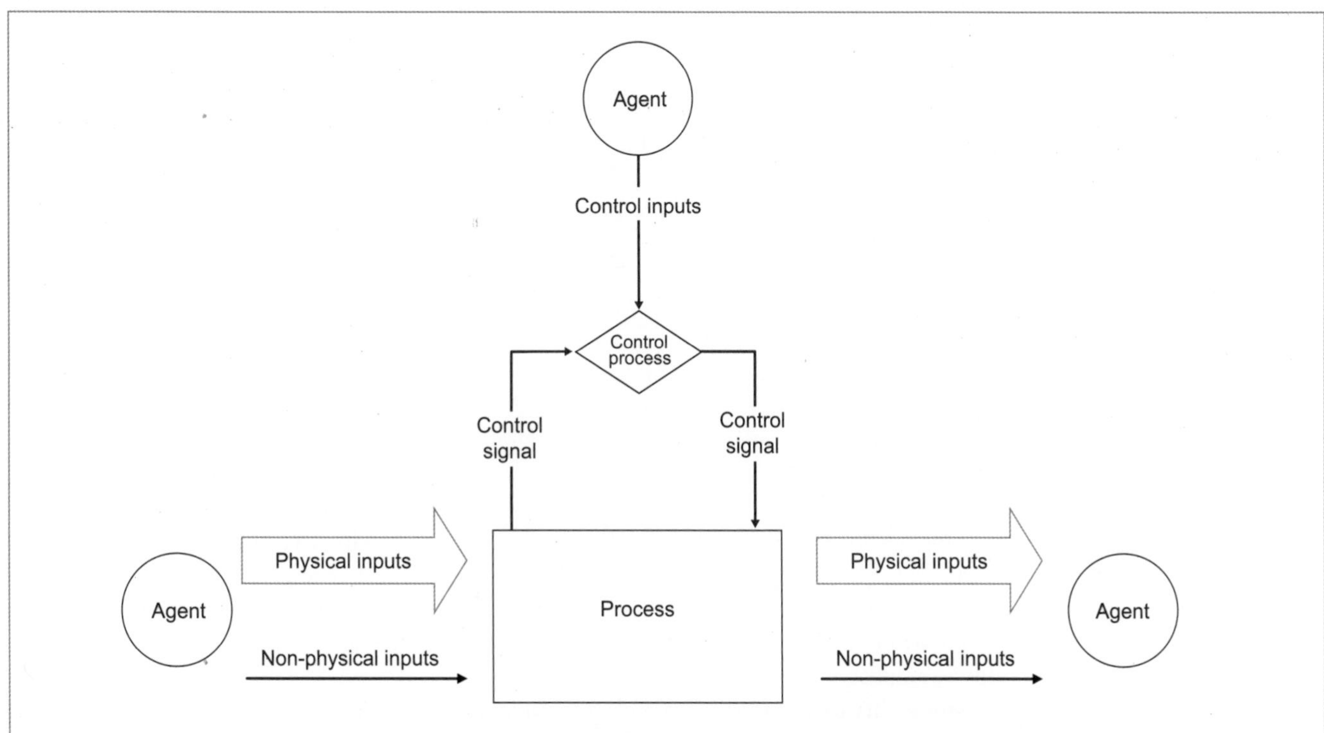

Figure 2.3: *System elements*

Process

Processes represent the dynamic elements of systems. A process is a mechanism of transformation. It consists of an interconnected set of actions (behaviour) necessary to transform input(s) into output(s). For example, a flower can be conceived of as a system that transforms water, carbon dioxide and light (inputs) from the physical environment into carbohydrates and oxygen (outputs).

There are two major types of processes in systems, operational processes and control processes. **Operational processes** achieve the defined purpose or transformation of some system. **Control processes** (discussed below) maintain the behaviour of operational processes in desired directions and hence maintain the overall identity of the system.

State

State: The state of a system is defined by the values appropriate to the systems' attributes or state variables.

The behaviour of a system can be defined in terms of its STATE, or more precisely changes of state. The state of a system is defined by the values appropriate to the system's attributes, or **state variables**. At any point in time a value can be assigned to each of a system's state variables. The set of all values assumed by the state variables of a system at one time defines a system's state.

For instance, in the system illustrated in Figure 2.2 (Beer, 1966), one state of the system is when the line A → B is open and all the other lines are closed. Another state is when B → C is open and all other lines are closed, and so on.

Variety

Variety: A measure of the complexity of a system; the number of states a system can assume.

VARIETY is a measure of the complexity of a system (Beer, 1972). Using the idea of a system's states, variety can be defined as the number of possible states of a system. Since there are two possible relations between each of the six nodes in the network in Figure 2.2, it can be shown that there are $n(n-1)$ possible relations between nodes, which is 30 possible relations. If each line on the figure can take two possible states, then there are over 2^{30} possible states for the entire system. This is a measure of the variety inherent in this simple system. For many systems, particularly those involving human activity, the variety of the system may be incomprehensibly large, in the sense that the number of possible states may not be precisely countable.

Subsystems

Hierarchy seems to be an inherent property of most systems. In viewing systems we frequently use a recursive lens. In other words, we can view a system on various levels, each level of which can be conceptualised in terms of a system. Hence, the environment of a system may be viewed as a system in its own right, a process that is part of one system may be treated as a system in its turn, and so on. Therefore in Figure 2.4 system S can be resolved into two SUBSYSTEMS S1 and S2. In turn, system S2 can be resolved into subsystems S2.1 and S2.2.

Subsystem: A coherent part of a system.

For example, an automobile can be viewed as composed of subsystems such as an electrical subsystem and a transmission subsystem. In medicine, the human body is typically seen as consisting of a number of subsystems such as the nervous system, the circulatory system and the digestive system. The operation and interaction of such subsystems contribute to the 'health' of the individual.

In the 1960s, Arthur Koestler (1967) proposed the term **holon** (which has the same root as holistic) to describe an identifiable part of a system, which is made up of subordinate parts and is in turn part of a larger whole. The hierarchical arrangement of holons has also been referred to as holarchy. The strength of holarchy is that it enables the construction of highly complex systems, highly resilient to disturbance and adaptable to changes in the environment.

This ability to consider a system at a number of levels is critical to avoiding cognitive overload on the part of the observer of a system. In other words, the observer does not need to understand all of the system at one time; they can focus on the operation of one particular subsystem. It is sometimes useful to think of organisational systems such as activity systems as containers for processes, which in turn are containers for activities, which in turn are containers for tasks.

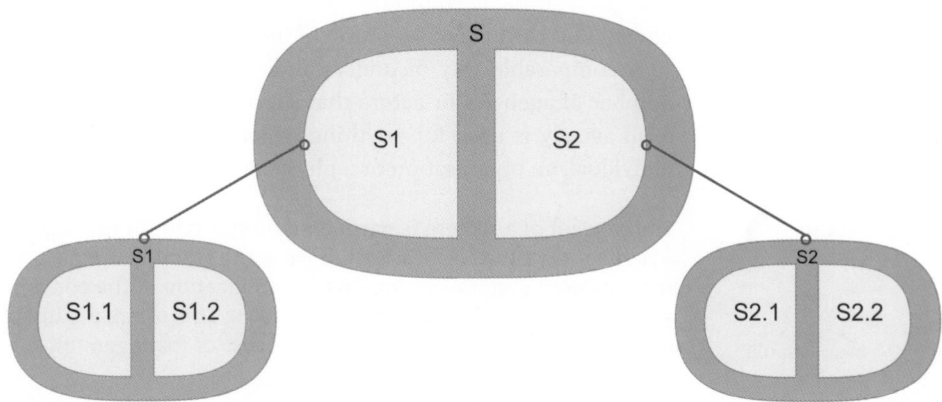

Figure 2.4: *Resolving a system hierarchy*

Within a complex organism such as a human, a single cell can be conceived of as a holon. It comprises more basic units such as plasma and nucleus, while at the same time it forms part of a larger unit of organisation such as muscle tissue. A nuclear family unit can also be conceived as a holon. It comprises more basic units such as parents and siblings, while at the same time it forms part of a larger unit of organisation such as the extended family or a community.

Inputs and outputs

The **inputs** to a system are the resources it gains from agents in its environment, some of which may be other systems. The **outputs** from a system are those things that it supplies back to agents in its environment.

The idea of a system interacting with its environment was originally given precise formulation in thermodynamics. In this view a system exchanges flows of energy with its environment. Since all matter can be described in terms of some energy equivalent, it is possible to consider the inputs and outputs from a system as consisting of two types of flow, physical and nonphysical flows. Physical flows consist of the flow of physical or material things to and from the environment, such as plant, machinery and foodstuffs. Accompanying the flow of physical material there will be a flow of information. Information is used to describe what is currently happening in a system, what has happened in the past or what is likely to happen in the future. Hence, in a manufacturing organisation data will record the flow of resources such as raw materials used by the organisation or goods distributed to customers.

Environment

Defining a system means deciding what is to be included in it and what in its environment. This means defining a boundary for the system. It means drawing the figure (the system) against its ground (the environment).

The decision on what to include in a system and what to exclude is one for the system modeller. A system is a key 'tool for thought' (Waddington, 1977), and systemic thinking is necessarily a process of abstraction – a process of resolution of what is environment, system and subsystem.

For example, if we consider an organisation as a system, we might define its boundary in terms of activities performed by its members. We might decide that the activities of its customers and suppliers do not form part of the system, but are part of the system's environment.

It is frequently useful to consider a system, particularly a complex system, as a **black box**. This is a concept from a branch of systemics known as **cybernetics** (see below), and is defined as a box to which inputs are observed to enter and from which outputs are seen to emerge. Nothing need be known about the internal operation of the box. Its behaviour can be understood through observation of the relationship between its inputs and outputs.

Agent: Something (usually a person, group, department or organisation but possibly some other information system) that is a net originator or receiver of system data.

A comparable way of understanding or representing the environment is in terms of a number of agencies or actors that supply inputs to a system or receive outputs from it. The term agency is used for anything which interacts with a system. The AGENT might be an individual, an organisation or a physical or technological system such as an ICT system.

Recap

The concept of a system is particularly important for managers because of the way it integrates a number of critical issues. Systemics is the study of the nature of systems. Organisational or management systemics concerns the application of the concept of a system to organisation and management problems (Jackson, 2003). This offers a number of lessons for understanding the nature of organisations and the process of management.

Organisations as systems

Now let us apply the concepts from systemics to the issue of organisations in more detail.

Considered as a whole, an organisation can be seen as a complex system of human activity. Applying the concept of hierarchy or holarchy, an organisation consists of a collection of interrelated and interdependent subsystems, each of which could also be considered as an organisation in its own right.

Activity systems by their very definition are systems, so we can use the toolkit of systems concepts to help us model existing activity systems and design new ones. We should be able to define the key processes of the system, inputs to each process, outputs from each process and the transformation undertaken by each process. Activity systems in this sense constitute sets of logically related activities by which organisations accomplish goals. For instance, a manufacturing organisation can be considered as a system. It uses inputs (supplies) such as raw materials and labour to produce products which it outputs (sells and distributes). Production as a process consists of a logical set of activities for transforming raw materials into final product.

Case check: Case 20, Tesco plc

Tesco plc can be considered in systems terms. The company originally specialised in food retail. It has now diversified into areas such as discount clothes, consumer electronics, consumer financial services, selling and renting DVDs, compact discs and music downloads, Internet service provision, consumer telecoms, consumer health insurance, consumer dental plans and budget software.

As a food retailer the physical inputs to the organisation are the foodstuffs it receives from its suppliers. Physical outputs consist of foodstuffs sold on to customers. Payments made by customers and to suppliers are examples of data inputs and data outputs respectively. Its key transformation consists of those activity systems involved in supporting the sale of foodstuffs. These activity systems can be considered in a hierarchical fashion. The company will have systems of supply, supermarket operation and financial management which all contribute to the overall purpose of the organisation, which is making a profit for its shareholders. The environment of the organisation consists of the retail industry generally, and specifically supermarket retail. This is illustrated in Figure 2.5.

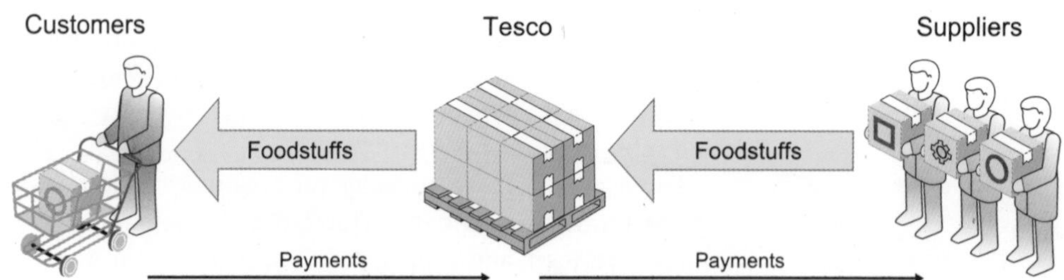

Figure 2.5: *Tesco as a system*

Modelling systems

The language of systemics is useful for building models of reality. It gives us a toolkit of concepts and components which we can use to engage with and make sense of the complexity of reality. We use modelling for a number of reasons.

- It allows the modeller to abstract certain features of some situation or phenomenon, and in this sense **simplify** a real-world situation.
- It enables the modeller to **represent** these key features in an agreed formal way.
- The model helps people to **communicate** and share a set of common understandings about a phenomenon.

A good example is a tube or metro map. The first diagrammatic map of the London Underground was designed by Harry Beck in 1933. Beck was an employee of the London Underground who realised that the exact physical locations of stations were irrelevant to travellers who just wanted to know how to get from one station to another. They are interested in the topology of this system; in other words, how the stations are connected. So he drew up a map which was effectively a **model** of the actual underground railway network. It highlights or abstracts the key features, and represents them as a series of circles (for stations) and coloured line segments (for tube lines). It does not show in proportion the distances between stations, but it does show the features that many users want.

Systemics uses the language of systems to build what artificial intelligence (AI) researchers and software engineers call ONTOLOGIES. An ontology is a term borrowed from philosophy: it means a systematic account or model of an area of existence, which logicians often call the **universe of discourse** or domain of discourse. In organisations, for instance, the universe of discourse might consist of employees, products, customers and suppliers, and the relationships and flows between these elements (see also Chapter 3).

Ontology: That branch of philosophy concerned with theories of reality. Also used as a specification for a domain or universe of discourse.

There are three main activities of modelling systems in this way:

- First, defining the boundary of a system: what is considered part of the system and what is considered part of its environment.
- Second, defining the hierarchy in the system: assigning structure and behaviour to subsystems, sub-subsystems and so on.
- Third, defining the elements of the system, such as processes, control and flows, as well as the relationships between elements.

Before we consider these issues in the modelling of activity systems, let us consider the relationship between models and reality.

Models and reality

There are two alternative positions which define the relationship between a model and reality, which are sometimes called objective and subjective positions.

In an **objective position**, reality is assumed to be independent of the observer. Also, reality displays systemic characteristics. A model in this view is an abstraction of reality; it is a representation of objective features: that is, features that are agreed on by all observers. The aim for the modeller is to achieve as close a correspondence as possible between the model and reality. We have already described this position as characteristic of the institutional perspective on organisations.

In a **subjective position**, reality is assumed to be different for different persons. Reality is necessarily subjective, it is argued, because systems do not exist in the world as such; they are a concept, a lens through which we see the world. A system model in this perspective is therefore a tool or lens for debating reality. The aim is to achieve intersubjective agreement, mutual understanding and possible joint action. This position is particularly adopted in the action perspective on organisations.

These positions can be appropriate for different forms of reality. Generally speaking, an objective position has proved appropriate for modelling the physical world, and an intersubjective position for modelling the social world. Since organisations are social constructions, we take a broadly intersubjective position in this book. So it is assumed here that modelling activity systems, information systems and ICT systems involves negotiation between the differing worldviews (see below) of the stakeholders in a system.

Stakeholders

It follows from this that organisational systems are defined through an intersubjective agreement between stakeholder groups (**stakeholders**, for short). Mason and Mitroff (1981) provided one of the earliest definitions of 'stakeholder': 'all those claimants inside and outside the organisation who have a vested interest in the problem and its solution.' What they call a **problem**, Checkland (1987) calls a problem situation: a situation in organisational life that is regarded by at least one person as being problematical. Facing up to the problem situation are some 'would-be improvers' of it: that is, people looking for a solution. These are the stakeholders for the system in question.

Reflect
How important is modelling to the effective management of organisations? Suggest some ways in which having a good model of an aspect of an organisation helps decision making.

Stakeholders and worldviews

Defining a system, and deciding what is in it, and what in its environment, depends on the viewpoint of the stakeholder. Stakeholders are normally groups of people to whom a particular system is relevant. As well as having different ideas about the boundaries of the system, they can also differ about its key elements and its intended purpose. These differences tend to reflect their differing worldviews.

Consider a manufacturing enterprise (Wilson, 1990). A customer might see it as a system to meet customer demand for a particular range of products, within resource constraints. A shareholder might see it as a system for transforming business needs into a satisfactory return on investment. A shop-floor employee might describe it as a system to achieve maximum utilization of resources while maintaining secure employment and acceptable working conditions.

Soft system: Collections of people undertaking activities to achieve a purpose.

Soft systems methodology: The approach to organisational analysis created by Peter Checkland.

Organisations as soft systems

A human activity system (or activity system for short) is what Checkland (1987) refers to as a SOFT SYSTEM. It is a type of social system that is 'designed' to meet certain defined objectives. Activity systems are soft because:

- their boundaries or scope may be fluid
- their purpose is likely to be open to interpretation, depending on the stakeholder viewpoint or worldview
- the definition of precisely what control (see below) means in the context, and therefore exact measures of performance, depend on the worldviews of stakeholders.

Systems are inherently processes of organisation (order) in a universe of disorganisation (disorder). Systemic thinking is interested in the process of organising as well as the **entity of organisation**. This entity of organisation (that is, a noun) arises from the process of organising (that is, a verb). Like a river, an organisation as entity is in a continual state of flux. Organisational actions continually recreate the organisation. Organisational action is also the motor for organisational change.

In a typical organisation, actions are to some degree predictable, because they are based on a defined structure of organisational roles and procedures for doing things. In the process of performing their roles and sticking to the procedures, organisational actors recreate the organisation. However, there is always a degree of innovation, particularly in times of environmental disturbance, when the organisation has to change or adapt if it is to remain viable. For instance, technological changes evident in the rise of eCommerce (see Chapter 5) have caused some industries (such as the music industry) to totally reassess their actions.

Organisations are different from mere collections of people, or social groups in general, in the sense that they are normally established for a purpose: usually to produce value of some form. Organisations are typically seen as needing clear identities to establish a context for action. However, organisational purpose is a dynamic, not a static issue. Purpose is continually negotiated, understood and disseminated throughout the organisation by its stakeholders.

The purpose of an organisation is typically formulated in terms of its **mission**. One popular way to define this is to list the key **competencies** the organisation needs: that is, those things the organisation must do well. The idea is that these define critical levers for ensuring the viability and sustainability of the organisation.

As should be evident from this, identifying the stakeholders in a system is critical to understanding the system itself. However, building a coherent and intersubjective worldview or appreciative system (in management-speak, a **vision**) is important to the organisation.

Let's take a sawmill, and consider how different stakeholders might see it. An industrial engineer might view it as a production system, and a management scientist as a profit-maximising system. The industrial engineer will be interested in how it transforms logs into finished products using resources such as plant and machinery, and will probably be studying it to determine effective control procedures for the production process: to decide where machinery is placed, the way in which products are handled and so on.

The management scientist would probably be less interested in the physical activities of the sawmill than in their financial consequences. They might see it as a series of subsystems such as a log handling and storage subsystem, a finished goods and warehousing subsystem, a marketing subsystem and a financial control subsystem, and be interested mostly in the way each subsystem communicates its needs to other subsystems, and how the flow of goods and information affects the financial performance of the firm. The system's environment in this case consists of the market for logs, the market for finished wood products and other elements such as the financial, labour and legal environment of the firm.

Wright (1989) defines an important property of open systems such as organisations as **equifinality**. This means that an open system can achieve its goals or purpose in a number of different ways. So there are likely to be several different ways of designing and organizing an activity system to meet defined objectives (or in other words to optimise performance against established measures). One consequence is that it should be possible to set **objectives** (or goals, or targets) for an activity system, and establish clear criteria for measuring performance.

The objective in most organisations is to design activity systems to support core organisational competencies. A general assumption is that most organisations consist of a limited number of activity systems which contribute to fulfilling their key mission or strategy. So there is a clear link between the design and operation of activity systems, and the planning of organisational strategy (see also Chapter 10).

Key skill 

Modelling problem situations and worldviews

Checkland (1987) suggests that the starting point for modelling activity systems is to consider the problem situation as the context for the system, and represent the environment, stakeholders, concerns and issues in this problem situation as a 'rich picture'. **Rich pictures** are deliberately loose or informal. They attempt to capture the essence of a complex situation within which some stakeholders perceive a problem, and some form of organisational analysis work needs to take place.

There is no standard notation for rich pictures: it is up to the modeller. Figure 2.6 is an example, an attempt to represent at a high level a rich picture of universities as problem situations. The stakeholders include academics, students and administrators, and the rich picture reflects some of their contrasting viewpoints or worldviews. It also tries to include environmental trends such as recruitment patterns and funding issues, which are likely to have an impact.

Root definition: A way of specifying organisational processes in the soft systems method.

The ideas that stakeholders hold of a particular activity system can be modelled more precisely using a ROOT DEFINITION. This expresses the core purpose of an activity system, in terms of the classic input–process–output model (see page 38). Checkland has suggested that most useful root definitions consist of six elements which make up the acronym CATWOE:

- **Customers**: the victims or beneficiaries of the transformation.
- **Actors**: those who would do the transformation.
- **Transformation**: the conversion of input to output.
- **Worldview**: the worldview which makes the transformation meaningful.

- **Owners**: those that could stop the transformation.
- **Environmental constraints**: elements outside the system which it takes as given.

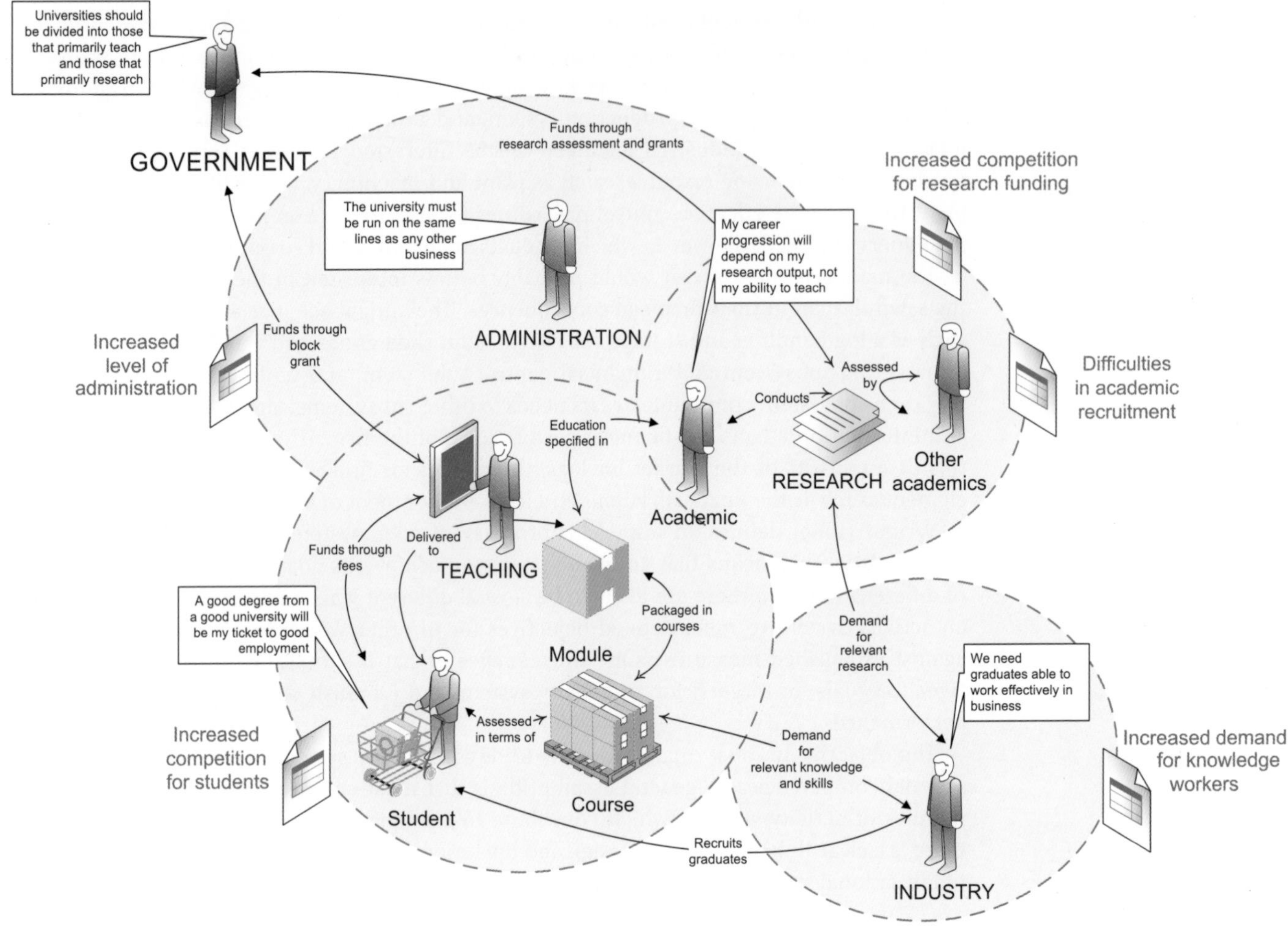

Figure 2.6: *A rich picture of a university*

The core of CATWOE is the pairing of transformation with the worldview, which makes it meaningful. There will always be a number of different transformations through which any activity system can be expressed, derived from different interpretations or worldviews of its purpose. The other elements of the mnemonic add ideas of key stakeholder types and their role in the system: someone must undertake the purposeful activity, someone could stop it and someone will be its victim or beneficiary. The system will also take some environmental constraints as a given.

As an example, from our rich picture of a university we know that its stakeholders include students, academic staff and administrative staff. Each will potentially hold a different worldview about the purpose of this 'system'. For example, a student's worldview of a university might be:

- Customer = Myself as a student.
- Actors = Other students, academic staff and administrative staff.
- Transformation = The process of education: attending modules, achieving satisfactory assessments and getting a degree.
- Worldview = That higher education is a passage to better job prospects.
- Owners = The academic and administrative staff.
- Environment = The higher education system: other universities and higher education institutions.

Case check: Case 20, Tesco plc

Tesco is primarily in the business of selling foodstuffs to customers. Its declared mission is to 'create value for customers to earn their lifetime loyalty'. Its strategy is based on offering a range of different types of stores, understanding its customers and treating its employees well. Tesco introduced its loyalty card for customers a number of years ago. Value for this company might therefore include the additional value services available to loyalty card customers, such as discounting of goods.

Reflect
What different stakeholders are involved in Tesco as a system? What differing worldviews might these stakeholders hold of the company?

We can demonstrate the equifinality characteristic of activity systems by considering two alternative models for food retail. Tesco supermarkets operate a traditional model of supermarket retail designed to manage the flow of physical goods from suppliers to customers. This involves maintaining a large floor-space stocked with products. Customers travel to the supermarket, pick products from the shelves and transport them home themselves (see Figure 2.7). Recently Tesco has introduced online retail. This uses a different design for the activity system. Customers order goods through a website. A picking list is produced for a store operative who walks around a store and picks products to satisfy the customer order. The customer shopping basket is crated and delivered by van to the customer's home, in return for a delivery charge. A limited service is available whereby customers can avoid the delivery charge by picking up crated goods from the local store themselves.

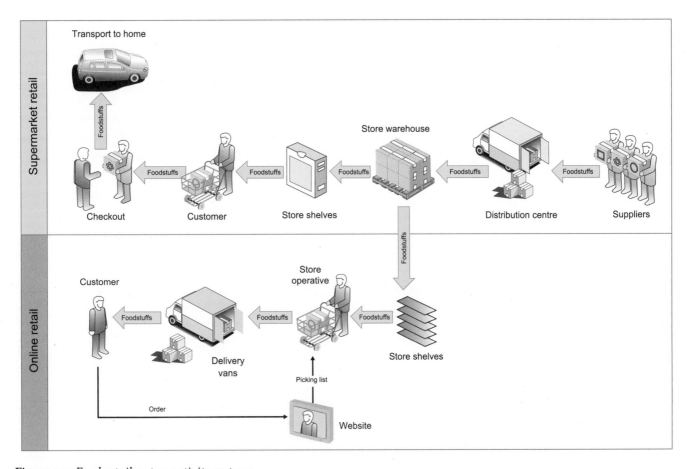

Figure 2.7: *Food retail as two activity systems*

Control

Control is the process by which a system ensures continuity through time. So it is the means by which system identity is sustained and the system maintains its viability as its environment changes.

Viable system: A term used by Stafford Beer to describe a system capable of surviving in a volatile environment.

Viability and sustainability

Beer (1972) argues that the key aim of any system is survival in a volatile environment – he refers to this as a VIABLE SYSTEM. The *Oxford English Dictionary* defines **viable** as being able to maintain a separate existence. Therefore, a viable system is one that is able to maintain a separate identity and is able to survive in a particular environment. Ensuring viability is a concern of control. Control can be conceived as a process of both regulation and adaptation applicable to systems.

A system is said to be viable if it survives in its current environment; it refers to the ability of a system to maintain identity in the present. **Sustainability** has become a popular but highly emotive term in recent times, particularly in relation to adapting to changes in the physical environment such as climate change. Peter Senge's book *The Fifth Discipline* (2006) is interested in the sustainability of organisations. In systemic terms we can define sustainability in terms of viability over an extended period of time. A system is sustainable if it has characteristics that allow it to maintain its identity through time.

Regulation and adaptation

To many people, 'control' involves stability and conservation. This side of control is frequently referred to as **regulation**. This conservative side of control is typically concerned with the internal operations of a system. It ensures that a system will recover some stability after a period of disturbance and maintain its viability over time.

Control also involves the principle of organising, what is frequently referred to as **adaptation**. This evolutionary side of control is concerned with the external relationships between the system and its environment. Systems generally exhibit some form of control that enables the system to adapt to changes in its environment, ensuring a degree of 'fit' between system and environment.

A manufacturing plant has to regulate the supply of raw materials to match production levels, to ensure the smooth running of production. This is fundamentally a process of regulation. A retail outlet must ensure that its product lines fit with changes in market demand if it is to remain competitive. This is primarily a process of adaptation.

Control processes

We can think of CONTROL as a monitoring SUBSYSTEM that 'steers' the behaviour of other operating subsystems. This is frequently referred to as a **control mechanism**, subsystem or process. The control process ensures defined levels of performance for the system through use of a number of control inputs.

Control subsystem: The subsystem that regulates the behaviour of a system it is monitoring. Also known as a control process or mechanism.

For systems designed by human beings such as organisations, control can be considered as an imposed process. It is necessary to establish processes of control for regulation in the process of system design and construction. In contrast, control in natural systems is not designed but emerges through processes of self-organisation. In complexity theory (Stacey, 1991), 'control' (although it is not referred to as such) is seen as emerging from the system itself. Coherent patterns of order or control emerge from the complex interaction of the multiple parts of a system.

For example, a concept of emergence familiar in classical economics is price. The price of a good or service (such as the price of oil in a pure economic market) is not fixed or designed, but emerges from the interaction of supply and demand.

Wilson (1990) argues that any coherent element of a system (what we earlier called a holon) has a control mechanism embedded within it. In other words, a system with operational processes must have at least one controller for those processes.

For a control process to work effectively it must have three things:

- resources that can be used to regulate the behaviour of the system in a particular direction
- CONTROL INPUTS which implement the 'purpose' of the system
- control signals enabling the process to monitor and instruct operational processes.

Control inputs: Special types of input to a control process that define levels of performance for a system.

For reasonably well-defined systems, the control inputs can be expressed as decision rules or a decision strategy. The rules are initially supplied to the control subsystem from outside the system, and are used to steer a system in a desired direction.

For example, in a heating system, thermostats normally act as control subsystems. A thermostat is set at a desired temperature (the control input). It then monitors the temperature of its environment, and when this reaches the set level, it activates to switch off the heating components (such as radiators). Once the temperature in the environment drops back below a defined range, the thermostat activates again, to switch the heating components back on.

Key skill 

Modelling business rules

Decision making: The activity of deciding on appropriate action in particular situations.

A decision strategy can be modelled in a number of ways. For instance, if it is suitably well formalised it could be represented as a series of If–Then statements or decision **rules**. For example, these are the decision rules for the decision strategy embedded in a thermostat:

> IF sensed temperature < desired temperature THEN open heating valve to increase flow of heat.
>
> IF sensed temperature > desired temperature THEN shut heating valve to reduce flow of heat.

Another way of representing a decision strategy is through a **decision table** or **decision tree**. For instance, Table 2.1 shows a set of business rules – that is, rules that regulate behaviour in a business process. They control the process of awarding discounts to customers renting compact cars. You can tell what discount is due by following the path down, from the appropriate type of car group to the status of an advance booking. So someone renting a compact car for a month with loyalty membership and booking at least three days in advance is entitled to a 20 per cent discount.

Table 2.1: *A set of business rules for car rentals*

Car group	Compact											
Rental period	D				W				M			
Loyalty member	Y		N		Y		N		Y		N	
>3 days in advance	Y	N	Y	N	Y	N	Y	N	Y	N	Y	N
0%			X	X				X				
5%		X					X					X
10%	X					X					X	
15%					X					X		
20%									X			

Reflect
Business strategy can be considered as a form of control used in organisations. It might be expressed in a mission statement. Can a mission statement be considered as a control input, and if so, how is it used to regulate organisational behaviour?

Control and performance

Control inputs implement the purpose of a system, as they effectively represent defined measures of performance for it. The performance levels are defined by higher-level systems.

For instance, a manufacturing plant's level of performance might be defined as productivity level per manufacturing unit. A general hospital's levels of performance might be defined as the size of waiting lists for specific medical treatments.

Checkland (1987) defines three main types of performance measure: efficacy, efficiency and effectiveness, sometimes referred to as the three Es of performance.

- **Efficacy** is a measure of the extent to which a system achieves its intended transformation. Measures of efficacy consequently tend to focus on its outputs.
- **Efficiency** is a measure of the extent to which the system achieves its intended transformation with the minimum use of resources. Efficiency is therefore primarily an attempt to address the balance of inputs to outputs in systems terms.
- **Effectiveness** is a measure of the extent to which the system contributes to the purposes of a higher-level system of which it is a subsystem. Effectiveness is therefore always an attempt to relate the goals of some super-system to the output from the subsystem.

We can also see the three Es in terms of how a transformation process might fail. It might fail to produce desired output: this is a problem of efficacy. It could produce the output but consume excessive resources: this is a problem of efficiency. Finally, the output might not make the required contribution to the wider system: this is a problem of effectiveness.

Let's take a sales department. We might measure its efficacy by examining the number of products sold over a chosen time span. To measure its efficiency we could use productivity measures such as the number of sales per salesperson. Its effectiveness is determined in relation to its contribution to overall company profitability. The key role of the sales department management is to define and operate measures such as these in order to control its work successfully. This example illustrates that specialist performance management systems in organisations are effectively control systems.

There are of course other ways of defining and measuring the performance of activity systems. For instance, it is important to consider ethical issues. The emerging area of **corporate social responsibility** can be seen as an attempt to develop baselines of performance for ethical business activity. For example, many clothing companies have been criticised for their use of child labour from the developing world: it would be possible to set a control standard below which this falls, so that it is seen as an ethical failure.

Case check:
Case 20, Tesco plc

In terms of the three Es, Tesco **efficacy** measures are likely to include sales for product groups across different supermarkets. **Efficiency** measures are likely to include profit margins against product lines, or measures of stock fulfilment against orders in warehouses. **Effectiveness** measures might include the degree to which new customers are attracted to Tesco supermarkets, old customers continue to come to the stores, and the levels of satisfaction expressed by customers with the level of service they receive.

Reflect
It is sometimes difficult to specify precise performance measures for an activity system. What difficulties might be experienced in attempting to specify efficacy, efficiency and effectiveness measures for a business?

Cybernetics

The discipline of **cybernetics** is founded on the study of control systems (Wiener, 1948). Norbert Wiener defined cybernetics as the 'entire field of control and communication theory, whether in the machine or in the animal'. The ancient Greek work *kybernetes* means the art of steersmanship. At the time, the word was naturally used to refer to the art of piloting a maritime vessel. However the philosopher Plato used it to refer to steering the ship of state. The English word 'governor' is derived from the Latin word *gubernator*, which in turn is derived from the Greek *kybernetes*. In modern English it is used for both a mechanical mechanism and a political role. A governor is part of a steam engine, which uses a self-adjusting valve mechanism to keep the engine working at a constant speed under varying conditions of load. A governor of state is a public steersman or political decision maker.

Did you know? The term *cybernetics* underlies many popular words such as cyberspace and cybermen.

Regulation

The idea of a governor suggests a control process designed to steer a system in a certain direction. If the focus is on continuity, an internal focus, a control process can be cast as a regulatory process.

Homeostasis: The process of ensuring that a system remains regulated within defined limits.

Homeostat: A mechanism for ensuring homeostasis.

In terms of regulation, the direction of steering is defined by the idea of HOMEOSTASIS or steady state. To maintain homeostasis, the control system attempts to maintain the system it is monitoring within parameters defined by its control inputs. This form of control system is generally referred to as a HOMEOSTAT, a control mechanism for holding a state variable or variables within defined limits. Homeostasis is the process of achieving control in this manner, and is the essential principle underlying the self-regulation of systems.

Norm: An expectation of human behaviour.

The exercise of a homeostat normally leads to oscillation: the system moves first above, then below, a target measure. The use of a control mechanism such as a negative feedback loop (see below) is generally characterised by the oscillation of process behaviour around the established NORM – frequently upper and lower limits expressed by control inputs. This is sometimes caused because of lags or delays (see below) in communication between control and operational processes. Generally speaking, the closer the controller is to the process being controlled, the less delay there is in sending and receiving control signals. Consequently the behaviour of the controlled process is less subject to oscillation.

Adaptation

A control process may also be designed, or may emerge, to ensure that a system **adapts** to changes in its environment. If the focus is on change – an external focus – a control process is cast as an adaptive process. The control signals to an adaptive process are likely to consist of sensory data from monitoring of the environment. The control inputs in this case are likely to consist of a model of the fitness of the relationship between the system and this sensory data.

Kaufmann (1995) portrays some of the complexities in this adaptive process. We can think of the overall environment of a system as a 'heaving landscape'. This is not unlike a natural landscape of hills and valleys, except that the shape of the landscape is subject to continuous change over comparatively short periods. The system cannot predict the behaviour of the environment because (in this analogy) the landscape is continually shifting around, throwing up peaks of different heights separated by valleys. So it has to attempt to navigate this landscape. Perhaps a system finding itself on a peak would be highly adapted (that is, well suited to the conditions); in a valley it would be poorly adapted. However, as more systems come to occupy a particular peak, their collective 'weight' pushes the peak downwards, causing other peaks to develop elsewhere – and meaning the system would be better off elsewhere. So adaptation is a continuous process of adjustment between the environment and the system.

The more detailed discussion of the organisational environment in Chapter 5 uses this image to discuss competitive position.

Did you know?

Much of the literature on organisational adaptation makes an analogy between organisations and organisms. In this sense, organisational adaptation is seen as similar to the process of natural selection.

Control and information

The process of control and the concept of information (Chapter 3) are inherently interlinked. For instance, in order for a homeostat to work effectively it must continually monitor the state of the system it is attempting to control. This involves information transmission. The control process must also contain a model of the system it is attempting to control. Critical to this model are defined measures of performance. Information transmitted from the monitoring process is compared with the model, and signals are transmitted back to the system to maintain the system's performance within defined parameters.

Control elements

Sensor: A mechanism that monitors the changes in the environment of a system.

Comparator: A mechanism that compares signals from sensors with control inputs.

Effector: Components that cause changes to a system's state.

Applying the idea of systems hierarchy, we can refine the idea of a control process in a system as consisting of three specialised forms of subprocess or subsystem. Any control process is likely to be made up of sensors, comparators and effectors. SENSORS are processes that monitor changes in the environment of a system, or in the system itself, and send signals to the system representing such changes. COMPARATORS compare signals from sensors with control inputs, and on the basis of a decision strategy send signals to effectors. Sometimes referred to as actuators or activators, EFFECTORS cause changes to a system's state. In other words, they introduce changes to system variables.

For instance, in a security system sensors are likely to be placed at points of entry into a building such as windows and doors. If a window is opened when the system is activated, a sensor sends a signal to the control unit. This unit identifies the point of entry, and send signals to effectors such as alarms.

Reflect
In a business organisation or within a business process, what are the likely comparators, sensors and effectors?

Organisations, control and management

To maintain identity an organisation needs to be controlled. This implies that there must be some identifiable control element within the activity system. However, control is not only a process of regulation; it is also a process of adaptation. Control in this dual sense is the essence of the process of organising within activity systems.

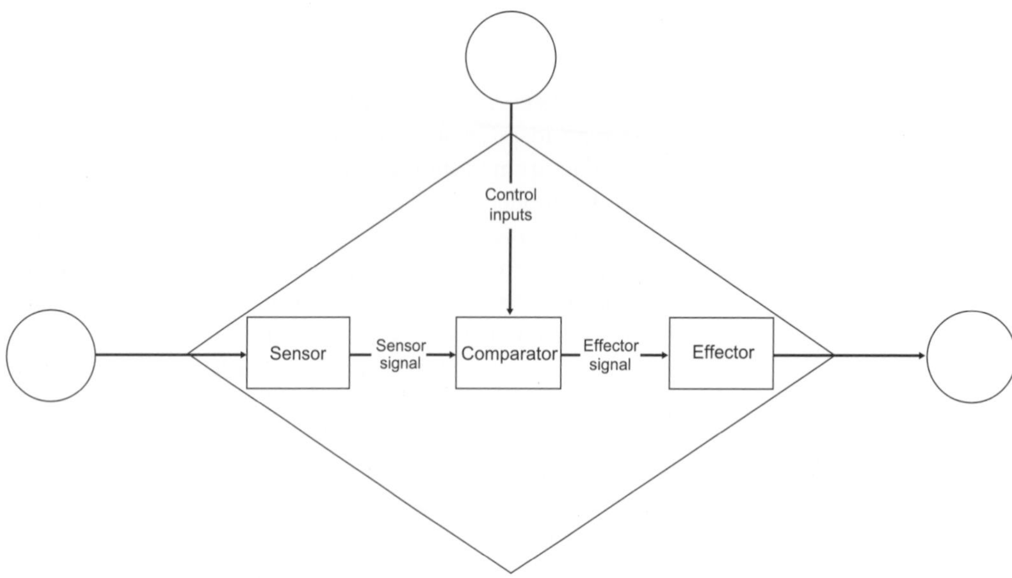

Figure 2.8: *Elements of a control process*

For effective control a controller needs a model of the system being controlled, so modelling is useful to deal with the complexity of problem situations. Models make explicit assumptions in the problem situation that are normally implicit. Organisational models are useful for management in a number of ways. They help managers better understand the organisation they are responsible for, they aid decision making and they are useful for managers in learning the effect of their decisions.

However, managers should not make the mistake of assuming that the model *is* the system. The model is always an approximation or representation of the system. Generally, it will have much less variety than the system itself. The art of management frequently consists of trying to draw out sufficient essential details of the operation of the system for the purpose of effective control.

Managerial control relies on the effective establishment of organisational sensors, effectors and comparators, which implement performance measurement and monitoring. Information about business processes needs to compared with standards set for performance. If there is substantial variation, adjustments need to be made to reduce it.

Modelling activities and control

Conceptual model: A model that represents a universe of discourse at a high-level. Used within soft systems approaches to refer to a high-level model of key activities.

Root definitions provide the material for constructing CONCEPTUAL MODELS of purposeful activity for managers. They specify the minimum activities needed to support the key transformation process, and their key relations can be shown graphically, as we shall see.

The modeller starts with the key transformation of the system. Let's use once more the example of an university, where this is 'the process of education'. This transformation is shown as an activity or process (or a series of activities or processes) in a diagram (see Figure 2.9).

The modeller works outwards from the central activity to consider activities that provide input to the central transformation, and those that are output from it. Process boxes are joined with dotted arrows to indicate dependencies or precedence of activities. So Figure 2.10 shows that to educate students we first need to recruit students and enrol students on courses and modules. These are input activities. To progress students we need to assess their educational experience against modules and award degree classifications for the whole course of their study. These are output activities.

The modeller might then in turn consider the inputs and outputs for each of the processes added. However, a conceptual model at this stage is a high-level model of the activity system. The usual rule is to limit the number of processes or activities shown to a maximum of seven.

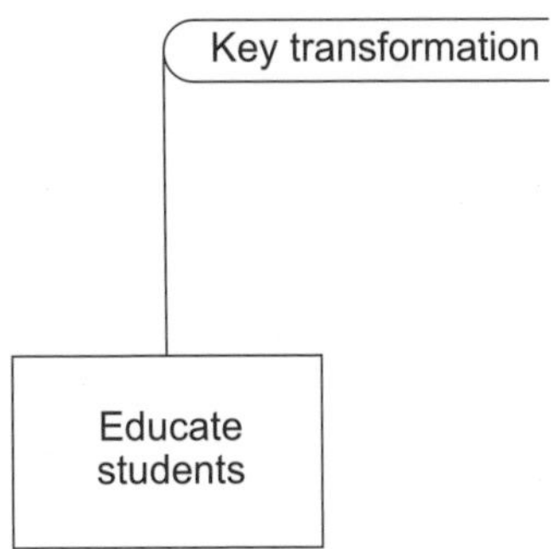

Figure 2.9: *The key transformation*

We next need to consider the issue of control. This means answering the question, how do we assess the key purpose of the activity system? And how do we implement this purpose in terms of the three Es of performance? This involves specifying four additional types of activity or process to the model:

- Planning activities which supply criteria for assessing performance in terms of the resources to be used and how they will be measured (that is, control inputs).
- Control processes (comparators) which need to be in place to assess performance against criteria set. Such processes put into practice the decision-making strategies that are necessary to assess the performance of an operational process.
- Monitoring processes (sensors) which collect measurements of activities against performance criteria set. These are necessary to supply performance information to control processes.
- Change processes (effectors) that are needed to regulate operational activities.

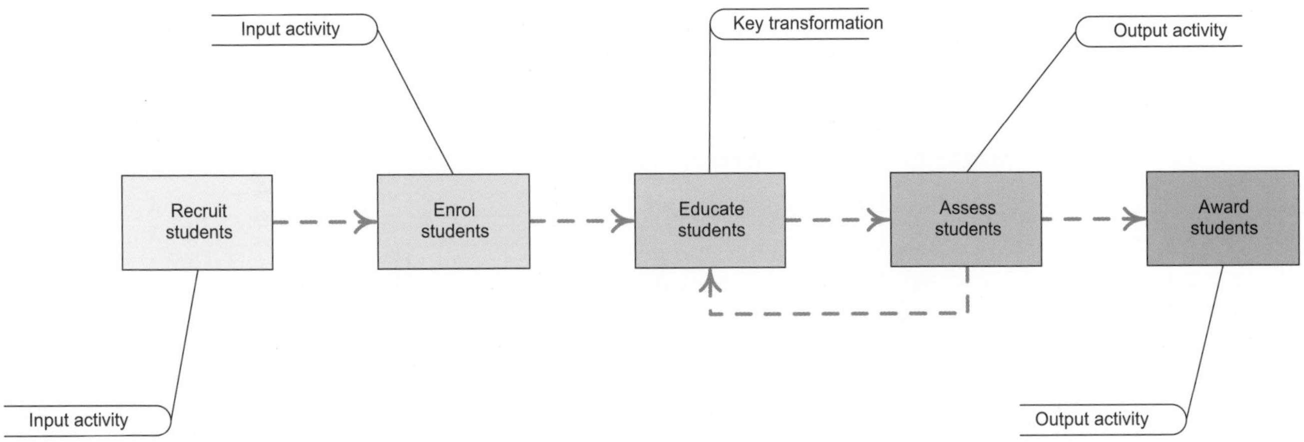

Figure 2.10: *Inputs and outputs*

These processes need to be joined together with appropriate dependencies. In our example (see Figure 2.11), each of the main operational activities might need to be controlled. For instance, the university might set recruitment targets for each of the schools or faculties under its umbrella. It will take action if actual levels of recruitment do not match the targets: perhaps greater investment in recruitment campaigns for particular courses.

The complete model for this example is shown as Figure 2.12. This could be used as the basis for a more detailed process analysis and design exercise (something that is looked at later in the book).

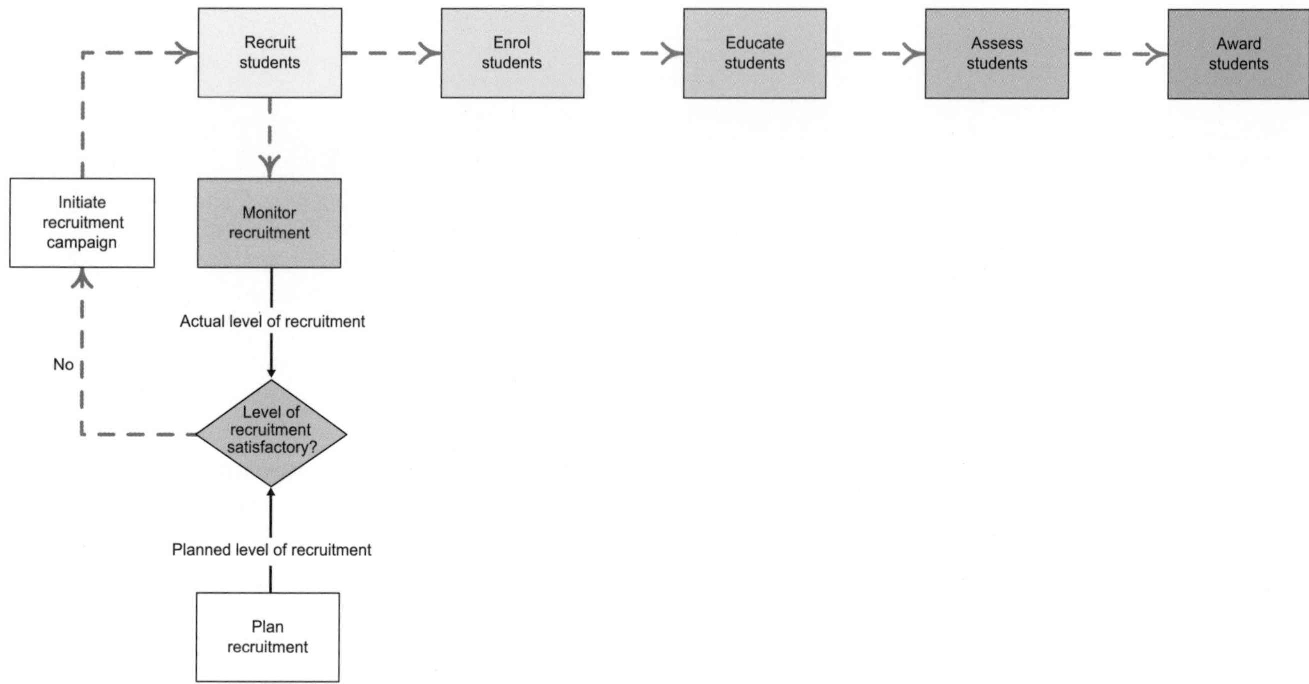

Figure 2.11: *Adding control*

Feedback

Peter Senge (2006) believes that one the most important characteristics of systems thinking is its ability to handle cycles of cause and effect. In this light the concept of feedback is critical. Control is normally exercised in a system through a form of feedback. Control outputs from the process of a system are fed back into the control process. The control process then adjusts the control signals to the operating process on the basis of the information it receives.

Feedback has two major forms, positive and negative. There is no value connotation here.

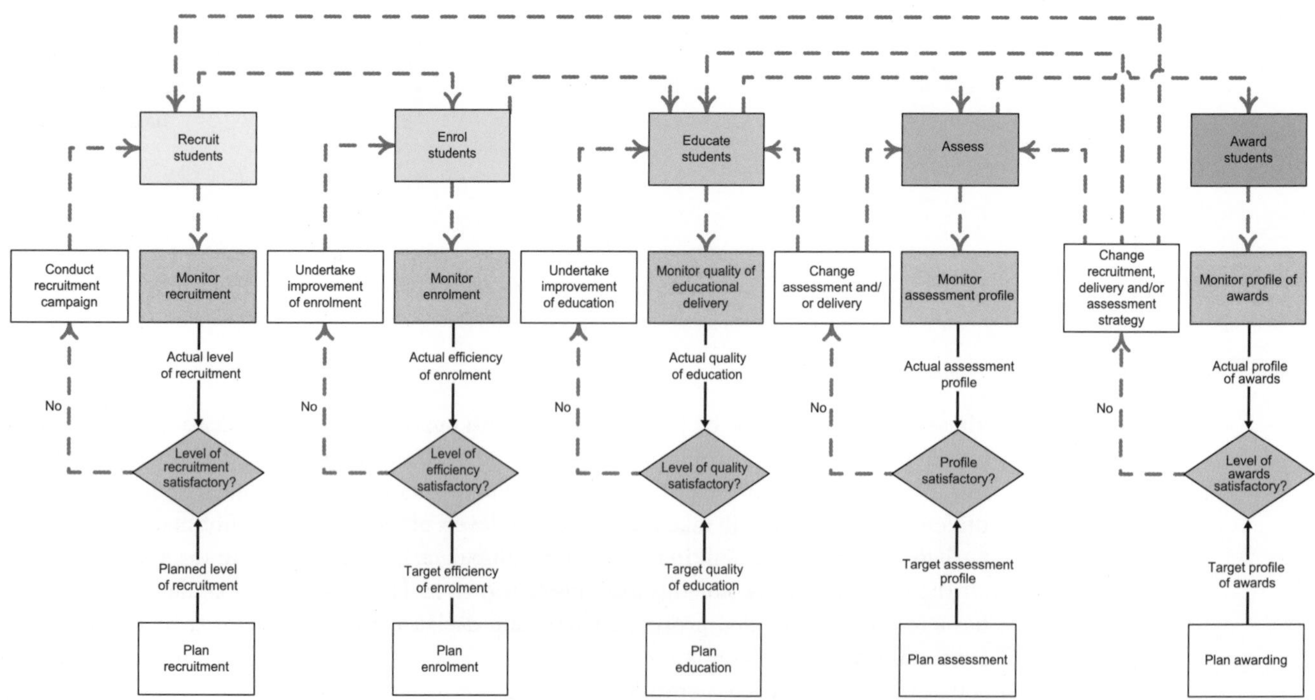

Figure 2.12: *A sample conceptual model*

There is also an important distinction between feedback processes involved primarily with regulation (single-loop feedback) and those involved with adaptation (double-loop feedback).

Negative feedback

Negative feedback: Process in which a monitoring subsystem monitors the outputs from a system and detects variations from defined levels of performance. If the outputs vary from established levels, the monitoring subsystem initiates actions to reduce the variation.

Control is normally exercised through a NEGATIVE FEEDBACK loop. Sometimes known as a balancing loop or damping feedback, it involves the control process monitoring the outputs from the operational process through its sensors. The comparators in the monitoring system detect variations from defined levels of performance provided by control inputs. If the outputs vary from the established levels, the monitoring subsystem initiates actions that reduce the variation through its effectors.

For example, in a thermostat, if the temperature falls below a specified level, the thermostat might open a hot water valve. We can also think of a company maintaining cash flow as a system with negative feedback, in which the cash balance continually influences company decisions on expenditure and borrowing. All the control loops added to the conceptual model in Figure 2.12 are forms of negative feedback.

Positive feedback

Positive feedback: The process in a which a monitoring subsystem increases the discrepancy between desired and actual levels of performance.

Commonly known as a 'vicious circle' or reinforcing loop, POSITIVE FEEDBACK involves the control process monitoring the outputs from the operational system through its sensors. The comparators in the monitoring system detect variations from defined levels of performance provided by control inputs. If the outputs vary from established levels, the monitoring subsystem initiates actions that *increase* the discrepancy.

Viewpoints vary on the issue of positive feedback. For some, it is a deviant form of control because of its ability to push systems beyond states of equilibrium. However, complexity theorists argue that positive feedback is essential to drive evolutionary and adaptive processes, and is the version of feedback driving the control evident in many natural systems.

Complexity theorists like Stacey (1991) argue that short-term control, for purposes of either regulation or adaptation, is characterised by negative feedback, but long-term control is much more subject to positive feedback. The movement away from equilibrium is punctuated by important changes in organisation.

The arms race that occurred during the cold war period is a classic example of a system characterised by a positive feedback loop. At the time, the United States increased its level of armament to improve its security. This prompted the Soviet Union to increase its level of armament too, because of the perceived greater threat to its security. The United States responded by increasing its level of armament, and so on. This positive feedback loop was eventually terminated with the collapse of the Soviet Union, and a new form of international political world order emerged.

In large business investment projects such as information systems development, there is a tendency to escalate decision making so that more resources are thrown at an ailing project in the hope of preventing failure. What tends to happen is that costs escalate, and even more resources have to be thrown at the project. This loop typically ends with the abandonment of the project (see Chapter 9).

Feedforward

Whereas feedback is a reactive form of control, **feedforward** is a proactive form of control. Feedforward controls predict how changes in inputs are likely to affect system behaviour, and send control signals to the system that will maintain its behaviour as close as possible to the desired course.

Most organisational planning is a form of feedforward control. For instance, managers attempt to predict the likely short-term future orders for their products, and on this basis decide to increase or decrease production and stock levels. The Bank of England attempts to control the level of inflation in the UK economy through a form of feedforward control. Using statistics on areas such as consumer spending and indices such as inflation rates, it projects a future level of inflation and uses changes to interest rates as a means of influencing it.

Reflect
In an economic market how is feedback likely to work? How is feedback used to help control market activity?

System lag: A delay between the issuing of a control signal and the adjustment of the system process to it.

System lags

However, in most systems there is a time LAG or delay in the exercise of control. It is such lags that cause the oscillating behaviour evident in many systems. Lags may be experienced for the three elements of a control process (see Figure 2.11). Comparators may be affected by a delay in the receipt of control inputs from a super-system. Sensors may be affected by a delay in the receipt of information from a monitored process. Finally, there may be a delay between the issuing of a control signal through effectors and the adjustment of the system process to the signals. The lags might be seconds, minutes, days, weeks, months or even years.

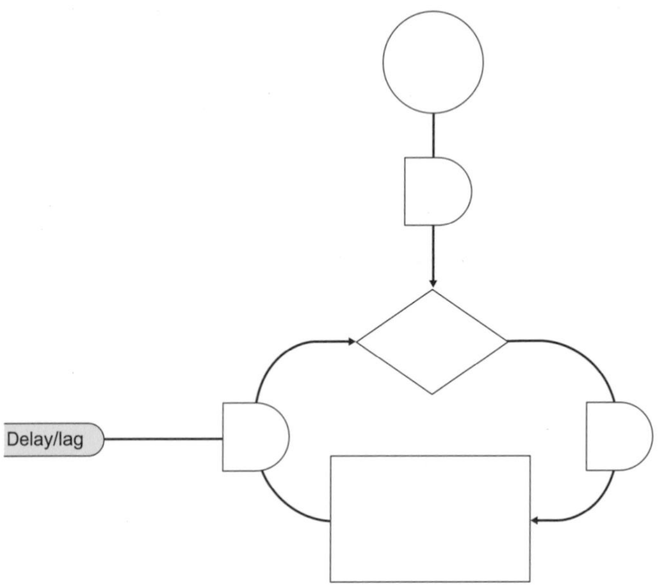

Figure 2.13: *System lags*

Think of a shower in which a person controls the temperature by turning a tap. Usually there are several seconds between turning the tap and the water reaching the required temperature. When the Bank of England changes interest rates there is a likely delay of months before the rate of inflation is affected. Lags in business systems are frequently the cause of managerial problems in areas such as the supply chain (see Chapter 7).

Requisite variety

Requisite variety: Only variety can absorb variety. For full control of the system it is monitoring a control subsystem should contain variety – a number of states – at least equal to the system under control.

There is an inherent limit placed on the operation of control systems. This is expressed as what Ashby (1956) calls the law of REQUISITE VARIETY, which states that only variety can absorb or destroy variety.

Humans and organisations typically deal with variety (the complexity of a system) by forming categories of things and rules appropriate to governing behaviour relevant to particular categories. However, categories and their associated rules attenuate or reduce variety but do not *have* requisite variety. A bureaucracy, for instance, cannot create sufficient rules and regulations to fit all the environmental states it is likely to experience now or in the future.

Variety (see page 40) is a measure of the number of states a system can take. For full control of the system it is monitoring, a control process should contain variety – a number of states – at least equal to the system under control. The consequence of this is that relatively simple control systems cannot be expected to control the multitude of activities characteristic of complex systems, so manual intervention is frequently required. In organisations, managers frequently need to intervene in the face of exceptional circumstances or non-standard situations. This kind of intervention may be an important trigger for organisational change.

Single and double-loop feedback

Feedback is critical to processes of both individual and organisational learning. In this context we can distinguish two other major forms of feedback which correspond to the two streams of control necessary for regulatory and adaptive behaviour. These two types, following the work of Argyris (Argyris and Schön, 1978), are generally referred to as single-loop and double-loop feedback.

Single-loop feedback: A simple feedback process in which the performance plans for a system remain unchanged.

SINGLE-LOOP FEEDBACK is primarily concerned with regulation. In this type of feedback a single control process monitors variations in the state of a process, compares this state with planned levels of performance, and takes corrective action to bring performance in line with plan. In single-loop feedback the plans for performance (the control inputs) remain relatively unchanged (see Figure 2.14). Sensors only monitor the behaviour of internal processes, and effectors only act upon these internal processes.

Closed system: A system that does not interact with its environment.

Inventory management, production control, budgetary control and standard costing are all examples of activity systems in organisations that tend to use single-loop feedback. This form of feedback is characteristic of control processed at the operational and tactical levels of management in business (see Chapter 3). Such systems are relatively CLOSED in that they do not interact with the environment, and since their performance plans do not change they are relatively easy to automate. In fact, much ICT automation in organisations has focused on replacing or supplanting elements of activity which implement aspects of single-loop feedback with technology.

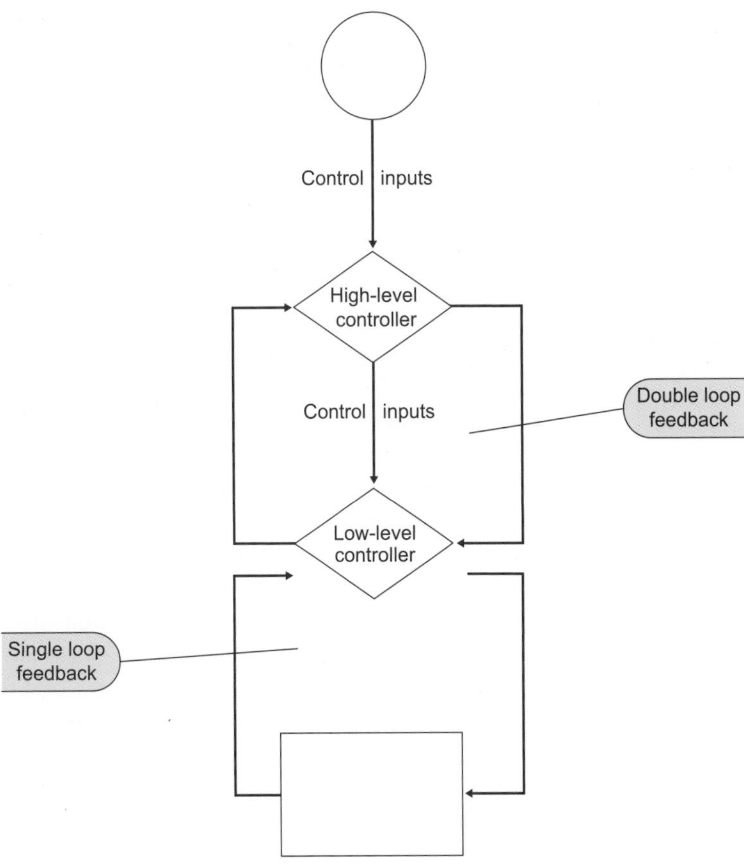

Figure 2.14: *Single and double-loop feedback*

Double-loop feedback: A system in which monitoring of single-loop feedback systems and the environment triggers examination and possible revision of the principles upon which a control system is established.

DOUBLE-LOOP FEEDBACK is primarily concerned with adaptation. In this type of feedback the control process must not only monitor variations in the state of an internal process, it must also monitor changes in its environment. Hence, there are two control loops involved and the feedback from the higher-level controller will cause adjustments to the decision strategies of lower-level controllers.

Double-loop feedback is consequently a higher-level form of control. Ashby (1956) insists that double-loop feedback is essential to ensure that a system adapts effectively to changes in its environment. In double-loop feedback, monitoring lower-level single-feedback control systems as well as the environment triggers examination and perhaps revision of the principles on which the control process is established. Colloquially, it is sometimes referred to as 'thinking outside the box'. At the simplest level, double-loop feedback may cause revisions to the control inputs of lower-level systems. At its most complex, it will involve redesigning the processes and structures on which the lower-level systems are established.

Imagine what would happen if an organisation did not set up double-loop feedback systems for its inventory management. Whatever happened to demand for its products, it would keep on using the same reorder levels and quantities. When demand changed, it would suffer from either excessive levels of stock or stocks running out so that it could not fulfil orders quickly.

Not surprisingly, double-loop feedback is an important characteristic of strategic management in organisations (see Chapter 10). Just as individuals continually learn, organisations need to continually learn.

Recap 

The concept of a system is fundamental to the discipline known as systems thinking or systemics. Systemics studies the general characteristics of all systems. A system is an organised collection of things with emergent properties and with a defined purpose. Different stakeholders need to be considered in defining the characteristics of a system. Critical features or components of all systems include subsystems, input–process–output, an environment and control. Control is the process through which a system regulates itself, but also the process by which a system adapts to its environment. Feedback is critical to processes of control.

Organisations and feedback

Regulator: A key type of organisational stakeholder. Groups or agencies that set environmental constraints for an information system.

Organisations are open systems since they interact with their environment. Business organisations interact with a number of agencies in the economic environment, including customers, suppliers, partners, competitors and REGULATORS. So organisations are continuously organising – engaging in a continuous process of interaction with this environment.

Control within systems relies on feedback, both single-loop and double-loop, so cause and effect in organisational life are frequently circular in nature. Understanding feedback loops is critical, particularly to understanding the unintended consequences of managerial action (Senge, 2006). Negative feedback is particularly associated with stability, regulation and the maintenance of equilibrium in organisations. Positive feedback is particularly associated with instability, change and adaptation to changing circumstances.

This means that organisations need to institute mechanisms for not only single-loop control (focused on regulation) but also double-loop control (focused on adaptation). Chapter 10 argues that various forms of analysis of the environment are critical to double-loop control.

However, just like the organisation itself the environment is not a static entity. It is in a state of continual flux – it is a 'heaving landscape'. Actions the organisation takes affect this landscape. In turn the organisation changes to improve its 'fit' with the environmental landscape. For instance, an organisation might pursue a strategy that changes the competitive landscape of its market. Competitors will naturally react, and their actions will cause the organisation to reflect on its strategy, and probably make further changes.

Organisations, systems and information

Information is critical to the effective operation and control of activity systems. It is critical for staff who need to coordinate their work with others, and it is critical to the effective monitoring of performance and the exercise of managerial control. So information and information systems are essential for both internal and external activity. To generalise, the effective performance of every activity system in organisations relies on effective information systems. Information systems are also needed for recording transactions between an organisation and its environment, and for managing relationships with external stakeholders.

ICT can be used in the design or redesign of systems, as well as playing its part in system operation. For many years the tendency was to replace existing activity systems, automating

Suboptimisation: Optimising the performance of a component subsystem independently will not generally optimise the performance of the system as a whole.

them in whole or in part. More recently the emphasis has been on seeing ICT as an agency to innovate new forms of activity system. But we must take note of a key principle of systemic thinking, SUBOPTIMISATION. Optimising the performance of one subsystem – such as an ICT system – will not necessarily optimise the performance of the system as a whole; it could even worsen it. So improvements in technology do not guarantee improvements in activity. This means, importantly, that activity systems, information systems and ICT systems should be designed in parallel to achieve optimal performance (see Chapter 12).

Case check:
Case 20, Tesco plc

Tesco operates a number of information systems which contribute to both operational control through single-loop feedback and strategic control through double-loop feedback. For instance, sales of products are recorded at checkouts, and the information updates the data on shelf stock levels, which in turn prompts staff to refill the shelves from the storeroom. This is an example of operational control. Sales to loyalty card holders provide valuable information to the company about which people buy what. This is used for determining which products to sell at which stores at which times of the year. This is an example of strategic control.

Organisation structure and organisation culture

Culture: The set of behaviours expected in a social group.

Two other viewpoints on the organisation complement the systems viewpoint: structure and CULTURE.

A systems viewpoint generally implies a dynamic perspective on organisational life. In contrast, a **structural view** tends to be static. A structural model of an organisation normally means a map of the relationships between its employees. Of particular interest are relationships of power and authority.

Organisation structure: The set of objects of relevance to an organisation plus the relationships between these objects.

Chain of command and control: Refers to the relationships of power and authority established in the organisation between its members.

The term ORGANISATIONAL STRUCTURE generally refers to the formal aspects of how an organisation functions. Three aspects of formal structure are important to most organisations: division of labour, chain of control and formal procedures:

- The **division of labour** refers to the way in which tasks and responsibilities are bundled into defined roles and assigned to people.
- The CHAIN OF COMMAND AND CONTROL refers to established relationships of power and authority: who is whose boss, in other words.
- Most medium to large-scale organisations have explicit **rules and procedures** which set down the expected ways of working.

All these aspects are found at their most extreme in bureaucracies. Bureaucracies have rigid formal structures with clearly defined roles, clearly defined procedures for action and clearly delineated chains of command and control. Often these are summarised in organisation charts or organograms, like Figure 2.15.

One important characteristic of the chain of command is the **span of control:** in other words, the number of staff a manager can successfully supervise. Research suggests that for most organisations the number is between four and 12. Obviously, the fewer people on each level, the more levels there will need to be. An increased span of control can lead to communication problems.

Large organisations have historically maintained **unitary structures**, in which there is a direct chain of command and centralised control of operations. This makes for a rigid hierarchy in which decisions flow downwards and information flows upwards. More recently many large organisations have changed over to **multidivisional structures**, in which each division runs as a semi-autonomous operation. This is particularly true for multinational and global organisations. Often their divisions are set up on national lines.

Modern organisations have decentralised even further. The trend has been to introduce **business units** within divisions, which act as semi-autonomous profit centres. They tend to be structured around either functions such as marketing and finance, or products and services, such as different manufacturing plants producing different automobile models.

These forms of organisational structure are illustrated in Figure 2.16.

Since modern organisations tend to operate in fast-changing environments, they frequently need to restructure rapidly. This is often seen as a way of maintaining competitive position.

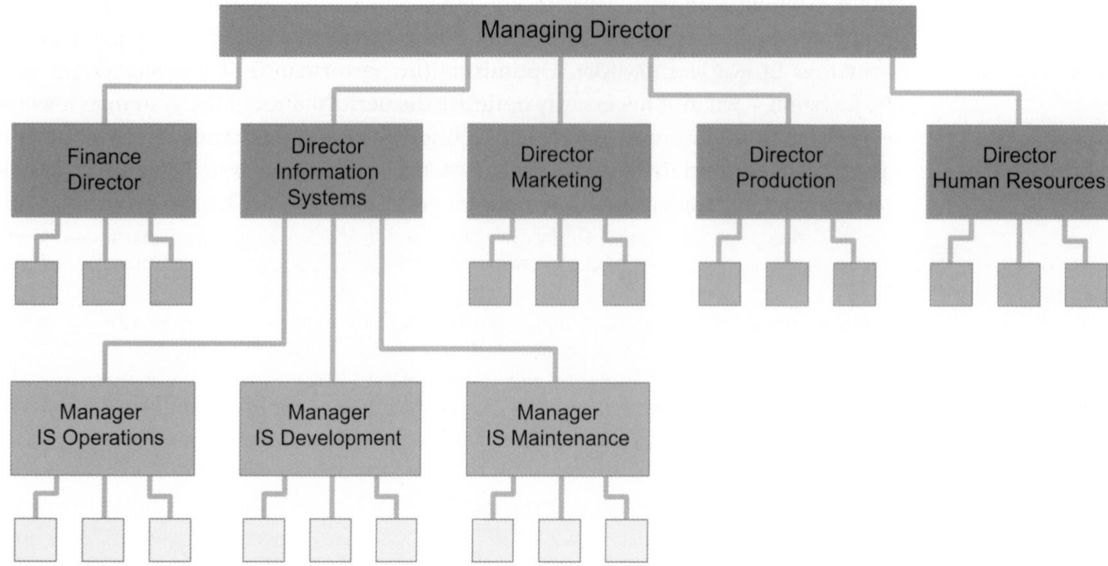

Figure 2.15: *An organisation chart*

On page 44 we introduced the key systemics concept of a **worldview**: that is, the set of underlying assumptions used by individuals and groups in understanding and constructing the world. This has much in common with Vickers' concept of an **appreciative system** (1965). This is 'the interconnected set of largely tacit standards of judgement by which we both order and value our experience'. He argues that decision making depends on the different appreciative systems that decision makers bring to bear on a problem, and that the stability of organisations depends largely on shared appreciative systems.

Organisation culture: The set of behavioural expectations associated with an organisation.

Appreciative systems in turn have much in common with the concept of ORGANISATIONAL CULTURE. A culture is the set of behaviours expected in a social group. We all know that any long-standing social group develops its own set of expected behaviours or norms, and people frequently speak of differences of culture between nation-states or regions. More recently commentators on organisations have suggested that differences in organisational culture are important.

Since an organisation is (or should be) a coherent social group, there grows up an organisational culture which exists within the larger societal culture. Management writers often suggest that top managers need to create 'strong' organisational cultures. This demand makes several assumptions:

- that organisational culture is open to manipulation
- that it can be designed by business leaders
- that it is a unifying force
- that it is linked to organisational effectiveness and performance via employee motivation.

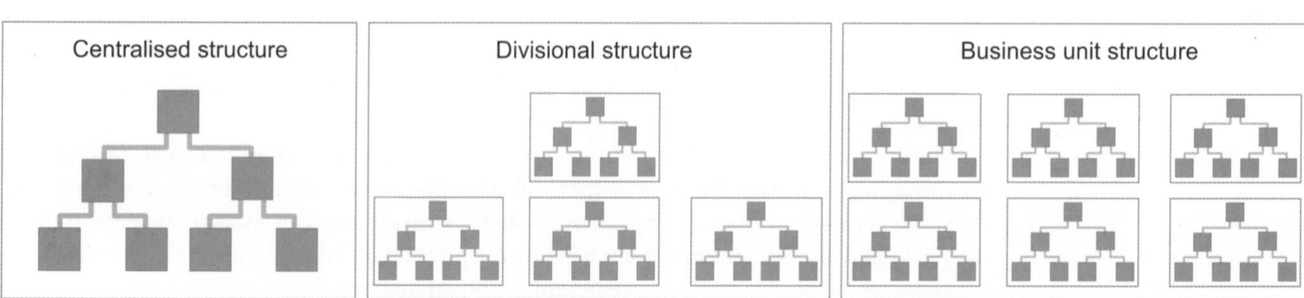

Figure 2.16: *Forms of organisational structure*

Each of these is open to question. Sociologists argue that groups do develop strong cultures if they have stable and homogeneous membership and stay together for long periods, but this is not always true of work organisations. A culture forms and changes slowly, if only because it takes time for new members to be socialised into the culture; to learn and accept its norms. And as well as possibly being a way of prompting change, organisation culture can be a major conservative force, preventing improvements in work practices and the adoption of new forms of technology.

It is also a dangerous simplification to assume that all organisations have a single 'culture'. In practice, medium to large-scale organisations are likely to feature a number of interacting subcultures. 'SUBCULTURE' refers to a subgroup within a broader social unit (such as an organisation), who share sets of meanings (a worldview) that is not the same as, and distinguishes its members from, the wider group and culture around them. Subcultures can grow up in structural units (such as departments) or within different stakeholder groups (managers, shop-floor employees, shareholders).

Subculture: The set of behavioural expectations associated with a part of a larger social grouping.

I experienced this myself in an utility company, where two distinct groups of workers had quite different subcultures, although they both carried out very similar work, and worked near each other in the company headquarters. They both consisted of 'linespeople' – that is, workers with responsibility for inspecting, maintaining and repairing parts of the utility network – but one group serviced low-power electricity lines while the other group serviced high-power lines.

The low-power linespeople worked as a group, and decisions about which lines should be serviced and what maintenance should be conducted were made at the centre. In contrast the high-power linespeople worked very much as individuals, and maintenance decisions were normally delegated to them. It was claimed that this was at least partly because the high-power workers had more dangerous jobs, so they needed to have delegated authority in deciding how to carry them out. This is an example of the kind of ways in which organisational cultures and subcultures carry through into individual expectations and operating procedures.

Reflect
Consider an organisation known to you. How would you describe its culture in terms of one of the dimensions listed in Hofstede?

Geert Hofstede (1991) introduced an influential model based on dimensions of cultures, and this is a convenient way of describing how they differ. Some of the dimensions he suggested were individualism/collectivism, risk-taking/risk aversion, masculinity/femininity and equality/inequality. Each individual culture will be located at some point on each of these dimensions.

In some organisations people expect to work and be rewarded as individuals (**individualism**), while in others they tend to work and be rewarded in teams (**collectivism**). In the utility company there was clearly a difference between the subcultures on this dimension.

In some organisations people feel encouraged to take risks as individuals (**risk-taking**) while in others they are discouraged (**risk aversion**) and prefer to play safe and pass decisions to their managers.

Masculinity refers to a set of values including assertiveness in personal relations, acquisitiveness (of money and possessions) and a lack of thoughtfulness about others. **Femininity** refers to a set of values focused around people and the importance of nurturing interpersonal relationships.

In some organisations **inequalities** in the distribution of power between individuals and groups are accepted, while in others power tends to be distributed more **equitably**.

Key skill 

Process modelling

Modelling is important, not only for understanding how organisations work now, but for designing new ways of working. We use the systems concept in modelling, in a hierarchical way: in other words, we can specify the system's working at a high or low level of detail. On page 53 we discussed building high-level models of purposeful activity. Now let us look at the application of process modelling to organisational problems. Process modelling allows us to represent in detail the important current or intended features of organisational systems.

Modelling approach: Constructs, notation and principles of use for modelling.

Any form of modelling needs three elements:

- **constructs**: the components of the model
- **notation**: the way we choose to represent the constructs in the model, which could be textual, graphical and/or mathematical (although it is usually graphical in informatics work because graphics are easy to use and a good way of communicating with others)
- **principles**: the formal and informal rules for constructing the model correctly.

Although modelling is essential in informatics work, there is no agreement on the most appropriate way of modelling organisational systems. We have hinted at one way of doing it through many of the figures in this chapter, though, and now we shall look at this more closely and completely. It is based loosely on Business Process Modelling Notation (BPMN), which was developed by the Business Process Management Initiative and is now maintained by the Object Management Group. Its aim is to provide a standard notation that is readily understandable by a variety of business stakeholders, including business analysts who create and refine business processes, technical developers responsible for implementing the ICT systems they need, and business managers who manage and control them. (The BPMN notation has been modified in this book to fit better with the modelling techniques discussed in other chapters.) It is summarised in Figure 2.17.

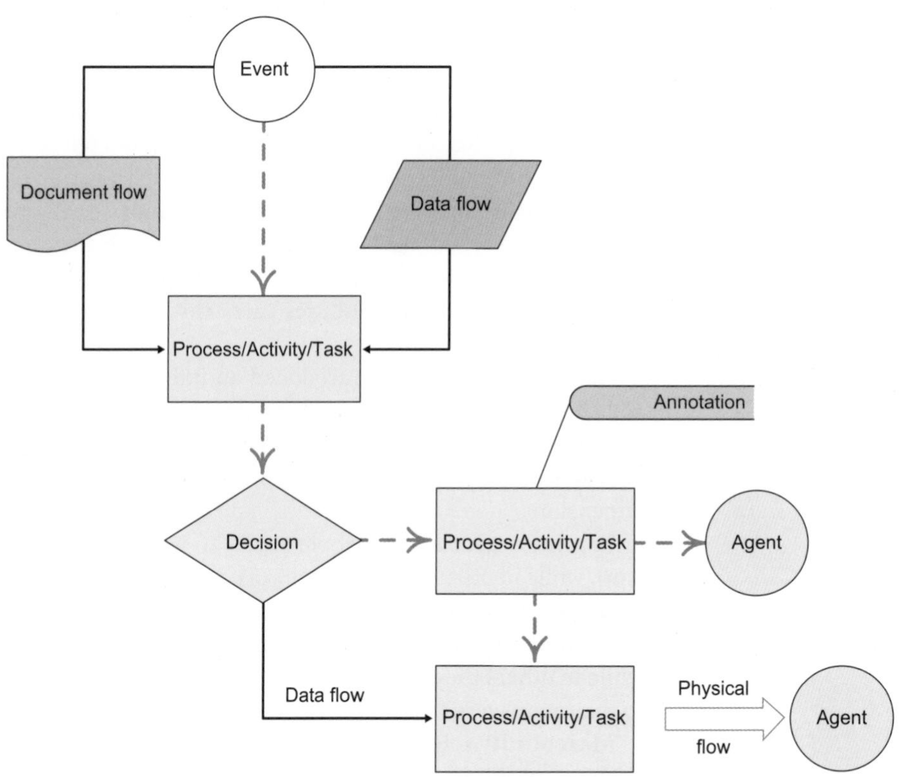

Figure 2.17: *Process modelling constructs*

- **Process/Activity/Task**. This defines a coherent piece of work, and is represented by a box labelled with a description of the process, activity or task performed.
- **Agents/Events**. These act as triggers for processes. They may act as the start or end-point of a process, or as an anchor for an intermediate result within a process. Events or agents in the external environment are represented as circles in the process model.
- **Sequence.** It is important to represent the sequence or precedence of activities. Sequences are represented as dashed or dotted lines with open arrowheads to indicate their direction.
- **Decisions.** These represent key control points in a process, and are also used to fork, join or merge different flows in a process. Decision points are represented by labelled diamonds.
- **Messages.** Two types of message flow in support of activities can be represented on a

process model. A labelled solid but narrow arrow with a solid head is used to indicate the direction of information flow. It is sometimes useful to distinguish between non-physical flow of information and the physical flow of paper documentation. Slanted boxes on the flow indicate non-physical information, and document symbols indicate physical forms of information.

- **Physical flows.** It is sometimes important to include the flow of physical items such as raw materials or finished goods. For this purpose a broad, labelled arrow is used.
- **Annotations.** These provide additional information about a process, sequence, decision or data flow. They are represented as bubbles attached by a line to the appropriate construct.
- **Functional band**. All the above elements are normally contained in an enclosing and named box known as a functional band. It provides a name for the process or sub-process. A series of functional bands can be used in a diagram to indicate communication between processes or subprocesses.

As an example, a possible process for managing inventory is illustrated as a process model in Figure 2.18. The entire process is made up of a workflow of defined activities. The control processes are embedded, as key decision points. You can see a clear feedback process at the decision point *stock level > re-order level*: if false (that is, the answer is no), this generates an order for new stock. It should also be clear that the activities both rely on information and generate information.

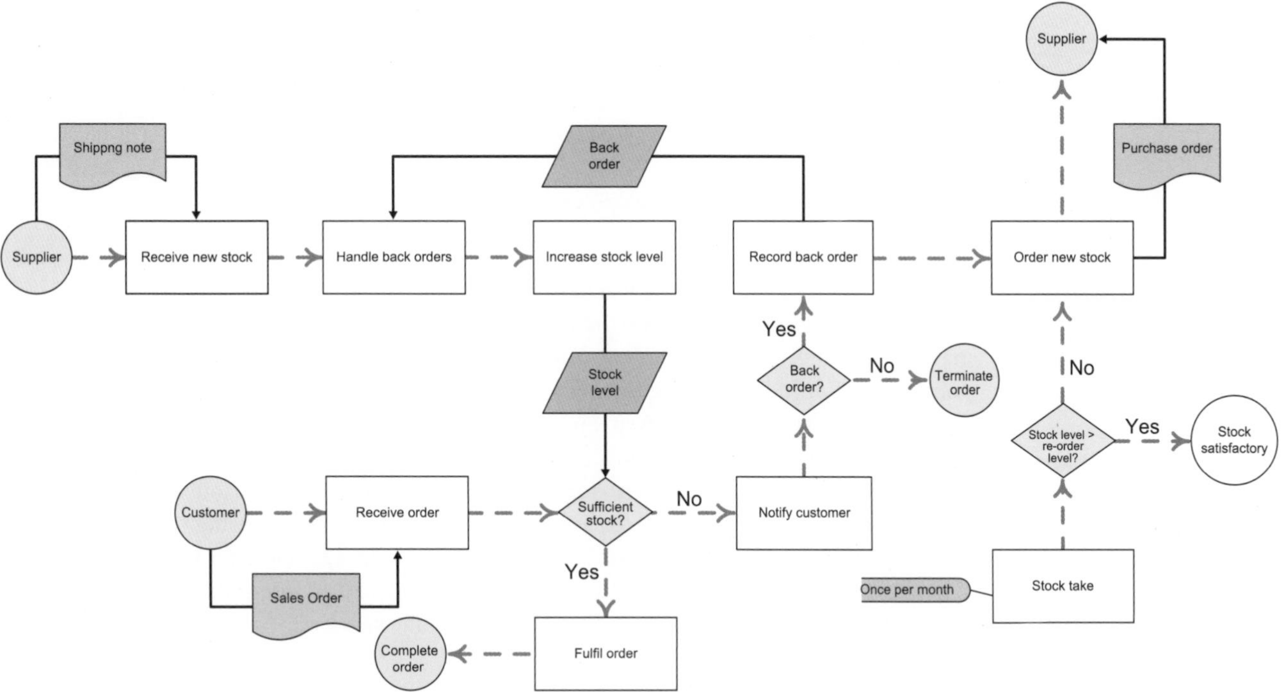

Figure 2.18: *Inventory management process*

Figure 2.19 is an example of process modelling from the public sector, dealing with the apparently simple issue of conducting a civil marriage, and showing how it has cross-organisational and inter-organisational consequences. Deciding to get married sets off a train of information-handling and other activities. First, details of the two partners need to be set down on an application form, then this is verified against approved documentation such as birth certificates and passports. Once the application is approved, a ceremony is booked and conducted. After the ceremony, a further train of information-handling takes place. The couple need a marriage certificate, and they are likely to need to update other records because of their change of status, and perhaps too of name and/or residence.

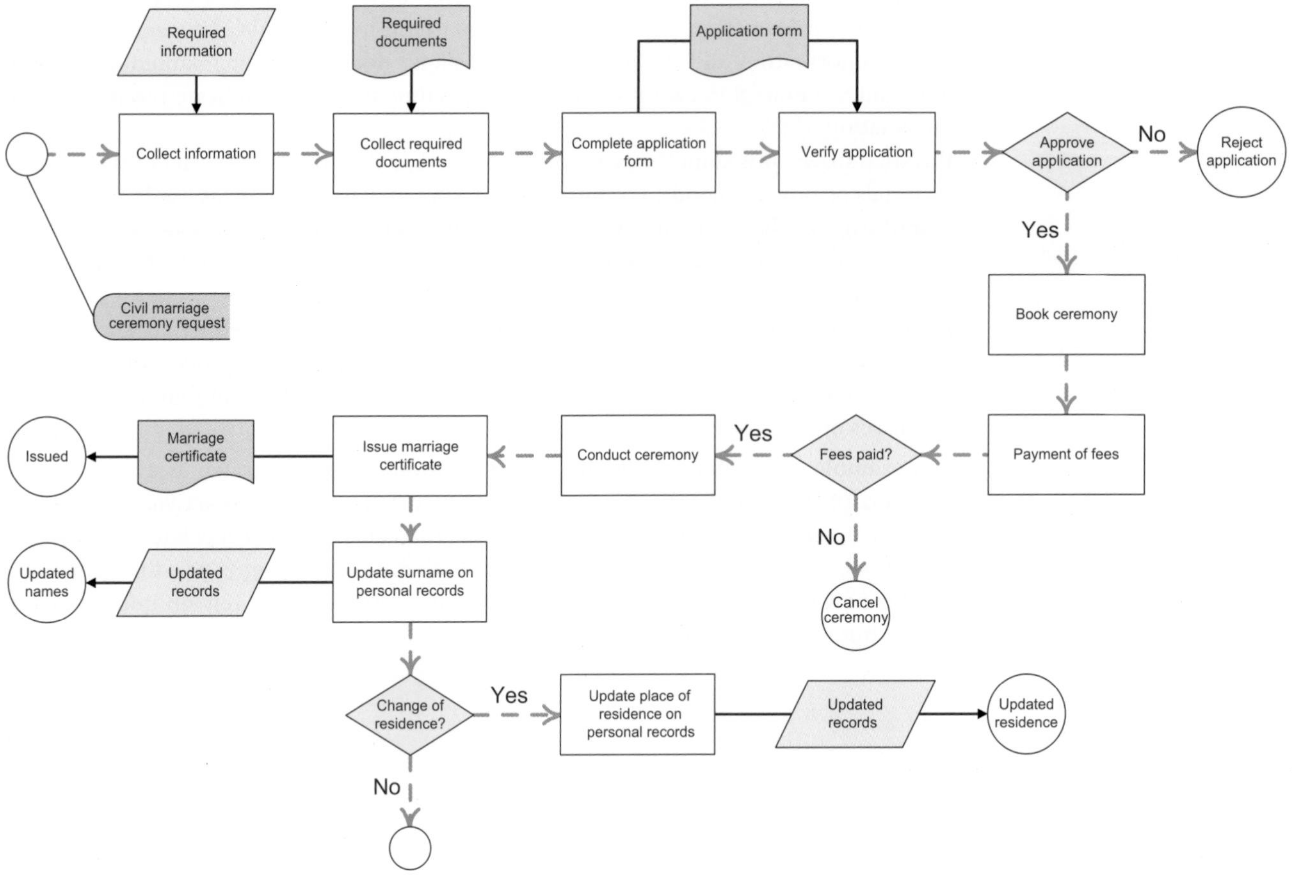

Figure 2.19: *Civil marriage process model*

The model is useful because it makes many aspects of this process explicit. First, it details the flow of activity: planning for the ceremony, conducting it, and all the post-marriage formalities. Second, it details the control embedded in the process, by a number of decision points. Third, it highlights the important way in which the input of information is critical. It also shows information outputs at various points.

It is also interesting to note how many organisations are involved in this model. Although a civil registrar (in the UK system) deals with much of the activity, various other public sector organisations are also involved: for example, driver and vehicle licensing (if there is a change of name or address), voting registries and tax collection agencies. So we could use this as a first step in considering how these agencies could better integrate their processes and information systems to provide a more effective public service.

Key skill 

Process design

The terms organisational or **business analysis** are used in a number of different senses. They can refer to the analysis of the informal systems of organisations: those systems of activity that are not formalised in the sense of being written down. They can refer to the process of analysing the overall objectives and needs of an organisation, and placing it in its environment. Here we focus on organisational analysis as concerned with analysing the different ways in which an organisation or part of an organisation works, and identifying the most fruitful role for information systems and ICT.

Business process re-engineering: An organisational analysis approach to redesigning business processes.

The 1990s saw the emergence of BUSINESS PROCESS RE-ENGINEERING or **business process redesign** – BPR for short (Hammer and Champy, 1993). One of its major premises is that ICT in and of itself delivers little value for most organisations. The value comes when it enables changes to activity that have the potential to deliver increases in organisational performance.

There are several implications here for the way in which organisations approach activity systems, information systems and ICT:

- ICT systems should initiate organisational change, not solidify organisational structure. BPR sees many of the problems of traditional ICT as arising from the tendency of the industry to 'pave over the cow-paths': to automate existing processes, not ask whether they are appropriate to the wider system. Management theorists like Davenport, Hammer and Champy have argued that when business processes are automated without first improving them, organisations will not achieve significant benefits from their investment in ICT.
- Activity systems must be designed in parallel with information systems. This is much the same as an established principle in the sociotechnical design movement mentioned earlier, that work systems and technical systems need to be designed together.
- Radical redesign of major business processes is likely to generate the greatest benefit. This is because of the danger of suboptimisation (see page 59). Information systems cannot work in isolation. The most effective use of ICT frequently involves redesigning entire business processes across the organization.

The essential features of process redesign are shown by a classic piece of research that Hammer (1990) conducted at IBM. IBM Credit (Hammer and Champy, 1993) was a subsidiary dealing with the financing of purchases of IBM hardware. In the old process, a salesperson called in with a request for financing. One of 14 people logged the request on a paper form. The form was then sent to a department where staff entered details of the request into a computer system and determined the customer's creditworthiness. Credit check details were written on the form and it was passed to the business practices department, which modified the standard form of loan to suit the customer. Any special terms were attached to the form and it was passed to a pricer who determined the appropriate interest rate with the help of a spreadsheet. This person then delivered this form to a clerical department which turned the information into a quote. This entire process took six days on average, long enough that many would-be customers gave up in despair.

The new process replaced specialists with generalists. A new role was created, of a deal structurer, who would deal with the entire order provided it was straightforward. An ICT system was developed to support the deal structurer. This led to a reduction in turnaround time from six days to four hours.

The typical elements of process redesign this illustrates are:

- Several jobs are combined into one. Jobs evolve from being narrow and task-oriented to being multidimensional. A case manager provides a single point of contact for customers.
- Workers make decisions. Work units change from functional departments to process teams. Processes cross traditional departmental boundaries.
- The steps in a process are performed in a 'natural' order. Work is performed where it makes the most sense, not to suit traditional boundaries or divisions.
- Control is sited as close to the point of work as possible. The focus is still on performance measures but reward shifts from activity to results.
- ICT is a key enabler, and particularly enables traditionally fragmented activities to be stitched together.

In a typical redesign process there are five phases. The first three consist of **unfreezing** activities, in the sense that they involve studying inadequacies in the current system and planning new ways of doing things. The last two stages consist of **freezing** activities, in the sense that they involve specifying a new process in some detail, then implementing it.

Process mapping

This first stage involves constructing a high-level map of organisational processes and indicating key process boundaries on it. A form of modelling notation is normally used; we have used conceptual maps for this.

From the process map, the designer needs to prioritise the importance of redesign of particular processes or subprocesses. Three sets of criteria can be used to rank processes:

Redundancy: A measure of the degree to which data is unnecessarily replicated across information systems.

- The 'health' of the process: does it work well, or is it dysfunctional? The key question is, which processes are in the deepest trouble? Indicators include extensive information exchange, REDUNDANCY of work and information, and unnecessary iteration of tasks.
- The criticality of the process: how important is it to the core competencies of the organisation? The key question here is, which processes have the greatest impact on performance? The aim is to find processes that offer the greatest potential for improving efficiency and effectiveness.
- The feasibility of redesign. This may involve questions of cost, or issues such as whether redesign is politically and culturally feasible in the organisation.

Process redesign

This involves the re-engineering team identifying problems with the existing process, challenging assumptions about ways of doing things, and brainstorming new approaches to organisational activity. Design workshops are held and various system stakeholders participate.

Process specification

This generally involves both modelling of existing processes and designing new ones, using the kind of modelling we discussed earlier.

Process implementation

This is probably the most difficult phase of process re-engineering, and involves introducing new work practices and associated technologies.

Summary

1. This chapter considered the important context for informatics work, the organisation. It began by considering some classic viewpoints on the organisation, and distinguished between the institutional perspective and the action perspective. It focused on considering organisations as complex, adaptive systems. This unifying perspective allows us to see an organisation as both an institution and a collection of individuals collaborating to achieve a common purpose.
2. The concept of a system has had a profound influence on informatics. This is seen, for instance, in the label 'information system': the primary bridge between human activity and ICT. The system concept is applied both to technology such as hardware and software ('hard' systems) and to human activity ('soft' systems). Information systems today are key examples of hybrid or sociotechnical systems (Emery and Trist, 1960).
3. Systems concepts have heavily influenced the design of modern computer technology. Systems thinking also influenced the creation of the communications revolution that underpins the Internet and the World Wide Web.
4. Systemic thinking underlies much contemporary thinking and work on business organisations, because it offers practical ways of engaging with organisational life. Most organisations can be modelled or analysed in systems terms. The aim of this is to identify deficiencies in current systems, then design new systems that can improve organisational performance. From this perspective, both information systems and ICT are key enablers for organisational change.

In Chapter 3 we consider another of the foundation concepts for informatics, information. We relate this concept to a number of issues arising from our treatment of organisations: the relationship of information to data and knowledge, the role of information in decision making and action, and the relationship of management to all these issues.

Focus on Value 

This chapter has showed the value of the concept of systems for considering organisations as both institutions and complex networks of individuals engaging in action. From either perspective, an organisation can be seen as a value-creating system, but how we identify and describe it depends on the worldviews or different appreciative systems of stakeholders both within and outside the organisation.

Worldviews or appreciative systems are essentially ways of valuing the world. For instance, our view of the purpose of the organisation-as-system will colour how we assess its performance, and how we design and implement processes of control.

All managers work with models, but these are frequently tacit or implicit. This book argues that it is important to model organisations explicitly. It introduces a number of different techniques or approaches for this. Modelling makes plain our understanding of how organisations work or should work. This can then be communicated and it can also be criticised.

Review test

1	Which are the two major perspectives on organisational life? Select two. ☐ Institutional perspective ☐ Bureaucratic perspective ☐ Action perspective ☐ Social perspective
2	Select the two statements that most accurately reflect the concept of structuration: ☐ Social structures never change. ☐ Through human interaction social structures are reproduced and may also change. ☐ Social structures do not exist independently of people ☐ Social structures constrain and inform human interaction.
3	A ____________ is an organised collection of things with emergent properties and some defined purpose. Fill in the blank.
4	Systemics considers phenomena by dissecting a problem into its smallest parts, attempting to understand the workings of parts, and building up a conception of the whole from this understanding. True or false? ☐ True ☐ False
5	A bicycle considered as a set of bicycle parts would be regarded as a system. True or false? ☐ True ☐ False
6	Modelling approaches can be distinguished by their levels of abstraction. Put the models in order from highest to lowest level of abstraction. Order using 1 for the model at the highest level of abstraction and 3 for the lowest. Logical model Physical model Conceptual model
7	Feedback has two major forms, positive and ____________ feedback. Fill in the blank.
8	The key elements of any system are inputs, outputs and what else? Select one. ☐ Process ☐ Agent ☐ Subsystem
9	Systems generally can be seen as being composed of ____________. Hierarchy seems to be an inherent property of most systems. Fill in the blank.
10	Variety refers to how flexible a system is. True or False? ☐ True ☐ False
11	Control enables a system to: Select all that apply. ☐ Regulate its behaviour. ☐ Improve its performance. ☐ Adapt to its environment.
12	A control process is composed of: Select all that apply. ☐ Sensors ☐ Processes ☐ Comparators ☐ Effectors
13	The UK is a parliamentary democracy and hence is reliant on an effective electoral system. The key inputs into the electoral system are ballot poll cards and ballot papers provided by the key agents, voters. The key outputs are a set of election results for each constituency. The key control process is electoral monitoring, which establishes guidance on expected electoral practice and monitors the actual election to determine any deviation from it. The environment of the electoral system is the overall political system of the UK. On a seperate sheet, draw a high-level conceptual map of this system.
14	Organisations are best described as what type of system? Select one. ☐ Closed ☐ Open ☐ Deterministic
15	The performance of any system is frequently expressed in terms of the three Es. Select the three most appropriate. ☐ Efficiency ☐ Effectiveness ☐ Enabling ☐ Efficacy
16	A business process is a set of ____________ cutting across functional areas of a business. Fill in the blank.
17	Match the name of the information systems modelling construct to the most appropriate symbol. Sequence ☐ Activity ⟶ Message flow - - ➝ Data ◇ Decision ▱
18	A ____________ is the set of behaviours expected in a social group. Fill in the blank.

Exercises

1. Consider an organisation known to you. Use one or more of the perspectives from organisation theory to characterise the organisation. For instance, would you class it as bureaucratic (mechanistic) or organic?
2. Identify one activity system known to you, and identify its key components.
3. Investigate the control processes you would expect in an organisation such as a university. What are the appropriate sensors, comparators and effectors in this control process?
4. Consider an educational organization such as a school or university as a system. Try to identify some possible subsystems.
5. There are various ways of classifying systems besides open or closed. Try to identify a number of other system types and give examples of each type.
6. Investigate a process of interest to a university such as the enrolment of students. Develop a simple process model for this process.
7. Attempt to draw high-level process models for the business process re-engineering examples described in this chapter.
8. Consider university teaching as a process and suggest some appropriate measures for assessing the efficacy, efficiency and effectiveness of it.
9. Negative feedback is frequently used to maintain the homeostasis of a system. Investigate the term homeostasis in greater detail and report on your findings.
10. Identify an example of positive feedback in some organization known to you.
11. Provide an example of the process of structuration (other than those given in this chapter) and discuss its importance.

Projects

1. Examine the literature on business information systems. Determine which of the models of organisation discussed in this chapter features the most in this literature.
2. Attempt to apply some aspect of systems thinking to a nontrivial problem in business or commerce. For instance, consider the problem organisations such as Tesco have in managing their supplies and suppliers. Attempt to model this supply chain as a system, and analyse the usefulness of applying a systems approach to this area.
3. The systems approach has been criticised by a range of authors in the areas of organisation theory and organisation behaviour. Investigate this literature and use it to critically determine the degree to which it is appropriate to use a systems model for describing and understanding organisations.
4. The whole is greater than the sum of its parts or the system is greater than the sum of its subsystems. What do you think is meant by this in terms of the three levels of business systems (activity systems, information systems and ICT systems) examined in this book? Provide some examples of the way in which these principles reflect organisational life.
5. Attempt a small project in process redesign within an organisation known to you. For instance, consider the admissions process at a university. How could this process be improved, and how important is ICT to your redesign?
6. There are a number of different graphical notations for specifying activity models and process models. Investigate two distinct notations for specifying either activity models or organisational processes. Develop some criteria of comparison (such as number of constructs or ease of drawing) and analyse each approach using these criteria.
7. Models are useful as a means of joint understanding not only within a particular organisation but also between organisations. Some have proposed the development of high-level or generic process models that may be applicable across organisations within the same industrial sector. Suggest some of the benefits and problems of this proposal. Determine to what degree it is possible for organisations to reuse existing generic process models to help in organisational analysis and design.

Further reading

There are many books on organisational theory and organisational behaviour. Bratton et al. (2007) provide a recent and comprehensive review of the field. This chapter has provided an overview of systems theory as applied to organisations, which is particularly designed to act as foundation to our consideration of informatics. Checkland (1999) provides the definitive account of soft systems work upon which the approach to activity systems described in this chapter is based. Jackson (2003) provides a more general but comprehensive overview of the range of systems thinking applied to management practice. Unfortunately there is not one central book on process modelling that can be recommended. Yeates et al. (2007) provides a high-level overview of business analysis within which process analysis takes its place.

References

Argyris, C. and Schön, D. A. (1978) *Organizational Learning: A theory of action perspective*. Reading, Mass., Addison-Wesley.

Ashby, W. R. (1956) *An Introduction to Cybernetics*. London, Chapman Hall.

Beer, S. (1966) *Decision and Control: The meaning of operational research and management cybernetics*. Chichester, John Wiley.

Beer, S. (1972) *Brain of the Firm: The managerial cybernetics of organisation*. London, Allen Lane.

Bertalanffy, L. V. (1951) 'General Systems Theory: a new approach to the unity of science', *Human Biology* 23(Dec.): 302–61.

Boulding, K. E. (1956) 'General Systems Theory – the skeleton of a science', *Management Science* 2(April): 197–208.

Bratton, J., Callinan, M., Forshaw, C. and Sawchuk, P. (2007) *Work and Organisational Behaviour*. Basingstoke, Palgrave.

Burns, T. and Stalker, G. M. (1961) *The Management of Innovation*. London, Tavistock.

Capra, F. (1996) *The Web of Life: A new synthesis of mind and matter*. London, Flamingo.

Checkland, P. (1987) *Systems Thinking, Systems Practice*. Chichester, John Wiley.

Checkland, P. (1999) *Soft Systems Methodology: A thirty year retrospective*. Chichester, John Wiley.

Churchman, C. W., Ackoff, R. L. and Arnoff, E. L. (1957) *Introduction to Operations Research*. New York, Wiley.

Durkheim, E. (1936) *The Rules of Sociological Method*. Glencoe, Ill., Free Press.

Ellis, W. D. (1938) *A Source Book of Gestalt Psychology*. London, Routledge & Kegan Paul.

Emery, F. E. and Trist, E. L. (1960) 'Socio-technical systems', in C. W. Churchman and M. Verhulst (eds), *Management Science, Models and Techniques*, Vol. 2. New York, Pergamon.

Fortune, J. and Peters, G. (2005) *Information Systems: Achieving success by avoiding failure*. Chichester, John Wiley.

Garfinkel, H. (1967) *Studies in Ethnomethodology*, Englewood Cliffs, N.J., Prentice-Hall.

Glieick, J. (1997) *Chaos: The making of a new science*. London, Vintage.

Goffman, E. (1990) *Stigma: Notes on the management of spoiled identity*. Harmondsworth, Penguin.

Hammer, M. (1990) 'Re-engineering work: don't automate, obliterate', *Harvard Business Review* July–August: 18–25.

Hammer, M. and Champy, J. (1993) *Reengineering the Corporation: A manifesto for business revolution*. London, Nicholas Brearley.

Heims, S. J. (1991) *The Cybernetics Group*. MIT Press, Boston, Mass.

Hofstede, G. (1991) *Cultures and Organisations*. New York, McGraw-Hill.

Jackson, M. C. (2003) *Systems Thinking: Creative holism for managers*. Chichester, John Wiley.

Johnson, S. (2002) *Emergence: The connected lives of ants, brains, cities and software*. London, Penguin.

Katz, D. and Kahn, R. L. (1966) *The Social Psychology of Organisations*. New York, Wiley.

Kaufmann, S. (1995) *At Home in the Universe*. New York, Oxford University Press.

Koestler, A. (1967) *The Ghost in the Machine*. London, Hutchinson.

Lovelock, J. (2000) *Gaia: A new look at life on Earth*. Oxford, Oxford University Press.

Mason, R. O. and Mitroff, I. I. (1981) *Challenging Strategic Planning Assumptions: Theory, cases and techniques*. New York, John Wiley.

Maurer, J. G. (1971) *Readings in Organisation Theory: Open systems approaches*. New York, Random House.

Mayo, E. M. (1933) *The Human Problems of an Industrial Civilisation*. New York, Macmillan.

Morgan, G. (1986) *Images of Organisation*. London, Sage.

Polanyi, M. (1962) *Personal Knowledge*. Anchor Bay Books, New York.

Senge, P. M. (2006) *The Fifth Discipline: The art and practice of the learning organisation*. New York, Doubleday.

Silverman, D. (1982) *The Theory of Organisations*. London, Macmillan.

Simon, H. A. (1976) *Administrative Behavior : A study of decision-making processes in administration*. New York, Free Press.

Stacey, R. D. (1991) *Chaos Frontier: Creative strategic control for business*. Oxford, Butterworth-Heinemann.

Stacey, R. D. (2003) *Strategic Management and Organisational Dynamics: The challenge of complexity*. Harlow, Pearson Education.

Taylor, F. W. (1911) *Principles of Scientific Management*. New York, Harper and Row.

Vickers, G. (1965) *The Art of Judgement*. London, Chapman and Hall.

Waddington, C. H. (1977) *Tools for Thought*. St Albans, Herts, Jonathan Cape.

Walsham, G. and C.-K. Han (1991) 'Structuration theory and information systems research', *Journal of Applied Systems Analysis* 17.

Weber, M. (1946) *Essays in Sociology*. Oxford, Oxford University Press.

Whyte, W. H. (1956) *The Organization Man*. Simon and Schuster. New York.

Wiener, N. (1948) *Cybernetics*. New York, Wiley.

Wilson, B. (1990) *Systems: Concepts, methodologies and applications*. Chichester, John Wiley.

Wright, R. (1989) *Systems Thinking: A guide to managing in a changing environment*. Dearborn, Michigan, Society of Manufacturing Engineers.

Yeates, D., Paul, D., Jenkins, T., Hindle, K. and Rollason, C. (2007) *Business Analysis*. London, BCS Publications.

CHAPTER 3 Data, information and knowledge

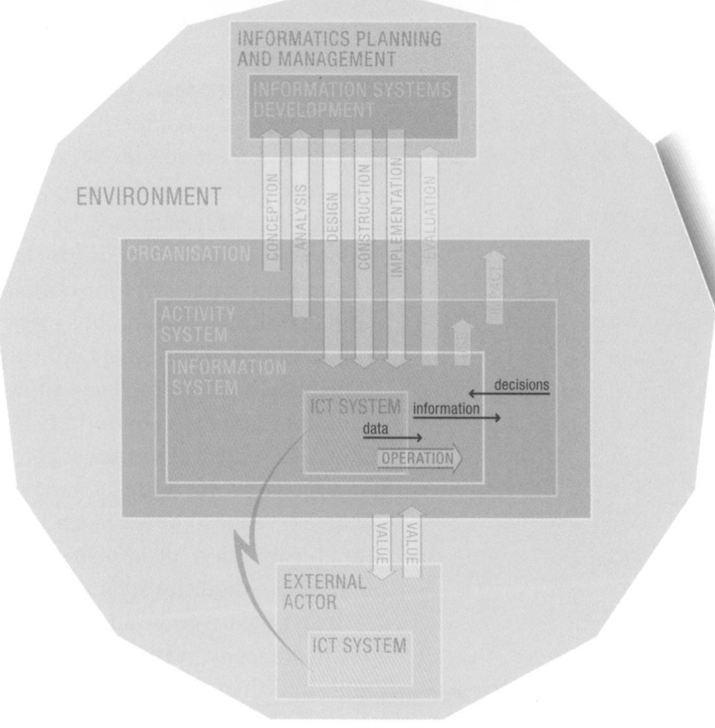

It is a capital mistake to theorise before one has data. Insensibly one begins to twist facts to suit theories, instead of theories to suit facts.

Sir Arthur Conan Doyle (1859–1930, A Scandal in Bohemia (1890)

Take care of the sense, and the sounds will take care of themselves.

Lewis Carroll (1832–1898). Alice's Adventures in Wonderland (1865), Chapter 9

LEARNING OUTCOMES	PRINCIPLES
Understand the relationship between signs and information and describe the place of information within the process of communication.	The concept of information is difficult to define because of its multi-faceted nature. The concept of a sign and the discipline of semiotics provide a useful framework for explaining the layered way in which information occurs in communication of any form.
Define differences between data, information and knowledge and describe the relationship between information, decision making and action.	An understanding of the principles of semiotics allows us to clearly distinguish between data, information and knowledge in organisations. It also provides a straightforward way of explaining the relationship between business information, business decision making and organisational action.
Relate the importance of modelling data, information and knowledge to informatics and construct simple data, information and knowledge models.	The structure of data, information and knowledge underlies business systems of many forms. It is therefore important to model data, information and knowledge in preparation for the design, operation and management of such business systems.

CHAPTER OUTLINE

Introduction

Chapter 1 argued that information is a critical concept for the twenty-first century. Information is vital to the competitiveness of the private sector globally. It is an important 'commodity' in modern economies. It is even developing as an important issue in the natural sciences, particularly physics and biology, causing some to refer to information as the new language of science (Von Baeyer, 2003).

But what is meant by 'information' in these contexts? In the natural sciences it tends to be defined quite narrowly: for example, as the transmission of bits of data. Management writers claim that it is important, but often do not define it at all. Therefore, although information is critical 'stuff', it is extremely difficult 'stuff' to pin down. It is probably not even 'stuff' at all.

Here are some examples to show how difficult it can be to define information.

If information is a commodity it is a very strange commodity. As Stamper states, 'Information is a paradoxical resource: you can't eat it, you can't live in it, you can't travel about in it, but a lot of people want it' (2001). If somebody sells information the commodity does not pass from seller to buyer like a traditional commodity such as food; the seller still retains it. The 'consumption' of information is therefore radically different from the consumption of physical commodities such as food, wine and electronic goods.

Much modern communication and hence information transmission uses technology. Take a telephone conversation. When two people talk on the phone, a lot less information is communicated than if they were talking face to face. The electronic signal travelling down the telephone line conveys only a percentage of the sound frequencies of normal human speech, but more importantly, because the people (often) cannot see each other, they cannot read each other's facial expressions and gestures.

Person A looks across at Person B, who is at the opposite end of a room. He holds up a hand and points a finger upwards, clenching his other fingers in a fist. What will B take this to mean? Is it perhaps an insult, a command to provide one of something, or a message that there is something stuck on the ceiling?

We need to consider issues like the ones these examples raise if we are to think seriously about what information is. They highlight that information is particularly associated with human communication, that communication involves signs, and that signs involve human interpretation. They also demonstrate that information is bound closely with language, action, logic and technology, and other phenomena too. So in thinking about the place of information in organisations, we need a multi-layered or multi-levelled perspective.

This chapter tries to provide that. It is also worth giving information a chapter to itself because it is undoubtedly an important topic in its own right. It is the catalyst of modern society, economy and polity. It is embodied directly in many of our modern technologies. It is an emerging central concept in our understanding of the natural world. Indeed, unpacking the concept of information reveals the interconnectedness of many areas of the contemporary social and physical world.

Understanding the concept of information provides a bedrock for building an effective understanding of the place of information systems, in both organisations and the wider environment. We need to make clear distinctions between data, information and knowledge, and understand how these distinctions help place technology and people within organisational systems. Broadly, we define information as an increment of knowledge which can be inferred from data.

Did you know?

A typical nurse, working on a hospital ward, spends up to 60 per cent of their time in information-handling activities during an average working day.

Signs and communication

Ronald Stamper wrote a seminal work on *Information in Business and Administrative Systems* (1973) more than 35 years ago. Here we build on his definition of information, and use the framework of semiotics to help understand its multifaceted nature. The chapter uses this approach as a unifying thread for fields as disparate as telecommunications, natural language, and management and organisations. The study of information is necessarily a boundary-spanning activity since information infiltrates a multitude of areas, all of which are important to organisational informatics.

Semiotics: The study of signs and sign-systems.

Sign: Anything that is significant. Normally made up of symbol, concept and referent.

Broadly, SEMIOTICS or semiology is the study of SIGNS. Signs act as a core concept to link issues of human intentions, meaning, the structure of language, forms of communication, transmission and collaborative action.

Modern semiotics developed from linguistics and the philosophy of language. Ferdinand de Saussure, one of its founders, wrote a pioneering work on general linguistics in 1916. The American philosopher Charles Morris built on Saussure's ideas and gave them more sophistication. Claude Lévi-Strauss used semiotic approaches in anthropology in the late 1950s. You may be familiar with some of the discussions of semiotic ideas in popular as well as academic literature: for example Umberto Eco's *The Name of the Rose* and Dan Brown's *The Da Vinci Code*. Brown's hero Robert Langdon is a professor of religious symbiology, which (as Brown portrays it) has much in common with semiotics.

Signs

Reflect
Humans use signs every minute of every day. Think about the signs you use in your everyday life. What are they used for?

A sign is anything that is significant. In a sense, everything that humans do is significant to some degree. Sometimes not having or doing anything is regarded as significant too, so our world is resonant with systems of signs.

The linguist and cognitive scientist Steven Pinker (2001) argues that our genetic makeup predisposes humans to be excellent manipulators of sign-systems. A sign-system is any organised collection of signs. Everyday spoken language is probably the most readily accepted and complex example of a sign-system, but signs also exist in most other forms of human activity, since they are critical to the processes of human communication and understanding (Stamper, 1973). Our species is sometimes referred to as *Homo habilis* – man the toolmaker. One of the most effective tools people make and use is signs, so perhaps *Homo signum* would be an equally appropriate label for us.

Although semiotics came out of linguistics, the concept of a sign is not exclusive to written or spoken language. Body language – facial movements and other forms of bodily gesture – also consists of signs. For example, if you use your first two fingers to create a V, and turn your palm towards someone, then (in Britain, at least) you are conveying the idea of 'victory' or possibly 'peace'. If you turn your hand round so your knuckles face them, it means something entirely different!

The English words *sign* and *significant* have the same root, so when we say that a sign is significant, we are really just saying that it is a sign. 'Significant', though, is perhaps a better word to bring home the fact that a sign is bound up with the ideas of communication and human beings. Only a person finds something significant. Different people find different things significant. So there is much that is subjective about signs: we interpret them in different ways, depending on the context and our culture and knowledge.

Levels of semiotics

Charles Morris originally proposed three branches of semiotics – pragmatics, semantics and syntactics. Stamper (1973) considered signs and sign-systems by identifying instead *four* interdependent levels, layers or branches of semiotics: pragmatics, semantics, syntactics and empirics. These layers serve to connect the social world with the physical or technical world (see Figure 3.1) (Stamper, 2001). In other words, we can say that information is necessarily a sociotechnical phenomenon which is interposed between the three different levels of system that were introduced in Chapter 2. This layered conception particularly allows us to locate human activity systems, information systems and ICT systems against the critical distinction between data and information.

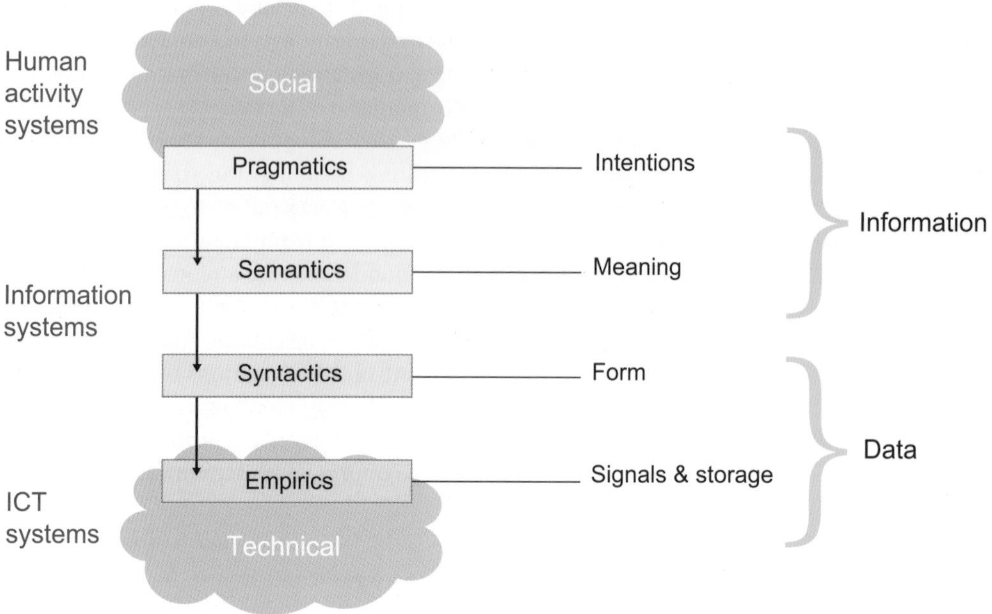

Figure 3.1: *Levels of semiotics*

Signs are used in **social systems**. The social layer is important because it forms the general context and culture of communication: it provides the shared assumptions underlying human understanding. For communication to occur between human beings, signs must exist in a context of shared understanding. So we study culture as it affects communication – the common expectations underlying human communicative behaviour in a particular context. The reverse is also true: the way in which signs are used in social systems both produces and helps to change those social systems.

Human activity system: A logical collection of activities performed by a group of people.

This was explained in Chapter 2, where we identified our particular interest in a sub-type of a social system which Checkland (1999) refers to as a HUMAN ACTIVITY SYSTEM. Human activity systems are an interrelated set of activities designed to fulfil a purpose. Signs are used in activity systems as a means of supporting collaborative action.

The various paper forms that were used by Goronwy Galvanising, in the case study discussed in Chapter 1, are examples of signs. Delivery advices, dispatch advices and job-sheets were used to support its activities.

Pragmatics: The study of the general context and culture of communication.

PRAGMATICS is concerned with the *purpose* of communication. It links signs with *intention*. When people communicate, their intentions link language to action. When the staff at Goronwy Galvanising filled in forms, these made up a kind of 'language' for indicating intentions within the activity system. When a customer sent a delivery advice note to Goronwy with a batch of steel products, this was a representation of its *intention* that Goronwy should galvanise them.

Semantics: The study of the meaning of signs.

Syntactics: The part of semiotics devoted to the study of the structure of signs and sign-systems.

Grammar: Rules that control the correct use of a language.

Syntax: The operational rules for the correct representation of terms and their use in the construction of sentences of a language.

SEMANTICS is concerned with the *meaning* of a message communicated. It is the content of the communication. Semantics is the study of the meaning of signs – the association between signs and behaviour. Semantics can be considered as the study of the link between symbols and their referents or concepts, and particularly the way in which signs relate to human behaviour.

SYNTACTICS is concerned with the formalism used to represent a message. Syntactics as an area studies the logic and GRAMMAR of sign systems. It is devoted to the study of the form rather than the content.

The discussion of Goronwy's forms in Chapter 1 covered both their SYNTAX and their semantics. For instance, it described how the form is made up of a series of elements such as order lines. It also described the meaning of these elements, in the sense that a given order line relates to a particular batch delivered on a trailer.

Empirics: Branch of semiotics concerned with the physical characteristics of a communication channel.

EMPIRICS is the study of the signals used to carry a message; the physical characteristics of the medium of communication. It is devoted to communication channels and their characteristics: sound, light, electronic transmission and so on. For Goronwy's manual information system, the communication channel involved the use of the written word on the printed page. It depended on people being able to see and read the words, which in turn depended on an adequate level of light.

Each sign has a physical or material form independent of the observer. Because of this physical form, each sign generates costs for its storage, transmission and processing. This is the level of technology for data storage, transmission and processing. In broad terms we can refer to this as information and communications technology (ICT), a term used in this book to refer to a variety of historical and technological forms, from the clay tablet to the modern computer (see also Chapter 4). Many organisations use computer hardware and software to reduce the costs of storage, transmission and processing, just as Goronwy came to do.

Figure 3.1 also indicates the subtle distinction between data and information. Data are concerned with the *form* and *representation* of symbols in storage and transmission. Information is concerned with the *meaning* of symbols and their use within human action. Hence, information is data plus sense-making.

Considering information in terms of signs in this manner allows us to identify information in unexpected places. It also provides us with a critical lens for unpacking this information in terms of its purpose, representation and use. For example, let us think about how we deal with time. The concepts of seconds, minutes, hours, days, months and years are clearly invented and culturally based: they derive from human beings, not from anything in nature. If we standardise our talking about time by using concepts – units – like these, we have a common reference framework, and that makes it possible for people to coordinate their activities. For human beings to come to measure the passing of time using accurate clocks, and to calibrate them using standards such as Greenwich Mean Time, was critical to their developing other concepts: longitude, for instance. And this in turn contributed to the development of naval exploration, merchant shipping and world trade (Sobel, 1996).

Did you know?

At the heart of every computer processor there is a clock. This clock is used to coordinate all the actions of the processor.

Communication

In short, information is related to the process of communication, and signs are the tools of such communication. The characteristics of communication as a process are outlined in Figure 3.2:

- It involves two or more parties whom we shall refer to as agents.
- One or more of the parties in a communication process is a sender with intentions to convey.
- The sender conveys their intentions in a message using elements from a particular language, with an agreed syntax.
- The message is sent using signals along a communication channel.
- One or more of the other parties is a receiver, with the ability to interpret signals as a message in the sense that the meaning becomes apparent.

The key elements of communication are therefore agents (senders and receivers), intentions, messages, language (with an agreed syntax and semantics), signals and communication channels. It is evident that there is a clear relationship between the layers of semiotics (illustrated in Figure 3.1) and this model of the communication process.

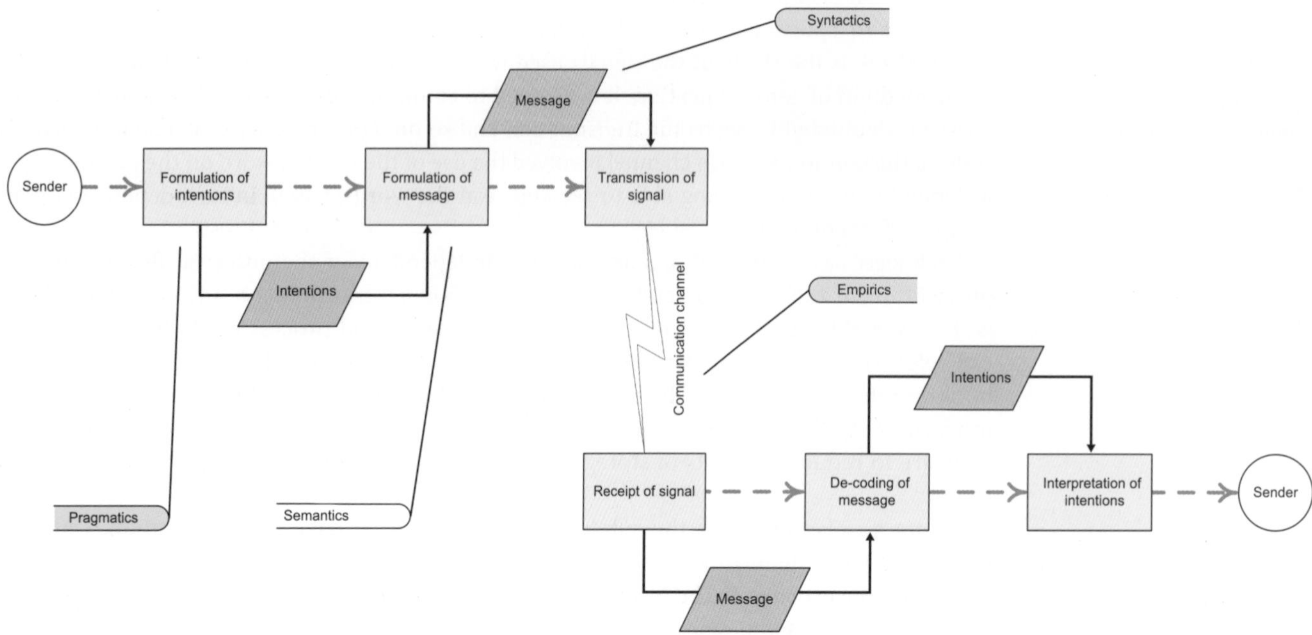

Figure 3.2: *The process of communication*

Message: A stream of symbols that is coded as a signal.

Communication normally exists in the context of a social situation. This sets the context for the intentions conveyed (pragmatics) and the form in which communication takes place. In a communicative situation, intentions are expressed through MESSAGES, which consist of collections of interrelated signs, which are taken from a language which is mutually understood by the agents involved. By mutual understanding, we mean that the agents understand both the syntax (syntactics) and the semantics. The sender codes the message in the language and sends the message as signals along a communication channel (empirics). This channel will have inherent properties which determine the outcomes, such as the speed with which communication can take place and over what distance.

Another way of looking at this is that the four levels of semiotics define elements of a *protocol* between agents or actors in communication activity. A protocol is a convention or a set of conventions which controls the communication process. This means that both sender and receiver must agree a protocol for communication before communication can occur. In terms of a communication protocol, *pragmatics* concerns the intentions conveyed in a message, *semantics* the meaning of a message, *syntactics* the formalism used to represent the message and *empirics* the signals used to code and transmit the message.

In normal face-to-face conversation, both sender and receiver are humans, and the communication channel is air. The signal involves the transmission of sound through air. However, much modern communication occurs remotely in the sense that the sender and receiver are not found in the same location, and possibly do not act at the same time. Remote communication is therefore more accurately referred to as **tele-communication**. Telecommunication refers to the electronic transmission of signals for communications, usually at a distance. In fact, ICT systems generally utilise a subset of telecommunications known as **data communications.** Data communications refers to the electronic collection, processing and distribution of data over communication networks (see also Chapter 8).

Recap 

Information can be seen as embodied in signs and the process of signification, which are essential elements of the area known as semiotics. Semiotics or semiology is the study of signs, and consists of four sub-areas: pragmatics, semantics, syntactics and empirics. Signs are tools used in the process of communication along defined communication channels. The key elements of communication are senders and receivers, intentions, messages, language, signals and communication channels.

Empirics

The lowest level at which we can describe information is that of empirics. **Empirics** is the study of the physical characteristics of the medium of communication: that is, communication channels and their characteristics. It is particularly concerned with the nature of signals used to code and transmit messages.

This area of semiotics is normally associated with the work of Claude Shannon (1949) on the statistical theory of signal transmission – generally called **information theory**, although this implies a restricted view of information, or more accurately, **communication theory**. As Shannon himself stated, 'the fundamental problem of communication is that of reproducing at one point, either exactly or approximately, a message selected at another point'.

Communication theory is thus concerned solely with the physical problems involved in transmitting messages and the properties of the communication channels used. It deals with messages carried along a communication channel in some form of 'carrier' signal. In this context, information is equated with variety (see page 40), or different forms of modulation of this signal.

Communication channels

A communication channel is a defined medium used for communication between two or more agents. In other words, there is a distinction between communication channels and their defined media. Human speech utilises sound generated by the human vocal organs and received by the human ear. Written English uses symbols written on the page transmitted to the human sight organ through light transmission. British Sign Language uses physical gestures generated by the sender and seen (using the human sight organs) by the receiver. Note that in each of these cases there are three parts to the definition of the communication channel: the characteristics of the sender, the physical medium used for transmission, and the characteristics of the receiver.

The important point of Shannon's theory is that it led to the definition of a number of generic properties of all communication channels, including writing, human speech and modern digital communication lines. Communication theory can thus be seen to be the foundation of modern communications engineering.

We can describe a communication channel in various ways. Some relevant properties are its modulation, capacity, direction and synchronisation.

Modulation: The process by which variety is introduced into a signal.

MODULATION is the process by which variety (see Chapter 2) is introduced into a signal. If the signal cannot be varied, it cannot carry information. If we can vary the signal, we can use its different states to code messages (see below).

Communication theory generally works with binary states or decisions. Logarithms to the base 2 are used as a measure of the order or **negentropy** of a message. Entropy is a measure of disorder, and negentropy of order, so in communication theory, negentropy equates to the presence of information and entropy the lack of information. Most telecommunication channels nowadays use a form of binary coding (conceived as 0s or 1s similar to the dots and dashes of Morse code) so they are known as binary communication channels.

Generally speaking there are two types of signals, digital and analogue. A **digital** signal has a small number of possible values: two for a binary digital signal, ten for a decimal signal. An **analogue** signal has values drawn from a continuous range. The value of the signal varies over this range. Modern telecommunication channels tend to use binary digital signals.

Bandwidth: A measure of the amount of data that can be transmitted along a communication channel in a unit of time. Normally measured in bits per second.

Bit: An abbreviation of binary digit – one of the two digits (0 and 1) used in binary notation.

Capacity refers to the amount of data that can be transmitted along the channel in a given period of time. The BANDWIDTH of a channel refers to the minimum and maximum frequencies allowed along a channel. Bandwidth is related to baud rate, which is a measure of the amount of data that can be transmitted along a channel in a unit of time. In a digital channel baud rate corresponds to BIT rate: the number of binary digits (bits) that can be transferred per second between sender and receiver.

Did you know?

Shannon believed that the human voice could be adequately handled by a communication channel with as little bandwidth as 500 bits per second.

Direction refers to the data flow between sender and receiver. In a simplex channel the flow is in one direction only. In a duplex channel data may flow in both directions simultaneously. In a half duplex channel flow can occur in both directions but not at the same time.

Synchronisation: A property of a communication channel. The degree to which the sender and receiver of messages participate in the process at the same time.

SYNCHRONISATION refers to whether the messages between sender and receiver are synchronised. In an asynchronous channel a message can be sent at any time. In a synchronous channel the receiver has to wait to receive the message from the sender before it can respond with its message.

Coding a signal

Reflect
Bandwidth is typically measured in terms of millions of bits per second or Megabits per sec (Mb/Sec). What is the typical bandwidth of your home or work Internet connection?

To help understand importance of this conception of communication as signal transmission, let us look at a simple example (Stamper, 1973). Suppose a factory in London wants to transmit a message to a factory in Cardiff. The message is carried in a signal travelling down a communication channel. (Since we are looking at the coding, the type of communication channel used is not the focus here.) Imagine that the signal that can be sent has only one state, one value. What information can be transmitted using this signal? The answer is none at all. The signal is just a steady stream of energy.

It is only when we can modulate the signal in some way that we can transmit information. Now let us assume that the signal has two possible values, which we might think of as on and off, a dot or a dash, or a zero or a one. (Each choice of what we call the values represents a different **code**. Each individual value transmitted is one **bit** of information.) Now we have the ability to code messages as signals.

Suppose the factory produces two lines each consisting of four products: one with products coded as A, B, C and D, and the other with products coded as W, X, Y and Z. At the start of every working day an administrative worker at the London factory reads through a pile of orders. Each order form contains an order for one product type. The administrator sends one message for each order. To do this, the administrator has to convert the alpha codes (A, B and so on, of which there are 26 possible alternatives, as you know) into binary codes, consisting of a sequence of bits, each of which has only two alternatives, since this is a binary system.

A, B, C and D might be coded as;

A	B	C	D
11	10	01	00

These are all the two-digit variations of 0 and 1, so it should be apparent that using only two digits, we can convey one of these four alternative messages (and no more). If each signal takes one second to transmit, one of these two-bit codes can be transmitted every two seconds. Thus, 30 messages can be transmitted in a minute.

However, we might be able to do better than this. Perhaps an analysis of past orders would show that that statistically some product types in the second line of products are ordered a lot more frequently than others. Let us assume that half of all orders are for W, a quarter for X and an eighth each for Y and Z. We could use this statistical analysis to formulate a more efficient code for the product line, using shorter codes for the most popular letters and longer codes for the least popular letters. Here is one possibility:

W	X	Y	Z
1	10	100	1000

If you work through the maths, you'll see that this coding makes it possible to send more than 30 messages per minute. (Sending 30 messages would take 15 seconds for the W messages, 15 seconds for the X messages, 11.25 seconds for the Y messages, and 15 seconds for the Z messages; 3.75 seconds remain out of the minute.)

Shannon's theory allows us to compute the capacity of a communication channel in terms of transmission of the most economical form of coding for messages. His theorems are defined using the concept of entropy – the degree of uncertainty associated with a message. Fundamentally this is a measure of probability based on the relative frequency of messages. Therefore, the more infrequent a message, the more information it conveys.

Shannon's work is particularly useful for providing ways of answering some basic questions about communication. How do we know that a signal is conveying information? How much information is being conveyed in a given signal? What is the most efficient way of transmitting a message in a signal?

Shannon was particularly interested in the question of how to measure the information content of a signal. This measure is based on the degree of order or variety in a signal. A statistical measure of the variety in a signal provides an indication of the level of communication being conveyed by it. First, translate the message into a binary code, then count the binary digits in the message string; this gives you a measure of the information content of the message. Binary code is used because it uses up the smallest amount of bandwidth in communication channels.

During the Napoleonic Wars the British Royal Navy set up a communication system consisting of a series of flags hoisted on the rigging of warships. A sequence of flags could be used to code a particular message such as 'England expects'.

Suppose a sailor wanted to signal a number between 0 and 127 using flags. Using a single flag of a distinctive design for each number he would need 128 flags to achieve this. (This assumes there is one flag of a distinct design for each distinct number between 0 and 127.) If he decided to use a decimal system to code the numbers being transmitted, he would need 21 flags – ten for the units, ten for the tens and 1 for the hundreds. Using a binary system he would require just 14 flags – seven ones and seven zeros.

Here are two communication problems which could be solved by this approach. In the search for extraterrestrial intelligence (SETI) you need some means of identifying whether an alien civilisation is trying to communicate with you using a particular signal. In zoology scientists need to prove that the clicks and whistles used by dolphins are a form of communication.

George Kingsley Zipf, an American linguist and philologist, studied statistical occurrences in different languages. He noticed that a small collection of elements (such as letters and words) in natural languages are used very frequently, but the vast majority of elements are used infrequently. This insight hints at an appropriate method for determining whether a signal consists of a code based on a language (rather than, say, a series of numbers, or a random succession of states). If you count the number of times particular letters appear in written extracts of English, you get a graph with a -1 (negative) slope. The same is also true of most other human written languages. A random string of letters (not conveying any meaning) appears as a flat slope on the graph (see Figure 3.3).

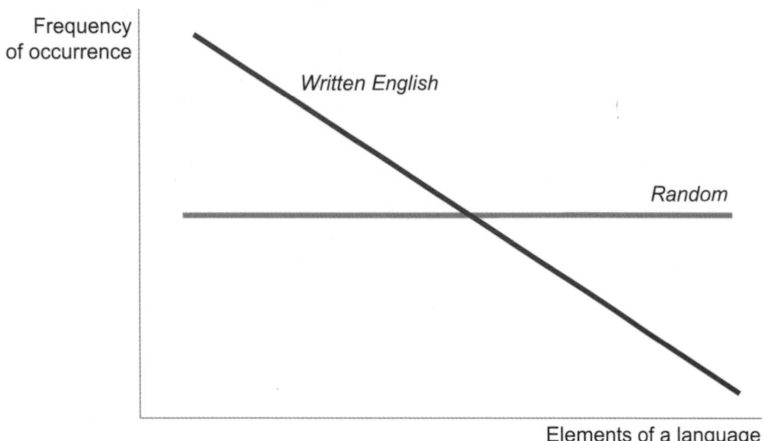

Figure 3.3: *Plotting language elements against frequency of occurrence*

Interestingly if we plot all the elements of radio signals received from outer space to date, they approximate to the random or flat slope. This implies that, at least in terms of the signals received, no alien life form out there has been trying to communicate with us.

In contrast, if we plot the strings of squeaks and whistles produced by dolphins, the line approaches the -1 slope. This is evidence that something is being communicated between these non-human species. But to know what is being communicated we would need to interpret the signal or decode the message. For this we would need to know the syntax and semantics of dolphin 'language'.

Syntactics

So we can see language as a tool to code information as messages in communication activity. Communication activity is important because it is the glue of collaborative and cooperative action. However, the concept of a message presupposes that there is a 'language' for expressing the message. Hence, language can be conceived of as a system of signs used for coding the intentions (the meaning) of the message. This begs the question of how we validate that intentions have been conveyed in a message. Frequently, it is done by checking whether the receiver did what they were asked to do. This implies that the activity system is the context for both messages and action.

Syntactics is the study of the logic of sign systems. Syntactics is devoted to the study of the physical form, rather than the content, of signs. In terms of a communication process, syntactics concerns the formalism used to represent the message.

Language

In its broadest sense we have used the term **language** to refer to an agreed system of signs used to convey messages between a set of agents. Language is important because, as Steven Pinker states, 'a common language connects the members of a community into an information-sharing network with formidable collective powers' (2001).

We can classify languages in a number of different ways, such as whether they are natural or artificial, formal or informal, and what medium of communication they use.

Languages such as English and Welsh are described as **natural languages.** They have grown naturally amongst a speech community. Certain other languages are **artificial**, invented or created – Esperanto is a particular example of an attempt to create an expressive language which would be easy to learn and so might act as a universal human language.

Most natural languages have a complex and continually (if slowly) changing syntax and semantics. As such they are **informal languages**. Other languages have a highly specified and limited formal syntax and semantics. Hence, they are referred to as **formal languages.** The most notable examples are programming languages used in the construction of ICT systems, such as Java or Perl.

It is conventional to distinguish between spoken and written languages. Frequently the conventions of spoken and written language are considerably different (as is the case for spoken and written Welsh). We also need to add to this categorisation nonverbal or body languages, consisting of nonverbal cues and gestures which convey meaning.

Vocabulary: A complete list of the terms of a language.

All languages of whatever form have a vocabulary, grammar and syntax. VOCABULARY is a complete list of the terms in a language. **Grammar** is the rules that control the correct use of a language. **Syntax** is concerned with the operational rules for the correct representation of terms and their use in the construction of sentences.

In the natural language Welsh, the words 'Ydych chi yn mynd i sinema heno?' can be translated into the English sentence 'Are you going to the cinema tonight?' The correct grammatical response to this question is either 'ydw' (yes, I am) or 'nac ydw' (no, I am not). The word *heno* (in English, tonight) is an example of vocabulary. Syntax relates to the structure of the sentence. Welsh syntax determines that starting the sentence with 'ydych chi' indicates a question, while 'rydych chi' would indicate a statement.

Key skill 

Modelling data

Empirics traditionally considers problems of data communication, and that is what we have just discussed. However, empirics should also logically concern the issues of data representation and storage, since in the modern world ICT relies on effective ways of representing and storing data. For these purposes we need to consider the concept of a data model.

The term **universe of discourse** (UoD) (also known as domain of discourse or ontology

– see Chapter 2) is sometimes used to describe the context within which a group of signs is used continually by a social group or groups. For work in informatics it is important to develop a detailed understanding of the structure of these signs. In this context the structure is known as a **schema.** A schema is an attempt to develop an abstract description of a UoD, usually in terms of a formal language.

To build a schema we must have a system of signs, or a language, with an agreed vocabulary, grammar and syntax. The formal language used for defining schemas is generally described as a DATA MODEL. Therefore, a data model establishes a set of principles for representing and organising the storage of data.

Data model: An architecture for data or a blueprint of data requirements for an application.

In general terms, the syntax of any data model can be described in terms of a hierarchy of data items, data elements and data structures (Tsitchizris and Lochovsky, 1982). A **data item** is the lowest level of data organisation. It is the atomic construct in any data model: a construct that cannot be divided any further. Hence, data values are stored against data items. A **data element** is a logical collection of data items, and a **data structure** is a logical collection of data elements.

The most common data model that has been employed for data storage in organisations is file-based. This data model uses the interrelated constructs of fields, records and files. Fields are data items, RECORDS are data elements and files are the data structures in this data model.

Record: A physical data element composed of fields.

The file-based (sometimes referred to as the records-based) data model has existed for many thousands of years in numerous human civilisations. In a sense, records by their very nature involve the use of signs to act as a persistent record of something. For example, in ancient Sumeria scratches on clay tablets were used effectively as an asset register. The scratches were signs which signified tallies such as the amount of grain held in various storehouses.

So the syntax of a typical record consists of a series of data items which serve to represent an instance of something. For instance, a business organisation might create a typical record for each of its customers, with fields such as customer name, customer address and customer telephone number.

Records are typically collected into the data structure of a FILE. This normally implies some association between these data elements. For instance, a **customer file** assembles a series of customer records. Various different customer files might be created, with a specific criterion used to decide which record goes in which file: customers located in different areas of the country, or handled by different account managers, for instance.

File: A physical data structure

Some of the meaning associated with data is therefore bound together with the way in which data are organised in terms of data structures, data elements and data items. Other semantics in the file-based data model are provided by the format of the data contained in the data item. This is often called its DATA TYPE. Some of the meaning of a data item is embodied in its data type, since this defines not only the appropriate form of data, but also the range of valid operations on it. For example, one data item might be a person's age. It might be defined an integer data type (in other words, it consists of a whole number such as 21 or 43). It is possible to conduct a range of arithmetic operations on integers, although not all of them will necessarily be appropriate in the context. Two integers such as 1 and 2 can be added, but it doesn't necessarily make sense to add one customer's age to another, or a customer's age to their house number. In contrast, it would hardly even seem to be an option to add the character A to the character B. So a number data type might allow addition but a text data type will not.

Data type: A categorisation of data defining the format and operations for it.

Most data needed in commercial information systems are what we might call **standard data**. Standard data are defined in terms of a number of standard data types used by most information systems, such as text – strings of symbols made up of characters from the alphabet and a range of other characters – numbers (including integer, decimal and real numbers) and units of time including dates, seconds, minutes and hours. However, information systems are now being used to capture, store and manipulate far more complex data types than these. This is to enable such systems to handle different media. Such complex data types include images (such as graphics and photographic images), audio and various forms of sound data and video (various forms of moving image).

These forms of complex or multimedia data need different coding schemes or formats to enable them to be represented in digital form. For instance, images are coded in pixels. A pixel is a picture element. A high-resolution computer monitor can be considered as a 1024 by 768 grid in which each cell is a pixel. To represent an image we therefore need to store information about its colour for each pixel in the image. For a complete monitor over 700,000 pixels are needed.

Information systems are now required to handle complex data structures as well as complex data items or elements. Organisations want to be able to define the structure of documentation that they use for communication. A document such as an invoice or a contract is a complex data structure in that it may be made up of text, numeric data and images. Different organisations may also use different formats for such documents. Hence, there is pressure on organisations in the same industrial sector to develop standards for their documentation. This issue is considered in Chapter 5.

Data are symbols. They must be represented in some way for storage and manipulation by computer hardware and software, and for transmission by communication technology. Most of the data types described above are coded in modern ICT systems using bits, although the quantity stored is typically expressed in bytes (a BYTE consists of 8 bits). Capacities of storage devices used in ICT systems are normally described in terms of KILOBYTES (Kbytes: 1 thousand bytes – 10^3), MEGABYTES (Mbytes: 1 million bytes – 10^6), GIGABYTES (Gbytes: 1 billion bytes – 10^9), or TERABYTES (Tbytes: 1 trillion bytes – 10^{12}).

Data are actually represented in a computer by strings of characters coded using a character set: a uniform type of coding scheme. The symbols coded are referred to as characters, or WORDS, and in the case of text consist of letters, digits, punctuation and non-printing characters such as control characters.

One of the most popular standard CHARACTER SETS is ASCII – American Standard Code for Information Interchange. In ASCII the capital A is represented by the binary string or word 10100001.

Byte: A set of eight binary digits/bits.

Kilobyte: 1000 bytes.

Megabyte: 1,000,000 bytes (million).

Gigabytes: 1,000,000,000 bytes (billion).

Terabyte: 1,000,000,000,000 (trillion) bytes.

Word: One or more bytes treated as a unit.

Character set: A scheme for representing symbols in binary notation.

Did you know? The word byte is a contraction of 'by eight'.

New measures of the volume of data are becoming required as ICT becomes more and more embedded in modern-day life. For instance, Google's whole data storage was estimated as being 5 petabytes (10^{15} bytes) in 2004. It was also estimated that print, magnetic and optical storage media produced about 5 exabytes (10^{18} bytes) of data in 2002. Of this data 92 per cent was stored on magnetic media, mostly in hard disks. 5 exabytes is equivalent to the size of data contained in 37,000 new libraries the size of the Library of Congress book collection (Floridi, 2007).

Modelling syntax

In a sense a data model is a formal language for organising data. It is possible to define the syntax of a formal language using Backus Naur Form (BNF). Consider the 'syntax' of a data structure for storing details of a postal address. In English we might define this data structure in terms of:

- A postal address consists of a house-part, followed by a street-address part, followed by a postal-identifier part.
- A house-part consists of either a house name or a house number.
- A street address consists of a street name followed by a location name.
- A location name consists of a village name, town name or city name.
- A postal-identifier is country-specific. In the United Kingdom a postcode is used; in the United States a zip-code is used.
- A postcode consists of postal district followed by postal town followed by a delivery area followed by a house group.
- A zip-code consists of a sectional center facility code (SCF code) followed by a postal-zone number followed by a hyphen followed by an add-on code.

Reflect
Consider an everyday item you come into contact with on a regular basis such as a supermarket till receipt. In what way could this be considered as representative of a data structure? Could you specify it in BNF?

A BNF specification is a set of derivation rules, written as <symbol> ::= <expression with symbols> where <symbol> is an element of the language, and the expression consists of sequences of symbols and/or sequences separated by the vertical bar, '|', indicating a choice. The sequence on the right of the ::= symbol is taken as being a possible substitution for the symbol on the left. Hence, a postal address might be defined in BNF as:

<postal-address> ::= <house-part> <street-address> <postal-identifier>
<house-part> ::= <house-name> | <house-number>
<street-address> ::= <street-name> <location-name>
<location-name> ::= <village-name> | <town-name>| <city-name>
<postal-identifier> ::= <post-code> | <zip-code>
<post-code> ::= <postal-district> <postal-town> <delivery-area> <house-group>
<zip-code> ::= <SCF-code> <postal-zone-number> '-' <add-on-code>

Recap

Empirics is the study of the physical characteristics of the medium of communication. Syntactics is the study of the logic and grammar of sign systems. Both empirics and syntactics can be considered as interested in data and the ways in which they are stored and transmitted. Symbols are equivalent to data. A datum, a single item of data, is a set of symbols used to represent something. In terms of data storage a data model defines the ways in which symbols are structured as data.

Semantics

The American philosopher John Dewey suggested that a word is three things: a fence, a label and a vehicle. The same could be said more generally of the concept of **sign**. A sign is a 'fence' in the sense that it sets a conceptual boundary around something and is used to distinguish one thing from another. A sign is a 'label' in that it acts as a convenient reference for something else. Finally, a sign is a 'vehicle' in the sense that, used with other signs as a language, it is a means for describing and debating with the world as well as acting upon it.

Semantics is particularly interested in the idea of the sign as label, and as such is the study of what signs refer to. Communication involves the use and interpretation of signs. When we communicate the sender has to externalise their intentions using signs. In face-to-face conversation this involves the use of linguistic signs: spoken words. The receiver of the message must interpret the signs. In other words, they must assign some meaning to the signs of the message. Semantics is concerned with this process of assigning meaning.

The meaning triangle

In a simple model of semantics, often called the meaning triangle, a sign is broken down into three component parts (see Figure 3.4) (Ogden and Richards, 1923):

- **Designation**: the symbol (or collection of symbols) by which a concept is known. The designation of a sign is sometimes referred to as the **signifier**, that which signifies something.
- **Extension**: the range of phenomena that the concept in some way covers. The extension is sometimes known as the REFERENT or the **signified**: that which is being signified.
- **Intension**: the collection of properties that in some ways characterise the phenomena in the extension. The intension is the idea of **significance**.

Referent: That which is being signified. The range of phenomena referred to.

Symbol: That which is signifying something.

SYMBOLS are equivalent to data. A datum, a single item of data, is a set of symbols used to represent something. Information particularly occurs in the 'stands for' relations between the symbol (designation) and its concept (intension), and the concept and its referent (extension).

For example, in a manufacturing system the symbols 43 might be a designation. A possible extension is a collection of products. The intension may be the quantity of a product sold. The symbols M and F might be significant in some other context. To speak of information we must supply some intension and/or extension for the symbols. M might have as its extension the male population; F might have as its extension the female population. Taken together, the meaning of these symbols is supplied by the intension of human gender.

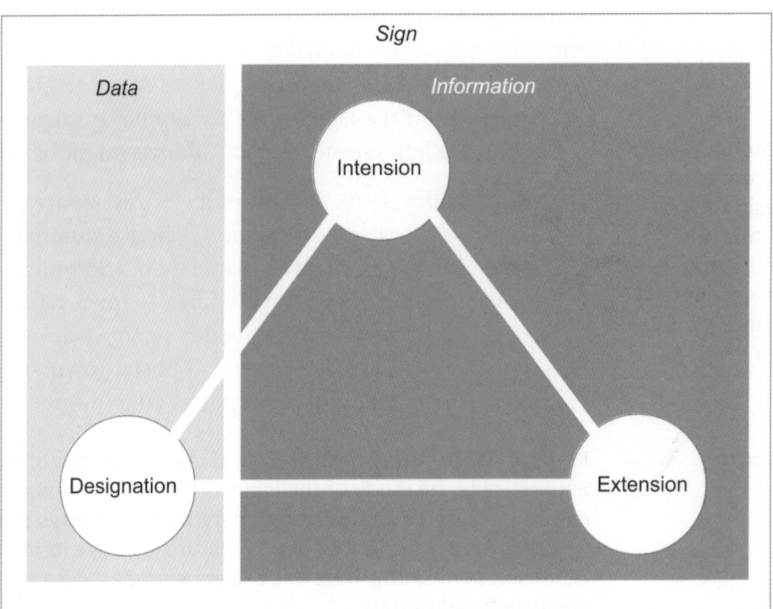

Figure 3.4: *The meaning triangle*

Did you know?

In many senses money is information. Money is a record of value. Within the global economy, money is essentially data held in the information systems of financial institutions. Money is transferred between such systems electronically, and accompanies the exchange of goods and services.

A particularly important example of a sign in information systems is the **identifier**. Identifiers are common in our information society primarily because information systems of various forms are used so widely. The identifier is a symbol or set of symbols (a designation) that can be used to authenticate an object such as a product, a place or a person (an extension).

Take the example of a barcode. This is a machine-readable representation of information. Normally it is a pattern of dark ink printed on a light background to create areas of high and low reflectance which can be converted into bits by optical scanners known as barcode readers. Barcodes are widely used to identify products – for instance, in a supermarket – and are particularly useful because the information can be captured electronically by information systems. This automated capture improves the speed and accuracy of data entry.

Reflect
How many forms of identification do you regularly carry around with you? How many of these are surrogate identifiers?

More controversially people are now identified to information systems in a number of different ways. Traditionally, people were identified by, for example, their physical appearance, personal names and knowledge (for example, of a PIN number). These are best described as natural identifiers, in that they are the conventional identifiers used in well-established interactions in society. However, they do not always provide the uniqueness demanded by organisations and their information systems, so surrogate identifiers tend to be used increasingly, particularly for remote interaction with organisations. These have additional features such as codes (alphanumeric strings which stand for the individual) and tokens (such as credit cards and passports) used to uniquely identify individuals. More recently, interest has shifted to the possibilities of identifying individuals through features of natural physiography (such as fingerprints, retinal scans and DNA profiles) readable by machine. These are known as biometric identifiers.

Pragmatics

A communicative act involves a person in formulating an intention and communicating that intention to another person in the form of a sign.

You should not assume from the meaning triangle that signs have an inherent meaning. A sign can mean whatever a particular social group chooses it to mean. The emphasis here is on *social group*. Humpty Dumpty in Lewis Carroll's *Through the Looking Glass* says that a word 'means just what I choose it to mean – neither more or less'. In reality people cannot define their meanings and intentions in isolation: the very act of communication implies a *mutual* understanding of associations between signs, meanings and intentions between the members of some social group, what was referred to earlier as a communication protocol.

The same sign may mean different things in different social contexts. As interpreters of signs humans are extremely proficient at assigning the correct interpretation for a sign in a particular context. They need to be. For instance forming an 'o' with the first finger and thumb of the hand and holding it up with palm facing outwards means A-OK in the United States. In France it means zero. In Japan it means money. In Tunisia it means 'I'll kill you!'

Likewise the same intention can be communicated using a number of different signs. For instance, the intention 'I love you' can be communicated with a verbal message, a blown kiss, or a written message containing a graphic representing a heart – '♥'.

Signs and action

Signs are used in various ways in human life, but in informatics we are interested in the way in which signs are used to generate action. The American philosopher Charles Morris created a sophisticated model of signs founded on the notion of action. More recently another American philosopher, John Searle, has built on Morris's work and created a detailed theory of **speech acts**.

Semiosis: The process of using signs.

For Morris, SEMIOSIS, the process of using signs, consists of five elements. The first element is the **sign** itself, which sets up in the **interpreter** the disposition to act in a certain kind of way (which he referred to as the **interpretant**) in relation to a certain kind of object (the **signification**) under certain conditions (the **context**).

Consider these elements in relation to a case of non-human communication – what is now referred to as animal or zoo semiotics. In the 1950s and 1960s the Austrian ethnologist Karl von Frisch carried out a series of studies which revealed evidence of communication amongst European honey bees. When a honey bee scout discovers a useful source of nectar, it flies back to its hive and performs a dance, which is watched by the other bees. The details of the dance vary depending on the distance to the source of nectar and on the particular species and variety of bee. In the most publicised case the bee performs a tail-wagging dance in the form of a squashed figure 8 with a straight middle section. It signifies to other bees where the nectar is by varying a number of the elements of the dance (see Figure 3.5). In other words, it modulates the signal.

The time the dancing bee takes to complete the figure 8 indicates the distance to the nectar source. The longer the time, the longer the flight to the source. The bee's level of excitement indicates the quantity of nectar: more excitement means more nectar and more bees needed to collect it. The orientation of the straight part of the figure 8 represents the direction of the source with respect to the position of the sun. For instance, if it is at 80 degrees to the left of straight up, it is telling the bees to fly towards a point 80 degrees to the left of the sun.

Charles Morris portrays this example in terms of the process of semiosis:

> Karl von Frisch has shown that a bee which finds nectar is able on returning to the hive to 'dance' in such a way as to direct the other bees to the food source. In this case the dance is the sign; the other bees affected by the dance are interpreters; the disposition to react in a certain kind of way by these bees, because of the dance, is the interpretant; the kind of object toward which the bees are prepared to act in this way is the signification of the sign; and the position of the hive is part of the context.
>
> (Morris, 1964)

In the human sphere, signs are used in information systems in a similar manner. At the semiotic level of pragmatics, information systems are used in organisations to create, control and maintain social action. From this perspective, an information system consists of different groups of people communicating using signs which are stored, manipulated and transmitted via ICT. The 'language' of an information system includes formal messages with a correct syntactic structure, a meaningful semantic context and a significant pragmatic use.

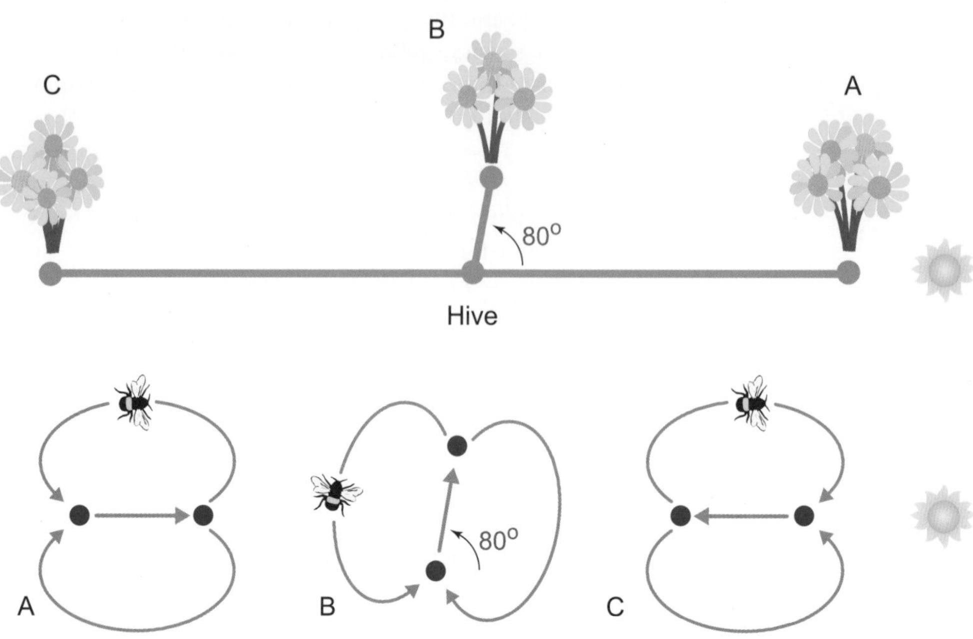

Figure 3.5: *The signification of bees*

Take the example of a system which records information on customers' orders for particular products. We can see it as a number of discrete acts of communication between customers and the organisation. By placing an order the customer commits to receiving the goods and paying for them. The company in turn commits to delivering the goods in an agreed time period and in a satisfactory state for an agreed price. These various commitments are likely to be stored in records maintained by both the customer and the supplying organisation. The values in the records act as a persistent memory of the commitments negotiated.

Did you know?

A vast range of jobs in the modern economy are information jobs in the sense that the majority of people's working life is devoted to information handling. For example, supermarket checkout work fundamentally involves data capture, and a stock market trader makes rapid purchasing or selling decisions based on current prices of stocks and shares and profiles of performance.

Key skill 

Modelling information

The practical focus of organisational informatics is on designing information systems to support activity in organisations. To do this, we need to model a system's information requirements. This section describes a commonly used approach for modelling information.

Organisations need to understand what information they require to perform effectively. This enables them to build data structures for the storage and manipulation of data, as well as to relate information to organisational activity. **Information modelling** gives us the means for understanding and representing information structures. It builds what was referred to in Chapter 2 as an ontology – a systematic account of an area of existence. Unlike the modelling of data considered earlier, which is focused primarily at the level of empirics and syntactics, information modelling is particularly concerned with issues of meaning (semantics) and the relationship of meaning to action (pragmatics).

Take for instance a university. Universities need to record information to help in the activities of teaching and learning. This includes details of students and lecturers, the courses and modules on offer, which lecturers teach which modules, which students take which modules, which lecturer assesses which modules, and which students have been assessed in which

Reflect
Consider your own average working day. How much of it is typically taken up with information-handling activity?

modules, as well as the grades they receive. Staff enter data about all this into data structures such as those available in a database system. For instance, data relevant to courses and modules might be entered by administrators in academic departments, course leaders might enter data about lecturers, and data relevant to students, particularly their enrolments on courses and modules, might be entered by staff at a central registry.

Entity–relationship–attribute modelling

This is a common approach for information modelling. It uses the three constructs of entities (classes), relationships and attributes to model the universe of discourse relevant to an organisational area.

An **entity** can be defined as a thing that an organisation recognises as being capable of an independent existence and which can be uniquely identified. It is an abstraction from the complexities of some universe of discourse. When we speak of an entity we normally speak of some aspect of the real world which can be distinguished from its other aspects. It can be a physical object such as a house or a car, an event such as a house sale or a car service, or a concept such as a customer transaction or order. Although the term *entity* is the one most commonly used, we should really distinguish between an entity or **instance**, and an entity-type or **class**. An entity-type or class is a *category* of something. An entity, strictly speaking, is one of the things in this category. There are usually many instances of a given class. So for example, *Lecturer* is an entity-type or class, and Paul Beynon-Davies is an instance of this class: in other words, an entity.

Because the term entity-type is somewhat cumbersome, we shall use the term *class*. Classes are by their very nature interesting because they normally refer to logical data groupings. In conventional technical jargon the term *logical data grouping* normally means a **file**. So one rule of thumb in identifying suitable classes for a given domain is: *if you need to store data about many properties of something, that thing is likely to be an information class.*

Relationship: An association between entities or classes.

A RELATIONSHIP is an association between information classes. Typically we work with binary relationships: associations between two classes. However, it is possible for more than one relationship to exist between any two classes. For instance, the classes *House* and *Person* can be related by *ownership* and/or by *occupation*. In theory, if we have a set of say six classes, there could be up to 15 relationships between them. In practice, it will usually be obvious that many classes are not related.

The object of the approach is to document only direct relationships: that is, relationships between two classes, with no intervening class. For instance, there are direct relationships between the classes *Parent* and *Child* and between *Child* and *School*. The relationship between *Parent* and *School* is indirect; it exists only through the *Child* class.

As an aspect of the real world, a class is characterised by a number of properties or **attributes.** Values assigned to attributes are used to distinguish one class from another. So in an information model for a university, school name and location are both attributes which define the class *Academic School.*

Let us look at this universe of discourse (UoD) in more detail. For a university, things of interest might include modules offered to students and students taking modules, so modules and students are classes in this context. We are particularly interested in the phenomenon that students take offered modules. This is a relationship between classes. We normally define a class such as *Module* or *Student* because we wish to record some information about its occurrences. In other words, classes have properties or attributes. For instance, students have names, addresses and telephone numbers; modules have titles and credit points.

Figure 3.6 illustrates a graphic notation for each of the three modelling constructs used in information modelling. Classes are represented by labelled boxes, attributes by labels within the class box, and relationships by labelled lines drawn between boxes.

Association: An association relationship establishes a connection between the instances of classes and is defined by cardinality and optionality.

We can model some of the constraints on information in the UoD using two sets of rules known as **cardinality** and **optionality**. In a sense, these rules model some of the pragmatics of the UoD. Each end of a relationship is annotated with a set of two symbols indicating which rules apply.

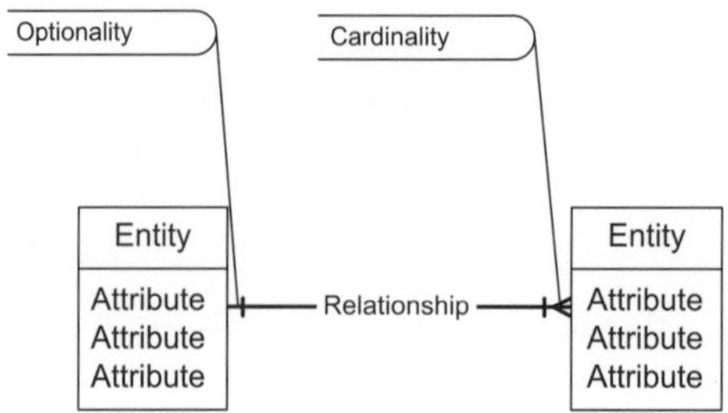

Figure 3.6: *Information modelling constructs*

Figure 3.7 stays with the university example, and shows the various options that apply in modelling cardinality and optionality between lecturers and modules.

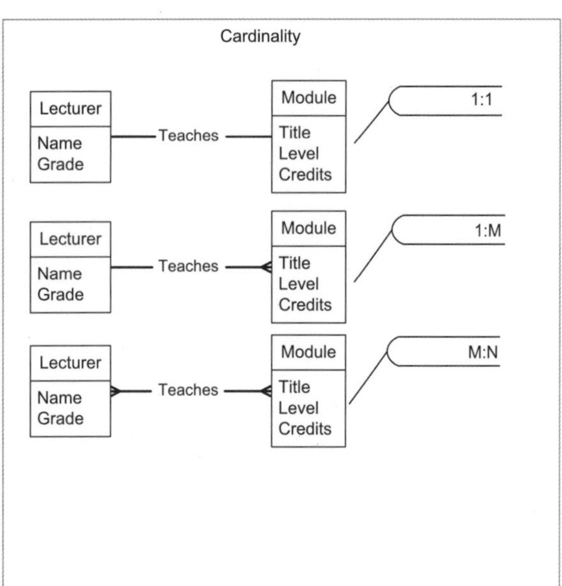

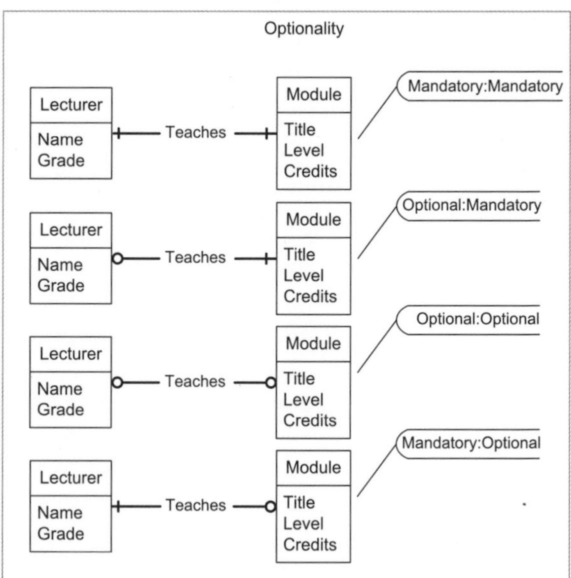

Figure 3.7: *A simple information model*

Cardinality: Establishes how many instances of one entity are related to how many instances of another entity.

CARDINALITY establishes how many instances of one class are related to how many instances of another class. The relationship might be one-to-one (1:1), one-to-many (1:M) or many-to-many (M:N). One to one means that one instance of one class is always associated with one instance of the other class. One to many means that one instance of one class is associated with more than one instance of the other class. Many to many means that many instances of one class are associated with many instances of another class. The many end of a relationship is indicated by a crowsfoot.

A modeller expressing the cardinality of a relationship makes two assertions about the UoD. On the left-hand side of Figure 3.7 three examples of cardinality are given for the relationship between the classes *Lecturer* and *Module*, so there are three sets of two assertions. (Obviously, just one of these examples will be used in the model, since they are mutually exclusive.)

- A lecturer may teach at most one module and a module is taught by at most one lecturer.
- A lecturer may teach many modules but a particular module is taught by at most one lecturer.
- A lecturer may teach many modules and a module may be taught by many lecturers.

Optionality: Establishes whether all instances of an entity must participate in a relationship or not.

OPTIONALITY establishes whether all instances of a class must participate in a relationship. It is either mandatory or optional for each class to participate. A O (zero) represents optional and a vertical line mandatory. For instance, on the right-hand side of Figure 3.7 there are four combinations of optionality for the *teaches* relationship between *Lecturer* and *Module.* Reading from top to bottom these embody the rules:

- Every lecturer must teach at least one module. A module must be taught by at least one lecturer.
- A lecturer need not teach any modules. A module must be taught by at least one lecturer.
- A lecturer need not teach any modules. A module need not have any lecturers assigned to teach it.
- Every lecturer must teach at least one module. A module need not have any lecturers assigned to teach it.

Again, in a specific model the modeller will of course determine which of these rules should apply.

Hence, when we build an information model we attempt to represent elements of the pragmatics and semantics appropriate to an area of information handling in organisations. Figure 3.8 is a simple information model, again based on the university example. Take the relationship between the class *Student* and the class *Course.* Its optionality indicates that a course must have at least one student and a student must register on at least one course. The cardinality of the relationship is one to many, indicating that many students take a course, but any given student may register for only one course at one time.

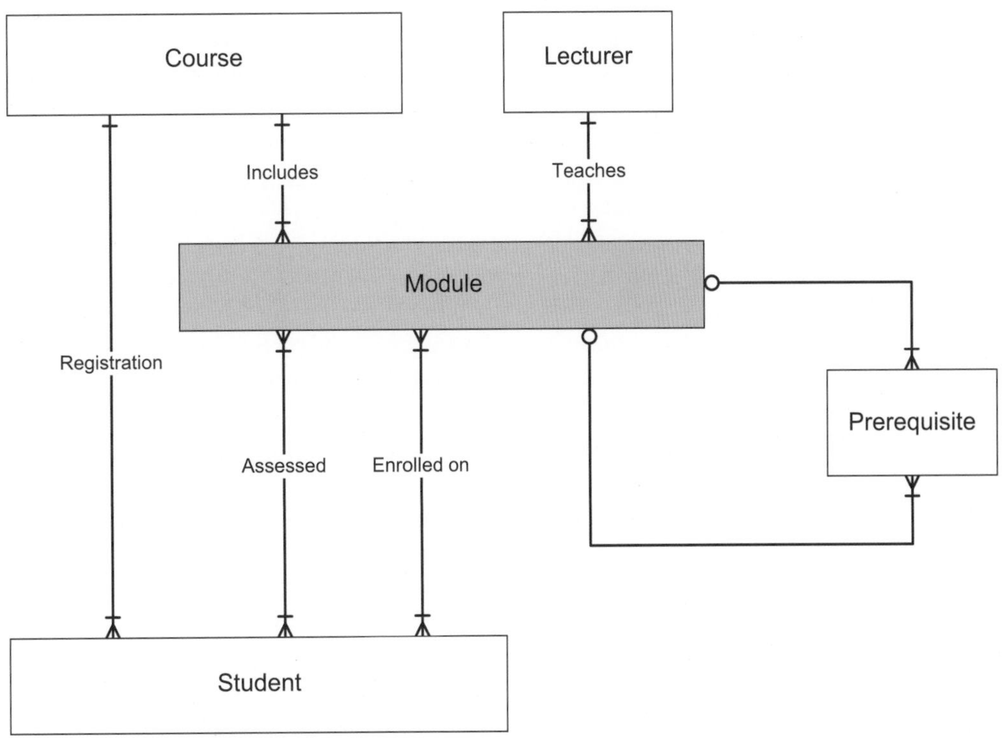

Figure 3.8: *Information model of a student information system*

Recap 

Semantics is the study of the meaning of signs. Pragmatics is the study of the general context and culture of communication, and the relationship between information and action. Both semantics and pragmatics are therefore interested in information and how it is used. An information model is an attempt to specify the semantics relating to the information required to support a human activity system.

Information, decision making and action

As we have seen, pragmatics is interested in the way people formulate intentions and communicate them to other people using signs. The reverse of this process is the way in which people use information to make decisions and take action. This is what we consider next.

Information supports human activity in the sense that it enables decisions to be made about appropriate actions in particular circumstances. Decisions and decision making therefore fall in between information and action.

We can think of management as a control process in an organisation (see Chapter 2), in as far as it is an activity system that controls other activity systems. Management's main function is to make decisions about action that needs to be taken in the organisation, particularly at the strategic and tactical level. Effective management decision making depends on good information, so the issues of management, decision making and information are necessarily intertwined.

Decision making is the activity of deciding upon appropriate action in particular situations. It relies on information because information reduces uncertainty. But on what basis does decision making take place? Simon (1960) argued that there are four general stages in any decision-making process:

- **Intelligence**. In this phase information in the decision-making area is examined. This might lead to the specification of a problem, or the recognition of an opportunity.
- **Design.** The problem is formulated, and solutions are developed and tested for feasibility.
- **Choice.** The decision maker selects from the alternatives.
- **Implementation**. The chosen alternative is carried out.

This model contains several explicit feedback loops, which suggests that most decision making is iterative. For instance, at the design phase additional questions might arise, and the decision maker will then need to go back to the intelligence phase to find out the answers.

For example, if an academic school at a university is making decisions about which new modules to run, the intelligence phase will involve gathering data about (for example) possible staff interests and skills, modules run by other institutions and requests made by commerce and industry. The design phase will involve writing descriptions for a number of key modules, and assessing their feasibility. A choice will then be made on which of these to proceed with, and the chosen modules will be passed on to other organisational processes such as validation.

Classic models of decision making assume it to be a rational process. This implies, for each phase:

- **Intelligence:** the decision maker gathers all relevant information and interprets it in an unbiased manner.
- **Design**: the decision maker identifies all feasible alternatives and draws up an explicit set of criteria for selecting between them.
- **Choice**: the decision maker's choice is based on a systematic assessment using explicit weightings of the importance of key criteria.

Close studies of actual human decision making make it clear that this ideal is not usually achieved. This is not surprising when we realise that rational decision making requires unlimited time within which to make a decision, all the information relevant to the problem and an information processor that is able to handle all of the information and alternatives. Most human decision making is satisficing rather than rational (see page 34):

- It is done in a finite amount of time.
- A limited rather than exhaustive amount of information is gathered.
- People are limited too in their information-processing capability. The make-up of our short-term memory means the average person can handle only seven items of information at any one time, and all of us are inclined to make emotive as well as rational judgements.

Any sizeable organisation will have a number of layers of management, and although managers at all levels make decisions, they do so in different ways. Three levels of management are often identified: STRATEGIC MANAGEMENT, TACTICAL MANAGEMENT and OPERATIONAL MANAGEMENT (see Figure 3.9). They differ in:

Strategic management: The top level of management, concerned with making unstructured decisions based on heavily summarised data.

Tactical management: Middle management which interfaces between strategic and operational management.

Operational management: The lowest level of management, involved with making structured decisions with detailed data.

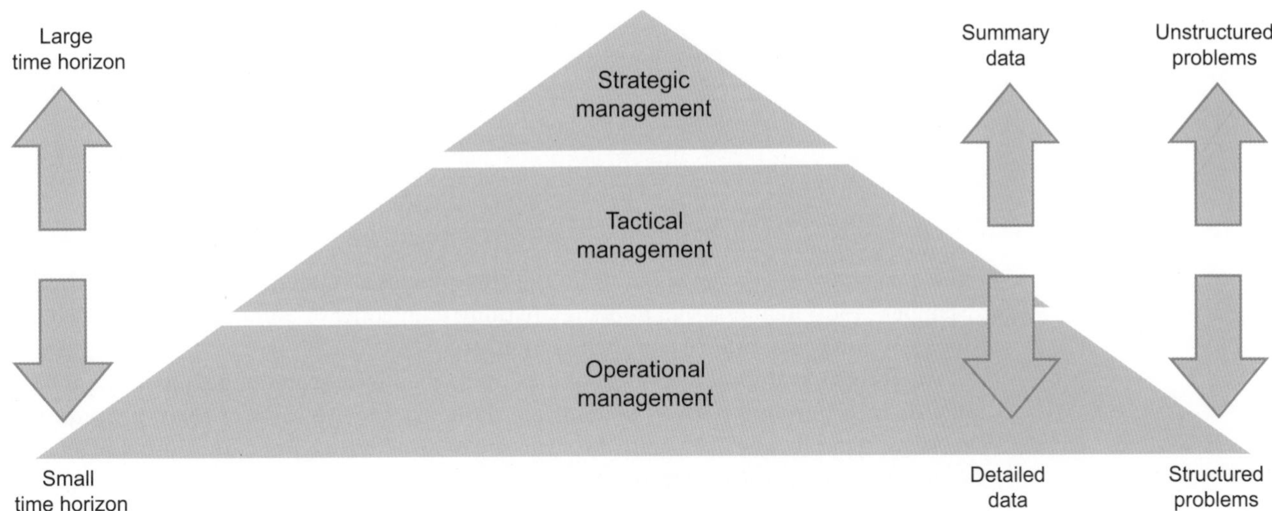

Figure 3.9: *Levels of management*

- **Decision-making characteristics.** The higher up the management hierarchy, the less structured problems and decisions become. Structured decisions are known as **algorithmic decisions**: we can draw up an explicit procedure for making them. Unstructured decisions are known as **heuristic decisions**: no set procedure can be established but some rules of thumb can be suggested.
- **Information needs**. The higher up the management hierarchy, the greater need there is for summary information and information concerned with the external environment. Operational managers need detailed information on operational activities. Strategic managers need information which summarises aspects of organisational performance and compares it with competitors.
- **Time horizon**. The higher up the management hierarchy, the larger the time horizon is for both decisions and information. Operational managers need information to help them make decisions on an hour-by-hour basis. Strategic managers are more likely to think in months and years.

Because technical ICT system use algorithms, it is of course algorithmically based operational decision making that can best be automated. For example, let's take people using their credit cards. A credit card number is typically made up of three elements. The first part of the number codes the card type, the second part identifies the card issuer, and the third part is the owner's account number. The last digit is a check digit, set so that when a particular algorithm is applied to the number, it produces a figure divisible by ten. This is used as a check on whether the number has been entered correctly: if the algorithm does not give a number divisible by ten, the transaction is rejected.

This Luhn algorithm (called after its inventor) works like this:

- Take the original credit card number.
- Reverse the numbers in the string.
- Double every second number.
- Add all three rows of digits together. If any result is more than nine, subtract nine from the number.
- Add together the final string of digits.

Table 3.1 gives an example. Adding up the final string of digits gives 80, so the number was entered correctly.

Reflect
Try out the Luhn algorithm on one of your own credit cards. Think too about decisions that affect your daily life. How many of them are algorithmic in nature?

Table 3.1: *The Luhn algorithm for checking credit card numbers*

Credit card number	3	7	7	9	5	6	5	7	0	9	4	4	7	2	6
Reverse number	6	2	7	4	4	9	0	7	5	6	5	9	7	7	3
Double every second digit		4		8		18		14		12		18		14	
Add numbers	6	4	7	8	4	9	0	5	5	3	5	9	7	5	3

Signs and systems

The concept of a sign serves to unify the three forms of system we consider in this book. Stamper (2001) defines a sign as being 'anything that "conveys" information because it stands for something else within a community of users'.

An **activity system** is a set of activities performed by a group of people in the fulfilment of a defined purpose. Activity systems are designed systems. Sets of roles, procedures and rules are typically used to specify the structure of an activity system. The output of an activity system is action (see Chapter 2).

Not surprisingly, in Figure 3.1 human activity systems are located in the realm of the social. Signs are used in activity systems to support collaborative and coordinated action. In one direction they are used to encode intentions. In the other direction they are used as key inputs into decisions made about action.

For example, information (about, for instance, students, staff and modules) is important to a university's successful operation. A module description is a critical sign-system in this environment. We can analyse it on a number of levels. At the level of pragmatics, key assumptions surrounding the use of module descriptions are that the educational experience can be packaged or chunked into modules, and delivered and assessed in discrete units. Modules effectively become the building blocks of the higher education experience. They are the educational products delivered by universities.

Reflect
Is it possible to conceive of any situation where information occurs without the participation of people?

An **information system** is a communication system used to support a given human activity system. The output of an information system is information. In Figure 3.1 information systems are located against the semantic and syntactic levels of signs. Information systems use agreed 'languages' to represent meaning.

At the level of semantics, in a university setting, students and staff tend to treat module descriptions as informal contracts. They define what is to be covered in the course, for instance. They also define the mechanism for assessment.

At the syntactic level a module description can be considered as a data structure. Normally an university will draw up a standard format for module descriptions, including data elements such as a module code, module name, level, learning outcomes, syllabus, assessment pattern and suggested reading. Many of the data items in these elements will be text-based.

An **ICT system** is a designed system of artefacts used to collect, store, process and disseminate data. The output of an ICT system is data. In Figure 3.1 ICT systems are located at the technical level. They are concerned with the physical representation of signs for STORAGE, transmission and manipulation. so they work at the level of empirics.

Storage: The part of a system concerned with the representation of data.

A module description may be made available in a physical form, on paper or as part of a student or module handbook. In the modern university it may also be made available electronically over a university intranet, and may be stored in a database system for easy retrieval and maintenance.

Case check: Case 17, Quipu

The human use of information in signs can be thought of as universal, in the sense that it is characteristic of all human time-periods and civilisations. This case demonstrates this by considering an artefact used in the successful Amerindian empire of the Inca for data storage and information transmission. The Inca, who did not have a written language, used an assemblage of coloured, knotted cotton cords known as a *quipu* (which means 'to knot') to record their messages and keep their records.

We can identify various types of system in the Inca civilisation – activity systems, information systems and ICT systems. Inca administration seems to have been organised and efficient. The activity systems in the Inca Empire included tax collection, the administration of workforces for public buildings and the distribution of goods. We can judge the usefulness of the information system and the technology it used by assessing the contribution it made to the Inca imperial activity systems.

Key skill 

Knowledge and modelling

The word *knowledge* is derived from the Ancient Greek word *gignoskein,* which can be roughly translated as to decide upon, determine or decree. Epistemology, or the philosophical theory of knowledge, is at least as old as the term itself, and knowledge, or the problem of knowledge, has been of intensive interest to sociologists and psychologists for centuries. More recently there has been an emphasis on organisational knowledge: how organisations learn and to what degree they can manage their knowledge.

There is a vast literature on what knowledge is, but a simple working definition should suffice at this point. (It also acts as a basis for the discussion on the distinction between data, information and knowledge management in Chapter 11.) Tsitchizris and Lochovsky (1982) define information as being 'an increment of knowledge which can be inferred from data'. Information therefore increases a person or group's knowledge of something. This definition relates the concepts of data, information, knowledge and people.

Individuals clearly acquire knowledge which improves their performance in specific fields. But does it make sense to think of groups and organisations as having knowledge, and if so, to what extent? The concept of **organisational memory** has been suggested for what an organisation knows about its processes and its environment. This knowledge is a critical resource for business organisations, helping them operate effectively in economic markets.

Types of knowledge

We can categorise types of organisational knowledge on three dimensions: accessibility, level of abstraction and purpose (see Figure 3.10).

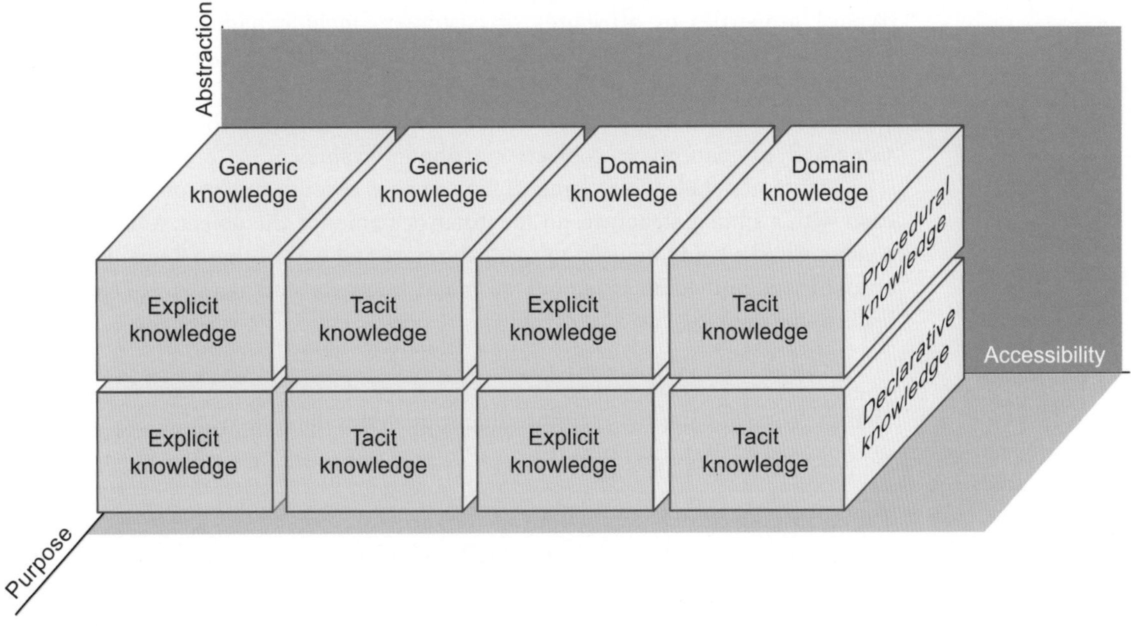

Figure 3.10: *Types of knowledge*

Explicit knowledge: Readily accessible, documented and organised knowledge.

Implicit knowledge: Knowledge accessible through querying and discussion but needing communication.

For accessibility, we can distinguish between explicit and tacit knowledge (Liebowitz, 1999). EXPLICIT KNOWLEDGE is readily accessible, documented and organised. **Tacit knowledge** is IMPLICIT and internal. Polanyi (1962; see also Chapter 1) argues that much human knowledge is tacit, and by implication that much organisational knowledge is largely tacit. Nonaka and Takeuchi (1995) argue that it is increasingly important to convert internalised tacit knowledge into explicit codified knowledge in order to share it and reduce problems caused by staff turnover. Clearly to make this knowledge explicit it must be translated or converted into data and information. In other words, mind-stuff must be converted into symbol-stuff.

In terms of purpose, we can distinguish between **declarative knowledge** (knowing what) and **procedural knowledge** (knowing how). Declarative knowledge involves being able to recognise something as an instance of something else. Procedural knowledge tells us how to do something in specific circumstances.

Finally, we can distinguish between knowledge applicable to a narrow area of life (**domain knowledge**) and knowledge that is transferable between domains (**generic knowledge**). Much business activity relies on workers using domain knowledge, both declarative (such as knowing what an expense claim form is) and procedural (such as the process set down for appraising staff).

Business knowledge

Recent business information systems incorporate mechanisms for representing or automating aspects of both declarative and procedural domain knowledge that is explicit. This section introduces the topic of knowledge representation, and builds on the earlier discussion of information modelling.

Object classes: A grouping of similar objects.

We can represent or model declarative knowledge using five constructs: objects, OBJECT CLASSES, relations, attributes and values. These are the constructs introduced earlier (see page 87). An object is anything with an independent existence from the relevant universe of discourse (UoD). Objects are typically organised into object classes, which abstract the common features of their members. An attribute is a property of an object class. A relation (or relationship) is a connection between two object classes, or between object classes and attributes.

For example, let's take a financial institution which invests money that people save in savings accounts. In this UoD, two object (classes) of interest are customers and savings accounts. Typical properties or attributes of customers include names, addresses and telephone numbers. Typical attributes of savings accounts are start dates and current balances.

A datum, a unit of data, is used to represent a fact about a UoD. We referred to it as a data item earlier. A datum or data item can be defined in terms of the constructs introduced, and using BNF, as <datum> ::= <object> <attribute> <value>.

A record of details (data element) for a savings account might consist of a set of data items each with a similar structure: an identifier or name for the object; a name for the attribute; a value. Spaces could be used to mark the start and end of these items. Perhaps one savings account is identified as 4324, and we might know its start date is 12 February 2001, which leads to the data item as:

4324 Start Date 12/02/2001

That the current balance is £500 would produce this data item;

4324 Current Balance 500.

The entire collection of facts about savings accounts constitutes the extension of this concept in this particular domain, and corresponds to what we referred to earlier as a data structure.

Information (as we defined it earlier) is interpreted data, data placed in a meaningful context. Here the context is defined in terms of two types of relation between classes: the relationship between an object class and its attributes (an attribution relation) or an association between an object class and some other object class. This might be defined in BNF as:

<information-item> ::= <object-class> <attribution-relation> <attribute>
<information-item> ::= <object-class> <association-relation> <object-class>

Let us use HASA as a label to represent an attribution relation, and *owns* as an example of a label for a type of association relation. Then we can define the relationships between customers and savings accounts as:

Customer HASA Name
Customer HASA Branch
Customer HASA TelNo
Savings Account HASA Start Date
Savings Account HASA Current Balance
Customer Owns Savings Account

In essence we are building an information model using these statements. We can illustrate this by drawing a diagram for this domain: Figure 3.11 shows it.

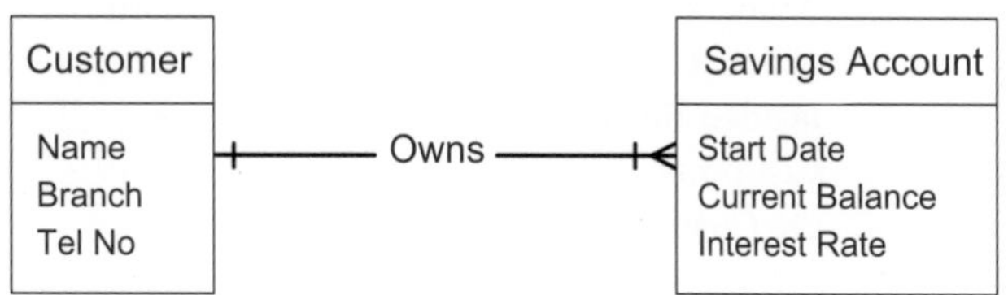

Figure 3.11: *An information model for the financial instution domain*

Abstraction relations

We derive knowledge from information by integrating it with existing knowledge. This is normally achieved through the process of abstraction, which we can represent as:

<knowledge-item> ::= <object-class> <abstraction-relation> <object-class>
<abstraction-relation> ::= ISA|AKO|PART OF

The process of abstraction is defined here using three types of abstraction relation: ISA, AKO and PART OF. An ISA relationship is a relationship between objects and object classes. Hence, when we state that [Paul Beynon-Davies ISA Customer], we are defining a particular object as being a member of the class of customers.

An AKO (A-Kind-Of) relationship is a relationship between an object class and its more general or abstract object class. It is sometimes referred to as a GENERALISATION relationship. When we state that an [Ordinary Account AKO Savings Account] we are defining the class of ordinary accounts to be a subclass of the class of savings accounts. An AKO or generalisation relation is represented on a diagram as a line terminating in a triangle (or an open arrowhead. This is illustrated in Figure 3.12.

Generalisation: This type of relationship establishes levels of abstraction between object classes.

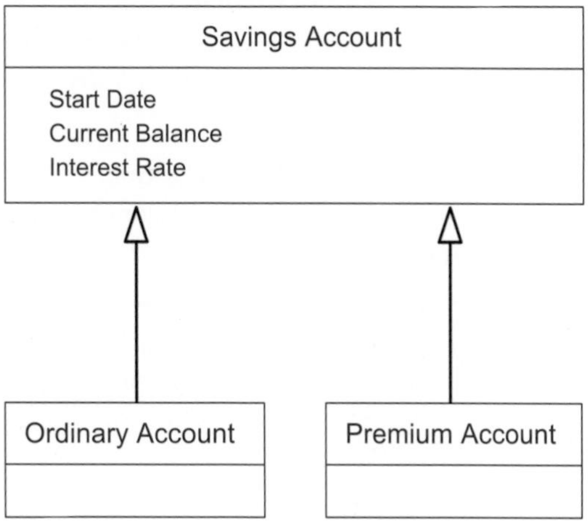

Savings Account
Start Date
Current Balance
Interest Rate
Ordinary Account
Premium Account

Figure 3.12: *Notation for generalisation*

For the financial institution example, we could define [4324 ISA Ordinary Share] and [Ordinary Account AKO Savings Account]. Suppose also we establish these two facts:

[Savings Account HASA Interest Rate] and [Ordinary Account Interest Rate 4]. Here we have established a fact, an interest rate of 4 per cent, relevant to all ordinary share accounts.

Establishing this fact allows us to infer another fact: [4324 Interest Rate 4]. Here we have an example of the application of existing knowledge to existing information to generate new information through a particular type of inference known as **inheritance**. In other words, if savings account 4324 is an ordinary account, it 'inherits' the properties of ordinary accounts.

Aggregation: This type of relationship serves to collect a set of different classes into one unit or aggregate.

PART OF relationships compose an object out of an assembly or AGGREGATION of other objects. When we state that [Railway Station PART OF Railway] and [Railway Line PARTOF Railway] we are specifying a railway as being made up of stations and lines. In terms of the financial domain we might define a Customer Portfolio class which aggregates all the financial products a particular customer uses. PART OF relationships are represented by diamond-headed lines on a diagram (see Figure 3.13). So we can specify [Current Account PART OF Customer Portfolio], [Savings Account PART OF Customer Portfolio] and [Mortgage PART OF Customer Portfolio].

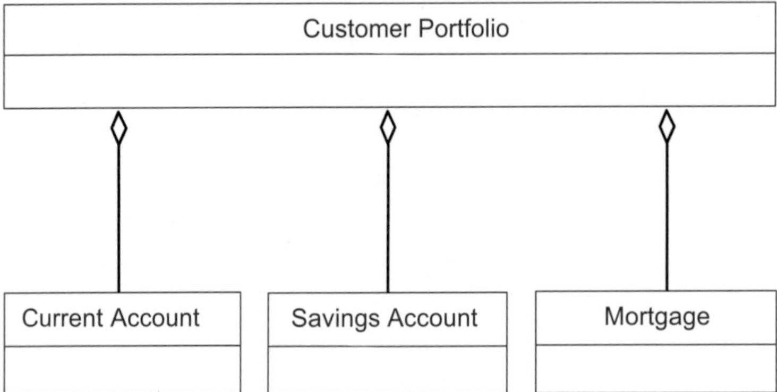

Figure 3.13: *Notation for aggregation*

Business rules

The word *inference* is derived from the Latin words *in* and *ferre*, meaning to carry or bring forward. So inference is the process of bringing forward new knowledge from existing knowledge. We can draw up rules for inference, and in the building society case one such rule is:

RULE*************************
IF Object ISA Object Class
AND Object Class Property Value
THEN Object Property Value

We described this rule above as an inheritance rule. Similar generic inference rules apply to AKO and PART OF relations.

We can generalise the concept of a rule to include rules specific to the domain of discourse, or domain-specific rules. For instance, we might write the following rule into our system:

RULE*************************
IF Object1 ISA Customer
THEN Object1 Holds Object2
AND Object2 ISA Customer Portfolio

In other words, this rule is that all customers can be assumed to hold a customer portfolio. We can use a rule such as this in a number of ways in an ICT system. For example, when a customer's access details are entered the system could automatically load data on that person's portfolio.

This is an example of a business rule: a rule that specifies an aspect of a business operation. Business rules have become an important part of the architecture of ICT systems. Typically they embed aspects of decision making in them: that is, given a rule that details which

Reflect
Consider the use of business rules in organisational life. Is it possible to capture much of the working of typical business processes using the idea of business rules? Is it desirable that businesses structure their activity like this? What problems are likely?

circumstances it must do one thing or another, the system can 'decide' what to do. Domain-specific rules can be used in this way to make changes to the data held in the system. Back on page 49 we used the example of a car rental company; let's go back to that now. Customers are given variable discounts which depend on the car rental group, period of rental, whether the customer is a member of a rental club and how far in advance the car has been booked. Here are two of the business rules relevant to this domain:

RULE************************
IF Customer rents Car
AND Car Rental Group ISA Compact
AND Rental Period ISA Day Rental
AND Customer ISA Club Customer
AND Booking > 3 Days in Advance
THEN Customer Discount = 10 per cent

RULE************************
IF Customer rents Car
AND Car Rental Group ISA Compact
AND Rental Period ISA Day Rental
AND Customer ISA Club Customer
AND Booking <> 3 Days in Advance
THEN Customer Discount = 5 per cent

Summary

1. Information is a central concept for organisational life in the twenty-first century. It is a multifaceted concept and difficult to define. This chapter used the core concept of signs as a way of approaching information. Signs mediate between the physical and the social world, and can be clearly related to the types of organisational systems discussed in Chapter 2. Signs also allow us to relate data, information, decisions and action.

2. A working definition of knowledge builds on the concepts of data and information. A datum, a single item of data, is a set of symbols used to represent something. When symbols are given context and meaning in a situation they become information. Information is therefore data placed in a meaningful context, and is used in organisations to make decisions and take action. Knowledge is derived from information by integrating it with existing knowledge. Declarative knowledge (knowing what) is normally acquired through a process of abstraction. Procedural knowledge (knowing how) typically involves the use of business rules.

3. The discipline of semiotics is devoted to the study of signs. Its four sub-areas – pragmatics, semantics, syntactics and empirics – cross both the distinction between data, information and knowledge, and the distinction between human activity systems, information systems and ICT systems. So these levels represent facets of the concept of a sign which span the social and the technical.

4. Pragmatics is concerned with the purpose of communication. It links signs with intention. Its focus is on the intentions of human agents underlying communicative behaviour. In other words, intentions link language to action.

5. Semantics is concerned with the meaning of a message. It considers the content of communications, and is the study of the meaning of signs: the association between signs and behaviour. It can be considered as the study of the link between symbols and their referents or concepts, and particularly the way in which signs relate to human behaviour.

6. Syntactics is concerned with the formal representation of a message: the logic and grammar of sign systems. In other words, it is devoted to form rather than content.

7. Empirics is the study of the signals used to carry a message; the physical characteristics of the medium of communication. It studies sound, light, electronic transmission and so on. Data representation and storage are also important issues at the level of empirics.

8. The four levels of information relate directly to the three levels of business system discussed in Chapter 2. Human activity systems are social systems and hence typically interact with the level of pragmatics. Signs are used in these activity systems to support collaborative and coordinated action. In one direction they are used to encode intentions. In the other direction they are used as key inputs into decisions. An information system is a communication system used to support a given human activity system, so it is located against the semantic and syntactic levels of signs. The output of an information system is therefore information; information systems use agreed languages to represent meaning. An ICT system is a designed system of artefacts used to collect, store, process and disseminate data. Since the output of an ICT system is data, such systems are located at the technical or empirics level of signs. ICT is concerned with the physical representation of signs for storage, transmission and manipulation.

Chapter 4 considers the concept of an information system in more detail. It distinguishes more clearly between the three types of business system introduced here. It also introduces the idea of infrastructure to help explain how systems are related in the organisational context. It discusses elements of a typical business information system infrastructure and explains how it supports decision making and business activity.

Focus on Value

Information has key value as a mediating force between technology and action or activity. It is the fundamental 'stuff' of communication, and can be understood on a number of different levels. A layered perspective allows us to distinguish between data, information and knowledge, and use this to understand the linkages between technology and activity systems in business organisations. Data consists of 'values' assigned to data items, but the true value of data arises in the use of data in the context of communication and coordinated activity. 'Quality' information has value to decision making and in support of coordinated activity. Knowledge involves connecting new information with established networks of information and is critical to organisational learning.

Review test

1 Semiotics is the study of ____________.

Fill in the blank.

2 Why is semiotics useful as a way of understanding the concept of information?

Write two sentences.

3 A sign is anything that is ____________.

Fill in the blank.

4 A datum, a single item of data, is a set of symbols used to represent something.

True or false? ☐ True ☐ False

5 Match the definitions to the terms:

Pragmatics	the study of the meaning of signs
Semantics	the study of the physical characteristics of the medium of communication
Syntactics	the study of the general context and culture of communication
Empirics	the study of the logic and grammar of sign systems

6 The three elements of the meaning triangle are designation, extension and intension.

True or false? ☐ True ☐ False

7 Claude Shannon's information theory consists of the study of information.

True or false? ☐ True ☐ False

8 The major elements of any communication process are:

Select all that apply.

☐ Sender
☐ Telecommunications device
☐ Communication channel
☐ Receiver
☐ Message
☐ Cable

9 Distinguish between natural and formal languages.

Write two sentences.

10 A data model consists of:

Select all that apply.

☐ Data structures
☐ Data elements
☐ Data flows
☐ Data items
☐ Data communications

11 <business-telephone-no> ::= <area-code> <telephone-no> <extension-no>

Write a full sentence that adequately describes this BNF specification.

12 Information modelling consists of these constructs: ____________, relationships and attributes.

Fill in the blank.

13 Match the name of the modelling construct to the most appropriate symbol:

Association relationship ☐

Entity/object class —

Aggregation (part of) relationship ◇

Generalisation (AKO) relationship ○

14

Describe the rules associated with the cardinality and optionality on this diagram as a number of sentences.

15 Information reduces ____________ in decision making.

Fill in the blank.

16 A decision is structured if the decision-making process can be described in detail before the decision is made.

True or false? ☐ True ☐ False

17	Herbert Simon identifies the stages in a decision-making process as intelligence, design, choice and ____________. Fill in the blank.
18	We can identify three levels of management in terms of decision making. What are they? Select the most appropriate three. ☐ Strategic ☐ Operational ☐ Middle ☐ Tactical
19	Good information is critical to: Select the most appropriate. ☐ Good data ☐ Good decision making ☐ Good data models
20	Provide one example of a business rule.
21	Produce an information model which represents the following domain of criminal court cases. Each judge has a list of outstanding cases over which they will preside. Only one judge presides over each case. For each case one prosecuting counsel is appointed to represent the Department of Public Prosecutions. Cases are scheduled at one Crown Court for an estimated duration from a given start date. A case can try more than one crime. Each crime can have one or more defendants. Each defendant can have one or more defending barristers. If a crime has multiple defendants, each defendant can have one or more defence counsel. Defendants may have more than one outstanding case against them.
22	Draw the diagram which represents the following statements: UndergraduateModule AKO module PostgraduateModule AKO module

Exercises

1. Take one example of data known to you. Try to separate out issues of data (representation) from information (interpretation). In other words, try to identify the context and use for the data.
2. Take a visual sign. Try to separate out what the sign is from what it represents. In other words, analyse its semantics.
3. Consider one contemporary facility on the Internet such as chat rooms or discussion boards in terms of the classic elements of a communication.
4. Consider texting as a communication system. What limitations are there to this medium?
5. All the inputs to and outputs from information systems can be regarded as signs. Give some examples of semantic problems that might arise in interpreting signs from information systems. Discuss the problems involved in individuals and groups misinterpreting signs.
6. Consider the Highway Code as a sign system. What human activity does it support? Provide some examples of signs, rules and behaviour.
7. Select and analyse a written communication in terms of the distinction between pragmatics, semantics, syntactics and empirics.
8. Investigate the way in which various forms of programming languages can be considered as formal languages.
9. Emails often use emoticons, signs such as -:) which convey emotional content. Investigate their range and use, and analyse them in terms of concepts from semiotics.
10. Consider a decision made in an organisation known to you. Work back from the decision to the information required to support it. What action resulted from the decision?
11. Select a decision and analyse it using Simon's model of the decision-making process.
12. Give an example of how human decision making in business suffers from limited time and information.

Projects

1. Using the approach described in this chapter, develop a detailed data model for an area known to you: for example, a specification of the data structures, data elements and data items relevant to student records.
2. Records have been maintained for many hundreds if not thousands of years in organisations of many different forms. Nowadays, records management is seen as a significant problem for organisations. Investigate the term 'records management'. Determine why it is a significant problem and why it is increasingly important for organisations.
3. Identify an information system supporting activity in an organisation known to you, such as a patient records system in a GP practice, a student records system at a school, an inventory management system at a retail store or a waste collection scheduling system at a local authority. Investigate and document the information model underlying your chosen information system using the approach in this chapter.
4. Determine the business rules underlying an information system known to you, such as those for student progression on university courses. Specify the business rules as a decision table or as a set of IF THEN statements.
5. The idea of speech acts and the theory of speech acts have been proposed as one way of understanding the essence of information systems. Investigate some of the literature and determine the relevance of speech act theory to informatics work.

6. Information theory has had a critical influence on the development of telecommunications, particularly data communications. Investigate the relevance of information theory to ICT. For instance, in what way can information theory be seen to underlie the modern conception of the Internet?

7. Electronic mail is a pervasive form of communication in many organisations. Investigate some of the literature in this area. What consequences does its increasing use have for organisational decision making and action?

8. Investigate the applicability of the three-layered management model (strategic, tactical, operational) to an organisation known to you. Try to identify who are the strategic, tactical and operational managers. What decisions to they typically take? What information do they use?

9. Consider Simon's model of the decision-making process in terms of a management activity such as project management. How do project management decisions and control fit with the stages of Simon's model?

10. Much literature has been published on organisational knowledge and its management. Consider a limited area of an organisation known to you (concerning, for example, the sale of products and services). Try to document some of this knowledge using the approach used in this chapter.

Further reading

Stamper (1973) provided the original motivation for considering information in terms of semiotics. It is now out of print but his position is summarised in a more recent book chapter (Stamper, 2001). Data, information and knowledge modelling are covered in some detail in Beynon-Davies (2004) on database systems.

References

Beynon-Davies, P. (2004) *Database Systems*. Basingstoke, Palgrave.

Checkland, P. (1999) *Soft Systems Methodology: A thirty year retrospective*. Chichester, John Wiley.

Floridi, L. (2007) 'A look into the future impact of ICT on our lives', *Information Society* **23**(1): 59–64.

Liebowitz, J. (ed.) (1999) *Knowledge Management Handbook*. Boca Raton, Fl., CRC Press.

Morris, C. (1964) *Signification and Significance*. Cambridge, Mass., MIT Press.

Nonaka, I. and Takeuchi, H. (1995) *The Knowledge-Creating Company*. New York, Oxford University Press.

Ogden, C. K. and Richards, I. A. (1923) *The Meaning of Meaning*. London, Routledge & Kegan Paul.

Pinker, S. (2001) *The Language Gene*. Harmondsworth, Middx, Penguin.

Polanyi, M. (1962) *Personal Knowledge*. New York, Anchor Day.

Shannon, C. E. (1949) *The Mathematical Theory of Communication*. Urbana, University of Illinois Press.

Sobel, D. (1996) *Longitude*. London, Fourth Estate.

Stamper, R. K. (1973) *Information in Business and Administrative Systems*. London, Batsford.

Stamper, R. K. (2001) 'Organisational semiotics: informatics without the computer?' In L. Kecheng, R. J. Clarke, P. Bogh-Anderson and R. K. Stamper (eds), *Information, Organisation and Technology: Studies in organisational semiotics*. Dordrecht, Netherlands, Kluwer.

Tsitchizris, D. C. and Lochovsky, F. H. (1982) *Data Models*. Englewood-Cliffs, N.J., Prentice-Hall.

Von Baeyer, H. C. (2003) *Information: The new language of science*, Weidenfeld & Nicolson.

CHAPTER 4 Information systems

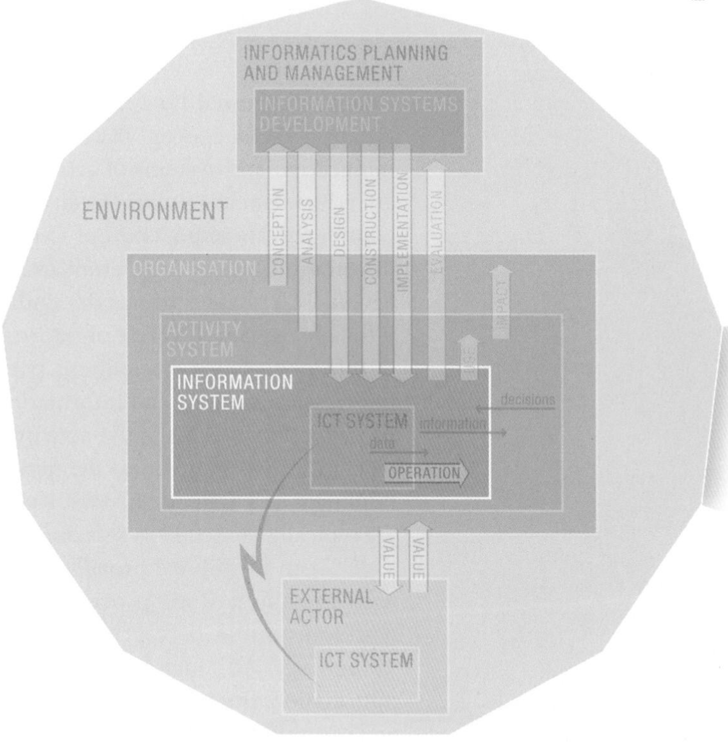

Knowledge is of two kinds. We know a subject ourselves, or we know where we can find information upon it.

Samuel Johnson (1709–1784). Quoted in the Life of Johnson (1791) by James Boswell.

CHAPTER OUTLINE

LEARNING OUTCOMES	PRINCIPLES
Explain the distinction between a human activity system, information system and ICT system, and in the process define in more detail the essence of an information system.	An information system is a sociotechnical system – a communication system using artefacts (ICT) in support of a given human activity system. It therefore spans the concepts of data, information, decision making and action discussed in Chapter 3.
Describe the concept of informatics infrastructure and distinguish between back-end and front-end information systems infrastructure.	The activity infrastructure of any organisation relies on a corresponding information, information systems and ICT infrastructure. Collectively this is referred to as the informatics infrastructure. For information systems infrastructure, which is the focus of this chapter, we can distinguish between information systems that directly interface with organisational stakeholders (front-end information systems) and those that form the organisation's core information-handling systems (back-end information systems).
Describe the high-level functionality of the key back-end and front-end information systems in a typical enterprise, and construct a simple information systems model based on this understanding.	Organisations in the private sector typically rely on a core set of back-end information systems. A range of front-end information systems are normally constructed around these core systems. It is important to represent the functionality of this information systems infrastructure as an aid to better management. For this purpose, information systems models are critical.
Describe the relationship between information infrastructure and information systems infrastructure, and identify some of the key information classes of relevance to the enterprise.	The information systems infrastructure of an organisation relies on an integrated information infrastructure. High-level information models are therefore important to recognising and managing the interdependencies between information systems in organisations.

Introduction

Chapter 2 showed how the concept of a system is core to organisational informatics. This is such a useful concept because it allows us to relate systems of activity to systems of communication and systems of artefacts. The relationships between these three levels of system are critical anchor points for any consideration of organisational informatics. Chapter 3 also considered the importance of the concept of information. Information arises in the process of communication, is different from data, and is critical in support of decision making and action. This chapter brings the understanding of systems and information together, and uses it to help explain the place of information systems in organisations.

Informatics as a discipline is particularly interested in questions relating to the value of information systems and information and communication technology (ICT). They can only be answered in terms of the activity systems in which these systems are embedded. In Chapter 2 an activity system was defined as a set of activities performed by a group of people in the fulfilment of a defined purpose. Activity systems are designed systems (Checkland, 1987), and are typically modelled as sets of processes with embedded control (see Chapter 2).

ICT can be defined broadly as a designed technical or technological system of artefacts used to collect, store, process and disseminate data. Hobart and Schiffman (1998) offer a useful historical perspective on the long-term nature of information and information 'technology'. Although both writing and speech are forms of communication and so impart information, they define the first information age as beginning with the invention of writing, and see writing as the first information technology: 'Both writing and speech constitute communication, but of the two only writing extracts the sounds of speech from their oral flow by giving them visual representation.'

This chapter focuses on the concept of an information system, a communication system using artefacts in support of an activity system. It can be seen as a sociotechnical system in that it forms a bridge between an activity system and an ICT system. Its essence does not lie not purely in the technology or the activity: it lies in the way in which technology is used in support of purposeful action.

As with ICT, we can broaden the definition of an information system by considering historical systems. Information systems date back almost 6000 years, and are particularly associated with the invention and refinement of ways of recording language. Of course, we can communicate information through speech and through our body language, but these are impermanent: there is no record. The invention of written language made it possible for the message to persist in the form of a record (see Chapter 3). This is particularly associated with the rise of agriculture and cities in human history.

Did you know?

Sumerian cuneiscript (used from the sixth to the third millennium BC) appears to have been invented to support early forms of financial administration. Some have even argued that without the need to record assets, written language might never have emerged.

Back-end ICT infrastructure: The ICT systems used to support the core information systems of the business.

Back-end ICT system: A core ICT system involved in manipulating the key data for the organisation.

Modelling continues to be used in this chapter as a tool to help understand and represent the nature of systems. This leads us to a consideration of diagramming as a tool for modelling information systems. The diagramming approach is used to help define some of the core information systems found in business: that is, the organisation's BACK-END INFORMATION SYSTEMS INFRASTRUCTURE. This provides the bedrock for contemporary business because it supports some key activity systems.

The core back-end information systems infrastructure is also typically the platform for many front-end information systems, which are critical to maintaining effective relationships between key organisational stakeholders. This includes external stakeholders such as suppliers and customers, as well as internal stakeholders such as employees and managers. So these information systems support the internal value chain as well as the supply and demand chains (see Chapter 7). A key challenge for the modern organisation is to successfully integrate back-end and front-end information systems to support new forms of activity (see Chapter 8).

Defining the concept of an information system

Activity systems, information systems and ICT systems are all systems, so they can be considered using the concepts described in Chapter 2. They have inputs, processes and outputs, and their behaviour relies on their effective control and performance.

Activity systems are social systems, so they are sometimes referred to as 'soft' systems. They consist of people engaging in coordinated and collaborative activities in fulfilment of a goal or purpose. ICT systems are technical systems, and are often called 'hard' systems because they consist of an assembly of artefacts, which are designed to support aspects of an information system. An ICT system takes data as input, manipulates it as a process and outputs it for interpretation in a human activity system.

Information systems are systems of communication. They involve people in producing, collecting, storing and disseminating information. Many systems in organisations are examples of sociotechnical systems: that is, systems of technology used in systems of activity, and information systems are prime examples of this. Information systems consist of ICT used in human activity systems, so they span ICT and human activity. They provide information which drives decision making, which in turn leads to action.

It is important to recognise that there were information systems in organisations before the invention of modern ICT, so information systems do not need modern ICT. It can be useful to consider non-ICT-based historical information systems, because it is sometimes easier to see in them the essence of what information systems are. But in today's complex global organisational world most information systems need and use hardware, software, data and communication technology (see Chapter 9).

Case check: Case 4, Early warning network

This case study gives an example of a historical information system, one that contributed to Allied victory in the Second World War. During the summers of the late 1930s, the Royal Air Force Fighter Command created an early warning network which played a part in a decisive battle against the German Luftwaffe – the Battle of Britain in 1940 (Holwell and Checkland, 1998). Hitler needed control of the skies if he was to invade Britain by sea, but the Battle of Britain gave it to the Allies, and caused him to abandon the planned invasion and turn his attention eastwards to the Soviet Union. This in turn made it possible for the Allies to invade continental Europe in 1944. Learning about systems such as this helps to prevent us from being over-concerned with ICT: information systems are not the same as ICT systems.

Table 4.1 provides some historical examples of human activity systems, information, information systems and information technology.

Table 4.1: *Examples of historical information, information systems, information technology and human activity systems* (continued overleaf)

Period	Activity system	Information	Information system	ICT
Approximately 4000 BC	Taxation collection and administration in the royal courts of Sumeria	Royal assets and taxes	Asset and taxation recording	Writing on clay tablets
1200–1500 AD	Administration of the Inca empire	Tribute, numbers of military, events	Road network, Chassqui, Quipucamaya	Quipu
1890	US Census production	US population characteristics	Census data collection, processing and reporting	Punched cards and tabulating machines
1940	Warning network: RAF command and control of fighter aircraft	Radar data, observation data, telephone communications	Collecting data from radar, organising this data for military-decision making and the dissemination of both decisions and data to airfields	Radar, telecommunications, totes

Table 4.1: *continued*

Period	Activity system	Information	Information systems	ICT
1951	Order processing, payroll, inventory management	Orders, payments, inventory	Lyons Electronic Office (LEO)	Early mainframe computer (EDSAC) and specially written software
2008	Customer relationship management	Customers, sales orders, enquiries, payments	CRM information system	Computer hardware (PCs and servers), software (CRM package), data (DBMS) and communication technology (wide and local area network)

We should not assume that information systems and ICT systems are in some way value-neutral. The use of technologies in wider information and activity systems is very much a value-laden activity. Information systems and ICT can support repugnant as well as generously intended activity systems. The design of information systems frequently involves a debate about the appropriate use of technology for information purposes in a particular system of activity. This means that ethical concerns as well as concerns of efficacy, efficiency and effectiveness have a part to play.

Case check: Case 27 W Herman Hollerith

In 1890 the first automated census was conducted in the United States, thanks to the tabulating machine, an innovation introduced by Herman Hollerith. This used cards, each of which was divided into a number of columns and rows to create small cells. Holes were punched through some of the cells to code data about an individual. The cards were then fed through a metal drum and a set of wire brushes, which briefly swept through the holes, making electrical contacts. These in turn would activate circuits which turned dials – one dial for each variable – making it possible to keep an automatic tally of each variable.

This led to massive efficiency savings. The original information system for the census consisted of making tally marks on small squares on rolls of paper, then adding them up by hand. For the 1890 census an army of 50,000 census takers posed 235 questions to 62 million Americans. It was estimated if they had done it by hand, it would have taken ten years to complete.

Hollerith eventually sold his machine to a company which changed its name to International Business Machines (IBM). Black (2002) tells how some of IBM's tabulating machines were used by Hitler's Nazi administration to compile two censuses of the German population in 1933 and 1939. They could not realistically have done this without Hollerith's invention (Biles, 1989), so it was this invention that allowed the Nazi regime to identify Jews and other groups for sending to the death camps. Tabulating machines were even used in the death camps themselves to process data about the extermination effort.

The quality of information

One key way to evaluate the value of an information system is by assessing the quality of the information it produces. Generally speaking the data stored needs to reflect the human activity system it models. So for example in the RAF's warning network, great efforts were made to ensure that its representations of enemy aircraft accurately reflected what was happening in the skies over Britain. Without quality information poor decisions are likely to be made, leading to poor actions. This is very clear for the warning network: if the RAF did not have clear information on where friendly and enemy aircraft were, they could not fight effectively.

This begs the question of what we mean by good or *quality* information. In 1967 the management scientist Russell Ackoff published an influential article which criticised some of the prevailing wisdom about the role of information and information systems in management decision making. Not least, he claimed it was a myth that more information necessarily leads to better decision making. Early designers had tended to assume this, and as a result had designed information systems which overwhelmed managers with their volume of information. Ackoff argued that what counts is the quality of information. Managers do not need

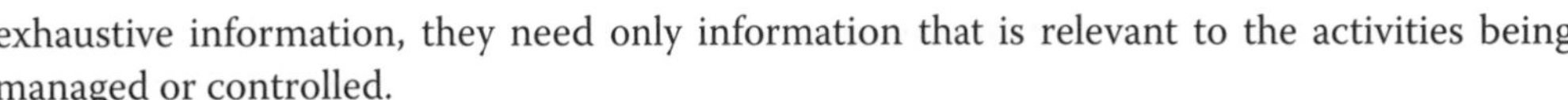

exhaustive information, they need only information that is relevant to the activities being managed or controlled.

Reflect
Consider how national statistics such as the census rate in terms of some of these properties. How are national statistics maintained as quality information?

So the quality of information relates to the use to which it is put. We also need to distinguish between issues related to collecting and processing information, and issues related to communicating and presenting it to users. The collection and processing operations need to focus on providing information that is:

- **accurate:** that is, free from errors
- **complete**, sufficiently covering the area for which it is required
- **current**: reflecting existing and not past circumstances
- **timely**: available in sufficient time for processes that need it
- **relevant** (to the situation in which it is required).

Presentation issues involve, for example:

- **clarity**: so it is easily understood for its intended purpose
- **detail**: which should be sufficient for its intended use
- **medium** (for instance a textual report, graph or table): this too should be appropriate for the type of information and its use.

Reflect
What data validation is required in a general hospital to ensure that the right patients receive the right treatments?

This concern with the quality of information leads to some practical considerations for organisations. First, collecting, processing and presenting information take both equipment and human time and effort, so there is a cost involved. Second, it is important to find ways to ensure that incorrect or invalid information is not entered. In other words, suitable methods of data validation and data verification need to be built into the system design.

Data validation is the process of ensuring that data captured and stored in an information system remains an accurate reflection of its domain or universe of discourse. Usually this is done by building a series of validation rules into the system. They will ensure, for instance, that dates are entered in a correct format: if someone enters, say, 30 February 2009, it will be rejected.

Data verification normally refers to the process of ensuring that data are both entered correctly and transmitted correctly. For instance, many commercial websites ask users when registering to enter their email address twice over. A verification routine checks that the two character strings match before storing customer details.

Recap 

The analysis of historical information systems is an extremely useful exercise for highlighting the essential features of information systems. Information systems are communication systems and are distinct from ICT. ICT supports communication within the information system. Good information systems are critical to efficient and effective action. Information and ICT systems rarely stand still; they evolve to support changes to human activity systems.

Key skill 

Modelling information systems

We need models in order to understand the behaviour of existing information systems or to represent the dynamics of new, designed information systems. One useful technique for creating these models is DATA FLOW diagramming. This modelling technique uses four main constructs. The names used for them here vary a little from those used elsewhere, to reflect the terminology established in Chapters 1 and 3:

Data flow: A pipeline through which packets of data of known composition flow.

Process modelling: The activity of analysing and specifying major organisational processes.

- **Agent** or **agency**: something (usually a person, group, department or organisation, but possibly another information system) that is a net originator or receiver of system information. In this sense it is similar to an event on a PROCESS MODEL, and it is represented in the same way, using a rounded shape (a circle or oval) with an appropriate name. Generally agents indicate something lying outside a system, which serves to define its key boundaries.
- **Information flow:** a pipeline through which packets of information of known composition flow. In the model this is shown by a labelled arrow. The label can be enclosed in an information symbol box (as we saw in Chapter 2), particularly if the modeller wants to distinguish abstract flow of information from actual flow of documents. Arrows at each end of an information flow mean that a process is both passing information to another process or information store, and receiving information from another process or information store.

- **Information store:** a repository for information. In a manual information system this might be a filing cabinet or card index. In an ICT system it is generally a database in a computer system (see Chapter 9). It is represented by a labelled open box.
- **Process**: on a process model, these are general activities. In an INFORMATION SYSTEM MODEL they are information-handling activities, so they consist of a transformation of incoming information flow(s) into outgoing information flow(s). A process is represented by a square or rectangle with a label explaining briefly what the process is.

Information system model: A representation of an information system.

Figure 4.1 illustrates the graphical notation for each of the information system modelling constructs. Figure 4.2 shows an actual model: it is an attempt to represent at a high level the main behaviour of the RAF early warning network.

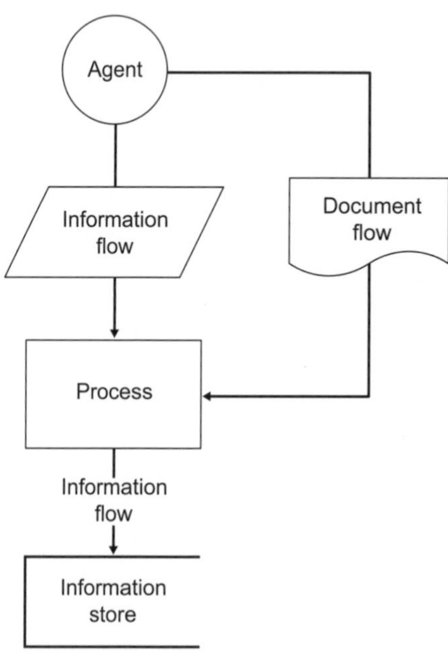

Figure 4.1: *Information system modelling constructs*

Did you know?

Data flow diagrams were invented by Larry Constantine in the 1970s as part of the structured design movement in information systems development (see Chapter 12).

Most real-life information systems are too complex to represent as a single diagram. The usual solution to this problem is to approach it in a top-down manner and decompose a system into subsystems, sub-subsystems and so on. Each process on an information systems model could be considered as a subsystem and at least theoretically could be modelled using a separate diagram (see Chapter 2). Later in this chapter this is done in showing some of the major information subsystems in a generic information systems infrastructure for a typical business organisation.

Levels of infrastructure

Organised activity of whatever form requires **infrastructure.** By this is meant systems of social organisation and technology that support human activity.

For example, we can think of travel using vehicles such as automobiles as an activity system, and the transport network which supports it as a sociotechnical infrastructure. The road infrastructure of motorways, carriageways and major or minor roads is its technological infrastructure.

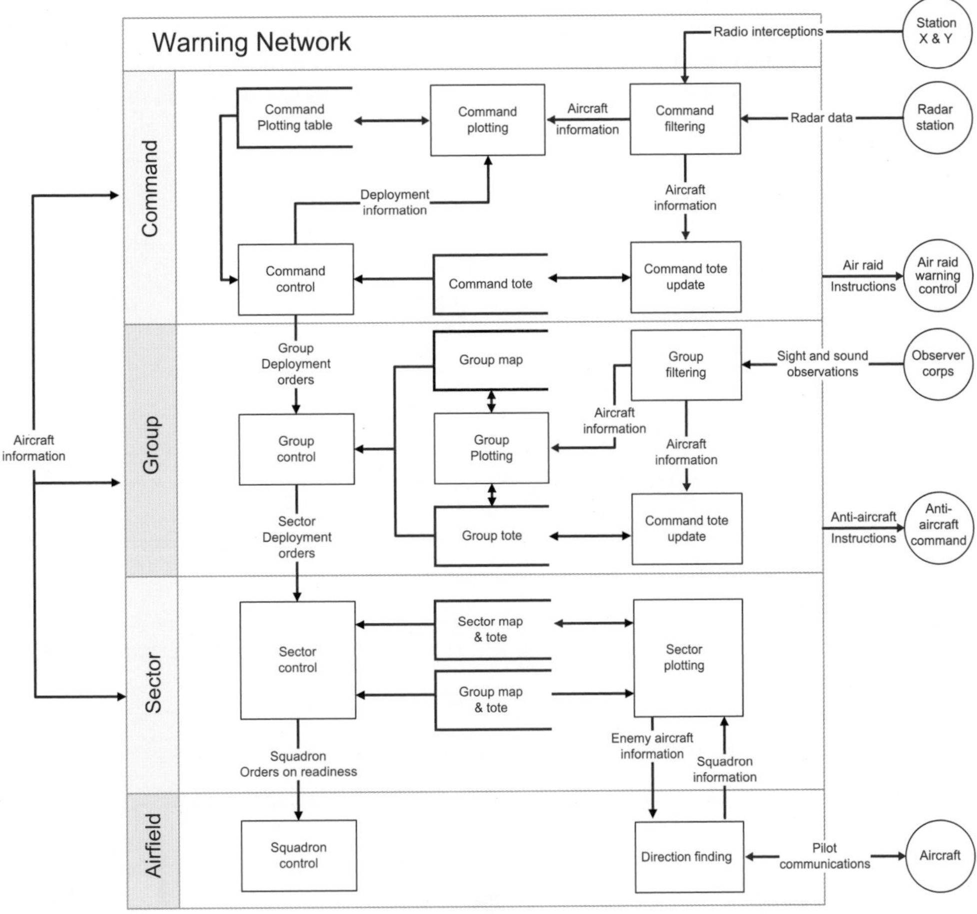

Figure 4.2: *An information systems model of the RAF early warning network*

In the business context we can identify four layers of infrastructure. Each of these layers is critically dependent on the layer below it:

- activity systems infrastructure
- INFORMATION INFRASTRUCTURE
- information systems infrastructure
- ICT infrastructure.

Information infrastructure: Definitions of information need and activities involved in the collection, storage, dissemination and used of information in an organisation.

We can think of organisations as complex collections of activity systems (see Chapter 2) and the wider environment within which they interact as a value network (see Chapter 7). Information is essential to the effective coordination of activity in organisations (see Chapter 3) and is supplied by information systems. Modern information systems rely on ICT (Chapters 5 and 6) to a greater or lesser extent. Figure 4.3 is a summary of this.

As well as having conventional competencies in areas such as sales and production, an organisation needs a specific set of activity systems that are concerned with the critical processes of planning, managing, developing and operating its informatics infrastructure. These activity systems form part of its informatics service, and are discussed in Chapters 10 and 11.

ICT plays a primary supporting role in organisations. It is also a catalyst for organisational change. The focus on infrastructure highlights the fact that ICT has the potential to change organisations in three ways (Heeks, 1999):

- **Supplanting**. ICT can be used to automate major parts of information systems, which involve the collection, storage, processing and dissemination of information. In other words, human agents, and particularly control processes, are supplanted by technology.

- **Supporting.** ICT can be used to assist human activity through efficient and effective data processing. This implies the use of technology to augment the capability of human agents.
- **Innovating**. ICT can be used to stimulate the design and implementation of new activity systems, which are likely to affect both the organisation's structure and its culture (see Chapter 2).

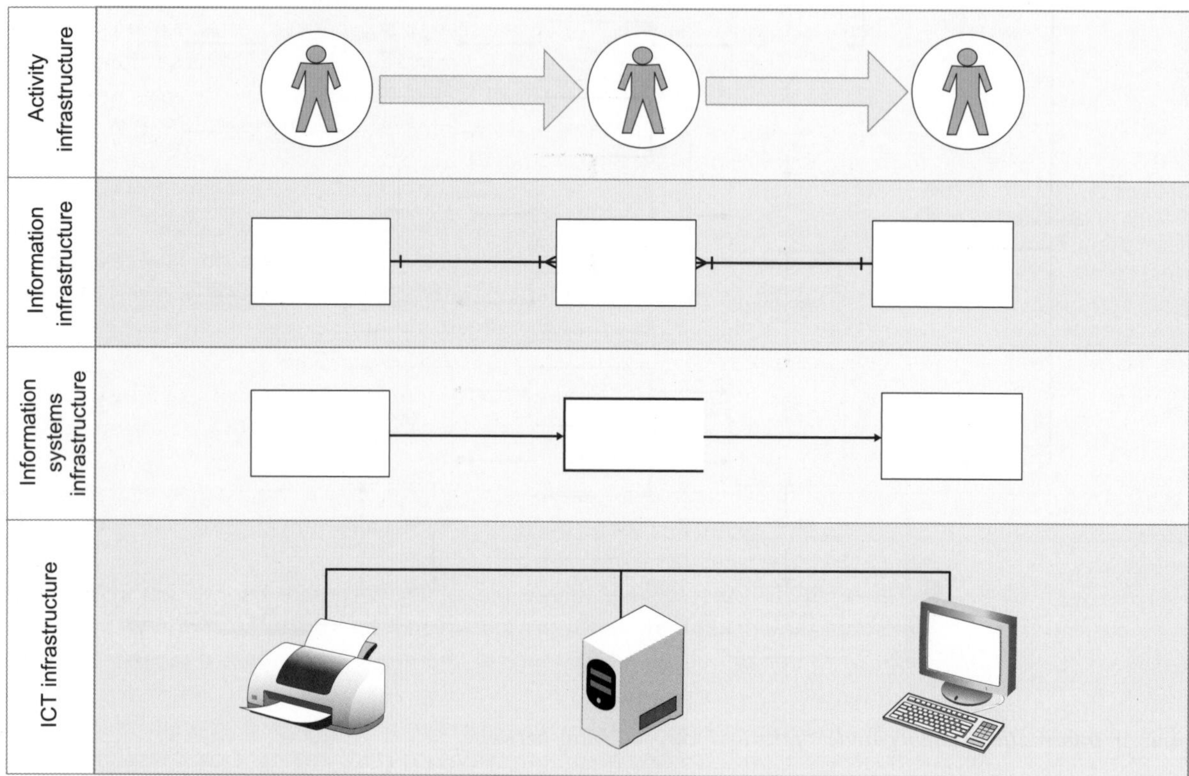

Figure 4.3: *Levels of infrastructure*

As was argued in Chapter 2, the traditional role for ICT has been to supplant or automate. More recently the emphasis has been on seeing it as an agency to informate (Zuboff, 1988) and innovate. It could be argued that this tendency is supported by that key principle of systemics, suboptimisation (which was discussed on page 89). (This is the thesis that optimising the performance of a subsystem such as an ICT system independently will not generally optimise the performance of the system as a whole, and could actually worsen it. So ideally activity systems and ICT systems should be designed in parallel (Hammer, 1996). For instance, ICT has been used to automate clerical processes in the public sector, such as making benefit payments. It has also been used to improve government decision making, communication and implementation. Finally, its use is fundamental to new forms of public service delivery. However, some have argued that until now, ICT has done little to transform the fundamental nature of government agencies (Fontaine, 2001): it has not been used substantially as yet to innovate.

Implicit and explicit infrastructure

Many organisations, both large and small, have an implicit informatics infrastructure. They have information needs, information systems for fulfilling these needs and technological systems to facilitate information dissemination and use, but they have not documented the information and data they collect, disseminate and use on a day-to-day basis. They also have little idea of which organisational activities use which information. There is no clear map of what information systems there are in the organisation and how they are interrelated. Often they also lack an inventory of their ICT systems: software, hardware, data management and communication technology.

Most medium to large-scale organisations have a mix of explicit and implicit infrastructure. Often this happens because there has not been a systematic planning process for informatics (see Chapter 10). Information systems have been built in a piecemeal manner and with little thought to how they interrelate with the rest of the business.

Reflect
One difficulty many businesses face is that their information systems are organised around transactions, products or services rather than customers. For instance, an insurance company might have an information system established for each financial product it sells, such as life insurance and car insurance. What difficulties do you think this form of information systems infrastructure might create for customer service?

There are clearly a number of advantages to a more explicit informatics infrastructure. Most of all, this makes it more feasible to integrate systems and make them interoperable, and that in turn makes their management and development more straightforward. However, as well as acting as an enabling force, an informatics infrastructure can be a constraining force, limiting what can be done in future.

Any application of informatics can leverage or extend the existing informatics infrastructure. An information system leverages the infrastructure when it draws on its resources. It extends the infrastructure when it contributes physical or non-physical resources that can be drawn upon by other applications. Strategic information systems (see Chapter 10) are one example of the way in which the informatics infrastructure can be enabling. These are designed to improve the organisation's competitive position.

An example of infrastructure as an enabling force is the Republic of Singapore's Tradenet information. Singapore is very reliant on foreign trade, and it looked to gain a competitive advantage over other ports in the Far East by developing a system that would significantly reduce the time required for shippers to clear customs. Tradenet leveraged existing governmental information systems by linking traders in to them. Introducing this system also extended Singapore's stock of informatics skills.

In contrast, legacy systems (large and ageing corporate information systems) generally constrain the organisation, in the sense that they determine the way in which much corporate data must be collected, manipulated and distributed. Often they have been so heavily maintained that they become difficult to change and interface to other systems.

The 'millennium bug' or Y2K (Year 2000) problem is a good example of the constraining influence of existing informatics infrastructure. Many systems created prior to the year 2000 (the millennium) were not designed to handle twenty-first century dates, and sometimes it was very difficult to carry out the necessary modifications. Major efforts had to be diverted to solving the problem, and around the turn of the millennium this put a brake on much new information system development in organisations worldwide.

Recap 

The dynamics of an existing information system or a designed information system can be represented as an information system model. Informatics infrastructure supports human activity systems infrastructure. It is composed of information, information systems and ICT infrastructures. It can be implicit or explicit, and is both an enabling and a constraining force in organisations.

Activity systems infrastructure

Each business is different. Some of the differences have developed because of the requirements in different sectors of the economy – retail, manufacturing, education and so on (see Chapter 7) – but even organisations in the same industrial sector operate in different ways. In part this is because they are trying to achieve a competitive advantage (Porter, 1985). They might achieve this, for example, through differentiation in human activity, efficiency of human activity and/or effectiveness in activity (see Chapter 10).

Figure 4.4 is a schematic of an **activity systems infrastructure** for a typical manufacturing company. It consists of a number of activity subsystems such as sales, after-sales, marketing, purchasing, receiving, warehousing, production, human resources, packing and shipping. These subsystems are related by flows of physical items (broad arrows) and information (narrow arrows).

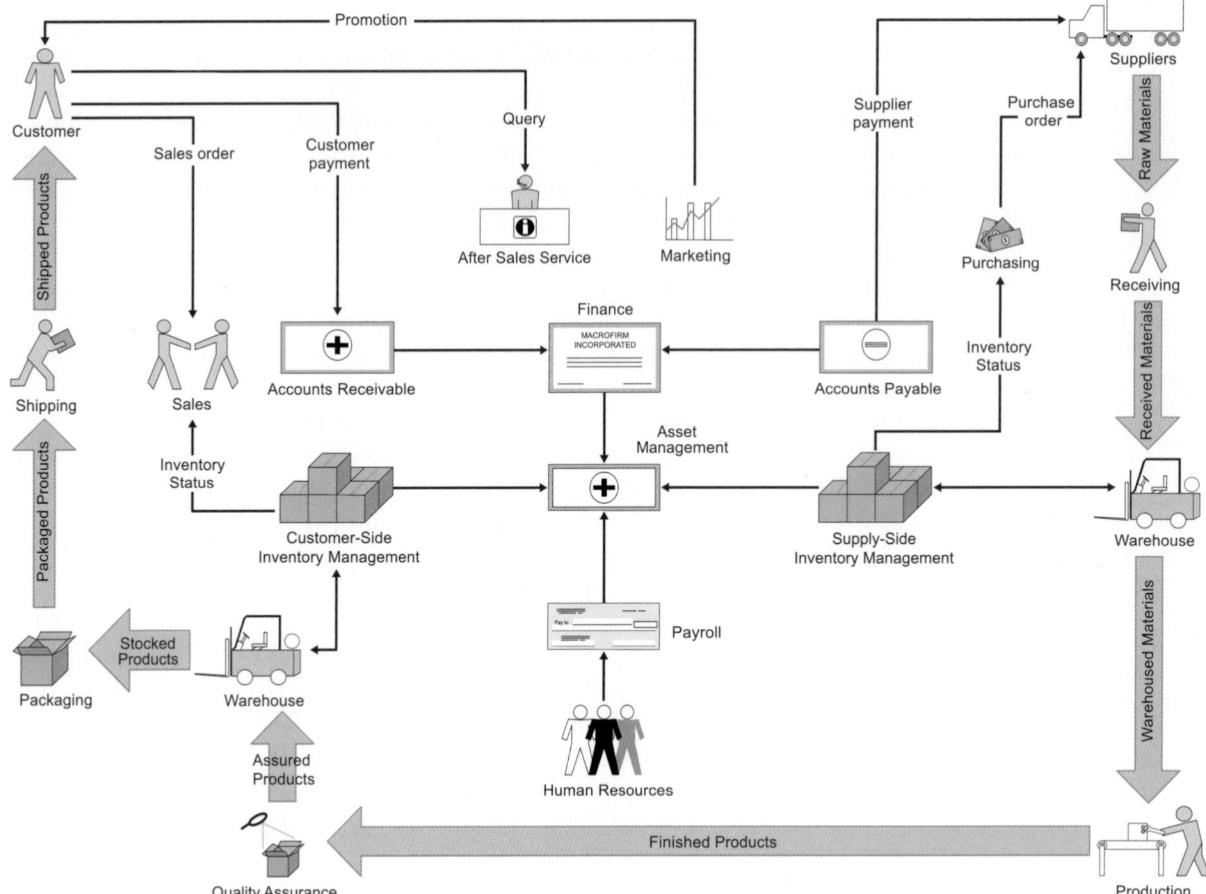

Figure 4.4: *Activity systems infrastructure of a typical manufacturing organisation*

Sales orders from customers act as the major input into the activity system. They trigger packaging and shipment of goods from the customer-side inventory. Marketing and after-sales service also engage in an attempt to build a long-term relationship with customers. On the other side, purchase orders from the company trigger the shipment of raw materials by suppliers, which is received into supply-side inventory management. This then drives production, which replenishes customer-side inventory with finished products. Finally, payments from customers are recorded in a central finance system, as are payments to suppliers and employees.

Back-end information systems infrastructure

Because companies vary in their activity systems infrastructure, their collections of information systems will also necessarily be different. There are many ways to implement operational procedures, and define units with which to parcel up the basic elements of information handling. The entire make-up of an organisation's information systems is known as its **information systems infrastructure** (Ciborra et al., 2000).

At a high level, most businesses have a number of core information systems in common. Financial systems are a good example. Organisations not only need financial data for their internal operations, they also need it to meet regulatory requirements. Not surprisingly, in most business organisations, ICT was first applied in the accounting or finance department, and financial information systems form the core around which other information systems are located.

Back-end information system: A core transaction processing information system concerned with supporting the internal processes of an organisation.

Back-end information systems infrastructure: The core set of transaction processing information systems in organisations.

These core information systems are known as BACK-END (or back-office) systems. They are critical to the performance of core activity systems such as sales and production. Around this core there will be a number of FRONT-END INFORMATION SYSTEMS: that is, systems that face the major stakeholders of the business (managers, employees, customers and suppliers). This leads us to identify four groups of information systems:

- management information systems
- EMPLOYEE-FACING INFORMATION SYSTEMS
- customer-facing information systems
- supplier-facing information systems.

> **Did you know?**
>
> The term *back office* comes from the building layout of early companies. The front office (which typically faced onto the street and had a public entrance) was where staff such as salespeople were visible to customers. The back office, which did not have a public entrance, was where staff worked on developing products or administration, without being seen by customers.

Front-end information system: An information system which interacts with internal or external stakeholders of the organisation.

Front-end information systems infrastructure: That part of the information systems infrastructure concerned with the core front-end information systems of the organisation.

Employee-facing information systems: Transaction processing systems that interact with employees of an organisation.

Sales-order processing information system: The information system that records details of customer orders.

Purchase-order processing information system: The information system that records details of purchase orders to suppliers.

Most companies, whatever their size, need systems for recording orders for products or services from customers, orders to suppliers for products or services, and the amounts paid or due to employees. These key information systems tend to be relatively standard in their design. For a company that deals in physical products, a SALES-ORDER PROCESSING system records details of sales orders from customers. An **inventory management** system maintains inventories of raw material and finished goods stored in warehouses. PURCHASE ORDER PROCESSING records details of orders and payments to suppliers. **Finance** systems record amounts owed and paid by customers, owed and paid to suppliers, and owed and paid to employees. Finally, **payroll** systems record details of wages and payments to employees. Service-based businesses have slightly different systems, but the principles behind them are much the same, and so are the principles in public-sector and other not-for-profit organisations. (This chapter uses product-based companies as an example.)

Figure 4.5 shows some of the flows of information (shown by labelled arrows) between these major back-end information systems.

Because all the companies operating in a country have to comply with the same system of external regulation, their financial information systems tend to be very similar, so software suppliers can build and sell standard ICT systems for supporting this activity. Standardised pieces of software like this are referred to as software **packages**. More recently, there has been a trend to offer integrated suites of ICT systems to help companies implement their back-end information systems infrastructure (see Chapter 9).

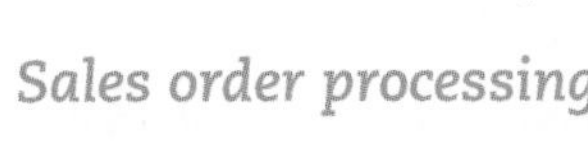

Sales order processing

In Figure 4.5 you will see a process box labelled **Sales Order Processing**. Figure 4.6 decomposes its elements: in other words, it outlines the subsystem that this comprises. Figure 4.6 in turn has a process box labelled **Sales Order Entry.** This subsystem is analysed in Figure 4.7. (Obviously, the more detail in which systems are analysed, the more difference there will be between organisations, so this is a generic model that will not exactly fit the processes in many companies.)

Sales order processing is an information system that communicates with a customer-side inventory management system. This is necessary because the system needs to check that finished goods are available before processing orders for them. It also passes processed orders to an outbound logistics system, which dispatches goods to customers, and handles liaising with the customers over the form and timing of deliveries.

Figure 4.7, which decomposes the order entry subsystem, shows information stores – repositories for information. This is to indicate the important reliance of information **systems** on information **resources**, such as the store of information on a company's products or customers.

Reflect

What contribution do the core information systems make to the business?

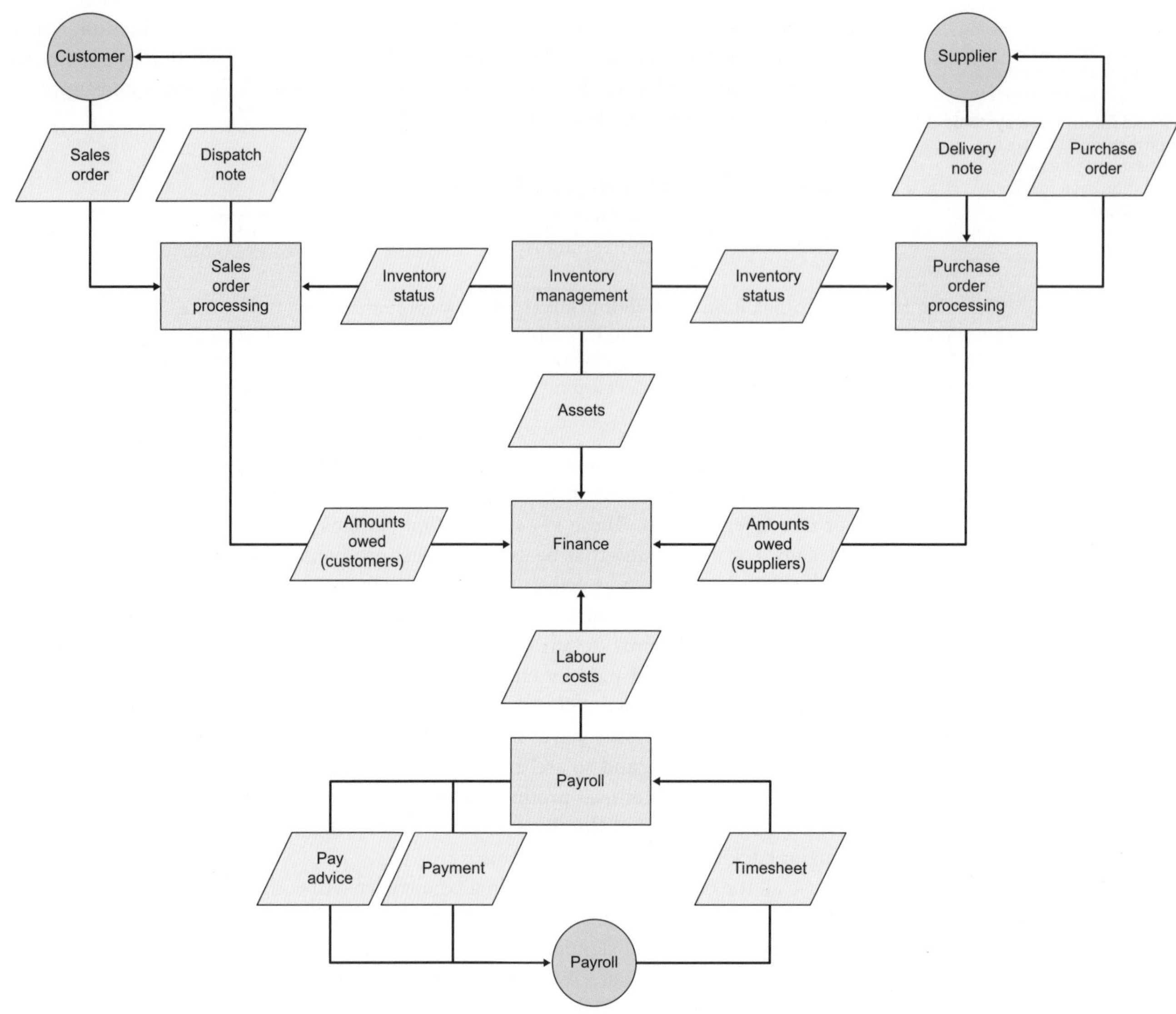

Figure 4.5: *Information flows between core back-end information systems*

Order entry is a key process which provides an interface with customers. It captures the key information needed to process a customer order. Traditionally, orders tended to be made by post or telephone. These days they are often sent electronically, over electronic data interchange (EDI) links or via the Internet (see Chapter 8).

Normally the order entry system makes an enquiry of the stock control system to check that the order can be filled from stock. If the goods ordered are out of stock, the system might suggest a substitute or generate a back order, to be filled when the stock is replenished. The system needs to notify the customer whether the order is confirmed, partially filled or will be kept as a back order.

Inventory management

Stock control information system: An information system for recording details of inventory.

Most businesses have several forms of stock or inventory. These include raw materials, materials for packing, finished goods and parts for maintenance of products. STOCK CONTROL or inventory management information systems are designed to record information about this material flow. The usual objective is to minimise the amount of stock held while ensuring optimal performance of other systems such as manufacturing or production.

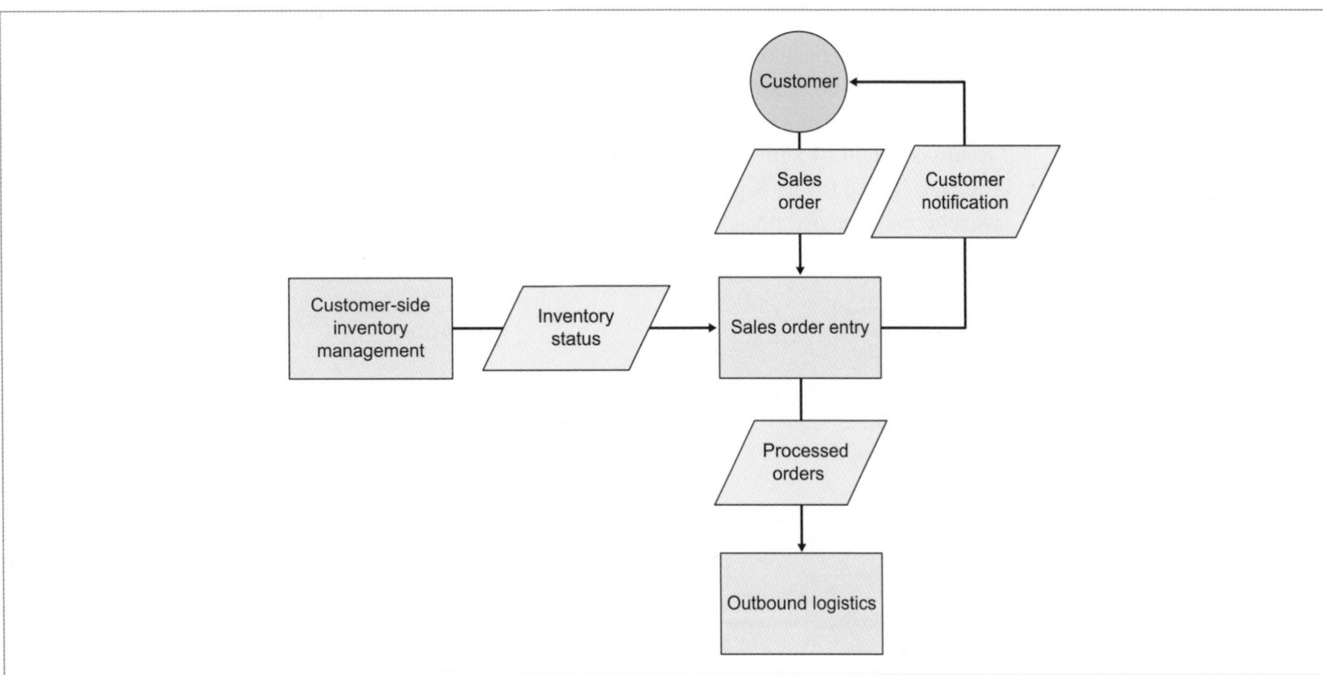

Figure 4.6: *Sales order processing*

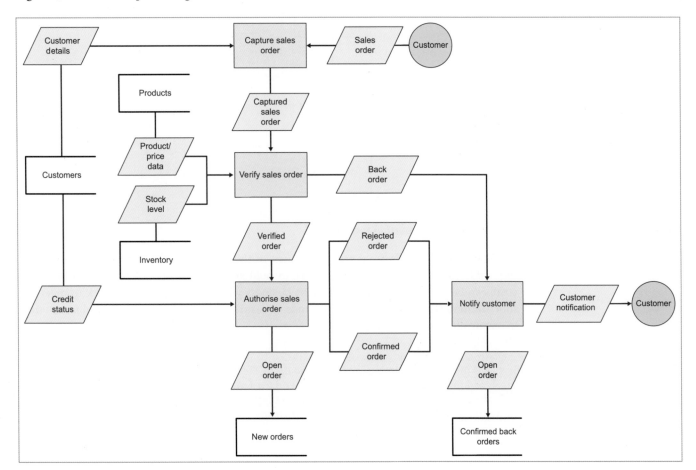

Figure 4.7: *Order entry*

Figure 4.8 shows a simple inventory management information system concerned with handling information about material received from suppliers. When raw materials or other goods (components, for instance) are received. the organisation normally checks them against the purchase order it issued. If the goods delivered are as ordered, the stock record is updated with the quantities supplied. (If not, obviously other systems are needed to resolve the difference.) The system then has to identify where the material is to go: this simple system assumes it will be sent to a warehouse, so it is concerned to determine the optimal place in the warehouse for it. A positioning report is generated for use by warehousing staff, and the warehousing record updated.

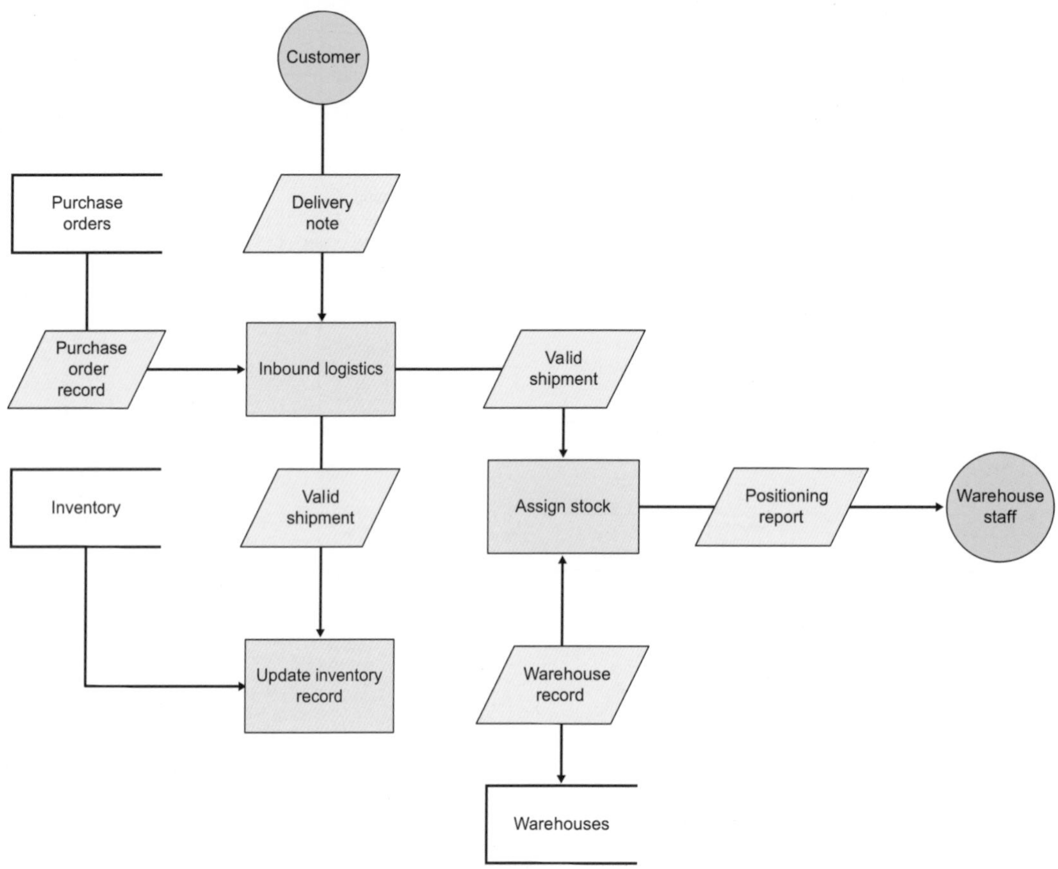

Figure 4.8: *Supply-side inventory management information system*

Minimal stock levels are a crucial element of the modern business philosophy of just in time (JIT) manufacturing. It is expensive to hold stock: it ties up capital, and warehousing costs can be considerable, so an efficient business will want only enough stock to meet the short-term needs of production. The aim is to ensure that materials are delivered *just in time* to ensure efficient production.

Did you know?

One of the first uses of computers in business was the Lyons Electronic Office (LEO). This system was designed for the British company J. Lyons and Co. Ltd (Mason, 2004). Lyons invested in the latest technology for the same reason that organisations do so today: it hoped to improve its performance and gain a competitive advantage.

Purchase order processing

Figure 4.9 outlines a standard purchase order processing information system. There are two basic ways of generating purchases: automatically (the inventory management system generates a purchase order if the level of a stock item falls below a certain level) or manually, by staff requesting that something not covered by the inventory management system be bought. Most medium to large organisations have a purchasing or procurement unit, whose staff

Reflect
How do supermarkets maintain sufficient stock on their shelves? What activities are needed to ensure this?

deal with purchase requests from both these sources. They ensure that purchase orders are produced and sent to the appropriate suppliers.

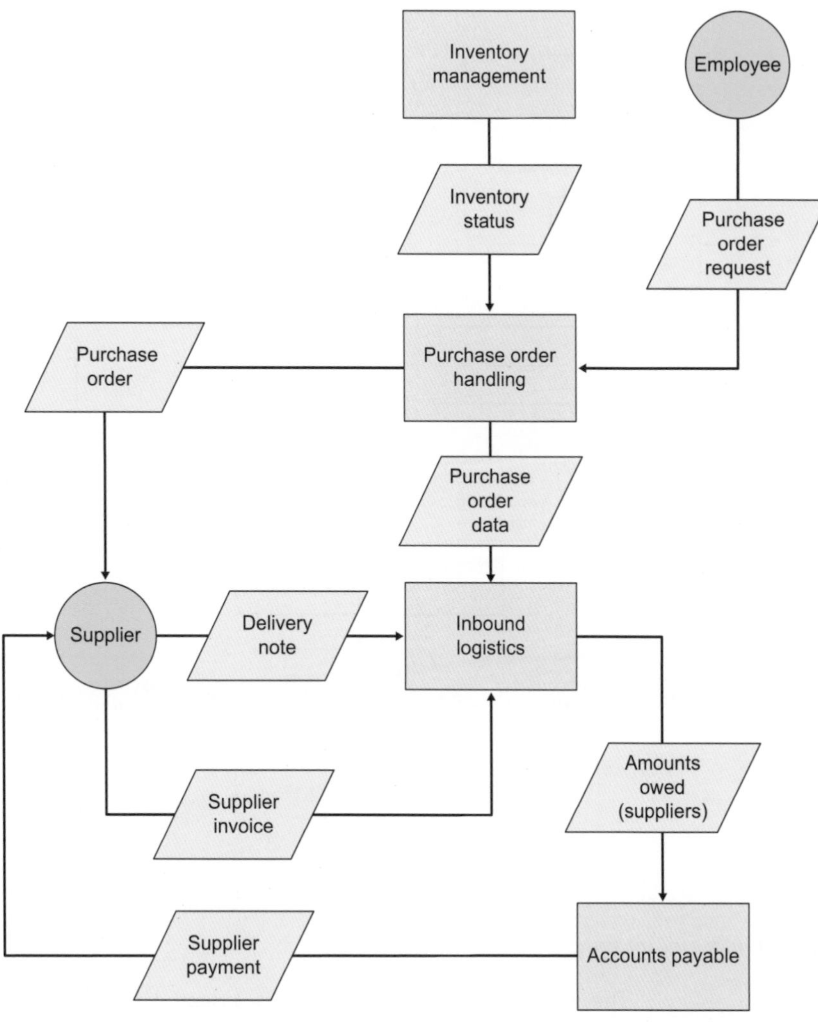

Figure 4.9: *Purchase order processing information system*

Inbound logistics: A primary process in the internal value chain involving the receipt and storage of raw materials and the distribution of them to manufacturing units.

The information from the purchase order is used to update an INBOUND LOGISTICS INFORMATION SYSTEM, which checks the information on them against invoices from suppliers. Provided the goods supplied and the prices tally, information about the amounts owed is passed to a major financial information subsystem, accounts payable.

Finance

Accounting information system: The part of the information systems infrastructure devoted to managing information concerning the financial state of the organisation.

Figure 4.10 outlines the functionality of a standard financial information system, or ACCOUNTING INFORMATION SYSTEM. Typically it is divided into three major subsystems: accounts receivable, accounts payable and general ledger. The information store used by the accounts receivable system is generally called a sales ledger, because it records details of the amounts owed by customers. The information store used by the accounts payable system is sometimes called the purchase ledger, because it details monies owed to suppliers.

The general ledger system is used to record details of all the financial transactions relevant to an organisation: income, expenditure and assets, so it receives information from accounts payable, accounts receivable and inventory management systems.

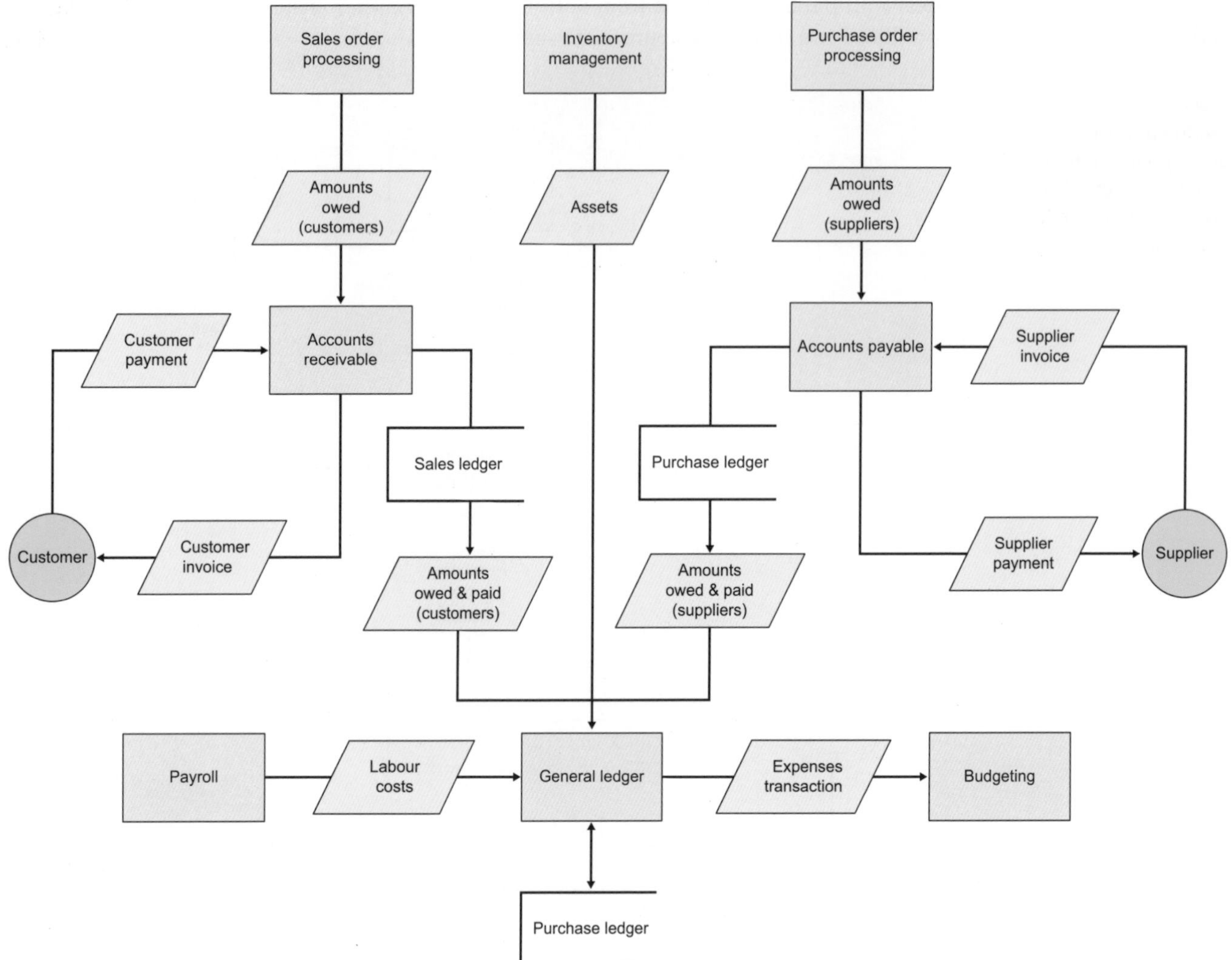

Figure 4.10: *Financial information system*

The accounts receivable system is essential for managing **cash flow.** When goods are shipped to customers, the system invoices them and updates their account with details of the amount owed. When customers send payments, their credit balance is reduced by the appropriate amount. The information about customer credit and amounts paid is regularly used to update the general ledger system.

The accounts payable system is also essential for managing cash flow. When goods are ordered from suppliers the system receives a record of the amount owed, and the supplier's account is updated. When payments are made against invoices received, the balance owed is reduced accordingly. This information too is regularly used to update the general ledger system.

The third key input into a general ledger system is a payroll system, which regularly updates the general ledger with the costs incurred in paying staff. There will also be an input into the general ledger from the inventory management system, so that a record is kept of the financial value of assets held.

Payroll

Figure 4.11 shows the elements of a standard payroll information system. This has two primary outputs: payments to employees (and to tax authorities and the like), and records of them (payslips or pay advice notes). The key input into a payroll system is information on the work undertaken during a given time period (a week or month). These details may be collected on time-sheets sent from operational departments or automatically generated from a production scheduling and control system. The payroll system also needs to access information stored on each employee, such as pay rates and tax details. Periodically, the payroll system updates the general ledger system with the financial costs of labour.

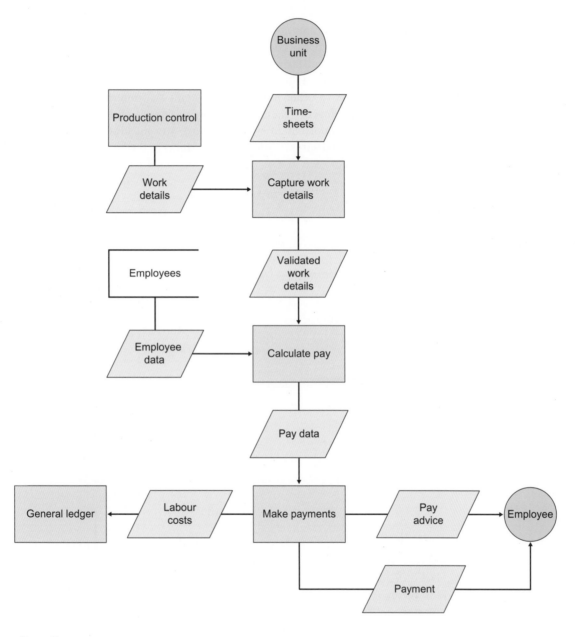

Figure 4.11: *Payroll system*

Recap 

Back-end information systems include finance, sales order processing, purchase order processing, inventory management and payroll. Most companies of whatever size need an information system for recording orders for products or services from customers, orders made to suppliers for products or services, and the amounts paid or due to employees. Sales order processing is an information system that records details of sales orders from customers. Inventory management is the information system that maintains an inventory of raw material and finished goods. Purchase order processing records details of purchase orders to suppliers. Finance systems record amounts owed and paid by customers, amounts owed to and paid to suppliers and amounts paid to and owed to employees. Finally, payroll is the information system that records details of wages and payments made to employees.

Front-end information systems infrastructure

The back-end information systems infrastructure acts as the foundation for a large number of other information systems. These are front-end systems in the sense that they interface directly with major stakeholders: managers, employees, suppliers and customers.

Various information systems feed off the information provided by back-end systems and provide analyses and summaries to aid effective management and planning. In effect this is a vertical extension to the back-end information systems infrastructure. These are the organisation's management-facing information systems.

Other extensions are made horizontally out from the core information systems: for example, connections to other information systems that interface to a company's customers, suppliers or employees. These are the organisation's customer-facing, supplier-facing and employee-facing information systems. Figure 4.12 illustrates some of the relationships between back-end and front-end information systems in the typical business.

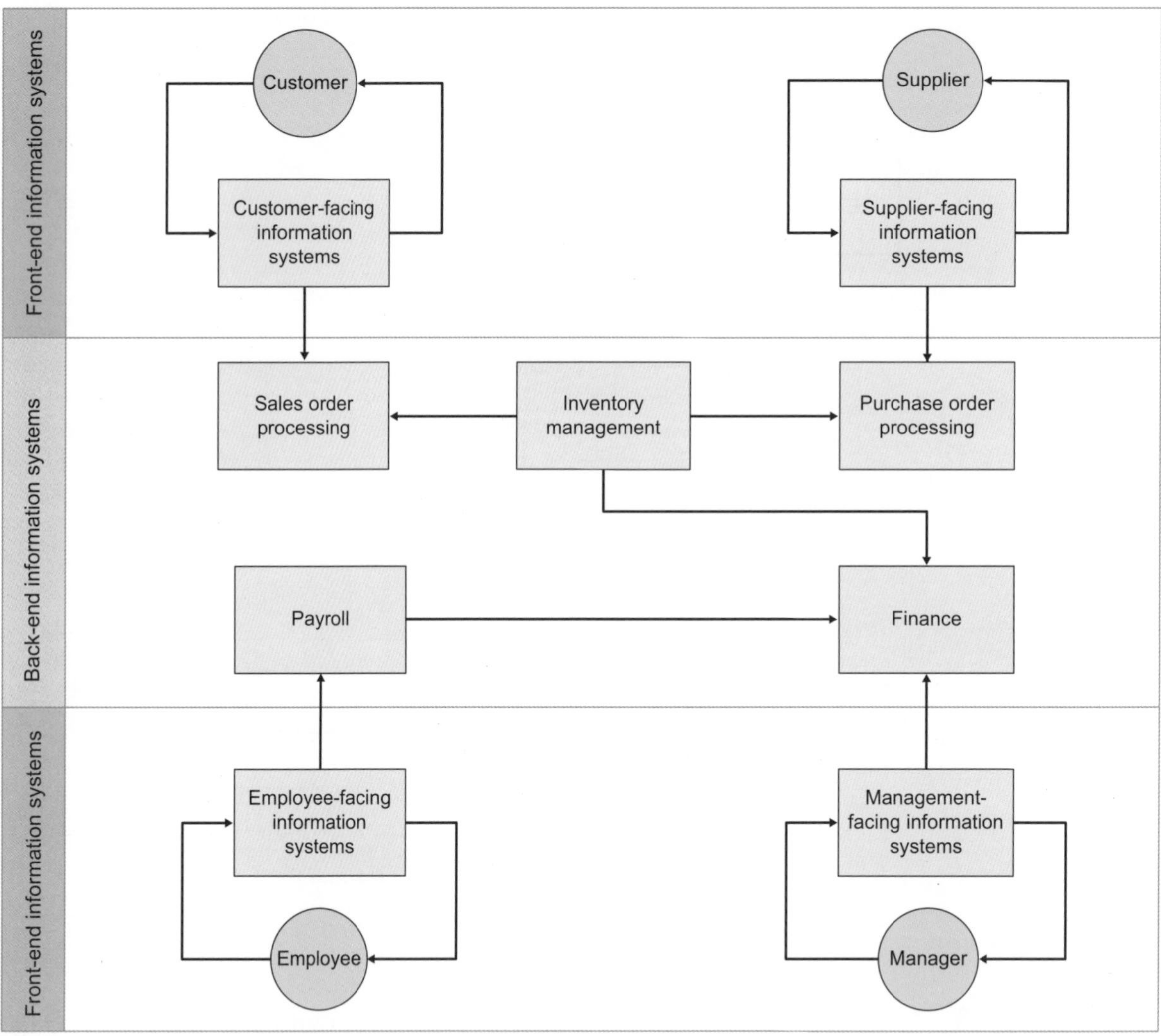

Figure 4.12: *Back-end and front-end information systems infrastructure*

In a university setting, a key back-end information system is the student information system which handles information concerned with students, courses and modules. A number of key front-end information systems will run off it. For example, academics might use a system to report on students enrolled on a particular module, administrators might use a system to manage student fees, and managers might use one to plan for several years of future student intake.

Management-facing information systems: Front-end information systems used by management.

Executive information system (EIS): An information system designed to support high-level, strategic decision making in organisations.

Transaction processing system (TPS): A type of information system supporting the operational activities of an organisation.

Management-facing information systems

The control processes of organisations make use of three major typ system: transaction processing systems (TPS), MANAGEMENT INFORMATIO and decision support systems (DSS), also known as EXECUTIVE INFORM (EIS).

TRANSACTION PROCESSING SYSTEMS are the operational information systems. For a business they include order entry, accounts payable and inventory management information systems, as described above. They process the detailed information generated during day-to-day operations. These TRANSACTIONS (as they are normally called) include customer orders, purchase orders and invoices. Information like this is essential to supporting operations that help a company add value to its products and/or services. Transaction processing systems are sometimes described as the lifeblood of the organisation because they are so essential to its effective operation.

> **Did you know?**
> The costs associated with information collection, processing and presentation are generally called *transaction costs* (Chapter 7). They can be significant, and one reason for using ICT is to attempt to reduce them.

Transaction: A logical unit of work. A transaction transforms a database from one consistent state to another consistent state. Transactions are major ways of recording service delivery.

Management information system (MIS): A type of information system supporting the tactical decision making of managers.

Chapter 2 described management as a key control process for organisations, and Chapter 3 described the place of decision making in management. As a system of human activity, management needs information systems to perform effectively. MANAGEMENT INFORMATION SYSTEMS (MIS) are used particularly by the operational layer of management to monitor the current state of the organisation. The MIS should provide managers with information about current production levels, number of orders achieved, current labour costs and so on.

Whereas MIS are generally used to enable effective short-term, tactical decisions to be made, DSS and EIS are generally expected to support longer-term, strategic decision making (see Chapter 10). DSS and EIS use the management information generated by MIS to model short-term and long-term scenarios of company performance. These are used to ask 'what-if' questions in business planning (Chapter 10) and to generate policy decisions in the area of business strategy. DSS and EIS are therefore critical to effective performance at the strategic level of management. They will probably need information from key environmental sensors (such as a range of other front-end information systems) to function effectively.

Major information classes such as employees, customers, orders, finance and inventory are important to the information systems infrastructure of our model organisation They are likely to form the key inputs into an MIS with which operational managers can continually monitor the state of the organisation. This is indicated in Figure 4.13 as one large MIS, but in practice there might be a number of integrated MISs, perhaps for particular business areas. One of the key outputs from the MIS will be summarised information on major trends affecting the company, such as labour costs, current levels of assets and current levels of spending. This information might be written to a planning information store for use by an EIS. The EIS is likely to be used to formulate high-level strategic decisions affecting the company (Anthony, 1988).

For example, in a supermarket chain an MIS will be used to monitor stock in warehouses and cash flow through the company. In a local authority, an MIS might be used to monitor revenues from local taxes and compare them with expenditure.

Reflect
Could management in the modern organisation be performed effectively without management information systems? In what way do these information systems provide models of the organisation?

Customer-facing systems

Customer-facing information systems support demand-chain activities, and typically interface between back-end information systems such as sales order processing and inventory management, and the customer. Traditional customer-facing information systems include sales, marketing, outbound logistics and after-sales systems. Recently there has been increased emphasis on integrating these systems to form a customer relationship management (CRM) or customer chain management (CCM) information system.

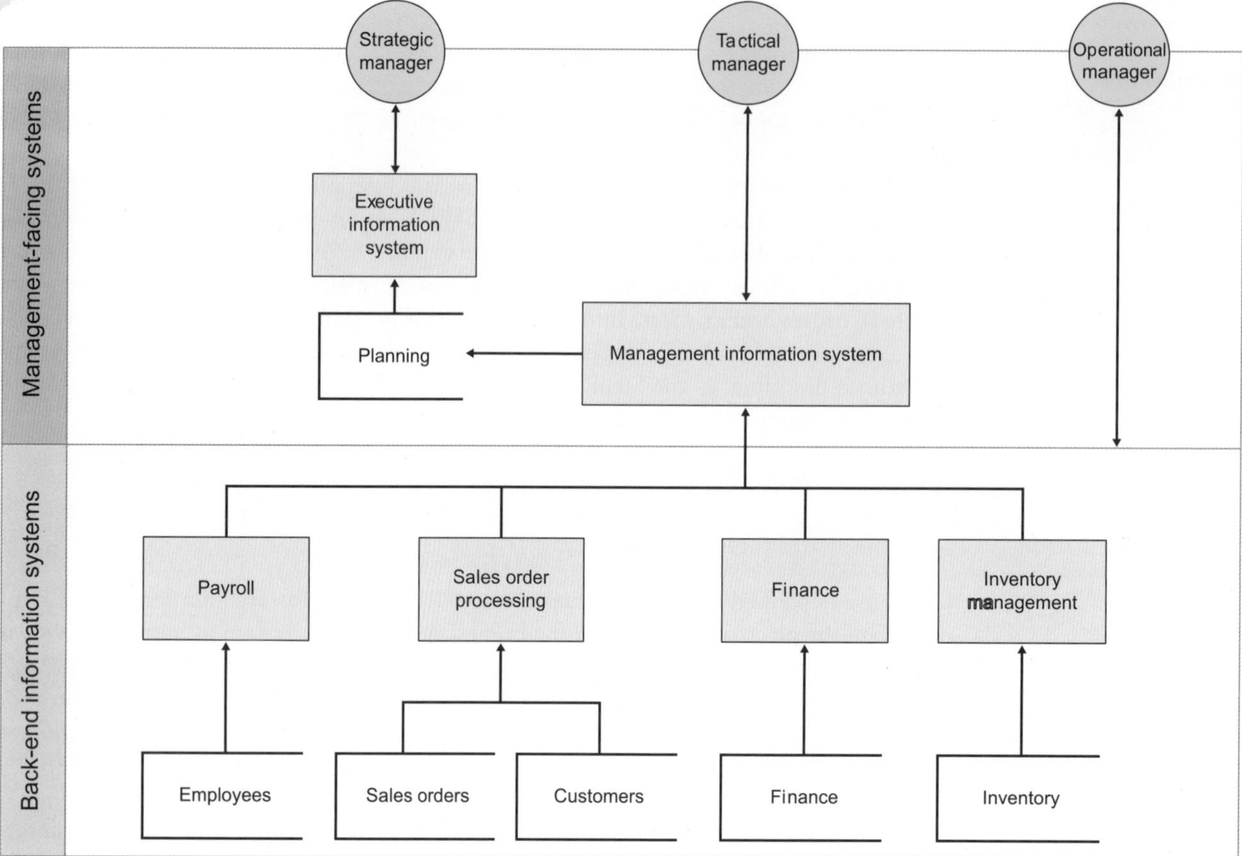

Figure 4.13: *Management information systems*

Sales

In some companies, particularly those that sell high-value products like automobiles and industrial equipment, customers place their orders via a salesperson. A sales information system is a common component of the information systems infrastructure here. It records the activities of the sales force: what sales have been made, to whom, by whom and when. This information is often used to calculate sales staff commissions.

Marketing

Marketing involves promoting the organisation's products and/or services, and depends on good customer information. It is likely to use the information held about existing customers in planning and managing advertising and promotional campaigns. It will also store details of promotions, customers contacted and the results, and so on.

Outbound logistics: A primary process in the internal value chain involving the storage of finished products in warehouses and the distribution of finished products to customers.

Outbound logistics

This is a term for the distribution of goods to customers (see Chapter 7). The OUTBOUND LOGISTICS or distribution system receives orders processed by a sales order processing system, and deals with their fulfilment. This is particularly important for medium to large companies with lots of customers, minimal stock and many points of distribution, because delivering products efficiently and effectively is critical to customer retention. As a result, aspects of this logistics system will be concerned with optimising the use of delivery channels. and this might involve managing intermediaries such as parcel post distributors.

Figure 4.14 shows this type of system. Shipment planning determines which orders will be filled and from where they will be shipped. The system produces two outputs: a shipment plan which indicates how and when each order is to be filled, and a picking list which is used by warehouse staff to locate the goods. Shipment execution supports the work of the shipping function, and is used to coordinate the flow of goods from the business to customers.

It produces a shipping note which is attached to each despatch of goods. It also passes on details of the shipment to invoicing. Invoicing systems take the information supplied on shipping, and produces invoices which are sent either with the shipment or shortly afterwards.

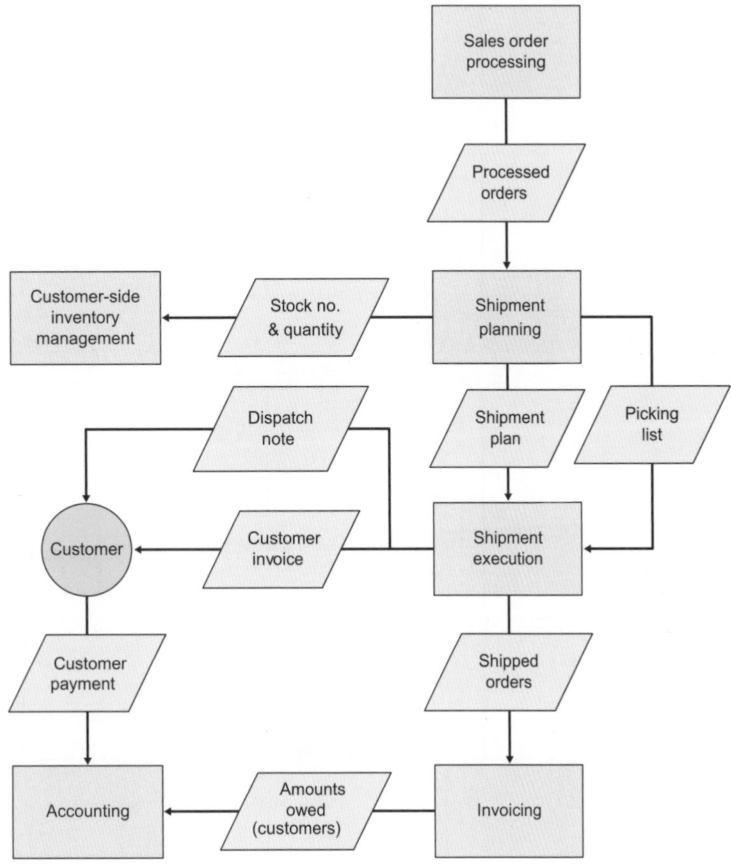

Figure 4.14: *Outbound logistics information system*

After-sales

An after-sales information system tracks customer support and product-maintenance activities following a sale, probably on a continuous basis for a number of years. Its complexity will vary depending on the type of product or service. For low-value goods such as books or CDs it will be concerned mostly with customer complaints and product replacements. For high-value goods such as automobiles it is likely to record maintenance or service schedules. For example, the lift manufacturer OTIS uses an after-sales system to proactively schedule maintenance by its engineers.

Customer relationship management

Each of the four systems of sales, marketing, outbound logistics and after-sales interacts with the customer in different ways and records different information associated with each interaction. CRM has become a popular philosophy because winning new customers and keeping existing ones happy is seen as critical to organisational success. Effective CRM demands a unified view of the customer, and this is what CRM information systems provide.

A CRM SYSTEM ideally tracks all customer interactions with a company, from initial enquiries through making orders to the whole range of after-sales services. It needs to integrate the range of front-end and back-end information systems that have a bearing on the customer. Some of the relationships between the key customer-facing information systems are illustrated in Figure 4.15.

Customer relationship management: The set of activities devoted to managing the customer chain.

Customer relationship management system: An information system devoted to managing all interactions of a customer with an organisation.

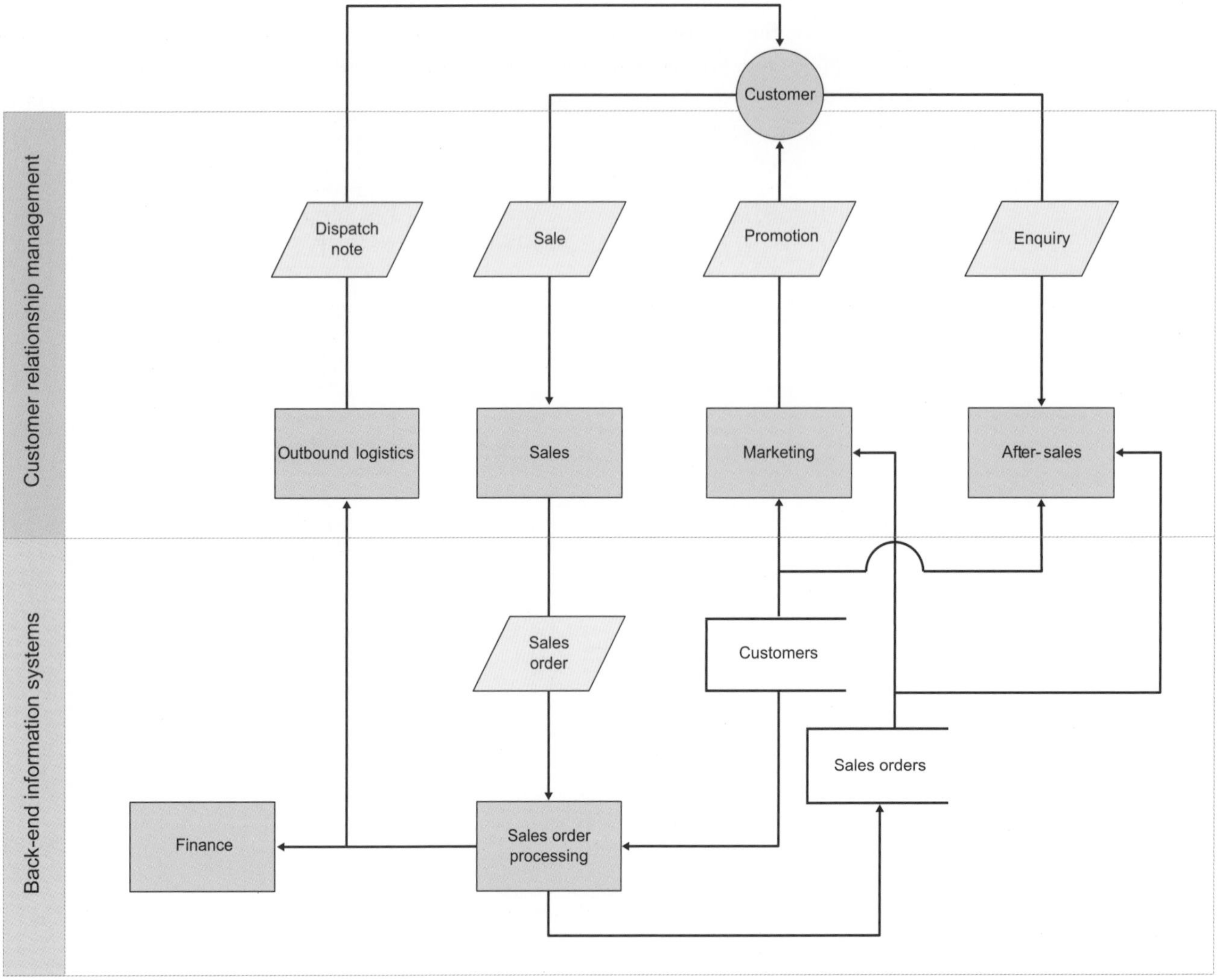

Customer
Dispatch note
Sale
Promotion
Enquiry
Customer relationship management
Outbound logistics
Sales
Marketing
After-sales
Back-end information systems
Sales order
Customers
Sales orders
Finance
Sales order processing

Figure 4.15: *Customer-facing information systems*

Many online sites (see Chapter 8) maintain forms of CRM system to log all the interactions between an established customer and the site. The information is used for a variety of purposes such as proactive marketing through email and the web.

Supplier-facing systems

Supply chain management: The collection of an organisation's activities devoted to management of the supply chain.

Supplier-facing information systems support supply chain activities. They include inbound logistics and procurement, and typically interface with back-end information systems such as purchase order processing, finance and inventory management. Not surprisingly, given the symmetric nature of buy-side and sell-side activities, there has been increased emphasis on integrating them to form an integrated SUPPLY CHAIN MANAGEMENT or supplier relationship management system.

Reflect
Is it true that the introduction of a CRM system will necessarily and automatically contribute to increased customer service?

Inbound logistics

This is devoted to managing the material resources entering an organisation from its suppliers and partners. In the retail sector for instance, large food retailers are likely to have fleets of vehicles involved in the delivery of goods to stores, each of which make up to 100 deliveries in a working week. Clearly, effective and efficient systems are needed to plan and schedule their routes.

Procurement: A secondary activity in the internal value chain. The process of purchasing goods and services from suppliers at an acceptable quality and price and with reliable delivery.

Supplier relationship management: The management of supply-chain activities. Sometimes referred to as supply chain management.

Supplier relationship management system: An information system devoted to managing all interactions of a supplier with an organisation.

Procurement

PROCUREMENT involves purchasing goods and services from suppliers at acceptable cost and quality. It is the sister process to sales. A procurement system is concerned with managing this process, and will interact with the purchase ordering information system and the inventory management information system.

Supplier relationship management

This is the sister system to CRM. It keeps track of all supplier interactions with the company, and integrates the information used by supplier-facing information systems such as procurement and inbound logistics.

Some of the relationships between the key supplier-facing information systems are illustrated in Figure 4.16.

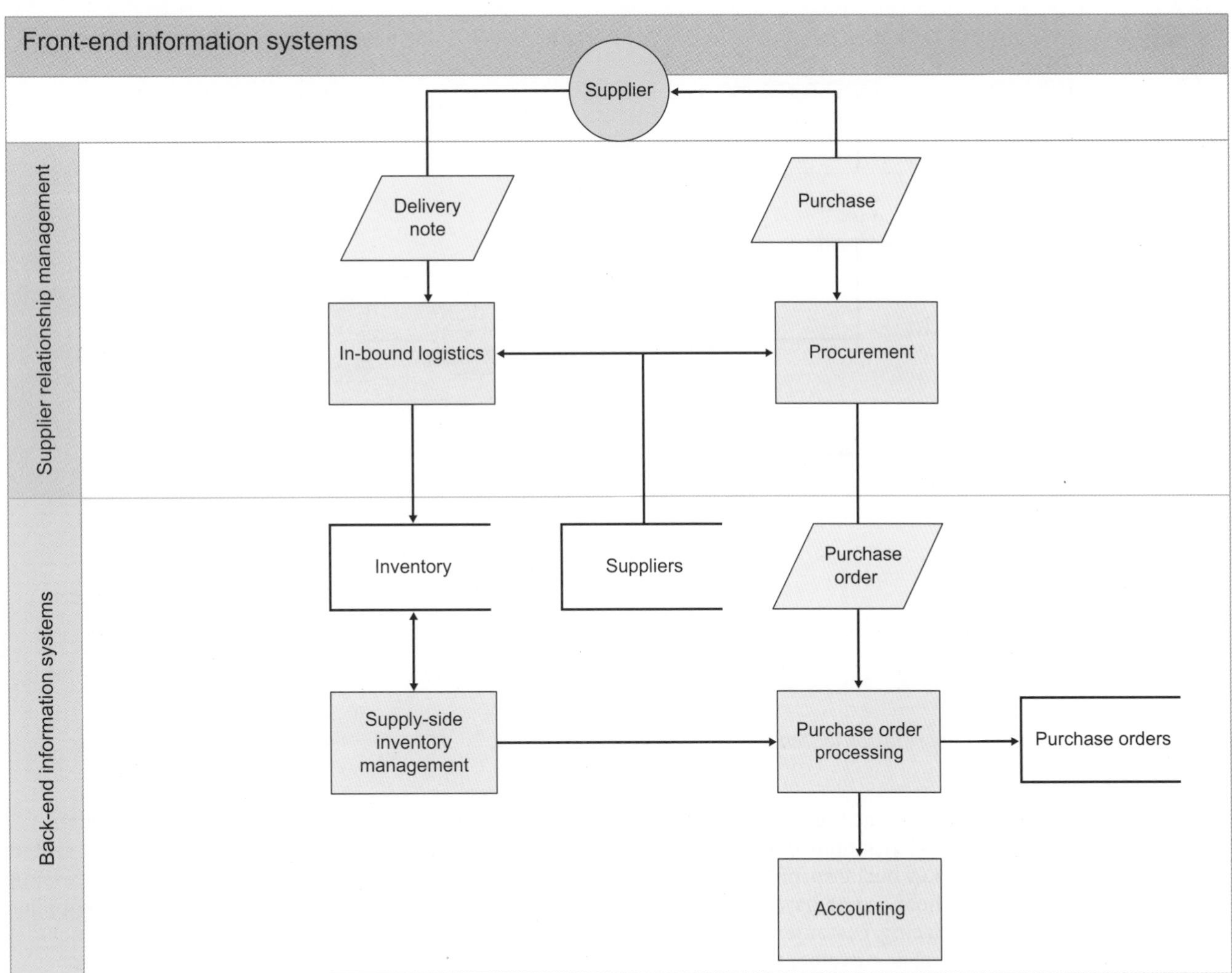

Figure 4.16: *Supplier-facing information systems*

Electronic procurement involves using ICT to integrate many supply-chain processes. Procurement information systems and supplier relationship MIS in general are important parts of it (see Chapter 8).

Employee-facing systems

Employee-facing information systems support the internal value chain. They include human resource management and production control systems, and are likely to interact with key back-end information systems such as payroll.

Human resource management: A secondary process in the internal value chain, involving the recruiting, hiring, training and development of employees.

Human resource management

A company is likely to need to build systems to record, process and maintain large amounts of information about its employees. Payroll information is only one facet of this; it will also include, for example, detailed employment histories.

Production control system

Reflect
How might the introduction of electronic procurement lead to cost savings for an organisation?

This is involved in scheduling future production, monitoring current production and interfacing with the inventory management information system, for requisitioning raw material for production and replenishing supplies of finished goods.

Some of the relationships between the key employee-facing information systems are shown in Figure 4.17. For example, human resource management systems and production or manufacturing systems are likely to integrate around activity information, so detailed employee work patterns can be integrated with production scheduling.

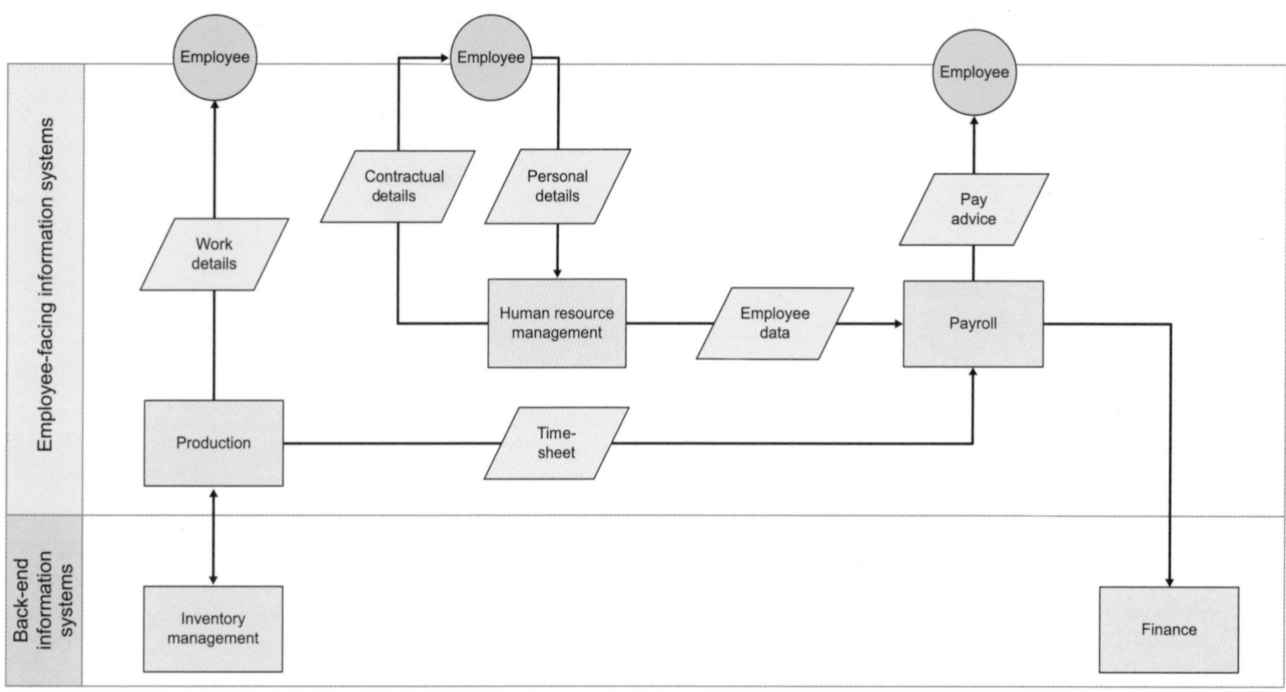

Figure 4.17: *Employee-facing information systems*

Recap  

Each business organisation's information systems will necessarily be different, although organisations in the same business sector will be more similar than those in different sectors. Key business information systems include sales order processing, purchase order processing, finance and payroll. Other key transaction processing systems can be categorised as supplier-facing, customer-facing and employee-facing. Customer-facing information systems include sales, customer relationship management, marketing and outbound logistics. Supplier-facing information systems include procurement and supplier-relationship management. Employee-facing information systems include human resource management and production management.

Information infrastructure

An organisation's back-end and front-end information systems support its **information infrastructure**. This mediates between the activity infrastructure and the information systems infrastructure. It can be expressed or represented as a series of interrelated information models, as discussed in Chapter 3.

Figure 4.18 illustrates part of the information infrastructure of a typical business. It relates directly to some of the back-end and front-end information systems already discussed.

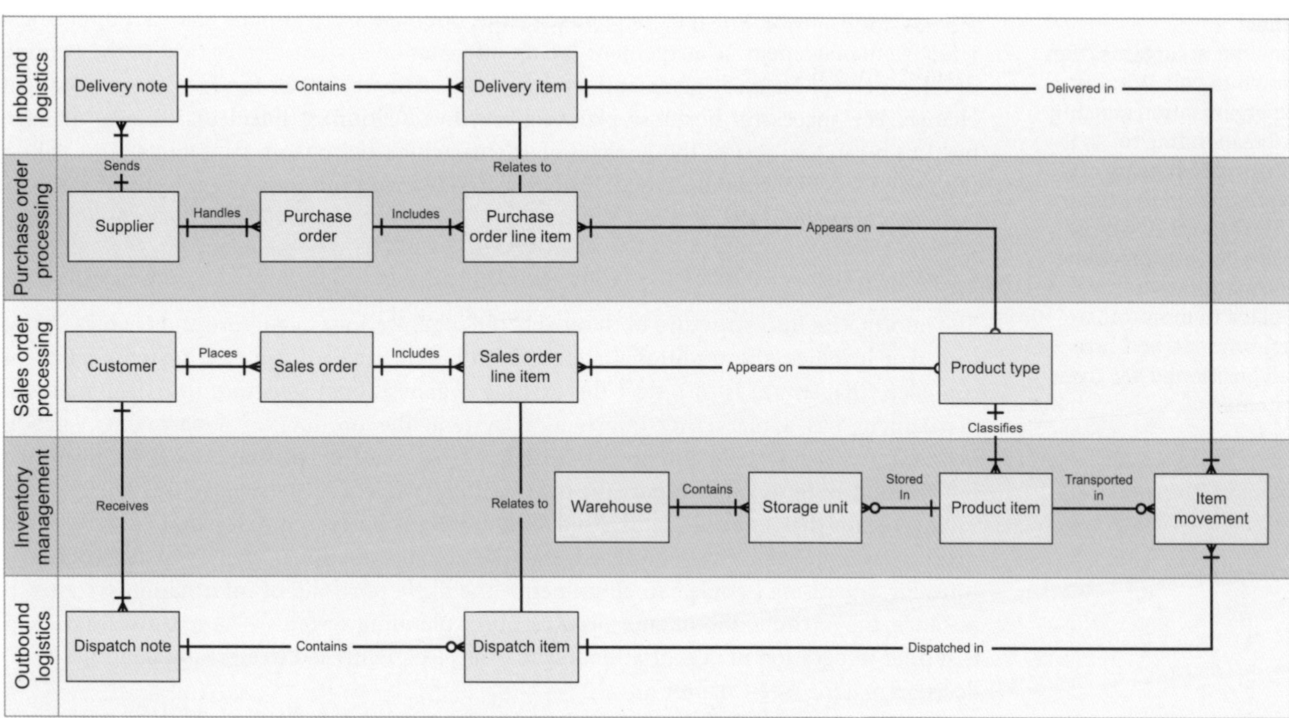

Figure 4.18: *Part of a company's information infrastructure*

The entities or information classes on the information model can be related directly to the information stores on the information systems models. For instance, in sales order processing the *customer* and *sales order* classes relate to the *customers* and *new orders* information stores on the sales order processing information systems model. So it is possible to use high-level models of information and information systems to form key elements of the documentation associated with explicit informatics infrastructure. This is a critical input into informatics planning, discussed in Chapter 10.

Informatics infrastructure and organisations

The information systems infrastructure of an organisation contributes to its activities by supplying information through an associated information infrastructure in support of activity systems within the activity infrastructure, so there is a close link between the informatics infrastructure and the organisation. Informatics infrastructure affects and is affected by its wider organisation in a number of ways. This section considers the relationship between the informatics structure and the issues of control, structure and culture raised in Chapter 2.

Sense and respond: A systems view of the organisation which emphasises adaptation to environmental change.

Chapter 2 argued that information is critical to the effective control of activity systems. This bears a close relationship to discussion of the modern business (Bradley and Nolan, 1998) (see Chapter 6) as a 'SENSE AND RESPOND' organisation. At heart this is a systems perspective. Sense and respond clearly refers to the control components that enable the organisation's various activity systems to adapt to changes in its environment. Successful adaptation relies on a combination of single and double feedback loops, consisting of appropriate sensors, comparators and effectors (see Chapter 2).

In this context we can see front-end information systems as key sensors. They collect information which triggers changes in other systems in the information systems infrastructure, and this in turn prompts changes in human activity. So successful organisational adaptation is critically dependent on the successful integration of front-end and back-end information systems.

Reflect
Consider an organisation known to you. What is the organisation sensing and responding to? Is it necessarily sensing and responding to the right things? In other words, does it have appropriate information systems in place to monitor its environment, and how well positioned are these systems?

To take a simple example, a change in the number of orders captured by customer-facing information systems should lead to a change in back-end systems, such as an increase in the production schedule. This in turn will cause an increase in the number of purchase orders.

Successful adaptation also depends on the double-loop feedback that is important for effective management. Management-facing information systems are critical to the continual development of business plans and strategies (see Chapter 10) in the face of environmental change. For successful business planning and formulation of business strategy, managers need to be able to model the environment with which the business interacts. This calls for the analysis of information trends, such as the differing purchasing patterns of particular customer segments.

Organisational structure

The informatics infrastructure both reflects the organisational structure and enables changes to it. For instance, the traditional approach to building an information systems infrastructure (see Chapter 12) is to reflect the existing organisational structure in it. The marketing department has a marketing information system, the production department a production information system and so on. This is perhaps not surprising, since the purpose of information systems is to support the organisation's work.

This means that a heavily centralised organisation is likely to develop quite different information systems from a decentralised one. Divisional, functional, matrix or network structures for organising people can all influence the likely portfolio of information systems. For instance, the introduction of enterprise resource planning systems – large software packages that offer integration of organisational data – has frequently led to a greater centralisation of decision making (see Chapter 6).

However, there are drawbacks to doing this. It has been argued that taking existing organisational structure as a baseline from which to build new information systems can guarantee only incremental improvements in organisational performance (see Chapter 2). The systems might make it possible to do the same things more efficiently, but they will not lead to more radical changes or improvements. For this to happen, information systems need to be used as a vehicle to support organisational restructuring. The problem is that implementing any information system is a risky process. Adding in substantial organisational change can make it even riskier. There are many examples of information system projects of this form that have failed (see Chapter 9).

Case check:
Case 25 W
The Child Support Agency

Electronic Data Systems (EDS) won a contract to develop an information system known as CS2 to support the work of the newly created UK Child Support Agency (CSA). A review by the UK Department of Work and Pensions claimed that the failure of this information system contributed to the closure of the CSA and cost UK taxpayers over £1 billion.

The ways in which informatics infrastructure can affect organisational structure include span of control, empowerment and newer organisational forms. A classic example is the use of information systems to reduce the number of layers of middle management, effectively increasing the span of control of top-level managers. Information systems are vehicles for improving communication flow. MIS often have the express purpose of improving managerial information and decision making. Middle managers have traditionally been involved in filtering information and decisions for strategic management, but MIS largely automated many of these functions, so there is less need for middle management.

Alternatively, information systems can push decision making down the organisation. For instance, workers can be encouraged to make decisions quickly with the aid of customer relationship systems, to improve customer satisfaction.

Information systems can facilitate the creation of virtual or network organisations. In a virtual organisation, people communicate and collaborate using ICT. Work is organised into loose projects which workers join and leave in a flexible way. This reduces the need for office space, for example. When they do need somewhere to work, workers are encouraged to 'hot desk' – to share office facilities on an as-needed basis.

Organisational culture

Organisational cultures and subcultures can influence the development, adoption and use of information systems. Different organisations may value information systems differently. For instance, Japanese companies seem to use significantly less ICT than western companies, perhaps because their culture puts a high value on face-to-face communication. It can also be difficult to introduce information systems designed to improve group work into an organisation where individuality is valued more highly.

Differences in national cultures affect the success of global information systems in different country units of global organisations. For instance, an information system designed around individualistic and masculine values could be met with significant user resistance in cultures that have a collectivist and feminine value orientation (Chapter 2).

The example on page 61 used two different work groups of linespeople (maintaining power lines) in a utility company. This company tried to build a single information system to service both groups, which included hand-held computing devices for the linespeople to capture information out in the field. The low-power linespeople were happy to accept this new technology but it was heavily resisted by the high-power linespeople. This was perhaps because the low-power linespeople were well used to collecting and sharing information, but in the individualistic culture of the high-power linespeople, they did not do this nearly so much, so they saw very little justification for the new technology.

Managers often use information systems as a way of trying to introduce changes to organisational culture: for example, encouraging group working rather than individual working. Stakeholder groups with distinct subcultures may use information systems to try to promote their own ideas. However, there are dangers in using information systems as levers for cultural change.

Summary

1. This chapter defines the book's final foundation concept, an information system. It is a sociotechnical system, a communication system in which humans use ICT in support of coordinated and collaborative decision making and action (that is, an activity system).
2. Information systems, like the human activity reliant on them, have been in existence for many thousands of years. Modern digital computers were invented over 50 years ago, and stimulated enormous growth in technologies associated with data capture, processing and communication. They rapidly came to be used in business organisations, and this stimulated rapid growth in the application of information and communication, both within and more recently between organisations.
3. Four layers of infrastructure are critical to the modern business: activity, information, information systems and ICT infrastructure. Each level supports the others. Every business organisation's information systems are necessarily different, but there are similarities, especially across organisations in the same business sector, so it is possible to develop generic descriptions of both back-end and front-end information systems infrastructure.
4. Key business back-end information systems include sales order processing, purchase order processing, inventory management, finance and payroll.
5. The sales order processing information system records details of customer orders, and supports activity systems such as sales and after-sales service.
6. The inventory management information system maintains an inventory of raw material and finished goods. It is important for providing sales staff with accurate information on quantities and pricing of products. It also supports procurement activity.
7. The purchase order processing information system records details of purchase orders and supports the procurement process.
8. The financial information system records amounts owed by and to, and paid by and to, customers, suppliers and employees. It supports other infrastructure activities such as management and planning. The payroll information system records details of wages and payments made to employees, and is a critical element of human resource management activity.
9. Front-end information systems interface directly with major stakeholder types: managers, employees, suppliers and customers.
10. Management-facing information systems are built on the foundation of back-end information systems. Management information systems are used by operational management to monitor the state of the organisation. Decision support systems and executive information systems generally support longer-term, strategic and tactical decision making.

11 Typical customer-facing information systems include sales, customer relationship management, marketing and outbound logistics. Typical supplier-facing information systems include procurement, inbound logistics and supplier-relationship management systems. Typical employee-facing information systems include human resource management and production control systems.

Chapter 2 considered systems of activity, and Chapter 3 the way in which information supports business activity. This chapter considered systems of information-handling activities which provide information to the business. The next couple of chapters switch attention to systems of technology. Part III of the book provides a high-level overview of the typical ICT infrastructure that supports current forms of business and offers significant potential for the design of new organisational forms. This is the growing area of electronic business, considered in Chapter 8.

Focus on Value

The key value of information systems lies in their role as producers of information. Information is critical in support of activity systems in organisations. Assessments of the 'quality' of information rely on the context of the information system. However information systems, like both systems in general and sociotechnical systems in particular, are not value-neutral. Values are necessarily embedded in the application of technology for particular purposes.

It is valuable to examine historical information systems, not only to gain a perspective on what an information system is in essence, but to see how information systems generate ethical issues. For the purposes of managerial control, single and isolated information systems in organisations have less value than integrated systems, so there is key value in having an explicit information systems infrastructure. However, the impact of information systems and their embedded technology depends on the organisational context. There is a necessary interaction between the value of information systems and the organisational structure and culture.

Review test

1	Information systems are distinct from ____________. Fill in the blank.
2	Information systems rarely stand still. They evolve to support ____________ systems. Fill in the blank.
3	Information systems are the same as human activity systems. True or false? ☐ True ☐ False
4	Write down three properties associated with the quality of information.
5	Match the term to the most appropriate definition. Data validation / Data verification / Information system / Process A transformation of incoming data flow(s) into outgoing data flow(s) Systems of communication that involve people in producing, collecting, storing and disseminating information The process of ensuring that data is entered correctly or transmitted correctly along particular communication channels The process of ensuring that data captured and stored in some information system remains an accurate reflection of its domain of discourse
6	Place the layers of informatics infrastructure in the order in which it supports human activity infrastructure. Indicate the order using 1 to 3. ICT infrastructure Information systems infrastructure Information infrastructure
7	MIS stands for: Choose one term. ☐ Management information system ☐ Modern information system ☐ Manufacturing information system
8	Match the name of the information systems modelling construct to the most appropriate symbol. Information flow ☐ Information store → Agent ⊏ Process ○
9	Core business information systems include: Select all that are relevant. ☐ Sales order processing ☐ Finance ☐ Inbound logistics ☐ Purchase order processing ☐ Payroll ☐ Customer relationship management
10	Good information systems are critical to: Select the most appropriate. ☐ Effective human action ☐ Stakeholder involvement ☐ The design of ICT systems

11	Sales order processing is the information system that records details of purchase orders to suppliers. It is likely to support major elements of the procurement process. True or false? ☐ True ☐ False
12	Typical management-facing information systems include sales, customer relationship management, marketing and distribution. True or false? ☐ True ☐ False
13	Customer-facing information systems include: Select all that are relevant. ☐ Sales ☐ Supplier relationship management ☐ Outbound logistics ☐ Procurement ☐ Marketing ☐ Customer relationship management
14	Supplier-facing information systems include: Select all that are relevant. ☐ Sales ☐ Procurement ☐ Sales order processing ☐ Human resource management ☐ Inventory management ☐ Supplier relationship management
15	Employee-facing information systems include: Select all that are relevant. ☐ Sales ☐ Human resource management ☐ Sales order processing ☐ Production management ☐ Marketing ☐ Customer relationship management

Exercises

1. Take a company known to you, and determine what are its core information systems. Determine the degree to which these systems are integrated.
2. Take a company known to you, and identify whether it uses any software packages for supporting finance, sales, procurement or payroll.
3. Provide three examples of accurate, timely and complete data.
4. Try to provide more detail on one chosen process from a system in the core information systems infrastructure, such as the calculate pay process in the payroll subsystem. Draw an information systems model for this process.
5. Draw a model of another information system associated with a process known to you, such as student admissions at a university.
6. Take an area of human activity known to you, and determine what form of information system supports it.
7. Take an organisation known to you, and determine the ways in which ICT has been used to supplant, support or innovate activity.
8. Identify a management information system in an organisation known to you and try to determine its functionality.
9. Take a public sector organisation such as a local authority. Try to identify the key front-end information systems relevant to it.
10. Try to identify the types of activity data that might be generated from an information system used to control manufacturing production. In what way might this information system update a human resource information system? What other information systems are likely to feed off a production system?
11. Try to identify some of the purposes that the data collected by a customer relationship management system might be used for.
12. Consider the management-facing information systems of an organisation known to you. Is it possible to identify distinct EIS and MIS? Develop a high-level information model of the information held in the EIS or MIS.
13. Investigate the distinction between EIS, DSS and MIS in more detail. Investigate the role of data warehousing and data mining within such systems.
14. Find a company close to you. Take along one or more of the generic information systems models discussed in this chapter. Compare the operations of the company to those described on the model. How closely do they match? In what ways are they different?
15. Consider a future situation in which corporations become involved in mining asteroids within the solar system. Would the information systems infrastructure of such corporations be different from the one discussed in this chapter?
16. Produce a brief description of the functionality of one or more of the customer-facing, supplier-facing or employee-facing information systems of a company in the services rather than the manufacturing sector.

Projects

1. Choose a historical information system and build a case description of its use. Some possible cases include Herman Hollerith's invention and use of his tabulating machine for running the US national census, the management of railway ticketing in the nineteenth century, and the operation of Lloyd's of London's insurance activities. Distinguish between the activity system, information system and the ICT used in each historical case.
2. Construct a high-level map of an organisation's information systems, perhaps using the modelling notation for information systems discussed in this chapter. Include both computerised (ICT) and

noncomputerised information systems, by using document symbols to indicate manual information systems. Consider the scope for extending ICT systems within the organisation.

3 Consider the diverse ways in which data is captured in an organisation such as a retail chain. Determine the ways in which it is validated and verified. Consider the extent to which the data collected by the organisation is of the necessary quality. You might use such criteria as the degree to which it is accurate and useful.

4 Choose an organisation and investigate the degree of integration between its information systems. Recommend ways in which the systems can be better integrated in the future. Use information systems models for this purpose.

5 Choose an organisation and investigate the relevance of the distinction between management information systems and transaction processing systems for it. In other words, is it possible to identify systems specifically used by management and those used by other workers? Identify clearly the current users of such systems. Try to determine whether they deliver the information required by such users.

6 Draw a detailed map of the information systems used in a business organisation known to you, using a hierarchical series of information systems models. Determine the extent to which they diverge from the systems described in this chapter. To what extent do they map onto the systems described in this chapter?

7 Choose an organisation and attempt to develop a case study of the way in which its ICT systems have been built up over the last 20 years. On the lines of the Goronwy Galvanising case in Chapter 1, try to determine how these systems were planned for and designed. Does it have explicit or implicit informatics infrastructure? Do people in the organisation describe such infrastructure as enabling or constraining?

8 Extend the information infrastructure model detailed in this chapter to include information of relevance to all the back-end and front-end information systems discussed.

Further reading

The concept of an information system is considered from a soft systems perspective in Holwell and Checkland (1998). Front-end and back-end information systems in business are also covered in Beynon-Davies (2004). Hay (1996) provides coverage of a range of 'patterns' or generic information models making up the information infrastructure of a typical company, on which the discussion of information infrastructure in this chapter is based.

References

Ackoff, R. L. (1967) 'Management misinformation systems', *Management Science* **14**(4): 147–56.

Anthony, R. A. (1988) *The Management Control Function*. Boston, Mass., Harvard Business School Press.

Beynon-Davies, P. (2004) *e-Business*. Basingstoke, Palgrave.

Biles, G. (1989) 'Herman Hollerith: inventor, manager, entrepreneur – a centennial remembrance', *Journal of Management* **15**(4): 603–15.

Black, E. (2002) *IBM and the Holocaust*, Time Warner.

Bradley, S. P. and Nolan, R. L. (1998) *Sense and Respond: Capturing value in the network era*. Boston, Mass., Harvard Business School Press.

Checkland, P. (1987) *Systems Thinking, Systems Practice*. Chichester, John Wiley.

Ciborra, C. U., Braa, C., Cordella, A., Dahlbom, B., Falla, A., Hanseth, O., Hepso, V., Ljunberg, J., Monteiro, E. and Simon, K. A. (2000) *From Control to Drift: The dynamics of corporate information infrastructures*. Oxford, Oxford University Press.

Fontaine, J. E. (2001) *Building the Virtual State: Information technology and institutional change*. Washington, DC, Brookings Institution.

Hammer, M. (1996) *Beyond Re-engineering: How the process-centred organisation is changing our lives*. London, Harper Collins.

Hay, D. C. (1996) *Data Model Patterns: Conventions of thought*. New York, Dorset House.

Heeks, R. (ed.) (1999) *Reinventing Government in the Information Age: International practice in IT-enabled public sector reform*. London, Routledge.

Hobart, M. E. and Schiffman, Z. S. (1998) *Information Ages: Literacy, numeracy and the computer revolution*. London, John Hopkins University Press.

Holwell, S. and Checkland, P. (1998) *Information, Systems and Information Systems*. Chichester, John Wiley.

Mason, R. O. (2004) 'The legacy of LEO: lessons learned from an English tea and cake company's pioneering efforts in information systems', Journal of the Association for Information Systems **5**(5): 183–219.

Porter, M. E. (1985) *Competitive Advantage: Creating and sustaining superior performance*. New York, Free Press.

Zuboff, S. (1988) *In the Age of the Smart Machine: The future of work and power*. London, Heinemann.

PART II

UNDERSTANDING ICT

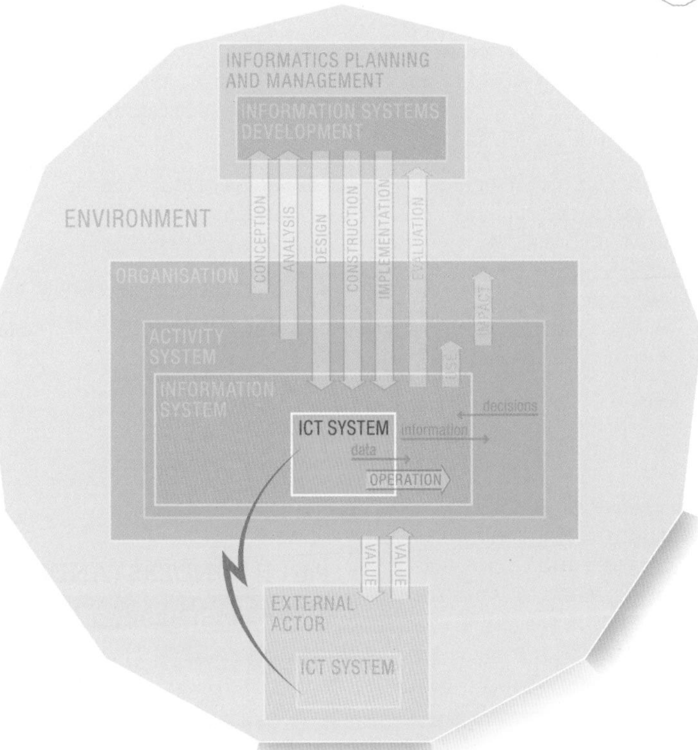

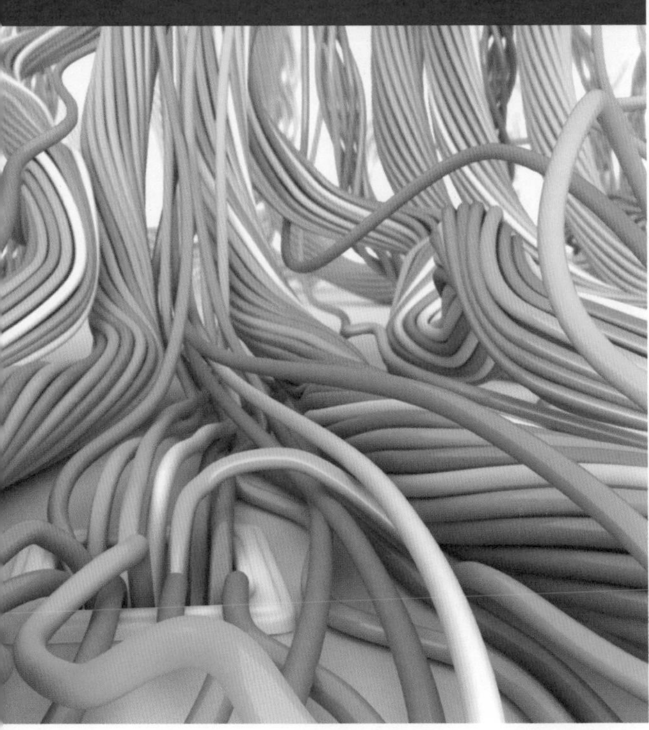

To use informatics in modern business, both technical and social infrastructure is needed. Technical infrastructure is made up of interdependent information and communication technologies. Social infrastructure is made up of good practices in planning, management and operations. This part of the book examines issues relating to technology, while Part IV considers issues relating to the social infrastructure for organisational informatics.

Chapter 5 first examines the way in which technical infrastructure is particularly designed to support electronic delivery of goods and services. This leads to a consideration of the range of access devices and communication channels through which it is possible to connect remotely to modern organisations. Communication technology tends to be equated with the separate but related concepts of the Internet and the World Wide Web, so both these issues are considered in some depth. Organisational communication is also particularly concerned with the transmission of transactions as data, and the chapter outlines a number of standards for managing the flow of transactional data between organisations.

Chapter 6 focuses on the concept of the ICT system in more detail. After a brief coverage of hardware and software it describes a layered model of a typical ICT system and the ways in which both processing and data tend to be distributed over communication networks. The chapter particularly considers the concept of front-end ICT and the place of websites in the technical infrastructure. It also considers back-end ICT issues and the critical importance of database technology to corporate systems. The chapter concludes with coverage of data security issues for ICT systems and communication networks.

OVERVIEW

The chapters in this part cover the following key areas:

Access devices and communication channels
Communication networks
The architecture of the Internet
The key elements of the World Wide Web
Standards for the transmission of transactional data
Component elements of hardware and software
Layered model of an ICT system
Front-end technologies such as websites
Back-end technologies such as databases
Data security

CHAPTER 5 Communication infrastructure

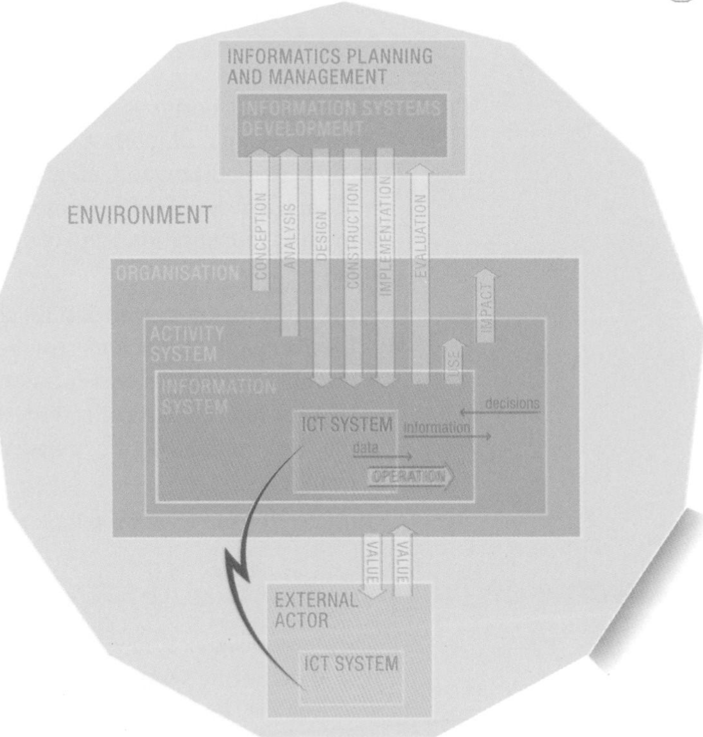

Man did not weave the web of life, he is merely a strand in it. Whatever he does to the web, he does to himself.

Chief Seattle (1786–1866)

LEARNING OUTCOMES	PRINCIPLES
Describe the concept of ICT infrastructure and explain its effects on modern business.	Modern business relies on ICT infrastructure consisting of access devices, communication channels, front-end ICT, back-end ICT and core data management. This infrastructure enables information systems used by both internal and external stakeholders to access data.
Distinguish between the Internet and the World Wide Web, identify some of the critical components of the Internet and explain some of the technologies underlying the Web and their relevance for business.	Modern communication infrastructure relies on two critical technologies: the Internet and the Web. The Internet consists of a set of technologies which enable data communication networks globally to interconnect. The Web is an application which runs on the Internet, and consists of standards for the transmission of hypermedia documents.
Discuss the importance of transactional data to business to business interaction and describe some approaches to handling this issue.	Data communication infrastructure connects business organisations through flows of transactions. These are typically documentation of various forms, and it is important for standards to be agreed for their electronic transmission.

CHAPTER OUTLINE

Introduction

Many texts on business information systems tend to skirt the issue of ICT, or provide a list of disjointed topics of interest. This book aims to provide a more holistic account, and it treats ICT as an important and integrated part of any modern business.

Chapter 4 discussed how modern business by its very nature relies on informatics infrastructure. Organisation activity systems need three mutually interdependent layers or levels of it:

- the information infrastructure, consisting of definitions of information need and activities involved in the collection, storage, dissemination and use of information (see Chapter 2)
- the information systems infrastructure, consisting of the information systems needed to support information collection, storage, dissemination and use (see Chapter 3)
- the ICT infrastructure consisting of hardware, software, data and communication facilities.

This chapter and Chapter 6 look at this last aspect of infrastructure.

Electronic delivery of goods and services

Chapter 7 discusses how ICT is being promoted in both the public and private sectors as a way of delivering services and goods more efficiently and effectively to internal and external stakeholders. Redesigning business processes to meet the challenges of electronic delivery relies on the creation of effective ICT infrastructure. Elements of this infrastructure are illustrated in Figure 5.1, and each one is discussed in this chapter and the next.

Investigating and using access channels

When people both inside and outside an organisation connect to its ICT systems, they do so using **access channels**. Two of the most common channels, particularly for customer use, are face-to-face contact and the telephone. Today, of course, there are also electronic channels, using devices such as Internet-enabled personal computers (PCs) and interactive digital television (iDTV). They enable people to order services and products 24 hours a day, 365 days a year. This is an essential part of the eBusiness and eCommerce agenda for many companies (see Chapter 8).

Front-end ICT for customer use

Front-end ICT infrastructure: The organised collection of ICT systems interacting with key stakeholders.

As was explained earlier, the stakeholder-facing part of a business's systems is known as its FRONT END. The technological infrastructure for modern front-end ICT relies on two critical technologies, the Internet and the Web.

The Internet is a set of interconnected computer networks distributed around the world. We can think of it on a number of levels. Its base infrastructure consists of packet-switched networks and a series of communication protocols. On this layer run a series of applications such as electronic mail (email) and more recently the World Wide Web (or just the Web). The Web is effectively a set of standards for displaying and distributing hypermedia documents over the Internet. Organisations set up their front-end ICT on the Web by creating websites. Many companies are investing heavily to make their WEBSITES more interactive. The aim is to provide fully transactional websites through which customers can carry out as much as possible of their interaction with the company. This chapter examines these important technological foundations for the electronic delivery of goods and services.

Website: A logical collection of HTML documents available on the WWW.

Delivering intangible goods and services effectively

Intangible goods: Goods that fundamentally can be represented as data and hence can be delivered to the customer electronically.

Information-based or INTANGIBLE GOODS and services (see also Chapter 7) are prime candidates for electronic delivery. Many of these are described today as **content**. Tangible goods and services in contrast cannot be delivered electronically, but customers can order them and pay for them electronically. This chapter discusses some of the standards supporting the electronic delivery of goods and services, as well as electronic payment systems.

Re-engineering or constructing back-end ICT

A key focus within the eBusiness agenda (Chapter 8) is on re-engineering service delivery around the customer. For example, when customers enter personal details such as their name and address into one system, this information should ideally be available to all other relevant systems. This kind of customer-focused strategy demands the integration and INTEROPERABILITY of ICT systems. Typically this relies on effective data management and data sharing. Chapter 6 focuses particularly on database systems as a critical back-end technology.

Interoperability: A measure of the degree to which information systems can be coordinate and collaborate.

Ensuring front-end/back-end ICT integration

Integration also involves establishing linkages between front-end and back-end ICT. For instance, to enable fully transactional websites, the information presented needs to be updated dynamically from back-end databases. The information entered by customers also needs to update company information systems effectively (this is also discussed in Chapter 6).

Ensuring secure data and transactions along communication channels

For effective eCommerce (see Chapter 8) people must trust electronic delivery. One important aspect of this is securing the privacy of electronic transactions, particularly payments. Chapter 6 examines the issues of securing data in ICT systems and ensuring secure electronic transactions along communication channels.

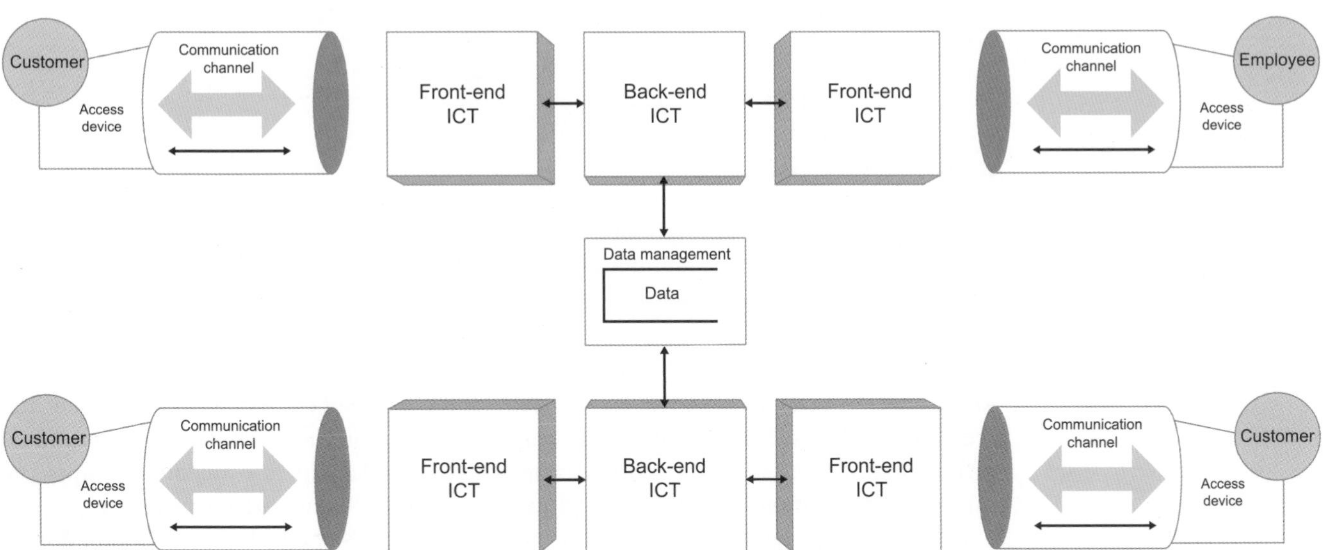

Figure 5.1: *ICT insfrastructure*

This chapter focuses on the first three aspects of ICT infrastructure mentioned above. It looks at the concept of an access channel, and explains the critical role that the Internet and the Web now play in supporting remote access to organisations. It examines standards for the electronic handling of transactional data, and concludes with an examination of electronic payment systems.

Chapter 6 covers the last three aspects of ICT infrastructure. It first looks at the component elements of ICT systems, and how they are both distributed and integrated across communication networks, in their processing and data storage. This leads us to a discussion of the centrality of data and content management systems, and the importance of enterprise-wide integration. The chapter concludes with an examination of the critical issue of data security.

Communication infrastructure

An organisation's services or products can be accessed in a number of different ways, each of which can be described as an **access channel**. Long-established access channels include face-to-face communication, postal services and telephones.

More recently, channels that involve remote and interactive electronic access have become popular. This is known as **electronic delivery**, and uses ICT. Customers can get hold of products such as digitised music directly via remote access channels. For more physical products they can get information and place orders, but the products are distributed through conventional physical channels (see Chapter 7).

Remote access relies on data communication (see Chapter 2). The basic model of communication described in Chapter 2 can be modified for data communication (see Figure 5.2). A sender unit formulates a message and transmits it as a signal to a telecommunication device, a piece of hardware that performs a number of functions on the signal and then transmits it along a communication channel to another telecommunication device, which reverses the process performed by the sending device and passes the signal on to a receiver unit, which interprets the signal as a message.

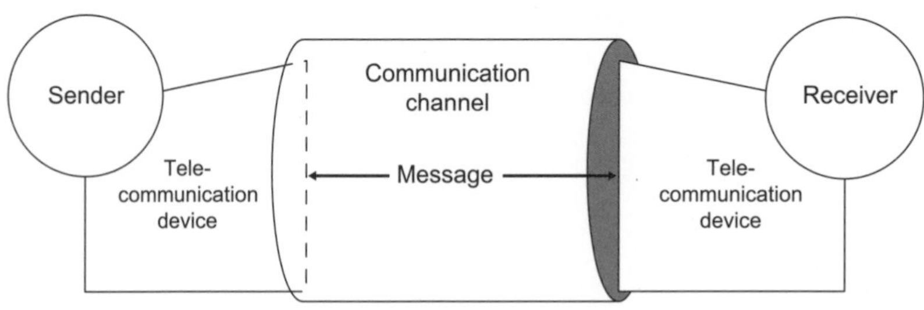

Figure 5.2: *Data communication*

For convenience, the sender unit and telecommunication device together are here called an **access device**. The telecommunication device and receiving unit at the organisation end are called a front-end ICT system.

Access devices and channels

Any access channel consists of an access device and associated communication channel. The **access device** is used to formulate, transmit, receive and display messages. The **communication channel** is used to carry the message between stakeholders – customers, suppliers, partners and employees – and the ICT infrastructure of the organisation (see Figure 5.1).

In the modern electronic business various remote access channels can be used (Whyte, 2001). Generally, there is an interdependence between certain access devices and channels. Access channels are conduits for the delivery of suitable goods and services and the recording of transactions. They are not mutually exclusive, and some electronic access devices and channels can be used together with traditional face-to-face access. Some organisations keep open traditional access channels because some customers prefer to use them (or will not use electronic channels), and it adds to overall effectiveness. However, it is usually cheaper for organisations to reduce the number of traditional channels and increase the number of remote channels.

For instance, when someone pays money into or withdraws money from a bank account over the counter, this costs the bank a few pence or cents. If they do it online, it costs a fraction of a penny or cent.

EBusiness and eCommerce (see Chapter 8) rely on individuals, groups and organisations being able to access electronic networks and systems. This applies particularly to customers, suppliers, partners and employees. Each of these types of stakeholder will have the option of using a variety of access devices and communication channels, and each type interacts with different front-end and back-end ICT systems.

This section considers various devices and channels, which include telephones, television, personal computers, multimedia kiosks and mobile devices (see Figure 5.3).

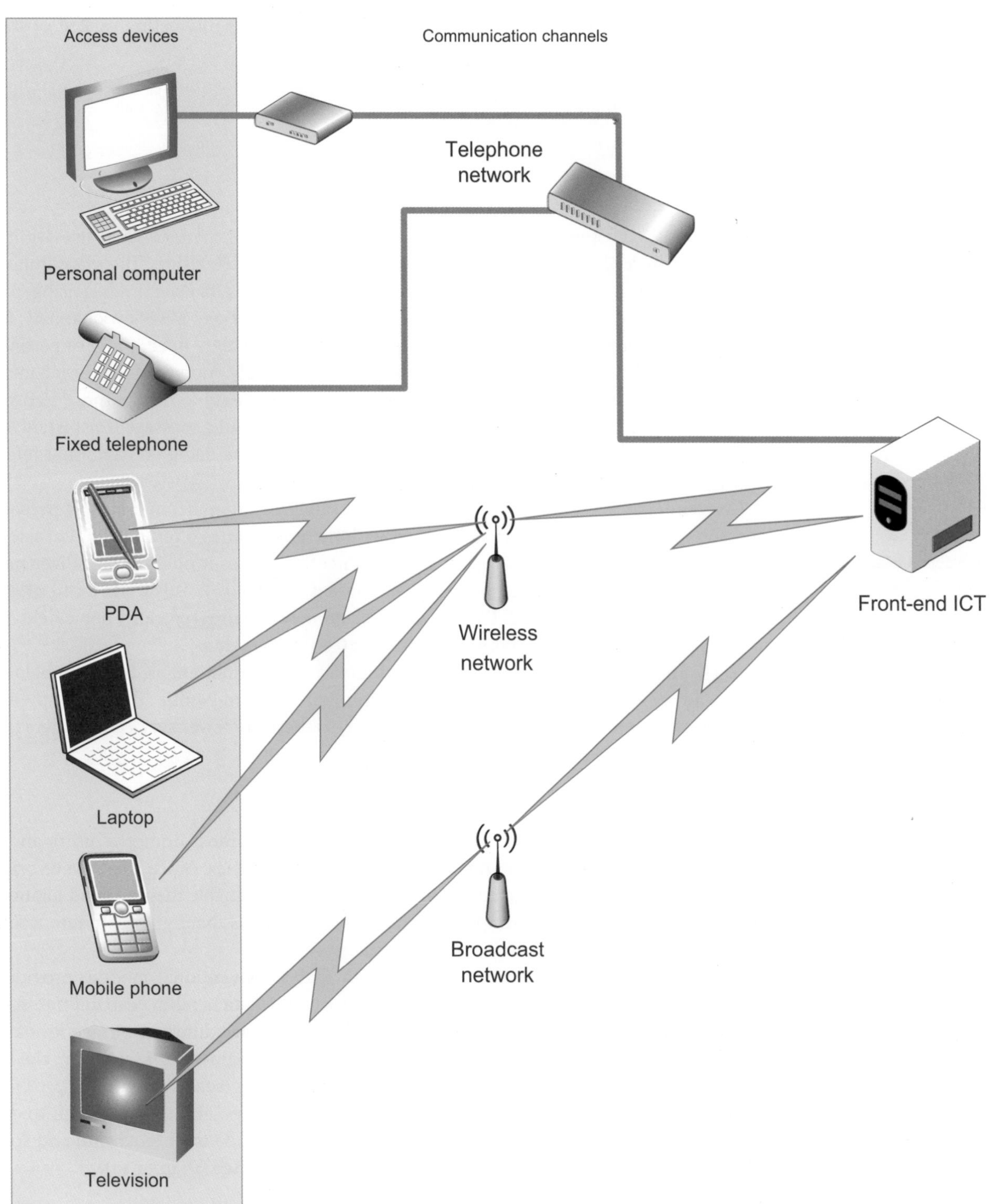

Figure 5.3: *Access devices and communication channels*

Telephony: A category of access device which includes fixed audio and video telephones as well as mobile telephones and fax machines.

Telephony

TELEPHONY includes conventional audio telephones, modern video telephones and the use of fax or telex for data transmission. For many years people have used telephones to order products and services, but the technology has developed recently, for instance with touch-tone services, intelligent networks and the growth of call centres. Telephony can be combined effectively with other access devices such as interactive television (see below) to provide a more complete electronic retail experience. Voice communication over the Internet through voice over internet protocol (VOIP) is a particularly interesting variant of standard telephony.

Did you know?

Music was sent down a telephone line for the first time in 1876, the year the phone was invented.

Television

Most domestic customers in Europe use analogue (see page 77) terrestrial television channels: they can receive a signal but not respond through the television. The main importance of analogue television as a form of electronic retail channel is its use for advertising. Satellite and more lately digital broadcasting have led to a number of pay-per-view channels, including specialist shopping channels. Pay-per-view service providers need a way of getting a fee for the use of the system, so the broadcasting signal is usually encrypted, with each customer getting decryption equipment, typically a set-top box. It is easy to design these to provide a backward channel to the service provider, so viewers can send a message (for instance, place an order) in response to what they see. This is usually done using conventional telephony services and modems.

Conventional television (both terrestrial and satellite) suffers from a lack of personalisation and interactivity, but this has changed with the possibilities offered by digital television. The change in the way the television signal is encoded makes it possible to deliver not only traditional television channels but also web content (see below). This leads on to INTERACTIVE DIGITAL TELEVISION **(iDTV)**, in which customers can use (typically) hand-held devices to navigate the Web, place orders and make electronic payments.

Interactive digital television: A remote access device. A combination of digital television and an up-channel using conventional telephony.

IDTV offers similar electronic retail capability to the Internet-enabled PC (see below), but often a lower level of actual content, reflecting its lower bandwidth. The start-up costs for companies using this medium are relatively high, so there are fewer service providers than on the Internet (see below).

Personal computers

Most people currently access the Internet using PCs, and most domestic users and small businesses connect to it via standard analogue telephone lines. Since these were originally designed to handle analogue speech, a **modem** is needed to enable them to send digital information of the kind used by computers. The modem converts the digital data into a series of analogue tones of different pitch and amplitude.

One key constraint is the limited bandwidth that a conventional modem provides, but technologies such as ADSL (see below) have improved the data handling capabilities. Another problem for those selling across the Internet is that there are difference usage levels across countries, regions and social classes. Between 20 and 66 per cent of households in the United Kingdom use PCs, while almost 100 per cent have televisions (see Chapter 9).

Most PCs use the same software and work in similar ways, and this is helpful to domestic users, but one problem is that people still need to upgrade their hardware and software relatively frequently, and that adds to the cost of ownership (see Chapter 12).

Multimedia kiosks

Multimedia kiosk: A remote access device. Specialist access points to services provided on the Internet.

PCs are used mostly in homes and offices, but people can readily access Internet services when away from home using specialist access points in the form of MULTIMEDIA KIOSKS (sometimes referred to as public internet access points, PIAPs) These tend to be in public places, and to offer services that people are likely to want in that particular location: so a kiosk in a shopping mall will give access to shopping services, and one in a hotel lobby to tourist information. These PIAPs are likely to become less common once most people have their own mobile Internet access.

Mobile devices

Wireless application protocol (WAP): An open international standard for **application** layer network communications in a **wireless** communication environment.

This includes WIRELESS APPLICATION PROTOCOL (WAP)-enabled mobile phones, palmtops (or personal digital assistants, PDAs) and laptop computers. The more powerful general-purpose devices are sometimes called 'fat' form, and the more dedicated, 'thin' devices. Their access channel is likely to be the cellular phone network, rather than the conventional fixed telephone network. At first WAP phones had very limited capability, and websites had to adapt to use over them, but their capabilities are fast expanding.

Many utility companies (gas and electricity suppliers and so on) use mobile devices: for example, to enter meter readings and to update customer billing services online.

Did you know?

Britons spend more time online than they do watching television (Floridi, 2007).

3.3 billion people, almost half the world's population, now subscribe to a mobile phone service (*Economist*, 2008). This is predicted to grow to 75 per cent of the world's population by 2011.

RFID tags

This automatic identification method stores and remotely retrieves data using devices called radio-frequency identification (RFID) tags (Angeles, 2005). These can be attached to, or incorporated into, a product, animal or person. Data from the RFID tag is transmitted using radiowaves, and some varieties can be read over a distance of several metres.

Reflect

The sociologist H. L. Dreyfus (2001) has questioned whether it is possible to provide a sufficiently rich experience for consumers of private and public services using remote access channels. He believes some face-to-face contact will always be required. Consider this in light of the increasing use of electronic delivery in the public and private sector.

Most RFID tags contain at least two parts. One is an integrated circuit for storing and processing data, modulating and demodulating a signal, and other specialised functions. The second is an antenna for receiving and transmitting the signal. A technology called chipless RFID allows for identification of tags without an integrated circuit. This enables tags to be printed directly onto things such as clothing at a lower cost than traditional tags.

RFID tags are now typically used in the supply chain to improve the efficiency of inventory tracking and management, but it has been suggested that the technology could be used more generally for tracking and monitoring, so this is likely to become a significant form of access device in the near future.

Multichannel access centres

Multichannel access centre: A organisational hub for various access mechanisms.

Few organisations would choose to use only remote access channels, because this would exclude some potential customers, so at least in the medium term, there is still a role for face-to-face contact and telephones. Even companies that began as entirely Internet-based businesses are beginning to establish a physical presence, to improve the quality of their service and gain a competitive advantage. Many organisations are also attempting to integrate access channels into MULTICHANNEL ACCESS CENTRES, which provide a common entry point for all customer interaction.

Many local authorities in the United Kingdom are doing this, for example. Cardiff City Council has created Connect to Cardiff, a large call centre capable of handling telephone and web-based enquiries, plus a number of 'one-stop shops' around the city where people can speak directly to its staff.

Communication networks

Communication technology: Technology used for communications.

Local area network (LAN): A type of communication network in which the nodes of the network are situated relatively close together.

Wide area network (WAN): A type of communication network in which the nodes of the network are geographically remote.

Access devices and channels are generally organised into **data communication networks**, a term used for any set of devices joined by a COMMUNICATION TECHNOLOGY that enables the transfer of data. There are several different kinds, defined by their coverage.

- In a LOCAL AREA NETWORK (LAN), the devices are situated near each other: often in one building, or a few buildings that are close together. These are often used to link a group of PCs and related devices such as printers, using either dedicated communication lines or wireless communication.
- In a WIDE AREA NETWORK (WAN), the nodes are geographically remote. WANs may consist of a mix of dedicated and non-dedicated communication lines as well as microwave and satellite communications.

Value added network (VAN): A type of communication network in which a third party creates and maintains a network for other organisations.

- A VALUE ADDED NETWORK (VAN) is a network that a third-party organisation sets up and maintains, selling the right to use it.

Figure 5.4 shows the components of a typical LAN. The PCs and the printer are linked to the cable via interface cards. These are pieces of **firmware** (a combination of hardware and software) which specify the data transmission rate, the size of message packets, the addressing information attached to each packet (see below) and the network topology. The cabling is likely to be coaxial or fibre optic. The **server** is likely to be a powerful PC which acts as a resource for programs and data used by other PCs in the network. The server will also run the **network operating system**, which operates the server facilities and manages communication on the network. A **gateway device** connects the LAN to other networks, and consists of a processor that translates between different communication protocols.

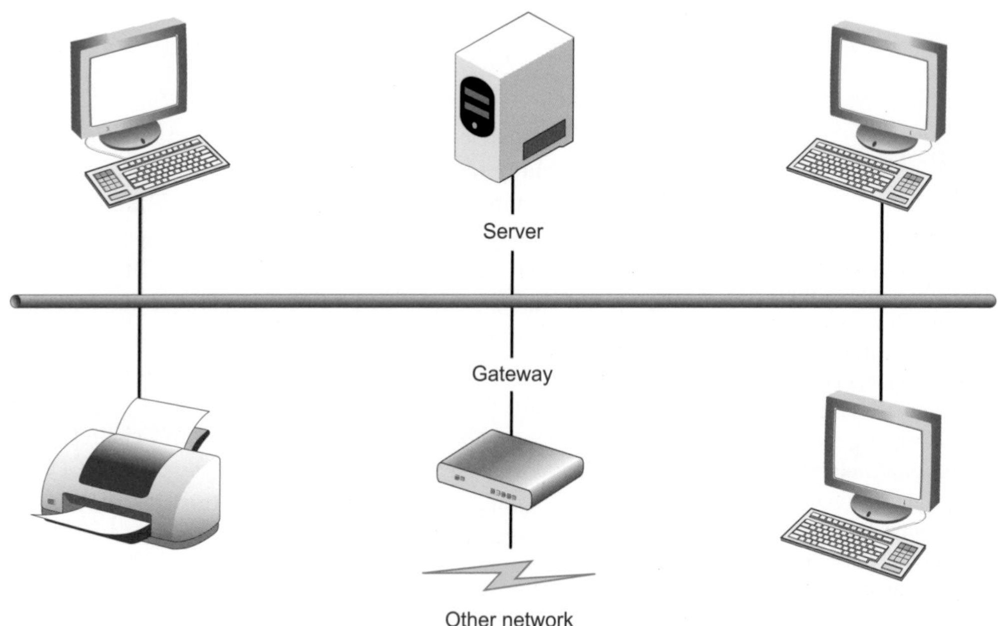

Figure 5.4: *A local area network*

A **topology** is a physical arrangement of objects. The topology of a data communication network refers to the arrangement of devices around the network. There are generally three main types of topology for a data communication network (see Figure 5.5).

Star network: A network topology in which network devices are connected to a central computer.

Ring network: A network topology in which network devices are connected in a loop.

Direction: A property of a communication which refers to the direction of the data flow between sender and receiver..

- In a STAR NETWORK, devices are all connected to a central computer, which acts as a form of 'traffic controller' for the other devices: all data communication passes through it, and it periodically polls other devices on the network.
- In a RING NETWORK devices are connected in a loop. A computer sends a message by grabbing a special bit pattern known as a token, which is recognisable as a message carrier by all devices on the network. (This type of network topology is also known as a token ring.) The message is added to the token along with the address of the destination computer. Messages are transmitted from computer to computer, flowing around a closed loop in a single DIRECTION. Since each device operates independently, if one fails the network is able to continue uninterrupted.
- In a **bus network**, also known as the **Ethernet** model, devices are connected to a main communication line called a bus along which messages are sent. Messages can be broadcast to the entire network through a single circuit, and messages may travel in both directions along the bus. Each computer checks all the messages and accepts those addressed to it.

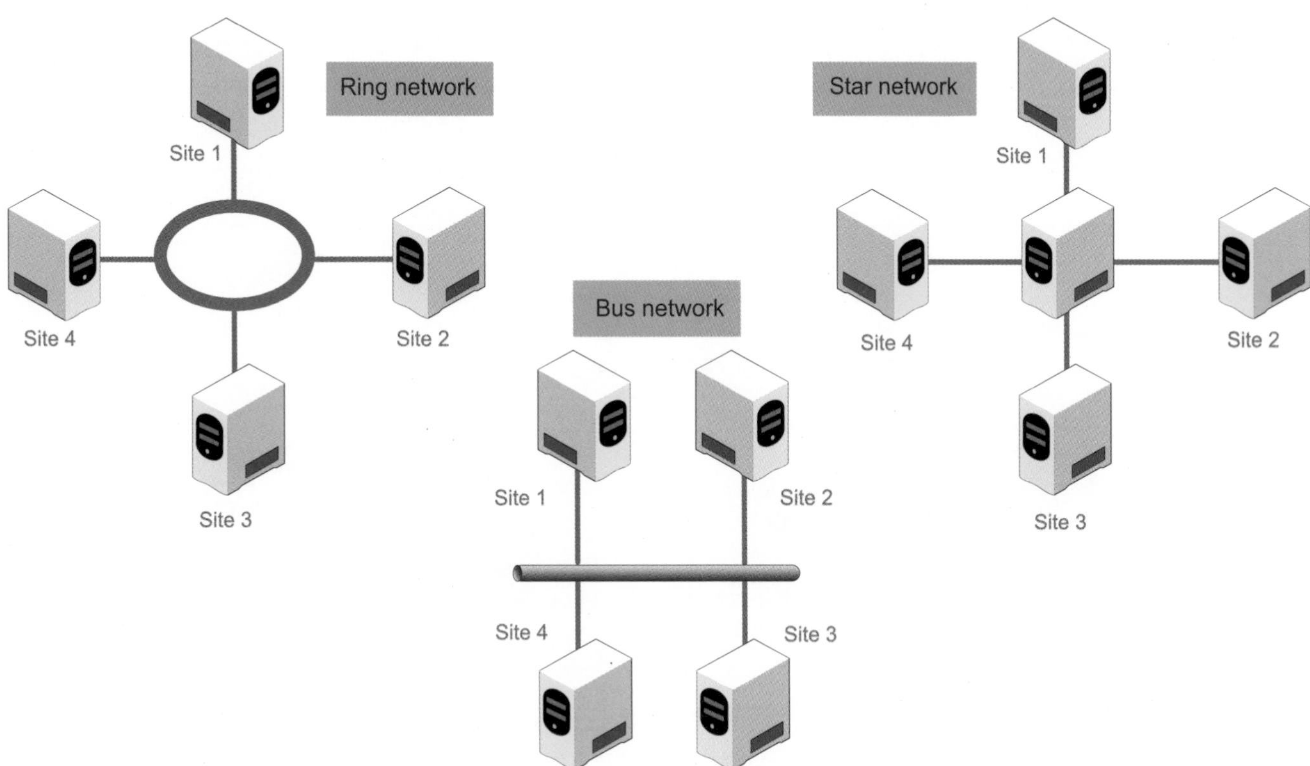

Figure 5.5: *Network topologies*

Reflect
How important is an efficient telecommunication network to international trade? Try to think of ways in which telecommunication networks facilitate trade between countries and regions.

Local loop: The communication channels between the local telephone exchange and the customer.

Telecommunication carrier: An organisation that provides the telecommunication infrastructure for communications.

Telecommunication device: A piece of hardware that permits electronic communication to occur.

Telecommunication media: Media used for the transmission of data in communication networks.

ISDN: Integrated service digital network, a broadband communication channel for the local loop.

In practice, many networks are hybrids, perhaps with part using a star topology while other parts use a ring topology. Most LANs tend to broadcast messages across the entire network, leaving each computer to check and receive those with its destination address. This approach would be extremely inefficient for WANs, which tend to use point-to-point protocols. This means that if a site wishes to send a message to all sites on the network it must send one for each destination computer.

Connecting access devices to front-end ICT

There are a number of major current alternatives for connecting home or office PCs to a front-end ICT system.

Telephone network

The telephone network in most countries is a wide-area telecommunication network. Its topology is a tapered star, with a relatively small number of main exchanges connected by long-distance trunk cables. Main exchanges are connected to a much larger number of local exchanges, which in turn connect directly to customers in the home or the office (see Figure 5.6).

The connections between main exchanges and local exchanges use cables that are designed for high-performance data transmission, typically of optical fibre and able to transmit many Mb/Sec (see Chapter 3). These can also be upgraded much more easily than the cabling between customers and the local exchange. But the network's data transmission performance is heavily reliant on the LOCAL LOOP: that is, the communication medium between local exchanges and customers, which typically consists of copper cabling.

Digital transmission

Telephone companies are interested in increasing the speed of data transmission (the bandwidth) over the telephony local loop. Digital services have been developed (primarily for businesses) that allow the simultaneous transmission of multiple voice circuits. This allows the business to treat their local telephone network as part of an **integrated services digital network (ISDN)**. The data rates available can be as large as the business requires.

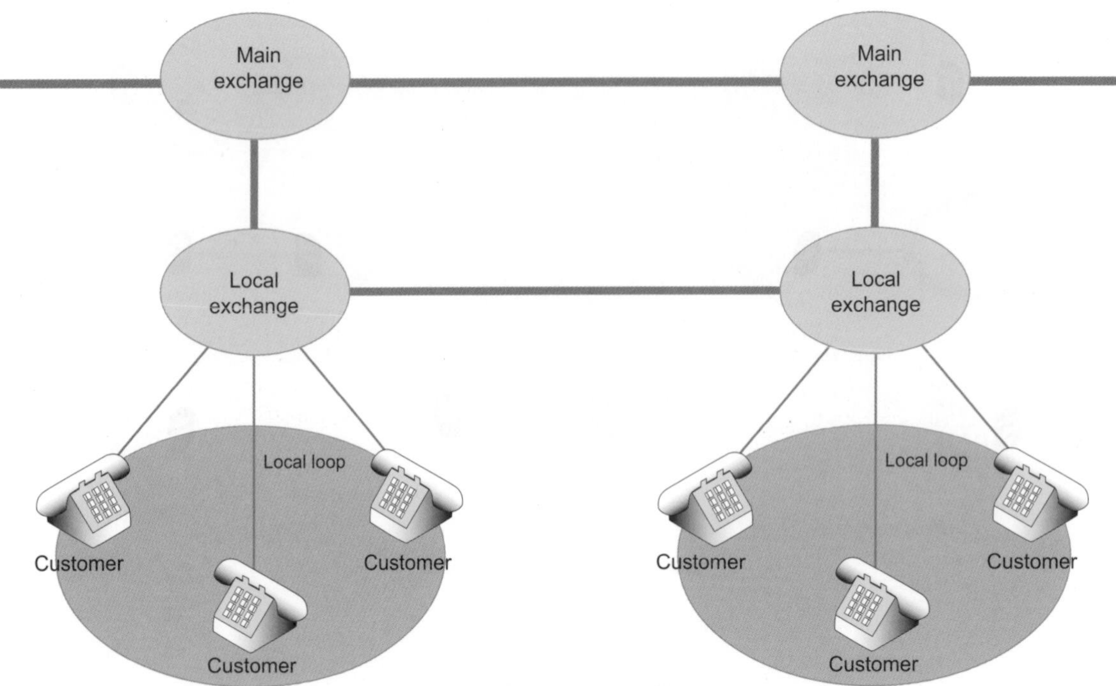

Figure 5.6: *The conventional telephone network*

Basic rate ISDN is a cheaper solution for smaller businesses and domestic users. It provides two-way digital communication over existing copper wires for usually twice the price of analogue telephony. The business gets two independent fully duplex 64Kb/sec channels. These can be combined for certain applications such as downloading higher-quality video at 128Kb/sec.

ISDN in turn has largely given way to the technology of the digital subscriber loop or digital subscriber line (**DSL** or xDSL), a family of technologies that provide digital data transmission over local telephone wires. DSL was originally developed as a means of providing video on demand services, but is now used as an effective means of providing fast, very high-quality access to the Internet. It is cheaper than ISDN and provides a permanent connection to the Internet.

The technology relies on short transmission distances between a local exchange and a domestic customer or business (typically below 10 km). The download speed of consumer DSL services ranges from 512 Kbit/sec to 51 Mbit/sec, depending on the DSL technology used, and the line conditions and service level implemented. Typically, upload speed is lower than download speed for ASYMMETRIC DIGITAL SUBSCRIBER LINES (ADSL) and equal to download speed for symmetric digital subscriber lines (SDSL).

ASDL: Asynchronous digital subscriber line. A broadband communication channel for the local loop.

Cellular networks

Radio networks are currently dominated by cellular mobile phones, which began as analogue devices capable of carrying only voice traffic. However, the development of digital standards led to integrated voice/data communications. **Third generation** (**3G**) technologies enable cellular network operators to offer users a wider range of more advanced services while achieving greater network capacity through improved spectral efficiency. Services include wide-area wireless voice telephony and broadband wireless data, all in a mobile environment. Typically, they provide services at 5–10 Mb/Sec.

Reflect
Many businesses choose to pay extra for symmetric bandwidth via SDL. Why is symmetric as opposed to lower-cost asymmetric bandwidth important to many businesses, particularly those involved in information work?

WiFi and WiMax

3G networks are wide area cellular telephone networks which evolved to incorporate high-speed Internet access and video telephony. In contrast, **WiFi** networks based on the IEEE 802.11 standard are short-range, high-bandwidth networks primarily developed for data. Typical bandwidth for WiFi varies between 10 and 54 MB/sec.

A WiFi enabled device such as a PC, mobile phone or PDA can connect to the Internet when it is in a hotspot: that is, within range of one or more wireless network connections. Hotspots can be as small as a single room, or when access points are dense and overlapping, cover many square miles. Some connections are provided free of charge: for example airports, hotels and restaurants often provide these as a customer service. Those who want to control their access point (either charge for it, or prevent others from using it) can make it secure through passwords and the like.

WiMAX, the Worldwide Interoperability for Microwave Access, is a telecommunications technology based on the IEEE 802.16 standard aimed at providing wireless data over long distances in a variety of ways, from point-to-point links to full mobile cellular type access. The bandwidth and reach of WiMAX makes it suitable for a range of potential applications, including connecting WiFi hotspots with each other and to other parts of the Internet, and providing a wireless alternative to cable and DSL for BROADBAND access within the last few kilometres. It has also been proposed as a technology for providing mobile connectivity. The actual bandwidth achievable through this technology depends on a range of factors, but it typically offers 2MB/sec rates over a few kilometres of distance between transmitters and receivers.

Broadband: A term generally used to describe a high-bandwidth communication channel.

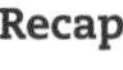
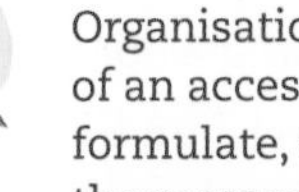

Recap

Organisations provide access to their services or products through **access channels**, consisting of an access device and associated communication channel. The access device is used to formulate, transmit, receive and display messages. The communication channel is used to carry the message between customers, suppliers, partners and employees and the organisation's ICT systems. Stakeholder access devices include telephones, interactive digital television, PCs and mobile devices. Major ways of connecting access devices to front-end ICT systems include telephone networks, digital transmission and radio networks. Communication networks tend to be organised as local area networks, wide area networks or value-added networks. The topology of a network generally follows one of three main models: star, ring and bus.

The Internet

At the moment, the dominant communication technology is the Internet (Whiteley, 2000). The Internet – short for inter-network – began as a WAN in the United States, funded by its Department of Defense to link scientists and researchers around the world (see below). It was initially designed primarily as a medium to exchange research data, but now it has become an essential part of the communication infrastructure of modern organisations in both the public and private sectors. Some have even claimed it to be the foundation of a global information society (Currie, 2000).

It consists at present of a set of interconnected computer networks distributed around the globe, and can be considered on a number of levels. The base infrastructure of the Internet is composed of packet-switched networks and a series of communication protocols. On this layer run a series of applications such as ELECTRONIC MAIL (email) and more recently the World Wide Web.

Email: Electronic mail. The transmission and receipt of electronic text messages using communication networks.

History

In August 1962 J. C. R. Licklider (the first head of the computer research programme at DARPA – the Defence Advanced Research Projects Agency in the United States) wrote a series of memos discussing his concept of a 'Galactic Network'. This constituted a global interconnected set of computers through which any person from any site in the network could quickly access data and programs.

Lawrence G. Roberts at ARPA (DARPA changed its name to ARPA and back again a number of times) took up the idea and published his initial plan for the ARPANET in 1967. This exploited the development of appropriate routing hardware using the proposed theory of packet-switching networks (see below). In 1969 the ARPANET was created by linking four US university computers. In October 1972 Bob Kahn gave the first large demonstration of it to the public at an academic conference. In 1972 the idea of electronic mail (email) was introduced for the first time as a viable application running on this network.

PART 2

The original ARPANET grew into the Internet, based around the idea that multiple independent networks of differing architectures could be made to work together through an open network architecture. Critical to this idea was the formulation of a meta-level 'internetworking architecture' which specified the interfaces required between networks. Also critical to the development of the Internet was Bob Kahn's development of a protocol that enabled end-to-end network communication in the face of environmental problems causing transmission error. The robustness and survivability of the network were critical to its design, including the capability to withstand losses of large portions of the underlying networks. The eventual protocol, which became known as TCP/IP (see below), enabled effective error control across an open network architecture.

Four principles were central to Kahn's thinking:

- Each distinct network must remain autonomous and no internal changes should be required to enable a network to connect to the Internet.
- Communications should be on a best effort basis. If a data packet does not make it to the final destination, it should shortly be retransmitted from the source.
- 'Black boxes' (later called **gateways** and ROUTERS) were to be used to connect networks. They did not retain any information about the individual flows of packets, which kept them simple and avoided complicated adaptation and recovery from various failure modes.
- There would be no global control of the Internet at the operational level.

Routers: Hardware and software technology that directs packets to their indicated destination along a communications network.

Part of the motivation for the development of ARPANET and TCP/IP was to enable the sharing of computer resources across a network. These were referred to as **time-sharing** computers. When desktop computers first appeared, it was thought by some that TCP was too big and complex to run on a PC. A research group at MIT set out to show that a compact and simple implementation of TCP was possible. They produced an implementation, first for the Xerox Alto (the early personal workstation developed at Xerox PARC) and then for the IBM PC.

Widespread development of LANs, PCs and workstations in the 1980s allowed the Internet to flourish. Ethernet technology, developed by Bob Metcalfe at Xerox PARC in 1973, is now probably the dominant network architecture underlying the Internet. PCs are also the dominant forms of computing device on the Internet.

A major shift occurred as a result of the increase in scale of the Internet and its associated management issues. To make it easy for people to use the network, host computers were assigned names, so that it was not necessary to remember the numeric addresses or so-called IP addresses. Originally, there were a fairly limited number of hosts, so it was feasible to maintain a single table of all the hosts and their associated names and addresses. With the invention of LANs the shift to having a large number of independently managed networks meant that a single table of hosts was no longer feasible. Hence, the DOMAIN NAME System (DNS) was invented by Paul Mockapetris. The DNS provided a scalable distributed mechanism for resolving hierarchical host names (such as www.acm.org) into an Internet address (see below).

Domain name: A hierarchical naming convention for identifying host computers on the Internet.

Thus, by 1985, the Internet was already well established as a technology supporting a broad community of researchers and developers, and was beginning to be used by other communities for daily computer communications. Electronic mail was being used broadly across several communities, often with different systems, but interconnection between different mail systems was demonstrating the utility of broad-based electronic communications. In 1984 the British JANET and in the following year the US NSFNET programmes explicitly announced their intention to serve the entire higher education community, regardless of discipline. This was a major stimulus to the idea of inter-networking.

On 24 October 1995, the Federal Networking Council (FNC) unanimously passed a resolution defining the term Internet. This definition was developed in consultation with members of the Internet and intellectual property rights communities:

> RESOLUTION: The Federal Networking Council (FNC) agrees that the following language reflects our definition of the term 'Internet'. 'Internet' refers to the global information system that – (i) is logically linked together by a globally unique address space based on the Internet Protocol (IP) or its subsequent extensions/follow-ons;

(ii) is able to support communications using the Transmission Control Protocol/Internet Protocol (TCP/IP) suite or its subsequent extensions/follow-ons, and/or other IP-compatible protocols; and (iii) provides, uses or makes accessible, either publicly or privately, high level services layered on the communications and related infrastructure described herein.

From initially connecting a handful of nodes on the ARPANET the Internet has grown astronomically. Some estimates for the number of users worldwide are:

- 1997: 100 million
- 1998: 200 million
- 2001: 390 million
- 2003: 640 million
- 2005: 1 billion
- 2008: 1.5 billion.

Let us now look in more detail at a number of the technical concepts that make up this communication infrastructure.

Did you know?

In 1972, Ray Tomlinson sent the first electronic message which used the @ symbol to indicate the location or institution of the email recipient.

Packet-switched networks

The early computer networks were modelled on the local and long-distance telephone networks which dated back to the early 1950s. Computer networks during the period tended to be composed of leased telephone lines. A connection between a caller and the receiver was established through telephone switching equipment (both mechanical and computerised) selecting specific electrical circuits to form a single path. Once the connection was established, data travelled along the path. This is known as a **circuit-switching** network.

Circuit-switching works well for voice communication but proves expensive for data communication because of the need to establish a point-to-point connection for each pair of senders and receivers. Most modern computer networks therefore use a form of network technology known as PACKET-SWITCHING. Here, the data in a message or file is broken up into chunks known as packets. Each packet is electronically labelled with codes that indicate its sender (origin) and receiver (destination). Data travel along the network from computer to computer until they reach their destination. Each computer in the network determines the best route forward for the packets it receives and must transmit. Computers that make these decisions are known as **routers**. The destination computer reassembles the packets into the original message.

Packet-switched network: A communications network which employs packet-switching protocols and technologies. Data is broken into individual packets which are disseminated over a communications network through the application of routers.

There are a number of advantages to packet-switching networks for data communication. Long streams of data can be broken up into small, manageable chunks. This means that the packets can be distributed efficiently to balance the traffic across a wide range of possible transmission paths in a data communication network.

TCP/IP

One of the key objectives of most computer networks is to achieve high levels of connectivity: the ability of computer systems to communicate with each other and share data. This means that standards must be defined to enable communication between sender and receiver, and embodied in communication software.

One approach to developing higher connectivity uses **open systems**, built on public domain operating systems, user interfaces, application standards and networking standards. One of the oldest examples of an open systems model for data communication is the Transmission Control Protocol/Internet Protocol (TCP/IP). This was developed by the US Department of Defense in 1972. TCP/IP is the communications software model underlying the Internet. A **protocol** is a statement that explains how a specific networking task such as the transmission

TCP/IP: Transmission control protocol/Internet protocol is the communications model underlying the Internet.

of data should be performed. TCP/IP divides the communication process into five layers of networking tasks:

- **Application**: the closest layer to the network user, which provides data entry and presentation functionality to the end-user.
- **Transport/TCP**. This layer breaks application data up into TCP packets known as datagrams. Each packet consists of a header comprising the address of the sending computer, data for reassembling the message and error-checking data.
- **Internet protocol.** This layer receives datagrams from the TCP layer and breaks the packets down further. An IP packet contains a header with an address, and carries TCP information and data in the body of the packet. The IP layer routes the individual packets from the sender to the receiver.
- **Network**. This handles addressing issues within the operating system as well as providing an interface between the computer and the network. Each device on a network will normally have a unique identifier (an IP number) assigned to it. This is represented in the network interface of each device.
- **Physical**: this layer defines the basic characteristics of signal transmission along communication networks.

The advantage of this approach is that two different computer systems using TCP/IP are able to communicate with each other even if they are based on different hardware and software platforms. Data sent from one computer pass down through the five layers of the protocol. Once the data reach the receiving computer they travel up through the layers. If the receiving computer finds a damaged data packet it requests the sending computer to send again. This process is illustrated in Figure 5.7.

Email protocols, FTP and HTTP

Email protocol: A communication protocol for the transfer of electronic mail

FTP: File transfer protocol, a protocol for transferring files over communication networks.

In addition to the TCP/IP protocol, other communication protocols are used to provide file transfer, email and Web applications on the Internet. FILE TRANSFER PROTOCOL (**FTP**) enables the transfer of files between computers. **Simple mail transfer protocol** (**SMTP**) enables email transfer between computers. **Multi-purpose internet mail extensions** (**MIME**) enable email transfer in complex organisations. This is particularly used by the Web to specify the media type contained in a message such as text, images or video. **Hypertext transfer protocol** (HTTP) is a protocol that defines how information can be transmitted between web clients and web servers in a network (see below).

IP addresses

IP address: Internet protocol address, a unique identifier for the computers on a communications network using TCP/IP.

An IP ADDRESS is the fundamental way of identifying uniquely a computer system on the Internet. It is constructed as a series of up to four numbers each delimited by a period, so it can be described as a dotted quad. In a 32-bit IP address each of the four numbers can range from 0 to 255. Generally the first four numbers identify a computer network. The remaining numbers usually identify a node on this network. For example, 126.203.97.54 might be an IP address for a computer on the local area network at my university.

> Did you know?
>
> Because of the explosion in Internet usage more computers are being added to the global network. Hence, the 32-bit IP system will eventually run out of unique addresses. To offset this, a 128-bit IP address will be introduced globally.

Universal resource locators

Internet users generally find IP addresses difficult to remember, so more memorable identifiers have been introduced. These map to IP addresses (that is, each one refers to one IP address).

Universal resource locator (URL): A unique identifier for a document placed on the Web.

HTML documents resident on computers attached to the Internet (see below) are identified by UNIVERSAL RESOURCE LOCATORS (**URLs**), so URLs can be used to provide a unique address for each document on the Web. Links between documents are activated by 'hotspots' in the document: a word, phrase or image used to reference a link to another document.

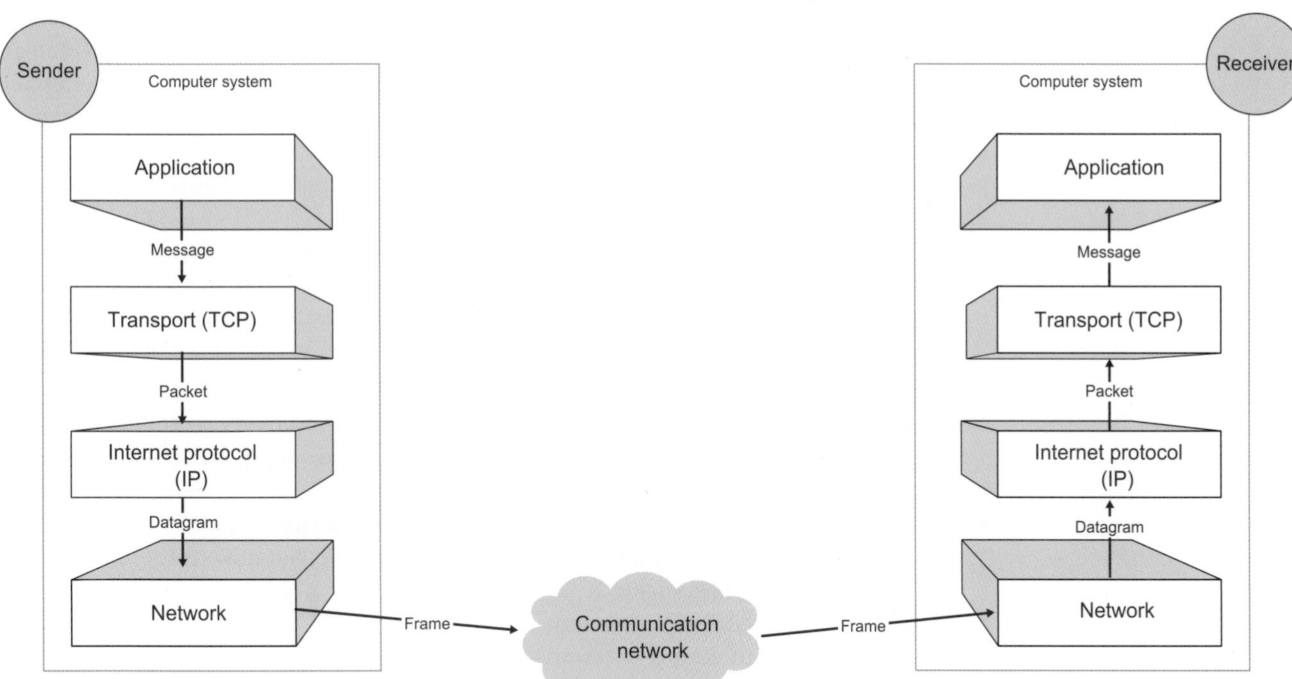

Figure 5.7: *TCP/IP layers*

The syntax of a URL consists of at least two and as many as four parts. A simple two-part URL consists of the protocol used for the connection (such as HTTP) and the address at which a resource is located on the host. In the URL below, the protocol – HTTP – is placed before the symbols ://. The address after these symbols identifies a specific web page on the host computer, in this case the home page of Cardiff University.

HTTP://www.cardiff.ac.uk

Domain names

The 'cardiff' in this URL is short for 'Cardiff University', the 'ac' for academic and the 'uk' for United Kingdom. Together these make up a **domain name**, an agreed string of characters that is used to provide greater meaning to a URL. In practice, a domain name identifies and locates a host computer or service on the Internet. It often relates to the name of a business, organisation or service, and must be registered in a similar way to a company name.

A domain name is typically made up of three or more parts referred to as domain levels. Levels therefore provide structure to the domain name. In a particular URL, domain levels read from right to left.

- **Top-level domains** consist of either generic names (such as .com) or country codes (such as .uk). Generic domain names are also referred to as first-level domain names.
- **Second-level domains** further refine the top-level domain name by typically suggesting the type of provider. For instance, .ac indicates an academic institution based in the United Kingdom.
- Domains below the second level are referred to as **sub-domains** and are typically used to refer to a specific content provider: in the example, Cardiff University.

The regulation of domain names

Internet protocol addresses are mapped to domain names by **domain name servers.** These are computer systems in the inter-network that perform this transformation. For such domain servers to work effectively standardisation is needed in domain names.

Such standardisation has traditionally been in the hands of the US government. During the late 1980s and early 1990s, the responsibility for allocating domain names was given to the Internet Assignment Number Authority (IANA). Then a company – Network Solutions

Inc. (NSI) – was set up and started charging customers for the registration of domain names. In 1997, IANA and a number of other organisations advocated self-governance in the domain name service, and a year later the Internet Corporation for Assigned Names and Numbers (ICANN) was created. Its main role is to oversee the allocation of domain names and the distribution of addresses by domain name registrars. Domain name registrars are public and private organisations in different countries, tasked with maintaining registries (databases of domain names and addresses).

ICANN has responsibility for a number of naming conventions, including generic top-level domain names such as .com and .org, country codes such as .uk and .fr, sponsored domain names such as .coop and .museum and unsponsored domain names such as .biz.

Generic top-level domains consist of strings of three letters, which were originally one of:

- .com, signifying a commercial organisation
- .org: although it can be any type, typically a public sector or voluntary sector organisation
- .gov, initially used to signify government establishments generally, but now restricted to refer to US government establishments
- .edu, used generally to signify an educational institution internationally
- .mil, initially used to signify military establishments generally but now restricted to refer to US Armed Forces establishments
- .int, initially conceived to denote international entities
- .net, initially used to signify 'networks' and therefore to denote a generic free usage domain.

Did you know?

At the end of 2006 there were 120 million unique registered domain names in the world, and of these, 80 million were generic top-level domain names. The most commonly used generic top-level domain name is .com, with 62 million domains. There was a 32 per cent increase in domain name registrations from 2005 to 2006.

Case check: Case 26 W dotCYM

The dotCYM campaign is a not-for-profit pressure group attempting to promote a distinct Internet domain for the Welsh linguistic and cultural community. The campaign believes that the Welsh language and culture represents a community that should be identified and enhanced by having its own sponsored top-level domain (sTLD) on the Internet – .cym. If successful this would mean that 'those organisations, companies and individuals throughout the world that express themselves in the Welsh language and/or wish to encourage Welsh culture will be able to be registered and identified with the .cym domain'.

Because Wales is a constituent part of the United Kingdom, it does not meet the criteria established by the United Nations for being an independent country. This means that Wales cannot qualify for a two-letter country code top-level domain such as .uk or .ne. Consequently, the dotCYM campaign is hoping to follow the precedent set by the puntCAT campaign, which made a successful application for a sTLD representing the Catalan cultural community – .cat.

Connecting to the Internet

Long-range data communications are rapidly moving off conventional telephony-based architectures to those based on the architecture of the Internet.

Layer 3 of the TCP/IP communications model described above – the transport layer – uses the internet protocol (IP) (Norris and West, 2001). Using this protocol data is split up into autonomous packets each carrying the address of the sender and receiver. The packets find their way across a range of interconnected sub-networks. These might be either LANs or WANs, and are connected to other networks by routers. The routers manage naming conventions for the sending and receiving units. This is illustrated in Figure 5.8.

Internet service provider (ISP): A company supplying connections to the Internet.

Domestic users and small businesses generally do not have LANs, so they are connected via a modem and a conventional telephone line to an INTERNET SERVICE PROVIDER (**ISP**). The customer achieves connection as a standard telephone call to a bank of modems held at the ISP. For the duration of the call the ISP provides a unique but temporary IP address to the customer's computer. It informs the computer of this address, which is used by the customer's browser in any communication with the Internet during the duration of the connection. This temporary binding of IP address to computer is typically achieved through a **point-to-point protocol** (**PPP**). This situation is illustrated in Figure 5.9.

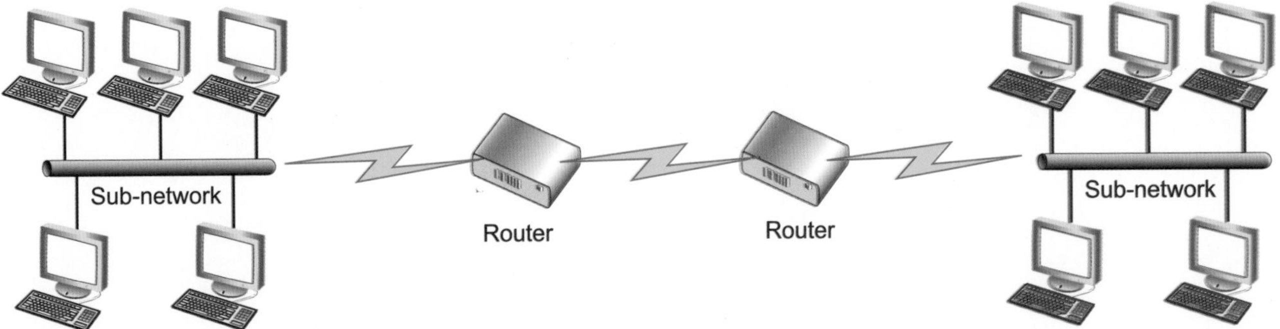

Figure 5.8: *Sub-networks and routers*

PART 2

Figure 5.10 displays graphically the primary architecture of the Internet. The Internet is supported by a high-speed communications backbone. Users access the Internet by connecting to an ISP via the local telephone loop. The ISP is connected to an **internet access provider** (**IAP**), which has permanent access to a **network access point** (**NAP**). This is an interconnection point that exchanges data traffic from a number of IAPs at high speed. Smaller ISPs may connect to the backbone via larger ISPs.

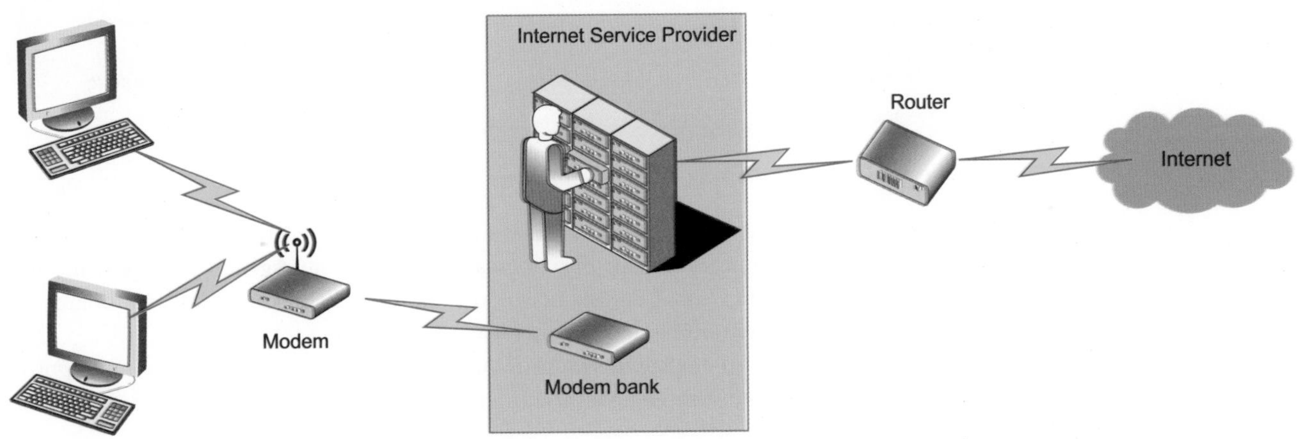

Figure 5.9: *Connection to an ISP*

Applications that run on the Internet

Chat: Technology enabling near-synchronous many-to-many communication over the Internet.

Newsgroup: Technology for enabling threaded discussions between many-to-many users.

The Internet is an inter-network on which a number of applications currently run, including WWW, email, NEWSGROUPS and CHAT.

- The **World Wide Web (WWW)** is effectively an application that allows the use and transmission of hypermedia documentation (see below) over the Internet.
- **Electronic mail** (email) was one of the first applications to run on the Internet. It uses email servers and email software to enable people to communicate primarily through the asynchronous one-to-one transmission of messages. It requires email addresses to be assigned to users.
- A **mail list** is a collection of email addresses. Using this technology the same message can be distributed precisely to the persons that need the information. Mail lists are therefore important for enabling one-to-many asynchronous communication. List servers permit the easy maintenance of mail lists.

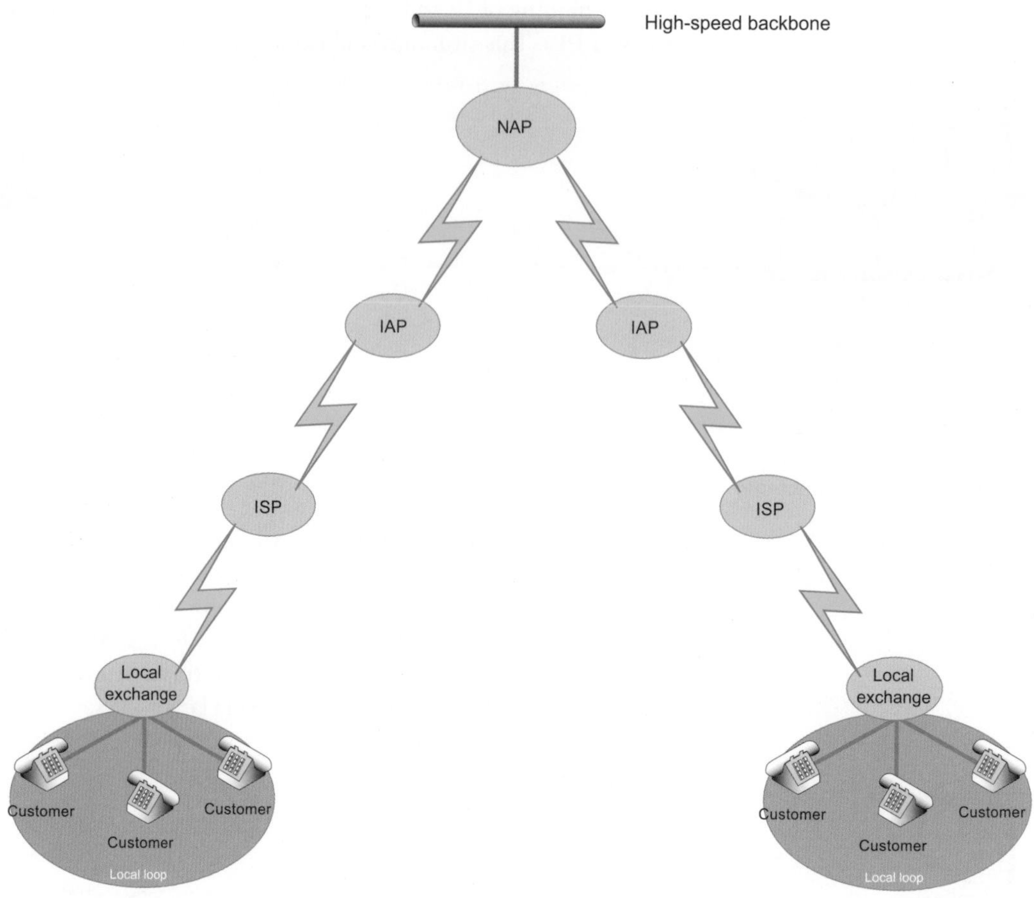

Figure 5.10: *Primary architecture of the Internet*

- **Newsgroups** consist of threaded discussions and enable many-to-many asynchronous communication. Participants can post messages onto the newsgroup using email. Other participants can then thread comments or replies to each message. Bulletin boards and online fora are variants of the newsgroup idea.
- **Chat** enables people to engage in synchronous many-to-many communication in approximate real-time using messaging over the Internet.

Recap 

The most prevalent current example of the application of communication technology is the Internet, short for inter-network. The TECHNICAL INFRASTRUCTURE of the Internet includes packet-switched networks, TCP/IP, HTTP, email protocols and FTP, IP addresses, universal resource locators (URLs) and domain names. Packet-switching networks employ protocols in which data in a message or file are broken up into chunks known as packets and distributed around the network. TCP/IP is an open systems model for data communication that employs a number of layers. In addition to the TCP/IP protocol, other protocols are used to provide file and email applications on the Internet, including FTP, SMTP, MIME and HTTP. Computers attached to the Internet and the HTML documents resident on them are identified by universal resource locators (URLs). A domain name provides more meaning to a URL, and identifies and locates a host computer or service on the Internet. Internet protocol addresses are mapped to domain names by domain name servers. A variety of applications run on the Internet, including the WWW, email, mail lists, newsgroups and chat.

Technical infrastructure: The supporting infrastructure of ICTs for eBusiness.

The World Wide Web

The Web dominates any discussion concerning the communication infrastructure for modern business. People often confuse the Internet with the Web. The Internet is the backbone communication infrastructure as described above. The Web is effectively an application that runs on the Internet, and forms a set of core standards for most contemporary front-end ICT systems. This section considers the history of the Web and its basis in the technology of hypertext and hypermedia, then describes hypermedia, HTML, websites and web portals.

History

Tim Berners-Lee (1999), the creator of the concept of the Web, has claimed that one major motivation was the inability of computers to store random associations, in the way the human brain does. A number of researchers in the academic community had proposed setting up networks of loosely connected nodes of textual material – referred to as hypertext (Conklin, 1987) (see below) – in a way that copied the brain's associative capacity. In 1989, while working at the European Particle Physics Laboratory, Berners-Lee proposed that a global hypertext space might be created in which any information on the network could be accessed by a single 'universal document identifier' (UDI). His employers gave him the opportunity to write a program in 1990 called 'WorlDwidEweb'. This constituted a point and click hypertext editor which ran on the 'NeXT' machine, a hardware platform of the time. This hypertext editor and an associated specification for a web server were released to the high-energy physics community at first. In the summer of 1991, this technology together with an early browser (see below) written by a student was released to the hypertext and NeXT communities. The specifications of UDIs (now URIs), HyperText Markup Language (HTML) and HTTP (see below) were also published on the first server in order to promote widespread adoption.

Between the summers of 1991 and 1994, the load on the first web server (info.cern.ch) rose steadily by a factor of 10 every year. The first three years of the development of the Web were devoted to attempts to get the technology adopted first by academia and then by industry. For this to prove successful web clients were needed for other hardware platforms (as the NeXT computer was not commonplace), and eventually an array of browsers – Erwise, Viola, Cello and Mosaic – emerged.

Berners-Lee was under pressure to define the future evolution of the Web. After much discussion he decided to form the World Wide Web Consortium (W3C) in September 1994, based at MIT in the United States, INRIA in France, and now also at Keio University in Japan. W3C has assumed responsibility for evolving the various protocols and standards associated with the Web since that time.

Components of the Web

Figure 5.11 illustrates the primary components of the Web: hypertext/hypermedia, HTTP, HTML web browsers, websites and web portals.

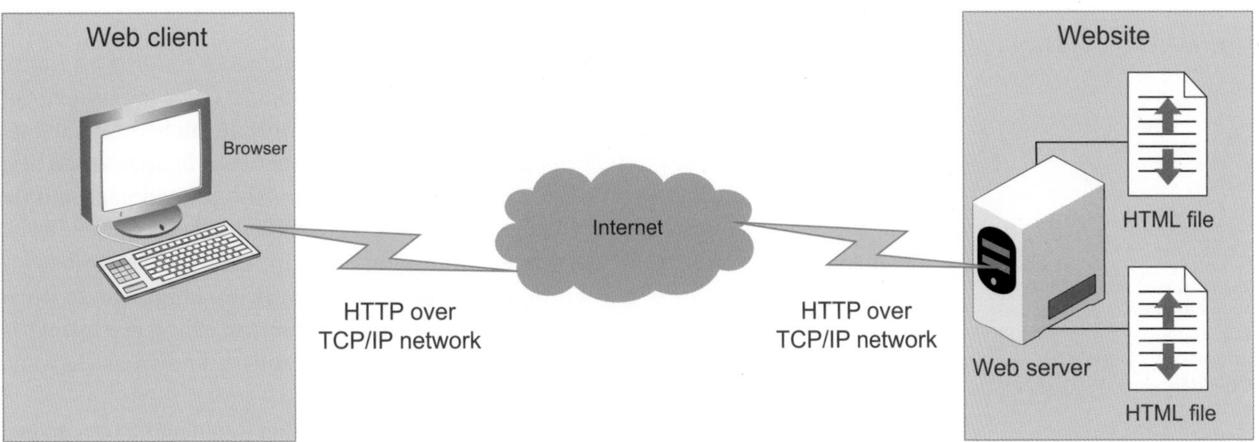

Figure 5.11: *Components of the Web*

Client-server: An applications architecture in which the processing is distributed between machines acting as clients and machines acting as servers.

Client: A key type of organisational stakeholder. Clients sponsor and provide resources for the construction and continuing use of an information system.

The Web is effectively a CLIENT-SERVER application (see Chapter 6) running over the Internet. Web CLIENTS run pieces of software known as browsers. This enables connection to web servers using two communication protocols, HTTP and TCP/IP. Web servers deliver hypermedia documents in HTML format over the Internet to web clients.

Hypertext/hypermedia

Vannevar Bush (1945) envisaged hypertext/hypermedia systems in the 1940s. In a groundbreaking paper he discussed the concept of a memex (memory extender), a device capable of storing and retrieving information on the basis of content. In 1968, Douglas Englebart demonstrated the Augment system. Augment was an online working environment designed to augment the human intellect. It could be used to store and retrieve memos, research notes and other forms of documentation. Ted Nelson extended Bush's original idea in his Xanadu environment. Xanadu was designed to be an ever-expanding workspace that could be used to create and interconnect documents containing text, video, audio and graphics. Nelson actually coined the term **hypertext**, and described it as being 'non-linear reading or writing'. A number of prominent hypermedia prototypes were developed during the 1980s. However, a software tool bundled with the Apple Macintosh computer did most to popularise the concept. In recent times hypertext and hypermedia form the bedrock for the Web.

Text can normally be organised in three major ways. The first is **linear** text, as in a conventional novel. The reader is expected to start at the beginning and progress steadily to the end. Most textbooks and reports are organised as **hierarchical** text: it is divided into chapters, sections, subsections and so on. The reader can use the hierarchy to find the text that interests them. Dictionaries and encyclopaedias are examples of **network text.** This does not have a hierarchical structure: each entry has an independent existence but is linked to a number of other entries via references.

Hypertext: A subset of hypermedia concentrating on the construction of loosely connected textual systems.

Hypermedia: The approach to building information systems made up of nodes of various media (such as text, audio data and video data) connected by a collection of associative links.

HTTP: Hypertext transfer protocol, an object-oriented, stateless protocol that defines how information can be transmitted between client and server.

HYPERTEXT is an electronic or online version of network text. A hypertext document is made up of a number of textual chunks connected with associative links called **hyperlinks**. HYPERMEDIA is a superset of hypertext, including text, graphics, audio and video.

Hypertext transfer protocol (HTTP)

HTTP is a protocol that defines how information can be transmitted between web clients and web servers, typically over a TCP/IP network. In a HTTP transaction, the client establishes a connection with a web server; the client sends a request message to a web server; the web server sends a response to the client; and the connection is closed by the web server.

HTTP is said to be a stateless protocol. This means that when a server provides a response and the connection is closed, the server has no memory of any previous transactions. This has the advantage of simplicity, in that clients and servers can run with simple logic and there is little need for extra memory.

Hypertext markup language (HTML)

The Web can be thought of as a collection of hypermedia documents residing on thousands of servers or websites situated on computers around the world. Electronic documents of any form are made up of two types of data: data that represents **content**, such as text and graphics, and data that describes to ICT applications how the content is to be **processed**. Typical processing involves formatting the document on media such as the printed page and the PC screen. The process information normally consists of a set of embedded tags that indicate how the content is to be presented. This process of tagging text with extra information is known as marking up, and the set of tags for doing this comprise a **mark-up language**. In the 1960s work began on developing a generalised mark-up language for describing the formatting of electronic documents. This work became established in a standard known as the standard generalised mark-up Language (SGML).

SGML: Standard generalised markup language, a generalised markup language for describing the formatting of electronic documents.

SGML is in fact a meta-language: a language for defining other languages, so it can be used to define a large set of mark-up languages. Tim Berners-Lee used SGML to define a specific language for hypertext documents known as HTML. HTML is a standard for marking up or tagging documents that can be published on the Web, and can be made up of text, graphics,

HTML: Hypertext markup language, a standard for marking up documents to be published on the WWW.

images, audio clips and video clips. Documents also include links to other documents stored on either the local HTML server or remote HTML servers.

HTML has undergone a number of versions since it was first introduced in 1991. A major part of the work of W3C has been to produce standard versions of HTML with increased functionality.

As suggested above, a HTML document contains both content and tags. The document content consists of what is displayed on the computer screen. The tags constitute codes that tell the browser how to format and present the content on the screen. The general form of this relationship between tags and content is expressed as:

<tagname properties> content </tagname>

The tagname is taken from an established set of keywords established in the particular version of HTML. Tags are embedded in angled brackets. Certain tagnames and the grammar with which they are used convey specific meanings to Web browsers. For instance, in the tag <P align="right">, *P* is the tagname and acts as an abbreviation for the word paragraph, so this tag is designed to be placed at the start of a chunk or paragraph of text. The word *align* is a property which can be assigned a number of values from a limited list. One of these is *right,* which specifies that the paragraph in question should be right-justified on screen. An end-tag </P> is placed at the end of the chunk of text.

The hyperlinks between pieces of text are established using **anchor tags**. The hyperlink can be to a textual element in the same document or to another document. This anchor tag has the form:

<A HREF="address">visible link text</A>

The letter *A* stands for anchor. *HREF* is a property that is used to specify the address of the document or piece of text to be linked to. The visible link text establishes what is displayed on the screen as a **hot spot.** When you move the cursor over a hot spot (which is usually formatted in some way so that it stands out on the screen), it typically changes from an arrow to a pointing hand, to show that if you click on the hot spot with the mouse, it will transfer you to the document specified in the address.

For example, if you saw **http://www.cardiff.ac.uk** formatted as a hotspot, it would have been set up using the anchor tag:

<A HREF="http://www.cardiff.ac.uk">Cardiff University</A>

and it would take you to the home page of Cardiff University.

Table 5.1 lists some commonly used tag-names. Note that most of them must be used with a corresponding end-tag.

Browser: A program that allows users to access and read Web documents.

As you probably know, to access the Web you need a web BROWSER, a program that lets you read web documents, view any inbuilt images or activate other media and hotspots. After the invention of the concept of the Web the idea became established quickly in the scientific community. However, few people outside this community had software capable of reading HTML documents. In 1993 the first program that could read HTML documents and display them on a graphical user interface was written at the University of Illinois. It was called Mosaic.

It soon became apparent that there was an opportunity to sell a good browser, and members of the Illinois team formed the company Netscape Communications. Their key product, Netscape Navigator, became an immediate success. Microsoft entered the market with its Internet Explorer soon afterwards, and these two browsers still dominate this niche in the software market.

Websites, pages and portals

Web page: Generally used to refer to the presentational aspect of a web document.

A **website** is a logical collection of HTML documents normally stored on a web server. We can distinguish between the content and presentation of a WEB PAGE. The content consists of the text and other media bundled as HTML documents. The presentation concerns the way the content is displayed on the user's access device. As was explained above, this is controlled by HTML tags. The term web page really describes how a HTML document is presented on a website.

Table 5.1: *Some common HTML tags*

Tag name	Functionality
<HTML>	Start of a HTML document
<HEAD>	Establishes the header of a page
<BODY>	Establishes the body of a page
<TITLE>	Can be used within the page header to indicate the text to appear in the title bar of the browser
<H1> <H2> ...	Used to establish various levels of headings in the text
<P>	Start of a paragraph
<B>	Embolden text
<I>	Italicise text
<U>	Underline text
<LI>	An item in a list
<CENTER>	Centre text
<FONT>	Used to establish the font, size and colour of some text
<IMG>	Short for Image – used to refer to a graphics file for insertion within the text
<A HREF>	A tag for linking to parts in or outside a document
<UL>	Start of an unordered list
<OL>	Start of an ordered list
<TABLE>	Start of a table definition
<FORM>	Start of a form definition

As the explanation above should show, web pages can be used both to display information and as sophisticated data entry and query interfaces to ICT systems, so in many ways web page design is a hybrid activity. From one perspective, it is not dissimilar to designing newspaper or magazine pages: good graphic design capability is desirable. From another perspective, since web pages can interface with both front-end and back-end ICT systems, it is important for the designer to understand the principles of good user interface design (see Chapter 9).

Web portal: A web page designed to be an entry point for users into the WWW.

Portal: An entry point for users into the WWW.

Horizontal portal: Portal that attempts to serve the entire Internet community, typically by offering search functions and classification for the whole of Web content.

Vertical portal: An entry point to the WWW, that provides the same functionality as a horizontal portal but for a specific market sector.

Search engine: A system that allows users to locate websites by matching keywords.

In the *Oxford English Dictionary*, a **portal** is defined as a door, gate or entrance, especially one of imposing appearance. WEB PORTALS are specialised websites designed to act as an entry point for users into the Web. They can be seen as a form of electronic reintermediation (see Chapter 8). A PORTAL tries to attract users through a range of value-added services such as information, news, eShopping, directories and searching, making it an anchor site for them. There are two major types of portal. HORIZONTAL PORTALS attempt to serve the entire Internet community, typically by offering search functions and classification for the whole of Web content. VERTICAL PORTALS normally provide the same functionality but for a specific market sector, so they target a niche audience.

Typical examples of horizontal portals are Lycos.com and Yahoo!com. Examples of vertical portals are the ones supplied by Dell (dell.com) and Cisco (cisco.com) (see Chapter 8).

A number of other software applications are heavily associated with the Web and its use, and enhance its functionality, although they are independent of it. For example, because of the information explosion on the Web, one major problem is knowing how to find the exact information you want. A SEARCH ENGINE lets users specify a combination of keywords using logical operators such as AND, NOT and OR. It then looks up the keyword combinations in what is effectively a large index linking keywords to URLs, and displays a set of results. Search engines are typically offered by information intermediaries or **infomediaries**, normally organisations maintaining horizontal portals. One of the most used at present is google.com (Vise, 2005).

Bulletin board: Web facilities that permit users to post items to a central access area.

BULLETIN BOARDS are virtual versions of physical bulletin boards: you can post news of events, products or services on them. Discussion fora are pages typically attached to a website that allow users to add comments to a long thread of discussion about a specific topic.

Case check:
Case 8, Google

Google Inc. is perhaps the best known of the recent American companies specialising in Internet search and online advertising. When they were first introduced, search engines matched a series of search terms entered by the user against the terms found in web pages. They provided a list of web addresses, ordered according to how often the search terms appeared in them.

The founders of Google produced an algorithm called PageRank which improved on this, by analysing the links emanating from and pointing to web documents. It then assigns a numerical weighting to each element of a set of documents, with the purpose of measuring each document's relative importance in the set. In this sense, the PageRank algorithm treats links much in the way that academics treat citations. Generally, the larger the number of citations an academic paper receives, the more important it is considered to be. Similarly, the more links made to a HTML document, the higher its rank in a Google search.

Web 2.0

The phrase **Web 2.0** tends to suggest a new version of the Web. The second generation it refers to is not a new set of technical specifications, though: it is a second generation of Web-based communities and hosted services which facilitate collaboration and sharing. These include RSS feeds, social bookmarking, weblogs, folksonomies and wikis.

- **RSS** stands for 'Really Simple Syndication' and consists of a family of web feed formats used to publish frequently updated content such as blog entries, news headlines or pod-casts to subscribers.
- The **social bookmarking** technology enables users to store lists of Internet resources that they find useful. These lists are then made accessible to the public by users of a specific network or website. Other users with similar interests can view links by topic, category, tags, or even randomly.
- A **weblog** (or **blog**) is a website where entries are written in chronological order and commonly displayed in reverse chronological order. Blogs typically provide commentary or news on a particular subject such as food, politics or local news. Some blogs operate as personal online diaries. A typical blog combines text, images, and links to other blogs, web pages and other media related to its topic. The ability for readers to leave comments in an interactive format is an important part of many blogs.
- A **wiki** is a shared web page or site that can be updated using easy-to-use tools through a browser. This means they can be directly edited by anyone with access to them, so their main use is in collaborative content production: creating articles about subjects, combining information from many different sources.
- **Folksonomies** are sets of tags developed and used collaboratively by a community of users to classify and retrieve content such as web pages, photographs and web links. Folksonomic tagging is intended to make a body of information increasingly easy to search, discover, and navigate over time.

Did you know? There were over 112 million blogs worldwide in March 2008.

Case check:
Case 22, Wikipedia

Wikipedia is a multilingual project which offers a free encyclopaedia on the Web. The name is a combination of the words wiki and encyclopedia. Wikipedia uses wikis as tools for its members to collaboratively produce content.

Registered users of Wikipedia are able to create new articles, then once an article is on the site anyone with access to it can change its content. Changes made to pages are instantly displayed. The consequence of this is that Wikipedia does not declare any of its articles to be complete or finished.

This process of so-called collaborative content production is built upon the premise that collaboration among users will improve articles over time, in much the same way that open-source software develops (see Chapter 12). Some of Wikipedia's editors have compared this process to Darwinian evolutionary processes, where the 'fitness' of content improves over time.

The semantic Web

The semantic Web is seen by many to be a natural extension to Web 2.0. The traditional Web consists of content connected via a multitude of hyperlinks. The essential property of the Web is its universality, achieved through the power of links that can relate any content to any other content. The key limitation imposed by this universality is that links do not contain any semantics (see Chapter 3) over and above their ability to associate content items.

The semantic Web (Berners-Lee, Hendler and Lassilo, 2001) is by definition an attempt to build semantics into the essence of Web architecture. It is proposed to do this using XML, a resource description framework (RDF) and the notion of an ontology described in Chapter 3. RDF will code the semantics of links in sets of triples (similar to the discussion of knowledge representation in Chapter 3). These triples will relate URIs using typed links which convey their relationship. Ontologies will consist of taxonomies of objects and relations plus sets of inference rules. Software agents will then traverse the Web and will need to share ontologies to enable them to perform tasks such as searching databases in multiple formats.

Recap 

The (World Wide) Web is an application that runs on the Internet. Its primary elements are the concept of hypertext/hypermedia, its implementation in HTML and the use of web browsers. Hypertext is an electronic or online version of network text. A hypertext document is made up of a number of textual chunks connected using associative links called hyperlinks. Hypermedia is a superset of hypertext which allows the distribution of multimedia content. HTTP is a protocol that defines how information can be transmitted between nodes in a network. HTML is a standard for marking up or tagging documents that can be published on the Web, and can be made up of text, graphics, images, audio clips and video clips. People accessing the Web need a browser, a program that lets them read documents, view inbuilt images and activate other media and hotspots. The nodes of the Web are generally made up of websites and web portals. A website is a logical collection of HTML documents normally stored on a web server. Web portals are specialised websites designed to act as an entry point for users. Software applications that enhance use of the Web include search engines, bulletin boards and discussion fora.

Transactional data

To enable the effective flow of transactions, there need to be defined standards for the format and the transmission of electronic messages. Electronic messages are forms of data transmission. For any transactional flow along electronic communication channels three conditions must be satisfied:

- The electronic message comprising the transaction must have a defined format.
- The receiver and sender of the message must agree on its format.
- The message must be able to be sent and read by electronic devices.

EDI: Electronic data interchange. A set of standards for the transfer of electronic documentation between organisations.

XML: Extensible markup language, a metalanguage for the definition of document standards.

Historically, a standard for transactional flow was based on ELECTRONIC DATA INTERCHANGE (EDI). More recently, standards have been defined using a web-based technology known as EXTENSIBLE MARKUP LANGUAGE (**XML**). Both EDI and XML are attempts to define standard data formats for the transmission of electronic messages between organisations.

EDI

EDI provides a collection of standard message formats and an element dictionary for businesses to exchange data through an electronic messaging service (Norris and West, 2001). It mainly supports the execution and settlement phases of commercial transactions (see Chapter 7).

Documentation such as sales orders, delivery notes, invoices and payment advices, which would once have been on paper, can instead be coded up as EDI messages. Each message consists of a number of data segments, each made up of a tag and a number of data elements. The tag identifies the data segment and the data elements include the codes and values required in the message. For example, in a purchase order a data element might detail shipment dates and times, and be given the code DTM (short for Date/Time).

The main benefits of EDI arise from its ability to streamline key business processes, particularly those associated with managing external stakeholders. For instance, if it is introduced for purchase orders, it should mean they are placed more rapidly, with fewer errors in data entry and transmission, reducing the staff time needed and improving inventory management and delivery times.

The main problems with EDI are that standardisation has never been sufficiently broad and technical implementation has proved expensive. For this reason organisations are looking to the next generation of business documentation standards based on Internet and Web technology. Standards are developing in Internet EDI that enable EDI to be implemented at lower cost through virtual private networks or over the public Internet. However, most contemporary interest is in the use of an extension of the Web known as XML for document specification and transmission.

XML

One of the main advantages of HTML (see above) is its simplicity. This enables it to be used effectively by a wide user community. However, this is also one of its disadvantages. Sophisticated users want to define their own tags, particularly for functionality involved with the exchange of data. The World Wide Web Consortium developed XML in 1998 (W3C, 2000) to meet these needs. The term *extensible* means that new mark-up tags can be created by users.

Like HTML, XML is a restricted descendant of SGML. Whereas HTML is used to define how the data in a document is to be displayed, XML can be used to define the syntax and some of the semantics of a document. So it can be used to specify standard templates for business documents such as invoices, shipping notes and fund transfers. XML is seen as a major way in which EDI could be replaced for electronic document transmission between organisations.

An XML document consists of a set of elements and attributes. Elements or tags are the most common form of mark-up. The first element in an XML document must be a root element. The document must have only one root element but this element may contain a number of other elements.

Suppose your company is a coffee wholesaler. You might wish to create XML documents for the exchange of shipping information to your customers. An appropriate root element might therefore be the tag <PRODUCTDETAILSLIST>.

An element begins with a start-tag and ends with an end-tag. The start tag in our document for the root element would be <ProductDetailsList>. The corresponding end-tag would be </ProductDetailsList>. Note that tags are case-sensitive in XML. Hence <PRODUCT DETAILSLIST> is a different tag from <ProductDetailsList>.

Elements can be empty, in which case they can be abbreviated to <EmptyElement/>. Elements must also be properly nested as sub-elements within a superior element. So this XML element might be used to define a particular coffee product:

```
<ProductDetails ID='1234'>
  <ItemName>Kenya Special</ItemName>
  <CountryOfOrigin>Kenya</CountryOfOrigin>
  <WholeSaleCost>20.00</WholeSaleCost>
  <Stock>4000</Stock>
</ProductDetails>
```

Here we have a ProductDetails element with a number of sub-elements. Definitions for these sub-elements such as ItemName, CountryOf Origin, WholeSaleCost and Stock are properly nested within ProductDetails.

In traditional database terms this would constitute a row in a products table (see Chapter 6). This row is made up of a number of columns including an identifier for the product, the name of the item, the country of origin of the product, the cost of the product and the number of product items in stock.

Attributes are name-value pairs that contain descriptive information about an element. The attribute is placed inside the start-tag for the element and consists of an attribute name, an equality ('=') sign and the value for the attribute placed within quotes. In the coffee producer example the tag <ProductDetails ID='1234'> contains the attribute ID and the value '1234'.

The ordering of elements is significant in XML. However, the ordering of attributes is not significant. Hence, the two orders for the product information below would be regarded as different elements:

```
<ProductDetails ID='1234'>
  <ItemName>Kenya Special</ItemName>
  <CountryOfOrigin>Kenya</CountryOfOrigin>
  <WholeSaleCost>20.00</WholeSaleCost>
  <Stock>4000</Stock>
</ProductDetails>
```

```
<ProductDetails ID='1234'>
  <ItemName>Kenya Special</ItemName>
  <WholeSaleCost>20.00</WholeSaleCost>
  <Stock>4000</Stock>
  <CountryOfOrigin>Kenya</CountryOfOrigin>
</ProductDetails>
```

However, we might have represented this information as attributes of the element Product:

```
<Product ID="1234" ItemName="Kenya Special" CountryOfOrigin="Kenya" Stock =
"400" WholeSaleCost="20.00"/>
```

In this case the following element is regarded as being identical.

```
<Product ID="1234" ItemName="Kenya Special" WholeSaleCost="20.00" Stock =
"400" CountryOfOrigin="Kenya"/>
```

Two other mechanisms are important for an XML document. First, a document type definition (DTD) defines the valid syntax for an XML document. It lists the names of all elements, which elements can appear in combination and what attributes are available for each type of element. Second, an extensible style sheet (XSL) is a definition that is used by a browser for the presentation of a document.

Electronic payment systems

Payments are a special form of transactional data. Any payment system is effectively a mechanism for recording exchanges of monetary value.

In earlier times goods and services were exchanged using barter: swapping one good or service for another. A major characteristic of this form of economic exchange is that the value of an item or a service varies with the negotiated basis of the exchange.

A leap forward occurred with the invention of tokens that held their own intrinsic value: what we call money. This meant that tokens could be exchanged in place of goods and services. Money performs four functions: it is a medium of exchange, a means of accounting for amounts owed by actors in an economic exchange, it provides a standard of deferred payment and it is a defined store of value.

Money traditionally has taken a tangible physical form, as first coinage, then banknotes. However, in the electronic world money assumes an intangible form (see Chapter 7). It is essentially data held in the information systems of financial institutions. Money is transferred between such systems electronically, and accompanies the exchange of goods and services.

EMarket: Electronic market, a market in which economic exchanges are conducted using information technology and computer networks.

Forms of eCommerce such as B2C eCommerce (see Chapter 8) rely on the concept of an electronic market (eMarket) (Bakos, 1997). An EMARKET is one in which economic exchanges are conducted between businesses using ICT. In an eMarket, electronic transactions enable the efficient and effective flow of goods and services along the value network (see Chapter 7) (Malone, Yates and Benjamin, 1987).

The essential features of an eMarket are illustrated in Figure 5.12. The eMarket is the domain in which buying companies and selling companies meet. The exchange of goods and services is enabled through electronic transactions between buyer, seller and the financial institutions of each. The market handles all the transactions between companies, including the transfer of money between banks. Banks are effectively intermediaries in any trading relationship in the eMarket.

EFT: Electronic funds transfer, a means for transferring money between financial repositories such as banks or bank accounts.

EFTPOS: Electronic funds transfer at point of sale, a form of EFT where the purchaser is physically at the point of sale.

ELECTRONIC FUNDS TRANSFER (**EFT**) and ELECTRONIC FUNDS TRANSFER AT THE POINT OF SALE (**EFTPOS**) are electronic mechanisms for the monetary flows accompanying the exchange of goods and services. EFT uses ICT to supply and transfer money between financial repositories (such as banks or bank accounts). EFTPOS is a form of EFT where the purchaser is physically at the point of sale such as at a supermarket checkout.

Electronic markets are reliant on efficient and effective ePayment systems. These are effectively information systems for monetary exchange. The forms of ePayment system tend to vary between forms of eCommerce. In B2C and C2C eCommerce (see Chapter 8), there are two types, credit-based and non-credit-based systems.

Non-credit based payment systems: Systems designed to encourage the exchange of micro-payments electronically.

Most NON-CREDIT-BASED SYSTEMS are designed to encourage the exchange of micro-payments: small amounts of money used for the purchase of goods such as access to online newspapers. They use a pre-paying principle. A purchaser must have a ready supply of funds built up in a mechanism that they can use to buy goods and services. These are effectively electronic tokens, and people can buy them using traditional payment mechanisms such as credit cards or funds transfer from a personal bank account.

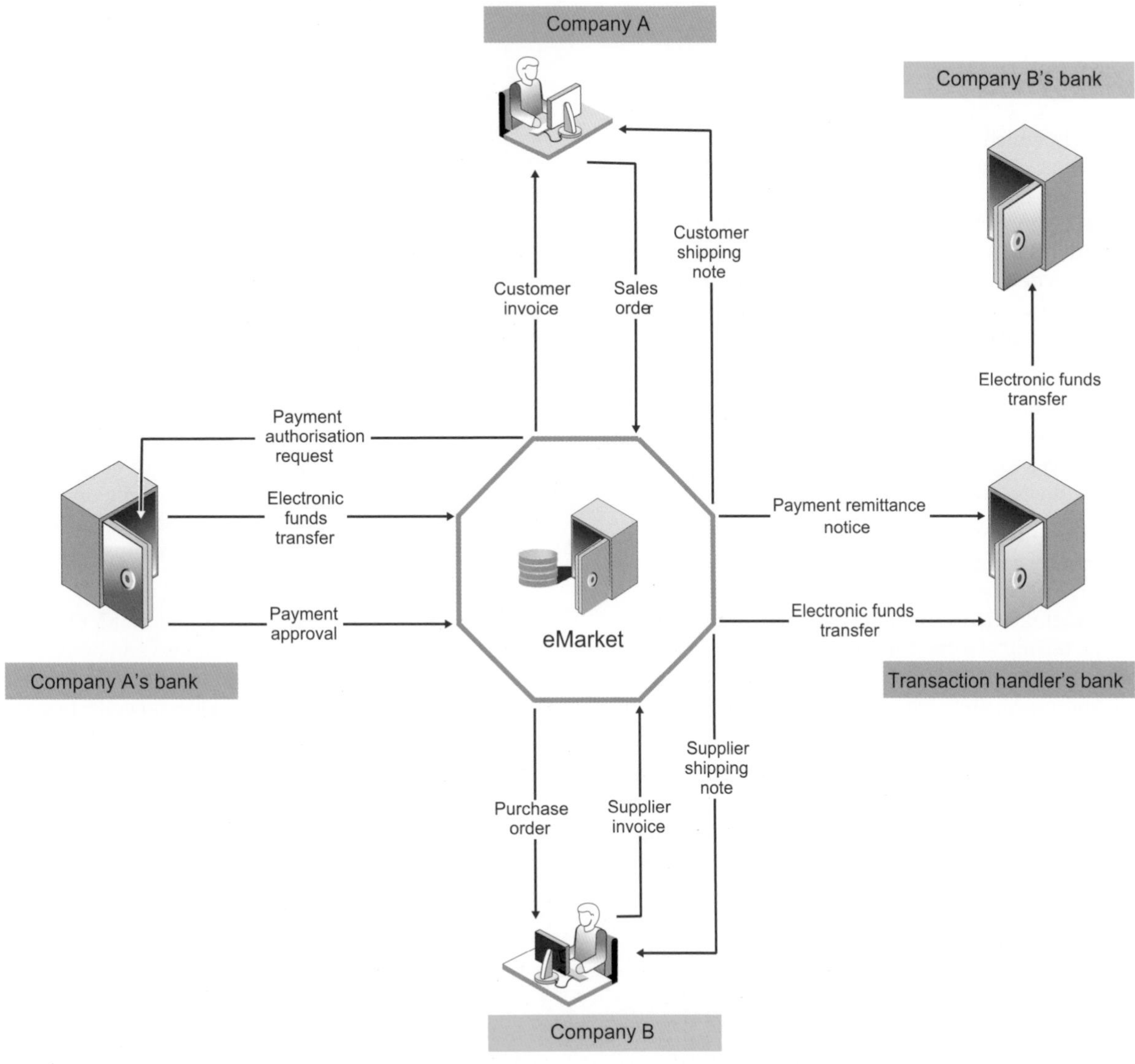

Figure 5.12: *Electronic markets*

Digital cash: A type of non-credit-based payment system.

Some companies have attempted to establish payment systems that share the anonymity of traditional cash payment (DIGITAL or electronic CASH) (Clemons, Croson and Weber, 1996), but to date these have suffered from poor take-up. Micro-transactions or micro-payments systems permit the transfer of small amounts of money between the buyer's and seller's accounts. Because the amounts transferred are small, the levels of electronic security can be lower than for major transactions. Cards such as debit cards issued in association with conventional bank accounts can be used for cash eCommerce. Smartcards are physical cards with embedded chips that allow the storage of significant amounts of data. Because they need card readers (sited in stores or connected to PCs in the home) their use has been restricted so far to a few major experiments. One of the most notable was the trial of the Mondex card in the British city of Swindon.

Credit-based systems are modelled on conventional payment mechanisms such as the cheque and credit card, except that signatures are digital rather than physical. The most popular method of paying for goods and services in B2C eCommerce is currently the credit card. Secure payment systems are required for this.

There are no standard payment mechanisms for B2B eCommerce, because businesses tend to engage in repeat commerce in which purchases are repeat orders, and are frequently complex, with many items. These would need highly specialised or bespoke systems. Also, the value of payments is likely to be significantly larger than for B2C transactions and the associated levels of security must also be higher.

Summary

1. The ways in which people access services or products are known as channels of access. The access channel is used to carry messages between stakeholders such as customers, suppliers, partners and employees and the organisation's ICT systems. Any access channel consists of an access device and associated communication channel. The access device is used to formulate, transmit, receive and display messages.

2. Stakeholder access devices come in many forms including telephones, interactive digital television, personal computers and mobile devices. Major ways of connecting access devices to front-end ICT systems include telephone networks, digital transmission and radio networks.

3. The Internet – short for inter-network – dominates contemporary communication technology. It began as a wide area network funded by the US Department of Defense to link scientists and researchers around the world. Its technical infrastructure includes packet-switched networks, TCP/IP, HTTP, email protocols and FTP, IP addresses, universal resource locators (URLs) and domain names.

4. Packet-switching networks employ protocols in which data in a message or file is broken up into chunks known as packets and distributed around the network using TCP/IP: an open systems model for data communication that employs a number of layers. In addition to the TCP/IP protocol, other protocols used to provide file and email applications on the Internet include FTP, SMTP, MIME and HTTP.

5. Computers attached to the Internet and the HTML documents resident on them are identified by URLs. A domain name provides more meaning to a URL and identifies and locates a host computer or service on the Internet. Internet protocol addresses are mapped to domain names by domain name servers. A variety of applications run on the Internet, including the WWW, email, mail lists, newsgroups and chat.

6. The (World Wide) Web is an application that runs on the Internet. Its primary elements are the concept of hypertext/hypermedia, its implementation in HTML and the use of web browsers.

7. Hypertext is an electronic or online version of network text. A hypertext document is made up of a number of textual chunks connected by associative links called hyperlinks. Hypermedia is a superset of hypertext. HTTP is a protocol that defines how hypermedia documents can be transmitted between nodes in a communication network. HTML is a standard for marking up or tagging documents that can be published on the Web, and can be made up of text, graphics, images, audio clips and video clips.

8. Web users need browsers, programs that let them read web documents, view inbuilt images and activate other media and hotspots. The nodes of the Web are websites and web portals. A website is a logical collection of HTML documents normally stored on a web server. Web portals are specialised websites designed to act as an entry point for users. A number of software applications enhance use of the Web, including search engines, bulletin boards and discussion fora.

9. To enable the effective flow of transactions, standards have to be defined for the format and transmission of electronic messages. Electronic data interchange (EDI) is well established, but more recently standards have been defined using a web-based technology known as XML. Both EDI and XML are attempts to define standard ways of specifying data formats for the transmission of electronic messages. The related technologies of electronic payment

systems support monetary exchange in electronic markets. Technologies in this area include electronic funds transfer and electronic cash.

The next chapter shifts attention from the connective tissue that links individuals and organisations to the technologies underlying the internal ICT infrastructure of the typical business organisation. It defines the concept of an ICT system in more detail, and considers ways in which its functionality is distributed across communication networks.

Focus on Value

ICT as a technology has no inherent value in and of itself to organisations. The value of ICT arises in its application to organisational problems. One key way in which ICT is applied is in facilitating communication, not only within the organisation, but more recently between it and its external stakeholders. The value of communication infrastructure for customers is that it gives them remote access to goods and services. The technologies of the Internet and the Web open up a larger variety of access channels to the organisation, on a global scale. Communication infrastructure is also particularly important in managing transactions as records of value between two organisations, and between organisations and stakeholders such as customers and suppliers.

Review test

1	The four primary components of the technical infrastructure supporting eBusiness are: Select all that apply. ☐ Access devices ☐ Communication channels ☐ Front-end ICT systems ☐ Messages ☐ Back-end ICT systems
2	An access channel consists of an access device and what else? Select the most appropriate term. ☐ Communication channel ☐ Telecommunications device ☐ Receiver ☐ Message ☐ Cable
3	An ____________ is used to formulate, transmit, receive and display messages. Fill in the blank.
4	Remote access devices include: Select all that apply. ☐ Personal computer ☐ Satellite communications ☐ Mobile phone ☐ Multimedia kiosk ☐ Interactive digital television
5	Communication channels include: Select all that apply. ☐ Conventional telephone network ☐ ADSL ☐ Cellular network ☐ Satellite communications ☐ Modems
6	How would you distinguish between a wide area network (WAN) and a local area network (LAN)? Write two sentences.
7	The Web is different from the Internet. True or false? ☐ True ☐ False
8	What is meant by packet-switching in the context of the Internet? Write two sentences.
9	An ____________ address is the fundamental way of identifying uniquely a computer system on the Internet. Fill in the blank.
10	Internet protocol addresses are mapped to domain names by ____________ servers. Fill in the blank.
11	A Web browser is: Choose the most appropriate description. ☐ A piece of security software. ☐ A piece of software used for accessing hypermedia documents stored on the Web. ☐ A form of search engine.
12	HTML stands for: Choose the most appropriate description. ☐ Hypertext Markup Language ☐ Hypermedia Translation Language ☐ Hot-spot Tracking Language
13	What is a universal resource locator and why is it important to the Web? Write two sentences.
14	XML stands for: Choose the most appropriate description. ☐ Extra manipulation language ☐ Extensible markup language ☐ Extensible manipulation language
15	Is Web 2.0 different to Web 1.0 and if so how? Write two sentences.

16	EFT stands for:
	Choose the most appropriate description. ☐ Electronic Funds Transfer ☐ Extensible Funds Transfer ☐ Extra Funds Transfer

Exercises

1. In face-to-face communication, what are the access device and channel?
2. Does a company known to you use any mobile devices to access systems? What type of systems are accessed through them?
3. Consider a computer network known to you. Identify the types of communication media used to connect it.
4. Investigate the communication networks used by an organisation known to you. Are there elements of LANs, and WANs in their communication infrastructure?
5. Determine the topology and coverage of a computer network known to you.
6. If you use a computer on some network try to determine the IP address of the computer.
7. Investigate some of the other common tags used in a HTML document.
8. Consider an organisation known to you and whether it utilises Web 2.0 in any way. For instance, does it use blogging, and if so, for what purpose?
9. Consider an organisation known to you and identify two distinct forms of transation handled by the organisation.
10. Find an example of the use of EDI in a key industrial sector.
11. Find an example of the use of XML in a key industrial sector.
12. Try to determine the volume of monetary transactions occurring within a nation such as the United Kingdom in any one day.
13. Investigate the degree to which 'content' such as television programmes will be delivered over the Internet into the home over the next decade.
14. Investigate the uptake of non-credit-based payment systems in an area of interest to you.
15. Investigate how academic material such as a textbook may be presented via the Web.
16. Determine how many distinct browsers there are in existence and how they differ in their functionality.

Projects

1. HTTP is a stateless protocol. Determine more precisely what 'stateless' means in this context. Also determine some of the problems of this stateless nature in relation to building information systems on the foundation of such a protocol.
2. Bandwidth was defined in Chapter 3 as a key property of a communication channel. Concerns have been raised over the level of bandwidth required not only in the workplace but also in the home over the next decade. Investigate the limitations of bandwidth in supporting the information superhighway in the near future.
3. Choose an organisation and a remote access channel that it uses, and investigate the key costs of maintaining the channel. For instance, what access devices are supported? How much does the communication channel cost to run and maintain?
4. Attempt to determine the current penetration of a chosen access device such as interactive digital television (iDTV) into your nation's homes. Also investigate the degree to which such an access channel is being used to conduct interaction with businesses.
5. Every device on the Internet needs its own IP addresses. Not surprisingly, with exponential growth in the Internet and devices connected to it, concerns have been expressed over the adequacy of the current addressing scheme. Investigate this issue and proposed solutions to any problems that become apparent.
6. Search engines such as Google are beginning to act as user's main portal into the Internet and the Web. Investigate some of the consequences of this for traditional web portals. Does it mean that they are no longer required, or what is their likely future role?
7. The Internet and the Web have created what is sometimes called a global marketplace. Define precisely what globalisation means in relation to communication technology. What consequences does communication technology play in globalisation? Would globalisation happen without communication technology?
8. Technology does not stand still. Investigate likely changes to the technology of the Internet over the next decade. What are the likely trends and what effect will such trends have on global business?
9. Investigate the likely effect of Web 2.0 on business organisations. For instance, business organisations are grappling with both the potential and the pitfalls associated with so-called social networking sites. Some businesses are using them as means of enhancing collaboration amongst organisational members. Other businesses see social networking as a large security risk.
10. Investigate the use of blogs for business purposes. Do they offer a distinctive new channel of communication with customers? How are blogs managed within the overall communication strategy of a company? Are blogs considered part of the content management process or are they managed separately?
11. Investigate the idea of mobile computing and its relevance for organisational informatics. What proportion of the workforce now work on the move, and how many workers are likely to do so over the next decade? What practical problems will organisations face in managing a mobile workforce, and what consequences does this have for informatics infrastructure?

Further reading

A vast range of material, both offline and online, has been published on the technologies of the Internet and the Web. Berners-Lee (1999) provides the definitive account of the creation of the Web and has recently published on the continued progression of the idea in areas such as the semantic web (Berners-Lee, Hendler et al., 2001).

References

Angeles, R. (2005) 'RFID Technologies: supply-chain applications and implementation issues', *Information Systems Management*, Winter.

Bakos, J. Y. (1997) 'Reducing buyer search costs – implications for electronic marketplaces', *Management Science* **43**(12): 1676–92.

Berners-Lee, T. (1999) *Weaving the Web: The past, present and future of the World Wide Web by its inventor*. London, Orion Business.

Berners-Lee, T., Hendler, J. and Lassilo, O. (2001) 'The semantic web', *Scientific American* **284**(5).

Bush, V. (1945) 'As we may think', *Atlantic Monthly* 176: 101–3.

Clemons, E. K., Croson, D. C. and Weber, B. W. (1996) 'Reengineering money: the Mondex stored value card and beyond', *International Journal of Electronic Commerce* **1**(2): 5–31.

Conklin, E. J. (1987) 'Hypertext: an introduction and survey', *IEEE Computer* **2**(9): 17–41.

Currie, W. (2000) *The Global Information Society*. Chichester, John Wiley.

Dreyfus, H. L. (2001) *On the Internet*. London, Routledge.

Economist (2008) 'Nomads at last: a special report on mobility', 12 April.

Floridi, L. (2007) 'A look into the future impact of ICT on our lives', *Information Society* **23**(1): 59–64.

Malone, T. W., Yates, J. and Benjamin, R. I. C. (1987) 'Electronic markets and electronic hierarchies', *Communications of the ACM* **30**(6): 484–97.

Norris, M. and West, N. (2001) *eBusiness Essentials*. Chichester, UK, BT/John Wiley.

Vise, D. A. (2005) *The Google Story*. New York, Random House.

W3C (2000) *XML 1.0 2nd Edition*. World-Wide-Web Consortium.

Whiteley, D. (2000) *E-commerce: Strategy, technologies and applications*. Maidenhead, Berks, McGraw-Hill.

Whyte, W. S. (2001) *Enabling E-Business: Integrating technologies, architectures and applications*. Chichester, John Wiley.

CHAPTER 6

ICT systems infrastructure

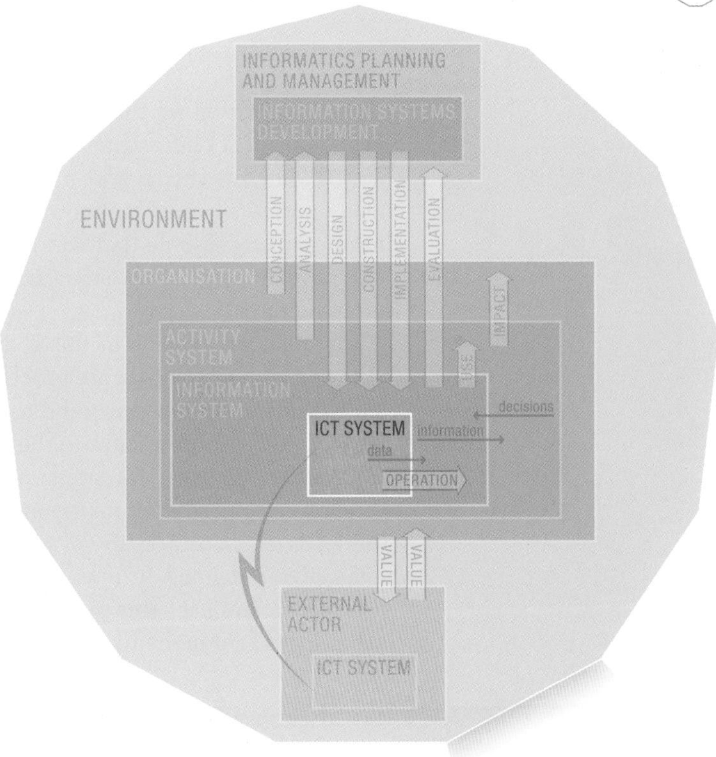

All programmers are playwrights and all computers are lousy actors.

Anonymous

You never know till you try to reach them how accessible men are; but you must approach each man by the right door.

Henry Ward Beecher (1813–1877)

LEARNING OUTCOMES	PRINCIPLES
Define the concept of an ICT system in terms of both technological components and interacting functional layers.	An ICT system may be defined in one of two ways: as hardware, software, communication and data technology, or as three interdependent functional layers.
Explain the ways in which processing and data are distributed across communication networks, and describe the importance of process and data integration to the ICT infrastructure.	With the rise of data communication networks, functional parts of the ICT system such as interface, business rules and data tend to be distributed. However, an effective ICT infrastructure depends upon the integration of processing and data.
Distinguish between various types of web application in the interface layer of an ICT system.	Web standards dominate contemporary approaches to the interface layer. Most corporations have websites, intranets and extranets.
Explain the idea of update functions, business rules and transactions and their relevance to the business tier.	Much of the logic of the ICT system is situated in the business layer, which consists of interrelated update functions, business rules and transactions.
Explain the importance of database systems to the data management layer, and describe related technologies.	The data management layer relies on database systems technologies. A database system consists of a database and associated database management system, both of which are defined by a data model.
Identify the place of data security in the ICT infrastructure, and explain some of the major ways in which it is achieved in ICT systems and communication networks.	As more business moves online, the issue of data security assumes increasing significance. Security technologies and approaches need to protect both stored data and transmitted data.

CHAPTER OUTLINE

Introduction

Chapter 5 focused on the communication aspects of the information and communication technology (ICT) infrastructure, particularly the architecture of the Internet and the (World Wide) Web. The media and much popular literature sometimes imply that these two elements are all we need to know to understand the modern business relevance of ICT. For instance, many assume that web developers are *the* ICT professionals. This is a big mistake. Web development forms only a small – albeit important – part of a modern business's ICT infrastructure.

The organising theme of this chapter is the central position data plays in ICT. It focuses on the ways in which data are processed and stored. It reviews the concept of an ICT system and considers the modern trend to distribute both processing and data storage around the network. This brings us back to the distinction between front-end ICT systems and back-end ICT systems. Websites, intranets and extranets are critical front-end concerns. Databases, data warehousing and content management are critical aspects of the back-end ICT infrastructure. This leads to a consideration of securing data that is stored and communicated.

Chapter 4 defined ICT as any technology used to support data gathering, processing, distribution and use. This makes it possible to define an ICT system in one of two ways: as technological components (what it consists of) or as functionality (what it does).

The technology of an ICT system

Modern ICT consists of hardware, software, data management technology and data communication technology. Hardware comprises the physical (hard) aspects of ICT: processors, input devices such as keyboards and output devices such as monitors. Software comprises the non-physical (soft) aspects of ICT. It is essentially programs: sets of instructions for controlling computer hardware, which come in various forms such as operating systems, programming languages and office productivity packages. Data management technology consists of hardware artefacts for storing data on peripheral devices such as hard disks, managed by software technologies such as database management systems. The data are manipulated by programs and transmitted via data communication technology. Communication technology is the interconnective tissue of ICT, and includes such components as cabling, transmitters and routers used to build communication networks between computing devices, as well as software that codes communication protocols (see Chapter 5).

Communication technology was considered in Chapter 5. Data management technology is considered later in the chapter, as part of the coverage of back-end ICT systems. This section concentrates on hardware and software.

Hardware

A modern computer can be considered as a system with five main subsystems: input, processing, storage, output and communications (see Figure 6.1).

Input subsystem: The part of a computer system concerned with the input of data.

Input to a computer is achieved through a variety of **input devices**, which make up the INPUT SUBSYSTEM of the computer system. Different input devices are designed to capture different types of data: character-based data, sound, images, graphics and movement.

Character-based input devices include keyboards and point of sale (POS) devices. Image-based input devices include digital cameras and scanners. Sound-based input devices include microphones and voice-recognition devices. Movement-based input devices include computer mice, touch sensitive screens and joysticks. Finally, graphics-based input devices include graphics tablets.

The processing subsystem is known as the **central processing unit** (**CPU**), and is the workhorse of a computing system. It can be subdivided (see Figure 6.2) into a control unit, logic unit, primary storage unit, registers and communication buses.

The **control unit** directs and coordinates the rest of the system in carrying out program instructions. The **logic unit** calculates and compares data, based on instructions from the control unit. The **primary storage unit** holds data for processing, instructions for processing and processed data waiting to be output. **Registers** are high-speed storage areas used to hold small units of program instructions and data temporarily, immediately before, after and during execution of the processing unit. These components communicate via physical connections known as **buses**.

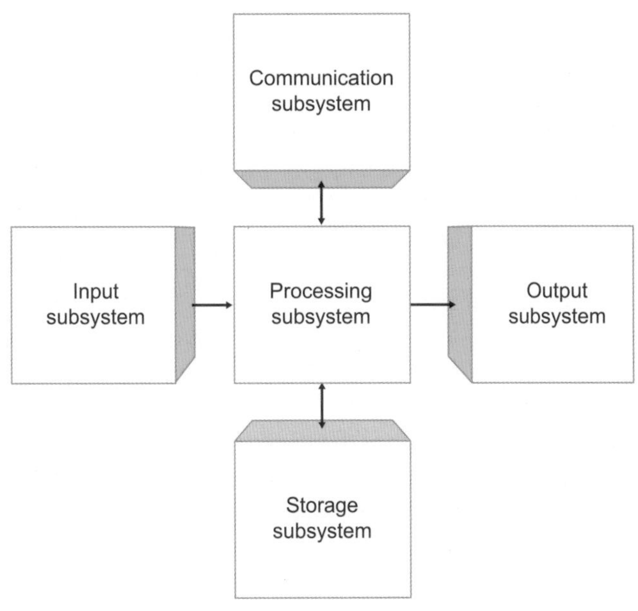

Figure 6.1: *Subsystems of a computer system*

Computers are controlled by programs, which consist of sequences of instructions. A computer operates by taking each instruction in turn and executing it. So there are two phases, an instruction phase and an execution phase. In the **instruction phase** the computer's control unit fetches the instruction from memory. Then the instruction is decoded to enable the central processor to understand what is to be done. In the **execution phase** the logic unit does what it is instructed to do, making either an arithmetic computation or a logical comparison. The results of the execution are then stored in the registers or in memory. A combination of the instruction and execution phases is called a **machine cycle**.

Storage subsystem: The part of a computer system concerned with the persistent representation of data.

Data store: A repository of data.

Primary storage: Storage of data in media that can be directly acted upon by the central processing unit (CPU) of the computer, such as main memory or cache memory. Primary storage usually provides fast access to relatively low volumes of data.

Secondary storage: Storage of data that cannot be processed directly by the CPU. It provides slower access than primary storage but can handle much larger volumes of data. Two of the most popular forms of secondary storage are magnetic disk and magnetic tape.

Output subsystem: The part of a computer system that outputs data to the user or to another device.

The STORAGE SUBSYSTEM is a repository for data used by the processing subsystem. DATA are stored there for both short-term and long-term use. Data for short-term use are stored in primary storage, and those for long-term use in secondary storage.

PRIMARY STORAGE includes media that can be directly acted upon by the CPU, such as main memory or cache memory. Primary storage usually provides fast access to relatively low volumes of data. Main memory is referred to as volatile memory because the data are lost when the power supply is switched off.

SECONDARY STORAGE cannot be processed directly by the CPU, so it provides slower access than primary storage, but it can handle much larger volumes of data. It is referred to as non-volatile storage because it persists after power loss.

Among the hardware devices for secondary storage are magnetic tape, magnetic disks and optical disks. Magnetic tape is similar to that used in audio cassettes. Magnetic disks include both' hard' and 'floppy' disk drives, so named because the magnetic media were originally made of hard and soft materials respectively. Optical disks include compact disk read only memory (CD-ROM) disks and DVDs (digital versatile disks).

A variety of **output devices** make up the OUTPUT SUBSYSTEM, depending on the type of data to be output. They include sound-based devices such as speakers, movement-based devices such as robotic devices or other forms of moving machinery, and character-based, image-based and graphics-based devices such as monitors and printers.

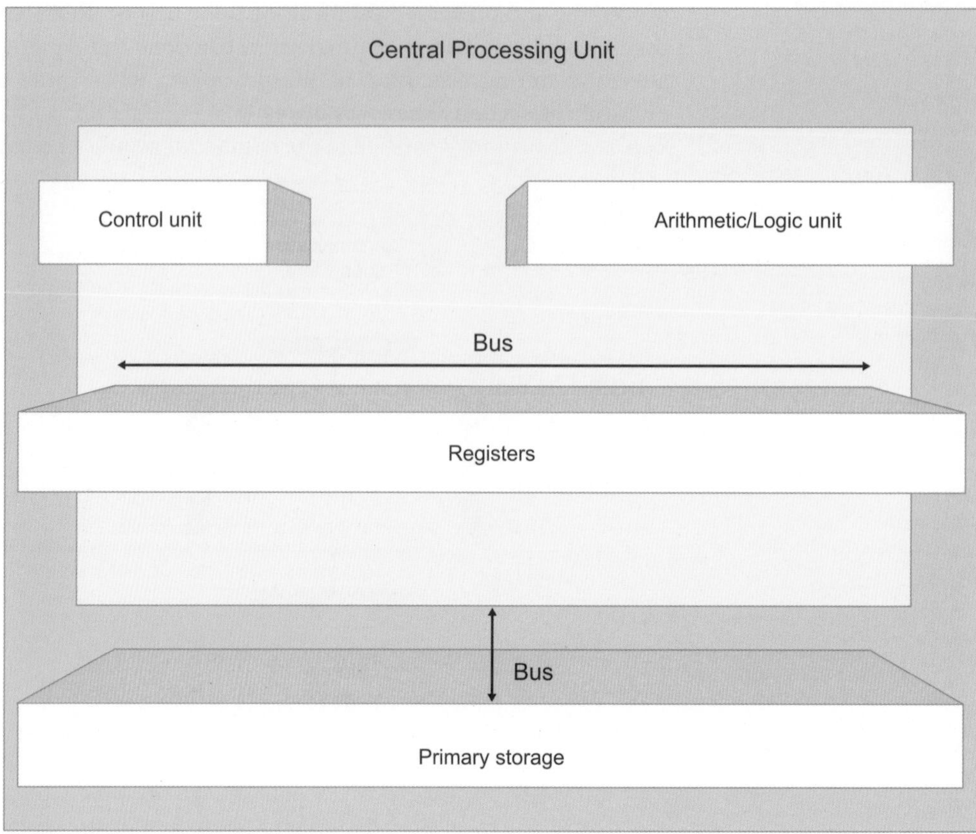

Figure 6.2: *Components of the CPU*

Did you know?

Douglas Englebart called his input device a mouse 'because the tail came out the end'.

Software

Application software: Software designed for a particular set of tasks in an organisation.

System software: The collection of programs that coordinate the activities of hardware and all programs running on a computer system.

Operating system: A piece of system software concerned with the management of all other applications on a computer system.

Software is a generic term for **computer programs**: that is, a series of instructions for hardware. They transform the universal machine embodied in computer hardware into a machine specialised for some task. Programs are written using a formal language. Suites of programs designed for specialised tasks form the software architecture of an ICT system.

There are three major types of software in ICT systems:

- APPLICATION SOFTWARE, discussed below.
- SYSTEM SOFTWARE manages the computer system's resources. It includes operating systems, programming language compilers and utility programs such as virus protection software. An OPERATING SYSTEM is a complex program that controls the execution of other programs. It also manages the use of other resources such as data storage. It can run several tasks simultaneously taking into account the priorities assigned to each task, service many different users working online at the same time and prevent interference between them, and interface to communication software enabling the computer to connect with other computers and computing devices such as peripherals. It also maintains file systems for the storage of data and programs, ensures the consistency of access to file systems and controls access to data and programs.
- COMMUNICATION SOFTWARE, enables intercommunication between different computing devices in a network.

Communication software: Software enabling the interconnection of computer systems.

Did you know?

It is estimated that the Windows XP operating system has 40 million lines of code. Versions of Linux such as Red Hat Linux are estimated to comprise around 30 million lines of code.

A software application, or **application system,** is another term for an ICT system. It is a system, normally written using a programming language or tool-set (see Chapter 12), designed to perform a particular set of tasks.

Application software is software designed to perform a particular business function, and can be categorised according to the number of people who use it.

Reflect
In what way is software information?

- **Personal productivity software** such as word-processing packages is designed for individual use.
- **Workgroup software** (sometimes known as **groupware**) such as electronic mail systems is designed to be used by groups of users working together.
- **Enterprise software** is designed to be used across all of, or a major part of, an organisation. Classic accounting systems are examples. Enterprise resource planning software (see below) is an integrated suite of enterprise software.

There is also a distinction between software that has been produced for the mass market, known as **shrink-wrapped software**, and software that has been produced specifically for an organisation, or **bespoke software**. Falling between these two poles is **packaged software**: software written to handle a generic organisational function such as sales order processing, but capable of being tailored to an organisation's specific needs.

Businesses are understandably interested in how software is distributed and priced. There are a number of different models. **Direct purchase software** is packaged and sold as a unit with a fixed price. This form of pricing is normally used for shrink-wrapped software. **Leased software** is paid for as it is used. The software remains the property of the producer but is hired for use. This is normally appropriate for enterprise software with a substantial cost. In APPLICATION SERVICE PROVISION (**ASP**), a software service is provided as an application. The application service provider runs the application for the customer. This is normally used for standard software services such as payroll. Finally, some software is available free from suppliers: this is known as **shareware**. Programmers develop this software out of interest, and usually distribute it via the Internet. The open source software movement (see Chapter 12) is a pressure group challenging cost models of software distribution in this manner.

Application service provider: A company supplying a software service as an application.

Case check:
Case 29 W
Linux

The classic example of direct purchase models is the range of shrink-wrapped software supplied by Microsoft, such as its Office suite. The classic example of shareware is the operating system Linux, which relies on a worldwide consortium of dedicated and enthusiastic developers for its development and maintenance.

Linux is a computer operating system, which is based on a popular operating system created in the 1960s known as UNIX. Linux is one of the most prominent examples of open source software and its development. The term **open source** is typically used to describe software in which the underlying source code can be freely modified, used and redistributed by anyone.

Functionality of an ICT system

It is useful to consider an ICT system as being made up of a number of subsystems or functional layers (see Figure 6.3):

- The INTERFACE SUBSYSTEM is responsible for managing interaction with users, and is generally referred to as the user interface, or sometimes the human–computer interface (see Chapter 9).
- The RULES SUBSYSTEM manages the logic associated with an application, using a defined set of update functions and business rules (see below).
- A TRANSACTION SUBSYSTEM acts as the link between the data subsystem and the rules and interface subsystems. Querying, insertion and update activity is triggered at the interface, validated by the rules subsystem and packaged as units (transactions) that will initiate actions (responses or changes) in the data subsystem.
- A DATA SUBSYSTEM is responsible for managing the underlying data needed by the ICT system.

Interface subsystem: The part of an ICT system concerned with managing the user interface.

Data subsystem: That part of an ICT system concerned with managing the data needed by an application.

Rules subsystem: The part of an ICT system concerned with application logic.

Transaction subsystem: The part of an ICT system concerned with communicating between the interface and rules subsystem and the data subsystem.

Take the example of an ICT system for storing details of research publications in a university. One part of the interface will be a data entry form to enter details of a publication. One of the rules or constraints used to validate data might be that the date entered must be less than or equal to that of today's date. A key transaction will involve insertion of new publication data into the system. Part of the data management layer will have data structures for the storage of publication data.

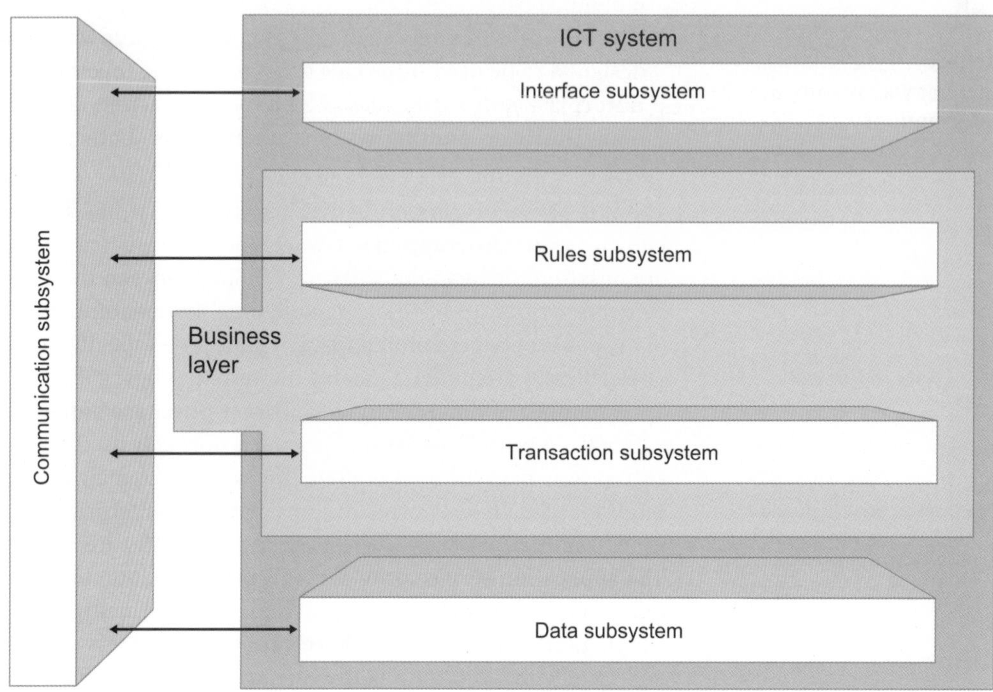

Figure 6.3: *Layers of an ICT system*

Distribution of processing

Communication subsystem: That part of an ICT system enabling distribution of the processing around a network.

Client–server: An applications architecture in which the processing is distributed between machines acting as clients and machines acting as servers.

In a contemporary ICT infrastructure each of these parts of an application might be on a different machine, perhaps at a different site. This means that the parts need to be stitched together via a communication backbone. For consistency, in this book it is called the COMMUNICATION SUBSYSTEM.

Figure 6.4 is divided vertically into client computers and server computers. Clients request services from server computers. The figure illustrates a number of different distribution patterns for processing or functionality amongst ICT systems.

Time-sharing

In the first phase of the development of ICT systems, all the component layers were on one machine. Large mainframe systems would run an application's data management, transaction management, rules management and much of its interface management functions. Users connected to them via 'dumb' terminals, so called because they contained very little functionality and primarily enabled operators to control systems via command-based interfaces (see Chapter 9). Most of the processing on this type of system was conducted in batch mode, which consisted of carrying out vast amounts of transactions in sequence with very little direct user input. Specialist staff carried out data entry, and the output was usually in the form of paper reports.

Fat clients

Over time, more and more functionality has been placed on client machines. Technological developments enabled the user interface layer and some of the rules management layer to be located on 'intelligent' terminals, so called because they were able to take some of the processing off the centralised mainframe or minicomputer. This advance enabled the development of online systems, which enabled users to enter data directly into the ICT system, and to some extent to query the data in the system. The rise of online systems enabled the development of management information system (MIS) and decision support system (DSS) applications (see Chapter 4).

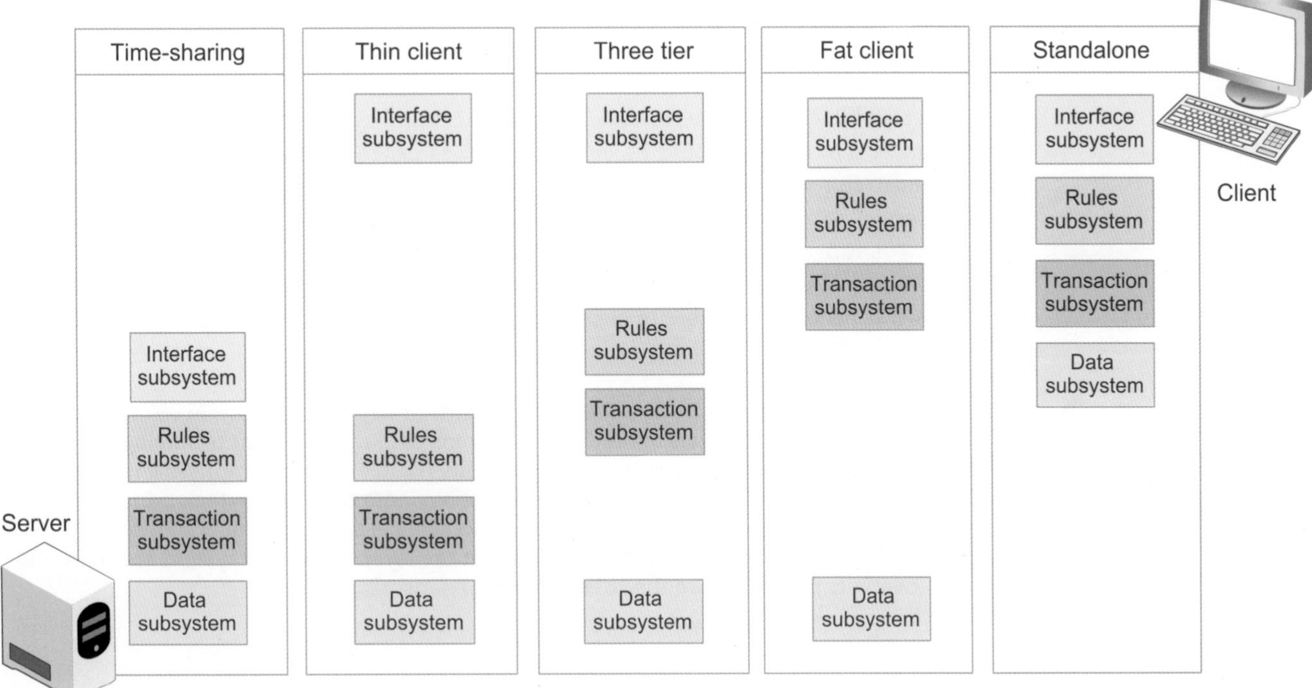

Figure 6.4: *Distributing functionality across the network*

Personal computer: A computer used on the desktop and normally devoted to individual computing use. Also used as a remote access device.

With the rise of PERSONAL COMPUTERS much more of the functionality of the ICT system began to be placed on desktop machines. The growing sophistication of graphical user interfaces (see Chapter 9) meant that more power needed to be available on the desktop to run them effectively. With the rise of software for the personal computer, slices from the total functionality of an ICT system could be built using application development tools available for the desktop.

Three tier

Three-tier architecture: A client–server architecture divided into three layers: interface, business and data.

Many current applications run on THREE-TIER CLIENT–SERVER ARCHITECTURES, which correspond closely to the layered model of an ICT system described above. The first tier runs the user-interface layer, the second tier runs the application logic (business rules and transaction management) and the third layer runs data management functions. In a web-based approach the client runs a browser, and the middle tier is a web server that interacts with a database server. Modern systems may extend this three-tier architecture to an *n*-tier architecture, in which more than three layers are involved. For instance, there could be a separation of business rules, web server and transaction management.

Reflect
Reflect on the degree to which many mobile access devices such as personal digital assistants could be considered as thin clients.

Thin clients

Some people have suggested that Internet technology could lead to a change from 'fat' clients to 'thin' clients. The corporate PC is currently a fat client. It requests information from a server and then processes and presents it at the client end using its own software. The thin client in its extreme form stores only a minimum of software (usually a web browser). Applications are resident on and accessed from the server. This means that each user has a desktop system that looks like a PC but has no secondary storage.

Advantages of an n-tier architecture

To summarise, a contemporary organisation's typical ICT infrastructure is built as a three-tier or *n*-tier client–server architecture with either thin or fat clients. The three tiers typically consist of the client or interface layer, the business or application layer and the data layer.

There are a number of advantages to constructing ICT systems in separate but interdependent layers:

- It makes for easier maintenance (see Chapter 12). Changes can be made to presentational issues separate from business rules, and changes to business rules can be made separately from data.
- *N*-tier architectures make for easier management and administration of ICT systems. For instance, thin clients should be considerably less expensive than PCs. Also, the network administrator will only need to buy and maintain one copy of each software application on the server. So an *n*-tier architecture in principle can reduce the costs of operating an ICT infrastructure and contribute to reducing the total cost of ownership (see Chapter 11).
- Separation of critical aspects of functionality permits easier integration of systems (see below). It becomes possible to share data structures and business rules across a range of separate systems.

Recap 

ICT systems can be defined using either key elements or key functionality. In terms of key elements, modern ICT consists of hardware, software, data management technology and data communication technology. In terms of functionality, an ICT system comprises a number of interacting subsystems: an interface subsystem, business rules subsystem, transaction subsystem and data management subsystem. Processing is likely to be distributed using an *n*-tier client–server architecture, which separates out the layers of the ICT system and distributes them at various points around the communication network.

The interface tier

Chapter 5 described how electronic delivery of goods and services demands effective ICT systems that interface directly with key stakeholders. Most contemporary business ICT systems have been designed so their **user interface** is accessed through a web browser and access channels are over a local area network or a wide area network. This is the client or interface layer. Front-end ICT is likely to consist of a series of web servers, providing electronic services to customers, suppliers, managers and employees. This is the business tier. Operational data is made available in response to requests from the business layer, and is typically stored in large corporate databases. This is the data tier.

Let's take a high-street bank which provides online banking services. The client end comprises the web browser run on the customer's PC or some other access device. The client requests access to a web server run by the bank, and interacts with a number of data entry screens whose dialogue is particularly concerned with authenticating him or her. The web server interacts with a series of large banking databases storing data about customers and accounts. The mediating business or application layer is likely to consist of business rules, such as 'customers should not be able to go overdrawn above their limit'. It will also contain update functions with embedded transaction types such as 'check an entered customer identifier against the identifier recorded in the customer database' and 'update an account balance by crediting or debiting an account'.

Internet and web technologies are therefore being used to produce standard interfaces to ICT systems in organisations. Interfaces and communication channels will vary with the type of stakeholder and access devices used. Customers are likely to access services through an Internet-enabled device which directs them to a general website on the Internet. Internal stakeholders such as employees and managers are likely to access ICT systems through a form of corporate INTRANET run on the organisation's local area network. External stakeholders such as suppliers and partners are likely to access ICT systems through a form of EXTRANET (see Figure 6.5).

Intranet: The use of Internet technology in a single organisation.

Extranet: Allowing access to aspects of an organisation's intranet to accredited users.

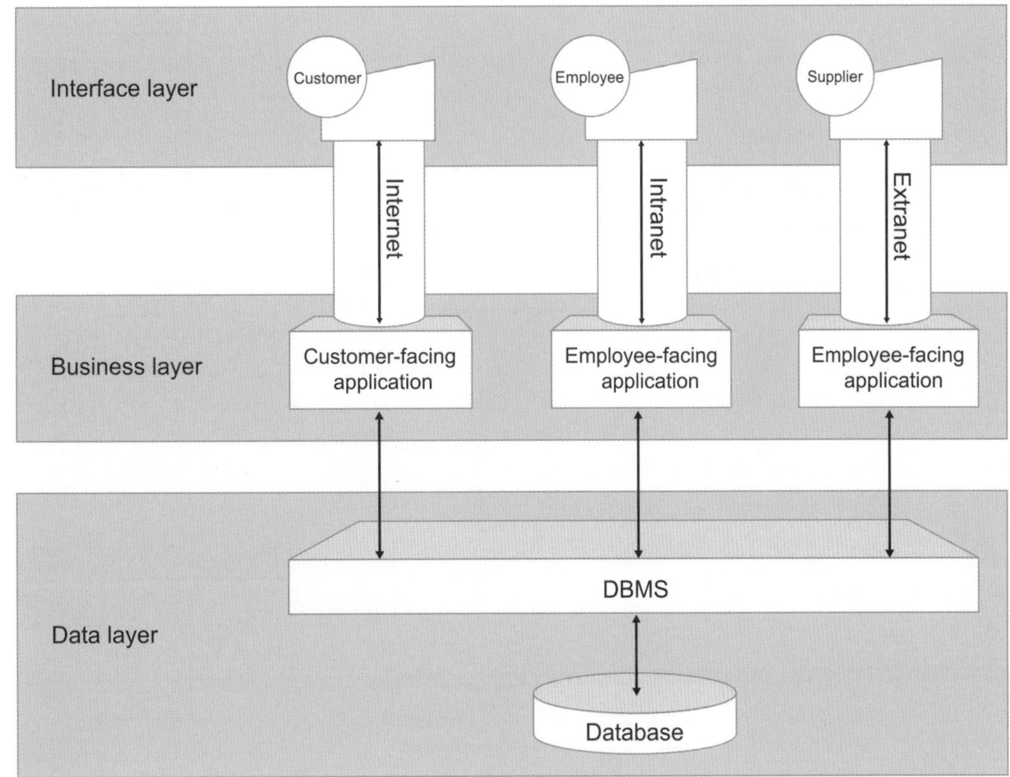

Figure 6.5: *Access via the three-tier architecture*

Websites and web content

Content management: The organisational process that manages the maintenance of Web-based material.

Websites are now regarded as the most important mechanism for presenting content. The term *content* was originally used for what was known as hypertext: networked text implemented through HTML (see Chapter 5). The term then expanded to include a growing range of media incorporated on websites (images, graphics, audio, video); hypertext became hypermedia. However, 'content' really came into its own with the rise of content management and CONTENT MANAGEMENT **systems** (see below), introduced because of problems in maintaining websites. Content is also now used as a term for websites that display dynamic content, refreshed at query time from back-end databases (see below). Over the last few years it has also been used to include traditional media, as the channels of delivery for this media were drawn into the Internet; magazines, television programmes, music, movies and so on are all now accessed through the Web.

Typically, a commercial website is organised hierarchically. The user enters at the home page, which for a commercial site usually establishes the range of products and services available (see Chapter 8). The user can then select a particular product or service by clicking on a hot spot or hyperlink, which navigates to another page (often on the same website). From here they might be able to access further detail or place an order, probably using a series of sub-forms. This hierarchical structure is indicated in Figure 6.6.

Many organisations are investing heavily in increasing the levels of interactivity on their websites. The functionality and 'quality' are assessed in terms of three major forms of content:

- **Publish content** is one-way content. It allows the user to retrieve general information placed on the website or web page.
- **Interactive content** is two-way content. It allows users to both retrieve information and communicate with people or systems in the organisation.
- **Transact content** is also two-way but allows users to transfer data to the organisation or receive personalised data from it.

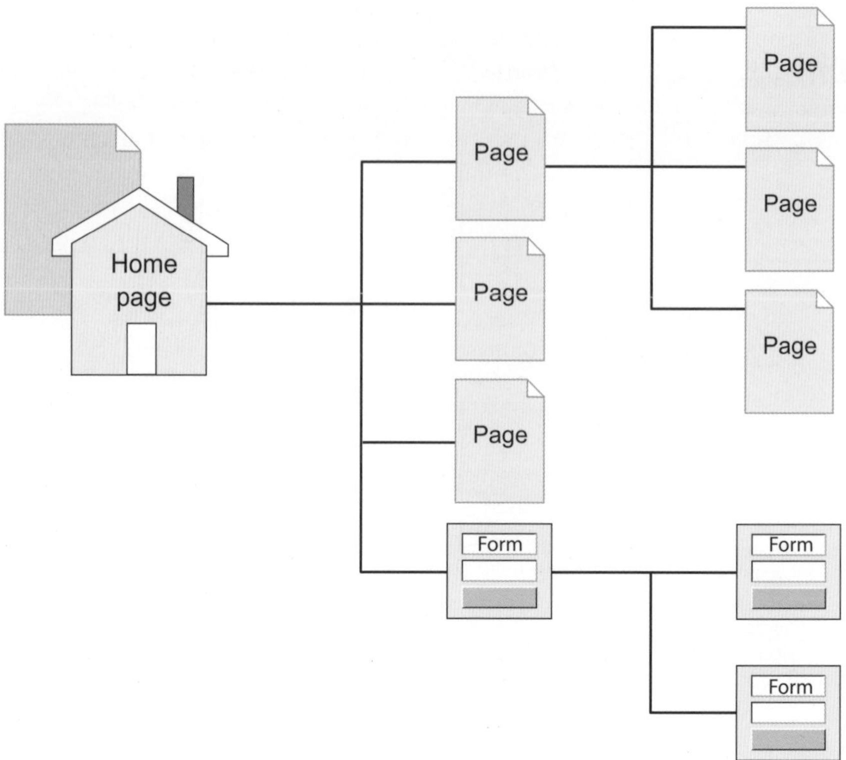

Figure 6.6: *Typical structure of a website*

Suppose a company sells toy soldiers. A *publish* site will provide simple details of the company and perhaps indicate how an order should be made. An *interactive* query site would allow the user to search an online catalogue of toy soldiers for sale. A *transaction* website would allow the user to place and pay for an order online.

Websites that primarily offer information content typically use static web pages, which are produced as standalone HTML documents. If any change is made, a new version of the page has to be posted to the website. In contrast, a dynamic web page consists of both HTML code and calls to back-end ICT systems such as database systems. A certain amount of the content may be retrieved from such back-end systems and displayed to the user.

For both static and dynamic web pages the process of content management and associated content management systems are critical to the effective maintenance of web sites (see below).

Case check: Case 9, IKEA

The website www.IKEA.com was launched in 1997. It includes a number of online planning tools to assist customers in improving their homes. Cost-effective customer support is provided by Anna, an automated customer service chat character driven by artificial intelligence. For example, if a customer finds that a part of the flat-pack they are assembling is missing, Anna will arrange for the part to be sent to them, or for them to collect the part from their local store. It is reported that in 2006, Anna provided support to UK customers generating cost savings of [e]10 million. The 'ask Anna' facility is being extended to the company's websites in other countries.

Intranets

An intranet is a corporate LAN or WAN that uses Internet technology and is secured behind firewalls. The Intranet links various clients, servers, databases and applications. It uses the same technology as the Internet, but is run as a private network: only authorised users from within the organisation are allowed to use it. At its most basic it involves setting up a web service for internal communications and coordination. At its most sophisticated, it involves using web interfaces to core corporate applications that rely on corporate-wide database systems.

Hence, an intranet can be considered as a special type of ICT system, and can be seen as comprising either horizontal or vertical components. Horizontally an intranet is made up of hardware, software, communication technology and data (see Figure 6.7). Computers acting as both clients and servers are required as well as communication 'lines' between them. Web browser software will be required on client machines and web server software on server machines. The role of the web server software includes processing requests from the client browser software and returning documents to clients.

An intranet may also have a domain server. This system translates between the numeric addresses assigned to each machine in the network under TCP/IP (chapter 5) and more meaningful names, so the intranet relies on a corporate communication infrastructure. This may be a LAN, WAN or a combination of both. Hardware and software will be required to run the TCP/IP communication protocol. Data will primarily be held in the form of HTML documents on servers in the network. Some data may be held in database systems accessible from web pages.

Vertically, we can consider an Intranet as a series of typical applications (see Chapter 5). Most intranets use both email servers and email software to enable users to communicate. They also use Internet technology such as browsers, HTML and TCP/IP to produce and disseminate information. They might also make available facilities such as mail lists, chat, FTP and online fora.

Firewall: A collection of hardware and software placed between an organisation's internal network and an external network such as the Internet.

Typically an intranet is connected to the wider Internet through a FIREWALL, which consists of hardware and software placed between the internal network and external networks. The firewall is programmed to intercept each message packet passing between the external and internal networks, examine its properties and reject any unauthorised messages, so it constrains the types of information that can be passed into and out from the organisation.

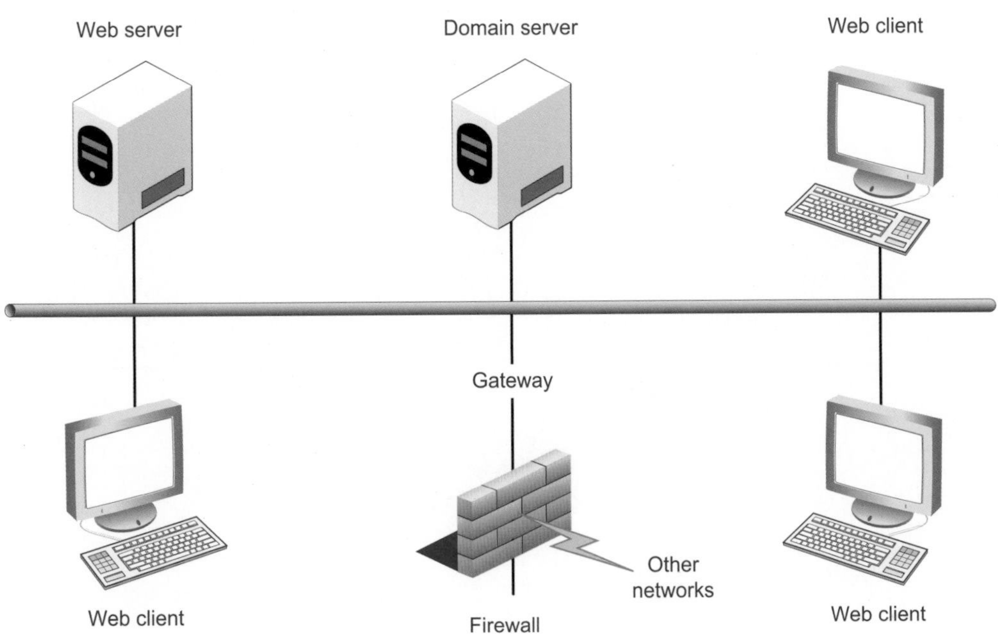

Figure 6.7: *Horizontal components of an intranet*

Extranets

Whereas an intranet is only accessible to the members of an organisation, an extranet provides a certain level of access to outsiders. An extranet is an extended intranet, and it too uses Internet technology, to connect a series of intranets. It secures its communications by creating 'tunnels' of secured data flows using encryption and authorisation algorithms (see below). The organisation will also use firewalls to protect its internal systems (see Figure 6.8).

The Internet with TUNNELLING TECHNOLOGY is known as a VIRTUAL PRIVATE NETWORK (**VPN**). Data on the extranet are shared with external stakeholders such as suppliers and other partners, so this enables collaboration between stakeholders. Access to it is restricted by agreements.

Recap 

Organisations use various front-end ICT systems to interface with their internal and external stakeholders. These typically involve some form of website accessible via the Internet or on an intranet or extranet. An intranet involves using Internet technology in the context of a single organisation. An extranet is an extended Intranet, that uses Internet technology to connect a series of intranets, providing secure communications.

The business tier

Tunnelling technology: Technology that involves the transmission of data over the Internet using leased lines to the local ISP. With the use of encryption, authentication and other security technologies such an approach can be used to produce a virtual private network (VPN) over a wide area network.

Virtual private network (VPN): A form of network which employs tunnelling technology to secure data transmission over the Internet.

The **business tier** of a typical business ICT application consists of three interrelated elements: update functions, business rules and transactions.

A **transaction** changes a database from one state to another. A new state is brought into being by asserting the facts that become true and/or denying the facts that cease to be true about some universe of discourse. For example, a university might want to enrol the student *Peter Jones* in the module *business information systems.* This is an example of a transaction and an instance of a particular transaction type.

There are four major types of transaction activities associated with a database, sometimes referred to as CRUD:

- **Create** transactions create new data elements within the data structures (see Chapter 2).
- **Retrieval** or **read** transactions access data in the data structures. They are often called query transactions, because they effectively answer user questions.
- **Update** transactions cause changes to values held in particular data items of data elements and data structures.
- **Delete** transactions erase particular data elements in data structures.

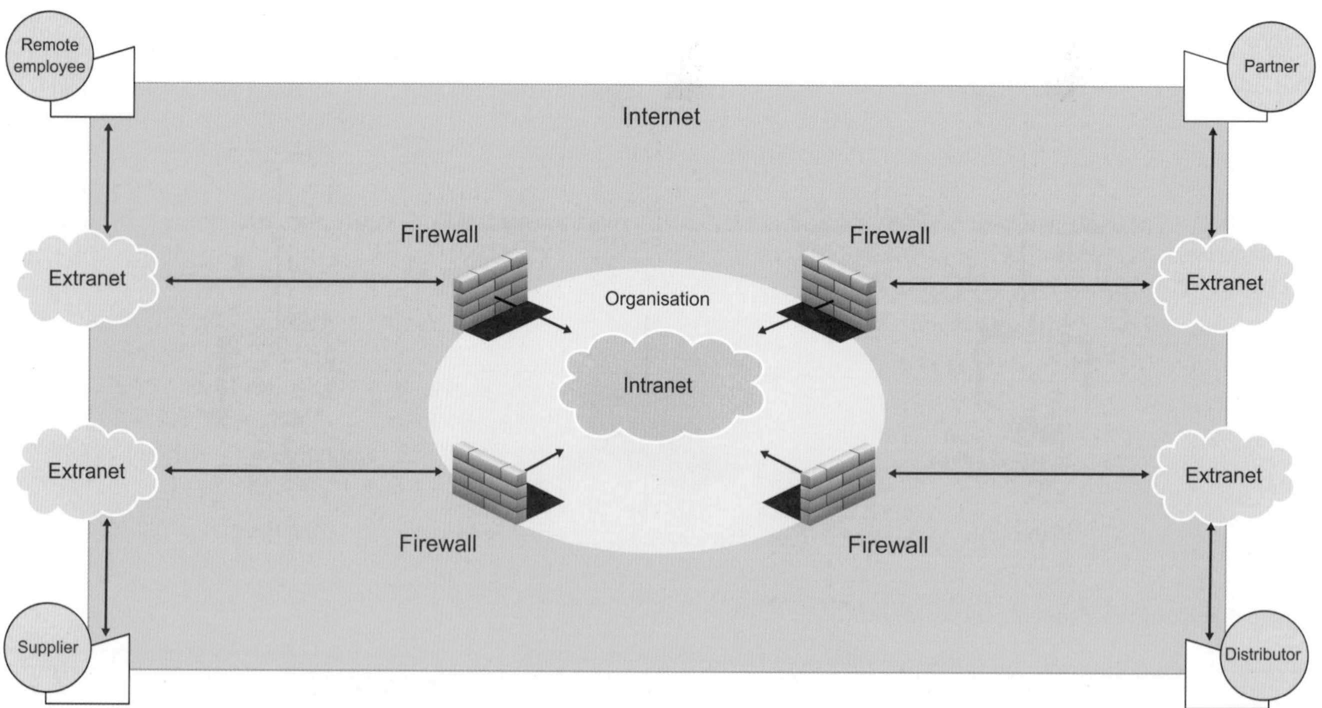

Figure 6.8: *Internet, intranet and extranet*

For example, in a banking application a *create* transaction might be used to enter a new credit or debit record against a particular bank account. A *read* transaction might be used to assemble a statement. An *update* transaction might be used to change a customer's contact details, and a *delete* transaction might be used to remove a standing order or direct debit.

A considerable amount of the functionality of an ICT system is taken up with **business rules**. These are found in both the rules management subsystem and the data management subsystem. They ensure that the data held in the data management layer of the ICT system remains an accurate reflection of its universe of discourse (the business or activity system it represents). In other words, the data should display integrity; it should accurately reflect what is happening in the real world.

In an university, for example, a student records system should provide accurate responses to questions such as, how many students are currently enrolled on a particular module? In online banking, customers should be able to get accurate current balances for their accounts.

Data integrity is ensured through integrity constraints. These are business rules that establish how a database is to remain an accurate reflection of its universe of discourse. There are two major types:

- A **static integrity constraint** is used to check that a transaction will not change a database into an invalid state, so it is a restriction defined on states of the database. For example, it might specify that students can only take currently offered modules. So if Strategic Management was not a currently offered module, it would not be possible to enter the data, John Davies takes Strategic Management.
- A **transition integrity constraint** is a rule that relates given states of a database. A transition is a state transformation, and can therefore be denoted by a pair of states, and a transition constraint is a restriction defined on a transition. An example is, the number of modules taken by a student must not drop to zero during a semester. If a user tried to remove the data that John Davies was taking a module, the system would first check that this would not leave him with no modules registered, and so cause an invalid transition. In banking, an example is that a customer should not be able to go overdrawn beyond an agreed limit, so before debiting an account the application would check that there were sufficient funds in it for this not to happen.

Reflect
Choose an organisation known to you, and reflect on the degree to which knowledge in the domain can be specified as a series of business rules.

Update functions represent individual elements of functionality associated with a particular business application. They encapsulate both business rules and transaction types. They are triggered by events, which are activated from the interface or client management layer, or sometimes from other update functions. The end-result of the activation of a particular update function is that transactions are fired at the data management layer of the ICT system.

An update function usually has a series of conditions associated with it, for example integrity constraints. There will also be a series of actions associated with the update function. These will specify what should happen if the conditions are true, and typically constitute transaction types.

For instance, we might specify an update function appropriate for a university application as:

```
ON Transfer Student X from module 1 to module 2
IF
student X takes module 1 AND
student X does not take module 2 AND
module 2 is offered
THEN
update student X takes module 2
```

Here, X, module 1, and module 2 are *place holders* for *values.* A transaction using this update function might assign the value *John Davies* to X, *Business Information Systems* to module 1 and *eBusiness* to module 2. This would record that student John Davies had transferred from the module Business Information Systems to the module eBusiness: but only if the data indicated that John Davies currently took Business Information Systems, did not currently take eBusiness, and that eBusiness was a currently offered module.

Update functions and business rules in the business layer used to be coded using a programming language as part of the wider application system. Today a business layer is often constructed using a **business rules engine**, which allows the developer to enter and maintain update functions and associated rules separately from interface and data management layers.

The data tier

Since front-end ICT in modern businesses is likely to use Internet and web technologies, the effective integration of front-office and back-office systems is critical to organisational effectiveness. For instance, fully transactional websites require information to be updated dynamically from back-end databases, and the information entered by customers needs to update company database systems effectively. This section focuses on the technology of data management, and gives an overview of how this is achieved. It also considers the related issues of data warehousing and content management.

Database management system: A suite of computer software providing the interface between users and a database or databases.

Data management

Data management in ICT systems used to be part of the file system managed by the operating system. During the 1970s a class of software known as DATABASE MANAGEMENT SYSTEMS (**DBMS**) started to be used for the higher-level management of data. These are software systems for managing databases, and they form the fundamental technology in the data management layer of most contemporary ICT systems. So a database system consists of a database and a DBMS, and both database and DBMS must conform to a given data model (Beynon-Davies, 2004) (see also Chapter 3). This section defines these terms in greater detail.

Database

A database is an organised repository for data. It has several important properties:

- It can be viewed as a model of its activity system.
- The data stored in a database is usually an attempt to represent the properties of objects in an activity system.
- A database is normally accessible by more than one person, perhaps at the same time.
- One major responsibility of database usage is to ensure that the data are integrated. This implies that a database should have no unnecessarily duplicated or redundant data.
- Another responsibility arising as a consequence of shared data is that a database should display integrity. In other words, it should accurately reflect its universe of discourse.
- Besides the integrity constraints discussed above, one of the major ways of ensuring the integrity of a database is by restricting access; in other words, securing the database. This is done mostly by defining in detail who can access and/or change all or part of it.

Let's take a database held by an insurance company. The data structures in the database reflect information classes of interest to the company's activities: in this case, for instance, insurance policies, policyholders and claims. Staff will need to access it to, for instance, create new policies and handle claims. This data must be consistent and accurate: a policyholder's record should accurately represent that person's dealings with the company. One way of ensuring that data has integrity is by restricting access to data to particular types of users. So for example, only employees in the claims department should be able to create and update a claim record.

DBMS

A DBMS is an organised set of facilities for accessing and maintaining one or more databases. It is a shell which surrounds a database and through which all interactions with it take place. Most DBMSs handle four main groups of interactions:

- **Structural maintenance** consists of adding new data structures to the database, removing data structures from it and modifying the format of existing data structures.
- **Transaction processing** typically involves inserting new data into existing data structures, updating data in them and deleting data from them.
- **Information retrieval** involves extracting data from existing data structures and presenting it for use by end-users and application systems.

- **Database administration** consists of creating and monitoring users of the database, restricting access to data structures and monitoring the performance of databases.

Data models

Chapter 3 used the term **data model** to refer to a model of the data required for a domain. The term is also used to denote the architecture for a particular database and DBMS, in that it describes the general structure of how data are organised, stored and accessed. A data model in this sense has three components: data definition, data manipulation and data integrity.

Data definition describes the way in which data can be represented in terms of the data structures, data elements and data items relevant to the data model. **Data manipulation** comprises a set of data operators for the insertion of data, the removal of data, the retrieval of data and the amendment of data in data structures: the CRUD operations as discussed above. **Data integrity** consists of a set of integrity constraints or rules that must form part of the database. Integrity is enforced in a database through the application of these integrity constraints.

One of the most popular forms of data model used in contemporary data management is the relational data model. Let us consider what data definition, data manipulation and data integrity mean within this particular data model.

Data definition consists of one and only one data structure in a relational database: the table. Each table is made up of a number of data elements called rows, and each row is made of a number of data items known as columns. The table in Figure 6.9 uses an university example again. It consists of four data items (Module name, Level, Course code and Staff no.) and five data elements corresponding to five rows in the table, one for each module.

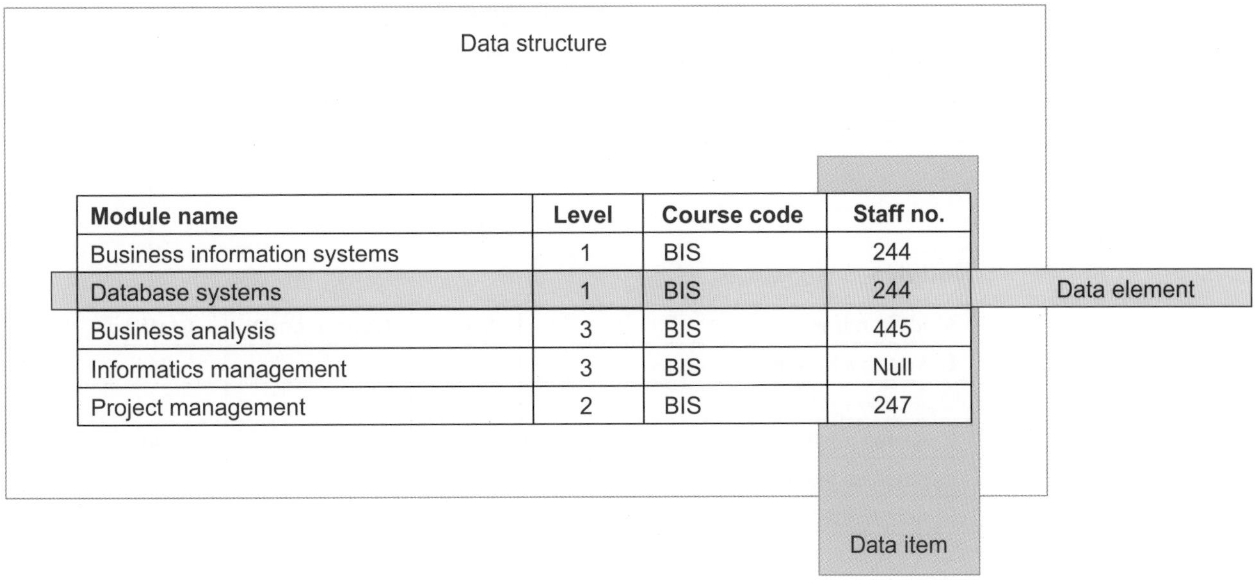

Module name	Level	Course code	Staff no.
Business information systems	1	BIS	244
Database systems	1	BIS	244
Business analysis	3	BIS	445
Informatics management	3	BIS	Null
Project management	2	BIS	247

Figure 6.9: *Tables as data structures*

Data integrity in the relational data model corresponds to three types of integrity rule: entity integrity, referential integrity and domain integrity.

Entity integrity establishes that each row in a table is identified by values in one or more columns of the table, called the table's primary key. The values of a primary key must be unique and not null. In other words, there must be a value for each element of the primary key, and each value must be unique in terms of other values of the primary key. For instance, in the *Modules* table the *Module name* data item is the only item having both these properties. It is therefore the most suitable candidate for a primary key for this table.

Referential integrity establishes that values in columns may also act as links to data contained in other tables. Such columns are called foreign keys. A value for a foreign key must either be the value of a primary key elsewhere in the database or be null. Suppose we add a *Lecturers* table to our relational database with the structure in Figure 6.10. The *Staff no.* column in the *Modules* table is now a foreign key to the primary key in the *Lecturers* table. This means that each value in the *Staff no.* column within *Modules* refers to a value which exists in the primary key column of the *Lecturers* table. If we were to enter a null value as a foreign key value for a staff number in *Modules* we would be indicating that no lecturer is assigned currently for this particular module, as is the case with Informatics management.

Domain integrity ensures that values entered into data items or columns are of the right type or from the same domain. Domains are therefore pools of values from which actual values appearing in the columns of a table are drawn. The idea of a domain in the relational data model is therefore similar to the concept of a data type defined in chapter 3.

Data manipulation involves functions for entering new rows into tables, deleting rows from tables and editing data held in the rows of a table. It also concerns ways of retrieving data from tables. Hence, in Figure 6.10 we might insert a new row in the modules table such as ['Information systems development, 2, 'BIS', 247]. We might also amend the Informatics management record by replacing the null value for the foreign key with the value 445, to indicate that Professor Evans has been assigned to teach this module.

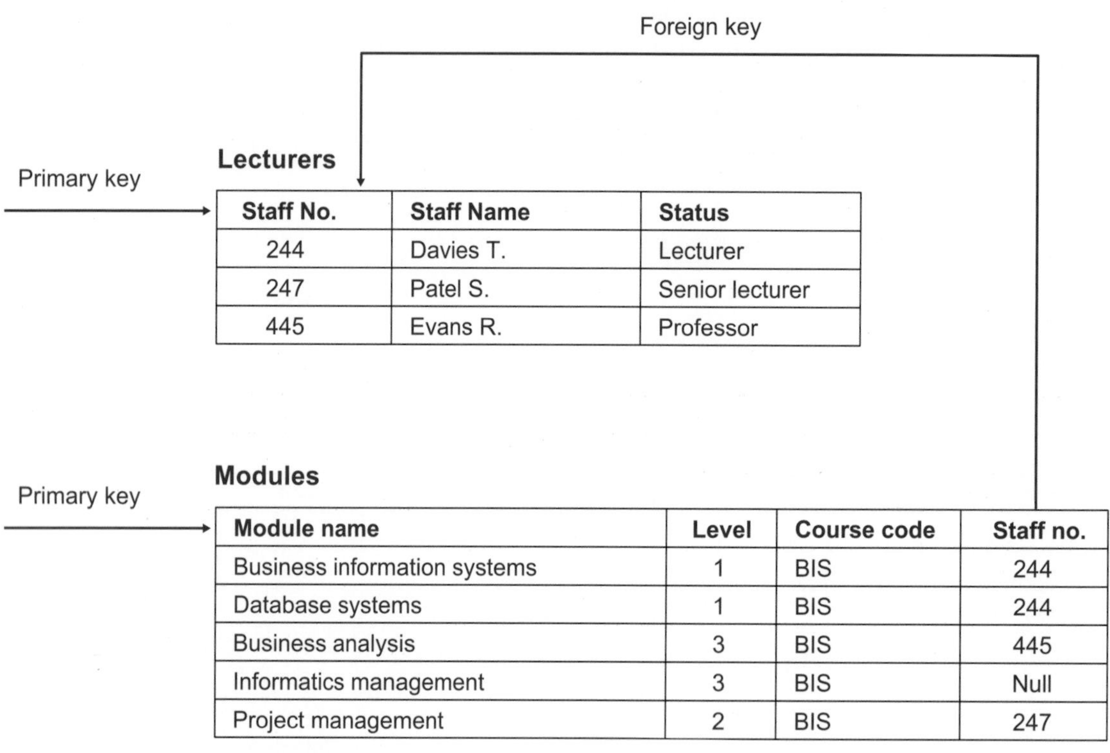

Staff No.	Staff Name	Status
244	Davies T.	Lecturer
247	Patel S.	Senior lecturer
445	Evans R.	Professor

Module name	Level	Course code	Staff no.
Business information systems	1	BIS	244
Database systems	1	BIS	244
Business analysis	3	BIS	445
Informatics management	3	BIS	Null
Project management	2	BIS	247

Figure 6.10: *A simple relational database*

Did you know?

The theory underlying relational databases was invented way back in the 1970s by Ted Codd.

SQL

SQL: Structured query language. A database sub-language. A standard for performing data manipulation, data retrieval and data control work with relational DBMS.

SQL is a database programming language standard which is used in most DBMS that follow the relational data model. As such, SQL contains commands for data definition, data manipulation and data integrity. It also contains some commands for administering or controlling data (see Chapter 11).

For example, the *Modules* table would be declared in SQL using the following statement:

```
CREATE TABLE Modules
    (moduleName CHARACTER(15),
     level SMALLINT,
     courseCode CHARACTER(3),
     staffNo INTEGER)
```

Note how each data item or column is given a data type (see Chapter 3), and in some instances is given a maximum length. This restricts the type of data entered and acts as part of the definition of a domain.

To define primary and foreign keys on this table we add appropriate clauses to the table definition, like this:

```
CREATE TABLE Modules
    (moduleName CHARACTER(15),
    level SMALLINT,
    courseCode CHARACTER(3),
    staffNo NUMBER(5) NOT NULL,
    PRIMARY KEY (moduleName)
    FOREIGN KEY (staffNo REFERENCES Lecturers))
```

To insert a new row into the modules table we would use an INSERT INTO command such as:

```
INSERT INTO Modules VALUES ('Information systems development', 2, 'BIS', 247)
```

To retrieve all the rows in the modules table we would use the command:

```
SELECT * FROM Modules
```

where the asterisk stands for 'all data items (columns) and all data elements (rows)' from the table.

Case check: Case 14, MySQL

First released in 1995, MySQL is a multi-user relational DBMS which has more than 11 million installations worldwide. This applications software is considered one of the most prominent examples of open source software. MySQL is popular for supporting Web applications and acts as the DBMS component of the LAMP stack for application development (see Chapter 12). The DBMS has been used to as part of the ICT infrastructure of organisations such as Wikipedia.

Distribution of data

Fragmentation: A measure of the degree to which data and processing are fragmented amongst information systems.

As well as distributing processing the modern ICT infrastructure involves the distribution of data. For large-scale applications this typically means distributed database systems. A distributed database system is a database system which is FRAGMENTED or replicated on the various nodes of a communication network in an organisation. A **data fragment** is a subset of the original database. A **data replicate** is a copy of the whole or part of the original database. Figure 6.11 illustrates the idea of a distributed database system. Here, four sites are connected by a communication network. Sites 1, 2 and 4 each run a database. Each database at these sites stores fragments and/or replicates from the global distributed database system. Site 3 stores no data but accesses the data stored at one or more of the other sites over the communication network.

A distributed database system is normally a representation of a single business information model (see Chapter 3). For example, one information model might reflect the practice of human resource management in an organisation. It could be set up as a distributed system so that the Edinburgh office maintains Scottish, the Cardiff office Welsh, and the London office English personnel data. However, the data at all three regions would be brought together periodically to provide a UK picture.

PART 2

Data warehousing, OLAP and data mining

Data warehouse: A type of contemporary database system designed to fulfil decision-support needs. It uses large amounts of data from diverse sources to fulfil multidimensional queries.

Data mining: The process of extracting previously unknown data from large databases and using it to make organisational decisions.

Decision-support database: Databases used to support organisational decision making.

Conventional database applications have been designed to handle high transaction throughput, and because of this are frequently called **online transaction processing** (**OLTP**) applications. The data available in them is important for running day-to-day operations, and is manipulated in the core transaction-processing information systems, such as those described in Chapter 4. The data are also likely to be managed by a relational DBMS as described above.

Contemporary organisations also need access to historical, summary data and to access data from other sources than the DBMS. This is where a DATA WAREHOUSE enters the picture. It requires extensions to conventional database technology, and a range of application tools for **online analytical processing** (**OLAP**) and DATA MINING. Together these two technologies are critical in support of modern MIS, DSS and EIS. Collectively with database systems, they are important to an area known as **business intelligence**.

A data warehouse is a type of contemporary database system designed to fulfil decision-support needs, and forms a major part of contemporary MIS and DSS (see Chapter 4). It differs from a conventional DECISION-SUPPORT DATABASE in a number of ways:

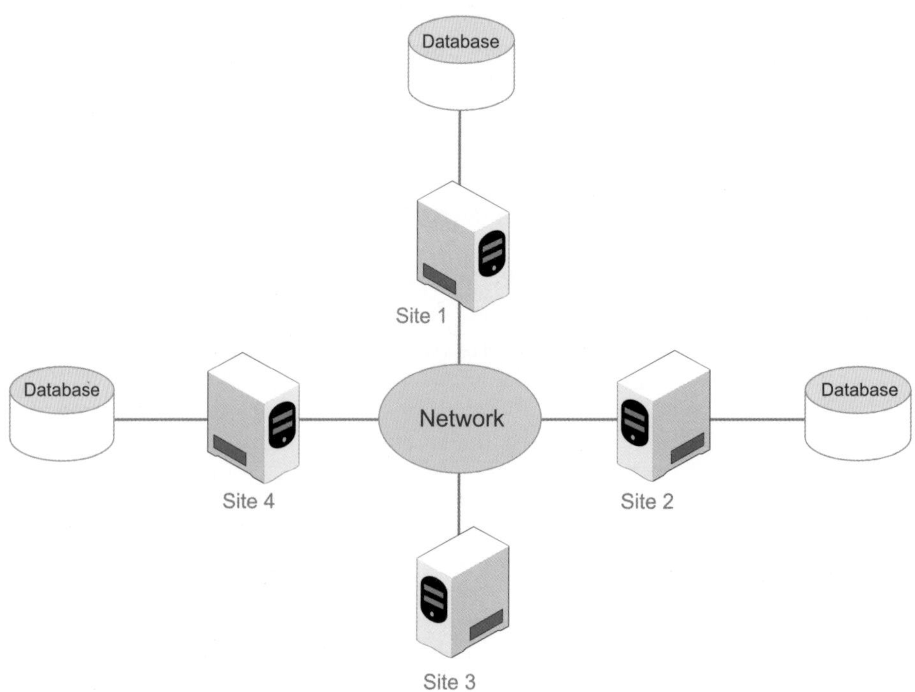

Figure 6.11: *An example of a distributed database system*

- It is likely to hold far more data than a decision-support database.
- The data stored are likely to have been extracted from a diverse range of application systems, only some of which may be database systems. These systems are described as data sources.
- It is designed to fulfil a number of distinct ways (dimensions) in which users may wish to retrieve data. This is sometimes referred to as the need to facilitate ad hoc query.

Did you know? Current estimates of brain capacity range from 1 to 1000 terabytes.

Modern database applications such as market analysis and financial forecasting require access to large databases for the support of queries which can rapidly produce aggregate data. These applications are frequently called analytical OLAP.

OLAP technology supports complex analytical operations such as consolidation, drilling down and pivoting. For instance, in a university, consolidation could mean that modules data

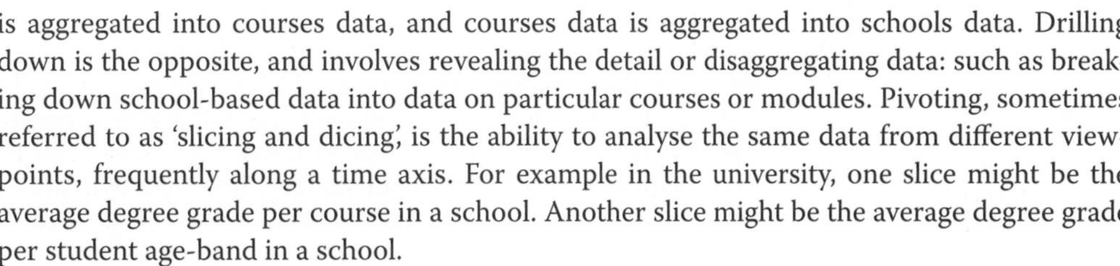

is aggregated into courses data, and courses data is aggregated into schools data. Drilling down is the opposite, and involves revealing the detail or disaggregating data: such as breaking down school-based data into data on particular courses or modules. Pivoting, sometimes referred to as 'slicing and dicing', is the ability to analyse the same data from different viewpoints, frequently along a time axis. For example in the university, one slice might be the average degree grade per course in a school. Another slice might be the average degree grade per student age-band in a school.

Reflect
What level of management is likely to get most value from the use of data warehousing, OLAP and data mining?

Data mining is the process of extracting previously unknown data from large databases and using it to make organisational decisions. It is concerned with the discovery of hidden, unexpected patterns within data, and usually works on the large volumes of data held in a data warehouse. As the size of a data warehouse grows, it becomes more difficult to find patterns using the conventional means of query and analysis. Also, large volumes are frequently needed to produce reliable conclusions. Data mining is useful in making strategic organisational decisions. For instance, in retail chains it has been used to identify the purchasing patterns of customers, and associate these with demographic characteristics such as their age and class profile. This is useful for deciding what products to sell in which stores and when. In the insurance industry data mining has been used to analyse the claims made against insurance policies, and feed into actuarial decisions such as the pricing of policies.

Content management

The face of the modern organisation is presented through its websites, so it is very important for their content to be well managed. **Content management** is the organisational process for the maintenance of web-based material. Two dimensions are critical to establishing the case for content management: the volatility of content and its visibility.

Let's take a website designed for the electronic delivery of services and products. It is likely to be highly volatile: its content will be updated continually, and will include products, prices and promotions. B2C sites like this are also highly visible, since their prime purpose is to attract and keep customers.

Now consider a website that is part of an extranet, designed for use by subcontractors. Its information is likely to be less volatile, as the content will be less subject to change. The content will be updated less frequently, and is likely to be less visible than a customer site.

The more volatile and visible the website, the more important it is to establish a content management process to ensure the content is accurate, relevant and timely. A content management process includes these activities:

- A team of content producers including technical staff and representatives of business units create the initial content and decide on its presentation.
- The proposed content is reviewed by stakeholders such as the web manager, marketing manager and legal department, to ensure that it complies with company standards and does not infringe any laws.
- The content is tested on a site which is not-live. Ideally, no content should be released until it has been thoroughly tested.
- The approved and tested content is published to a live site. This should only occur after full review and testing, and the release might be planned to coincide with other organisational activities.
- Timescales are established for the content management process. They will vary depending on the type of content.

Reflect
Reflect on the damage inaccurate content on a company website can have for the business.

A range of ICT tools are now available to support the content management process. These are often integrated to form a complete content management system. For example, tools such as Dreamweaver enable content and its presentation to be produced and updated rapidly. Workflow tools such as Lotus Notes automate to some extent the flow of producing, distributing and checking content. These tools help to establish a clear audit trail for the authorisation of content. Many volatile and visible websites are now also integrated with back-end database systems. When product descriptions and pricing are updated in the database, this is automatically reflected on the website.

Recap

The business tier of a typical business ICT application consists of three interrelated elements: update functions, business rules and transactions. Update functions are elements of functionality associated with a particular business application, and consist of business rules and transaction types. They are triggered by events which are typically initiated at the interface, and activate a set of business rules. Once these business rules have operated, transactions are fired at the data management layer of the ICT system. Back-end ICT systems include the core systems in the business, and tend to be located around databases storing important corporate data. Contemporary data management involves databases, DBMS and data warehouses.

Integration

We can look at the integration and distribution of ICT systems both vertically and horizontally. Vertically (as described above) this means cooperative and distributed processing. Horizontally, the aim of many ICT strategies is to integrate ICT systems across the organisation. This is generally focused around issues of integrated and distributed data.

We can see how important this is by thinking about piecemeal ICT systems. When organisations first began to use computers they adopted a piecemeal approach to information systems development (see Chapter 12). One manual system at a time was analysed, redesigned and transferred onto the computer, with little thought to its position in the organisation as a whole. This was largely unavoidable because of the difficulties in using a new and more powerful organisational tool.

However a set of a self-contained ICT systems, each with its own program suite, files and inputs and outputs, does not represent the way in which organisations work, which normally involves complex interacting and interdependent activity and information systems. When systems have been built up piecemeal, it is often necessary to use non-automated forms of communication to interface between them. For instance, one system might produce a report which has to be transcribed to make it suitable for another system. These 'workarounds' proliferate inputs and outputs, and create delays.

Information obtained from a series of separate files is also less valuable to personnel because it does not provide a complete picture of activity. For example, a sales manager reviewing outstanding sales orders might not get all the information they need from the sales system, but have to manually add in information about stock from the inventory management system.

Inconsistency: A measure of the degree to which data is held or processed differently across information systems.

This also leads to data duplication: for example, the human resources department and the payroll section might both maintain the same types of data about employees. This creates unnecessary maintenance overheads and increases the risk of INCONSISTENCY.

Although this is what happened historically, rather than the way in which new systems are designed today, many 'legacy' ICT systems, designed some time ago but still in essential use, suffer from these problems. It is also common for these systems not to have been explicitly documented (see Chapter 4). This makes them difficult to maintain (see Chapter 12).

In contrast, an integrated ICT system is designed as a whole, to avoid duplication and incompatibilities. Take for example a chain of supermarkets, such as Tesco. In each supermarket there are checkouts operating electronic point of sale (EPOS) equipment, which allows checkout staff to record sales by scanning barcodes, and transmits details of each sale electronically to a database.

The sales data automatically update data on shelf levels, which are compared against periodic stock checks by staff, and the system generates a report prompting staff to replenish the shelves from the supermarket's storage. The same thing happens with the storeroom: when stock falls to a fixed level, purchase orders are generated and sent electronically to the central supplies division. Data on sales, shelf and stock levels are also used by management to decide on marketing strategies: which goods to promote, how to site products on shelves and so on. In this example at least three effective uses are being made of the same integrated collection of data: the collection of customer transaction data, the management of stock and the marketing of goods.

Database/website integration

As mentioned above, many web pages are static: they just consist of HTML and associated graphics. Whenever a change is needed, the page has to be manually amended and republished to the website, a process that can be time-consuming and error-prone, so core technologies have been developed which enable application developers to link the data on web pages to the data held in corporate databases. There are three main ways in which database systems interact with web-based services (Beynon-Davies, 2004):

- In **static report publishing** the DBMS generates a report in static form (a display only form), or a response to a query in HTML format, and posts this onto the website automatically.
- In **query publishing** a HTML form is generated containing text boxes for users to fill in when making a query. Once the form is submitted it generates request to the DBMS. which returns matching data or an error.
- In **application publishing** the interfaces (both data entry and reports) are all web-based. This is clearly a web-based emulation of the traditional ICT system architecture.

An example of a static report application is a university website that updates the timetable from a core database timetabling system. A query publishing application is an enquiry about the availability of a specific room on campus. These applications need dynamic web pages, where the content is dynamically generated each time the page is accessed.

Enterprise systems

One intended benefit of an explicit informatics infrastructure (see Chapter 4) is a closer fit between an organisation's activities and its information systems. How is this fit measured? Four aspects of the informatics infrastructure can be measured and used to determine elements of fit: the levels of fragmentation, redundancy, inconsistency and interoperability.

Poor fit is evident when data are **fragmented** across information systems. This usually happens because information systems emulate structural divisions within the organisation. and organisational units put up barriers of ownership around key data sets. Fragmentation can also be evident in processing, where separate ICT systems communicate through manual interfaces.

Poor fit is also evident when large amounts of data are unnecessarily **replicated**. This usually happens because there are no interfaces between systems, so the same data is entered many times over. Redundancy also occurs when separate systems perform the same effective processing on data.

Poor fit is evident when the same data is held differently in different systems or processed differently by different systems, leading to **inconsistencies** in the ways in which information is produced, stored and disseminated.

The property of **interoperability** is related to the other three fitness criteria. Generally speaking systems that are fragmented, redundant and inconsistent are likely to suffer from poor levels of interoperability. This refers to the level at which systems communicate and cooperate within the ICT infrastructure.

Situations subject to fragmentation, redundancy and inconsistency creates a series of information 'islands', and these make it difficult to model the organisation's information. Operational managers then find it difficult to plan effectively on a day-to-day basis, and strategic managers find it difficult to plan for the medium and long-term future of the organisation.

The layered model of an ICT system we have discussed can be considered as the vertical integration, interoperability and distribution of ICT systems. This is described as cooperative and distributed processing. Integration, interoperability and distribution can also be considered in a horizontal sense. The aim of many strategies is to integrate ICT systems across the organisation. Generally speaking such integration is focused around issues of integrated and distributed data.

Enterprise resource planning system: A software package consisting of a set of ICT systems which are integrated to form an infrastructure for an organisation.

Traditionally integration has been achieved by effective planning and management of internally built ICT systems. More recently, many organisations have chosen to buy in large suites of ICT systems with in-built integration. This is an ENTERPRISE RESOURCE PLANNING

(**ERP**) package or mega-package (Davenport, 1998). The strategy of buying these systems can be seen as an attempt to buy in a complete ICT infrastructure (Shields, 2001).

An ERP system integrates a number of different organisational functions under one umbrella, and commonly consists of a series of packaged software modules feeding off a central database. Many were developed from manufacturing resource-planning (MRP) systems.

Figure 6.12 illustrates the typical suite available in a mega-package. These systems promise the seamless flow of information through an organisation: financial and accounting information, human resource information, supply-chain information and customer-chain information (Davenport, 2000).

Case check: Case 19, SAP

SAP AG is the largest European software company. Its main product is the SAP ERP package, an integrated suite of ERP software targeted at supporting medium to large-scale organisations in a number of industries and sectors. SAP ERP includes four individual modules that support key back-end functional areas: SAP ERP Financials, SAP ERP Human Capital Management, SAP ERP Operations and SAP ERP Corporate Services.

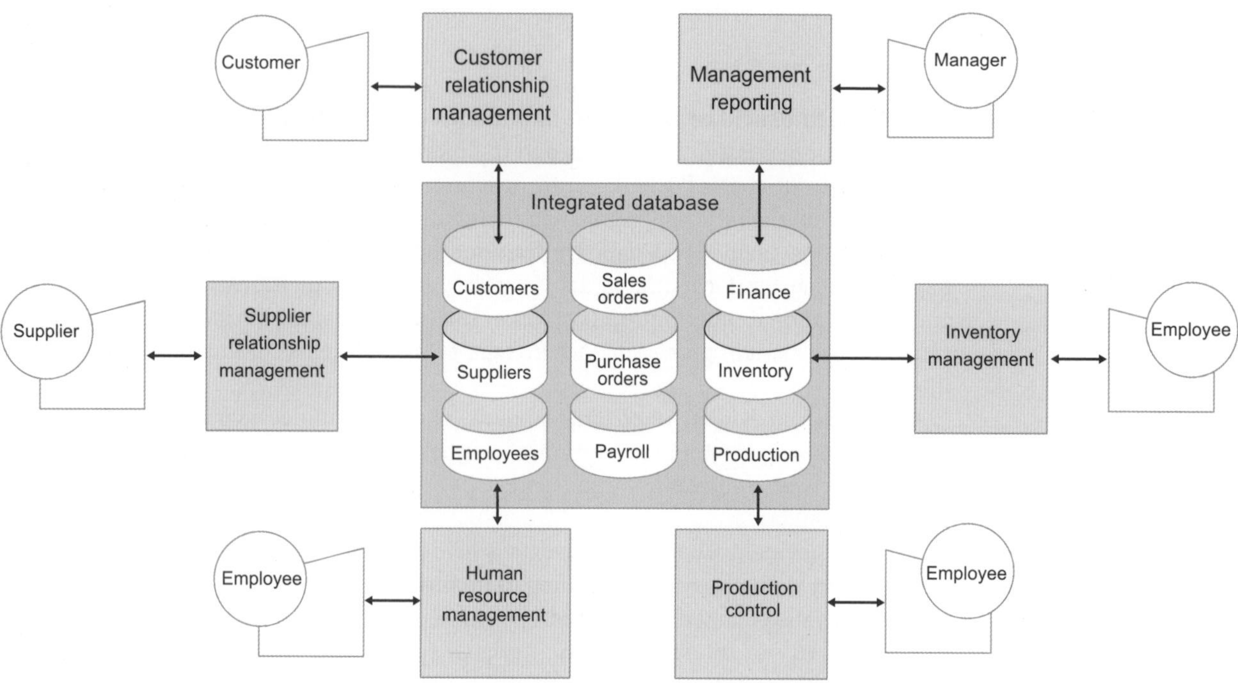

Figure 6.12: *A typical ERP package*

Web services

Web standards are starting to support interoperable systems across computer networks, particularly through the idea of a **service oriented architecture** (**SOA**) and the related idea of a web service. SOA represents a model in which ICT system functionality is decomposed into small, distinct units known as services, which can be distributed over a network and can be combined together and reused to create business applications. These services communicate by passing data from one service to another, or by coordinating an activity between one or more services.

Web services typically implement software functionality that most humans would recognise as a service, such as filling out an online application for a bank account, viewing an online bank statement, or placing an order for an airline ticket online. Instead of web services embedding calls to each other in their source code, protocols are defined which describe how one or more services talk to each other. This architecture then relies on a **business proc-**

ess expert linking services in a process known as orchestration, to meet a new or existing business system requirement.

Each element of a service-oriented architecture can play one or more of three roles: service provider, service broker and service requestor. The **service provider** creates a web service and possibly publishes its interface and access information to a service registry or broker. The **service broker** is responsible for making the web service interface and implementation access information available to any potential service requestor. The **service requestor** or web service client locates entries in the broker registry using various *find* operations, then 'binds' to the service provider in order to invoke one of its web services.

The World Wide Web Consortium (W3C) defines a web service as a:

> software system designed to support interoperable machine-to-machine interaction on a network. It has an interface defined in a machine-processable format (specifically WSDL). Other systems interact with the Web service in a manner prescribed by its description using SOAP messages, typically conveyed using HTTP with an XML serialisation in conjunction with other Web-related standards.

In this jargon, WSDL stands for web service description language. and is effectively a means to define the functionality of a web service in terms of XML grammar (see Chapter 5). SOAP stands for simple object access protocol, and consists of a framework for XML format messages sent between distributed ICT systems.

Cloud computing

Reflect
Some see the rise of the data centre as a return to a centralised model of computing in which a large 'mainframe' provides a computing resource for organisations. Reflect on whether this is an accurate picture of developments.

Recently, the demands of providing distributed processing and distributed data for organisations through the technology of web services have been given the name cloud computing. This derives from the common representation of the Internet on diagrams, such as the ones used in this book, as a cloud.

In this model, computing resources are typically owned and operated by a third-party provider located in one or more data centres. A data centre is a purpose-built facility which runs multiple computing servers, usually with associated infrastructure such as telecommunications, back-up power supply and security, although these are of less interest to consumers than the web applications or data storage it can offer.

This process generates a massive network of 'cloud servers' interconnected as if in a grid. The servers run applications in parallel, and sometimes use a technique known as **data virtualisation** to maximise computing power per server. This involves making multiple physical resources such as STORAGE DEVICES or servers appear as a single virtual resource to the user.

Storage device: A device that persistently represents data.

There are number of advantages of cloud computing. For producers, infrastructure such as data centres can be located in areas with lower property costs, close to water (for cooling purposes) and within easy access of electricity supplies. For consumers, cloud computing has the potential to make applications much more scalable. The application itself in terms of software and data can be separated from physical resources such as hardware. If more computing power is required to handle peak loads, additional cloud servers can be applied to the task on an as-needed basis.

Did you know?

Google is said to operate a global network of approximately 36 data centres needed to run its search engine. Microsoft's data centre in Chicago is reputed to need three electrical substations with a capacity of 198 megawatts to run effectively. The Environmental Protection Agency in the United States estimates that its 7,000 data centres consume 1.5 per cent of the country's electricity consumption.

Source: *Economist*, 24 May 2008.

Data security

Data security: The process and technologies associated with ensuring the security of data.

DATA SECURITY is a critical issue in modern societies and economies because of the increasing use of remote interaction. Among the problems this creates are the need to authenticate users, and the risks of unauthorised access to systems. eCommerce (see Chapter 9) cannot occur without the transfer of transactional data and the storage of data in ICT systems.

Data form the life-blood of much modern business and commerce (Stamper, 1985). There is an increasing level of computer-related crime, and there are an increasing number of measures, many of them technological, that organisations take in response. Data security is becoming a critical issue for most businesses, and involves a vast range of technical and non-technical solutions.

This section considers three major technological dimensions to the issue of data security:

- ensuring effective personal identity management
- securing stored data
- securing transactional data.

Personal identity management consists of three interrelated processes – authentication, identification and enrolment – that serve to connect people, identifiers and identity in the information society. The data in an organisation's ICT systems are a valuable resource and must be protected. We consider both computer-based and non-computer-based ways of achieving this. DATA PRIVACY needs to be maintained too, keeping sensitive data from both internal and external unauthorised users. We also consider some technologies for achieving this.

Data privacy: Ensuring the privacy of personal data.

The dimensions of data security

To provide a secure environment for the conduct of eBusiness and eCommerce three conditions must be satisfied (Schneier, 2000):

- Privacy of data should be ensured. In other words, only authorised people should have access to stored data. In data transmission only the parties to an electronic transaction should have access to the data about it.
- Users of ICT systems need to be authenticated, as do parties to an electronic transaction. In general messages should only be exchanged between parties whose identity has been confirmed in some way.
- Users of an ICT system should not be able to deny that they have used it, and the sender of a message cannot deny that they have sent it. This is known as NON-REPUDIABILITY.

Non-repudiability: A user of an ICT system should not be able to deny that they have used the system for a commercial transaction.

Some of the major components of the technical infrastructure for ensuring data security are illustrated in Figure 6.13.

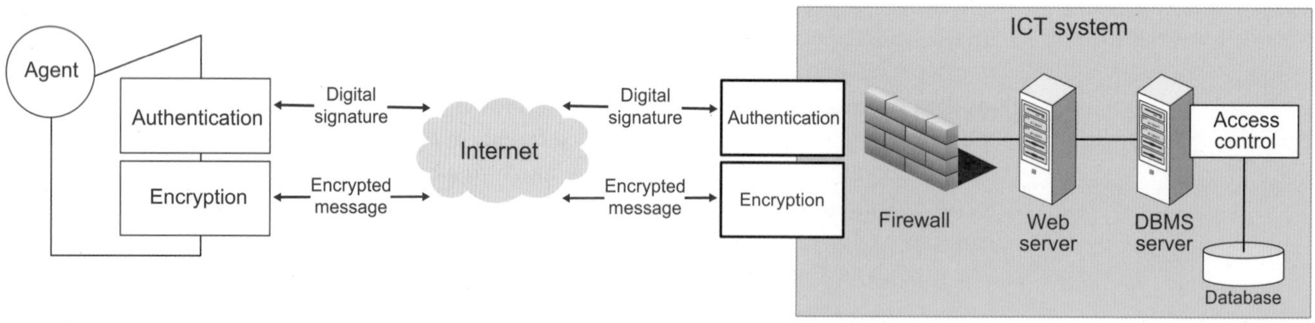

Figure 6.13: *The components of data security*

Let's take someone who wants to move money from one bank account to another. Let's say they use a PC to access their bank's online banking facility. They will be asked to authenticate themselves to the system by entering data such as a username and password, which are checked against an access control list. If the authentication is successful, they are given a secure connection to the bank's web server. Depending on the activity, messages from the access device will then be encrypted and bundled with a form of identification known as a **digital signature**. The message will be sent over the Internet using its inherent communication protocols, decrypted and unbundled at the organisation end, and examined by a firewall.

This validates the message in various ways and only allows access to particular web servers once security rules are satisfied. The personal bank account details are likely to be held in a database managed by a DBMS server.

Personal identity management

The issue of **personal identity management** has assumed importance because of the increasing complexity of the personal identity web we all need in our complex information society. We tend to accumulate a vast array of personal identifiers – user names and other significant data used for identification by various systems – as well as physical identifiers like credit cards, debit cards, a driving licence, passport, library card and so on.

In our context, personal identity management consists of three interrelated processes: authentication, identification and enrolment.

Authentication: The process of identifying an actor to a system.

AUTHENTICATION involves validating the association between an identifier and the person it stands for. The identifier is a symbol or set of symbols (see Chapter 3), and this is used as a check on whether someone is the person they claim to be. For online banking, for example, the identifiers typically consist of a customer number, a password and sometimes a piece of personal knowledge such as your father's first name.

Face to face, we use natural identifiers such as appearance and voice, but we need something else to use for remote interaction: an artificial or surrogate identifier such as a code. There has been much recent interest in biometric identifiers such fingerprints and iris scans: data on these can be captured and sent electronically to strengthen authentication processes.

Some banks now issue card readers to online customers, who have to swipe an identity token such as a debit or credit card to gain access to information.

Identification is the process of using an identifier to connect to a stream of data constituting a person's identity (an **intension**). In other words, personal identifiers are used to assign identities to individuals. For example, public sector employees frequently have to legitimate people as legal residents or taxpayers. In the private sector, financial institutions have to validate people's creditworthiness before offering a loan.

A validated identity serves to enrol the individual in a defined activity system. **Enrolment** in this sense involves answering the question, 'What am I expected to do and to receive?' For example, to be a taxpayer leads to a range of rights, responsibilities and expected actions: the obligation to pay tax and the right to access health care services, for instance.

Securing stored data

Data protection: The activity of ensuring data privacy.

Effective electronic service delivery demands the storage of much personal data, so it is very important to protect this stored data from external threats. This is important for both organisational and personal data.

The threats include:

- **Electronic theft and fraud**: for example, someone falsely updating corporate data with the aim of defrauding their employer, or a hacker making an illegal entry into a database system and extracting corporate data without permission.
- **Loss of confidentiality**: such as an unauthorised person viewing information on confidential corporate policies and disclosing it to outside agencies.
- **Loss of availability**: such as a database system becoming unavailable because of a natural disaster such as fire and flood, or a human-generated disaster such as a bomb attack.
- **Loss of privacy**: when an unauthorised person views data someone wished to be kept private.
- **Loss of integrity**: when data is corrupted, by a software virus or a software or hardware failure.

Any organisation needs to take both computer-based and non-computer-based measures to counter threats such as these.

Computer-based measures include an authorisation strategy for operating systems, ICT systems and database systems. This normally involves system administrators assigning user names and passwords to individuals and groups. As mentioned above, it can also include physical tokens such as a card with an electro-magnetic strip or a smart card with an embedded chip, which is read by a specialised input device, or a biometrics reader.

Non-computer-based measures include establishing a security policy and plan and enforcing it; establishing a policy on access to data (which can involve rethinking people's roles); positioning computer hardware in secure environments through physical access controls; and securing copies of data and software in offsite, fireproof storage (see Chapter 11).

Securing transactions

Encryption: The process of encoding and decoding messages to ensure their security in transmission.

Chapter 5 outlined how the increasing use of electronic data transfer leads to a need for security and privacy, and introduced key technologies which include ENCRYPTION, digital signatures and certificates, firewalls and tunnelling technology.

Encryption and decryption have been carried out for thousands of years (Singh, 2000). Figure 6.14 shows the essential elements. An unencrypted message is normally referred to as a plain text message because of its historical association with the written word. It is first encrypted using a particular algorithm –a method for producing something – and an appropriate key which provides data for the algorithm. At the receiver end the algorithm is applied as a decryption method using another key, and this reveals the plain-text message to the receiver.

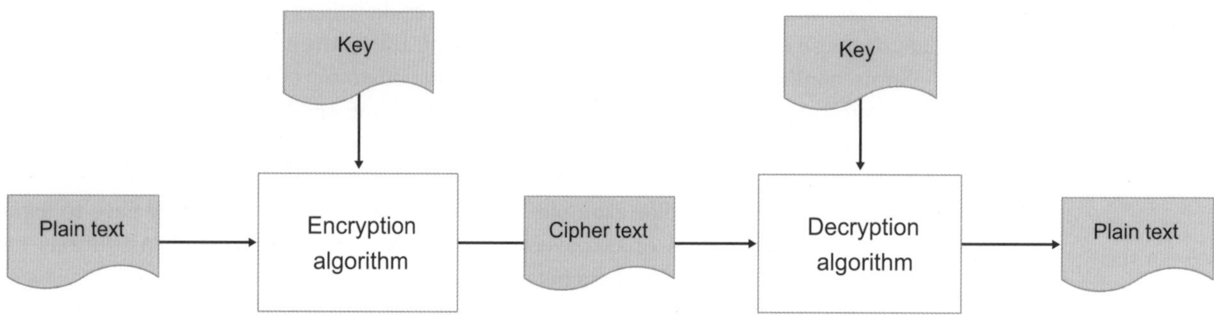

Figure 6.14: *Coding of messages*

A very simple form of encryption consists of taking the letters of the alphabet and replacing each one with a letter from a cipher alphabet. The cipher alphabet is the key. The encryption and decryption algorithms detail the method of substitution. For instance, if this key is used to encrypt 'et tu brute?':

Plain:	a	b	c	d	e	f	g	h	I	j	k	l	m	n	o	p	q	r	s	t	u	v	w	x	y	z
Cipher:	j	l	p	a	w	I	q	b	c	t	r	z	y	d	s	k	e	g	f	x	h	u	o	n	v	m

the coded message would read 'wx xh lghxw?'

Encryption ensures some privacy if only authorised people have access to the key, but a cryptologist can still use logic to decipher this kind of simple encrypted message, so more complex algorithms are used in practice.

Two types of algorithm employed in commercial data transmission are symmetric and asymmetric key encryption.

In **symmetric key encryption**, sometimes known as private key encryption, the same key is applied at both ends of the encryption process. The key is agreed in advance between the sender and receiver. The main problem is that messages can only be transmitted between parties known to each other and trusted to hold the private key.

Asymmetric key encryption, sometimes known as **public key encryption**, uses a pair of keys, one private and one public. A user with a private key can give a corresponding public key to anyone they wish. This then allows the user to send a message encrypted with the private key, safe in the knowledge that only users with the corresponding public key can decrypt it. There is no requirement for the sender to agree the keys in advance of sending a message since the user can place the public key in a register of selected users via encrypted messages.

Public key infrastructure: An infrastructure for ensuring the security of electronic transactions which includes procedures for managing the assignment and storage of digital keys, and ensuring they are used only by legitimate holders.

Digital certificate: Sometimes referred to as digital signature, used to authenticate parties in an eCommerce transaction.

Secure socket layer (SSL): Netscape's attempt to offer a secure channel of communication. It is a framework for transmitting sensitive information such as credit card details over the Internet.

Public key encryption provides the foundation for **digital signatures**. These are important in authenticating the senders of messages and for ensuring a degree of non-repudiability. The sender transmits a message using a private key. If the receiver of the message is able to decrypt the message successfully using the public key, this automatically acts as a way of authenticating the sender.

The management of encryption and digital signatures requires an infrastructure that includes ensuring that keys are used only by legitimate holders, and procedures for managing the assignment and storage of keys. This is referred to as the PUBLIC KEY INFRASTRUCTURE (PKI), and is provided by a trusted certification authority (CA). All legitimate users are required to register with the CA to use public key encryption. The CA issues a DIGITAL CERTIFICATE, sometimes called a digital passport, to users. This consists of an electronic document that keeps a record of users and their public keys.

Public key encryption is also important to securing data transmission over the Internet. SECURE SOCKET LAYER (SSL) is an attempt to offer a secure channel of communication. It is a framework for transmitting sensitive information such as credit card details. It involves using a sophisticated protocol between client and server systems that is transparent to the user and provides a secure connection. It exchanges a digital signature between a client (such as an individual using an Internet-enabled PC) and a server (an organisation's front-end ICT system).

Leading vendors of Internet browsers such as Microsoft use standards for digital certificates to implement SSL. Figure 6.15 illustrates the process of using digital certificates. The customer first has to request a digital certificate from the certification authority. They provide details of themself plus evidence of their identity to the certification authority. They also send their public key to the certification authority (that is, the key provided to them by the organisation they are trying to access). The certification authority produces a digital certificate and includes the public key within it. When the user later wants to engage in eCommerce, they use their digital certificate to prove their authenticity to the participating organisation.

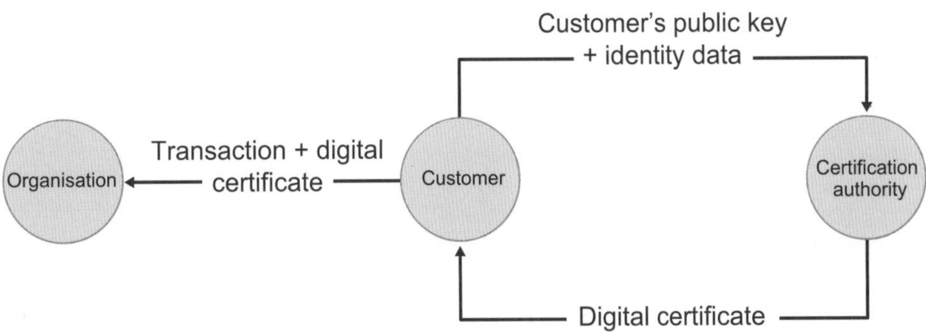

Figure 6.15: *Digital certificates*

A **firewall** is a system that attempts to protect a private network from hackers, software viruses, data corruption or unauthorised access. Effectively it restricts access to the private network by external users, and may also be used to prohibit internal users from accessing selected parts of the private network. For example, it is used to prevent public Internet users from accessing an organisation's private intranet.

Firewalls can be implemented in both or either of hardware and software. They typically comprise a proxy server, which examines all messages entering or leaving the private network, and blocks those that do not match particular security criteria. In a web environment a proxy server sits between a web browser and a web server. It runs routers, other communications software and special programs known as proxies. One proxy is normally assigned for each Internet service such as HTTP and FTP. When data packets from the external environment reach the firewall it checks the packets for details of their source and destination. It then makes a decision to accept or reject the packet depending on an inspection of an access control list and a set of associated security controls.

Tunnelling technology involves the transmission of data over the Internet using leased lines to the local ISP. With the use of encryption, authentication and other security technologies, this can be used to produce a virtual private network (VPN) over a wide area network (see Chapter 5). Data packets are encrypted and encapsulated into IP packets, then transmitted over the Internet using routers. At the receiver end the packet is decrypted and authenticity checks are made. This creates secure data tunnels between an organisation's systems and key external stakeholders such as suppliers and partners. This approach offers an inexpensive way for an organisation to extend the reach of its information systems, and is the key technology underlying extranets.

Case check: Case 21, the UK national ID card

In the United Kingdom, the issue of personal identity management came to the fore in 2002 when the then Home Secretary David Blunkett resurrected the idea of introducing a national identity card, as had been done during the First and Second World Wars. There was consultation for two years on draft legislation to create a national identity management infrastructure for the United Kingdom, consisting of a large central registry of personal identity data, and the issuing of biometric tokens to all UK citizens by 2013.

Summary

1. This chapter has defined at a high-level the important component elements of business ICT systems. Practitioners need this in order to understand the ways in which ICT systems 'encode' organisational practice in technologies such as interfaces, business rule engines and databases.
2. ICT systems can be defined in terms of key elements or key functionality. In terms of key elements, modern ICT consists of hardware, software, data management technology and data communication technology. In terms of functionality, an ICT system can be seen as being made up of a number of interacting subsystems: the interface subsystem, business rules subsystem, transaction subsystem and data management subsystem.
3. Processing in the contemporary ICT infrastructure is likely to be distributed in an *n*-tier client–server architecture. This separates out the layers of the ICT system and distributes them at various points around an organisation's communication network.
4. Various front-end ICT systems interface with internal and external stakeholders. They typically involve a website accessible via the Internet or on an intranet or extranet. An intranet involves using Internet technology in a single organisation. An extranet is an extended intranet which uses Internet technology to connect a series of intranets.
5. The business tier of a typical business ICT application consists of three interrelated elements: update functions, business rules and transactions. Update functions are elements of functionality associated with a particular business application, and consist of business rules and transaction types. They are triggered by events which are typically initiated at the interface and activate a set of business rules. Transactions are then fired at the data management layer.
6. Back-end ICT systems include the core systems in the business, and tend to be located around databases storing important corporate data. Contemporary data management involves databases, DBMS and data warehouses. The integration of back-end ICT infrastructure is now frequently achieved through ERP systems.
7. To provide a secure environment for the conduct of business activity over the Internet three conditions must be satisfied: authentication, privacy and non-repudiability. Security is needed for both stored data and transactions. Key approaches to ensuring the security of stored data include authorisation schemes such as user names and passwords. Key technologies for ensuring privacy and authentication of transactional data include encryption, digital signatures and certificates, firewalls and tunnelling technology.

This chapter concludes our look at the ICT infrastructure of modern business. The next three chapters examine the application of business systems and their impact on the internal operations of the business, and also on relationships and activities with external stakeholders. First we need to consider in more detail the idea of the business as a value-creating system that exists within and adapts to a wider value network.

Focus on Value

The value of an ICT system lies in its role as a producer of data. However, value also arises in the ability of the modern ICT infrastructure to integrate processing and data across the organisation, particularly for multinational and global organisations. Modern technology allows the distribution of processing and data around data communication networks, and the separation of the functionality of the typical ICT system into manageable layers. Organisations tend to rely increasingly on their data resources, and this means an increasing value for technologies that ensure the security of both stored and transmitted data.

Review test

1	Types of input devices include: Select all that apply. ☐ Character-based devices ☐ Image-based devices ☐ Sound-based devices ☐ Access-based devices ☐ Movement-based devices ☐ Graphics-based devices
2	A ____________ is a series of instructions for hardware. Fill in the blank.
3	Match the type of software to the most appropriate definition. System software — Software that is designed to perform particular business function Applications software — Designed to be used across the entire enterprise Enterprise software — Software that manages the computer system's resources
4	Front-end systems are information systems in an organisation which interact with the stakeholder through specified electronic services. True or false? ☐ True ☐ False
5	Back-end ICT systems are information systems in the organisation which interact with front-end ICT systems and provide key data services to them. True or false? ☐ True ☐ False
6	An ICT system can be considered to have five major layers or subsystems. Place in order, with the layer closest to the user first ☐ Rules subsystem ☐ Interface subsystem ☐ Data management subsystem ☐ Transaction subsystem ☐ Communications subsystem
7	Name the two types of integration of ICT systems. Select the most appropriate two. ☐ Data ☐ Transaction ☐ Process ☐ Physical
8	An ____________ is a corporate LAN or WAN that uses Internet technology and is secured behind firewalls. Fill in the blank.
9	Match the type of system to the most appropriate stakeholder type. Internet — Customer Intranet — Supplier Extranet — Employee
10	Internet protocol addresses are mapped to domain names by ____________ servers. Fill in the blank.
11	A database is the same as a DBMS. True or false? ☐ True ☐ False
12	An ____________ constraint is a rule which establishes how a database is to remain an accurate reflection of its universe of discourse. Fill in the blank.
13	Securing data in the ICT infrastructure involves: Select all that apply. ☐ Securing data in ICT systems ☐ Securing transactions ☐ Securing personnel
14	VPN stands for: Select the most appropriate description. ☐ Virtual private network ☐ Virtual positioning network ☐ Virtuous practical network
15	ERP systems integrate a number of different organisational functions under the umbrella of one system. True or false? ☐ True ☐ False

Exercises

1. Find an ICT system, and analyse it in terms of the four-layer model described in this chapter. Is the ICT system distributed in any way? Which model of distribution best approximates its architecture?
2. Consider an organisation's ICT infrastructure. How closely integrated are the systems? How much distributed processing and/or data is present in the infrastructure?
3. Classify a website known to you in terms of whether it solely provides information content, allows querying or enables transactions.
4. Try to find an organisation that maintains both an Internet and intranet website and determine how they differ.
5. Determine whether an organisation known to you uses an intranet. Attempt to determine its functionality.
6. Take one website known to you and attempt to determine whether database integration is used and in what way.

7. If you have made any payments online, determine how sites inform you that they are secure. Determine the confidence you place in the security of such sites.
8. Identify core database systems in an organisation known to you.
9. Determine whether an application known to you uses an n-tier client–server architecture.
10. Determine whether an organisation known to you uses an extranet. Attempt to determine the functionality of the extranet.
11. Determine how privacy is handled in a system known to you.
12. Determine how authentication is handled in a system known to you.
13. Determine the sort of access controls used in an ICT system known to you.
14. Investigate what software is available under the open software movement.
15. Consider an ICT system known to you. Attempt to estimate the volume of data stored in the system.
16. Investigate the range of contemporary DBMS used in a specific organisation.
17. Find an organisation that has adopted a mega-package. Why did the organisation decide to implement the package? What experience have they had of using it for their infrastructure?

Projects

1. Conduct an assessment of the hardware used by a particular organisation in terms of the typical desktop. Develop policy guidelines for a standard hardware profile for the organisation. What advantages arise from an organisation maintaining a standard hardware profile?
2. Conduct an inventory of the software used in an organisation known to you. Categorise the inventory in terms of the distinctions made in this chapter, such as operating systems and office productivity software. Use this inventory to determine the degree of standardisation of software in the organisation. Produce a brief for the organisation, highlighting the importance of standardisation to a successful ICT infrastructure.
3. Thin client technology has been proposed as a solution to managing ICT infrastructure for a number of decades. Define more precisely what thin client technology means for modern organisations, and investigate its penetration.
4. Open source software is now used by major organisations as part of their ICT infrastructure. Determine more precisely what open source actually means for these organisations. What benefits does open source software provide? Infer from this the likely success of the open software movement in the longer term.
5. Most modern information systems projects utilise database technology. Investigate why this is the case and to what purposes such database systems are put. What DBMS are used in association with corporate databases and what facilities do such systems provide?
6. Genetic sequences can now be determined and represented as data. Determine the precise characteristics of such data and the features of databases needed to handle such complex data. How important are applications in bio-informatics such as this to the developing biotech industries?
7. Investigate the prevalence of data warehousing as an organisational technology. To what purposes are data warehouses put? How critical is the effective use of data warehousing to modern management decision making?
8. Gather data on a limited range of ICT systems within a specific organisation. Analyse their functionality in terms of the layered model discussed in this chapter. How easy is it to assign aspects of their functionality to a three-tiered model? Is an *n*-tiered model more appropriate?
9. Build a high-level description of the functionality of a mega-package such as SAP. How much of a core information systems infrastructure as described in Chapter 4 does it provide for organisations? Investigate the penetration of ERP systems such as the one chosen into a particular industrial sector such as manufacturing and retail.
10. ERP systems are frequently introduced into organisations in an attempt to import integration of data and processes. However, many organisations have experienced problems in implementing such large-scale package solutions. Investigate the problems and pitfalls of ERP implementation.

Further reading

No one text covers all the material discussed in this chapter. **Schneiderman and Plaisant** (2004) covers the interface layer. **Graham** (2006) covers the business layer in terms of service-oriented architecture. **Beynon-Davies** (2004) covers the data management layer. **Shanks, Seddon and Wilcox** (2003) covers ERP systems and their implementation.

References

Beynon-Davies, P. (2004) *Database Systems*. Basingstoke, Palgrave.

Davenport, T. H. (1998) ‘Putting the enterprise into the enterprise system’, *Harvard Business Review*, July/Aug: 121–31.

Davenport, T. H. (2000) *Mission Critical: Realising the promise of enterprise systems*. Boston, Mass., Harvard Business School Press.

Graham, I. (2006) *Business Rules Management and Service Oriented Architecture: A pattern language*. London, John Wiley.

Schneiderman, B. and Plaisant, C. (2004) *Designing the User Interface: Strategies for effective human-computer interaction.* New York, Pearson.

Schneier, B. (2000) *Secrets and Lies: Digital security in a networked world.* Chichester, John Wiley.

Shanks, G., Seddon, P. B. and Wilcocks, L. P. (2003) *Second-Wave Enterprise Resource Planning Systems: Implementing for effectiveness.* Cambridge, Cambridge University Press.

Shields, M. G. (2001) *E-business and ERP: Rapid implementation and project planning.* New York, Wiley.

Singh, S. (2000) *The Science of Secrecy.* London, Fourth Estate.

Stamper, R. K. (1985) 'Information: mystical fluid or a subject for scientific enquiry?', *Computer Journal* **28**(3).

PART III APPLYING INFORMATION SYSTEMS TO BUSINESS

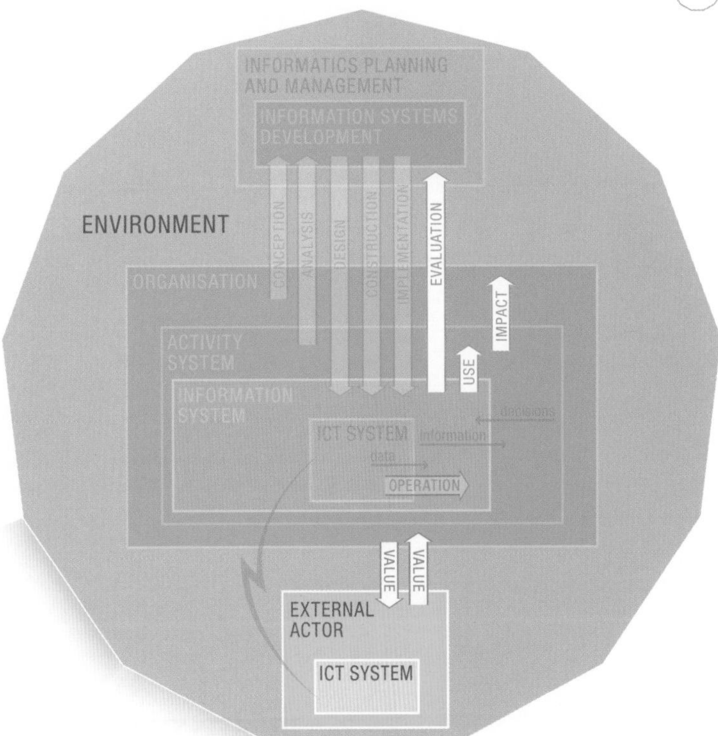

OVERVIEW

The chapters in this part cover the following key areas:

The value-chain and the value network

The place of organisations in the value network

Electronic business

Electronic commerce

The uses of information systems

The impact of information systems on organisations, groups and individuals

Evaluating the success or failure of information systems

Strategies for avoiding information systems failure

What distinguishes the field of information systems or organisational informatics from information technology or computing is its interest in the application of technology. This part of the book examines issues relating to the introduction of information systems into organisations, and the effect this has.

Chapter 7 examines the external environment within which an organisation operates, and considers the organisation as a value-creating system that operates in a wider value network. This makes it possible to define the elements of commerce in some detail, and consider the relationships between flows of value, the control of activity and the place of information.

Chapter 8 considers the rise of electronic business and electronic commerce. The term eBusiness is used to refer to all activity relating to the application of ICT in business, and eCommerce is used to refer to the use of ICT to support and enhance dealings with external stakeholders. Distinctions are made between forms of eBusiness which relate to different areas of the value network defined in Chapter 7.

Chapter 9 addresses directly the question of the value of ICT, which is considered through the related issues of use, impact and evaluation. As ICT impacts on more and more aspects of organisational life, issues of use assume significance not only for internal stakeholders such as managers and employees, but also for external stakeholders such as customers and suppliers. The use of information systems is a necessary precondition for the impact on individuals, groups and the organisation as a whole. Although the impact is usually designed to be positive, it can be negative for some individuals and groups. To assess it effectively it is necessary to evaluate it and determine the degree to which stakeholders regard information systems as successes or failures.

CHAPTER 7

The business environment

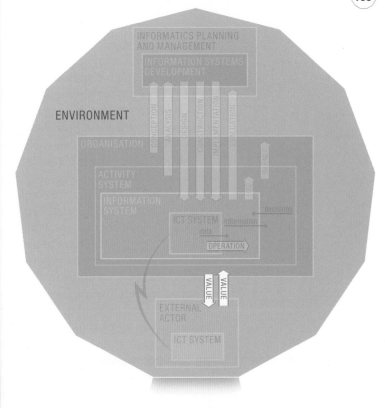

There can be no economy where there is no efficiency.
Benjamin Disraeli (1804–1881)

CHAPTER OUTLINE

LEARNING OUTCOMES	PRINCIPLES
Define the key elements of the economic environment of the organisation and describe organisations as value-creating systems existing within a wider value network.	An organisation as an open system exists within a wider economic environment, which can be considered as a value network. An organisation maintains relationships with various actors in the value network, and flows of value and transactions occur across it.
Distinguish between critical parts of the value network and describe their relationship to forms of commerce.	Porter describes the organisation as an internal value chain. This can be extended to a consideration of the supply chain and the customer chain, and is often also extended today to the community chain.
Identify the key forms of value travelling along the value network and distinguish between the different forms of control evident within it.	Value comes in three forms: goods, services and social capital. The distinction between tangible and intangible goods and services is important for understanding some of the recent changes to the value network. Social capital emerging in communities around the organisation is also important to modern commerce.
Explain the relationship between the concepts of a business model and the value network, and conduct a simple analysis of an organisation's value network.	Business models are useful because they highlight the important relationship between strategy, business processes and enabling technologies. Designing a business model implies analysing the most appropriate application of these three things within a wider value network.

Introduction

For well over a century people have been arguing about which has more effect on children's development : their environment or their genetic inheritance. The notable British geneticist and evolutionary biologist J. B. S. Haldane commented, 'We do not know, in most cases, how far social failure and success are due to heredity, and how far to environment. But environment is the easier of the two to improve.' In a sense the same is true for organisations. Organisational success cannot be guaranteed solely by improving internal operations: their prior history and inherited competitive position have a great influence too. In the long term organisational sustainability definitely relies on effective interaction with the wider environment.

This book takes a primarily process or systems view of the organisation. In this sense, organisations are viewed as a number of interdependent activity systems (Checkland, 1987) or business processes (Hammer, 1996). Information, information systems and information and communication technology (ICT) support activity in these systems. This entire complex system is affected by forces in its environment. Organisations are not isolated entities, they are open systems. The success (that is, both current viability and future sustainability) of any organisation will depend on how well it integrates with aspects of its environment. In other words, we can view an organisation as a system that builds and uses information systems to cope with environmental forces. The form of its information systems will also be shaped by environmental constraints.

This chapter focuses on the wider environment. It first considers it as four major environmental systems: an economic system (economy), political system (polity), societal system (society) and physical system (ecosystem). Because of its critical importance for business organisations we focus particularly on the wider economic environment.

The chapter describes how organisations can be considered as systems creating value that travels within and between organisations. Activity systems provide the supportive mechanisms for customer, supply and internal value chains. It outlines key elements of these value chains, and describes them as conduits within a wider value network for the flow of goods, services and transactions. It also introduces the concept of the community chain as a social network, and discusses how the value it produces (social capital) is increasingly important for business.

The concept of the value network is critical to understanding the place of eBusiness and eCommerce (discussed in Chapter 8) and the forms these contemporary trends take. The material in this chapter is also important for understanding the worth of ICT and information systems (considered in Chapter 9).

The external environment of the organisation

Environment is the general term for anything outside of the organisation with which it interacts (Worthington and Britton, 2005). The environment of most organisations can be seen as four major interdependent systems: an economic system, social system, political system and physical system (Figure 8.1). In this sense, it is made up of a complex network of activities and relationships between the organisation and other agencies.

Each of these systems has an impact on informatics activities, and the organisation's informatics activities in turn are likely to impact on the social, economic, political and even physical spheres.

Economic environment: The markets within which an organisation competes. An economic system is the way in which a group of humans arrange their material provisioning.

An **economic system** is concerned with the way in which groups of humans arrange their material provisioning, and essentially involves the coordination of activities concerned with this. An organisation's ECONOMIC ENVIRONMENT is defined by its activities and relationships with economic actors or agencies. It is particularly concerned with national and international commerce and trade, and is influenced by such factors as levels of taxation, inflation rates and economic growth. Information systems are critical to organisational performance in economic markets. Recently, there has been a lot of growth in the specialised markets focused around the use of electronic networks. Not surprisingly, eBusiness and eCommerce have become significant strategies for modern organisations to improve their performance (see Chapter 8).

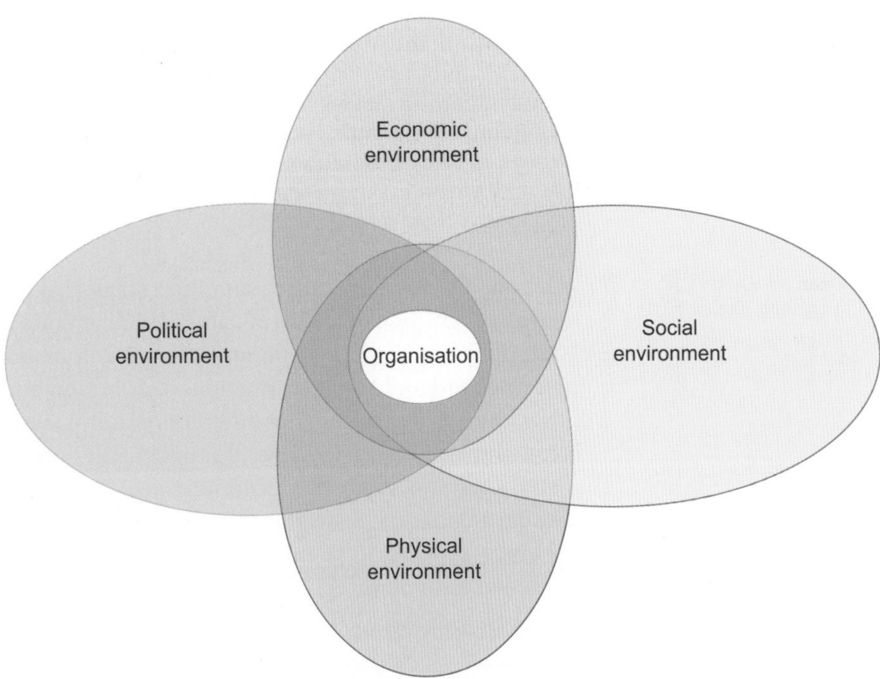

Figure 7.1: *The external environment of organisations*

Social environment: The external environment of the organisation concerned with society.

Political environment: The external environment of the organisation concerned with power and its exercise.

The SOCIAL ENVIRONMENT of an organisation concerns its position in the cultural life of a grouping such as a nation-state. We can think of it as a series of social networks consisting of activities and relationships that serve to bind various social groupings together. This chapter is particularly interested in the ways in which people relate to organisational activity through communities of consumption.

The POLITICAL ENVIRONMENT or system concerns issues of power. Political systems consist of sets of activities and relationships concerned with power and its exercise. This deals especially with government and legal frameworks, which are a major constraining force on organisational behaviour. Among the issues we can consider here, especially for western countries, is the influence of ICT on electronic government and electronic democracy.

The **physical environment** is the ecosphere surrounding organisational activity. In recent years there has been growing concern about organisations' impact on the physical environment, such as the effect of carbon dioxide emissions on the atmosphere and the resultant process of global warming. Businesses are increasingly expected to act to reduce their 'ecological footprint'. Information systems have a part to play here. For instance, ICT makes it possible for many people to work from home, which means they commute to work less often and do not need to use so much energy (for instance, petrol).

The relation of all four environmental systems to informatics is a huge subject, so the rest of this chapter focuses on the system of most interest to business organisations, the economic system. It also covers some aspects of the social environment – social networks, communities and social capital – to establish a basis for some of the discussion of virtual communities in Chapter 8.

Economic systems and actors

An organisation exists within a wider economic system. At the level of the nation-state this is known as an **economy**. It is concerned with the way that groups of people arrange their material provisioning, and essentially involves the coordination of these activities.

Three major processes are relevant to economic systems:

- **production**: the set of activities concerned with the creation of goods and services
- **distribution**: the associated process of collecting, storing and moving goods into the hands of consumers, and providing services for consumers
- **consumption**: the process by which consumers receive and use goods and services.

Case check: Case 12, The movie industry

The trend of putting movies into digital format affects their production, distribution and consumption. For example, movies used to be distributed via cinemas and broadcast television. Now they can be distributed on DVDs, or electronically by downloads from the Internet. Many people now access music, newspapers, television and radio via the Web; movies are rapidly coming to join them as digital content.

Economic actor: An agency that engages in economic exchange.

Production, distribution and consumption are activities that deliver value, so economies can be seen as a multitude of chains of value, which operate both within and between ECONOMIC ACTORS. In other words, economic actors (such as businesses) interrelate and interact in complex networks of value production, distribution and consumption. Any economic actor will take on roles in a number of different chains of value.

For example, take agriculture, the part of the economy that produces basic foodstuffs. Foodstuffs are the value this economic sector produces. This value is added to by food processing companies, distributors and retailers such as supermarket chains.

For our purposes it is useful to see economic systems as being composed of three fundamental elements:

Economic relationship: The relationships of exchange between economic actors.

- Economic activity occurs between economic actors – organisations, groups and/or individuals.
- It occurs within defined systems of RELATIONSHIPS between these economic actors.
- Information is essential to the coordination of activity in economic systems. Economic exchange, for instance, is typically managed by defined transactions between buyers and sellers.

Say, for example, that organisation A buys goods from organisation B. The relationship between organisation A and B is therefore one of trade. Organisations A and B are both economic actors. Along with the flow of goods between them there is a flow of information. Much of this is bundled into defined transactions such as invoices, shipping notes and payments.

Competitor: A key type of organisational stakeholder. Key organisations in the same industrial sector or market that compete with an organisation.

Partner: A key type of organisational stakeholder. Key organisations in the same industrial sector or market that participate in a partnership arrangement with an organisation.

Customer: A key type of organisational stakeholder. Consumers of an organisation's products or services.

So we can consider an organisation's economic environment as defined by activities and relationships between the organisation and a number of major types of economic actor or external stakeholder (see Figure 8.2). COMPETITORS are other organisations in the same fundamental area of business, looking to sell similar products or services to the same consumers. PARTNERS are other organisations that cooperate in the provision of goods and services. **Suppliers** are those organisations providing resources to the organisation. CUSTOMERS are individuals, groups or organisations purchasing products or services from the organisation. **Regulators** are groups or organisations that set policy for appropriate economic activity. They try to constrain the behaviour in economic systems within defined bounds.

Organisations take on different roles at different times: for instance, they are likely to be both buyers and sellers of goods and services. They may compete with other organisations, or perhaps set policy for the supply of particular goods and services from other, perhaps smaller, organisations and hence act as regulators.

For example, let's consider a supermarket chain. Its economic environment can be described as food retail. In the United Kingdom it is characterised by the dominance of four major firms, Tesco, Asda, Sainsburys and Morrisons. Each chain has many suppliers, ranging from farms providing fresh foodstuffs to factories providing processed foods and other products. Their customers are the general public. Food retail is heavily regulated by bodies such as the UK Food Standards Agency.

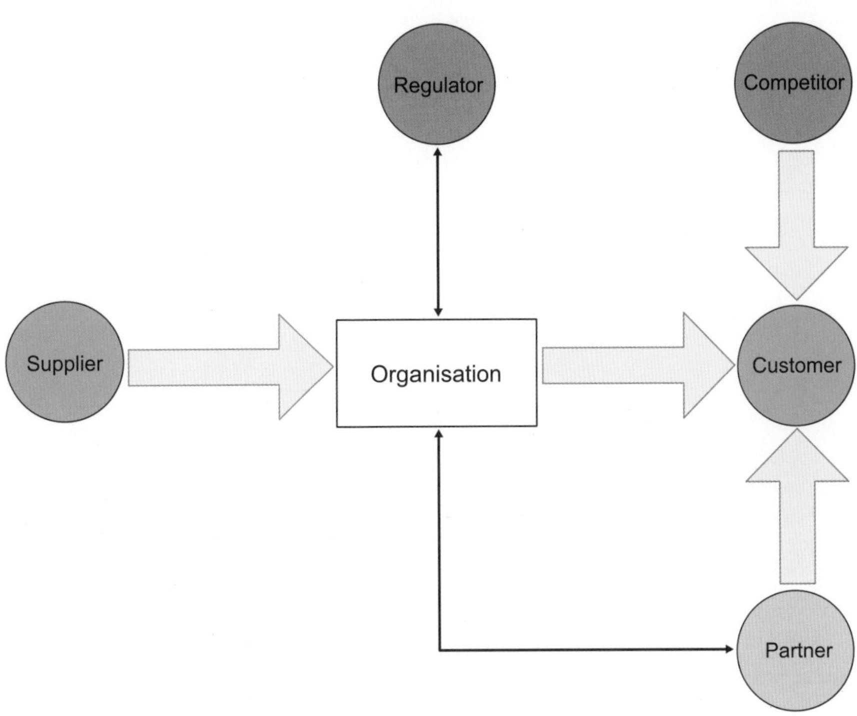

Figure 7.2: *Key economic actors*

Economic relationships

Michael Porter (Porter and Millar, 1985) defines an economic environment (or what he calls industry structure) using a number of dimensions which involve relationships between four of the main types of economic actors (Figure 7.3):

- **Competitive structure of the industry.** This really defines the relative power of competitors to determine issues like pricing policy.
- **Relative power of buyers and sellers.** This highlights the important position that customers and suppliers play in markets.
- **Basis of competition.** This means describing the main products or services sold and the main ways in which organisations compete in the economic environment.
- **State of regulation in the economic environment.** Regulation has a major impact on the activities that companies may perform in particular forms of commerce.
- **State of technological deployment in the environment**. In certain markets technology is essential to competitiveness and/or cooperation.
- **Industry growth**: whether the industry is growing, shrinking or stable. This is a reflection of the state of regulation, competition and demand in a particular market.

Each business takes a specific competitive position in this environment, and the ways in which it can get an advantage over its competitors are determined by the structure of the environment.

Case check: Case 20, Tesco

For example, it is possible to apply the model of the economic environment described above to the food retail industry. The dominance of big supermarkets in food retailing in the United Kingdom means that they have enormous power in determining what they pay their suppliers for key foodstuffs. However, the food retail industry is subject to quite heavy regulation (for example, environmental health legislation). The food retail sector is still growing in the United Kingdom. In recent years the major supermarkets have introduced much more technology, and used their information systems to enter new areas such as financial services. The basis of competition has traditionally been on price, although other bases such as quality (for instance, organic foodstuffs) have recently come into play.

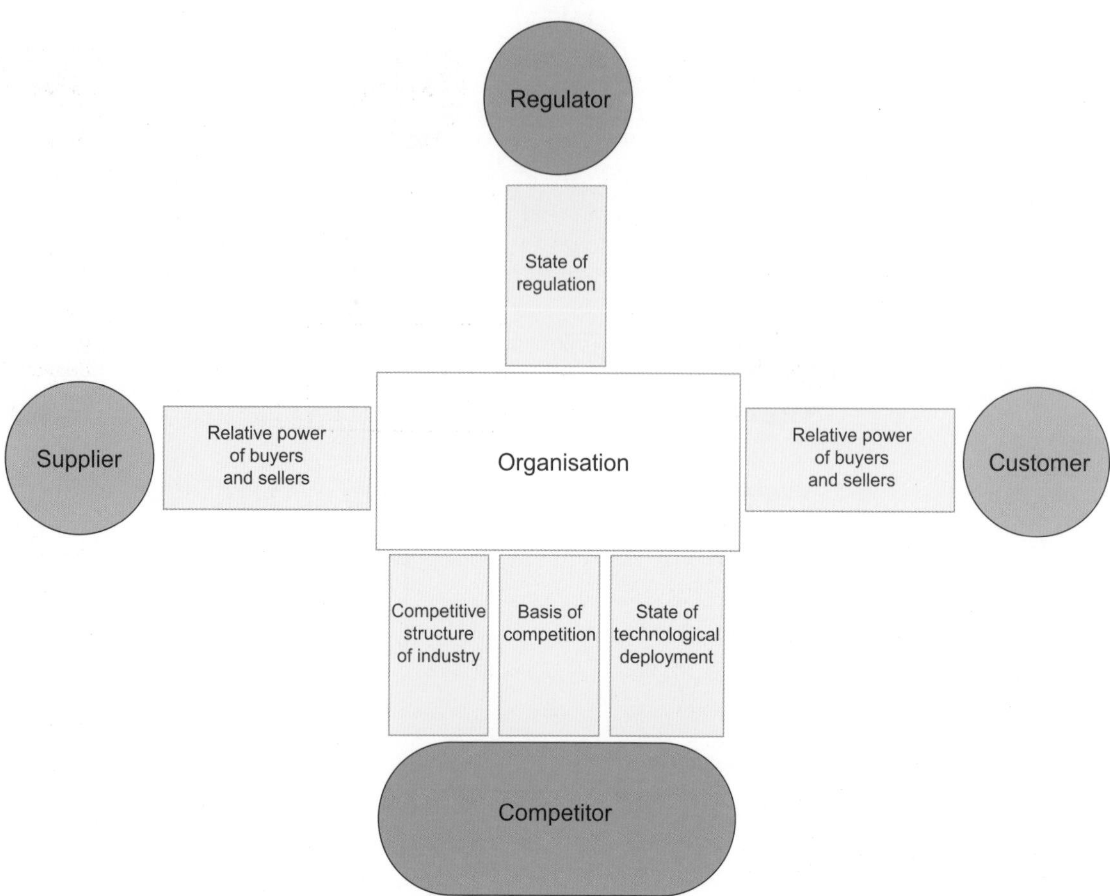

Figure 7.3: *Actors and relationships in a market*

Competitive position: An organisation takes up a particular position in a market defined by its activities and relationships with its competitors, suppliers, customers and regulators.

So we can define an organisation's position in an economic system by its activities and relationships with competitors, suppliers, customers, regulators and partners (Porter, 2001). Its strategy (see Chapter 10) normally aims to at least maintain, and more usually improve, its COMPETITIVE OR MARKET POSITION. In systems terms, strategy is a weapon of both current viability and future sustainability (see Chapter 2).

EBusiness strategy (see Chapter 8) is a specialised form of business strategy. This attempts to influence an organisation's position and relationships through its relative technological capability. For instance, consider a major book retailer. Part of its business strategy might be to increase the coverage of marketing campaigns for new books. It might be fulfilled in part by an eBusiness strategy to improve the company website. If it does so to a greater degree than its competitors, this will improve its position relative to them.

Porter's theory of industry structure and his notion of competitive advantage both come down to the idea of value:

> The threat of entry determines the likelihood that new firms will enter an industry and compete away the value, either passing it on to buyers in the form of lower prices or dissipating it by raising the costs of competing .... This means that industry structure ... determines who keeps what proportion of the value a product creates for buyers.
>
> (Porter, 1985)

Recap 

Any organisation exists within an economic system. Three major processes are relevant to economic systems: production, distribution and consumption. Production is concerned with the creation of goods. Distribution is the associated process of collecting, storing and moving them into the hands of consumers, and providing services for consumers, and consumption is the purchase and use of them. Production, distribution and consumption are activities that deliver value. We can think of an organisation's economic environment in terms of activities and relationships between it and a number of major types of economic actor.

The organisation's specific position in an economic system is defined by its activities and relationships with its competitors, suppliers, customers, regulators and partners.

Flows of value and transactions

Goods: Tangible or intangible objects produced by organisations.

Service: An activity delivered to a stakeholder.

Value traditionally comes in two forms: goods and services, although it can be argued that there is a third type, social capital. This section focuses on goods and services as the most prevalent forms of value relevant to the business organisation.

A GOOD is a product produced by an organisation and distributed to the customer. A SERVICE is an activity performed by an organisation for a customer. Goods and services are the end-points of business processes or activity systems performed in business organisations (see Chapter 2). They are outputs delivered to customers.

Porter uses the term value in its strictly economic or monetary sense. This means that non-monetary expressions of value have to be expressed in monetary terms:

> Value is the amount buyers are willing to pay for what a firm provides them. Value is measured by total revenue, a reflection of the prices a firm's product commands and the units it can sell. A firm is profitable if the value it commands exceeds the costs involved in creating the product.
>
> (Porter, 1985)

PART 3

Tangible goods: Goods that have a physical form and cannot be delivered to customers electronically.

Intangible goods: Goods that fundamentally can be represented as data and hence can be delivered to the customer electronically.

We can distinguish between physical or TANGIBLE GOODS, and non-physical or INTANGIBLE GOODS, corresponding to the idea of physical and non-physical system flows introduced in Chapter 2 (Anthony, 1988). Tangible goods have a physical form, so they cannot be delivered electronically. Intangible goods comprise some form of data, so they are capable of digitisation (and are sometimes called digital goods) and *can* be delivered electronically. This has a bearing on the degree to which a company can use eCommerce (see Chapter 8).

Did you know?

The management theorist Peter Drucker wrote that 'customers pay only for what is of use to them and gives them value'.

Tangible services: Services that have a physical form and cannot be delivered to customers electronically.

Intangible services: Services that fundamentally comprise information and hence can be delivered to the customer electronically.

Electronic government: The use of ICT to enable government administrative processes.

Examples of tangible goods are mechanical goods such as automobiles, electrical goods such as DVD players and perishable goods such as foodstuffs. Examples of intangible goods are text (as in books, magazines and academic papers), images such as prints or photographs, audio (such as music) and video (as in movies).

Similarly services can be classed as either TANGIBLE or INTANGIBLE. The inspection of goods, the ordering and delivery of them are information-based services that support the sale of tangible and intangible products. However, services such as health treatments (for instance, operations) and beauty treatments (for instance, hairdressing) are tangible in nature so they cannot be delivered electronically. Other services are intangible by nature: they are primarily communication or information services such as legal advice, news reports and monetary transfers. These are open to delivery through electronic channels.

For example, a typical unitary local GOVERNMENT authority in the United Kingdom is estimated to provide 70 different types of service. Among its primarily information-based services are maintaining a land and electoral register and collecting council tax. Other services, such as waste disposal, although not information-based nevertheless rely on effective and efficient transmission of information (in this case, on waste collection times, for example) to stakeholders.

Table 7.1 illustrates these distinctions.

Table 7.1: *Types of goods and services*

	Goods	Services
Tangible	Automobiles	Health care
	Foodstuffs	Waste disposal
Intangible	Music	Legal advice
	Movies	Monetary transfers

Reflect
Is software a good or a service?

Goods and services are not mutually exclusive categories; many tangible goods are sold with a range of associated services, both tangible and intangible. A car, for instance, is often sold in a package with regular servicing and inspection and/or motor insurance. And even a tangible good like this leaves plenty of scope for eBusiness: the buyer might use the website to look at photos and read its spec, order and pay for it.

Associated with the flow of any goods and services through production, distribution and consumption is a corresponding flow of transactions. A **transaction** is a data structure (see Chapter 2) that records a coherent unit of activity. Information is needed to support both internal activity and the exchanges between organisations and their suppliers and customers, so transactions are critical to the recording of organisational activity – past, current and future. Transactions typically write information to the information stores of an information system (see Chapter 4), and this information is important for the measurement of organisational performance.

For instance, a sales order records information in a sales order processing information system. It specifies who made the order, when, for what goods or services and in what quantities. This information then triggers activities such as picking the goods from a warehouse and delivering them to the customer. It is also important for measuring sales performance.

In any regular trading relationship, five main types of transaction flow between buyer and seller (see Figure 7.4). The buyer sends an order to the seller. The seller sends the goods and a delivery note, which is followed by an invoice. Finally, the buyer pays the invoice and sends a payment advice to the seller. Order, delivery note, invoice, payment and payment advice are all sets of transactions flowing between buyer and seller.

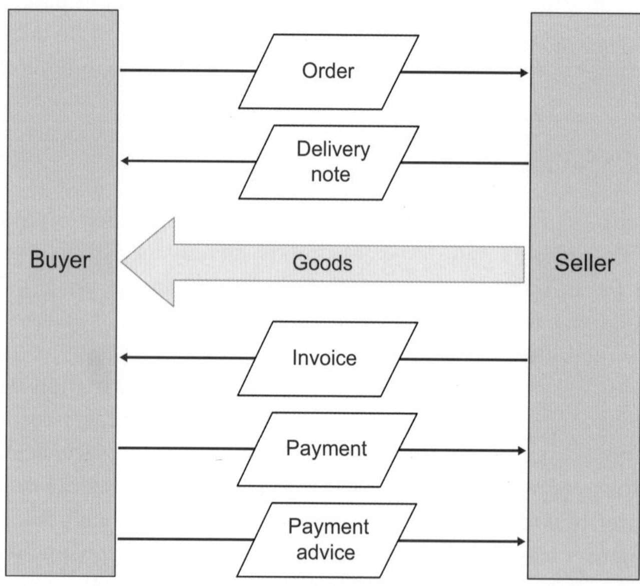

Figure 7.4: *Major transactions between buyer and seller*

For instance, a supermarket chain might order potatoes from an agricultural goods supplier. The supplier's delivery note would detail the number of sacks delivered to the distribution warehouse.

Did you know?

Many countries have followed the United States in counting the acquisition of software as not a current business expense but an investment. This has meant that software contributes to the Gross Domestic Product of a country in the sense that it is considered an intangible good (Floridi, 2007).

Case check:
Case 30 W
Napster

One of the most significant forms of intangible good to benefit from digitisation is music. The MP3 (which stands for Motion Picture Experts Group-1 Level 3) file format was developed by the Fraunhofer Institute in Germany in 1992. It uses an algorithm to compress a music file, achieving a significant reduction of data while retaining near CD-quality sound, so a three-minute song, which would normally require 32Mb of disk space, can be compressed to 3Mb. Using a modem with a bandwidth as little as 56Kb/sec, someone can download it from Internet in a few minutes rather than the two hours required if the file had not been compressed.

Napster: A software application that enables users to locate and share digital music in MP3 format.

The value chain

MP3: Motion Picture Experts Group-1 Level 3. A format that employs an algorithm to compress a music file, achieving a significant reduction of data while retaining near CD-quality sound.

Value chain: A series of interdependent activities that deliver a product or service to a customer.

Porter (1985) uses the concept of value as a way of considering an organisation's key activity systems, producing a generic model of an organisation known as the VALUE CHAIN. In this view organisations are seen as social institutions that produce and deliver value to customers through defined activities (Sawhney and Parikh, 2001).

In a manufacturing organisation, the value added is focused on the products manufactured, so a car manufacturer will be judged on criteria such as the price of its cars, their reliability and safety. In the public sector, the services an organisation delivers represent its value, so a university might be judged on the quality of the education it provides or the research it conducts.

The value chain is therefore a series of interdependent activities that deliver a product or service. Porter categorises them as primary and secondary activities. **Primary activities** are the core competencies of the organisation. **Secondary activities** are important to the successful operation of primary activities. This is illustrated in Figure 7.5. Porter's model is based on an ideal manufacturing organisation, but these key activity systems can be adapted to service-oriented organisations.

The primary activities in the value chain are:

- **Inbound logistics**, which involves receiving and storing raw material, and distributing it to manufacturing premises.
- **Operations**, which used to be called production or manufacturing, and involves transforming inputs (raw materials) into finished products.
- **Outbound logistics**: storing finished products in warehouses and distributing them to customers.
- **Marketing and sales**. Marketing is the process of planning and executing the conception, pricing, promotion and distribution of ideas, goods and services to create exchanges that satisfy individual and organisational goals. Sales is the associated activity of managing customers' purchasing activities.
- **After-sales service**: services that maintain or enhance product value and also work to establish a continuing relationship with customers. This includes installation, testing, maintenance and repair.

Operations: A primary process in the internal value chain involving the transformation of raw materials into finished products.

Marketing and sales: A primary process in the internal value chain. Marketing is the process of planning and executing the conception, pricing, promotion and distribution of ideas, goods and services to create exchanges that satisfy individual and organisational goals. Sales is the associated activity involved in the management of purchasing activities of the customer.

After-sales service: A primary process in the internal value chain. These are services that maintain or enhance product value by attempting to promote a continuing relationship with customers. They involve such activities as the installation, testing, maintenance and repair of products.

Secondary activities are:

- **Infrastructure activities**: support activities for the entire value chain, such as general management, finance, accounting, legal services and quality management.
- **Human resource management**, concerned with recruiting, hiring, training and developing employees.
- **Technology development**: designing and improving products and manufacturing processes. (This is also known as research and development.)
- **Procurement**: purchasing goods and services from suppliers at an acceptable quality and price, and with reliable delivery.

Case check:
Case 20, Tesco

Some of the key processes from the internal value chain can be mapped onto a supermarket chain such as Tesco. Inbound logistics involves receiving food and other supplies, and distributing them to warehouses. Operations involves unpacking bulk deliveries and putting the goods on the supermarket shelves. Outbound logistics involves distributing bulk stocks from warehouses to supermarkets. Marketing and sales consists of advertising and checkout operations. After-sales service includes handling customer enquiries, complaints and product returns.

Tesco's secondary processes include managing finances and producing company accounts. The company procures both goods to sell and other goods and services needed to enable it to operate effectively: for instance, building contractors build and maintain its stores.

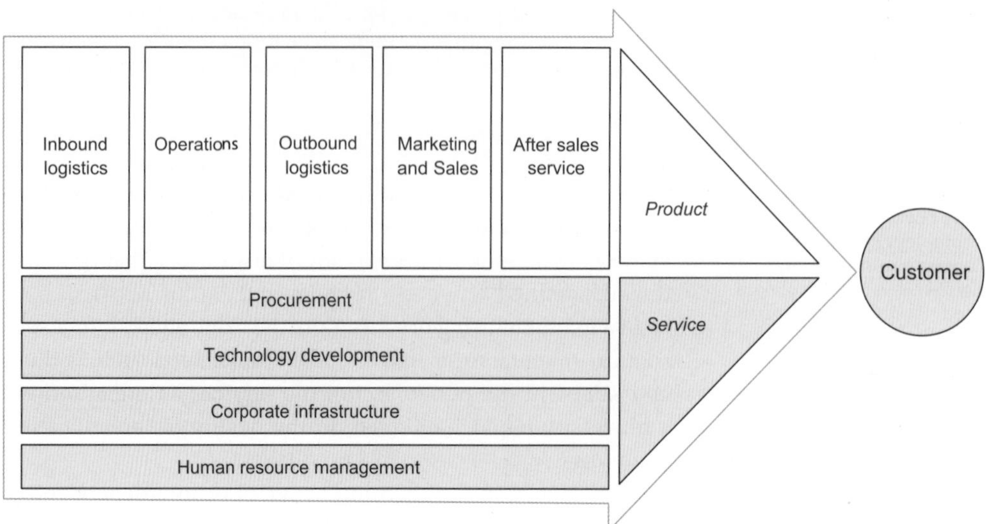

Figure 7.5: *The value chain*

Supply chain, customer chain and community chain

Reflect
Does the value-chain model cover all the activity systems discussed in Chapter 4 for the typical business?

Intermediary: Sometimes known as a channel organisation. An organisation that mediates between other organisations in the value network.

Intermediation: The process of introducing intermediaries or channel organisations into the supply or customer chain.

Porter's value chain focuses on internal processes, but two other chains of value extend the same concept to the wider competitive environment: the **supply chain** and the **customer chain.** An economic system consists of a complex network of chains such as these, which are known as the wider value network.

The supply chain for a typical business is illustrated in Figure 7.6. The broad arrows on the diagram indicate the flow of goods and services between organisations. It distinguishes between direct suppliers one step removed in the supply chain, and indirect suppliers that are two steps (or more) removed. The agents handling indirect suppliers are sometimes referred to as **channel organisations** or INTERMEDIARIES. They include warehousing companies, independent wholesalers, retailers and distributors.

The **customer chain** is the demand chain of the business. Figure 7.7 shows a typical one. It distinguishes between local customers and export customers in a global marketplace. Forms of channel organisation or intermediary (such as distributors and retailers) may provide links to both, and especially to global customers.

Clearly the value network, including the supply and customer chains, varies with the type of industry. Figure 7.8 shows value chains from three different industrial sectors. In automobile manufacturing components are produced by subsidiaries of the car manufacturers and external component suppliers. They are used in assembling cars which are passed on to a dealer network. In food retail, foodstuffs are supplied to supermarkets from warehouses and foodstuff suppliers, and sold on to the consumer. In insurance there is little in the way of a supply chain, but there is a customer chain consisting of agents and brokers.

Community chain: Based on informal social networks of individuals, a major force underlying C2C eCommerce.

Although the supply chain and customer chain define the immediate external environment, it can be argued that they overlap with another chain of value, which is frequently ignored but becoming increasingly significant. This is the COMMUNITY CHAIN. It is founded on social networks of individuals, and its value lies in its ability to generate social capital: the productive value of people engaged in a dense network of social relations. One indicator of high social capital is a high level of interpersonal trust in a social network. This is an increasingly important prerequisite for many forms of business and commerce and will be discussed in more detail in a later section.

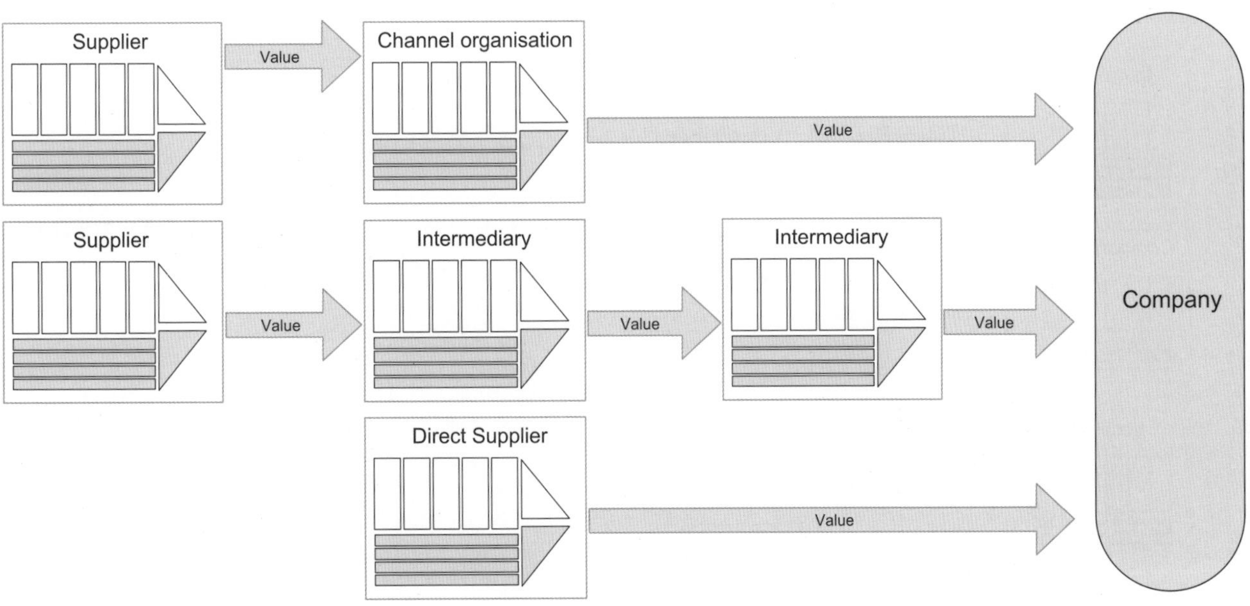

Figure 7.6: *The supply chain*

Recap Value comes in three forms: goods, services and social capital. Associated with the flow of value is a corresponding flow of transactions. The flow of value within and between the organisation and external stakeholders defines a number of distinctive elements of a value network. The internal value chain is made up of a series of interdependent activity systems. Linking the organisation to its environment are the supply chain, through which goods and services are delivered to the organisation to enable it to function effectively, and the customer chain, through which its value is distributed. The community chain consists of networks of individuals surrounding an organisation.

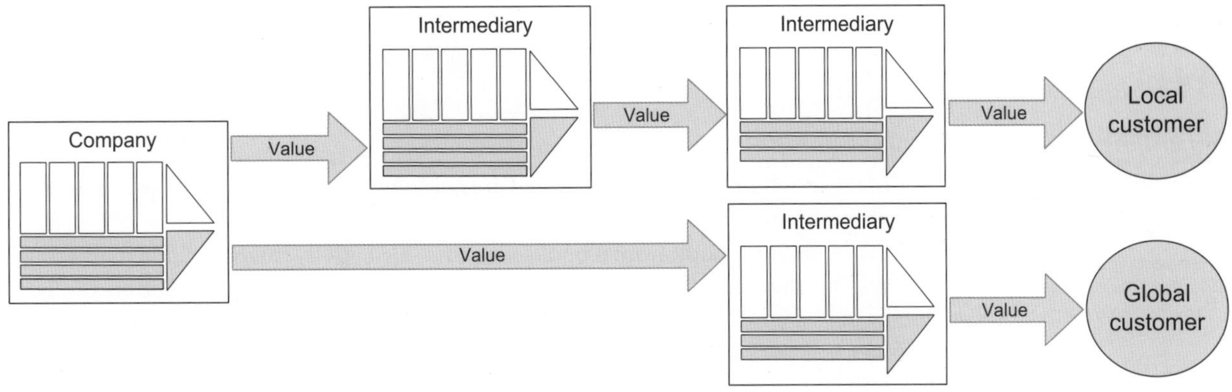

Figure 7.7: *The customer chain*

Commerce

Commerce: A process consisting of pre-sale, sale execution, sale settlement and after-sale activities.

COMMERCE is the economic process which deals with the exchanges of goods and services from producer to final consumer. It can be considered as a system or process involving a series of phases of activity:

- **Pre-sale activities** occur before a sale is made.
- **Sale execution** consists of the activities involved in the actual sale.
- **Sale settlement** involves those activities that complete the sale.
- **After-sale** activities take place after the buyer has received the product or service.

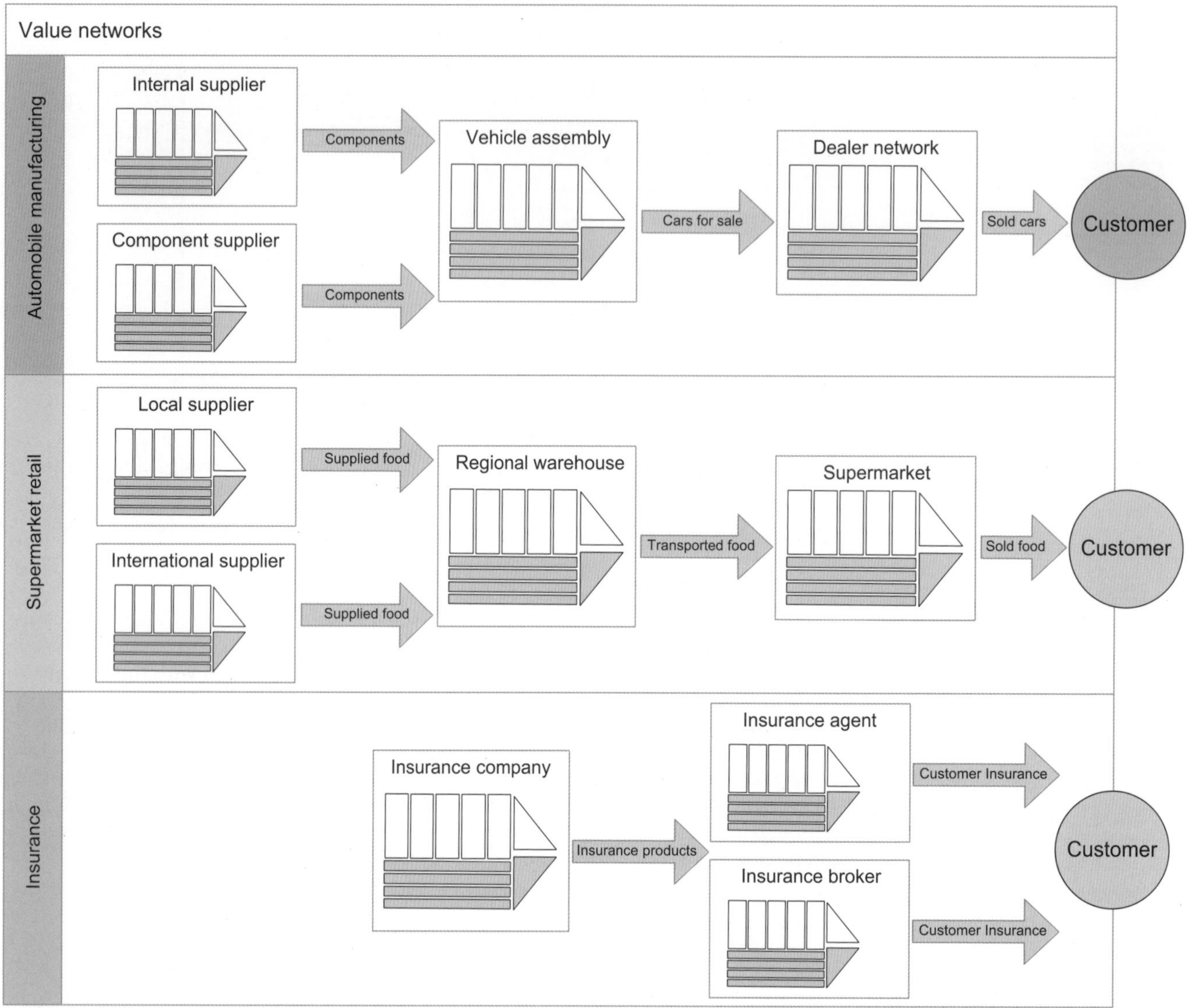

Figure 7.8: *Three value networks*

Each of these activities generates a range of transactions, one of the most prominent types of which is payments.

Think of buying a book from a bookseller. Pre-sale activity might include marketing books by including their details in online and offline catalogues. In sale execution the customer actually buys a book. This might mean walking into a bookshop and paying at the till, or if the customer is an organisation, it could mean that it places an order, the bookseller sends the book and an invoice, and the purchaser pays at a later date. After-sale service might include sales personnel making site visits to schools and universities to get feedback on textbooks, and perhaps initiatives such as discounting some book lines.

The precise form of this generic process of commerce will vary depending on the nature of the economic actors involved, the nature of the goods or services being exchanged and the frequency of commerce between the actors.

Distinctions are often made between individual actors and organisational actors, which can be broken down further into private sector or commercial organisations, public sector organisations and other not-for-profit organisations such as voluntary organisations.

An important feature of a product or service is its price. Hoque (2000) distinguishes between low-priced items, low to medium-priced items, medium to high-priced items and high-priced items. The price of an item is often related to what Malone, Yates and Benjamin (1987) call product complexity and asset specificity.

Repeat commerce: The pattern in which regular, repeat transactions occur between trading partners.

Credit commerce: Irregular transactions occur between trading partners and the processes of settlement and execution are separated.

Cash commerce: Occurs when irregular transactions of a one-off nature are conducted between economic actors. In cash commerce the processes of execution and settlement are typically combined.

Asset specificity is the degree to which an organisation has inputs that are specific to it, and cannot readily be used by another firm. This might involve its location, human knowledge or physical attributes. A specialised tool such as a machine tool is physically specific if it is designed for a specific purpose. Coal produced by a coalmine located close to a power station is site specific. A service provided by a consultant with specific knowledge of a company's processes is knowledge specific.

Product complexity refers to the amount of information buyers need to make a selection between rival products.

Another way of categorising goods and services is by their tangibility, as was discussed on page 205.

Whiteley (2000) categorises forms of commerce by their frequency and the point at which payment is made:

- In REPEAT COMMERCE there are regular repeat transactions between trading partners.
- In CREDIT COMMERCE there are irregular transactions and the processes of settlement and execution are separated.
- CASH COMMERCE occurs when there are irregular one-off transactions paid for at the time of purchase.

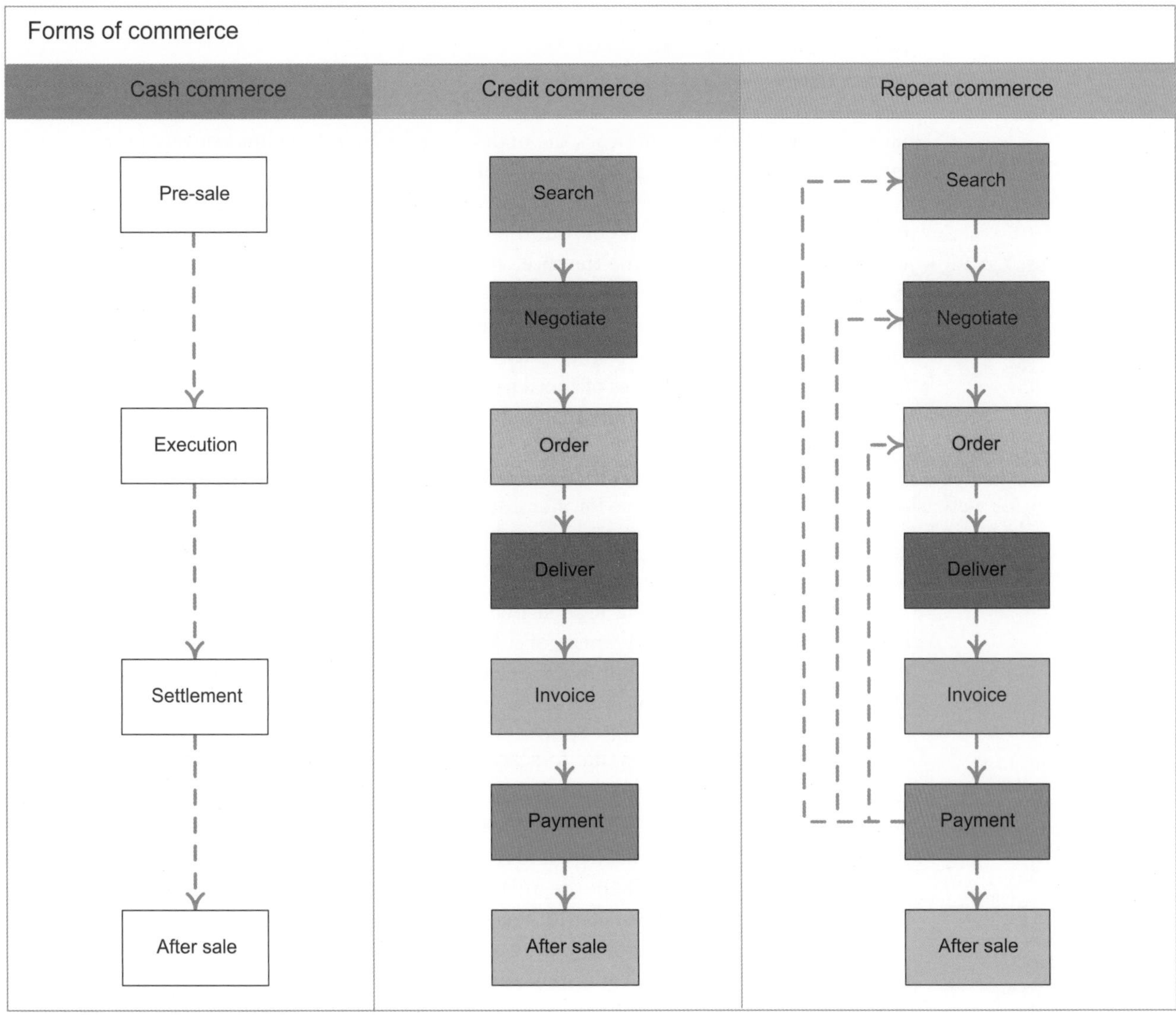

Figure 7.9: *Cash, credit and repeat commerce*

Cash commerce for low and standard-priced goods typically follows the four stages of the generic commerce model quite closely. Its sequence is see/buy/get. For medium to high-priced items credit commerce is more usual. Organisations (and individuals) search for a product, negotiate a price, place the order, receive delivery, are invoiced, make payment and receive after-sales service. For high-priced and customised goods traded between organisations, a repeat commerce model is more usual. The same processes occur as for credit commerce but the processes cycle around indefinitely in a trusted relationship between producer and consumer. These three forms of commerce are illustrated in Figure 7.9.

Most purchases of small items over the Internet occur in cash commerce mode. A good example is someone ordering food from a supermarket's website. Companies in established relationships tend to work with either a credit or repeat commerce model. For instance, when the supermarket chain itself makes purchases, it normally places a repeat order with an established supplier, receives an invoice after delivery, and pays its account on a regular basis.

Communities and social capital

Social network: A network of people and social relations.

It is widely accepted now that the wider community in which an organisation operates acts as a stakeholder in it, but what is meant by a community and what are its key features? People have argued over this for centuries (Tonnies, 1935). Here we can think of a community as being founded on SOCIAL NETWORKS.

A **network** is a set of nodes connected by links of some form. In communication networks (considered in Chapter 5) the nodes are usually computing devices and the links are communication lines. In a social network the nodes are people and the links or relations are various forms of social interaction and/or social bonds.

Figure 7.10 shows people as circles and their relationship links as lines. In this case the relationship is given as 'friend of' but there are other types of relationship, of course (works with, is related to, and so on). The three nets in the figure all show the same people, but the density of the connections between them changes from one to the next. Suppose we also overlay relationships of trust, collaboration and cooperation on these networks. In a community we would expect the connectivity – a measure of the interconnectedness of the nodes in a network – in all four types of social network to be high. So net 3 in Figure 7.10 is closer to most definitions of a community than net 1.

Did you know?

Managers spend a considerable amount of time networking. This is because a social network is a particularly valuable resource for them. Studies of personal careers shows that the higher people move up the managerial hierarchy, the more important are social networks to their promotional prospects.

Some recent authors have argued that communities generate value (that is, they have a chain of value) just like organisations. However, the value of a community lies not in its physical or financial capital but in its social capital. Putnam defines social capital as 'features of social organisation such as networks, norms and trust that facilitate coordination and cooperation for mutual benefit' (2000).

Social capital: The productive value of people engaged in a dense network of social relations. Social capital consists of those features of social organisation – networks of secondary associations, high levels of interpersonal trust, reciprocity – that act as resources for individuals and facilitate collective action.

Capital is traditionally defined as the financial assets available to a company, so it is a key resource for production. SOCIAL CAPITAL is the productive value of people engaged in a dense network of social relations. It consists of features such as networks of secondary associations, and high levels of interpersonal trust and reciprocity, which act as resources for individuals and facilitate collective action. Therefore, it is argued, a community rich in social capital is more likely to possess effective civic institutions and be effective at maintaining law and order.

This is similar to Metcalfe's law (proposed by the communication engineer Robert Metcalfe) of the value of a communication network: that its value for a particular user is proportional to the square of the number of users of the system (n^2). This can be directly related to the **variety** of a network. If there are n users in a network then there are a maximum of ($n*(n-1)/2$) possible unique connections between the members of such a network. Hence, the more members of a network the more potential there is for connections between members. So it can be suggested, through Metcalfe's and to a certain extent Putnam's work, that the variety of a social network has a bearing on the amount of social capital generated.

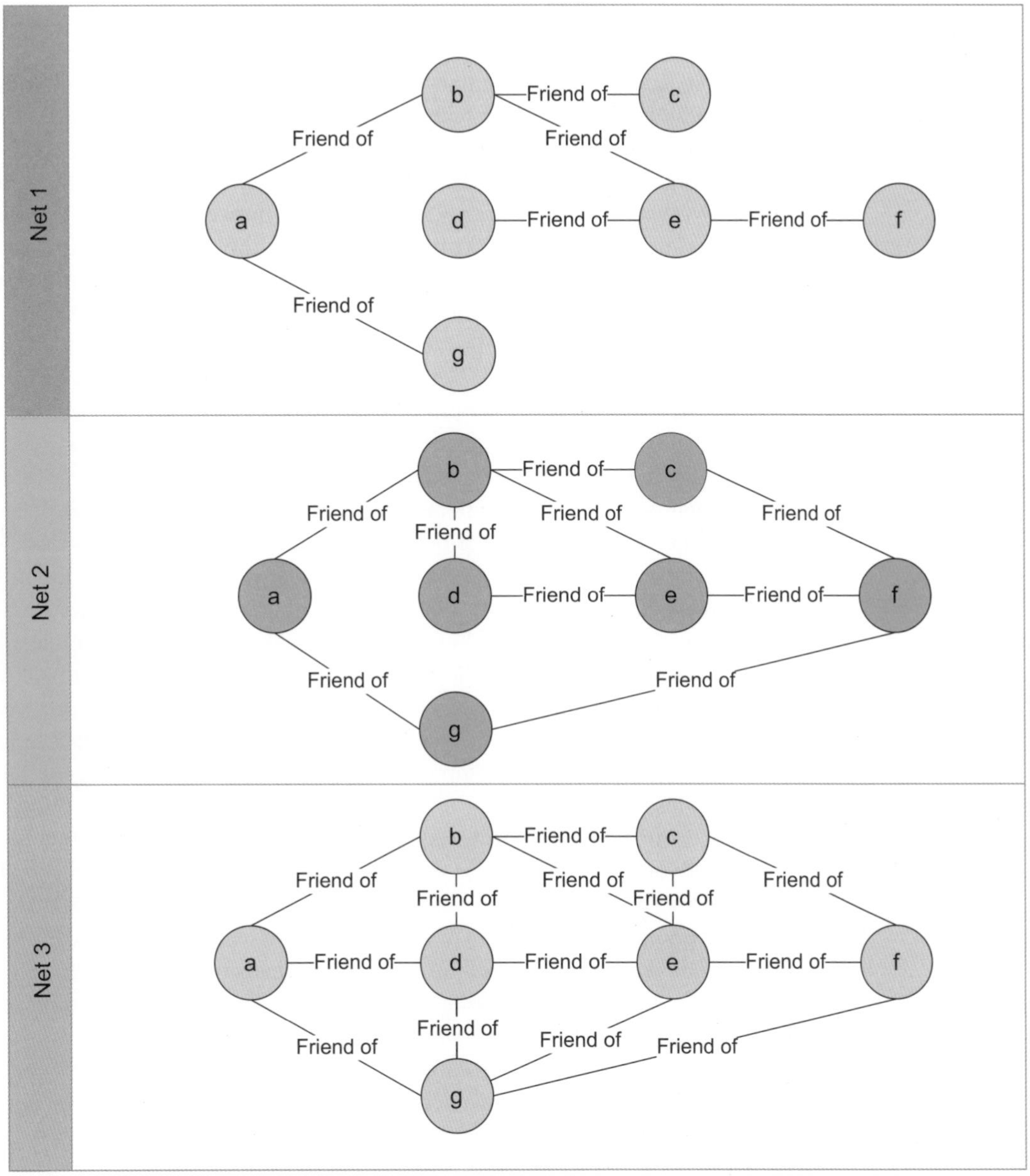

Figure 7.10: *Social networks*

Reflect
In the terms discussed what is the density or variety of the three nets illustrated in Figure 7.10?

An example which might make this clearer is a mobile phone network. If only one person possessed a mobile phone it would be useless. If a second person gets a phone, they can call each other. If three people have phones, each of them has two others they might call or text. And the more people acquire one, the more people each individual user has to send messages or make calls to, and the more value the network has. Likewise in a social network the value of the social network to the individual is a function of the variety of the network. The more connected a person is to others in a community, the more resources they are able to draw upon in collective action.

A scene from the film *Witness* demonstrates the power of social capital. Part of it is set in an Amish village, a close-knit community who come together one day to build a barn. People contribute their labour for free, and the barn is built from scratch in the day. Then when one of the builders finds they need help, they can assume they too will be able to call upon the collective resources of the community.

The value of a social network does not directly correspond to its density or connectedness. Of equal importance is the 'quality' of the links. It is often argued in literature on social capital and community that the moves to mass globalisation and urbanisation have led to a decline in community spirit and therefore a decline in social capital. This supposes that not only are social networks less dense or more widely dispersed, their links are in some sense less binding.

For example, trust between human beings is normally developed over time as individuals (actors) gain confidence in the reliability of other actors through a series of interactions. Social capital rests on the transitivity of trust as a human relation – A trusts C because B trusts C and A trusts B. This makes it possible for trust to exist between people in large social networks when there is not necessarily a close contact between them, but there is a dense web of connections surrounding them. Putnam documents the decline in civic life – membership of clubs, sports, voluntary and political associations – in the United States over the past three decades, and argues that this thinning of the web of contacts has led to a decline in social capital, which manifests itself, for instance, as falling levels of trust.

Granovetter (1973) distinguishes between strong links and weak links in a social network. There are strong links between people who are regularly in contact and have a lot in common: close friends, work colleagues or family members. Weak links exist between people in irregular contact: for instance acquaintances, occasional business contacts and distant friends. Strong links are important in people's support networks, particularly in the early and later stages of life. Weak links deliver new social and economic opportunities.

More recently it has been proposed that technology, particularly ICT, can be important to maintaining social networks with both strong and weak links. In the information society a large proportion of the interaction between individuals is conducted remotely: people email each other, contribute to bulletin boards, write and read blogs and so on. All of this activity creates and strengthens links in social networks. Many of these links are weak, but some become increasingly strong. The networks that grow up have a different shape from neighbourhood networks, because the interconnections are location-independent, but they are not necessarily any less valid.

For instance, most people send texts on their mobiles as a means of staying in touch with their social network. Academics use email lists to maintain loose networks of researchers. During the terrorist attacks on the World Trade Center on 11 September 2001, people used mobiles, fixed phones, PCs, all kinds of channels to contact loved ones and exchange information. On that one day around 30 million North Americans (one-third of all US Internet users) turned to email, chat rooms and online fora to write eyewitness descriptions, offer words of comfort and engage in debate about what had happened (Preece, 2002).

Adjunct community: An eCommunity fostered by a commercial operation.

Businesses are interested in the community chain and social networks because they can take advantage of the social capital such as increased levels of trust. Social networks spread information about goods and services, both good and bad, and this process can be used to try to grow sales. Many organisations have tried to establish ADJUNCT COMMUNITIES (see Chapter 8), online social networks of people who are interested in their goods and services, and can help to promote them.

Recap 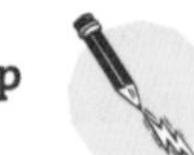

All kinds of commerce can be considered as a system or process with the phases of pre-sale, sale execution, sale settlement and after sale. The precise format varies depending on the nature of the economic actors involved, the frequency of their commerce and the nature of the goods or services. Organisations typically create value of three different forms: goods, services and social capital. Organisations exist within a wider community of social networks that generate social capital.

Control in economic systems

Systems need to be controlled or governed, as we have seen, and if we think of organisations and their environments in systems terms, we need to understand how their control and governance work. An economy can be seen as a system that controls the flow of goods and services along chains of value, and Thompson (2003) argues that there are three possible approaches to controlling and governing that flow: through markets, hierarchies and networks.

In a sense, these are types of economic control process (see Chapter 2), and are important for understanding why various parts of the value network, such as supply chains, develop as they do. These forms of control are also important in thinking about eBusiness; understanding how it has emerged, and predicting how it could develop further (see Chapter 8).

Markets, hierarchies and networks are mechanisms for both coordination and governance. **Coordination** concerns how elements are made to act together. **Governance** concerns the regulation of elements. Table 7.2 summarises the main differences between these three forms of control.

Table 7.2: *Hierarchies, markets and networks*

Type	System	Economic relationships	Order	Behaviour
Hierarchy	System of cooperation.	Managerial hierarchy consisting typically of one economic actor interacting with a limited number of others; one-to-many relationships.	Order is designed and consciously organised to achieve outcomes.	Rule-governed and involving bureaucratic monitoring and interventions.
Market	System of competition.	Many-to-many relationships between economic actors.	Order is emergent and develops from spontaneously generated outcomes.	Emergent from interaction of many private competitive decisions working with the forces of supply and demand.
Network	System of cooperation and competition: co-optition.	Both one-to-many and many-to-many relationships.	Order may be both designed and emergent. Networks may display both designed and spontaneously generated outcomes.	Both rule-governed and emergent.

Hierarchy: An important systems concept in which a system can be decomposed to various levels of detail.

Hierarchies

HIERARCHIES are a logical extension of the firm itself. They coordinate the flow of value by controlling and directing it at a higher level in management structures. In hierarchies, order is designed and consciously organised to achieve outcomes. This is the traditional form of control exercised within and between public sector organisations. In government it typically constitutes bureaucratic control (see Chapter 2) since behaviour is very much governed by rules and procedures. In hierarchies, the mechanisms of operation involve bureaucratic monitoring and interventions, and as a result hierarchies demonstrate overt, planned, purposeful governance.

Simplistically, hierarchies can be seen as systems of cooperation. A managerial hierarchy is a medium for exchanges between a limited number of buyers and sellers, and the buyers and sellers exchange goods and services in established patterns of trade. So hierarchies form the cooperative environment of organisations, and because of the established nature of relationships between economic actors, they tend to rely on smaller volumes of information flow than do markets (see below).

Most companies have established trading relationships with a limited number of suppliers, and these relationships are traditionally managed through managerial hierarchies. A car manufacturer, for example, is likely to build established trading relationships with a limited range of component suppliers, and distribute its cars to a specialised network of dealers. Both the supply chain and the customer chain will be organised as a series of hierarchies.

Markets

Markets coordinate the flow of value through forces of supply and demand, and external transactions between actors in an exchange relationship. In markets, order is not predefined; it develops or emerges from spontaneously generated outcomes. This is the form of control seen as typical in the private sector since in markets behaviour arises from private competitive decisions. Within markets operations are governed by price, competition and self-interest. So markets do not have any overt or planned form of governance: instead it is implicit and emergent.

Put simply, markets are systems of competition. A market is a medium for exchanges between many potential buyers and many potential sellers, and at least for larger companies, a series of markets forms the immediate competitive environment. However, because of its many-to-many nature a market is heavily reliant on large volumes of information flow. Participation in markets traditionally generates large transaction costs (see below).

The stock market is a specialised market that is important particularly for financial companies, but for other types of company too. It is a market for the exchange of shares and other forms of security. Companies trade shares through financial intermediaries to a vast range of financial consumers, many of which are other companies. The price of a share is determined by the forces of supply and demand: the more demand, the higher its price.

Networks

Networks are a mediating form of coordination and governance between hierarchies and markets. There are two distinct forms of economic control network:

- **Organised networks** involve conscious directive action to establish and sustain the network (and hence overlap with hierarchies).
- In **self-organising networks**, order arises from non-directive interactions between members (so they overlap with markets).

So networks may display both designed and spontaneously generated outcomes. Overall, the behaviour in networks is normally cooperative and consensus-seeking; the mechanisms of operation are loyalty, reciprocity and trust, and governance may be both formally organised and self-organised.

Many modern companies conduct trade or commerce in networks of partnerships. Participation in them reduces the costs and risks of operation. For instance, an airline might partner with a car hire company and a hotel chain. Each member of the partnership network agrees to promote the goods and services of the other organisations, and they may also share customer information. The key advantage of participation is the ability to provide end-to-end value to the customer. This in turn is likely to improve both customer acquisition and customer retention.

Did you know?

Networks are becoming very important as a control mechanism in the public sector in many countries, where for a number of years private sector organisations have been introduced to areas of service provision such as buildings maintenance and education. They have introduced aspects of competitive behaviour into what had traditionally been a system based upon cooperation and collaboration.

Reflect
In what way might the idea of a network as a form of economic control be seen as mediating between market forms and forms of managerial hierarchy?

Transaction costs, the nature of the firm and electronic markets, hierarchies and networks

One of the key questions that has concerned economics for many decades is why the economy is populated largely by firms rather than individuals. Simple classical models of economic exchange suggest it should be made up of independent, self-employed people who contract with one another, but in most sectors, firms win out. One reason is the impact of **transaction costs** (sometimes referred to as coordination costs). This also helps explain the increasing importance of ICT, and the ways in which it can be, and is being, used to transform economic systems.

In the 1930s Ronald Coase (1937) used the idea of transaction costs to develop a theory about when economic tasks would be performed by firms and when they would be performed by markets. A transaction cost is a cost incurred in making an economic exchange. For example, a transaction cost of undertaking a deal on the stock market (buying or selling a financial security) is a commission paid to a broker. When you buy a textbook, the 'costs' include not just the cover price, but the energy and effort you spent finding a bookseller that had the right book in stock at the right price.

Did you know?

It has been estimated that as much as 25 per cent of the healthcare budget in a country like the United Kingdom goes on transaction costs.

Coase suggested that one way for organisations to avoid transaction costs is to produce what they need (both goods and services) internally instead of finding it on the wider market. This theory has also been used to attempt to explain why firms engage in relationships with other firms, and what form (hierarchies, markets or networks) these relationships take.

Malone and colleagues (1987) argued that we can classify markets and hierarchies using the balance of production costs to coordination (transaction) costs, and the balance of asset specificity to the complexity of a product. Production costs include the processes necessary to create and distribute goods and services. Coordination costs or transaction costs include the costs of information processing necessary to coordinate the work of people and machines (Bakos, 1997). Markets are generally characterised by low production costs and high coordination costs, while hierarchies typically have high production costs and low coordination costs; markets also tend to be good for low product complexity and low asset specificity, whereas hierarchies are good for high asset specificity and high product complexity (see Figures 7.3 and 7.4).

Consider procurement (which is discussed in more detail in Chapter 8). Generally, companies perform two types of this major process in the supply chain (Chaffey, 2002): production-related and operating procurement.

Production-related procurement is geared to fulfilment of long-term needs, and generally deals with customised items (with high product complexity and high asset specificity). It normally involves building regular relationships with suppliers, and so it tends to be organised as hierarchies. Non-production or operating procurement mostly fulfils immediate needs for commoditised items (with low product complexity, and low asset specificity). Relationships with suppliers tend to be irregular and temporary, and therefore operating procurement is frequently organised via markets.

Table 7.3: *Production and coordination costs*

		Coordination costs	
		High	Low
Production costs	High		Hierarchy
	Low	Market	

Table 7.4: *Product complexity and asset specificity*

		Asset specificity	
		High	Low
Production complexity	High	Hierarchy	
	Low		Market

However, Malone and colleagues (1987) argued in the 1980s that the increased use of ICT would stimulate a trend towards electronic markets and electronic hierarchies. They also argued for the dominance of market forms because ICT would decrease the costs of coordination, and would enable companies to personalise goods and services more. This in turn would enable them to better handle issues of product complexity and asset specificity.

More recently Tapscott and Williams (2006) have proposed that the Internet and the Web (see Chapter 5) are critically changing the logic of the firm. This technological infrastructure is forcing a decline not only in transaction costs but also in the costs of 'production', because it is easier to work collaboratively using communication technology. Open-source software production is a case in point. They infer from this that network forms of governance and control will begin to overtake traditional pure hierarchy and market forms over the first quarter of the 21st century.

Recap

An economy is a system that controls the flow of goods and services along chains of value in three possible ways: hierarchies, markets and networks. Hierarchies are a logical extension of the firm itself, and coordinate the flow of value by controlling and directing it at a higher level in management structures. Markets coordinate the flow of value through forces of supply and demand, and external transactions between actors in an exchange relationship. Networks are a mediating form of coordination and governance between hierarchies and markets.

Case check: Case 33 W The UK stock market

The stock market is a classic example of an economic market. It is a market that does deals for the purchase and sale of blocks of securities (stocks and shares). It is essentially an information-intensive activity system. Securities are information assets (intangible products) and deals are effectively transactions recording economic exchanges. ICT systems and infrastructure are critical to the modern financial services industry and to trade in financial products.

Business models and the value network

Business model: Specifies the structure and dynamics of a particular enterprise, particularly the relationship between different stakeholders, benefits and costs to each, and key revenue flows.

The concept of a BUSINESS MODEL has become a popular way of thinking about business change, particularly when it involves technological innovation. Behind this concept is a model of the organisation as an open system (see Chapter 2). The equifinality characteristic of open systems (see page 45: that is, the concept that an open system can achieve its goals in a number of different ways) implies that systems of activity can be designed. This is the context in which business models often arise (Timmers, 1998). But is the concept useful? Porter, for instance, argues that its definitions are murky at best and that 'The business model approach to management becomes an invitation for faulty thinking and self-delusion' (2001).

From our perspective, the concept is very similar to that of a value-creating system (see page 45), and has explanatory power because of its basis in systems thinking (Jackson, 2003). This in turns ties in with the ideas of value chains and value networks.

A business model specifies the structure and dynamics of an organisation in terms of, for example, its major products and/or services, key stakeholders, costs and benefits of particular modes of operation and key revenue flows. Linder and Cantrell (2000) define a business model as the organisation's core logic for creating value, and from this angle it is useful in relating business strategy to business processes to information systems. Osterwalder and Pigneur (2002) describe a business model as the 'conceptual and architectural implementation of a business strategy [that] represents the foundation for the implementation of business processes and information systems'.

All this comes down to the fact that organisations have choices in how they do what they aim to do, and eBusiness and eCommerce multiply the options. Business strategies (see Chapter 10) specify how a particular business model can be applied to a particular market sector to improve competitive position.

A key part of the argument used for adaptive systems is that the model of the business must fit market circumstances. So it must be founded in its key value chains and be viable in this environment. Its activities must also be sustainable long-term.

Case check: Case 20, Tesco

Let's go back again to Tesco. It has relationships with customers and suppliers. Revenue flows into its value chain from its customers and on to its suppliers. Customers are mainly attracted to supermarkets by a combination of low prices and a large variety of goods on offer. The stores sell large volumes, so the company's business strategy is typically based on low-cost/high-volume operations with low profit margins on each product. Costs are minimised by, for instance, buying in bulk from suppliers and letting customers bear the costs of picking products from shelves, packing them and taking them home. A supermarket needs above all to attract plenty of customers to its stores, so their location is critical: they need a good catchment area.

An eCommerce site such as Tesco.com (see Chapter 8) changes the business model. Relationships with customers and suppliers change, as do costs and revenue. For example, it will cost the store if a member of staff takes the order list, walks around the store picking goods, packs them and hands them to a delivery driver who takes them to the customer's home. Many supermarkets pass on this cost as a delivery charge, as does Tesco.

However, with eCommerce it becomes an option to do away with stores entirely: instead the goods can be stored in and delivered from low-cost warehouses. So the additional order fulfilment costs can be balanced by lower operational costs (larger range, reduced inventory, larger volume, lower margins). In a slightly different market, this is the business model adopted by Amazon.com.

Key skill 

Value-chain, value-network and value-stream analysis

Although Porter's original value-chain model has been applied in many different settings, it has also received plenty of criticism. For instance, it is seen as more applicable to physical products than to services; it under-emphasises the role of informatics infrastructure in the delivery of value; it focuses on the internal value chain to the detriment of the value network. Here we focus on the last of these deficiencies.

The idea of the **value network** is that organisations interrelate and interact in complex networks of value production, distribution and consumption. A particular organisation will take on roles in a number of different chains of value. ICT can make it possible to deliver value along them more efficiently and effectively (Porter 1985). Porter now acknowledges that with the rise of eBusiness certain 'secondary activities' such as ICT offer far more than a support role. They have become critically embedded within primary activities.

PART 3

To deliver more efficiently and effectively requires organisational change. So the task is to analyse the existing value chain and see how aspects of it can be redesigned to improve performance. In the wider value network, similarly, it is to analyse activities and relationships with external stakeholders as preparation for redesigning aspects of that network.

Conventional value-chain analysis distinguishes between primary activities that relate directly to getting goods and/or services to the customer, and secondary or support activities (see page 207). Value-chain analysis involves analysing each activity in the value chain, such as procurement, manufacture, sales and distribution, and identifying ways in which redesign will lead to performance improvement (adding value to customers). Performance can also be improved by redesigning interfaces between the elements: for instance, between sales and outbound logistics.

Rayport and Sviokla (1996) refer to a virtual value chain which parallels the physical value chain. Here too, we conceive of the value chain as a series of both physical and non-physical flows. The virtual value chain consists of information flows, and involves the use of ICT to mediate traditional value-chain activities such as market research, new product development, marketing, procurement, production, and managing selling and fulfilment. Many of these have already been automated to some extent, and with the introduction of newer forms of ICT such as software agents many of them could become fully 'virtual' or automated in the near future.

Disintermediation: The process available though electronic markets of enabling companies to sell directly to customers.

Reintermediation: The process in electronic markets of new intermediaries developing between buyers and sellers.

The traditional retail chain consists of wholesalers, distributors and retailers, but eCommerce has cut out the intermediaries, in what is known as DISINTERMEDIATION. The Internet suffers, though, from being a large and complex medium for supporting a market. People often find it difficult to find the precise product or service they are looking for, so a new breed of intermediaries – electronic intermediaries – has emerged. They supply a service to consumers by locating companies that can fulfil their needs, and they supply a service to producers in identifying potential customers. This process is known as REINTERMEDIATION. Figure 7.11 illustrates the three processes of intermediation, disintermediation and reintermediation.

Value-network analysis is an extension of value-chain analysis which focuses on the activities and relationships of the business with external stakeholders. It looks for ways of disaggregating (Kalakota and Robinson, 1999) or deconstructing (Timmers, 1999) the value network, as well as ways of reaggregating (Kalakota and Robinson, 1999) or reconstructing (Timmers, 1999) it. Disaggregation involves segmenting out elements of the value chain and perhaps outsourcing them to partners. Reaggregation involves integrating elements of the value chain to streamline key processes.

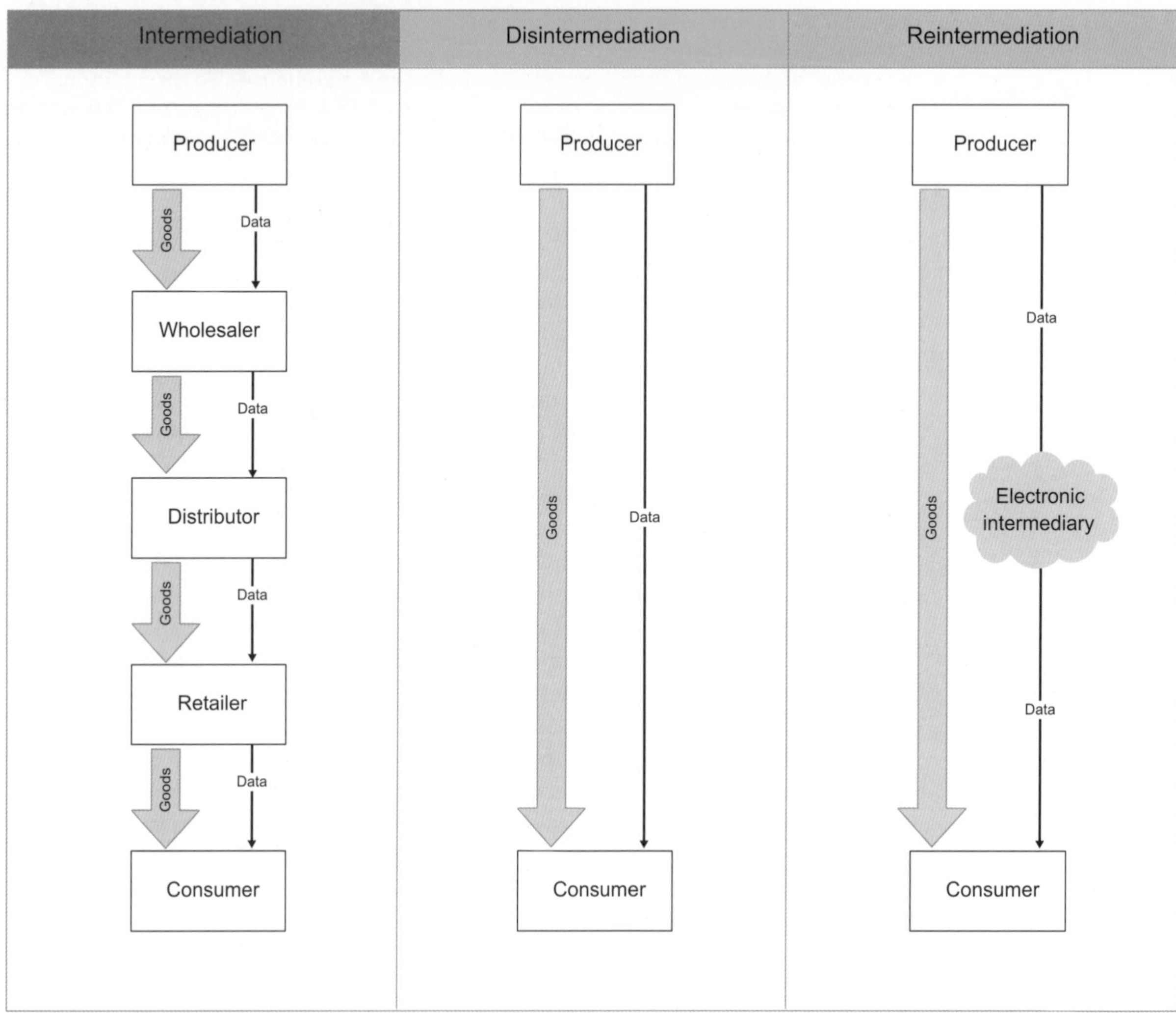

Figure 7.11: *Intermediation, disintermediation and reintermediation*

Deise and colleagues (2000) describe the importance of managing the value network of partners which might result from a reconstruction of the value network. It might include supply-side partners, primary activity partners, sell-side partners and value-chain integrators. On the supply side, partners are likely to include traditional suppliers (perhaps managed through hierarchies), business-to-business exchanges (managed in market terms) and wholesalers/distributors (perhaps managed in networks). On the sell side, business-to-business exchanges, wholesalers and distributors will also exist alongside traditional customers. Partners may also fulfil certain primary value-chain activities such as inbound logistics. **Value-chain integrators** are organisations that integrate aspects of the internal and external value chain for companies. An example is maintaining the informatics infrastructure (see Chapter 11).

A combination of process modelling approaches (see Chapter 1) and information systems modelling constructs (see Chapter 2) can be used to conduct both value-chain and value-network analyses. Collectively this is called **value-stream analysis,** and its objective is to improve the efficiency of both internal and external processes, frequently through the application of ICT.

For instance, Hammer (1990) describes a classic piece of value-stream analysis of an accounts payable process at the Ford Motor Company. The department originally employed 500 people while a competitor's department had just five. Ford closed the gap by removing what were seen as wasteful activities in its invoicing process.

In the old process the purchasing department wrote an order and sent a copy to accounts payable. Later, when the materials control department received goods, it sent a copy of the receiving document to accounts payable. Meanwhile the vendor sent an invoice to accounts payable. This is illustrated in Figure 7.12. The accounts payable department had to match up to 14 data items before it could pay the vendor. Staff spent most of their time trying to sort out mismatches between the order, despatch note and invoice.

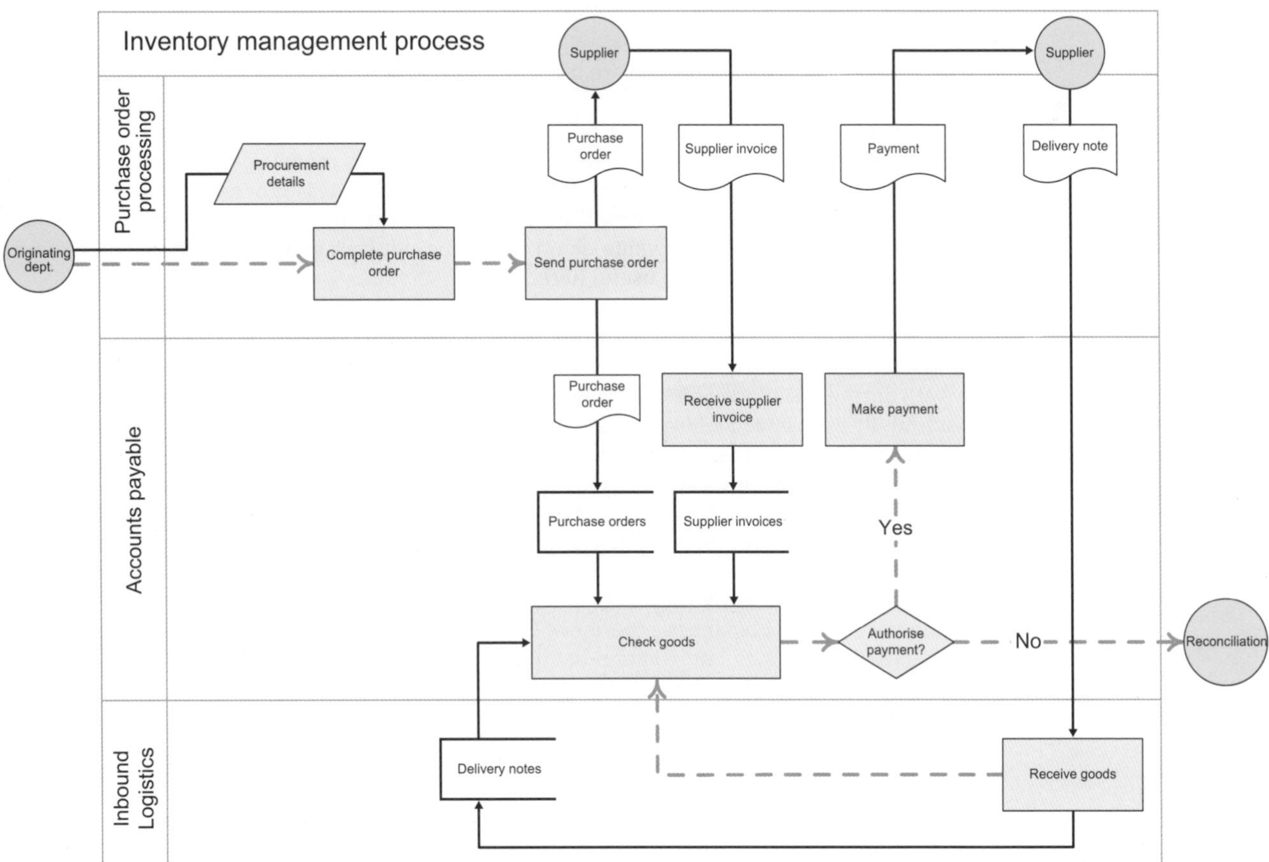

Figure 7.12: *The old payments process at Ford*

The new process was built using the principle of invoice-less processing. Now the purchasing department entered order information in a database, and did not send a copy of the data to anyone within the company. When goods arrived at the receiving dock, a receiving clerk checked the material against the outstanding purchase record in the database. If they matched, the clerk accepted the goods and payment was automatically sent to the vendor. If they did not match, the order was returned. Only three data items – part number, unit of measure and supplier code – had to be matched on a purchase order and a receipt order. This removed the jobs of 75 per cent of the accounts payable department.

Some stages for value-stream analysis are:

- Identifying in close detail the nature of the value produced by the organisation. Distinctions between tangible and intangible products and services can help highlight potential areas for change.
- Drawing a map of the current value stream. Techniques such as activity systems modelling, process modelling and information systems modelling come in here.
- Conducting an assessment of the existing value stream. This uses criteria such as the

three Es of performance (efficacy, efficiency and effectiveness). It should consider ways of improving the performance of activities and the flow of physical goods as well as the flow of information. From modelling it may become possible to identify problems with the value stream such as wastage in activities or delays in information handling.

- Considering ways of redesigning elements of the value stream to eliminate problems. This may involve looking at the role of intermediaries in supply and customer chains, and deciding whether to disaggregate or reaggregate. The role of ICT in improving the flow of information and integrating activities needs to be part of this process.
- Defining the new value stream, using a model or a series of models.
- Implementing the new value stream. This needs to take into account the scale of change that is both required and feasible. It may involve considerable organisational and technological change, and so the disciplines of project management (see Chapter 11) and change management (see Chapter 12) are likely to be critical to success.

Recap

The concept of business model can be related to the idea of the organisation as a value-creating system within the wider value network. A business model specifies the design for the organisation, and is a foundation for implementing business processes and information systems. It effectively specifies how the value chain of the company should operate and fit into its wider value network. Both value-chain and value-network analyses (collectively referred to as value-stream analyses) are useful here.

Case check:
Case 24 W
The beer distribution game

The key role of information in the value network can be demonstrated using a management simulation or game originally developed by Jay Forrester and his Systems Dynamics group at MIT during the 1960s. Sometimes known as the beer distribution game, it has been used continually ever since to demonstrate the important systemic nature of business activity and the importance of information to effective management. It is particularly used in Peter Senge's book *The Fifth Discipline* (2006) to illustrate how intuitive decision making is frequently wrong.

It provides a simplification of the typical business supply chain consisting of actors such as wholesalers, retailers and customers. This game has been run many thousands of times at management schools around the world. The experience is the same – systems oscillate more and more widely, in a way that is characteristic of many business activity systems. Players trying to control the business experience frustration and helplessness. This is mostly because they have detailed local information but a lack of information on the behaviour of the entire supply chain and their customers. They tend to react to the local information rather than considering the systemic interrelationship between the actions they take and the supply chain as a whole.

Summary

1. This chapter introduced the concept of value, and its production and distribution. It considered organisations as value-creating systems that interact with a wider value network. They have the option to design their internal activity systems and their relationships and activities with the wider value network to optimise their performance. Information is important for the support of both internal activity and activity with external stakeholders,. The concepts considered in this chapter therefore provide a context for considering the place of ICT and information systems in organisations.
2. The primary environment of any commercial organisation is the economy. Economies can be considered as systems for coordinating the production, distribution and consumption of value. Value traditionally comes in two forms, goods and services (that is, products produced or activities performed by organisations). Goods and services can be seen as the end-points of activity systems performed in business organisations.
3. Goods and services can be categorised in a number of ways. Tangible goods and services have a physical form. Intangible goods and services have a non-physical form and are amenable to representation as information. The flow of both tangible and intangible goods and services has a corresponding flow of information or transactions. A transaction is a data structure that records a coherent unit of activity, typically an event in an activity system or between activity systems.
4. Activity between economic agents is typically organised in one of three ways: hierarchies, markets or networks. Markets are systems of competition. They are media of exchange between buyers and sellers. Managerial hierarchies are systems of cooperation. Exchange within hierarchies is conducted on the basis of established trading arrangements. More recently, a third form of economic control has been proposed. Networks are intermediate forms of economic control in which both cooperation and competition are evident.
5. According to Michael Porter, an economic environment is determined in terms of: the competitive structure of

the industry, the relative power of buyers and sellers, the basis of competition, the state of regulation, the state of technological deployment and whether the industry is growing, shrinking or stable. An organisation takes up a position in an economic system that is defined by its activities and relationships with its competitors, suppliers, customers and regulators.

6 Porter has also proposed a template for the activity systems of the typical business, known as the internal value chain and consisting of a defined set of primary and secondary activities. Two other chains of value are also seen as critical to the competitive environment: the supply chain and the customer chain. These three value chains overlap with another frequently ignored chain of value of increasing significance to organisations: the community chain, founded on social networks of individuals. Its value lies in its ability to generate social capital, one indicator of which is a high level of interpersonal trust, an essential prerequisite for many forms of business and commerce.

7 The concepts of the internal value chain and the wider value network provide the business analyst with ways of considering potential changes to business systems. These involve not only competitive performance but improvements in managing networks of cooperative relationships with other organisations and the global network of potential customers. The effective management of information is critical to ways in which the organisation adapts itself continually to its environment.

The next chapter uses the material in this one as a platform to consider the rise of eBusiness and eCommerce. These are defined in terms of the value chain and the value network, and we consider the place of technological innovation in this mix. The role of ICT in reducing transaction costs is one crucial aspect. This is considered in Chapter 9. The concept of the value network also recurs in considering business strategy in Chapter 10.

Focus on Value

Michael Porter uses the term *value* to describe, at a high level, the key output of the business organisation. It also enables him to focus on the processes that produce value, collectively referred to as the internal value chain. But economies are systems not only of value production but also of value distribution and value consumption. An organisation's value is determined by its position in a wider value network. Typically, the value associated with organisations equates with the services and/or products they provide. However, value also emerges from dispersed forms of 'organisation' evident in social networks. This is related to social capital, the resource for mutual support available in forms of community. Social capital is the key value that members gain from participation in social networks.

Our emphasis on design focuses on the options an organisation has to do things differently, not only within its internal value chain but also in positioning itself in the wider value network. There is key value in the concept of a business model in that it relates issues of strategy, activities and technology.

Review test

1 Economic actors include:

Choose all that are relevant.

- ☐ Customers
- ☐ Suppliers
- ☐ Regulators
- ☐ Partners
- ☐ Controllers
- ☐ Effectors
- ☐ Competitors

2 In Porter's model of the competitive environment, match the force to the appropriate definition.

- Competitive structure of the industry
- Relative power of buyers and sellers
- Basis of competition
- State of regulation in the economic environment
- State of technological deployment in the environment
- Industry growth

- Highlights the important position that customers and suppliers play in markets
- Defines the relative power of competitors to determine things like the pricing policy in the economic environment
- Describes when irregular transactions of a one-off nature are conducted between economic actors and when the processes of execution and settlement are typically combined
- Describes the use of technology and the part it plays in competitiveness and/or cooperation
- Determines the activities that companies may perform in particular markets or hierarchies
- Describes the main products or services sold and the main ways in which organisations compete in the economic environment whether the industry is growing, shrinking or stable

3 A ____________ is some form of product produced by an organisation. A ____________ is some form of activity performed by an organisation.

Fill in the blanks.

4 Intangible goods are those that do not have a physical existence and are fundamentally information-based.

True or false? ☐ True ☐ False

5	A data structure that records a coherent unit of activity, typically an event in a human activity system. Choose the most appropriate terms for this definition. ☐ Database ☐ Transaction ☐ Value
6	Inbound logistics is a primary activity in Porter's value chain. True or false? ☐ True ☐ False
7	Human resource management is a primary activity in Porter's value chain. True or false? ☐ True ☐ False
8	Match the chain of value to the appropriate definition. Customer chain — The flow of goods and services from suppliers Supply chain — The flow of social capital between individuals Community chain — The flow of goods and services to customers
9	Commerce is the exchange of goods and services between businesses, groups and individuals. True or false? ☐ True ☐ False
10	The precise form of the process of commerce will vary depending on: Choose all that are relevant. ☐ The economic actors involved ☐ The type of technology ☐ The frequency of commerce ☐ The nature of the goods or services being exchanged
11	Commerce of whatever nature can be considered as a process with four main phases: Put in descending order using 1 for the first phase. ☐ After-sale ☐ Sale settlement ☐ Sale execution ☐ Pre-sale
12	Match the term for a type of commerce to the appropriate definition. Repeat commerce — Irregular transactions between trading partners and the processes of settlement and execution are separated Credit commerce — Regular, repeat transactions occur between trading partners Cash commerce — Irregular one-off transactions between economic actors with the processes of execution and settlement typically combined
13	Put the phases of the repeat commerce model in the correct order. Use 1 for the first phase. ☐ Delivery ☐ Search ☐ After-sale ☐ Negotiate ☐ Order ☐ Invoice and Payment
14	A ____________ is a network in which the nodes are people and the links or relations are various forms of social interaction and/or social bonds. Fill in the blank.
15	Match the term for economic control to the appropriate definition. Market — A system of competition Hierarchy — A system of cooperation and collaboration Network — A system of co-opetition
16	____________ capital is the productive value of people engaged in a dense network of social relations. Fill in the blank.
17	A ____________ cost is a cost incurred in making an economic exchange. Fill in the blank.
18	A ____________ specifies the structure of human activity systems appropriate for a particular business in terms of its market. Fill in the blank.
19	How does the value chain differ from the value network? Write two sentences.
20	Define disintermediation. Write a sentence.

Exercises

1. Service industries have been the largest growing sectors of western economies. Identify some such industries and the services they supply.
2. Identify the production and distribution processes in an industry known to you.
3. Identify the internal and external value chains relevant to a company or organisation known to you.
4. Provide one example of an economic market and describe what is exchanged in it.
5. Provide one example of an economic hierarchy and determine what established trading relationships exist in it.
6. Describe the actors, relationships, information and transactions in a segment of a market or hierarchy known to you.
7. Identify the competitors, customers and suppliers of an organisation known to you.
8. Describe some of the relationships between competitors, suppliers, customers and regulators in an industrial sector known to you. Determine the basis of competition and the state of technological deployment. Identify whether the industry is growing, shrinking or stable.
9. In relation to the commercial activities associated with a product or service known to you, try to jot down what the four phases of commerce represent.
10. Try to draw a value-chain model for the new accounts payable process at Ford Motor Company from the description supplied on page 221.
11. eMedicine is a developing area of medical practice, and involves the remote treatment of patients using ICT. Experiments have even been undertaken in performing surgical operations using robotic devices controlled across communication networks. How would you class this form of service – tangible or intangible?
12. Choose an example of a commercial activity known to you. List the economic actors involved, the frequency of the activity and the type of product or service offered.
13. Try to model a public sector organisation in terms of activities of the internal value chain.
14. Identify the elements of the customer chain and supply chain of an organisation known to you.
15. When you purchase a product through mail order, attempt to identify the flow of data transactions that accompanies the purchase.
16. If you live in what you would class as a community, investigate how much social capital exists in it. Determine the evidence for this.
17. List a number of the social networks in which you participate. How are you linked to other members? Would you describe the ties as strong or weak?

Projects

1. Select one industrial sector such as retail or finance. Investigate and detail the changes caused in the sector over the last 20 years through the application of ICT. What effect has this had on competitiveness in the sector and on the shape of the sector generally?
2. Take a specific company and develop a case study of the effects of the economic environment on its information systems. For instance, who are the major economic actors in its environment? How much bargaining power do customers have?
3. Develop a case study of the way in which a particular company has used information systems to improve its competitive position. How did the information system improve its profitability?
4. Investigate ways of measuring social capital in a community. For instance, develop some ways in which you might map the social network underlying a virtual community. What sort of bonds or links exist in this network? Are they strong or weak links, and what level of mutual support is provided to members of the social network through such links?
5. Investigate the relationship between transaction costs and consumer behaviour. For instance, what sort of transaction costs are involved in consumers changing their utility (gas, electricity, water, broadband) suppliers? Has the Web reduced these switching costs?
6. Investigate the degree to which music constitutes an information commodity (intangible good) and the consequences this has for the music industry. Try to treat the problem as one demanding a form of value-network analysis.
7. Investigate the degree to which movies constitute an information commodity (intangible good) and the consequences this has for the film industry. Try to treat the problem as one demanding a form of value-network analysis.

Further reading

Porter's original conceptions of the value chain and his model of the competitive environment of the organisation are reconsidered for the Internet age in Porter (2001). Sawney and Parikh (2001) consider the issue of value and ways in which value changes in a connected world. Paolini (1999) introduces the idea of the organisation as a value-creating system. Coase's (1937) work on transaction costs forms the basis for Malone et al's (1987) treatment of electronic markets and hierarchies, and the more recent popular discussion of this in Tapscott and Williams' consideration of new collaborative forms of working supported through ICT (2006). Value-stream analysis is a part of 'lean thinking', covered in the text by Womack and Jones (2003).

References

Anthony, R. A. (1988) *The Management Control Function*. Boston, Mass., Harvard Business School Press.

Bakos, J. Y. (1997). 'Reducing buyer search costs – implications for electronic marketplaces', *Management Science* **43**(12): 1676–92.

Chaffey, D. (2002) *E-Business and E-Commerce Management*. Harlow, Essex, Pearson Education.

Checkland, P. (1987) *Systems Thinking, Systems Practice*. Chichester, John Wiley.

Checkland, P. (1999) *Soft Systems Methodology: A thirty year retrospective*. Chichester, John Wiley.

Coase, R. H. (1937) 'The $$m', *Economica* **4**(16): 386–405.

Deise, M., Nowikow, C., King, P. and Wright, A. (2000) *Executive's Guide to E-Business: From tactics to strategy*. New York, John Wiley.

Floridi, L. (2007) 'A look into the future impact of ICT on our lives', *Information Society* **23**(1): 59–64.

Granovetter, M. (1973) 'The strength of weak ties', *American Journal of Sociology* 78.

Hammer, M. (1990) 'Re-engineering work: don't automate, obliterate', *Harvard Business Review* (July–August), 18–25.

Hammer, M. (1996) *Beyond Re-engineering: How the process-centred organisation is changing our lives*. London, Harper Collins.

Hoque, F. (2000) *E-enterprise: Business models, architecture and components*. Cambridge, Cambridge University Press.

Jackson, M. C. (2003) *Systems Thinking: Creative holism for managers*. Chichester, John Wiley.

Kalakota, R. and M. Robinson (1999) *E-Business: Roadmap for success*. Reading, Mass, Addison-Wesley.

Linder, J. C. and S. Cantrell (2000) 'Changing business models: surveying the landscape.' Working paper. Accenture Institute for Strategic Change.

Malone, T. W., Yates, J. and Benjamin, R. I. C. (1987) 'Electronic markets and electronic hierarchies', *Communications of the ACM* **30**(6): 484–97.

Osterwalder, A. and Pigneur, Y. (2002) 'An ebusiness model ontology for modeling ebusiness.' 15th ecommerce conference, Bled, Slovenia.

Paolini, C. (1999) *The Value Net: A tool for competitive strategy*. Chichester, John Wiley.

Porter, M. E. (1985) *Competitive Advantage: Creating and sustaining superior performance*. New York, Free Press.

Porter, M. E. (2001) 'Strategy and the Internet', *Harvard Business Review* **79**(3): 63–78.

Porter, M. E. and Millar, V. E. (1985) 'How information gives you competitive advantage', *Harvard Business Review* **63**(4): 149–60.

Preece, J. (2002) 'Supporting community and building social capital', *Communications of the ACM* **45**(4): 37–9.

Putnam, R. D. (2000) *Bowling Alone: The collapse and revival of American community*. New York, Simon and Schuster.

Rayport, J. and Sviokla, J. (1996) 'Exploiting the virtual value-chain', *McKinsey Quarterly* 1: 20–37.

Sawhney, M. and Parikh, D. (2001) 'Where value lies in a networked world', *Harvard Business Review* **79**(1): 79–86.

Senge, P. M. (2006) *The Fifth Discipline: The art and practice of the learning organisation*. New York, Doubleday.

Tapscott, D. and Williams, A. D. (2006) *Wikinomics: How mass collaboration changes everything*. London, Atlantic Books.

Thompson, G. F. (2003) *Between Hiearachies and Markets: The logic and limits of network forms of organization*. Oxford, Oxford University Press.

Timmers, P. (1998) 'Business models for electronic marketplaces', *Electronic Markets* **8**(1): 3–8.

Timmers, P. (1999) *Electronic Commerce: Strategies and models for business to business trading*. Chichester, John Wiley.

Tonnies, F. (1935) *Gemeinschaft und Gessellschaft*. Leipzig.

Whiteley, D. (2000) *E-commerce: Strategy, technologies and applications*. Maidenhead, Berks, McGraw-Hill.

Womack, J. P. and Jones, D. T. (2003) *Lean thinking: Banish waste and create wealth in your corporation*. London, Free Press Business.

Worthington, I. and Britton, C. (2005) *The Business Environment*. Englewood Cliffs, N.J., Prentice Hall.

CHAPTER 8

Electronic business and electronic commerce

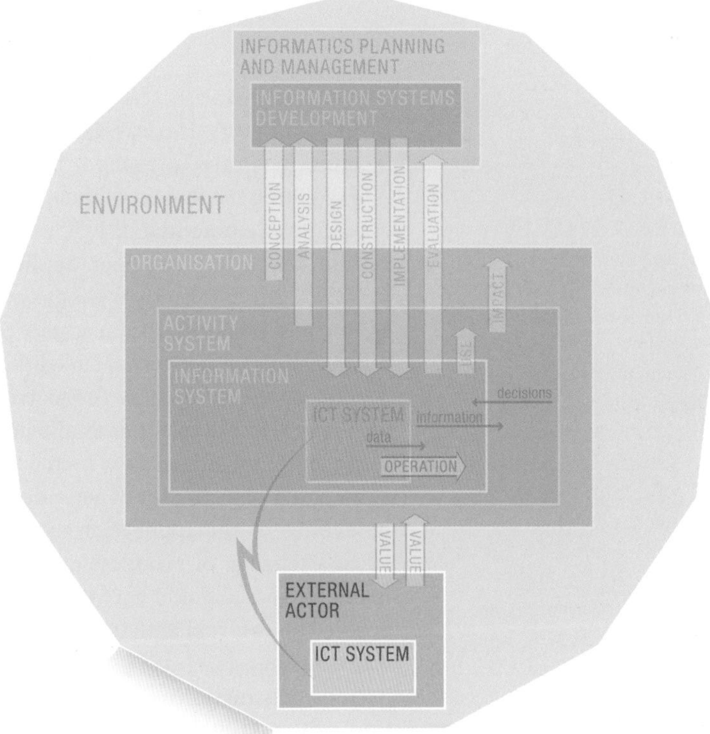

Half the money I spend on advertising is wasted, and the trouble is I don't know which half.

Lord Leverhulme (1851–1925)

CHAPTER OUTLINE

LEARNING OUTCOMES	PRINCIPLES
Define the concept of electronic business and distinguish between electronic commerce and electronic business.	ICT has been used in organisations for a number of decades to support the internal value chain. More recently it has been used to enable activities within the wider value network. Electronic business (eBusiness) is the term for the application of ICT in businesses. Electronic commerce (eCommerce) is the term for ICT enablement of activities and relationships with external stakeholders.
Describe the major forms of eBusiness and distinguish between them in terms of the features defined in Chapter 7.	Four major forms of eBusiness are discussed which link to parts of the value network discussed in Chapter 7. Internal eBusiness focuses on the internal value chain. B2C eCommerce focuses on the customer chain and B2B eCommerce on the supply-chain. C2C eCommerce focuses on developments in the community chain.
Identify the importance of electronic marketing to B2C eCommerce and describe key elements of it.	Electronic marketing is considered an important subprocess of B2C eCommerce. As more businesses move operations online, managing electronic communications with customers assumes greater significance.
Discuss the importance of electronic procurement to B2B eCommerce and describe the key elements of it.	Electronic procurement is considered an important subprocess of B2B eCommerce. Managing procurement of supplies through electronic channels is a major way in which organisations improve their efficiency.

Introduction

The eminent British scientist Michael Faraday once gave the (then) prime minister a tour of his laboratory He was asked what use the discovery of electricity could possibly have. 'I cannot say,' Faraday replied, 'but one day Her Majesty's government will tax it.'

Predicting the impact of technology is a tricky business. Of the many predictions about the revolutionary potential of ICT use in business, some have missed the mark and others have hit the target. ICT has been applied for the last 30 years to the change of internal business practices. More recently the focus on innovation in this area has shifted to outside the organisation, and it is now on the application of technology to external activities and in support of relationships with external stakeholders.

Organisational activity in electronic hierarchies, markets or networks (see Chapter 7) is generally referred to either as eBusiness or eCommerce. This chapter makes a clear distinction between these: eBusiness is seen a superset of eCommerce. Business can be considered either as an entity or as the set of activities undertaken by a commercial organisation. EBusiness can be defined as the application of ICT in support of all the activities of business. Commerce is the exchange of products and services between businesses, groups and individuals, so it is one of the essential activities of any business. ECommerce focuses on the use of ICT to enable the external activities and relationships of the business with individuals, groups and other businesses.

Intra-business eBusiness: The use of ICT to enable internal business processes.

Social infrastructure: The social infrastructure for eBusiness consists of those human activity systems central to supporting the conduct of eBusiness. These include competencies in planning, management, development and evaluation.

Consumer: An actor (individual, group, organisation) which consumes a good or service.

These distinctions allow us to distinguish between the use of ICT to enable communication and coordination between the internal stakeholders of the business such as employees (INTRA-BUSINESS EBUSINESS) and the use of ICT to enable communication and coordination with external actors such as suppliers and customers (eCommerce). By definition intra-business eBusiness has been around as long as ICT has been applied within business. Many eCommerce applications also have a history of 20 years or so. However, it should not be assumed that we have seen the end of innovation in this area. Both the technical and SOCIAL INFRASTRUCTURE of eBusiness are continually evolving to meet the challenges of an increasingly volatile and global environment (see Chapter 7).

Kalakota and Whinston (1997) define at least four perspectives on eBusiness, each of which effectively provides a different definition. From a *communication perspective*, eBusiness consists of the delivery of information, products/services or payments via communication networks. From a *business perspective*, it can be seen as the application of ICT in the automation of business transactions and workflows. From a *service perspective*, it is a tool that addresses the desire of firms, CONSUMERS and management to cut service costs while improving the quality of goods and increasing the speed of service delivery. Finally, from an *online perspective*, eBusiness provides the capability of buying and selling products and information on the Internet and using other online services.

In a sense, these perspectives correspond to the distinctions between activity systems, information systems and ICT systems made in previous chapters. EBusiness can be viewed in terms of the changes to organisational structures and processes made possible by ICT (business/service perspective), of the extension of information systems into the environment of organisations (online perspective) or of innovations in technology making interorganisational communication easier (communications perspective).

This chapter builds on the definitions in the generic model for commerce outlined in Chapter 7. Commerce of whatever nature can be considered as a system of exchange between economic actors with a number of generic phases or states. The precise form of the system of commerce will vary depending on the nature of the economic actors involved, the nature of the goods or services being exchanged and the frequency of commerce.

ECommerce refers to the use of ICT to enable aspects of this system of exchange. There are three distinct forms of eCommerce, based on the model of the value network: business to consumer (B2C), business to business (B2B) and consumer to consumer (C2C). Two key subprocesses of B2C and B2B eCommerce are also considered: electronic marketing (eMarketing) for B2C, and electronic procurement (eProcurement) for B2B. This is because of their contemporary significance as key process strategies for improving organisational performance.

B2B: Business to business

B2C: Business to consumer

To this discussion of B2C, B2B and C2C eCommerce there needs to be added a concern with the changing nature of internal activities. Intra-business eBusiness traditionally concerns the use of ICT to improve internal processes. Modern business is a global phenomenon, and businesses now use ICT to integrate their business divisions and units on the global scale. They also participate in complex partnerships with other businesses, using ICT to cooperate in the delivery of value. This is known as partner to partner (P2P) eCommerce.

eBusiness

Bricks and mortar businesses: Businesses in the sense that they have a physical presence, usually buildings where they can be located.

Clicks and mortar businesses: Businesses that still maintain a physical presence but also offer services and products that are accessible online.

Clicks-only businesses: Businesses that have emerged entirely in the online environment.

For a while, traditional businesses were known as 'BRICKS AND MORTAR' BUSINESSES in the sense that they have a physical presence: offices, factories, retail outlets. When they move into the world of eBusiness they are often called 'CLICKS AND MORTAR' BUSINESSES. They still maintain a physical presence but also offer services and products through websites (see Chapter 6). Businesses that have emerged entirely in the online environment are known as 'CLICKS-ONLY' BUSINESSES (Thomas, Ranganathan and Desouza, 2005). This chapter focuses on these last two areas. Decisions about a particular business's particular eBusiness strategy (see Chapter 10) rely on understanding the ways in which ICT can be used to innovate within the wider value network.

Figure 8.1 provides a framework for understanding the current make-up of eBusiness, based on the idea of the organisation as a value-creating system in a wider value network (see Chapter 7). The original Porter value-chain model (Porter, 1985) has proved useful for understanding the place of ICT. More recently the value-chain idea has been extended into the idea of the value network (Kalakota and Robinson, 1999), which is particularly useful as a means of distinguishing between distinct forms of eBusiness. This model also allows us to place some of the newer application areas for eBusiness (such as social networking sites) in relation to some of the more established areas.

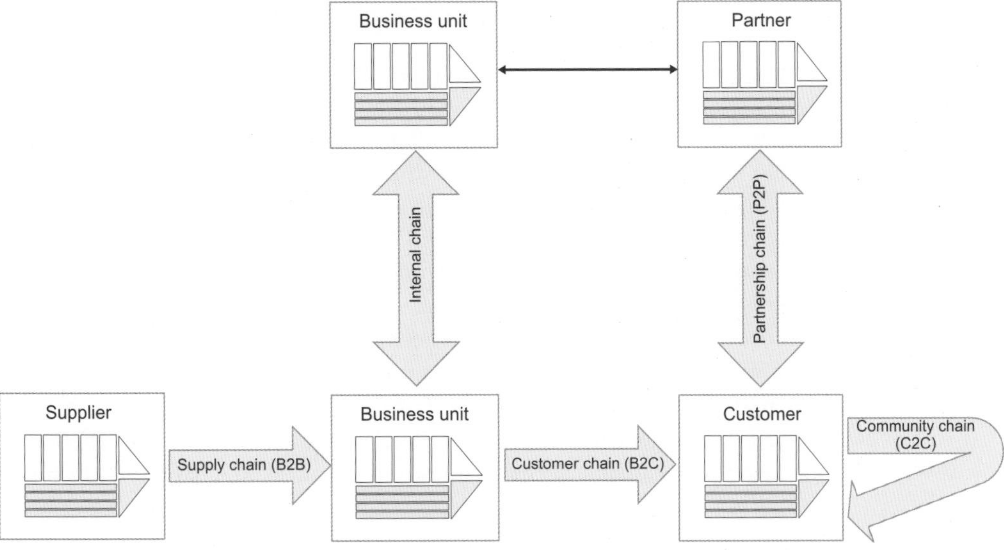

Figure 8.1: *The domain of eBusiness*

C2C eCommerce: Consumer to consumer eCommerce. ICT enablement of aspects of the community chain.

The traditional view of eCommerce mapped onto the value network is of ICT supporting external activities and relationships with two major stakeholder groups, suppliers and customers. B2C eCommerce is sometimes called sell-side eCommerce, and concerns enabling the customer chain with ICT. B2B eCommerce is sometimes called buy-side eCommerce, and involves supporting the supply chain with ICT. C2C ECOMMERCE also has a place in this model: it is a developing form of eCommerce recently linked to 'new media' services. This is potentially the most radical form of eCommerce since it overlaps with non-commercial activity in communities. It is therefore built on the 'community' chain, and a new range of business opportunities emerge, with virtual networking as a phenomenon driving new levels of content and services.

The massive levels of interest in eCommerce over the last decade have tended to devalue the importance of ICT to internal operations. This is a mistake. The model in Figure 8.1 emphasises that eBusiness is as much about internal operations as it is about external operations. It also highlights the increasing importance of integrating the internal and external, so Figure 8.1 includes two areas that extend both the internal and external forms of eBusiness.

First, any contemporary definition of eBusiness must include the growing range of issues associated with providing effective infrastructure for multi-part businesses spread geographically. The modern eBusiness is likely to be made up of numerous business units, some located close together, and others dispersed or even mobile. Modern ICT infrastructure acts as a critical backbone for this type of complex organisation.

Second, any modern conception of eBusiness must extend the notion of business cooperation and collaboration beyond the supply chain, to a network of business partnerships. Hence, eBusiness involves the application of ICT in both cooperative and competitive activity. A business can fulfil a number of different roles in the value network at the same time, such as being both a partner and a competitor. This is sometimes called co-optition.

Did you know?

One of the most important forms of P2P eBusiness involves the partnership between a company and another that supports the whole or part of its informatics services.

ECommerce

ECommerce is the use of ICT to enable external activities and relationships with individuals, groups and other businesses (Laudon and Traver, 2002). It supports supply chains, customer chains and community chains (see Chapter 7), and used to be conducted through eMarkets or eHierarchies. More recently networks have become more important as a control mechanism for electronic activity, and hence electronic social networks have become important for business activity.

There has been a lot of hype about eCommerce, particularly during the 'dot-com' boom, the investment bubble associated with Internet start-up companies during the late 1990s. Cassidy (2002) compared this with other financial booms and busts such as the South Sea Bubble in the 18th century. Much of the emphasis in this period was on B2C eCommerce, probably because it is the most visible form, but most of the business conducted electronically over the last decade has been B2B eCommerce. Much recent interest is in the business opportunities afforded by social networking sites, which has provided some renewed vigour to the phenomenon of C2C eCommerce.

There are a number of differences between the three major forms of eCommerce: the value chain supported, the economic actors involved, the direction of transactional/informational flow between economic actors, the form of commerce transacted, the nature of goods or services exchanged, and the typical model of economic exchange. These distinctions (which build on the discussion of the business environment in Chapter 7) are summarised in Table 8.1.

Table 8.1: *Forms of eCommerce*

	B2C	B2B	C2C
Value chain	Customer chain	Supply chain	Community chain
Economic actors	Company/consumers	Company/suppliers	Consumers/consumers
Direction of transactional flow	Consumer–customer	Company–supplier	Consumer– consumer
Nature of goods/ services	Standard-priced items	Customised/high-price items	Negotiated/low-price items
Form of commerce	Cash/credit	Credit/repeat	Cash
Model of economic exchange	Markets	Hierarchies	Networks

B2C eCommerce

B2C eCommerce: The use of eCommerce in the customer chain.

These concern the use of ICT to enable forms of cash and credit commerce between a company and its customers or consumers. So B2C ECOMMERCE generally focuses on sell-side activities in the customer chain, The primary difference between B2C and C2B eCommerce is the transactional/informational flow: in B2C it is from business to consumer, while in C2B it is from consumer to business. In this book the term B2C eCommerce refers to both directions of flow.

Customers or consumers are typically individuals, but sometimes other organisations. Cash commerce for low and standard-priced goods typically follows the four stages of the generic commerce model discussed in Chapter 7 quite closely, with a see/buy/get sequence. For medium to high-priced items a form of credit commerce will operate. Typically, B2C eCommerce uses a market model of economic exchange in which economic actors freely exchange goods and services in many-to-many interaction.

Tesco.com is an example of B2C eCommerce. People buy low-cost items such as groceries through a catalogue available on the website, pay for them using a debit or credit card, then have them delivered by delivery van.

B2B eCommerce

B2B eCommerce: The use of e-Commerce in the supply chain.

B2B ECOMMERCE supports the supply chain of organisations since it focuses on buy-side activities. Its organisational actors are public and/or private sector organisations, and it involves using ICT to enable forms of credit and repeat commerce.

For high-priced and customised goods traded using a repeat commerce model, a form of managerial hierarchy controls the operation of the commercial relationship. Interorganisational information systems such as extranets (see Chapter 6) have become popular as a technological vehicle.

Tesco, for example, manages aspects of its supply chain using ICT systems such as extranets, to support patterns of repeat orders, delivery and payment between the company and its major suppliers.

PART 3

C2C eCommerce

C2C eCommerce supports the community chain, so it can be seen as a commercial extension of community activities. It typically occurs between individuals, and involves forms of cash commerce generally for low-cost services or goods, so it tends to follow a market model for economic exchange. Other forms of value may also be generated in the communities or social networks engaged in C2C eCommerce, particularly social capital (see Chapter 7), so network forms of economic control are particularly applicable.

Auction: A form of commercial exchange involving bidding.

Internet auction: An auction conducted over the Internet.

EBay is the classic example of C2C eCommerce, with individuals typically trading low-cost items using its online AUCTIONS. The value of eBay as an eMarket lies in its ability to connect millions of sellers with millions of possible buyers worldwide. More recently interest has grown in the potential of social networking sites such as MySpace for commercial activity, particularly for encouraging users to make product referrals.

Benefits of eCommerce

Many benefits have been claimed from the adoption of eCommerce, generally related to improving activities and/or relationships in the value network:

- Reduced transaction or coordination costs. When sales and after-sales service operations replace paper-based communications with electronic communication, it should make their processes more efficient.
- More efficient external-facing activity systems such as outbound logistics: for example, enabling a company to manage its inventory better, and capture and process orders more quickly.
- Closer integration of suppliers into inventory systems, enabling just-in-time manufacturing.

Reflect
For a company such as Tesco, which type of eCommerce do you think provides most benefit, and why?

Information security: The process of protecting information systems from criminal or unwanted activity.

- Innovative ways of marketing new products and services, leading to a general improvement in customer relations. This might allow companies that traditionally traded on the local scale to do business on a global scale.

Problems with eCommerce

There are also a number of problems associated with eCommerce.

- Many people still do not trust eCommerce enough to use the Web to buy high-value goods or services. They are worried about the security of electronic transactions and reluctant to release personal information over the Internet (see Chapter 6). The first is an issue of INFORMATION SECURITY, the second an issue of information privacy.
- Technological standards are developing rapidly in support of electronic trade, and sometimes they are not particularly secure or not easily integrated with standards in other areas. Much work is being undertaken worldwide to create effective security standards for the transmission of electronic transactions.
- It can be difficult to find particular suppliers of goods and services on the Internet. E-brokers (or information brokerages) try to satisfy this need. This is effectively a process of reintermediation (see Chapter 7).
- Some people worry about the digital divide: the fact that older and more economically disadvantaged people are less likely to have a home internet connection so they are excluded from much eCommerce.
- Mistakes are very visible with online systems. For instance, the initial introduction of the cross-company loyalty card Nectar experienced problems because people were unable to register their details on a website established for this purpose. This was apparently because of the volume of traffic on the website in the first week. When Barclays Bank first introduced online banking, customers found they were able to access other customers' financial details, and the company had to apologise.

Recap 

EBusiness is a superset of eCommerce. Its forms can be mapped onto the value network. Two forms are focused on internal relationships (internal eBusiness) and relationships with partners. There are also three major forms of eCommerce: B2C, B2B and C2C. The benefits of eCommerce include cost savings and time savings. Its problems include issues of security and technological standards.

B2C eCommerce

Traditional business processes involving relationships between businesses and customers include sales, marketing and after-sales. They have all been changed by the use of ICT over a number of years, but two trends explain the current explosion of interest in ICT enablement of the customer chain. First, the rise of the Internet and the Web means people find it much easier to connect to electronic networks at home or in public places, and there is a push to make use of these new access channels. Second, although distant customers have communicated with businesses using the post and telephones for a long time, it is only more recently that organisations have been able to deliver a range of goods and services remotely.

This section describes some of the major ways in which the customer chain is being supported and restructured using ICT (De Kare-Silver, 2000). B2C eCommerce acts as an extension of the customer-facing information systems discussed in Chapter 4.

Credit-based payment systems: Systems modelled on conventional payment mechanisms such as cheques and credit cards except that signatures are digital rather than physical.

Database/website integration: The technologies associated with integrating database systems with websites.

Since the customer chain uses either a cash or a credit model of commerce (see Figure 8.2), B2C eCommerce applications can be used to support the pre-sale, sale execution, sale settlement and after-sale stages of operation. For instance, in the pre-sale phase, people can be made aware of products through banners on websites, inclusion in search engines and personalised marketing based on customer profiling. Online catalogues and portals also enable product comparisons to be made between vendors. In sale execution, websites make it possible to order products and services online. Sale settlement means that online payment can be made through secure B2C sites integrated with back-end information systems such as finance and distribution. After-sale may involve various forms of customer profiling and preferencing, and this information can be used to encourage further purchases. The use of this technology has stimulated interest in integrating information across all the phases of the customer chain, so eCommerce can be used to support the process of customer relationship management.

For example, take an online seller of art prints. Its pre-sale activities might include emailing past and potential customers with details of products and discounts. Sale execution is conducted through online ordering. Sale settlement is conducted through online payment using a financial intermediary. After-sale service includes the creation of a customer profiling system which automatically emails previous customers with details of new prints in their indicated areas of interest.

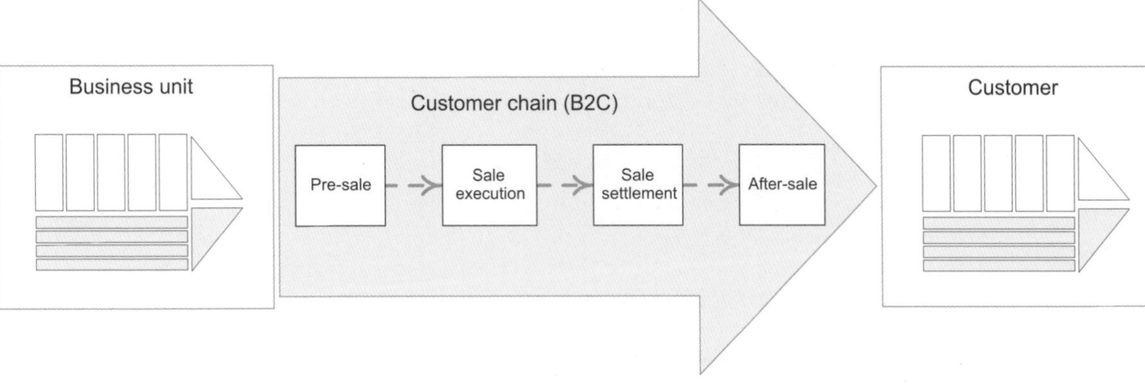

Figure 8.2: *The customer chain*

> Did you know?
>
> Estimates of the number of websites worldwide vary, but many reckon there are over 100 million distinct ones, and between 15 billion and 30 billion web pages.

The B2C eCommerce infrastructure

An organisation's experience of B2C eCommerce typically moves through a number of distinct stages, of increasing ICT infrastructure complexity, and increasing support for activities. These form extensions of the customer-facing information systems described in Chapter 4. They include:

- information-seeking and communication
- establishing an online marketing presence
- creating an online catalogue
- online ordering
- handling online payment
- offering online delivery
- customer profiling and preferencing.

For example, small and medium-sized enterprises (SMEs) (with less then 250 employees) might start by using a computer connected to the Internet to seek out information about competitors. They will also probably use it to email suppliers. Depending upon its business strategy, the SME might eventually reach the stage at which most of its business is conducted electronically.

Each of these stages supports a part of the model of commerce described in Chapter 7. Pre-sale activities include information seeking and communication, creating a marketing presence and establishing an online catalogue. Sale execution activities are online ordering and potentially online delivery. Sale settlement activities mean online payment, and after-sales activities are customer profiling and preferencing.

Information-seeking and communication

In the first stage, a company begins to engage with the Internet, probably using it primarily for **information seeking and communication** via email (Figure 8.4). The Internet and the

Web have provided a much more effective and efficient way to look for information than existed previously, and there are many software tools (such as search engines) to help with this (see Chapter 5).

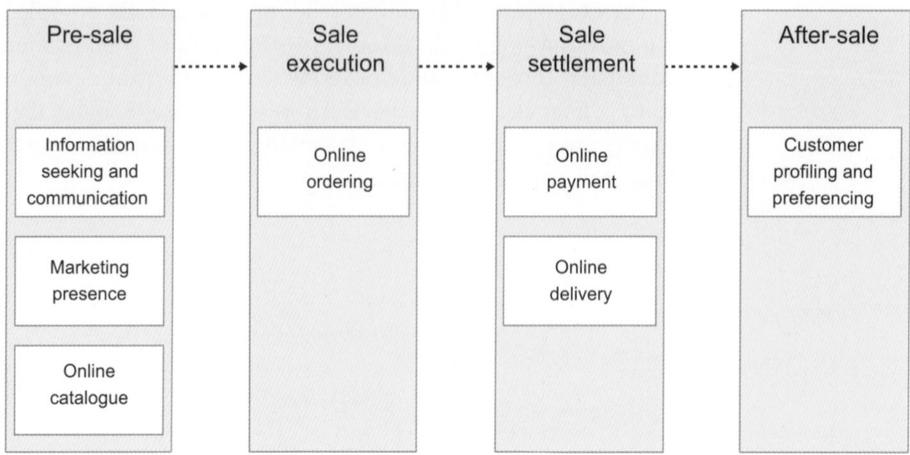

Figure 8.3: *Stages of B2C eCommerce systems*

Email is a significant technology for business because it allows asynchronous communication between stakeholders (unlike a phone call, say, both parties do not need to be communicating at the same time). It also enables the easy transfer of electronic files. If a company has an email address this makes it easy for customers to make enquiries and place orders.

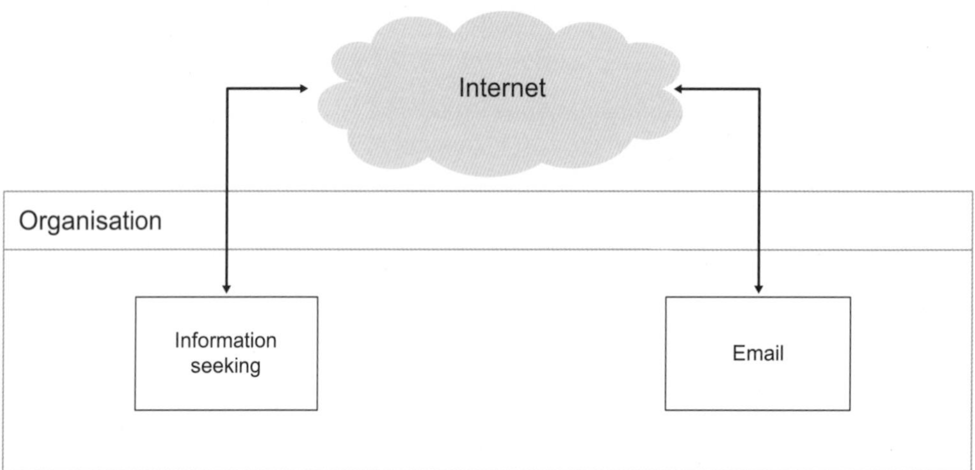

Figure 8.4: *Information seeking and communication*

Surprisingly perhaps, many SMEs are at this stage in the adoption of eCommerce, particularly micro-enterprises with less than ten employees.

Marketing presence

The next step is to establish a **marketing presence** on the Internet by setting up a corporate website (Figure 8.5). It will provide a company profile, most likely including a description of the main activities, the location and contact details. A simple website allows potential customers to communicate with the company through email.

Within the UK a number of portals have been produced specifically to act as gateways to the websites of SMEs within a particular region of the country.

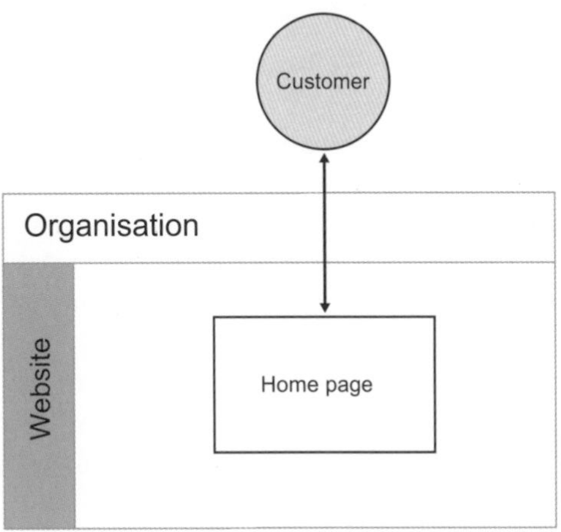

Figure 8.5: *Marketing presence*

Online catalogue

Here the company provides an **online catalogue** of its products or services, which could consist of a series of static web pages, or may be dynamic in the sense that it is updated from a database. More sophisticated sites allow dynamic pricing of product information, so that different types of market segment (such as irregular and regular customers) can be given different information. Customers still have to place orders through traditional channels such as over the telephone, through the post or potentially through email (Figure 8.6).

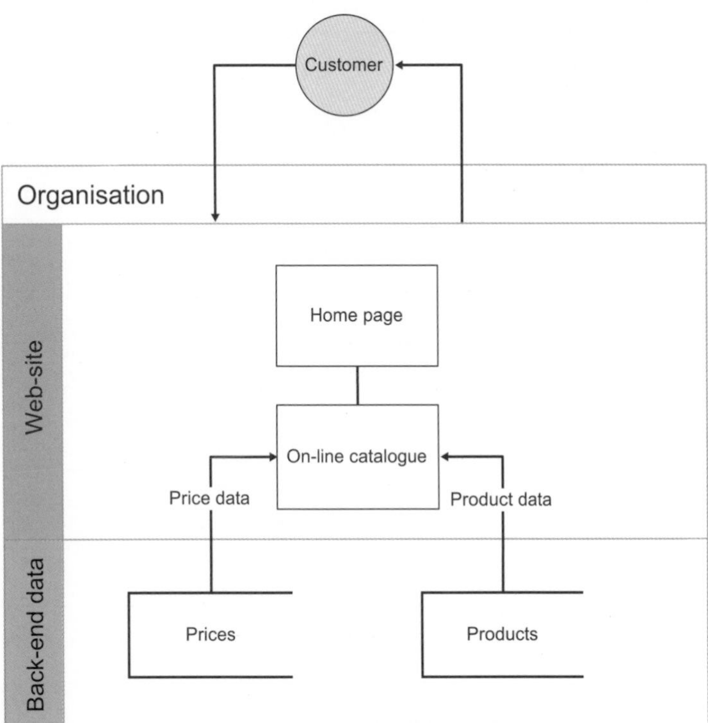

Figure 8.6: *Online catalogue*

For instance, a specialist music publisher produces an **online catalogue** of its range of specialist publications. For each publication there is a cover image, a short synopsis of the contents, and details of the price and delivery charges. To order publications customers have to telephone or send an order form through the post with payment.

Online ordering

The next logical step is to enable customers to place orders online. This is a key transition point for most businesses since it involves the integration of websites with back-end information systems. In forms of credit commerce the company invoices the customer for payment after delivery. This calls for integration between the website and the sales-order processing information system. The sales-order information system will trigger the outbound logistics information system that manages deliveries. Payment details will also ideally be passed to the organisation's finance system, which sends an invoice and receives payment (Figure 8.7).

For example, a bulk supplier of specialist stationery to the trade might provide an online catalogue of its range of products. This material can be ordered via the Internet site for established customers. The traditional outbound logistics, invoicing and finance systems of the supplier are used to support the B2C process.

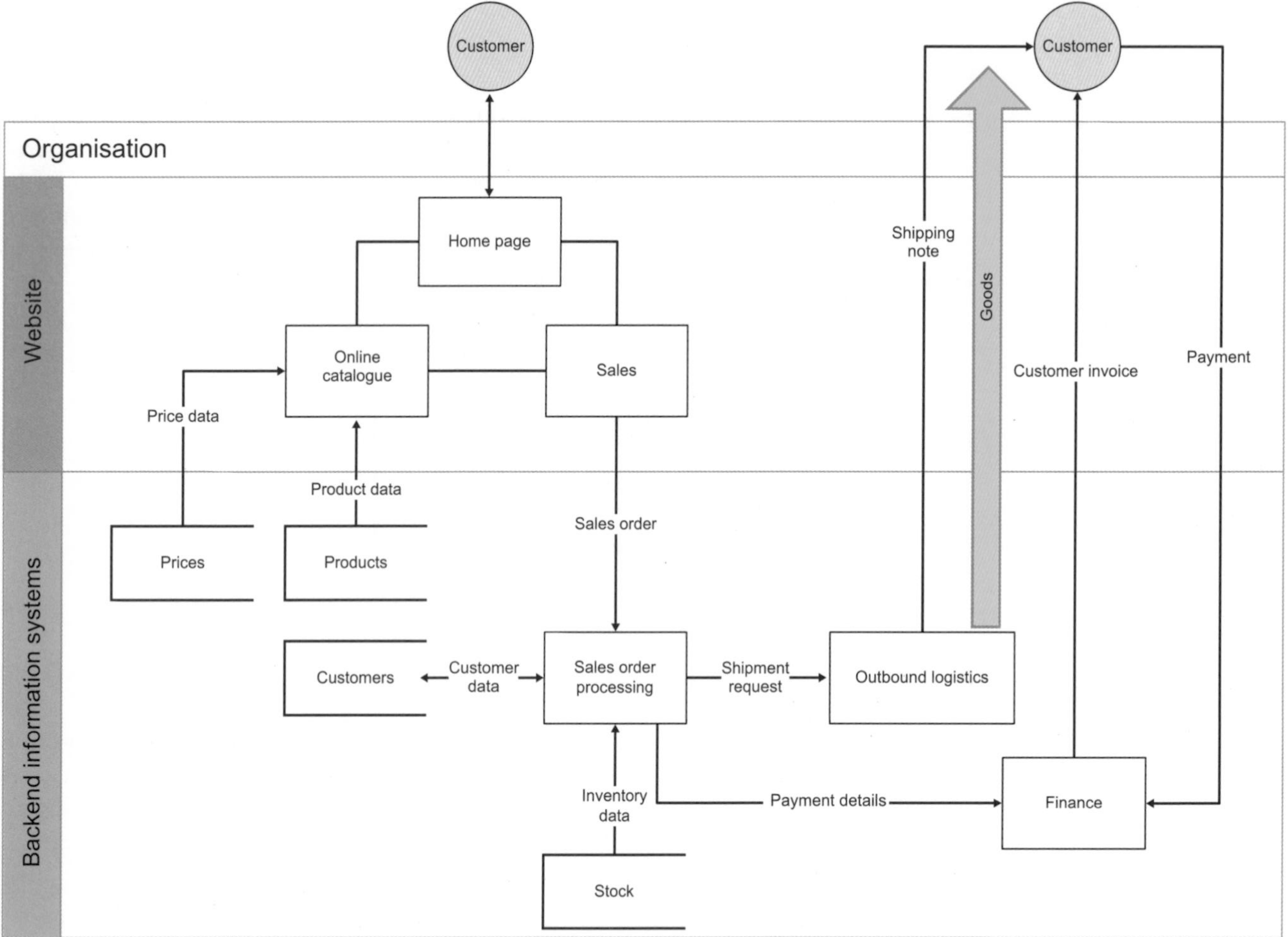

Figure 8.7: *Online ordering*

Online payment

In this scenario the customer both orders and pays for goods using the website. This is more usual for cash commerce in which the customer is an individual and the goods are standardised and relatively low-price, such as CDs or books. This form of B2C eCommerce demands a close integration between an organisation's front-end and back-end information systems.

Figure 8.8 outlines the typical functionality of many sites offering online ordering and payment. (Obviously, individual sites vary, and might not exactly fit this template.) The customer first orders goods using an electronic shopping facility in the sales system. The shopping

Electronic payment system: A system for the electronic transfer of monetary data.

facility calculates the total cost of the order and includes the delivery charge. The customer enters credit or debit card details, and completes the purchase via a secure PAYMENT SYSTEM.

Payment details are checked with a financial intermediary such as the customer's bank. Provided sufficient funds are available the intermediary makes an electronic funds transfer to the company's bank account, and details of the transfer are recorded in the company's finance system (Figure 8.8).

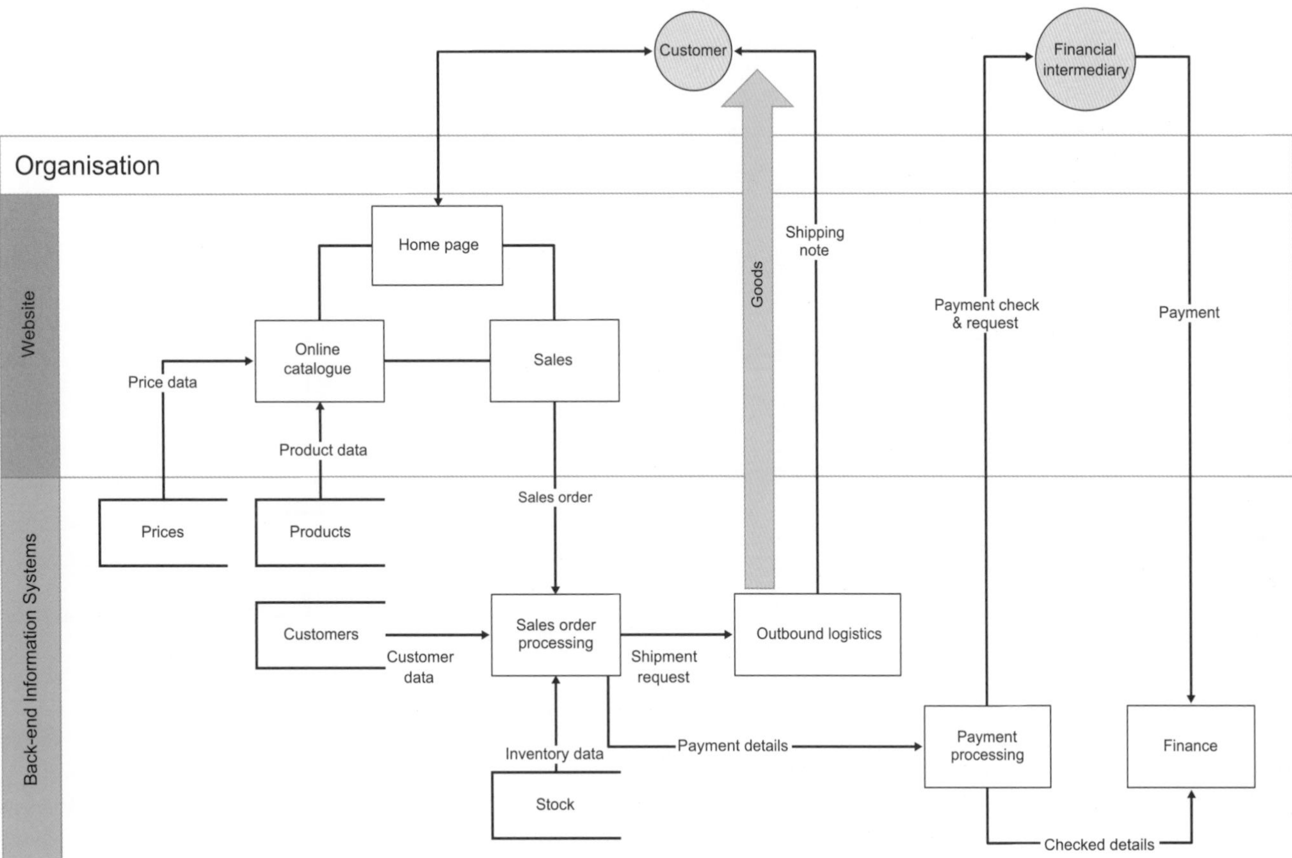

Figure 8.8: *Online payment*

For the company which supplies high-quality art prints, customers can search for prints by theme, period, artist and price. They can look at images of selected prints at various degrees of resolution, and order them in various sizes. They add their selected prints to a shopping trolley and pay online by credit or debit card. The site automatically confirms orders via email.

Online delivery

There are established digital standards now not just for textual and numeric data, but for audio and video as well, so an increasing range of intangible goods can be **delivered** electronically in digital format. This means that the outbound logistics system in Figure 8.8 is replaced by an online delivery system. There is also less likely to be a need for separate inventory and product databases, since one database can hold both product descriptions and the data that comprise the products themselves.

Sometimes intangible goods and services are paid for per item, but in other models there is a subscription system, perhaps with monthly payments. For instance, suppliers of virus protection software sometimes work on a subscription basis, in return for which they provide frequent updates. Music files are sometimes provided on a subscription basis too (either a set limit of downloads per month, or as much as the user requires), although others use a cash-based model, with a payment for each individual download.

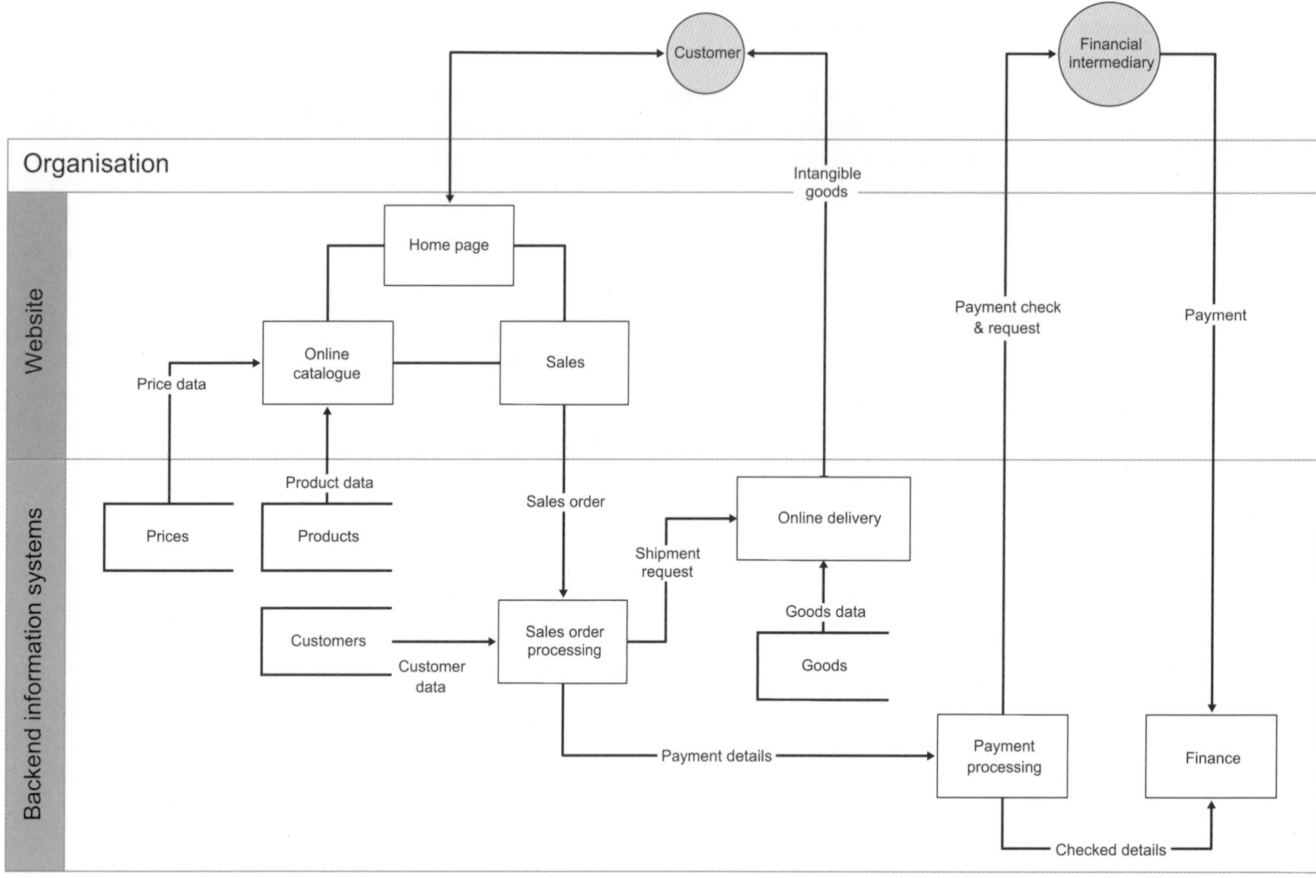

Figure 8.9: *Online delivery*

Global information system: An information system that operates across the globe.

Globalisation: The process by which organisations are operating across the globe.

Customer profiling and preferencing: A mechanism of customising online products and services for the customer based on detailed information captured about the customer.

Customer profiling and preferencing

In the modern business world, where GLOBALISATION means that companies face increasing competition, the customer is a key focus. Winning new customers and keeping existing customers satisfied is seen to be key to organisational success, and electronic systems can help to provide the efficient service that contributes to this.

Customer relationship management (CRM, sometimes known as customer chain management) comprises a set of activities that support the entire customer chain. In an electronic CRM system, an organisation's information systems track all customer interactions, from initial enquiries through orders to after-sales services. Often for larger companies, the customer-facing systems are integrated with a CUSTOMER PROFILING AND PREFERENCING system. This information system dynamically builds a profile of each customer, and adjusts it on the basis of new transactions. This profile is then used to offer the customer a targeted range of goods and/or services (Figure 8.10).

Many Internet booksellers such as Amazon now use customer-profiling systems. Stored email addresses combined with a previous purchase history enable the company to email customers with details of new books in their area of interest, perhaps offering special discounts as well.

Customer relationship management

CRM is an attempt to establish long-term relationships with customers. It comprise three interrelated processes: customer acquisition, customer retention and customer extension.

Customer acquisition is the set of activities and techniques used to gain new customers. For eBusiness this clearly involves attracting customers to websites, so eMarketing is a critical part of this aspect (see below). It also involves attempts to persuade the customer to engage in a dialogue with the company, through which its systems can construct a profile of

Consumer behaviour: The behaviour of consumers, and particularly their decision making, in the commercial process.

them: the products or services they have shown an interest in, their demographic profile and general purchasing BEHAVIOUR.

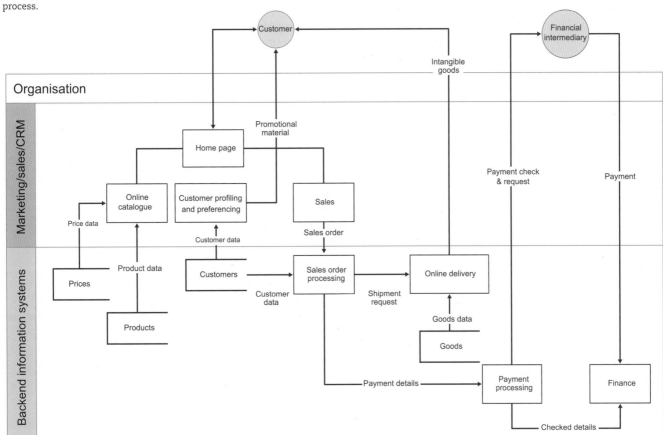

Figure 8.10: *Customer relationship management*

For a high-street bank, for instance, customer acquisition means persuading people to open an account or perhaps take up another financial product such as insurance or a loan. Online banking has become an expected part of the services offered, so it plays an important part in attracting new customers.

Customer retention is the set of activities and techniques designed to maintain relationships with existing customers. For eCommerce it has the related goals of retaining customers (repeat customers) and persuading them to keep communicating online (repeat visits). Two factors are critical to retention: customer satisfaction and customer loyalty.

One technique used in customer retention is the personalisation of email content. Customers receive alerts about products or services that their profile has suggested they will find particularly interesting: a new album by a musician whose previous work they have bought, for instance. These alerts may also offer discounts or other added-value services in a bid to persuade customers to return to a B2C website.

Reflect
Take an organisation known to you. At what stage would you describe it as being at in its B2C eCommerce?

For the bank, customer retention activities might include offering multi-channel access to accounts and aggregated products such as combined bank accounts and mortgages. Because online transactions are cheaper for the company, online customers are given inducements to keep on using electronic communications, such as higher interest on balances in savings accounts.

Customer extension activities and techniques encourage existing customers to increase their level of involvement with a company. This is made easier in the online environment as more targeted promotions can be offered to customers.

All these activities depend heavily on good information: knowing who the customers are, what they are purchasing, how satisfied they are with the company and what future services and products they want. Hence, there has been an increasing emphasis on information systems to support the CRM process.

It might be argued that B2C eCommerce in general and CRM in particular are a natural consequence of the increasing customer focus. Porter (1985) has argued that the value delivered to the customer is the key feature of contemporary business (see Chapter 7), so it is not surprising to find companies attempting to reorient their processes and systems around customers, instead of around business events such as orders and sales.

Take for example an insurance company whose products include life insurance, car insurance and home insurance. If it structured its information systems around policy types (as most such companies used to do), it would find it hard to work out which customers were purchasing more than one type of insurance. It would also not be able to integrate its communications, so that if, for instance, a customer's household insurance was renewed the same day as their car insurance, they would get separate communications about each one. With its systems restructured around customers, the company can tell which are its most valuable customers, and which customers for one type of policy have not as yet chosen the company for their other insurance needs. It can then initiate schemes such as discount packages, aimed at retaining and extending its business.

Recap

B2C eCommerce focuses on the ICT enablement of key processes in the customer chain. Customer chain processes include product identification, catalogue search, product comparison and purchase. An organisation's experience of B2C eCommerce moves through a number of stages of increasing complexity, including information seeking and communication, marketing presence, online catalogue, online ordering, online payment and customer relationship management.

Case check: Case 1, Amazon.com

Amazon.com provides a number of levels of functionality through its website such as search features, additional content and personalisation. The site also provides searchable catalogues of books, CDs, DVDs, computer games and other products. Customers can search for titles using keyword, title, subject, author, artist, musical instrument, label, actor, director, publication date or ISBN. Amazon's service to customers relies on a close integration of its website with its back-end information and activity systems. For instance, the company's streamlined ordering process relies on reusing previous billing and shipment details.

Did you know?

In 2007 it was estimated that US$170 billion was spent online. This is predicted to rise to $263 billion by 2010.

B2B eCommerce

It has been argued that B2B eCommerce is even more critical to business activity than B2C eCommerce (Cunningham, 2002), and it is estimated that B2B eCommerce transactions are typically ten times the value of B2C eCommerce transactions (Wise and Morrison, 2000). So ICT innovation has potentially enormous value for organisations engaging in B2B activities.

B2B eCommerce involves the use of ICT in the supply chain. Much discussion of it is directed at supporting the repeat commerce model, discussed in Chapter 7. Here a company sets up an arrangement with a trusted supplier to deliver goods of a certain specification at regular intervals (Figure 8.11). Each phase of this repeat commerce model can be affected by B2B eCommerce.

In terms of **search**, buyers in organisations might specify what products or services are needed by completing online forms, which they submit via the corporate intranet for requisition approval. After approval the purchasing department issues a request for quote to potential suppliers, perhaps using an online bulletin board or B2B hub that connects businesses as buyers and sellers.

After all bids have been received, in the **negotiate** phase, software can be used to rank them on the basis of chosen key features, supporting the decision to select a particular vendor. In the **order** phase, the supplier is notified that the bid was successful and a purchase order is electronically transmitted to them. After **delivery** of goods the inventory management system is automatically updated. After receiving the invoice from the supplier the company arranges an electronic funds transfer (in other words, a payment). Finally in the **after-sale** phase, supplier relationship management systems monitor all interactions with suppliers and can be used to check on the performance of particular suppliers.

This approach to B2B eCommerce is primarily modelled on the economic model of an electronic hierarchy (see Chapter 7) and can be considered to be an extension to the supplier-facing information systems described in Chapter 4. More recently, forms of market-based trading are infiltrating the B2B sector. leading to an overlap of B2B and B2C business models and ICT infrastructure.

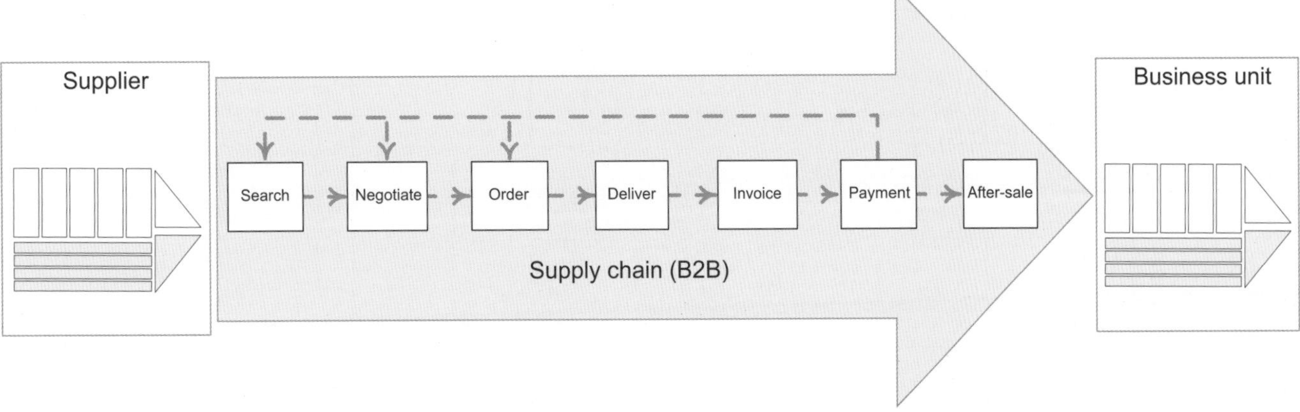

Figure 8.11: *The supply chain*

B2B eCommerce infrastructure

Supplier-facing information systems: Transaction processing systems that interface with suppliers.

B2B eCommerce is a natural extension of the informatics infrastructure of commercial organisations. Chapter 4 referred to these information systems as SUPPLIER-FACING INFORMATION SYSTEMS.

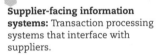

Purchase order processing and payment processing systems normally handle the settlement and execution stages of the commerce cycle. These are an established part of the information systems infrastructure of most medium to large organisations. The pre-sale and after-sale stages are the most open to innovation. Requisitioning, request for quote and vendor selection are part of what was called a supplier relationship management information system (see Chapter 4). It is in this area that most of the discussion of B2B eCommerce occurs.

Figure 8.12 illustrates the relationships between the supplier-facing systems of supplier relationship management, procurement and purchase order processing, and other infrastructure systems such as finance and inventory management. This serves to emphasise that successful B2B eCommerce relies on integration with back-end information systems.

Supplier relationship management

Supplier relationship management (SRM) is sometimes referred to as supply chain management (Meier, 1995), and involves the coordination of all supply chain activities. It is a generalisation of inbound logistics (see Chapter 7), the management of material resources supplied to the organisation. It is also sometimes used to encompass outbound logistics, the management of resources supplied by the organisation to its customers. Just as CRM can be seen to include eMarketing, SRM can be seen to include eProcurement (see below).

Reflect
Take an organisation known to you, Does it engage in B2B eCommerce? If so, what type of B2B eCommerce best describes its activity in this area?

Models of B2B eCommerce

B2B commerce traditionally relies on trusted relationships between a company and one or more established suppliers. Traditionally, management of the supply chain was organised through managerial hierarchies. With the rise of the Internet and the Web there has been an increasing trend for supply chain management to move more closely towards market-oriented models. In pre-sale activity the Internet has enabled four distinct models for B2B eCommerce to emerge: supplier-oriented B2B, buyer-oriented B2B, partnership-oriented B2B and intermediary-oriented B2B.

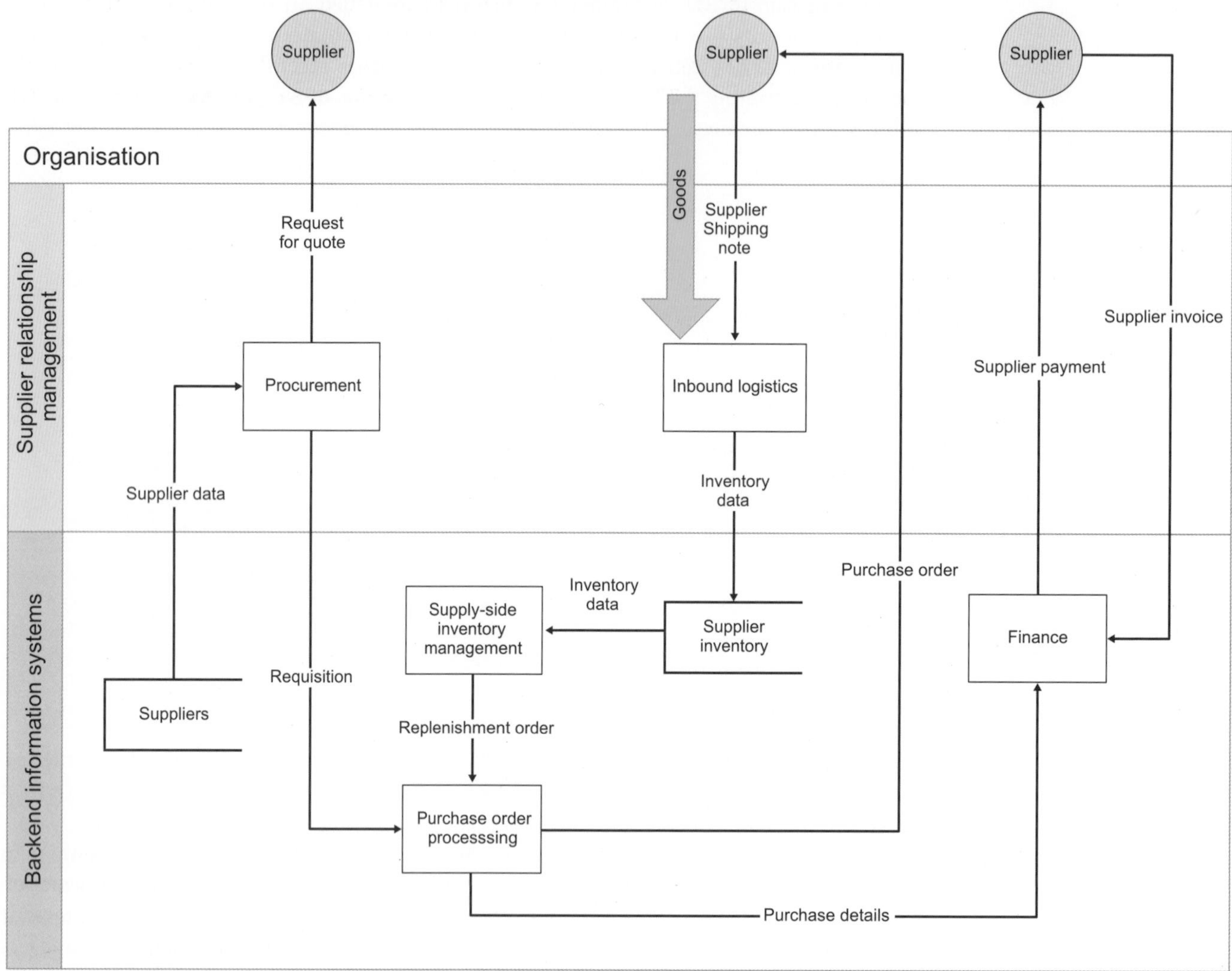

Figure 8.12: *Integration of B2B systems with the information systems infrastructure*

Supplier-oriented B2B: Producers and consumers use the same electronic marketplace. Essentially the same as B2C eCommerce.

Buyer-oriented B2B: The consumer opens an electronic market on its own server and requests bids.

Intermediary-oriented B2B: A process in which an intermediary runs an electronic market for buyers and sellers in a specific area.

SUPPLIER-ORIENTED B2B is sometimes referred to as sell-side B2B eCommerce, and effectively is a mirror-image of B2C or buy-side eCommerce. Typically, it involves one supplier and many potential purchasers, low-cost items and low-volume purchases. One of the most popular forms of supplier-oriented B2B is the eShop, which involves the promotion of the supplier's products or services through the Internet.

In BUYER-ORIENTED B2B, a consumer opens an electronic market on its own server. It then invites suppliers to bid on the supply information displayed. Hence, one buyer requests tenders for products from many potential suppliers. This is sometimes referred to as buy-side B2B eCommerce. The scenario can be expanded into eProcurement, in which the later stages in the supply chain are handled electronically.

In INTERMEDIARY-ORIENTED B2B an intermediary effectively runs a subset of an eMarket where buyers and sellers can meet and exchange products and services. This form of B2B eCommerce involves many-to-many exchanges and is also referred to as B2B eMarketplaces or B2B hubs.

These three models are all effectively market-oriented in the sense that they are designed for many-to-many exchange. The traditional model of B2B eCommerce is modelled on an electronic hierarchy, sometimes referred to as **partnership-oriented B2B**. Here an established relationship exists between a company and its supplier. The relationship is likely to be supported by integration of information systems using technologies such as extranets.

Intermediary-oriented B2B is a key form of reintermediation in the supply chain, and can be conducted in a number of ways. Vertical portals aggregate buyers and sellers around a particular market segment. They produce revenue through subscription, advertising, commission and transaction fees. B2B auction sites enable buyers and sellers to negotiate the price and terms of sales. The seller holds inventory but the auction site handles fulfilment of goods and the exchange of payment. EMALLS or eStores are general portals run by third parties offering a range of products/services from suppliers for customers. An eMall is effectively a collection of e-Shops.

EMall: Electronic mall. A collection of eShops.

Recap

Most discussion of B2B eCommerce is directed at supporting the repeat commerce model. Here a company sets up an arrangement with a trusted supplier to deliver goods of a certain specification at regular intervals. Changes to this business model tend to focus on pre-sales activity. Pre-sale activity can now be conducted using vertical portals, internet auctions or eMalls.

Case check: Case 3, Dell

Dell engages in supply-chain innovation including customisation of hardware and direct retailing to customers. Customers order personal computers through a website that provides an online catalogue of products. They can specify the exact configuration of hardware they require, and this is then built to order, using assembly plants around the world (Austin, Texas; Limerick, Eire; Penang, Malaysia) close to suppliers such as Intel (chips), Maxtor (hard drives) and Selectron (motherboards). Order forms follow each PC across the factory floor. Online customer support is provided. The Dell site provides order and courier-tracking and pages of technical support related to the tagging of machines. Dell associates a Service Tag, a unique alphanumeric identifier, with most of its products.

Dell sells all its products to both individual and business customers using a direct-sales model via online and telephone channels. The company receives payments for products before it has to pay for the materials, and practises just-in-time (JIT) inventory management.

C2C eCommerce

The Internet is not only a domain for B2B and B2C eCommerce, it is also a domain for C2C eCommerce: that is, ICT enablement of aspects of the community chain. In a way this is the most radical form of eCommerce since it overlaps with non-commercial activity in communities. Commercial and non-commercial organisations are attempting to incorporate aspects of the community chain into their operations, or to formulate new business models embedded in social networks.

As a form of exchange, many forms of C2C eCommerce revert to earlier models of markets and trade in which products and services are exchanged between individuals, where the fixed price model of products and services breaks down and in some instances trade reverts to earlier forms of economic exchange such as barter. It is a many-to-many commerce model. It typically involves the exchange of low-cost items and monetary transactions. With C2C eCommerce a form of trade that typically survives in local marketplaces is opened up to global access.

This section reconsiders the definition of a community given in Chapter 7 and uses it to distinguish between three forms of electronic community: an eNabled community, virtual community and adjunct community. Many businesses are now turning to adjunct communities to increase the levels of value associated with their products and services.

ECommunities

The concepts of a social network and social capital defined in Chapter 7 help us understand some of the different forms of ECOMMUNITY. ICT can be seen as an enabler or disabler of traditional forms of community: an eNabled community. It can also be seen as offering potential for newer forms of community based on communication networks, or virtual

eCommunity: Electronic community either a traditional community enabled with ICT or a virtual community.

communities. Virtual communities may exist separate from the organisation, or be built upon infrastructure provided by it, in what is known as an **adjunct community**.

ENabled community: A traditional community supported by ICT.

An ENABLED COMMUNITY is a traditional community enhanced by the use of ICT. Community is normally established on the basis of frequent and prolonged interaction between individuals resident in a clearly defined geographical area. This form of community chain addresses the rise of communication networks and considers whether they are vehicles for recreating community and social capital in local areas. Some argue that communication networks are a threat to existing forms of community; others that they provide a new basis for enhancing social capital.

The Internet and the Web were initially established for free information exchange between dispersed actors around the globe. Some have begun to consider such dispersed networks or individuals and organisations as examples of electronic communities. In such virtual communities social networks are constructed through electronic rather than face-to-face communication. Social networks based upon communication infrastructure may not only be dispersed geographically, they may also have a much more specific area of focus than traditional communities.

As a generalisation, public sector organisations have particularly been interested in making connections between their informatics activities and initiatives in the area of eNabled community. These forms of eCommunity are seen as offering the potential for the stimulation of local economies, particularly in disadvantaged areas.

In contrast, private sector organisations have particularly been interested in connecting to virtual communities. The idea is that various forms of value produced by the community chain may support and encourage commerce of various forms. It is only comparatively recently that the Internet and Web have been used as vehicles for commerce and trade/business purposes. C2C eCommerce mediates between pure forms of trade and pure forms of information exchange.

Virtual communities

Virtual community: A community consisting of a network of actors on a communication network.

Rheingold (1995) defines VIRTUAL COMMUNITIES as 'social aggregations that emerge from the Net when enough people carry on those public discussions long enough, with sufficient human feeling, to form webs of personal relationships in cyberspace'. For example, it could be argued that one of the first virtual communities was the community of academics that started to use the Internet (see Chapter 7) in the early 1970s to share data, exchange messages and collaborate on various research programmes.

Virtual communities are founded in social networks, and produce social capital just like traditional communities. However, there is still some question whether the bonds in the social network of a virtual community are as strong and the social capital as great as that produced in traditional communities. This is because there are a number of differences between virtual communities and traditional communities, including issues of space, form of communication and general focus.

In terms of space, traditional communities are normally established on the basis of long residence by individuals in a prescribed geographical region. In contrast, virtual communities break geographical boundaries and individuals are effectively nodes in a wide-area communication network.

Reflect
Companies are beginning to use the idea of social networking for internal collaboration between organisational members. Consider some ways in which these technologies might be used in this manner.

In traditional communities the dominant form of communication between community members is face-to-face conversation. In virtual communities various forms of remote communication are employed such as email, chat, telephone conversations and videoconferencing.

The focus of a traditional community is diverse but its members are all found in a particular geographical area. The focus of virtual communities is likely to be much more specific, but span the globe.

Various types of virtual communities have been defined. One categorisation is by the different types of content provided on websites, such as transactions, area of interest, industry or expertise. Many sites are established to facilitate the buying and selling of products and services, and to deliver information related to the completion of transactions. Many community websites focus on areas such as theatre, sports, science fiction or fantasy. Community websites are frequently located around key industrial areas such as accounting or manufacturing. Also, occupational groups may focus around key areas of expertise such as waste management.

Virtual communities are now being used to enhance conventional eCommerce activity by creating adjunct communities. Virtual communities also underlie forms of many-to-many eCommerce, or what are also known as C2C exchanges.

Social networking sites

Social networking is a misleading name for a website-based activity, because most social networks are not virtual. This phenomenon is really about using ICTs, particularly Web 2.0 technologies (see Chapter 6), to facilitate networking amongst dispersed individuals, and set up virtual communities.

Sites such as MySpace and Facebook are themselves businesses, so this is a new growth area in itself, but they are also of interest to other businesses, which are looking at the potential of using the technologies involved either internally and externally. For example, the Web 2.0 technologies on social networking sites (see Chapter 6) could foster and support collaborative working and information sharing in distributed organisations. In an external sense, virtual communities of this form could be used to improve CRM. For example, many companies are exploring the use of blogs as tools for marketing or CRM.

Case check: Case 13, MySpace and Case 23, YouTube

MySpace and YouTube are two of the most popular recent social networking sites. MySpace is reputed to be one of the world's most popular English-language websites. It describes itself as an 'online community that lets you meet your friends' friends'. It is pitched as a tool for creating a private community in which participants can share photos, journals and interests with a network of mutual friends. YouTube is a popular website which lets users upload, view and share video clips. Founded in February 2005, the wide variety of site content includes movie and TV clips and music videos as well as amateur content such as videoblogging.

Adjunct communities

Some electronic businesses are attempting to foster and support virtual communities as a means of adding value to their products and/or services. These focus around the development of relationships between customers and businesses (Armstrong and Hagel, 1996). By creating and supporting them, businesses aim to build membership audiences for their products and services. Certain features of social capital, such as increased mutual support amongst members of a virtual community, can be particularly beneficial to companies. These enhanced levels of member trust might lead to increase customer loyalty and trust in the company, and increased levels of trade.

Timmers (1999) argues that there are two business models appropriate for adjunct communities. A **communication exchange** model attempts to add value to products and services through communications between a community of members. The company provides an environment in which members can enjoy unedited communication and information exchange. Revenue is generated through membership fees, advertising revenue and cross-selling of products and services. **Collaboration platforms** tend to be much more focused on enabling collaboration between individuals and organisations, and typically provide a set of tools and an information environment for collaboration with a company.

C2C exchanges

Other business models for C2C focus more precisely on facilitating customer-to-customer relationships of exchange. C2C exchange involves trade of typically low-cost items between complex networks of individual actors. Revenues from C2C communities may be generated through advertising, transaction fees and/or membership fees.

Timmers (1999) details two main business models for this. Electronic auctions, the main form, are discussed in more detail below. **Information brokerages** are companies specialising in the provision of information to consumers and businesses, to help them make buying decisions. Revenue models in this area include membership fees, advertising fees and cross-selling.

C2C exchanges involve trade between complex networks of individual actors. Although typically the monetary value of each exchange is low, altogether billions of dollars are traded annually. C2C exchange is not a new phenomenon: it used to be (and still is) conducted through, for example, newspaper classified advertisements, flea markets and auction houses.

The small ads in local newspapers list items for sale. Buyers phone the seller, look over the items before purchase, and usually collect and pay for them in person. In a flea market, sellers stock and display items for sale at their own homes or at organised markets. Buyers browse, negotiate prices and collect and transport items themselves. The auction house model involves sellers taking items to specialist organisations that advertise them for sale. Buyers are able to inspect items before an auction. They often pay a registration fee to bid, and are required to be at an auction or to nominate a proxy bidder. The highest bidder wins the auction and pays the auction house. The auction house in turn takes a percentage of the sale and pays the balance to the seller.

The value and take-up of a C2C exchange is likely to be affected by Metcalfe's law (see page 213), that the community value of a network grows with the square of the number of users. So the more people who already use a network as buyers or sellers, the more likely it is that sales will take place, and that other people will participate.

Recap

C2C eCommerce is ICT enablement of the community chain. The community chain is founded in social networks, and the value it produces is social capital. ICT has been used to enable community in local areas. ICT is also the infrastructure underlying the rise in virtual communities and social networking. Forms of electronic community include virtual communities and C2C exchanges.

Case check: Case 6, eBay

EBay is probably the most significant contemporary example of a C2C electronic exchange. Essentially its business model is a simple one: it provides C2C auctions online. It relies heavily on collectors trading small-priced items such coins, stamps and militaria. Although the average items sold through markets like this cost only a few dollars, as a whole billions of dollars worth of goods are traded every year.

EMarketing

Marketing can be defined as the process of planning and executing the conception, pricing, promotion and distribution of ideas, goods and services to create exchanges that satisfy individual and organisational goals (Brassington and Pettit, 2000). This definition emphasises that marketing is not just an activity that occurs after a product has been produced or after a service has been formulated. In modern business practice, marketing input is important in the design of a product and in the after-sales process.

The Internet and ICT generally offer innovative ways of engaging in pre-sale activity with customers. One of the most significant is eMarketing of goods and services. In terms of CRM, EMARKETING is particularly directed at customer acquisition but is also relevant to customer retention and extension.

eMarketing: The process of planning and executing the conception, pricing, promotion and distribution of ideas, goods and services using electronic channels.

Not surprisingly, marketing strategy is typically an important part of organisational strategy, and eMarketing strategy is likely to be a critical component of any eBusiness strategy (see Chapter 10).

Marketing channels

Marketing channel: A channel for the communication of marketing messages.

Marketing used to focus on the transmission of messages to potential customers through CHANNELS such as television, radio, newspapers and magazines, and more recently through direct-selling approaches using the telephone. These approaches are push-oriented, passive, linear, event-driven and information-weak. A company disseminates (*pushes*) the material to a perceived market of potential customers, who have to find an advert either through browsing or through some more directed search. In other words, this is a *passive* activity on the company's behalf. The marketing material is scripted and is expected to be delivered in a *linear* sequence as a package. The material is *event-driven* in that it tends to be delivered at a specific point in time, and is typically 'broadcast' from one source to many potential customers. Because of such characteristics, it is typically difficult to gather direct data on the impact of marketing, so it is *information-weak*.

Take an advertisement in newspapers and magazines for a new model of car. The company pays to have the advertisement designed by a graphics company (scripting) and is likely to make a key decision on which newspapers and magazines to buy space in on the basis of the intended customer base (push). A multinational manufacturer will probably run separate marketing campaigns in each country it markets in (location-dependent). The assumption is that potential customers will come across the advertisement while reading their newspaper or magazine (passive). The company pays the publishers to print the advertisement in a particular edition of the publication, perhaps timed to coincide with a launch event for the car (event-driven). Since it appears in all copies, the advertisement is effectively broadcast. There is no automatic feedback on the reaction to the advertisement. Orders for goods will not be able to be related directly to an advertisement, so advertising agencies have to do research if they want to know what customers thought of it, for instance by interviewing a sample of consumers (information-weak).

Electronic delivery: The delivery of services and intangible products over communication networks.

In contrast, eMarketing uses ELECTRONIC DELIVERY and thus tends to be characterised by being pull, aggressive, interactive, time-independent and information-rich (Bickerton, Bickerton and Simpson-Holey, 2000). Potential customers themselves access the material using channels such as websites (*pull*). The advertising also involves actively seeking out customers through technologies such as email, and initiating a form of contact with them (*aggressive*). The potential customer can communicate with the company using channels such as email, and there is also potential for customising the marketing material for particular customers (*interactive*). The marketing material can be accessed 24 hours a day, 365 days a year (*time-independent*). It can also be accessed in different contexts: in a one-to-one or one-to-many relationship between the potential customer and the business, or in a many-to-many way within customer audiences. Because of the transaction-based nature of B2C eCommerce sites, a vast amount of data can be captured which relates customer searching to eventual purchase (*information-rich*). Finally, marketing via the Internet can be achieved on an international scale from one location.

However, a website will not prove effective as a marketing tool unless sufficient numbers of people access it, so eMarketing cannot be divorced from traditional promotional activities that are designed to persuade people to log on to the site. Once a sufficient level of traffic has been produced, a number of eMarketing techniques may be applied.

EMarketing strategy

Reflect
How important would you say eMarketing is to an organisation such as a university? How successful do you think universities are at eMarketing?

Good marketing is reliant on good planning, and planning for eMarketing is an important part of general eBusiness planning. It should include (Chaffey et al., 2000) an analysis of the environment for eMarketing, an assessment of current internal infrastructure available to the company for eMarketing, establishing a vision for eMarketing, specifying an eMarketing strategy, implementing the strategy and evaluating the contribution eMarketing makes to the business.

Market analysis involves determining the demand for eCommerce in particular segments of the market. It calls for close attention to the behaviour of competitors and partners such as intermediaries in this area. Market or customer segmentation is the process of identifying the characteristics of different segments of the target population. **Customer segmentation** is a concept frequently used in marketing strategy. The assumption is that members of a customer population can be distinguished on number of key dimensions. Different customer segments are likely to have different buying patterns.

Some key segmentation dimensions are socioeconomic group, age, sex and ethnicity (see Chapter 9). Customer segmentation may be an important part of a channel strategy, since different customer segments will have different profiles of interaction. It is also likely that different customer segments will need different website content.

On the basis of an analysis of segments it becomes possible to determine particular marketing requirements. Seybold (1999) argues that there are five key questions companies should ask themselves in relation to segmentation: Who are our customers? How are their needs changing? Which do we target? How can we add value? And how do we become first choice for the customer?

Assessment involves evaluating the performance of the current infrastructure and determining the feasible options for extending the eMarketing infrastructure.

Establishing a vision involves setting clear objectives for the use of eMarketing in terms of online contribution to company performance and the marketing mix of product, price, place and promotion (McCarthy, 1960).

Companies look to add value to **product**s sold through using electronic channels. This can be done, for example, by improving searching facilities to online catalogues or providing more personalised products.

Pricing strategies for products and services should reflect the capabilities of electronic channels. Companies might offer discounts for using online ordering, or differentiate pricing more dynamically by time of purchase or customer segment. For instance, easyJet.com and other low-cost airlines operate a dynamic pricing policy for their ticketing, where the prices change continually based on the level of advanced booking and customer demand.

Due consideration should be given to the most appropriate **place** to promote goods and services through electronic channels. Placing decisions involve consideration of whether to disintermediate or reintermediate in particular markets. Another decision is on the degree of integration between a company's promotional strategies and those of its partners.

Finally, **promotion** involves considering whether, and how, to integrate electronic and conventional promotional channels, and the appropriate mix of online with conventional promotion. The company must decide on the proportions of investment in eMarketing and traditional marketing. Low-cost airlines such as easyJet, for instance, have used newspapers to offer discounts for advanced booking. Potential customers collect tokens from the newspaper and then contact the company via telephone or the Web.

Specifying an eMarketing strategy involves detailing the part that eMarketing (Chaston, 2001) plays in general eBusiness strategy. Implementing an eMarketing strategy involves building a technical infrastructure for eMarketing and putting the associated human activity systems in place. Evaluating the eMarketing contribution means monitoring its performance in terms of defined objectives.

Key skill 

The techniques of web-based eMarketing

Websites are now the primary approach for eMarketing. The main techniques of web-based eMarketing include (Hardaker and Graham, 2001):

- **Banner adverts**, so called because they are usually displayed across the top of a web page. These are one-to-many passive advertisements which the user sees when they access the web page.
- **Target advertisements**, which are one-to-many active advertisements in the sense that the user must click on something in order to be taken to the detailed advert. Some banner advertisements are also click-through.
- **Email** can be used to directly contact existing customers with offers or promotions. Direct email is a one-to-one aggressive promotion strategy. Email can also be used to contact potential customers from purchased mail lists.

Banner advertising campaigns may involve placing the adverts on many different forms of website such as portals, generalised news services and special interest sites. Some large online companies use a large-scale network of affiliates which place small target advertisements on their websites encouraging users to redirect to the advertiser's home page.

Companies generally charge for advertisements on their websites, and this may form an important revenue stream for an intermediary such as a web portal or affiliate. Generally there are four main ways of charging for online advertising:

- Flat fee is a traditional model where a set fee is charged for placing the advertisement for a set time-period.
- Cost per thousand presentation model (CPM) is based on the number of advertisements viewed.

- Click through is relevant to target advertisements, and involves billing on the basis of the number of consumers who click on the link provided,
- Many companies offering advertisements on the Web, such as Google, are now using a cost per action/acquisition (CPA) revenue model. In cost per action the advertiser pays for each specified action such as a purchase or a form submission. Cost per acquisition is a related type in which the advertiser pays for new acquisitions such as new customers, prospects or leads achieved through online adverts.

Branding: The process of using some form of sign to identify a product or service.

One other important tool in the eMarketing armoury is the use of BRANDING in domain names. Brands are classic examples of signs (see Chapter 3). The logo or brand name of a company is an example of a symbol, which signifies a referent: particular products or company activity as a whole. Particular logos or brand names are also associated with a range of other connotations or concepts such as perceived company values and behaviour. In the online world it is particularly important to ensure that a brand is used to maximum effect. This may involve copyrighting the brand, registering an existing and well-recognised brand name as a domain name, registering the domain name with the most well-used search engines, ensuring that the domain name returns high in the lists of returned results to users of search engines, and monitoring access from search engines and adjusting strategies to maintain a presence.

Recap

Marketing can be defined as the process of planning and executing the conception, pricing, promotion and distribution of ideas, goods and services to create exchanges that satisfy individual and organisational goals. EMarketing is the use of electronic channels for the delivery of promotional material. Techniques for Web-based eMarketing include banner advertisements on websites and email to contact potential customers. Electronic marketing revenue can be achieved through flat fee, CPM, CPA or click-through. Branding domain names is a significant component of successful eMarketing.

PART 3

Case check:
Case 5, easyJet

EasyJet is one of the largest low-fare airlines in Europe, operating domestic and international scheduled services on over 300 routes between over 100 European and north African airports. Cost savings through the use of online booking helped to establish the business model for low-cost airlines.

EasyJet's early marketing strategy was initially based on 'making flying as affordable as a pair of jeans', and urged travellers to 'cut out the travel agent'. Its early advertising consisted of little more than the airline's telephone booking number painted in bright orange on the side of its aircraft. Initially booking was by telephone only.

In December 1997 the company created its first website for online bookings. The company now relies almost entirely on this website and associated eMarketing to promote its business.

Did you know?

Global spending on web advertising was estimated to be US$17 billion in 2006. This is estimated to rise to US$51.6 billion by 2010.

EProcurement

The pre-sale activities of search, negotiate and order in the supply chain are frequently given the umbrella term of procurement. Sometimes procurement refers to all the activities involved in the supply chain. It is an important business process in the value chain, and involves the purchasing goods and services from suppliers at an acceptable quality and price and with reliable delivery.

eProcurement: Electronic procurement. A term used to refer to ICT-enablement of key supply chain activities.

EPROCUREMENT is the use of ICT to enable the whole of the procurement process (Rajkumar, 2001). It is a specific and important feature of B2B eCommerce (Matin, Gerard and Lariver, 2001). This section considers some of the key differences between conventional procurement and eProcurement, and examines key areas of performance improvement. This leads to a discussion of various forms of eProcurement and suitable technologies for supporting this form of process strategy (see Chapter 10) for eBusiness.

The conventional procurement process

There are two basic types of procurement by companies (Chaffey, 2006), production-related and operating procurement.

Production-related procurement is designed to support manufacturing operations. It is geared to the fulfilment of long-term needs, generally involves customised items, and is frequently undertaken through established and regular relationships with suppliers. This procurement process tends to be organised as managerial hierarchies (see Chapter 7).

Non-production or operating procurement is conducted to support all the operations of the business. It is designed to fulfil immediate needs, typically for commoditised items. Relationships with suppliers tend to be irregular and temporary, so operating procurement is frequently organised via a market-based model of economic exchange (see Chapter 7).

Historically, procurement has been a human-intensive process involving activities such as requesting quotations, submitting purchase orders. approving and confirming orders, shipping, invoicing and payment. It used to be performed by a specialist purchasing department, typically employing many people using paper documentation, the telephone and fax to communicate with suppliers. Figure 8.13 is a model of a conventional procurement process.

Employees first search for a product matching a particular need. Details of the product are then entered on a requisition form, which is sent for authorisation to the purchasing department. This department receives the requisition, authorises production of a purchase order and sends it to an established supplier. The supplier despatches goods to the company with an attached shipping note. When the goods have been checked a payment authorisation is issued to the accounting department who pay the supplier. The goods are then despatched internally to the originating department.

This process can be analysed in a number of ways. One approach is to analyse the average time taken to conduct each activity. These are indicated on the diagram as annotations, and Table 8.2 shows the total lead time for the procurement process.

It is important to recognise that it takes so long because of delays, lags or waiting times embedded in the activity system. For instance, documentation such as requisitions can sit in a person's in-tray for up to 12 hours before receiving attention.

Figure 8.14 illustrates a process that has been redesigned with the use of ICT, of typical eProcurement where staff order directly from supplier websites.

We can do the same sort of analysis for this process, as shown in Table 8.3.

Table 8.2: *Activities and timings for a conventional procurement process*

Activity	Average time
Search for product and product identified	1 hour
Complete requisition	10 minutes
Send requisition	24 hours
Receive requisition	12 hours
Authorise and complete order	24 hours
Send order	24 hours
Delivery from supplier	24 hours
Receive goods	24 hours
Check goods	24 hours
Authorise payment	10 mins
Despatch goods	1 hour
Total	6 days 2 hours and 20 minutes

Table 8.3: *Activities and timings associated with a re-engineered procurement process*

Activity	Average time
Search for product and product identified	20 minutes
Complete order	10 minutes
Delivery from supplier	24 hours
Receive goods, check goods and authorise payment	20 minutes
Total	1 day 50 minutes

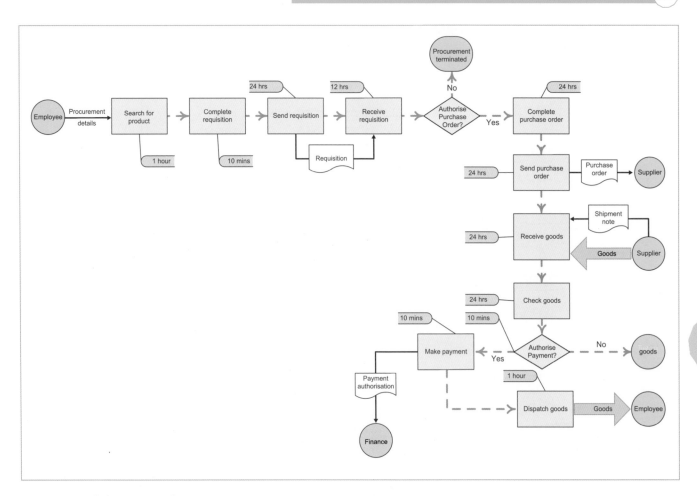

Figure 8.13: *The conventional procurement process*

The procurement process is much faster because there is more automation of activities and more electronic transmission and storage of data. Some activities are no longer required and there is less waiting time.

Reflect
Besides obvious efficiency gains such as cost savings, what other benefits might eProcurement provide, particularly for public sector organisations?

Forms of eProcurement

There are three broad categories of eProcurement, roughly corresponding to the interdependent activities found in all procurement processes: electronic sourcing, purchasing and payment.

Electronic sourcing typically involves the use of electronic tendering systems which enable organisational agents to create requests for quotation (RFQ). These electronic RFQs are then issued to suppliers, and forms of electronic auction are used to source best-priced contracts.

Once a contract is awarded, a number of tools may be used to search catalogues, select desired goods or services, place them in an electronic shopping basket and automatically raise a requisition or purchase order. This is **electronic purchasing**.

Invoices may be issued in XML format (see page 157) from a supplier once goods have been despatched. Once the buyer has received the goods an invoice can be automatically matched to the purchase order for price and to the goods received for quantity. Various electronic payment systems (see Chapter 5) may then be used to transfer payment to the supplier.

To facilitate standardisation of data and hence effective analysis for management information, many forms of eProcurement use standard commodity classification coding. These standard coding schemes may also enable faster searching for a particular item from a range of possible suppliers. Commodity coding is the assignment of standard codes to item records (at the part number level) and to purchase orders (at the purchase order line item level).

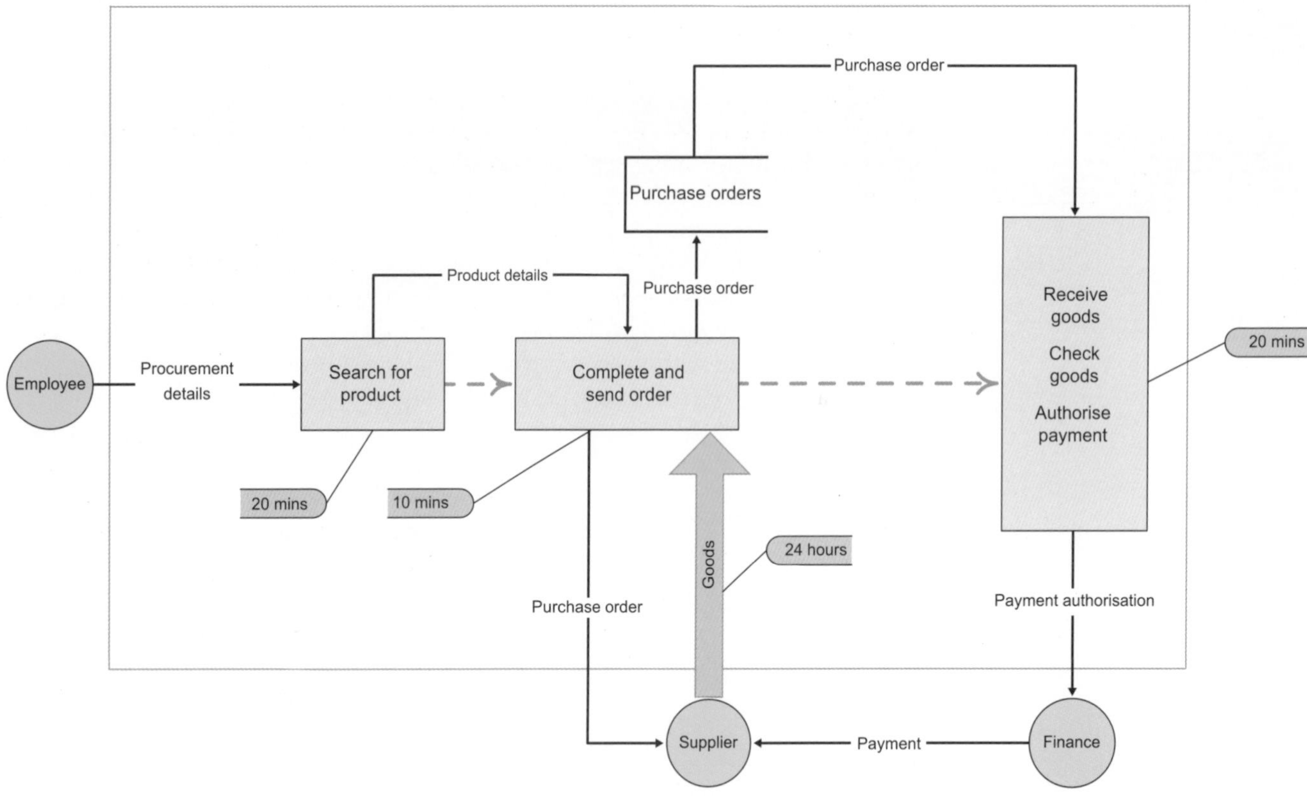

Figure 8.14: *A model of an eProcurement process*

There are various coding schemes. The common procurement vocabulary (CPV) is used in public procurement in the European Union to group products from similar producers. The European article number (EAN) is widely used in association with a standard for bar-coding. The United Nations Standard Product and Services Code (UN-SPC) provides a hierarchically organised product classification system. For example, a UN-SPC code for a mobile phone is 43.17.15.12. The 43 stands for Communications and Computing Equipment; 17 stands for Hardware and Accessories; 15 stands for Telephony equipment; 12 stands for Mobile Telephone.

Recap

The pre-sale activities of search, negotiate and order in the supply chain are jointly known as procurement, a term sometimes also used for all the activities in the supply chain. EProcurement is the use of ICT to enable the whole of the procurement process. Forms of eProcurement include eSourcing, ePurchasing and ePayment.

Intra-business eBusiness and the partnership chain

Figure 8.1 details two other forms of eBusiness: intra-business eBusiness and P2P eBusiness. Intra-business e-Business concerns enablement of the internal value chain with ICT. P2P eBusiness comprises the use of ICT to support the partnership chain: networks of organisations collaborating in the delivery of value to customers.

In a sense, all the material covered in previous chapters of this book is relevant to successful intra-business eBusiness. However, a number of issues are of particular relevance:

- the focus on organisational processes and the importance of re-engineering activity systems with the support of ICT to achieve improvements in efficacy, efficiency and effectiveness (see Chapter 2)
- the central importance of information as an organisational resource (see Chapter 3)
- the desire of companies to develop integrated and interoperable information systems infrastructure (see Chapter 4), for instance the use of mega-packages (see Chapter 6).

Further chapters also consider intra-business issues. For instance, Chapter 10 considers the importance of developing strategy for information, information systems and ICT in organisations.

From the discussion in Chapter 4 it should be evident that an effective information systems infrastructure is critical to the effective control of human activity in business organisations. Each of the five core information systems described in Chapter 4 supports an activity system or business process in the value chain. Sales order processing is likely to support sales activity as well as possibly after-sales service, so it is critical to the goals of gaining and retaining customers. Purchase order processing is likely to support major elements of the procurement process, ensuring the effective supply of raw materials. Inventory management is important for sales activity, providing sales staff with accurate data on quantities and pricing of products. It is also likely to support procurement activity by enabling the identification of stock levels of raw materials, so it concerns the effective maintenance of relationships with both suppliers and customers. Financial data is the lifeblood of most commercial organisations, so it is essential for supporting infrastructure activities such as management and planning. The payroll system is a critical element of any human resource activity in an organisation. For many service organisations labour is the major cost, so information that enables the effective control of this resource is vital for achieving the organisational mission.

The traditional structure of organisations was based on functions such as marketing, finance and manufacturing, and information systems were designed to echo this structure. Each functional unit tended to have its own information system. Martin (1996) refers to this type of organisational model as a series of functional silos, and the information systems infrastructure associated with it as stovepipe systems. These frequently use incompatible data structures, making communication across functional silos difficult. The systems were also likely to suffer from redundancy and fragmentation.

Value-chain models of organisations stress the importance of cross-organisational processes. The emphasis is on designing efficient and effective cross-organisational processes that deliver value to the customer. This model of the organisation encourages the design of integrated information systems to support key organisational processes. Martin argues that this form of information systems infrastructure not only provides more utility for organisations, it enables the organisation to adapt more easily to changing environmental influences. This is similar to Hoque's (2000) idea of building dynamic business models on the foundation of reusable process models and information system models.

Partnership chain and inter-organisational information systems

Electronic markets are founded on competition, since a market is a network of interactions and relationships by which products and services are negotiated and exchanged. However, businesses also indulge in cooperation and collaboration. Information systems support business cooperation through the concept of an INTER-ORGANISATIONAL INFORMATION SYSTEM **(IOS)** (Barrette and Konsynski, 1982). An IOS is an information system developed and maintained by a consortium of companies for the mutual benefit of member companies. Generally they provide infrastructure for sharing an application. IOSs can prove a particularly effective way of sharing the costs of developing and maintaining large and complex information systems. Therefore an IOS is a type of information system directed at collaboration.

Inter-organisational information system: A form of information system that is developed and maintained by a consortium of companies in an area of business for mutual benefit.

The automatic teller machine (ATM) networks run by major building societies and banks in the United Kingdom are key examples of IOSs. These networks are constructed and maintained by consortia of financial institutions, so the large costs of running the networks are distributed among the participating members. Another example is BACS, the clearing system of the major high street banks in the United Kingdom, which handles account debit and credit transactions.

Reflect
Airlines run major inter-organisational information systems. For what purpose?

An inter-organisational informatics infrastructure based on developments in service-oriented software architecture (see Chapter 6) has been proposed as a backbone for fostering what are sometimes called digital business ecosystems. The ideal is that businesses can flexibly utilise this backbone to develop new business models based on cooperation with other businesses.

Case check: Case 2, Cisco

A key component of Cisco's B2B eCommerce strategy is integration of its ERP systems with the information systems of its key suppliers. Suppliers use their ERP systems to run their Cisco production lines, allowing them to respond to demand from Cisco in real time. This is enhanced by the introduction of Cisco Manufacturing Online, an extranet portal that allows partners to access real-time manufacturing information including data on demand forecasts, inventory and purchase orders.

Cisco: A leading firm in the market for inter-networking equipment.

Summary

1. This chapter introduced the term electronic business or eBusiness, to encompass the entire range of ICT application in businesses, both to improve internal operations and to extend systems into the environment. Electronic commerce (eCommerce) is the term used for the use of ICT in the external activities and relationships of the business with individuals, groups and other businesses.

2. Different forms of eBusiness can be identified, related to the features of the value network discussed in Chapter 7. There are also three major forms of eCommerce: B2C, B2B and C2C.

3. B2C eCommerce concerns the attempt to support the organisation's customer chain with ICT, and involves the ICT-enablement of key processes in the customer chain: pre-sale, sale-execution, sale-settlement and after-sale. It moves through a number of distinct stages of increasing complexity. A company is likely to first use the Internet for information-seeking and communication, then establish a marketing presence on the Internet, and subsequently put an online catalogue of its products and/or services on a website. Online ordering and online payment are two additional levels of functionality likely to be provided on a company B2C site. At the highest level of sophistication forms of customer relationship management enable a company to better track its interactions with its customers.

4. B2B eCommerce represents the attempt by organisations to use ICT to improve elements of their supply chains. A typical supply chain includes activities such as search, negotiate, order, delivery, invoice, payment and after-sale. B2B eCommerce systems are likely to be built on bedrock of sound back-end information systems infrastructure. Supply chain management has arisen as a distinct philosophy which helps frame the objective of B2B eCommerce.

5. C2C eCommerce is the ICT enablement of the community chain, or social networks surrounding the organisation. Public sector initiatives have been interested in enhancing traditional communities with increased ICT use. Private sector initiatives have been particularly interested in the community chain as a new revenue source or as a means of adding value to traditional commercial activities.

6. EMarketing is the use of electronic channels for delivery of promotional material. Traditional marketing channels are characterised as push, passive, linear, event-driven, one-to-many, and information-weak. In contrast, electronic marketing channels are characterised as pull, aggressive, interactive, time-independent, one-to-many and many-to-many, and information-strong. Techniques for Web-based eMarketing include banner advertisements on websites and email to contact potential customers. Revenue is achieved through schemes such as flat fee, CPM, CPA or click-through.

7. The pre-sale activities of search, negotiate and order in the supply chain are given the umbrella term procurement, which sometimes also refers to all the activities involved in the supply chain. Electronic procurement (eProcurement) is the use of ICT to enable the whole of the procurement process. Significant performance improvement is possible through forms of eProcurement such as eSourcing, ePurchasing and ePayment.

8. Whereas recent interest has been directed at the ways in which networks of consumers generate value, there has also been interest in the ways in which networks of businesses can use ICT to collaborate as well as compete. Internally, organisations are beginning to manage collaboration across internal units and divisions globally. Externally, digital ecosystems of businesses are emerging. This is known as P2P eBusiness.

At a number of points this chapter touched on the benefits of eBusiness and eCommerce. Chapter 9 looks at benefit or worth in more detail. It considers the related issues of the use of information systems in organisations and the impact they have. It also considers approaches to evaluating this impact.

Focus on Value

The idea of a transaction cost helps explain the value of information to business. Some would argue that it explains the existence of business itself. Businesses continually have to balance and control the costs of production with the costs of coordination. The value of ICT lies in its ability to lower costs of coordination in business hierarchies, markets and networks. Hence, electronic business and electronic commerce are seen as being of value in a general business strategy. ICT has value in enabling internal coordination of activities within the business. More recently, ICT has been used to facilitate new forms of collaboration and coordination with external stakeholders, so in general, ICT has key value in both supporting and innovating organisational behaviour in value networks.

Review test

1 Match the type of value chain to the appropriate definition.

Customer chain	A series of interdependent activities that produce a product or service for a customer/consumer
Supply chain	A series of interdependent activities by which an organisation sources products or services from other individuals, groups or organisations
Internal value chain	A series of interdependent activities by which an organisation sells its products or services to customers

2 ECommerce is a superset of eBusiness.

True or false? ☐ True ☐ False

3 There are three main forms of eCommerce.

Select all that apply.

☐ B2C eCommerce
☐ B2B eCommerce
☐ I2I eCommerce
☐ G2G eCommerce
☐ C2C eCommerce.

4 Some of the benefits of eCommerce are:

Select all that apply.

☐ Cost savings
☐ Time savings
☐ Increased security
☐ Connection improvements

5 B2C eCommerce is an extension of customer-facing information systems.

True or false? ☐ True ☐ False

6 Place the stages of B2C eCommerce growth in increasing order of complexity.

Use 1 for the lowest level of complexity.

☐ Marketing presence
☐ Information seeking and communication
☐ Online catalogue
☐ Online payment
☐ Online ordering
☐ Customer relationship management

7 Customer relationship management is composed of which three main processes?

Select all that apply.

☐ Customer search
☐ Customer acquisition
☐ Customer satisfaction
☐ Customer retention
☐ Customer extension

8 B2B eCommerce is an extension of supplier-facing information systems.

True or false? ☐ True ☐ False

9 Match the type of B2B eCommerce to the appropriate definition.

Buyer-oriented B2B	In this approach a consumer opens an electronic market on its own server.
Supplier-oriented B2B	In this model, producers and consumers use the same marketplace.
Intermediary-oriented B2B	In this model an intermediary runs effectively a subset of an electronic market where buyers and sellers can meet and exchange products and services.

10 ____________ portals attempt to serve the entire Internet community, typically by offering search functions and classification for the whole of Web content.

Fill in the blank.

11 Vertical ____________ aggregate buyers and sellers around a particular market segment.

Fill in the blank.

12 C2C eCommerce is:

Select the most appropriate definition.

☐ ICT enablement of the community chain
☐ Connect to Cardiff
☐ Competitive eCommerce

PART 3

13	Match the type of community to the appropriate definition. eNabled community — A traditional community in which most interaction is conducted offline and some interaction is supported by communication networks. Virtual community — A community in which all interaction between members is conducted via communication networks. Social networking site — Using ICTs, particularly Web 2.0 technologies, to facilitate networking amongst dispersed individuals.
14	Marketing can be defined as the process of planning and executing the conception, pricing, promotion and distribution of ideas, goods and services to create exchanges that satisfy individual and organisational goals. True or false? ☐ True ☐ False
15	Market or customer segmentation is the process of: Select the most relevant definition. ☐ Identifying different segments of the population to which a company sells or wishes to sell. ☐ Offering differing discounts to different customers. ☐ Personalising the delivery of goods and services to customers.
16	Techniques for Web-based eMarketing include: Select all that apply. ☐ Use of banner advertisements on websites. ☐ Use of email to contact potential customers. ☐ Use of cookies. ☐ Use of pop-ups.
17	____________ refers to the use of ICT to enable the whole of the procurement process. Fill in the blank.
18	Forms of eProcurement include: Select all that apply. ☐ eSourcing ☐ ePurchasing ☐ ePayment ☐ eShopping
19	Match the type of procurement to the appropriate definition. Production-related procurement — Procurement designed to support manufacturing needs, typically for customised goods and consequently organised as a hierarchy. Operating procurement — Procurement designed to fulfil immediate business needs for commoditised items and hence typically organised as a market.

Exercises

1. Determine whether an organisation known to you has adopted eCommerce. If so, attempt to determine the benefits it derives from it. If not, determine what benefits it might derive.
2. Access a B2C site and attempt to assign the features you find to the phases of the customer chain.
3. Consider a company known to you. Determine at what stage it is in as far as B2C eCommerce is concerned.
4. Take a company known to you, and determine what information is searched for using the Internet.
5. Find a website for an SME in your local area. Determine how successfully it markets itself through the Internet.
6. Find a website with an online catalogue. Describe the features of the online catalogue.
7. Make a list of the types of goods you can order over the Internet and what you cannot. Reflect on the types of products characteristic of markets and hierarchies.
8. Visit the Amazon.com site and attempt to determine what forms of customer profiling it employs.
9. Investigate the range of CRM systems offered by vendors.
10. Try to find an example of a community website and determine what content is provided on it.
11. Produce a brief statement of the characteristics of a traditional promotional channel such as a television advert. Produce a brief statement of the characteristics of an eMarketing promotional channel such as a banner advertisement.
12. Generate a list of the efficiency and effectiveness improvements relevant to a particular organisation's use of eMarketing.
13. Access a particular web portal and determine what eMarketing techniques are used.
14. Select a particular eMarketing technique and try to determine the revenue model used.
15. Examine and analyse the whole of or part of some procurement process known to you in terms of the time taken to complete activities.

16 Determine what forms of eProcurement are suitable for operational as opposed to production-related procurement.

17 Find one example of an eMarket and describe its key stakeholders and features.

18 Find one example each of a vertical and horizontal Internet portal and describe their key features.

19 Find one example of an interorganisational information system and analyse some of the reasons for its creation.

20 Consider whether the costs and benefits associated with eCommerce differ with the size of company.

Projects

1 Investigate the take-up of eBusiness and eCommerce by companies in your local area. Attempt to determine the importance of eBusiness to their operations.

2 Choose an industrial or commercial sector. Investigate the degree with which B2B and B2C eCommerce has penetrated the sector. As a consequence how have the value-networks in such a sector been transformed?

3 Determine the levels of disintermediation and reintermediation amongst eCommerce conducted in a particular market sector, such as travel agencies or high-street banking. In other words, what sort of structural change has been caused to the market through ICT?

4 Interorganisational information systems are important to collaboration between business partners such as high street banks or major airlines. Determine the benefits associated with them for a particular partnership network. Also determine the costs associated with building and operating them.

5 Choose a market sector and determine the most appropriate organisational form for eBusiness. Can the business be run entirely online or is it important to maintain a physical presence?

6 Study the take-up of B2C eCommerce among a limited range of companies. Discover the degree to which the evolution of eCommerce in these companies corresponds to the growth model discussed.

7 The rise of online trading has caused a parallel increase in online theft and fraud. Investigate the impact this growth has on the issue of consumer trust. Will trust be a major brake on the continued growth in B2C eCommerce?

8 Customer relationship management is now a major philosophy for companies. Determine the degree to which it relies on customer relationship information systems. How do these information systems help improve organisational performance, and how can this be measured?

9 Consider the most effective ways of evaluating B2C systems. How can companies determine the value that B2C eCommerce provides for them? Does conducting B2C eCommerce inevitably make such measurement easier, and if so, why?

10 Among the various forms of B2B eCommerce described in this chapter, determine the most prevalent. For instance, determine the level of usage of intermediary-oriented B2B in a market sector known to you such as retail.

11 Those companies that survive in the e-economy will be those that integrate effectively their front-end information systems such as their B2B systems with their existing core information systems infrastructure. Investigate the degree to which such integration is critical to the success of eBusiness.

Further reading

Beynon-Davies (2004) covers the issues discussed in this chapter in more depth, as does Chaffey (2006).

References

Armstrong, A. and Hagel, J. (1996) 'The real value of online communities', *Harvard Business Review*, May–June: 134–41.

Barrette, S. and Konsynski, B. R. (1982)' Inter-organisational information sharing systems', *MIS Quarterly*, Fall.

Beynon-Davies, P. (2004) *E-Business*. Basingstoke, Palgrave.

Bickerton, P., Bickerton, M. and Simpson-Holey, K. (2000) *Cybermarketing: how to use the Internet to market your goods and services*. Oxford, Butterworth-Heinemann.

Brassington, F. and Pettit, S. (2000) *Principles of Marketing*. Harlow, Pearson.

Cassidy, J. (2002) *Dot.Con*. London, Allen Lane/Penguin Press.

Chaffey, D. (2006) *E-Business and E-Commerce Management*. Harlow, Essex, Pearson Education.

Chaffey, D., Mayer, R., Johnston, K. and Ellis-Chadwick, F. (2000) *Internet Marketing*. Harlow, Pearson.

Chaston, I. (2001) *E-Marketing Strategies*. Maidenhead, McGraw-Hill.

Cunningham, M. J. (2002) *B2B: How to build a profitable e-commerce strategy*. Cambridge, Mass., Perseus.

De Kare-Silver, M. (2000) *E-Shock 2000: The electronic shopping revolution; strategies for retailers and manufacturers*. Basingstoke, Palgrave Macmillan.

Hardaker, G. and G. Graham (2001) *Wired Marketing: Energizing business for e-commerce*. Chichester, John Wiley.

Hoque, F. (2000) *E-enterprise: Business models, architecture and components*. Cambridge, Cambridge University Press.

Kalakota, R. and Robinson, M. (1999) *E-Business: Roadmap for success*. Reading, Mass, Addison-Wesley.

Kalakota, R. and Whinston, A. B. (1997) *Electronic Commerce: A manager's guide*. Harlow, UK, Addison-Wesley.

Laudon, K. C. and Traver, C. G. (2002) *E-commerce: Business, technology, society*. Boston, Mass., Addison Wesley.

Martin, J. (1996) *Cybercorp*. New York, American Management Association.

Matin, A., Gerard, P. and Lariver, C. (2001) 'Turning the supply chain into a revenue chain', *Harvard Business Review* **79**(3): 20–2.

McCarthy, J. (1960) *Basic Marketing: A managerial approach*. Homewood, Ill., Irwin.

Meier, J. (1995) 'The importance of relationship management in establishing successful inter-organisational systems', *Journal of Strategic Information Systems* **4**(2): 135–48.

Porter, M. E. (1985) *Competitive Advantage: Creating and sustaining superior performance*. New York, Free Press.

PART 3

Rajkumar, T. M. (2001) 'E-procurement: business and technical issues', *Information Systems Management*, Fall: 52–60.

Rheingold, H. (1995) *The Virtual Community: Finding connection in a computerised world*. London, Minerva.

Seybold, P. (1999) *Customers.com*. London, Random House.

Thomas, D., Ranganathan, C. and Desouza, K. C. (2005) 'Race to dot com and back: lessons from ebusiness spin-offs and reintegration', *Information Systems Management*, Summer.

Timmers, P. (1999) *Electronic Commerce: Strategies and models for business to business trading*. Chichester, John Wiley.

Wise, R. and Morrison, D. (2000) 'Beyond the exchange: the future of B2B', *Harvard Business Review*, November–December: 86–96.

CHAPTER 9

Assessing the use and impact of information systems

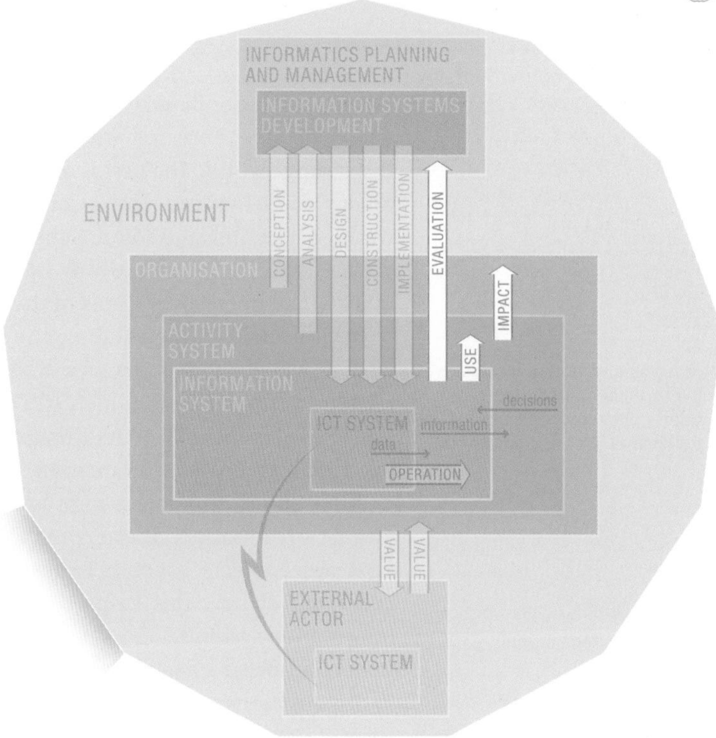

Just because something doesn't do what you planned it to do doesn't mean it's useless.

Thomas A. Edison (1847–1931)

Haste in every business brings failures.

Herodotus (485 BC–425 BC)

CHAPTER OUTLINE

LEARNING OUTCOMES	PRINCIPLES
Understand the relationship between the value of ICT and questions of its use and impact.	The value of ICT lies in the interaction of the technology with the activity systems of an organisation. Successful information systems rely on successful use, and successful use is a precondition of successful impact.
Describe elements making up the use context of an information system, and distinguish between the impact of information systems on the organisation at large, and on groups and individuals within organisations.	The use context consists of stakeholders of various types engaging with the interfaces to an ICT system. The usability of this interface and user satisfaction with the overall information system establish a good base for successful impact. The impact of information systems will be felt in terms of the jobs and work of particular individuals and groups. Impact also needs to be assessed in terms of performance improvement within activity systems in organisations.
Relate the importance of understanding the causes of information systems failure to achieving success in this area.	The failure of information systems is commonplace. Failure or success needs to be judged against the expectations of particular stakeholder groups. Avoiding failure and achieving success relies on understanding and managing the complex relationship between ICT, information systems and organisations.
Understand the importance of evaluation of information systems and explain the distinction between strategic, formative and summative evaluation.	Evaluation is an assessment of worth. Such assessments are important at a number of points in the life of an information system: before it is conceived (strategic evaluation), during its development (formative evaluation) and after it is delivered into its context of use (summative evaluation).

Introduction

Davenport (2000) makes an interesting analogy between ICT and plumbing. Imagine a world, he says, obsessed with the technology of plumbing. Only two things are missing in this strange world. The first is an interest in the qualities of the material handled by this technology, namely water. The second is an interest in the uses to which water is put: drinking, washing, cleaning and so on. Substitute ICT for plumbing and information for water, and you get an appreciation of the way in which technology, information and action are inevitably intertwined in considerations of the worth of ICT.

Use: A precondition of electronic delivery. Stakeholders must regularly use remote access mechanisms in core areas of life.

In other words, the value or the worth of ICT cannot be divorced from the question of what it delivers: that is, data for USE in information systems. The worth of ICT is also directly related to the degree to which ICT systems are used and the impact they have on organisations. Judgements of worth ultimately relate to assessments of success and failure, so they rely on critical processes of evaluation.

After an information system is introduced into an organisation, it begins to have effects on that organisation. These come in two forms, first-order effects and second-order effects. First-order effects concern issues of use. This chapter considers them in the use context, and looks at how this helps determine stakeholder commitment to and satisfaction with information systems.

Second-order effects concern the impact of the information system on activity systems in organisations; on individuals, groups and the organisation as a whole. To help explain the issue of organisational impact more clearly, we use the distinction between efficacy, efficiency and effectiveness measures of performance that was introduced in Chapter 2.

Both use and impact are critical inputs into any assessment of the success or failure of an information system. This chapter. therefore considers information systems failure in some detail. This helps to show the systemic relationship between a number of elements that affect the success of information systems.

The question of the worth of ICT and information systems raises the important issue of evaluation. The chapter concludes with discussion of a number of forms of evaluation appropriate to organisational informatics. These forms link directly to the processes needed to ensure effective informatics planning, management and development activities.

The worth of an information system

DeLone and McLean (1992) systematically reviewed the literature on the success of information systems in organisations, and produced a model of the factors influencing it (see Figure 9.1). This model has been much debated but it is still useful for highlighting some of the key variables, and has been used to organise some of the discussion here.

To the left of the figure are two issues of technical quality: the quality of the information system itself and the quality of the information it produces. Both are likely to influence the use of the system and perceptions of user satisfaction. The use of the system will have an impact on individuals in the organisation, which in turn will have an impact on the organisation as a whole.

In a later paper (DeLone and McLean, 2003), the authors suggested two amendments to the model. The concept of service quality was added alongside system and information quality. Service quality is meant to extend the focus from the products of the informatics function (see Chapter 11) to the service this function provides. The issues of individual impact and organisational impact were also brought together in the notion of net benefits achieved from information systems. This is meant to encompass the fact that multiple stakeholders, both inside the organisation (such as differing work groups) and outside it (such as customers and partners) are likely to benefit from the introduction of an information system.

Elements from the DeLone and McLean model can be overlaid onto a far simpler scheme of functionality, usability and utility (see Figure 9.2).

Information systems have to be designed in the sense that their key features need to be determined before they are constructed and implemented. These key features or properties provide core ways of assessing the system's worth or success. Since an information system mediates between technology and activity, we can consider it in terms of three properties: functionality, usability and utility.

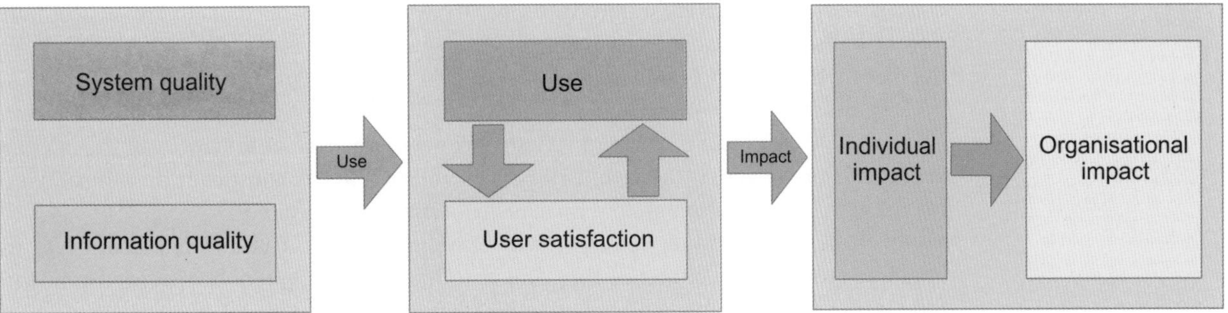

Figure 9.1: *The DeLone and McLean model*

Functionality: What a system does or should be able to do.

Usability: An information system's usability is how easy a system is to use for the purpose for which it was constructed.

Utility: The worth of an information system in terms of the contribution it makes to its human activity system and to the organisation as a whole.

The FUNCTIONALITY of an information system is normally determined by a close examination of organisational requirements. It is what the system does, or should do. Specifying the core functionality is a critical aspect of information systems development (see Chapter 12). For instance, to describe a system as an order processing system indicates that it in some way captures, stores and manipulates data associated with the processing of orders.

USABILITY is evident in the way in which an information system embeds itself in activity. It is a measure of how easy it is to use for the purpose for which it has been constructed. Usability is evident at the human–computer interface (see below), the point at which the user interacts with the ICT system. An order processing system's usability will be determined by how easy it is for users such as order clerks or customer service representatives to input and extract data about orders.

Whereas functionality defines what an information system does and usability defines how it is used, UTILITY defines how acceptable the information system is in terms of doing what is needed. It judges the system by the contribution it makes to its activity system and the organisation as a whole. An order processing system's utility might be defined as the contribution it makes to the efficient handling of customer orders. It might contribute to significant cost savings in order processing, and/or to improvements in organisational effectiveness. For instance, if it leads to customers getting an improved service, that should be apparent in their level of satisfaction, which feeds through into the level of customer retention.

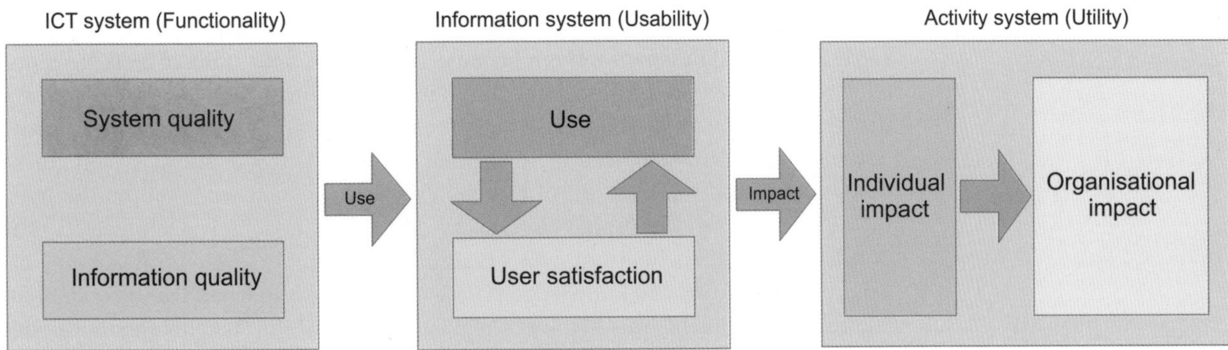

Figure 9.2: *The domains of functionality, usability and utility*

There is a clear relationship between functionality, usability and utility on the one hand, and an ICT system, information system and activity system on the other. Functionality is typically seen to be a property of the ICT system whereas utility emerges as a property of the activity system. Usability is a mediating feature between the technical system (the ICT system) and the social system (the activity system), and is evident at the user interface (see below).

In the Delone and McLean model, system quality, information quality and to a certain extent service quality are primarily issues of *functionality*. Functionality is established in the context of the informatics service (see Chapter 11), and in particular the process of information systems development (see Chapter 12). As a result these issues lie mostly in the domain of the ICT system (Chapter 6). Use and user satisfaction are primarily issues of *usability*, which is established in the context of use, and lies in the domain of the information system (see Chapter 4). Impact at a number of levels is primarily an issue of the *utility* of the information system within an activity system. Utility is established in the context of the consequences or impact of the information system on aspects of the activity system.

Put these together, and we have a way of judging the worth of an information system. It might be judged to lack functionality, and so to have failed. It might be regarded as adequately functioning but unusable, and hence to have failed. Or it could be judged that it is adequate in both functionality and usability, but has not delivered any key organisational benefit, so it has failed in terms of utility. This issue of information systems failure is revisited later in the chapter.

The context of use

The context of use of an information system is defined by a number of key issues including:

- usability
- the user interface
- the use setting
- stakeholder involvement
- stakeholder satisfaction.

Conventional conceptions of use see it in terms of the **usability** of ICT systems: that is, how easy the system is to use for the purpose for which it was constructed. So the definition of usability hinges on the activity system it is meant to serve.

Evidence suggests that for successful use, activity systems must be designed in parallel with the design of ICT systems. The identification and *involvement* of key system stakeholders is therefore essential for the successful development and use of ICT systems (see Chapter 12).

One of the key reasons for involving stakeholders in the development of information systems is that this involvement appears to increase levels of **user satisfaction** with the systems. Systems that are not accepted and do not have the commitment of system stakeholders are likely to be subject to stakeholder resistance.

These issues are neatly summarised in a series of propositions concerning ICT systems design expressed nearly two decades ago by Eason (1988):

> IT technical design is not enough because benefit can only come if these systems are effectively harnessed and exploited by their users. The achievement of this involves the creation of compatible social and technical systems to serve some important organisational purpose. This in turn means the design of a social system to serve this purpose and the creation of a technical system which will support the users in the social system. The design process by which this is achieved requires a process of planned change which not only creates the appropriate system but creates in the users a motivational and knowledge state where they are able and willing to exploit the technical capabilities. This involves the participation of the stakeholders in the design process and individual and collective learning processes.

The user interface

An **interface** defines how a given technology can be used. Every technology has an interface, and ICT is no different. An ICT system's interface is known as the user interface, or sometimes the human–computer interface. People use it to input data to the system and to receive data output from it. The use activities of the ICT system form part of the larger information system. Decisions are made on the basis of information interpreted from the information system, and action is taken in the encompassing human activity system (Figure 9.3).

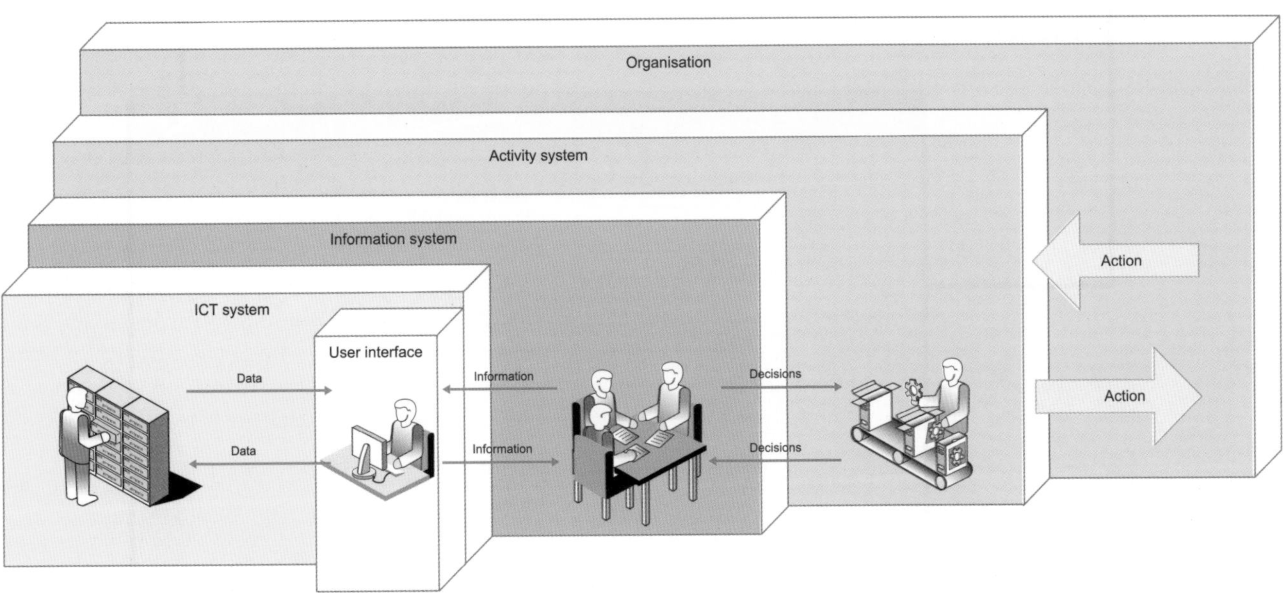

Figure 9.3: *The domain of use*

Reflect
What is the user interface for a car? How do you go about controlling or using it? How easy is it to learn to use its interface, and how transferable are the skills between different types of car? How does this compare with the interfaces that apply to ICT systems, in your experience?

For example, say a customer phones through an order for a certain quantity of products. The order clerk inputs details of the order into the order-processing ICT system through an order-entry screen. The ICT system might check automatically whether the customer is an existing one, and provide details of previous orders, which enables the clerk to decide whether to offer a discount.

In this example, the activity system might be described as the process of customer ordering. The ICT system is the order-processing system, and the interface is the order entry screen. To use this interface the clerk enters data using the keyboard and mouse, and receives feedback of the entry on the computer monitor. The data output by the ICT system is interpreted by the clerk as existing customer details and previous orders. The ICT system plus this context of use therefore forms the information system in support of customer ordering.

A user interface can be seen as a collection of dialogues, each made up of a series of messages between the user and the ICT system. As such, the user interface is the technology supporting human–machine communication (see Chapter 3).

There are three major aspects to these dialogues:

- the content of messages between the user and the ICT system
- control, which refers to the way the user moves between aspects of one dialogue or from one dialogue to another
- the layout or format of messages and data on input and output devices.

Dialogues can also be seen in terms of the four areas of semiotics described in Chapter 3: pragmatics, semantics, syntactics and empirics. Format and control are largely aspects of the syntax, and empirics of signs: the way signs are stored, transmitted and represented on the devices of a computer system. Some aspects of control, and certainly content, relate to the pragmatics and semantics of signs: how they are given meaning in various layers of context.

Take the interface to the Goronwy Galvanising ICT system first described in Chapter 1. Control will involve aspects such as the navigation between the main menu and a Jobs data entry screen. Format refers to the structure of menus and data entry screens. Content refers to the actual data entered and retrieved via these screens (Figure 9.4).

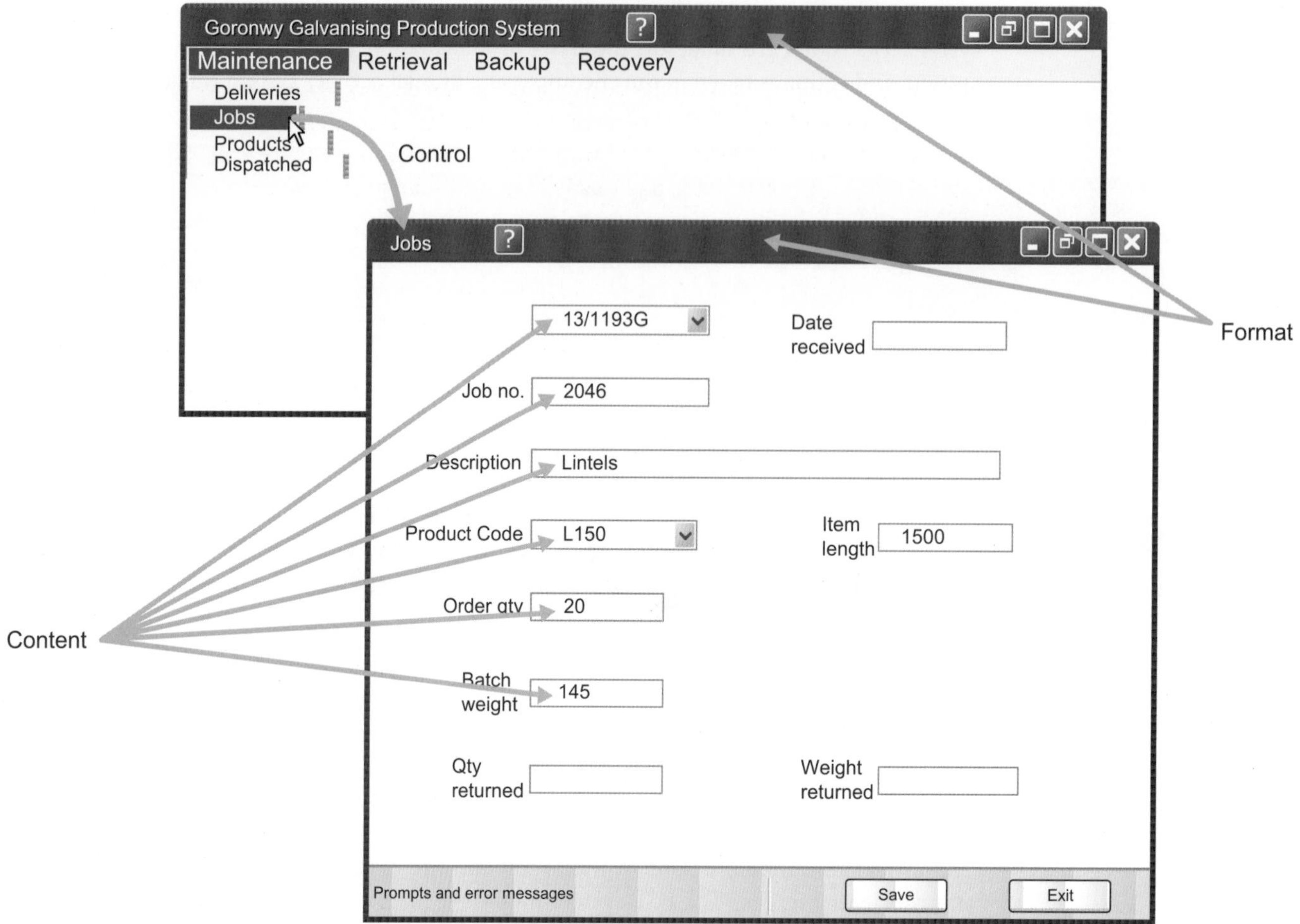

Figure 9.4: *Format, content and control*

Did you know?

Interfaces to technologies tend to get locked after a period of time in which a substantial number of users learn to use them. There are switching costs involved in learning to use a new interface. For example, the arrangement of keys on most computer keyboards was designed and patented in 1874 by Christopher Scholes, and appeared in typewriters of the time. It is known as the QWERTY keyboard after the first six letters in the top alpha row. On Scholes' first design the characters of the alphabet were arranged alphabetically, but when typists typed at speed, the hammers (the devices moved by the keys, which struck the paper through a ribbon impregnated with ink) had a tendency to jam. A colleague suggested to Scholes the idea of separating more widely the keys for letters that were commonly used together, and this was what he did. When keyboards began to be used as input devices to computers the design was transported over, and it has remained dominant ever since, even though there is no question of jamming with modern electronic keyboards. The layout has been modified slightly to meet the needs of particular linguistic groups. For instance, the AZERTY layout is used in several French-speaking countries, including Belgium, and includes the accented letters needed in French, such as é, à and ô.

Types of interface

There are five broad categories of interface format: menus, forms, command language, natural language, direct manipulation, multimedia and virtual reality interfaces. They can be used in combination: for instance, the interface to an order processing system might be made up of menus, data entry forms and elements of direct manipulation.

Menus are interfaces consisting of a displayed list of choices. The user selects an item from the list by pressing a key combination, moving a cursor to the choice and clicking the mouse, or typing in a value and pressing 'enter'.

Forms are used for data entry and retrieval. A form is simply a set of fields laid out on a screen, or more readily these days in a window. The data entry fields are normally labelled, and there is also usually a header and an area for the display of error messages or prompts.

In a **command language interface** the user enters statements in a formal language. Historically, command level interfaces were the first type of online interface. Operating systems typically have command language interfaces, and many database management systems also offer command-level interfaces to the database sub-language SQL (see Chapter 6).

Natural language interfaces are slightly misnamed because they will not generally accept everyday English input as character strings. They are more accurately described as being restricted language interfaces. The system is programmed to decipher a range of statements and commands, but it is limited in the grammar and vocabulary that is accepted. So the statement, 'give me all the salaries of my employees' might be acceptable, but 'list my employees' salaries' might not. Natural language statements can be either typed via the keyboard or spoken through a microphone with associated voice recognition software. These interfaces have achieved some success as front ends to database systems (see Chapter 6).

Direct manipulation interfaces are generally associated with icon-based, windows environments, and are referred to as direct manipulation because the user causes events to happen by manipulating graphic objects using a mouse or similar input device. They are now dominant in most areas of ICT systems.

Multimedia interfaces are a direct extension of the direct manipulation interface, in that they employ the same mechanisms for controlling input, but rather than having menus and data entry forms, a full range of media types is used to build the interface. The prevalence of the Web has caused an explosion in the types of media used in interfaces, which often include animation, video and audio. However, adding multimedia to interfaces does not always improve their usability.

In some applications, such as simulations, it is important for the user to experience feedback through an interface that closely resembles the real-world situation being simulated. For instance, aircraft simulators are used to train commercial and military pilots, and their controls are copies of actual aircraft control panels. Aspects of this form of **virtual reality interface** have now become feasible on the desktop, and organisations have experimented with the use of such immersive interfaces in the domain of information systems.

Use setting

It is important to recognise that increasingly interfaces to systems will differ depending on the access channel used by stakeholders (see Chapter 5). For example, both a customer service employee and a customer might have access to a CRM system, but their interfaces are likely to be significantly different in both functionality and usability. Interfaces are also likely to differ depending on the access device used and the place of use. There are four major types of location for remote access devices: at home, in public spaces, while on the move (mobile) or in the workplace. Particular access channels are associated with particular places of access and use. For example, as a means of improving access to electronic services, governments have put more access devices in public places such as schools, libraries, community centres and museums. An increasing range of WiFi hotspots are also being offered in cafés and other public spaces.

Use setting: A concept that includes the information-handling behaviours of stakeholders using a particular access device in a particular place.

These three issues of stakeholder type, access device used and place of use together make up a USE SETTING, a concept which also includes the information-handling behaviours and practices established in a context, particularly in the workplace. For instance, Marchand, Kettinger and Rollins (2000) make the important point that what they call the **information orientation** of people in organisations has a bearing on the success of information and ICT systems. This means a set of positive practices and behaviours established in relation to information handling, and is a facet of organisational culture (see Chapter 2).

In some organisations the information orientation is focused on individuals rather than groups. The organisational culture encourages people to build and maintain their own information repositories. There is little incentive for people to share information, which might even be thought of as bringing a potential loss of power. In other organisations people are encouraged to collect information about customers but not given any incentive to enter it in the core information system. This makes coherent customer resource management difficult.

Usability

Reflect
Do you text regularly on your mobile phone? Reflect on the interface available for texting in terms of Nielsen's dimensions of usability.

Usability normally considers both a defined user group and a defined set of tasks. The design of a user interface must consider the roles of its users, and what tasks they will need to carry out. For the interface in Figure 9.4, for example, the defined user group is likely to be production controllers at Goronwy. The tasks to be performed are the entry of new job sheets, the retrieval of existing job sheets and the amendment of data on existing job sheets.

The **usability** of an ICT system is how easy it is to use for the purpose for which it has been constructed. Nielsen (1993) suggests that it can be evaluated on five dimensions:

- **Learnability**, or how easy it is to learn to use the interface.
- **Rememberability,** or how easy it is for the user to be able to remember learned operations.
- How **efficient** it is to use. For instance, users should not face delays when they try to input data.
- The interface should promote **reliable** human performance in the sense that it should lead users to make fewer errors.
- The interface should satisfy the users in the sense that it leaves them subjectively pleased with using it. This is known as **user satisfaction** (see below).

Since the interface is now an increasingly large part of the structure of most ICT systems, its design has become an established part of information systems design (Chapter 12). There is also an increasing emphasis on assessing, evaluating and testing the usability of systems. The discipline devoted to these activities is now frequently known as USABILITY ENGINEERING.

Usability engineering: An approach that focuses on assessing, evaluating and testing the usability of ICT systems, with the aim of improving the design of the user interface.

The quality of the user interface

Whichever combination of formats is chosen for the user interface, a number of design guidelines have been shown to improve usability:

- It is important to use consistent and meaningful terminology. This fundamentally means applying a consistent and relevant semantics to a particular domain. For instance, if menus are used, it is important to provide a consistent way for the user to select options, to title every menu, to align options and to have no more than seven options per menu. Menus also need a consistent way of displaying error messages, and it is useful to organise menus in a hierarchy which emulates the division of tasks in the system.
- A different user interface should be designed for each distinct user group. The terms used should be familiar to the proposed group of users. Naive users will need different interfaces than experienced users. For instance, naive users might prefer menu selection because of ease of use, whereas sophisticated users might prefer a command-line interface because of speed of use.
- Feedback should be provided for users: when they do something right, they need to see a result; when they do something wrong, help should be provided.
- Dialogues should be designed with a well-defined start, middle and end. This and feedback are sometimes discussed under the concept of 'closure', because they both concern the importance of showing users whether or not they have successfully completed an operation.
- Simple, meaningful error messages should make it easy to correct a mistake. It is also useful to allow users to backtrack to a previous state.
- Information overload should be avoided. Interfaces should not be cluttered with too much information. Also, images and other media should be used only when they contribute to usability.

Stakeholders

Use implies a user, a term often used to refer to everybody in an organisation except the ICT developers. So it might include, for instance, top-level managers, middle managers and operational staff.

As in Chapter 2, this book prefers the term stakeholder group or **stakeholder** rather than user, to help distinguish between different groups inside and outside an organisation who might have an effect on the system's use and impact. A number of major types of stakeholder relevant to this context can be distinguished at a high level.

Producer: A key type of organisational stakeholder. Teams of developers that have to design, construct and maintain information systems for organisations.

Client: A key type of organisational stakeholder. Clients sponsor and provide resources for the construction and continuing use of an information system.

End-user: That stakeholder group that uses an information system to conduct work.

First there are the stakeholders that form the development context for an information system (Chapter 12): producers, clients and end-users. PRODUCERS are the people tasked with developing the information system. CLIENTS sponsor and provide resources for the project: they are normally managers. Users, or more accurately END-USERS, are the people involved in using the information system, and are only rarely managers: most information systems are designed to support other workers, as was described in Chapter 4.

Since information systems are increasingly being used to support external relationships and activities, stakeholder groups such as customers, suppliers, regulators and partners are increasingly important. Some of these groups, such as customers and suppliers, may even overlap with end-users for certain classes of front-end information systems. Partners and regulators are likely to have a key influence on the design of an information system.

For Goronwy Galvanising, for instance, the clients are the managers in the company's headquarters. Producers are the developers brought in to construct the ICT system for the company. The end-users are various workers at Goronwy, including inbound and outbound logistics staff, production controllers and shift foremen. As the system developed into an extranet, customers such as Blackwalls were involved in the design of aspects of it.

A stakeholder is a political concept in that it is related to issues of power and its exercise (see Chapter 2). Stakeholder groups are social groups that have a 'stake' in and potentially a degree of influence over the development of an information system. An organisational group can also be defined in terms of a set of shared meanings – in other words, a subculture. Each stakeholder group might form a distinct subculture (see Chapter 2) in an organisation. In this chapter, the main interest is in the set of assumptions, expectations and knowledge a group might use to frame technological change.

Technological frames

Technological frame: A collection of underlying assumptions, expectations and knowledge that people have about technology and its use.

Orlikowski and Gash (1994) suggest that people approach technology on the basis of their TECHNOLOGICAL FRAME: a collection of underlying assumptions, expectations and knowledge about technology and its use. Managers, technologists, users and other stakeholders have significantly different technological frames, which influence how they understand the development, use and change of technology.

Orlikowski and Gash use the example of a project which attempted to introduce the ICT package Lotus Notes into a consulting organisation:

- **Nature of technology**: the technologists saw Notes as an information-sharing and group-work tool, but users framed it more as an individual productivity tool.
- **Technology strategy:** technologists expected the package to leverage the work of the firm. Users tended to see Notes merely as a substitute for existing ICTs such as fax and telephone.
- **Technology in use:** technologists assumed that Notes was an end-user tool which needed little support from the informatics service (see Chapter 11). But users did not really know how they were expected to use it or what it could do for them, and felt they should have been given demonstrations by the technologists.

Stakeholder involvement and satisfaction

A number of critical principles affecting use arise from the concept of a stakeholder group. First, it is important to identify stakeholder groups that are likely to influence the development process as part of the planning (see Chapter 10) for an information system. Second, it is important to involve representatives of various stakeholder groups in the development process (see Chapter 12). Third, it is important to identify differences in meanings assigned to technology by different stakeholders.

Stakeholder involvement: Involvement of stakeholder representatives in the development of an ICT system.

Stakeholder satisfaction: The state of satisfaction expressed by a stakeholder group in an information system.

STAKEHOLDER INVOLVEMENT in the development of information systems is seen to improve system acceptance and satisfaction with systems (Newman and Sabherwal, 1996). STAKEHOLDER SATISFACTION refers to a subjective assessment of the success of an information system, so determining its levels is an important part of assessing the worth of a system. It can be assessed at a number of levels. Satisfaction with the interface may serve as a measure of usability. Satisfaction with the ICT system itself may serve as a measure of functionality. Finally, satisfaction with the information system may serve as a measure of utility.

This section on usage issues concentrates on user interface satisfaction, although this is difficult to separate out from issues of functionality. User satisfaction criteria with systems include output assessments such as accuracy, quality, completeness and relevance of output, process assessments such as availability of service, mean time between failure, down-time and number of security breaches, and input assessments such as ease of use and response time.

Often satisfaction is measured using questionnaires with a series of attitude questions. One popular approach is QUIS (Chin, Diehl and Norman, 1988) – Questionnaire for User Interface Satisfaction – consisting of 27 items using a nine-point Likert scale. Figure 9.5 provides an example of the questions that are asked.

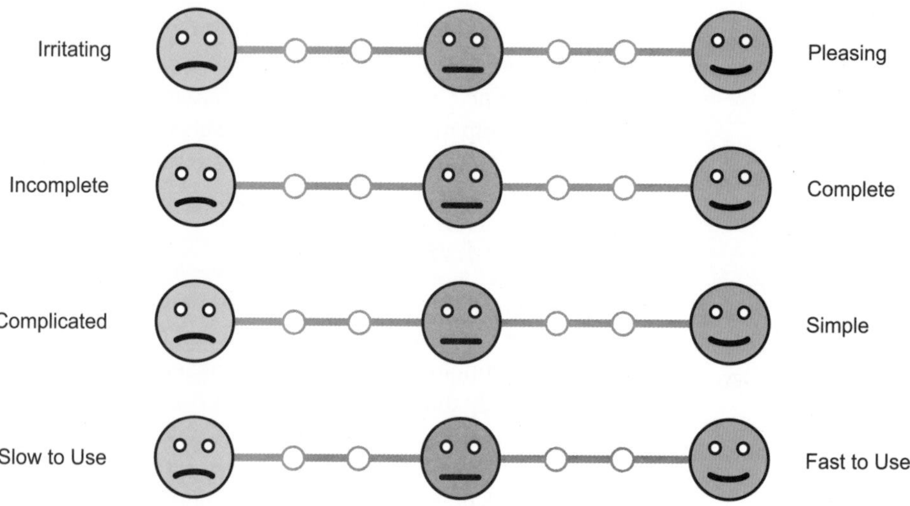

Figure 9.5: *Examples of questions from a user satisfaction questionnaire*

Stakeholder resistance

After delivery, an information system is subject to use and maintenance (Chapter 12). The further development and maintenance of a system is known as its **post-implementation trajectory**.

Stakeholder resistance: The resistance of stakeholder groups to the introduction of an information system.

One of the key ways in which organisational politics may affect the post-implementation trajectory is through user or STAKEHOLDER RESISTANCE. Hirschheim and Newman (1988), for instance, provide a case study that illustrates how user resistance depended on the amount of stakeholder involvement in implementation. Keen (1981) details a number of counter-implementation strategies that users may take to impede the development of an information system. One of these strategies is to lay low or to be too busy to be involved. In other words, if a stakeholder does not wish a system to succeed, then keeping out of the way and not giving help and encouragement can help make it a failure. Another strategy is to exploit the development team's lack of inside knowledge. The technical staff in particular will probably know very little about the detailed nature of the work involved in a particular business area, and if users do not help by telling them what goes on, the system they design will probably prove to be inadequate.

Recap

After information systems are introduced in an organisation, the context of use begins to affect the activity system. Information systems may be closely aligned with their activity system, through design or by accident, generating both intended and unintended positive effects. If they are misaligned they can have a negative effect on organisational activity. They are more likely to be well aligned if the developers identify the stakeholders, understand the differences in their technological frames, and involve representatives of stakeholder groups in the development process.

Impact

Once introduced, information systems have immediate effects in their context of use, which is largely determined by the activity system into which they are placed. The effects can be positive or negative depending on how well the system is aligned with its context.

Second-order effects, or impact, can be separated into impact on individuals, on groups and on the organisation as a whole. All these can be either positive or negative. At the level of groups and individuals, perceptions of the positive or negative nature of impact will relate to people's organisational position: for instance, the system might bring about shifts in power and influence. Of the impacts on the organisation as a whole, the relationship between information systems and productivity has been hotly debated (see Figure 9.6). Some of the impact will have been predicted and designed for, but much of the impact of information systems can be unintended.

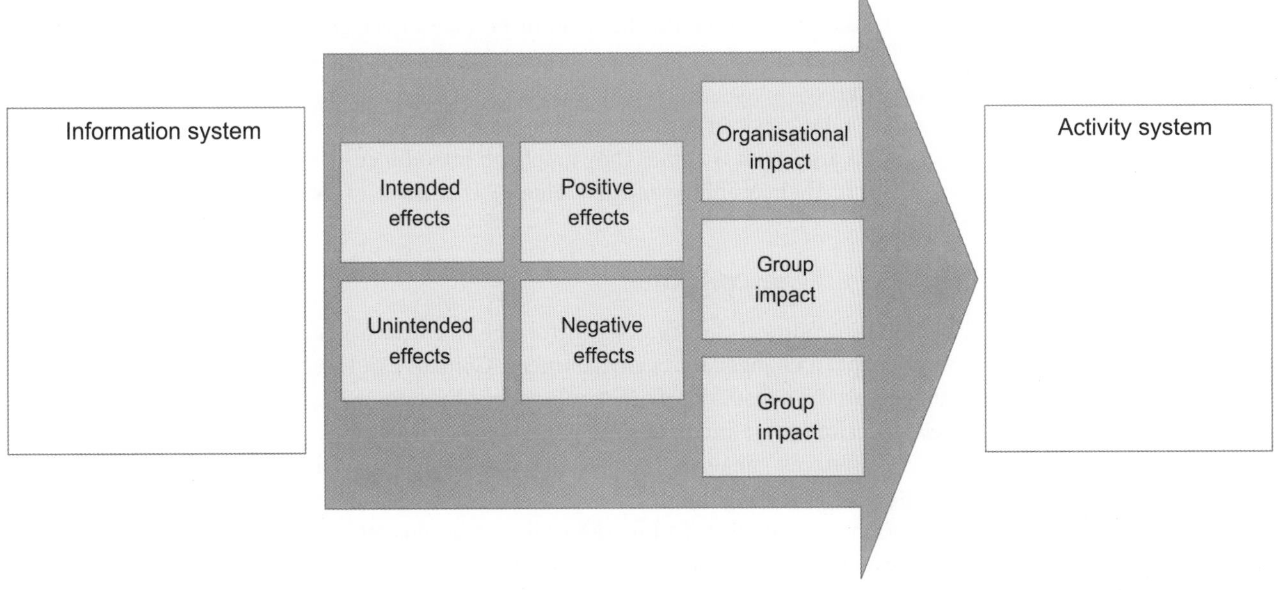

Figure 9.6: *Dimensions of impact*

Case check: Case 25 W Child Support Agency

The UK Child Support Agency's information system CS2 is a good example of a system with unintended negative impacts. It failed so disastrously that it contributed to the closure of the Agency, and cost the UK taxpayer over £1 billion.

Orlikowski (1996) made a second study of the introduction of Lotus Notes in a company selling marketing software, and noted how it changed planned ways of working. Initially, the technology was intended to help manage a large increase in phone calls to software support staff at local offices. The idea was that the individual call-handlers would use the package to document calls electronically, so they could track and respond to them more effectively.

What actually happened, Orlikowski noticed, was that people started to use the system to proactively respond to other people's calls for which they had a ready solution during downtime periods in their work. This change was so successful that managers began to assess support specialists in terms of their ability to collaborate proactively with their colleagues. Eventually the system began to be used as a way of training new support staff in 'appropriate' ways of performing support work.

Less successful was the example Button and Harper (1993) give of the introduction of a computerised order-processing system in a foam manufacturing company. It upset existing work practices to such a degree that it interfered with effective fulfilment of orders – 'It slowed things down.' Likewise, Sachs (1995) demonstrated how the introduction of a centralised work-scheduling system in a telephone-engineering organisation disrupted the effective 'troubleshooting' work of maintenance engineers.

Landauer (1995) compiled an impressive list of evidence against the usefulness and usability of many computer systems, providing examples of misalignment at organisational, individual and group levels. He maintains that there was little evidence that computer systems actually contributed to organisational effectiveness, and particularly to increases in productivity. There were examples of effective use of computer technology to improve business performance, such as computer-aided telephony, but he believed they were in the minority.

Landauer made a distinction between phase one and phase two computer applications. In phase one applications, computers are used to automate functions that had either previously been performed by humans, or that no human would be capable of. These applications exploit the computer's calculating power: examples are missile control and accounting systems. Because of their inherent deterministic and limited context, phase one applications proved relatively successful. Landauer argued, however, that there were fewer and fewer areas left for them to penetrate. Phase two applications are about augmentation, encompassing that range of tasks that people do that cannot be taken over entirely by numerical calculations. It was in this field that it was hard to be clear whether the systems were making a positive contribution.

Landauer did however believe that computer systems can be used to improve performance; much of his argument was that they had been introduced with little formative or summative evaluation of their usability and usefulness. This issue of evaluation is discussed in a later section.

Impact on the organisation

Chapter 2 introduced the idea of control, the need for a system to be able to regulate itself and to adapt to changes in its environment. Control can be seen as a monitoring subsystem that controls the behaviour of other subsystems by comparing their behaviour against defined levels of performance and acting appropriately.

Performance: The degree to which a system reaches specified levels.

What systems analysts see as control, business theoreticians tend to see as PERFORMANCE **management**: the process of measuring past action (Neely, 1998). The assumption is that past action determines current performance. In a systems context, performance can be measured in terms of efficacy, efficiency and effectiveness (see Checkland, 1999 and Chapter 2). The level of performance an organisation attains is a function of the efficacy, efficiency and effectiveness of the actions it has undertaken. The difference between these performance measures is illustrated in Figure 9.7.

Efficacy is a measure of the extent to which a system achieves its intended transformation. Porter would argue that for any company this transformation involves delivering greater value to customers (see Chapter 7). So efficacy is primarily focused on the outputs from the organisation, or producing the appropriate value. Efficacy gains are typically measured as improvements in the volume or quality of a service or product.

Efficiency tends to correspond, at least for commercial organisations, to an economic model of the firm. It is a measure of the extent to which the system achieves its intended transformation with the minimum use of resources. Efficiency gains can be achieved in an activity system through doing more with the same resources or the same with less resource, so they can be measured by comparing inputs against outputs using a systems model of the organisation. If inputs and outputs can be expressed in numeric terms, efficiency can be expressed as the ratio of inputs to outputs: Efficiency = Inputs/Outputs.

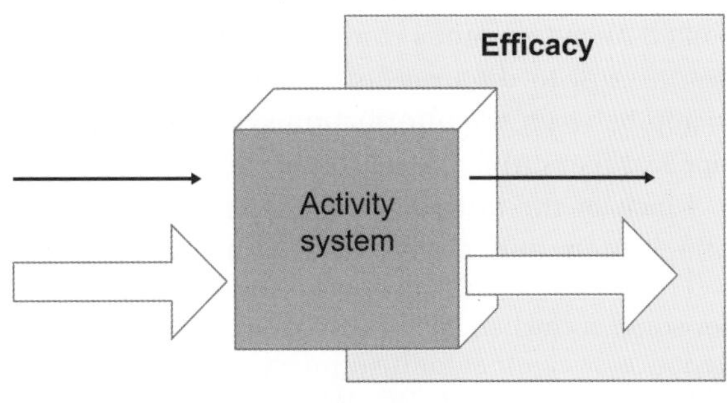

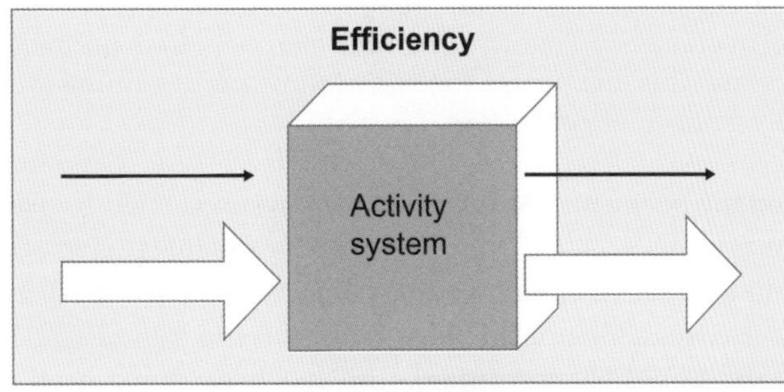

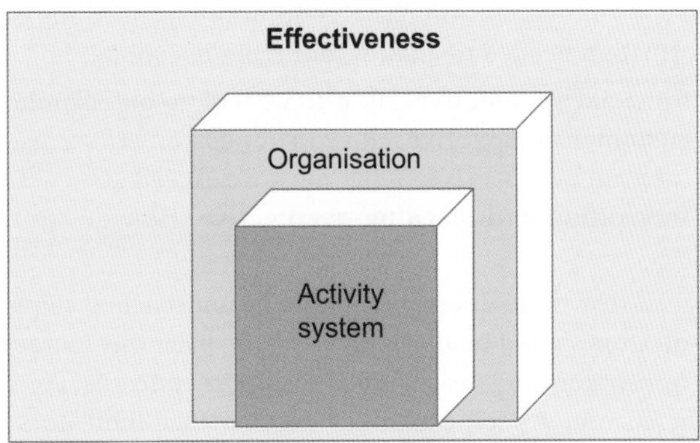

Figure 9.7: *Efficacy, efficiency and effectiveness*

In the traditional open systems model of organisations, capital and labour are the two inputs that the organisation takes from its environment. A microeconomic model of the firm permits capital to be freely substituted for labour to produce similar levels of output or production. Such models predict that ICT can be freely substituted for labour through the automation of processes, thereby introducing cost savings.

Another type of economic model of the firm is based around the idea of transaction costs (see Chapter 7). These are the costs incurred by the organisation when it buys in the marketplace. Firms seek to reduce transaction costs particularly by reducing the costs associated with using markets, such as locating and communicating with suppliers, maintaining contracts and obtaining information on products. ICT can help in these ways.

For commercial organisations, improving efficacy and efficiency are strategies to make more money: that is, to increase profitability. Efficacy and efficiency gains will lead to more customers and improve the competitive position of the company.

Efficacy, efficiency and consequently profitability all have to be measured and monitored. Successful companies institute both single and double-loop learning (Chapter 2) through single and double-loop feedback mechanisms. These rely on information collected, stored and disseminated through information systems, so information systems and their associated ICT systems are critical to modern organisational performance. The key question is how to measure the effectiveness of the information and ICT systems in organisations?

Effectiveness is a measure of the extent to which the system contributes to the purposes of a higher-level system of which it may be a subsystem. For example, a company that was a member of a larger business group would be judged on the contribution it made to group profitability. An autonomous company's effectiveness might be assessed through competitive BENCHMARKING, to discover its competitive position in its key markets. In terms of the relationship between the information system and the activity system it supports, effectiveness concerns measuring the impact of the information system on the purpose of the activity system. Much of the discussion of the effectiveness of information systems is directed at attempting to determine the strategic advantage they offer to businesses (see Chapter 10).

Benchmarking: Sometimes called competitive practices benchmarking. The process of comparing performance against other comparable organisations or processes.

Case check:
Case 20, Tesco

Consider some of the benefits of Tesco maintaining its online arm, Tesco.com. The site offers a different access channel for its primary value flow, the sale of foodstuffs. This is a gain in efficacy. The online channel also offers the company the possibility of reaching a larger base of customers and selling a wider range of products to them for little additional resource. This is a gain in efficiency. Finally, the online channel offers improvements in market position for the company. It is able to use the site as a means of gaining greater market share. These are primarily gains in effectiveness.

Traditionally performance measurement systems tried to use financial measures to measure tangible efficiency gains. More recently companies have attempted to build more holistic performance measurement systems that encompass the broad range of efficacy, efficiency and effectiveness. One of the most famous is the BALANCED SCORECARD invented by Robert Kaplan and David Norton (1992). This has been much used in business consulting. It maintains that if an organisation has a good, well-balanced measurement system, it should have the information needed to answer four main questions:

Balanced scorecard: A popular form of organisational evaluation which benchmarks against an holistic measurement system.

- **The financial perspective.** How do we look to our shareholders?
- **The customer perspective.** How do our customers see us?
- **The internal perspective.** What must we exceed at?
- **The innovation and learning perspective.** How do we continue to innovate and create value?

It is argued that these questions should be approached sequentially, and a few key performance indicators should be used for each. The balanced scorecard has been proposed as a useful instrument for the assessment of eBusiness concerns. For example, to assess CRM systems from the customer perspective key performance indicators might be customer acquisition rate, customer retention rate and customer satisfaction measures.

The productivity paradox

But does the introduction of an information system always have a positive impact? Evidence suggests that there are some inherent paradoxes or contradictions involved with their introduction. One of the most significant is the PRODUCTIVITY PARADOX.

Productivity paradox: The paradox that organisations that have invested significantly in ICT do not appear to have experienced significant improvements in productivity.

Organisations expect new information systems to raise the productivity of their workforce, but over a number of years, this link between information system usage and productivity has been questioned. This is illustrated by graphs produced by Brynjolfson (1993), shown in Figure 9.8.

Brynjolfson's early paper examined the literature on the relationship between productivity and the application of ICT for office-based (white collar) organisations in the United States. The evidence suggested that whereas delivered computing power had increased by two orders of magnitude between the 1970s and 1990s, productivity, particularly in the service sector (the heaviest users of ICT), had stagnated. Figure 9.8 shows that spending on computers reached its peak in the mid-1980s, but although productivity (measured in terms of service transactions handled per worker) increased rapidly during the early 1960s, it remained relatively stable up to 1990.

Brynjolfson considered four main explanations for the productivity paradox:

- **Mismeasurement of inputs and outputs.** A proper indicator of ICT impact has yet to be formulated and analysed. Measures such as the number of service transactions multiplied by their unit value tend to ignore sources of value such as increased quality and speed of customer service.

- **Lags due to learning and adjustment.** The long-term lag between cost and benefit may be the result of the extensive learning required for individuals, groups and organisations to fully exploit ICT.
- **Redistribution and dissipation of profits.** This explanation proposes that those investing in technology benefit at the expense of others in a particular industry, Hence, there is no aggregate benefit to an industrial sector such as financial services.
- **Mismanagement of ICT.** This is the basic informatics argument, and is given greater credence by subsequent work by Brynjolfson (Brynjolfson and Hitt, 1998). It proposes that companies have systematically mismanaged and have not planned systematically for the introduction of ICT, so they have not reaped benefits in terms of productivity.

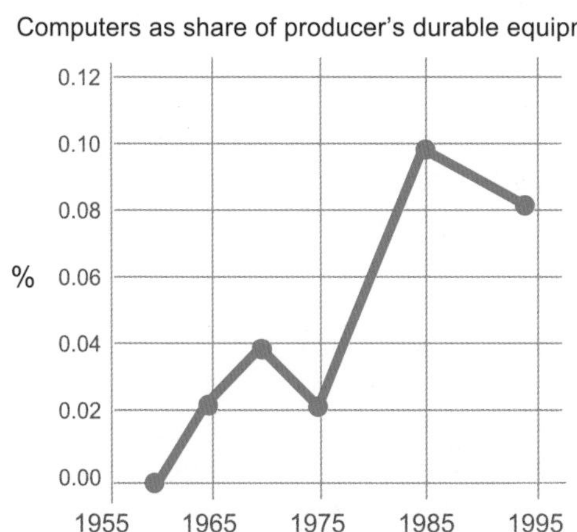

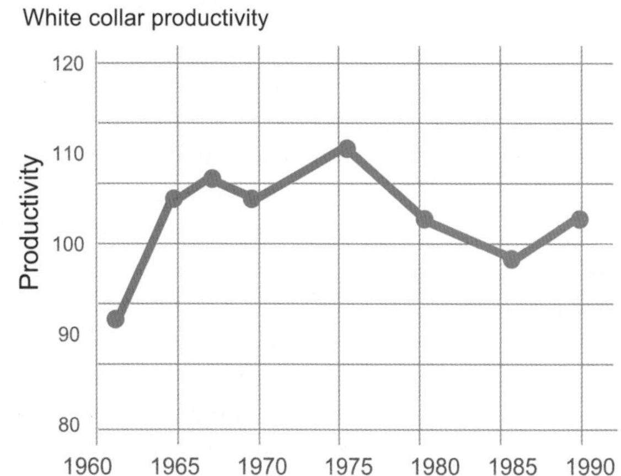

Figure 9.8: *Productivity plotted against ICT spending*

Impact on groups and individuals in the organisation

At a more micro level, as well as having an impact on organisations as a whole, information systems have an impact on the work of groups and individuals. Again, the impact may be positive or negative. The assessment of the value of the impact depends on the position of the stakeholder group within the organisation. Some potential consequences for groups and individuals are discussed below.

The introduction of ICT systems may increase levels of work monitoring and permit greater control of work by managerial groups. ICT systems may enable large amounts of transactional information to be captured about the day-to-day activities of the workforce. This could be used, for instance, to decide on promotion and redundancy strategies.

In contrast, ICT systems can be used to enrich jobs and provide greater degrees of worker empowerment. They could be used to remove many burdensome administrative activities, freeing up workers to devote more time to issues such as customer service. One key way in which customer service can be improved is by letting front-line personnel make instantaneous decisions (for example, on how to handle customer complaints) with the aid of ICT systems.

The introduction of ICT systems typically causes changes in forms of collaboration and coordination between groups. For instance, email is now extensively used in organisations as a means of scheduling meetings, and this could mean there is less face-to-face contact.

ICT systems may change the patterns of power and influence in and between groups. For example, when information systems were first introduced to replace typical secretarial skills such as typing, it had a major impact on secretaries, and on their bosses too.

Zuboff (1988) has argued that ICT makes work more visible. There is the potential for workers to establish more clearly what is happening in their organisation, identify problems with work processes and suggest alternative ways of doing things. Hence, ICT systems have significant potential as vehicles for learning in organisations.

All this should make it clear that the design of information systems (see Chapter 12) is not a value-neutral activity. Decisions made particularly about the shape of an activity system to be used in association with an information system can affect a number of dimensions of work in a positive or negative way, including the levels of the skills required and the variety of the tasks undertaken. Information systems can increase (upskill) or decrease (deskill) the levels of skill required in a particular work setting. They can increase or decrease the variety of tasks required of workers. They can increase or reduce the size of a task relative to the overall purpose of the organisation. They can be designed to increase the autonomy of workers in the sense that they are given responsibility for planning and controlling their own work, or to control their work, sometimes in minute detail. Finally, information systems can be designed to encourage or decrease levels of social interaction between workers.

Reflect
Are you personally able to list the benefits of electronic delivery? What strategies are needed to raise the awareness of such benefits? Are low levels of awareness a concern for business, and if so, why?

Impact on groups and individuals outside the organisation

Information systems and the ICT embedded in them do not only affect internal stakeholders, they also affect external stakeholders. Two particular issues are considered here: the relationship between the use of systems and data protection, and unequal access to electronic delivery of goods and services.

The definition of the information society considered in Chapter 3 relies on a critical mass of the populace using electronic delivery as their preferred method of accessing services and products from public and private-sector organisations. Many organisations are producing strategies to encourage this, but there are a number of preconditions to the successful uptake of remote access channels. These represent the interaction of a range of social factors including awareness, interest, access, skills, use and impact (see Figure 9.9).

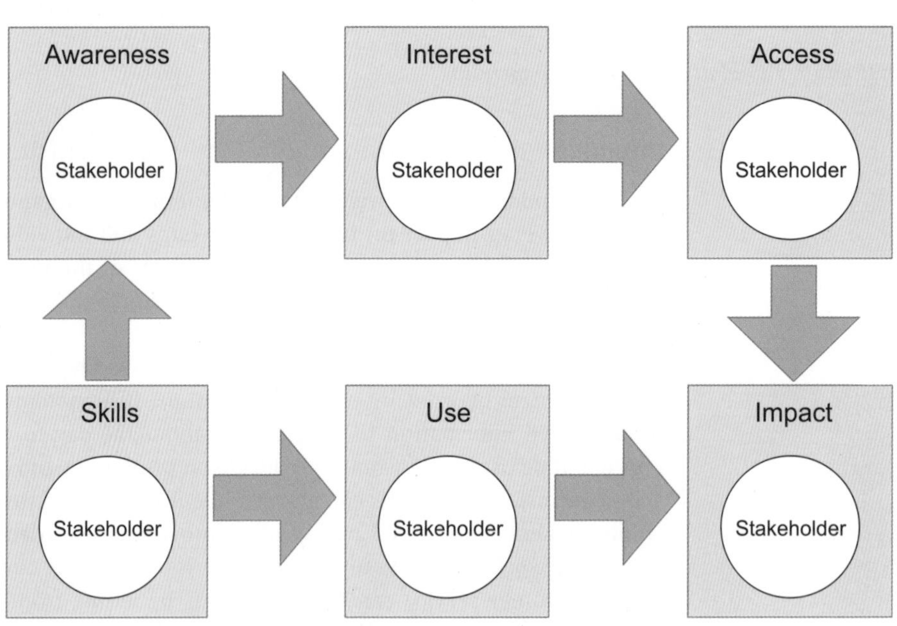

Figure 9.9: *Preconditions for electronic delivery of products and services*

Preconditions for electronic service delivery: A range of social factors, expressed in a sequence, which affect the likely take-up of the electronic delivery of goods and services.

Awareness

Stakeholders must be aware of the benefits of using various remote access channels, and such benefits must outweigh the costs in their minds.

Crabtree, Nathan and Reeves (2002) argue that there are three useful stereotypes of people's reactions to ICT. **Enthusiasts** are naturally enthusiastic about ICT and are usually early adopters of innovations. **Aversives** are naturally averse to any new technology and hence unlikely to adopt it. **Pragmatists** are likely to be adopters of a technology but only once there is a critical mass of users and they have seen the benefits. Therefore, the typical diffusion of awareness is likely to be through enthusiasts to pragmatists to aversives. However, AWARENESS in and of itself is not guaranteed to lead to take-up.

Awareness: A precondition of electronic delivery. Stakeholders must be aware of the potential benefits.

Even enthusiasts can show concern about two interrelated features of electronic delivery: the trust placed in electronic transactions and the privacy of them. Evidence suggests that low levels of trust and concerns over the privacy of information critically affect the take-up of electronic delivery in certain sectors.

Interest

Interest: A precondition of electronic delivery. Stakeholders must be interested in using remote access channels for electronic delivery.

Stakeholders must be INTERESTED in using remote access channels for their purposes. Margetts and Dunleavy (2002) argue that when people change to ICT mechanisms there is a substantial and immediate set of transaction costs, which include the costs of finding relevant information, the costs of learning new ways of conducting interaction and the costs of correcting mistakes. These are all part of the **switching cost**. Evidence suggests that small, up-front transaction costs of this nature may discourage people from making the switch. They will only be outweighed if customers perceive substantial added value from electronic access.

Access

Stakeholders must have **access** to remote access devices from the home or another convenient location. A common measure of this is the penetration of forms of connectivity to the Internet. This access depends upon a number of factors, particularly income, since a computer and Internet access are not cheap for most people. There is no such thing as 'free' access to the Internet, although some people feel that it is free to them because their university, company or another institution pays the costs (Sardar and Ravetz, 1996). Other people need to meet the initial costs of the hardware and software, payments to the internet service provider (ISP), and telephone line rental, then to pay out fairly regularly to upgrade their equipment and replace obsolete software.

Many of the heaviest users of local authority services are in disadvantaged groups, but they often do not have Internet access at home, so to widen access there have been many initiatives to provide personal computers with broadband access in public spaces such as libraries, community halls, job centres and even supermarkets.

Reflect

1. How would you persuade a customer of your organisation, or an organisation you are familiar with, that there is significant added value in electronic delivery of its products and services? What is the added value in this case?
2. At what level do you think that access to the Internet will stabilise amongst the general population? Do you think public Internet access points actually increase levels of access?
3. Are there any specific skills associated with using transactional websites? Is it easy to switch between using say one flight-booking service on the Web and another?

Skills

Stakeholders must have the **skills** to use access devices such as Internet-enabled PCs effectively. This is frequently cast as the problem of eLiteracy: the low-level skills required to use ICT effectively. They include being able to use a keyboard and a mouse, conduct basic operations with operating systems, use productivity packages such as office software, and use Internet and Web tools such as browsers. All of this takes effort for those who do not already have the skills.

Use

Margetts and Dunleavy (2002), for example, argue that initiatives in electronic government have to be capable of **domestication.** In other words, people accept technological innovations if they become domesticated into their personal, everyday routines, as have telephones, televisions, fridges, washing machines and microwave ovens. They then get used to **using** them.

Although there are Internet-enabled PCs in many homes in First World countries, not everyone yet uses them as their first point of call for doing things such as accessing bank account details, registering a birth or taking an educational course.

Impact

Use of various access channels must approach a threshold that encourages the provision of more content and services delivered electronically. The hope for many organisations is that a virtuous cycle of positive IMPACT is established in which better content and services, perhaps directed at particular social, economic or political groups, will encourage greater awareness of, interest in and use of remote access channels as the preferred method of contact with organisations.

Impact: A precondition of electronic delivery. Use of remote access mechanisms must reach a critical threshold driving a virtuous cycle.

The digital divide

Digital divide: The phenomenon of differential rates of awareness, interest, access, skills and use of ICT for different groups in society.

There has been a lot of publicity about an aspect of the information society known as the DIGITAL DIVIDE: that is, the different levels of awareness, interest, access, skills and use of ICT of different social groups. There is a lot of evidence that the lower socioeconomic groups in Western societies are the least aware, the least interested, have the least access to ICT, the lowest levels of eLiteracy and use electronic services the least.

This relates to issues of social exclusion, processes by which some social groups cannot participate in key social activities, and limits the potential for ICT to improve economic, social and political processes (Tapscott, 1998). Economically, many people in disadvantaged groups cannot afford ICT equipment and to maintain a connection to the Internet. Socially, they cannot do so if they have a low level of eLiteracy. Politically, governments might want to impose levels of political or state control of the communication infrastructure that prevent or discourage some opinions from being aired or activities from being undertaken through electronic channels.

Reflect

In your own country, how extensive do you think the digital divide is at the moment? What policies might have an impact on it?

Did you know?

The European Union's official statistics body showed that in 2004, 85 per cent of European students used the Internet compared with only one in eight retired people.

As well as the digital divide between social groups in Western societies, there is concern over the divide between developed and less developed countries. This forms the background to initiatives such as the **one laptop per child** non-profit organisation, which aims to 'create educational opportunities for the world's poorest children by providing each child with a rugged, low-cost, low-power, connected laptop with content and software designed for collaborative, joyful, self-empowered learning' (www.laptop.org).

In the United Kingdom it took several years to bring a Regulatory of Investigatory Powers Act into force because companies such as ISPs were concerned over the powers given to security agencies to monitor the traffic passing through them. A human rights organisation, the Freedom House (www.freedomhouse.org), believes that countries around the world are increasingly censoring content on the Internet. In a large list of countries access to the Internet is tightly controlled by governments.

A key concern is that information elites will be able to exploit the economic, social and political advantages of the information society. For businesses a key concern is that major sectors of their potential customer base will miss out on electronic delivery of services and products.

Reflect

1. Have you engaged in any of the online activities listed above? If so, what persuaded you to do this online? If not, why not? Do some of the personal reasons for not engaging with online services that have been mentioned apply to you?
2. Try to log on to one of the many government websites. What did you think of the content? Do you regard it is useful? How might it be improved?

Privacy and data protection

There are also some major privacy concerns associated with people using the Internet for eCommerce. These include the collection and storage of personal data by companies, its disclosure to third parties, and its use by companies or other agencies in ways that people might feel invades their privacy.

Cookie: A data file placed on a user's machine by a web browser. Used by an organisation's ICT system to monitor interaction.

For example, COOKIES are data files placed on Internet users' machines by web browsers, which the browser uses to store information like passwords and when a site was last visited. This is particularly useful to companies because they can identify particular customers, monitor their surfing behaviour and use the information to tailor the user's interaction with their site. However, many people feel that the use of cookies is an invasion of privacy, because it is not apparent to them when they are created or what data is held in them, and of course, they might not choose for the company to have access to this kind of detailed record of their activities.

Spamming: The process of sending unsolicited emails to large numbers of people.

SPAMMING is sending unsolicited emails to large numbers of people whose data is held on address lists. This is seen by many to be both an inconvenience and an invasion of privacy. During the 1990s thousands of Usenet news groups were spammed by the US legal firm Canter and Siegel, offering to help potential US immigrants get green cards.

The UK Data Protection Act (1984) laid down a number of principles to enforce good practice in the management of personal data by organisations. In 2000 the UK government implemented new legislation to bring the Act in line with the EU Data Protection Directive.

Reflect
How concerned are you over the privacy of data held about yourself? Are you in favour of a national identity card for each citizen? What consequences would one have for data protection?

Data protection in the European Union is based upon five main principles (Zorkadis and Donos, 2004):

- Personal data should be collected for a specific and declared purpose.
- The collection and processing of personal data should be adequate, relevant and not excessive in relation to the declared purpose.
- Organisations should maintain accurate and current data on people, and inaccurate or incomplete data should be erased or rectified.
- Personal data should be preserved in a form that permits identification of individuals for a period no longer than is required for the purposes for which the data is stored.
- Appropriate security measures, technical and organisational, should be taken to protect personal data from unintended or unauthorised disclosure, destruction or modification.

European countries have generally legislated on data protection and privacy. In the United States the strategy has been to rely more on self-regulation by organisations. This makes it difficult for many multinational companies to transfer data internationally, because actions that are permissible in one country might not be in others. In order to ease data transfer, the US Department of Commerce and the European Union have created the Safe Harbour Framework. Companies which sign up to this framework, such as Microsoft, are seen as having adequate data protection procedures for cross-border data transfer.

In the United Kingdom, all organisations that maintain personal data must register details of it with the Data Protection Registrar, and are obliged to ensure that their use of it conforms with the law. Many other countries, such as those in Scandinavia, have stronger data protection legislation in place.

Recap

Information systems have an impact on individuals, groups and organisations as a whole. The impact of introducing them can be either positive or negative at each of these levels, and different stakeholders will have different views on which it is. Most common assessments of ICT focus on the effects ICT has on organisational efficiency and/or effectiveness, but ICT does not deliver performance gain in and of itself. Rather, it can contribute to changes in activity systems which in turn can affect the performance of organisations.

Success and failure

The two issues of the use of information systems and the impact of them are tied up with assessments about their worth or value. In very broad terms, assessments of worth or value focus on considerations of their success or failure.

In many ways the success or failure (and so the value) of information systems is the key dependent variable for the discipline of organisational informatics. This section concentrates on the issue of information systems failure, using the assumption that analysing failures can provide important lessons for formulating successful strategies for the planning, management, development and operation of information systems.

Dimensions of failure

Development failure: Failure of an information system project while in development.

Use failure: Failure of an information system after a period of use.

Information systems failure, and strategies for avoiding it, have both horizontal and vertical dimensions. Horizontally there is a distinction between DEVELOPMENT FAILURE and USE FAILURE. Vertically failure can be explored at the level of ICT systems, information system projects, organisations or the external environment. These two axes are illustrated in Figure 9.10.

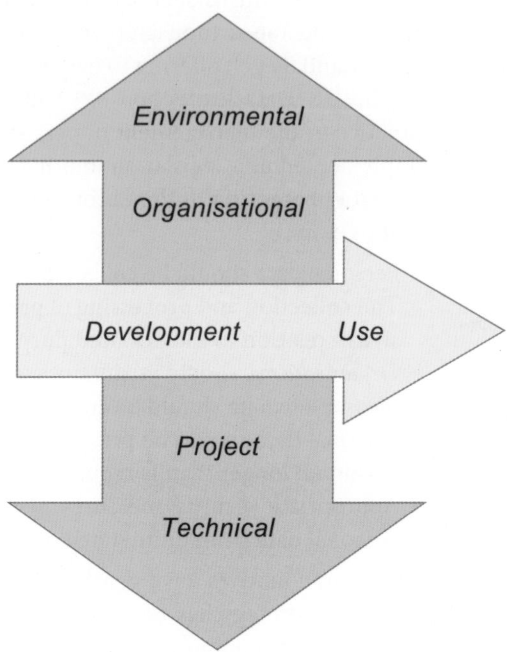

Figure 9.10: *Dimensions of failure*

Vertically, we can address information systems failure on a number of levels: technical, project, organisational and environmental. In very general terms these form a hierarchy of problem complexity:

- **Technical failure** is the failure of hardware, software and communication networks such as system crashes.
- **Project failure** involves failures in project management and control, such as cost or time overruns.
- **Organisational failure** is the failure of a system to deliver organisational benefits such as an increase in efficiency or effectiveness.
- **Environmental failure** is caused by changes in environmental factors, such as regulations and labour relations.

There are two important phases in the way human beings approach problems, problem *setting* and problem *solving*. In some areas of human activity it is relatively easy to set problems, but in other areas there is vast disagreement on how to define key problems.

Technical problems tend by their nature to be relatively easy to define. At this level we can usually identify quite precisely what the problem is, which leads to a search for suitable solutions. These problems are described as 'hard'. Problem setting is uncontentious, and most effort is devoted to problem solving.

At the opposite end of the scale lie organisational and environmental problems. These are frequently difficult to identify, not least because different stakeholder groups perceive the problems differently. These 'soft' problems are sometimes also called 'wicked' problems, and they are characterised by a focus on problem setting rather than problem solving. This distinction is illustrated in Figure 9.11.

Problems at the project level tend to lie between the poles of hard and soft. Some, such as forming project teams, are relatively tractable. Other aspects of project management are less clearly definable. A good example is the frequent difficulty in estimating the scale of an information system project and the resources needed to complete it (see Chapter 12).

There is also a distinction between failure during development and failure in use. **Development failure** occurs when the whole or part of a system is abandoned prior to implementation. **Use failure** occurs during the post-implementation trajectory. It is apparent when a system is abandoned after a period of use, or needs large amounts of adaptive maintenance (see Chapter 12). This distinction is illustrated in Figure 9.12.

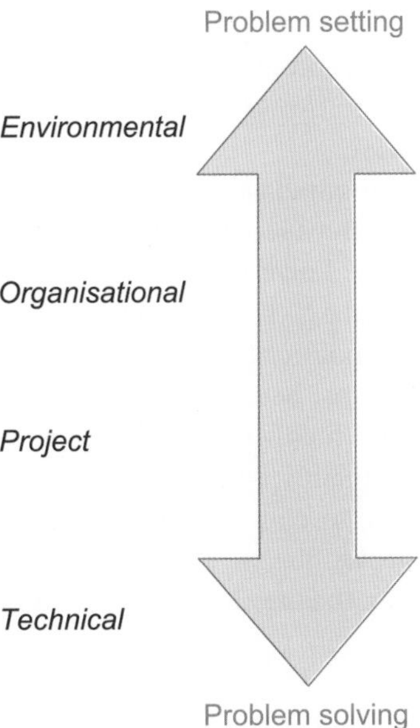

Figure 9.11: *Problem solving and problem setting*

Studies of failure

Studies of information systems failure fall into four categories: anecdotal evidence, theory building, case studies and survey research.

For a number of years the Association for Computing Machinery (ACM) collected anecdotal descriptions of information system failures in its Software Engineering Notes. McKenzie (1994) analysed this material and found that of the computer-related accidents (examples mainly of use failures) reported, 92 per cent involved failures in what he called human–computer interaction: 'More computer-related accidental deaths seem to be caused by interactions of technical and cognitive/organisational factors than by technical factors alone.'

Lyytinen and Hirschheim (1987) also explored the literature on failures, and put them into four categories: correspondence failure, process failure, interaction failure and expectation failure.

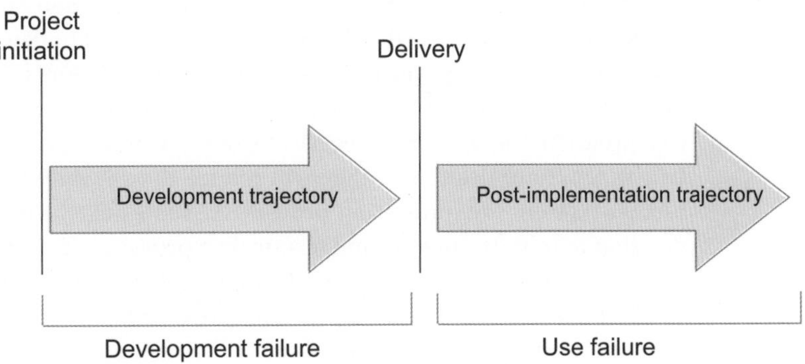

Figure 9.12: *Development and use failure*

Correspondence failure: Lack of correspondence between objectives and evaluation.

Process failure: This type of failure is characterised by unsatisfactory development performance.

Interaction failure: The argument that if a system is heavily used it constitutes a success; if it is hardly ever used, or there are major problems involved in using it, it constitutes a failure.

Expectation failure: The inability of an information system to meet a specific stakeholder group's expectations.

Project organisation: The structuring of staff activities in projects to ensure maximum effectiveness.

CORRESPONDENCE FAILURE is the most common, and typically reflects a management perspective on failure. It is based on the idea that design objectives are first specified in detail. When the system is evaluated against these objectives, if it does not match up, it is regarded as a failure.

PROCESS FAILURE is caused by unsatisfactory development performance. Usually this means either that the development process has failed to produce a workable system, or that it has overrun its cost or time budget.

In INTERACTION FAILURE the emphasis shifts to system use. The argument is that if a system is heavily used it constitutes a success; if it is hardly ever used, or there are major use problems, it can be judged a failure. Lucas (1975) clearly adheres to this idea of failure.

Lyytinen and Hirschheim describe EXPECTATION FAILURE as a superset of the three other types. It is a more encompassing, politically and pluralistically informed view of information systems failure than the other forms, because in their model, correspondence, process and interaction failure are all based on a highly rational image of information system development, seeing an information system as mainly a neutral technical artefact (Klein and Hirschheim, 1987). Expectation failure is seen, in contrast, as the inability of an information system to meet a stakeholder group's expectations. So for particular stakeholders who see the system as a failure, there is a gap between the existing situation and their desired situation, although their judgement might not be entirely reasonable from the viewpoint of other stakeholders such as developers.

Sauer (1993) criticises Lyytinen and Hirschheim's model for its plurality. He points out that this last category means that all information system projects would rate as failures to some extent. His model uses a more conservative definition of failure: that an information system should only be deemed a failure when development or operation ceases, leaving supporters dissatisfied with the extent to which the system has served their interests. This means that a system should not be considered a failure until all interest in progressing the project has ceased, leading to what he calls **termination failure**.

Sauer uses this concept to develop a model of information system failure based on exchange relations. In this, the development of an information system is seen as an innovation process based on three components: the project organisation, the information system and its supporters (see Figure 9.13). PROJECT ORGANISATION in this sense means the producers or developers of the system, and supporters means various stakeholder groups, particularly clients and end-users.

Each of the components in the model is arranged in a triangle of dependencies. The information system depends on the project organisation, the project organisation depends on its supporters, and the supporters depend on the information system. The information system requires the efforts and expertise of the project organisation to sustain it; the project organisation is heavily dependent on the provision of support in the form of material resources and help in coping with contingencies; supporters require benefits from the information system.

One key way in which Sauer distinguishes termination failure from expectation failure is the concept of a flaw. The development process is open to flaws, and every information system is flawed in some way, but flaws are different from failures. They can be corrected at a cost, or accepted at a cost. So a flaw is what someone perceives as a problem to be solved, such as a program bug, a shortfall in hardware performance, or a need for organisational change. Unless flaws are dealt with they will reduce the capability of the system and could lead to further flaws in the innovation process. At some stage, the volume of flaws might trigger a decision to remove support and terminate a project, and that brings us back to failure.

The London Ambulance Service Computer Aided Dispatch System (LASCAD) project (see Chapter 13) is often quoted as an example of information systems failure. Beynon-Davies, Owens and Williams (1995) argue that it has gained this profile more because of its 'safety-critical' nature and the claim that 20 to 30 people may have lost their lives as a result of its failings than because of the scale of the project or its failure. Indeed, LASCAD (which cost £1.1–£1.5 million) is dwarfed by other British information system 'failures' such as Wessex Regional Health Authority's RISP project (£63 million) (HMSO, 1993) and the UK Stock Exchange's TAURUS settlement system (£75– £300 million) (Flowers, 1996).

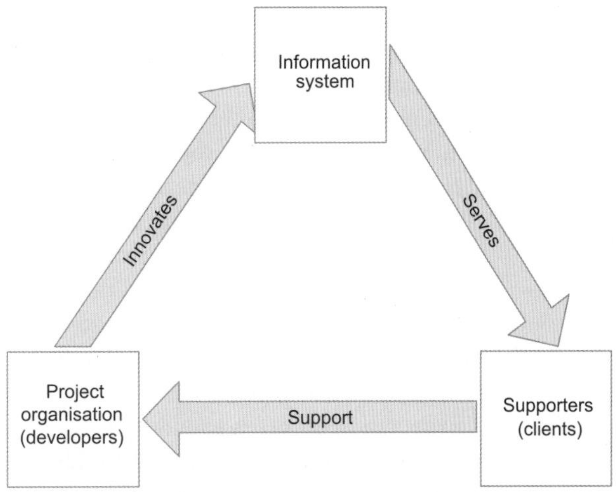

Figure 9.13: *Sauer's model of information systems failure*

Information system failure is of course not specifically a British malaise. Accounts of failures elsewhere in the world are provided for example by Oz (1994), on the CONFIRM reservation system in the United States ($125 million), and Sauer (1993) on a large Australian government information system project, Mandata (A$30 million), abandoned during the 1970s.

Lyytinen (1988) describes an exploratory study of systems analysts' perceptions of information systems failure. This major stakeholder group has a rather different view of information systems and their failure than do users or management. He found they believed that only 20 per cent of projects were likely to prove failures, and preferred to explain failures in highly procedural and rationalistic terms. The reasons they gave for them included inexact development goals and specifications, inadequate understanding of users' work and inadequate understanding of system contingencies. He put this down to their professional expectations of the information system development process, which conceived of it as a rational task involving high technical and professional competence.

Ewusi-Mensah and Przasnyski (1994) make a slightly different distinction, between project abandonment and system failure. In their terms information system failure is the failure of usage and/or operations, whereas project abandonment is concerned with the system development process. This is similar to Lytinnen's distinction between development and use failure. In Ewusi-Mensah and Przasnyski (1996) they distinguish between three types of project abandonment, all of which take place prior to full implementation. **Total abandonment** involves complete termination of all activities on a project. **Substantial abandonment** involves major truncation or simplification of the project to make it radically different from the original specification, and **partial abandonment** involves reducing the original scope of the project but not significantly changing the original specification. They suggest from their small survey that total abandonment is the most common type of development failure in the United States. They also found that organisational factors, particularly the amount of senior management involvement and the degree of end-user participation in the project development, were the most widespread and dominant factors in success or failure.

Case check: Case 31 W the UK Passport Agency

In July 1996 the UK Passport Agency announced its planned introduction of digital passports, to minimise the risk of fraudulent use. This meant it needed to replace its existing ICT system. In October 1998 the new information system (ICT system and procedures, including those outsourced) was introduced in the Agency's Liverpool office.

In summer 1999 there were a number of problems. Over a half a million British citizens were less than happy to discover that they would not get their new passports in time for their holidays. In June passport applications were taking up to 50 working days to process. In July the Home Office introduced emergency measures including a free two-year extension to passports. It had to pay millions in compensation to citizens and in staff overtime required for managing the backlog of applications.

Lessons from the evidence on information systems failure

- Information system failure is commonplace. A survey conducted by the US Government Accounting Agency in 1979 (US 1985) found that less than 3 per cent of the software the US government paid for was actually used as delivered. More than half was never used at all. Gladden (1982) reported in a similar survey that 75 per cent of all system development undertaken is either never completed or the resulting systems are not used. In an international survey conducted by Coopers and Lybrand (Coopers 1996), 60 per cent of organisations internationally and 67 per cent of organisations in the United Kingdom had suffered at least one systems project that had failed to deliver planned business benefits or had experienced cost and time overruns.
- Failure and success are intersubjective, not objective concepts. Their definition depends on the position and perspective of the definer. Lyytinnen and Hirschheim's (1987) concept of expectation failure is useful here.
- It is important to identify stakeholders and judge what views and impact they will have on the project. It is their expectations and desires that define some types of failure.
- Understanding and monitoring project trajectory is important. This is defined as the historical shaping of an information system both before and after delivery. Often this is affected by the power play between different stakeholder groups (Hirschheim and Newman, 1988; Keen, 1981). An information system project, and the resulting system, are significant power resources.
- Failure can occur prior to the delivery of an information system. This is the notion of project abandonment, or what Lyytinnen and Hirschheim (1987) call development failure. Sauer (1993) makes it clear that as well as termination failure and total abandonment of a project, there are partial failures which lead to rethinks of the project scope. Failure can also occur after delivery: this is the idea of use failure (Lyytinen, 1988), often because although the system works after a fashion, it does not match stakeholders' needs or expectations (Kling and Iacono, 1984).
- Information system projects are frequently the subject of escalation in decision making. Drummond (1994) defines escalation as 'the predicament where decision-makers find themselves trapped in a losing course of action as a result of previous decisions. Costs are incurred; there is an opportunity to withdraw or persist; and the consequences of withdrawal or persistence are uncertain. Typically the response to such dilemmas is irrational persistence.' This means that major stakeholders might continue to support a project even in the face of major system flaws, because of the heavy investment in personnel and other resources (Newman and Sabherwal 1996).
- It is important to evaluate information systems and projects. Evaluation is the process of assessing the worth of something, which ties in with definitions of success or failure. There is a distinction between the worth of the product (the information system) and the worth of the process (the activities involved in producing the information system). In practice, it is clearly difficult to separate the two. The worth of the information system development process is normally evaluated by assessing the worth of the product.

Avoidance strategies

Since the value of information systems is a key dependent variable for the discipline of organisational informatics, strategies for ensuring success or avoiding failure are important. This section briefly examines some conventional and extended strategies for preventing failure and ensuring success, and gives pointers to relevant material elsewhere in the book. It is obviously easiest to employ solutions or avoidance strategies in lower levels of the hierarchy of failures. This issue is revisited in Chapter 13.

First, at the level of ICT systems the appropriate selection and use of tools can significantly reduce the risk of failure. Appropriate use of information system development methods (Chapter 12) and analysis and design techniques also reduces the risk of failure.

Second, at the level of projects, good and effective management and control of informatics personnel (Chapter 11) and their activities can significantly reduce the occurrence of failure. Success is also more likely when stakeholders participate in development projects.

Third, at the organisational level, effective planning of the information system development portfolio and the structure and activities of the informatics service can affect risk of failure (see Chapter 12). Proper management of the informatics services function (Chapter 11) is also crucial to the long-term health of organisations.

Informatics strategy: A definition of the structure within which information, information systems and information technology are to be applied in an organisation.

Fourth, at the environmental level, effective alignment of INFORMATICS STRATEGY with business strategy is critical to the performance of the informatics services function and the information systems under their development and control. Effective organisational analysis (see Chapter 2) needs to be conducted to guide this alignment.

In summary, ideally an organisation wishing to avoid failure would do well to engage in many of the best practices described in this book: organisational analysis, informatics planning, informatics management, project management, information system development. Many years of experience have been accumulated in the development of information systems, and many lessons have been learned on how, for instance, to manage information system projects. Yet information system failures are still commonplace. Perhaps in part this is because although most medium to large-scale organisations do a lot of information systems management, development, operation and maintenance, few seem to take organisational analysis, informatics planning and particularly the evaluation of information systems seriously.

Recap 

Perhaps the most extreme example of negative impact is the abandonment of an information system either during development or during use. This might be done because of technical reasons, problems with a development project, problems of an organisational nature or unintended effects of the business environment. Information systems failure appears commonplace. However, analyses of previous failures suggest a number of strategies for avoiding failure at the technical, project, organisational and environmental levels.

Key skill 

Evaluation

General managers often ask a number of questions about information systems and ICT, including:

- How much is currently spent on information systems and ICT?
- What value results from this spending?
- How should information system alternatives be justified/prioritised/financed?
- Why do information system projects continually experience cost and time overruns?
- Why do informatics budgets continue to rise while ICT unit costs continue to fall?
- How can we regain our belief in the return provided by information systems?

All these relate to the issue of evaluation. This section focuses on evaluation, and discusses its importance. It highlights the different forms of evaluation and indicates some of the problems in the way it is conducted. A model of information systems evaluation linked to the development process (see Chapter 12) is used to structure the discussion.

Figure 9.14 is a model of information systems evaluation fitted to the life-cycle of information systems development (Beynon-Davies et al., 2004). This illustrates the importance of evaluation to organisational learning. Organisations need to conduct evaluation for a number of reasons: to assess and prioritise investment in information systems and ICT, to control information system costs, to determine the value arising from information systems and ICT, to determine changes needed to the organisation's information systems portfolio and to learn successful strategies for information systems management and development.

Information systems evaluation can be defined as the attempt to assess the success or failure of an information system and the associated process by which it is developed and implemented. Although evidence suggests that organisations do not conduct evaluation of their systems and projects very effectively, systematic evaluation is critical to improvements in both development and organisational success (Farbey, Targett and Land, 1998).

Figure 9.14 makes a distinction between four types of information systems evaluation activity: strategic evaluation, formative evaluation, summative evaluation and post-mortem evaluation.

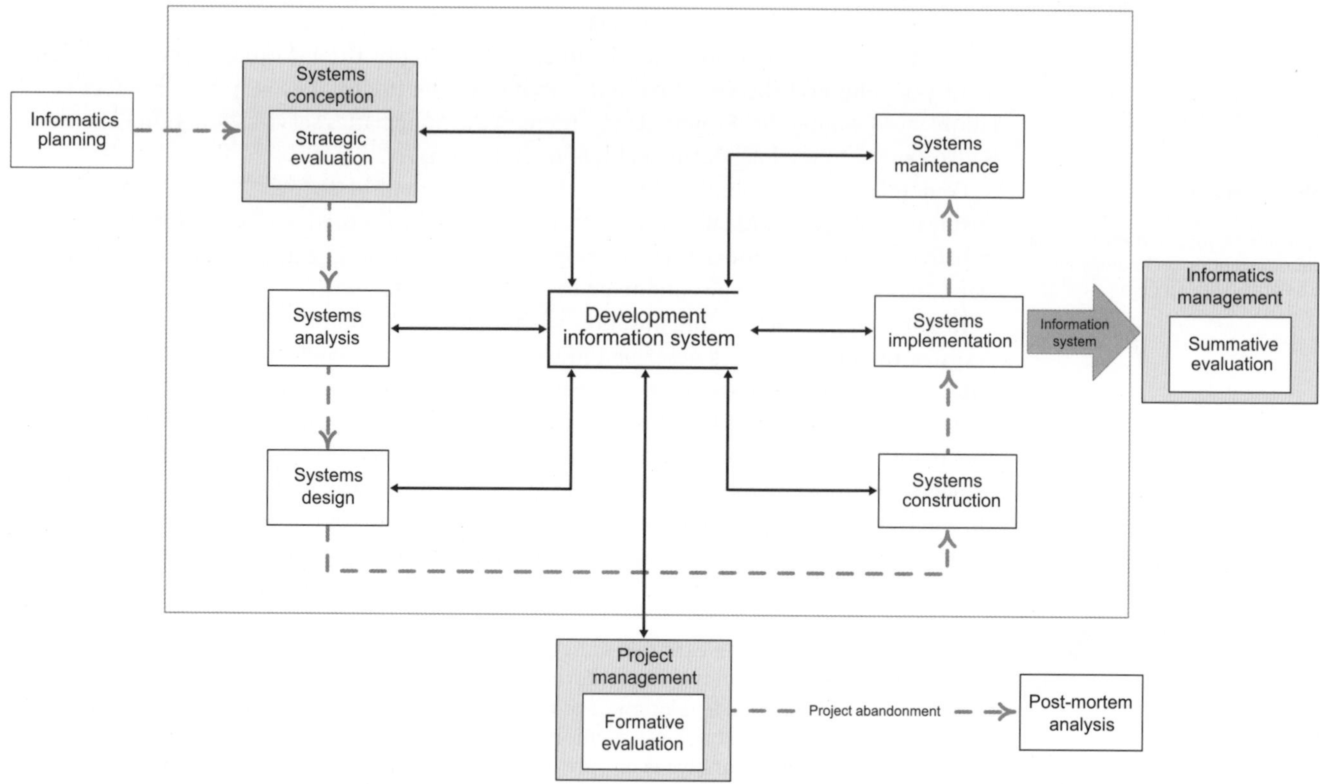

Figure 9.14: *Information systems evaluation and the development process*

Strategic evaluation: The form of IS evaluation concerned with assessing the utility of an information system prior to development.

Systems conception: The part of the development process devoted to eliciting and representing the requirements for systems.

Return on investment (RoI): The benefit gained from investment in a project. It is calculated using the equation: RoI = average (annual net income/annual investment amount).

Payback period: Payback is calculated on the basis of Payback = Investment – cumulative benefit (cash inflow)

Formative evaluation: A form of information systems evaluation concerned with monitoring the developing functionality and usability of a product.

Strategic evaluation

Most organisations conduct some form of STRATEGIC EVALUATION or pre-implementation evaluation of information system projects. This type of evaluation involves assessing or appraising an information system investment. This is usually achieved by assessing the balance of costs and benefits of an intended project, and leads to a go/no-go decision. It may also be used to prioritise potential investments.

Strategic evaluation is fundamentally part of the SYSTEMS CONCEPTION phase in the process of information system development (see Chapter 12). The most popular techniques are RETURN ON INVESTMENT and PAYBACK PERIOD. These are effective ways of evaluating tangible costs against tangible benefits. One of the most popular frameworks, which includes an assessment of intangible costs and benefits, is Information Economics (Parker, Benson and Trainor, 1988, and Chapter 11).

Formative evaluation

FORMATIVE EVALUATION involves assessing the shape of an information system within the development process itself. It is an inherent part of the process of project management (see Chapter 12). In iterative approaches to development, it can used to make crucial changes to the design of an information system. It is also critical to effective decisions on the degree of project abandonment.

Development projects should be assessed continually against objectives, and careful attention should be paid to this activity to avoid project escalation: that is, continued commitment to a project in the face of continual negative information from formative evaluation exercises. Major stakeholders might be reluctant to withdraw support when it would be reasonable to do so, if there has already been heavy investment in personnel and other resources.

Summative evaluation

Summative evaluation: The form of IS evaluation that assesses the worth of a system after implementation.

The model also contains an important organisational learning feedback loop. Even if a project reaches completion, it might fail in some sense when it is delivered. Therefore, at a suitable time after delivery the organisation should engage in a SUMMATIVE EVALUATION of the system and project. This is sometimes called post-implementation evaluation. Ideally, summative evaluation involves returning to the costs and benefits established in strategic evaluation after a period of use. Hence, it is a critical activity in effective informatics management (see Chapter 10).

Kumar (1990) reports on a US empirical study of the prevalence and form of evaluation of information systems after they have been implemented. He found three major results:

- The major reason for performing post-implementation evaluation is the formalisation of the completion of the development project. Summative evaluation is thus a major tactic in a project disengagement strategy.
- Much of the evaluation is managed and performed by those who have designed the system being implemented.
- The most frequently evaluated criteria seem to be information quality criteria (accuracy, timeliness, adequacy and appropriateness) along with facilitating criteria such as user satisfaction and attitudes. Sociotechnical criteria such as the system's impact on users and the organisation are evaluated much less frequently.

One framework proposed for the summative evaluation of information systems is benefits management (Ward, Taylor and Bond, 1996). Even at this point it is possible that the system may be wholly or partially abandoned, in which case there should also be a post-mortem analysis (see below).

It must be emphasised that no system is ever complete. A summative evaluation is likely to suggest a number of ways in which it could be modified or extended. These are normally both classed as systems maintenance (Chapter 12). The conclusion is that effective evaluation leads to effective management of system maintenance.

Post-mortem evaluation

Post-mortem evaluation: A variant of summative evaluation concerned with assessing the reasons for and lessons from information systems failures.

If a system is abandoned prior to implementation or after a period of use, then a variant of summative evaluation needs to be performed on the project not only to determine the reasons for failure, but to consider and suggest changes to organisational practice. This is known as POST-MORTEM ANALYSIS.

The results are important for suggesting ways in which the organisation might improve its development practice, so the report of the analysis needs to be disseminated to senior management, project management and members of the project team. It is important to assure all project participants that there will be no recriminations, or this cannot be done effectively. Ideally, the analysis should be conducted by a reputable senior executive not involved in any way with the project. Alternatively, it should be undertaken by an external body or consultant.

Wherever possible, post-mortem information should be made public outside the organisation. This is important in enabling the validation of information system development and management practice, and the effective progression of the profession of informatics.

Case check: Case 15, OGC Gateway Process

Large-scale ICT in government agencies in the United Kingdom is now procured from external vendors rather than being built in-house. To manage this process effectively, acquisition programmes and procurement projects in central civil government are subject to a process known as Office of Government Commerce (OGC) Gateway Reviews. The OGC Gateway Process examines a project at critical stages in its life-cycle to look for assurance that it can progress successfully to the next stage. Hence, there are similarities between this process and the model of information systems evaluation discussed in this section.

PART 3

Summary

1. Previous chapters touched on the issue of value in a number of ways, but this chapter considered the worth of information systems directly. When information systems are introduced they have immediate effects in the context of use, which is largely determined by the activity system in which they are placed. Information systems may be closely aligned with their activity system, through design or by accident, and generate both intended and unintended positive effects. They might also be misaligned with their activity systems, which normally has a negative effect on organisational activity.

2. Close alignment is made more likely if the project team identify the stakeholders, understanding the differences in their technological frames and involve representatives of stakeholder groups in the development process. Misaligned information systems are likely to be subject to user resistance, which can take numerous forms.

3. There can be an impact on individuals, groups and the organisation as a whole, which is either positive or negative at each of these levels. Judgements about the impact are frequently subjective. Most common assessments of ICT are concerned with its effects on organisational efficiency and/or effectiveness, but ICT does not deliver performance gain in and of itself. It contributes to changes in activity systems which in turn can affect performance.

4. At the most extreme, a system's negative impact is seen as its failure. Information systems failure can be analysed on the technical, project, organisational and environmental levels. Technical problems tend to be 'hard' while environmental problems tend to be 'soft' . There is also a distinction between failures during development and during use. Information systems failure appears commonplace, and has been much studied, producing anecdotal evidence, theory-building, case studies and survey work. This work offers lessons and suggests strategies for avoiding failure and ensuring success.

5. One key lesson is that it is important for organisations to evaluate their ICT systems and their impact on activity systems. Strategic evaluation involves assessing the system's potential for delivering benefit against estimated costs. Formative evaluation involves assessing the shape of an information system during the development process. Summative evaluation involves returning to the costs and benefits established in strategic evaluation after a period of use. A variant of this is post-mortem analysis, summative evaluation of a failed information system project to determine lessons for organisational practice.

The effective planning, management and operation of informatics have a critical bearing on the use, impact and success or failure of information system. The next part of the book covers these topics.

Focus on Value

Evaluation is the process by which assessments of worth or value are made. Informatics evaluation can focus on the relationships between the three distinct forms of business systems discussed in this book. Functionality is fundamentally an assessment of the value of an ICT system. Usability is an assessment of the use of an ICT system within its wider information system. Utility is an assessment of the impact of the system on its wider activity system. An alternative focus is based on the position of the assessment in the system life-cycle: during its conception, as it is being built, while it is being used, or when it has failed. The question of value is therefore embedded in judgements of the success and/or failure of information systems. These judgements are normally relative to stakeholder position.

Review test

1	The context of use is largely determined by the ____________ into which the information system is placed. Fill in the blank.
2	The ____________ of an ICT system is how easy an ICT system is to use for the purpose for which it has been constructed. Fill in the blank.
3	The identification and involvement of key system ____________ is essential for the successful development and use of ICT systems. Fill in the blank.
4	A technological frame is a collection of underlying assumptions, expectations and knowledge that people have about technology and its use. True or false? ☐ True ☐ False
5	Systems that are not accepted and do not have the commitment of system stakeholders are likely to be subject to stakeholder ____________. Fill in the blank.
6	A user interface can be seen as a collection of dialogues between the user and the ICT system. Each dialogue is made up of a series of messages. It is useful to distinguish between three major aspects of such a dialogue: content, control and format. Match the appropriate definition to the term. Content — The actual messages travelling between the user and the system. Control — The layout of messages and data on input and output devices. Format — The way in which the user moves between aspects of one dialogue or from one dialogue to another.
7	The impact of introducing ICT systems may be either positive or ____________. Fill in the blank.

8	How would you distinguish between efficiency gains and effectiveness gains in terms of the organisation? Write two sentences.
9	ICT does not deliver efficiency or effectiveness gains in and of itself. True or false? ☐ True ☐ False
10	The productivity paradox is: Select all that apply. ☐ The poor productivity of ICT workers ☐ The mismatch between investment in ICT and improvements in productivity ☐ The difficulty of building productive ICT systems
11	Information systems failure can be analysed on four major levels. Identify them. Select all that apply. ☐ Technical ☐ Vertical ☐ Project ☐ Horizontal ☐ Environmental ☐ Organisational
12	Match the type of failure to the definition. Use failure — Failure occurs when the whole or part of a system is abandoned prior to implementation. Development failure — Failure occurs during the post-implementation trajectory of an information system.
13	Distinguish between problem setting and problem solving. Write two sentences.
14	Evaluation involves assessing the ____________ of something. Fill in the blank.
15	There are three types of information systems evaluation, What are they? Select all that apply. ☐ Strategic evaluation ☐ Technical evaluation ☐ Formative evaluation ☐ Summative evaluation
16	____________ analysis involves the summative evaluation of some failed IS project. Fill in the blank.
17	What is meant by alignment in terms of information systems? Write two sentences.

Exercises

1. Take an information system known to you and try to identify the major stakeholders that affected the project trajectory. Use the taxonomy of producers, clients, end-users, customers and regulators.
2. Were representatives of any stakeholder groups involved in the project? In what ways were they involved? Is it possible to assess the effect this involvement had on the success of the project?
3. Consider an organisation or part of an organisation known to you, and in what ways an information system has been used to improve either the efficiency or the effectiveness of a human activity system in the organisation. How might you measure the improvements in efficiency and effectiveness?
4. In terms of strategic, summative and formative evaluation, what are we evaluating – usability, functionality or utility?
5. Provide an example of strategic, formative and summative evaluation.
6. Try to estimate the percentage of projects in an organisation known to you that are regarded as successes. What percentage are regarded as failures? What are seen as the major reasons for failure? What are seen to be the major features of success?

Projects

1. Identify the stakeholders relevant to an information system known to you. From their viewpoints, generate an analysis of the negative and positive effects of the information system on each stakeholder group.
2. The usability of an information system is critical to its success. Investigate in more detail the issue of usability as a property of an information system. Determine appropriate ways of assessing usability.
3. Apply some established technique such as QUIS to the assessment of user satisfaction with the interface of some information system known to you. Try to evaluate not only the interface itself but also the technique used, in terms such as the degree to which it is easy to administer.
4. User resistance is a frequent contributor to information systems failure. Try to determine the levels and forms of user resistance to the introduction of information systems in a particular sector such as the health service.
5. The impact of information systems on organisational performance can be measured in a number of ways. Decide on one simple and straightforward measurement of organisational performance such as level of sales of products. Try to trace the effect of any information systems innovations on the chosen measurement.
6. The productivity paradox was initially identified in the financial services sector in the United States. Investigate whether the productivity paradox holds in another sector such as manufacturing or government, or in another nation-state.

7. All information systems projects fail to some degree. Develop a natural history of one or more information systems development projects. Assess the degree to which they can be considered as a success or failure, using any published accounts from the organisations themselves. What measurements did they use to evaluate success and failure?

8. Information systems failure is frequently a result of their not meeting expectations. Investigate why expectations are an important facet of the phenomenon of information systems failure. Consider appropriate ways of managing expectations and try to identify the likely effects of these approaches.

9. Investigate a range of published case studies of failure, and classify them as development or use failure. In other words, how many were abandoned prior to use and how many were abandoned after implementation? How many projects engaged in effective information systems evaluation? Besides post-mortem evaluation, what sort of evaluation was conducted?

Further reading

The original Delone and McLean paper (1992) provides a good review of information systems use and impact. The user interface and principles of good design is covered in Schneiderman and Plaisant (2004). Chan and Reich (2007) review the issue of alignment of information systems with organisations. Fortune and Peters (2005) provide one of the most recent accounts of information systems failure and strategies for avoiding it. Beynon-Davies et al. (2004) provide more detail on the various forms of information systems evaluation.

References

Beynon-Davies, P., Owens, I. and Williams, M. D. (2004) 'IS failure, evaluation and organisational learning', *Journal of Enterprise Information Management* (formerly *Logistics and Information Management*) **17**(4): 276–82.

Brynjolfson, E. (1993) 'The productivity paradox of information technology', *Communications of the ACM* **36**(12): 67–77.

Brynjolfson, E. and Hitt, L. (1998) 'Beyond the productivity paradox', *Communications of the ACM* **41**(8): 49–55.

Button, G. and R. H. R. Harper (1993) *Taking the Organisation into Accounts. Technology in Working Order: Studies of work, interaction and technology*. London, Routledge.

Chan, Y. E. and Reich, B. H. (2007) 'IT alignment: what have we learned?' *Journal of Information Technology* **22**(4): 297–315.

Checkland, P. (1999) *Soft Systems Methodology: A thirty year retrospective*. Chichester, John Wiley.

Chin, J. P., Diehl, V. A. and Norman, K. L. (1988) *Development of an Instrument for Measuring User Satisfaction of the Human–Computer Interface*. CHI'88 Conference on Human Factors in Computing Systems, New York, ACM.

Coopers (1996) *Managing Information and Systems Risks: Results of an international survey of large organisations*. Coopers & Lybrand, London.

Crabtree, J., Nathan, M. and Reeves, R. (2002) *Reality IT: Technology and everyday life*. Work Foundation. London

Davenport, T. H. (2000). 'Putting the I in IT', in D. A. Marchand, T. H. Davenport and T. Dickson (eds), *Mastering Information Management*. Harlow, Essex, Pearson.

DeLone, W. H. and McLean, E. R. (1992) 'Information systems success: the quest for the dependent variable', *Information Systems Research* **3**(1): 60–95.

DeLone, W. H. and McLean, E. R. (2003) 'The DeLone and McLean Model of Information Systems Success: a ten year update', *Journal of Management Information Systems* **19**(4): 9–30.

Drummond, H. (1994) 'Escalation in organisational decision-making: a case of recruiting an incompetent employee', *Journal of Behavioural Decision-Making* 7: 43–55.

Eason, K. D. (1988) *Information Technology and Organisational Change*. London, Taylor and Francis.

Ewusi-Mensah, K. and Przasnyski, Z. H. (1994) 'Factors contributing to the abandonment of information systems development projects', *Journal of Information Technology* 9: 185–201.

Ewusi-Mensah, K. and Z. H. Przasnyski (1995) 'Learning from abandoned information system development projects', *Journal of Information Technology* 10: 3–14.

Farbey, B., Targett, D. and Land, F. (1998) *Hard Money Soft Outcomes*. London, Nelson Thornes.

Flowers, S. (1996) *Software Failure, Management Failure: Amazing stories and cautionary tales*. Chichester, John Wiley.

Fortune, J. and G. Peters (2005) *Information Systems: Achieving success by avoiding failure*. Chichester, John Wiley.

Gladden, G. R. (1982) 'Stop the lifecycle I want to get off', *Software Engineering Notes* 7 (April) (2): 35–9.

Hirschheim, R. and Newman, M. (1988) 'Information systems and user resistance: theory and practice', *Computer Journal* **31**(5): 398–408.

HMSO (1993) *Wessex Regional Health Authority Regional Information Systems Plan: Report of the public accounts committee*. HMSO. London

Kaplan, R. S. and Norton, D. P. (1992) 'The Balanced Scorecard: measures that drive performance', *Harvard Business Review* January–February: 71–9.

Keen, P. (1981) 'Information systems and organisational change', *Communications of the ACM* **24**(1).

Klein, H. K. and Hirschheim, R. A. (1987) 'A comparative framework of data modelling paradigms and approaches', *Computer Journal* **30**(1): 8–14.

Kling, R. and Iacono, S. (1984) 'The control of IS developments after implementation', *Communications of the ACM* **27**(12): 1218–26.

Kumar, K. (1990) 'Post implementation evaluation of computer-based information systems: current practices', *Communications of the ACM* **33**(2): 236–52.

Landauer, T. K. (1995) *The Trouble with Computers: Usefulness, usability and productivity*. Cambridge, Mass., MIT Press.

Lucas, H. C. (1975) *Why Information Systems Fail*. New York, Columbia University Press.

Lyytinen, K. (1988) 'The expectation failure concept and systems analysts view of information systems failures: results of an exploratory study', *Information and Management* 14: 45–55.

Lyytinen, K. and Hirschheim, R. (1987) 'Information systems failures: a survey and classification of the empirical literature', *Oxford Surveys in Information Technology* 4: 257–309.

Marchand, D. A., Kettinger, W. J. and Rollins, J. D. (2000) 'Company performance and information management: the view from the top', in D. A. Marchand, T. H. Davenport and T. Dickson (eds), *Mastering Information Management*. Harlow, Essex, Pearson.

Margetts, H. and Dunleavy, P. (2002) 'Cultural barriers to e-government: academic article in support of better public services through e-government.' National Audit Office. London.

McKenzie, D. (1994) 'Computer-related accidental death: an empirical exploration', *Science and Public Policy* **21**(4): 233–48.

Neely, A. (1998) *Measuring Business Performance*. London, Economist Books.

Newman, M. and Sabherwal, R. (1996) 'Determinants of commitment to information systems development: a longitudinal investigation', *MIS Quarterly*: 23–54.

Nielsen, J. (1993) *Usability Engineering*. Boston, Academic Press.

Newman, M. and R. Sabherwal (1996) 'Determinants of Commitment to Information Systems Development: a longitudinal investigation. *MIS Quarterly*, **20**(3): 23-54.

Orlikowski, W. T. (1996) 'Realising the potential of new technologies: an improvisation model of change management.' Business Information Technology Conference, Manchester Metropolitan University, October.

Orlikowski, W. T. and Gash, T. C. (1994) 'Technological frames: making sense of information technology in organisations', *ACM Transactions on Information Systems* **12**(2): 17–207.

Oz, E. (1994) 'When professional standards are lax: the confirm failure and its lessons. *Communications of the Association for Computing Machinery* (ACM) **37**(10): 29–36.

Parker, M., Benson, R. and Trainor, H. (1988) *Information Economics: Linking business performance to information technology*. New Jersey, Prentice-Hall.

Sachs, P. (1995) 'Transforming work: collaboration, learning and design', *Communications of the ACM* **38**(9): 36–45.

Sardar, Z. and Ravetz, J. R. (eds) (1996) *Cyberfutures: Culture and politics on the information super-highway*. New York, New York University Press.

Sauer, C. (1993) *Why Information Systems Fail: A case study approach*. Henley-On-Thames, Alfred Waller.

Schneiderman, B. and Plaisant, C. (2004) *Designing the User Interface: Strategies for effective human–computer interaction*. New York, Pearson.

Tapscott, D. (1996) *The Digital Economy: Promise and peril in the age of networked intelligence*. New York, McGraw-Hill.

US (1985) 'US Government Accounting Office Report FGMSD-80-4', *ACM Sigsoft Software Engineering Notes* **10**(5).

Ward, J., Taylor, P. and Bond, P. (1996) 'Evaluation and realisation of IS/IT benefits: an empirical study of current practice', *European Journal of Information Systems* **4**(1): 214–25.

Zorkadis, V. and Donos, P. (2004) 'On biometric-based authentication and identification from a privacy-protection perspective: deriving privacy-enhancing requirements', *Information Management and Computer Security* **12**(1): 125–37.

Zuboff, S. (1988) *In the Age of the Smart Machine: The future of work and power*. London, Heinemann.

PART IV

MANAGING INFORMATION SYSTEMS IN BUSINESS

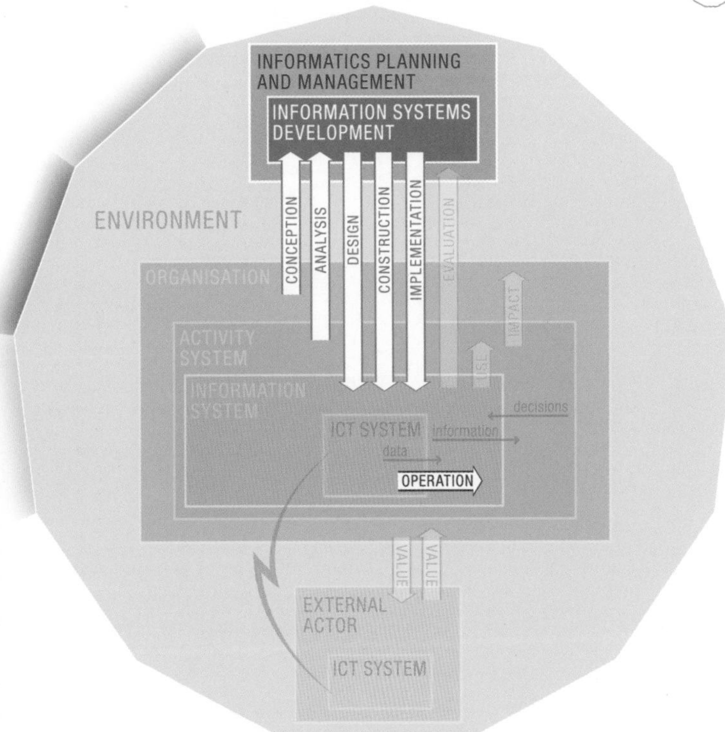

Because the informatics infrastructure is so important to modern organisations, they need to invest in effective practices for planning, managing, developing and operating it. This part of the book introduces a number of best practices in each of these areas.

Chapter 10 considers the importance of planning to effective informatics infrastructure. Planning is particularly concerned with the development of informatics strategy and its alignment with organisation strategy. Management involves putting plans into action. Both informatics management and informatics strategy can be viewed on the three levels of information, information systems and ICT.

Chapter 11 considers the informatics industry in terms of major producers and consumers. The structure of the industry has a critical bearing on the ways in which informatics infrastructure is not only developed but also operated by organisations. The informatics service is the term used for the organisational function devoted to planning, management, development and operation of the informatics infrastructure for an organisation. Parts of, or the whole of it, including operation, may be outsourced to vendors in the wider informatics industry. These operations tend to be considered today as ICT services management. Under this heading a number of important issues for the modern business organisation are discussed, such as provision of helpdesks, disaster recovery and managing the total cost of ownership associated with ICT infrastructure.

It is impossible to understand the processes of planning, management and operations without a high-level understanding of how organisations procure or build new information systems. **Chapter 12** considers approaches to this development process. Since information systems are sociotechnical systems, activity systems and ICT systems need to be looked at together. The chapter begins with a consideration of the development process and the supporting 'technology' of methods, techniques and tools. Each of the phases of the development life-cycle is then considered in some detail: conception, analysis, design, construction, implementation and maintenance.

OVERVIEW

The chapters in this part cover the following key areas:

Informatics planning
Informatics strategy
Informatics management
Project management
Informatics industry
Informatics service
Operating the ICT infrastructure
Development life-cycle
Development methods, techniques and tools

Chapter 1	Introduction: The domain of business information systems
Part I	KEY CONCEPTS
Chapter 2	Organisations and systems
3	Data, information and knowledge
4	Information systems
Part II	UNDERSTANDING ICT
Chapter 5	Communication infrastructure
6	ICT systems infrastructure
Part III	APPLYING INFORMATION SYSTEMS TO BUSINESS
Chapter 7	The business environment
8	Electronic business and electronic commerce
9	Assessing the use and impact of information systems
Part IV	**MANAGING INFORMATION SYSTEMS IN BUSINESS**
Chapter 10	Planning, strategy and management
11	Services, projects and operations
12	Development
Chapter 13	Successful informatics practice

CHAPTER 10

Planning, strategy and management

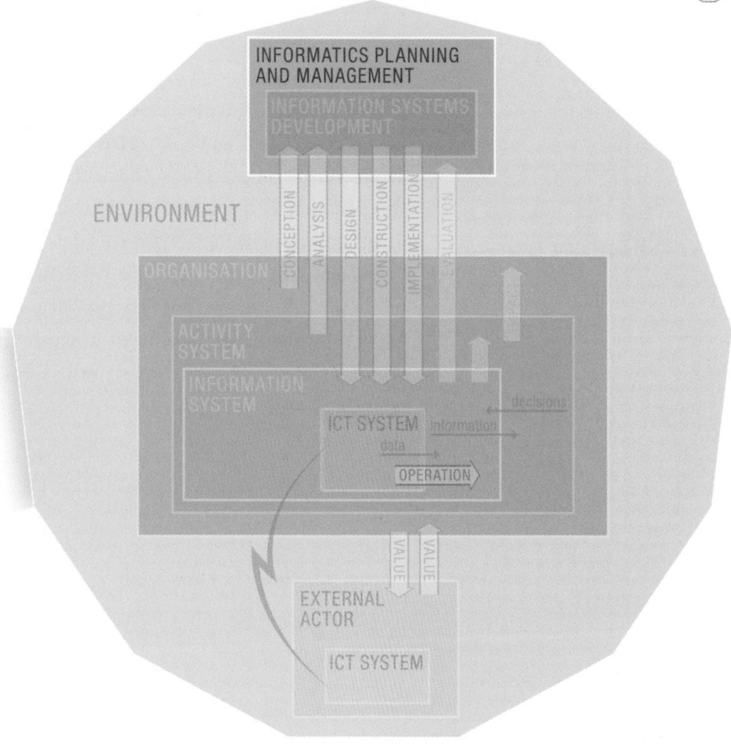

There is nothing more difficult to take in hand, more perilous to conduct, or more uncertain in its success than to take the lead in the introduction of a new order of things.

Niccolo Machiavelli (1469–1527) The Prince (1513), Chapter VI

To conquer the enemy without resorting to war is the most desirable. The highest form of general-ship is to conquer the enemy by strategy.

Sun Tzu (544–496 BC), The Art of War

LEARNING OUTCOMES	PRINCIPLES
Define and describe the critical organisational processes of planning and managing the informatics infrastructure	Planning and managing the informatics infrastructure are two critical processes for the modern organisation. Planning is the process of producing an informatics strategy. Management is the process of implementing it.
Distinguish between organisational strategy and informatics strategy, and discuss ways in which informatics strategy can be built.	Informatics strategy consists of the interdependent layers of information strategy, information systems strategy and ICT strategy. Informatics strategy exists in a mutually dependent relationship with organisational strategy. Organisational strategy typically drives informatics strategy but the implementation of informatics strategy is likely to cause changes to organisational strategy.
Define some of the critical activities of informatics management.	Informatics management not only involves managing the development of future informatics infrastructure, it involves managing the operation and maintenance of current informatics infrastructure.

PART 4

CHAPTER OUTLINE

Introduction

A classic management theorist, Henri Fayol, described the process of management as being 'to forecast and plan, to organize, to command, to coordinate and to control' (Gray, 1984). This chapter considers the activities of planning, commanding and control in relation to the eBusiness infrastructure: that is, the interdependent activity systems infrastructure and informatics infrastructure of an organization.

Figure 10.1 illustrates the relationships between the critical processes of planning, management and development. In systems terms, these can be seen as a hierarchy of control: informatics planning is a control system for informatics management, which in turn is a control system for project management, which in turn is a control system for information systems development.

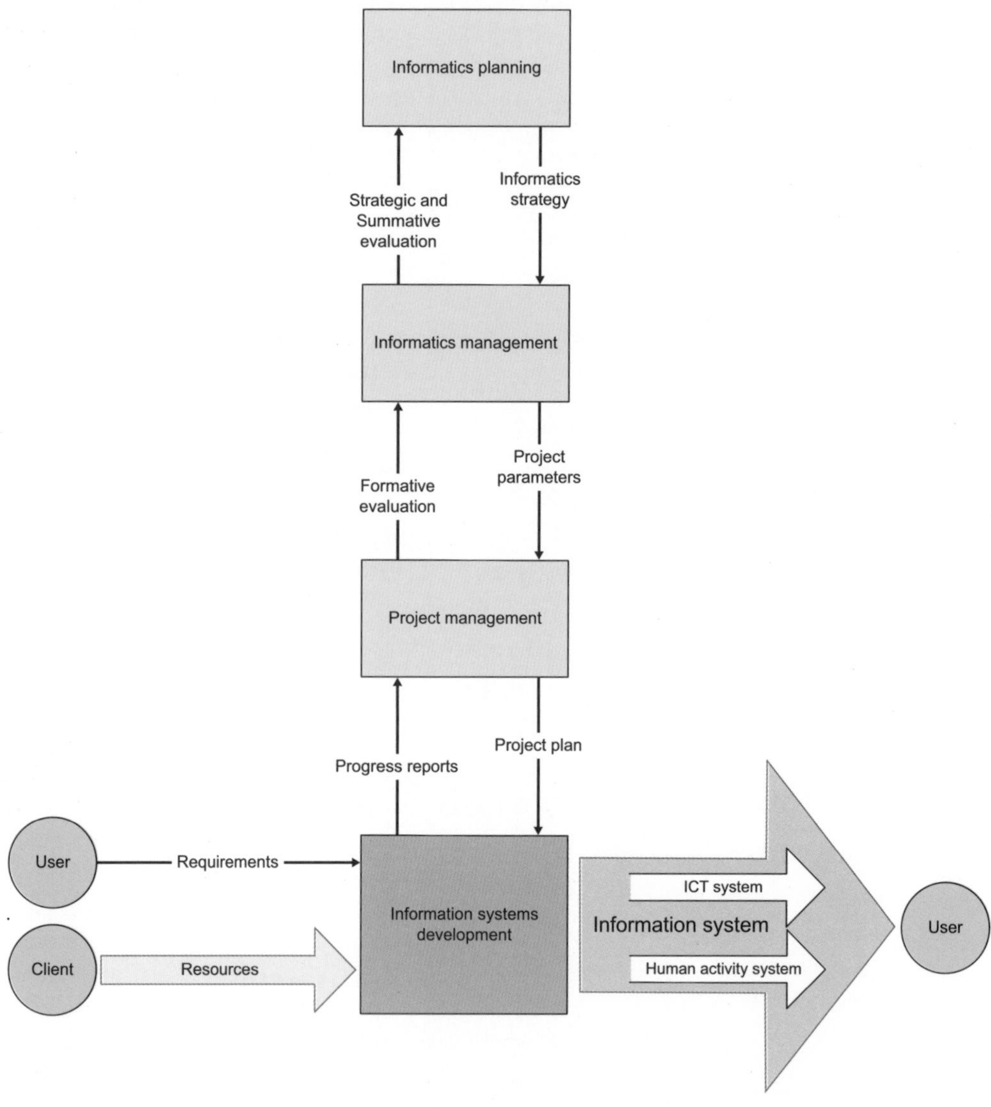

Figure 10.1: *The hierarchy of control*

Planning here is the processes of deciding on the optimal informatics infrastructure for an organisation, and engaging with the transformation of one informatics infrastructure into another. The key output from informatics planning is informatics strategy. The planning process also typically includes performance monitoring – information fed back from the management process – which is critical to the ongoing evaluation of strategy.

Two forms of management are outlined on Figure 10.1, general informatics management

Informatics management: The process of putting information, information systems and information technology plans into action.

and project management. INFORMATICS MANAGEMENT is the process of putting into action joint plans for organisational and technological change, and monitoring performance against plans. Management typically define, resource and implement a portfolio of projects. Individual projects need to be managed as autonomous fields of activity, and progress is reported to general management processes. General informatics management is covered in this chapter; **project management** is considered in Chapter 11.

Development organisation: That specialist form of organisation charged with producing an information system.

Development is the process of implementing the plans documented in strategy and resourced from management. Information systems are sociotechnical systems which bridge between ICT systems and the activity systems they support. They are constructed by a DEVELOPMENT ORGANISATION, using detailed requirements provided by potential users and key resources supplied by clients of the development organisation, usually managerial groups. This process is the topic of Chapter 12.

Informatics strategy, project parameters and project plans are all control inputs in this hierarchy of control. Development progress, project reports (formative evaluation) and strategy evaluations (summative and strategic) are all forms of control signal in feedback processes. Figure 10.1 is meant to emphasise that planning, general informatics management, project management and development are continuous processes. As in any activity system, it is important that the feedback loops work effectively for the infrastructure of an eBusiness to be a viable system. Information systems are just as critical to these processes as they are to conventional business processes such as sales and manufacturing.

Key skill 

Informatics planning

Informatics planning needs to take place in the context of general business planning, since there are a number of advantages to doing this. It is important to ensure that there is a close match between the proposed direction of an organisation and its information services. Informatics planning can be used to ensure that information system projects correctly balance business objectives with technical objectives. Planning helps with effective resource allocation. It makes it easier to estimate the effect (and the risk) of proposed information system projects, in terms of their contribution to business objectives, and to evaluate the effectiveness of current systems. Planning should lead to greater integration of both current and future information systems. Good planning is a necessary part of good management of information systems, and is likely to improve the ability of an organisation to react to unforeseen circumstances.

PART 4

The value of informatics planning

However, the value of informatics planning varies depending on the type of organisation. Cash, McFarlan and McKeney (1992) provide a useful way of assessing the importance of both existing and potential information systems to the strategy of organisations. If we consider importance along the two dimensions of existing systems and future systems, we come to the four organisational possibilities illustrated in Figure 10.2.

Strategic organisations are those in which smooth functioning of existing informatics activity is critical to their daily operation. Applications under development are also critical to the organisation's future competitive success. Since strategic companies are so dependent on the smooth functioning of their informatics infrastructure both now and in the future, they benefit from considerable amounts of well-considered informatics planning.

Many organisations in the financial industry are clearly in this sector of Cash's taxonomy. ICT is at the heart of modern banking, for instance. Developments in the area of online banking have had a major effect on the industry and are likely to continue to be very important to its future.

Turnaround organisations require considerable amounts of informatics support, but their activities are not absolutely dependent on the uninterrupted, cost-effective functioning of informatics infrastructure to achieve their short-term or long-term objectives. Applications under development however are absolutely vital to their long-term health. Turnaround companies also need a substantial informatics planning effort since although current organisational effectiveness is not critically dependent on informatics, future performance is likely to be.

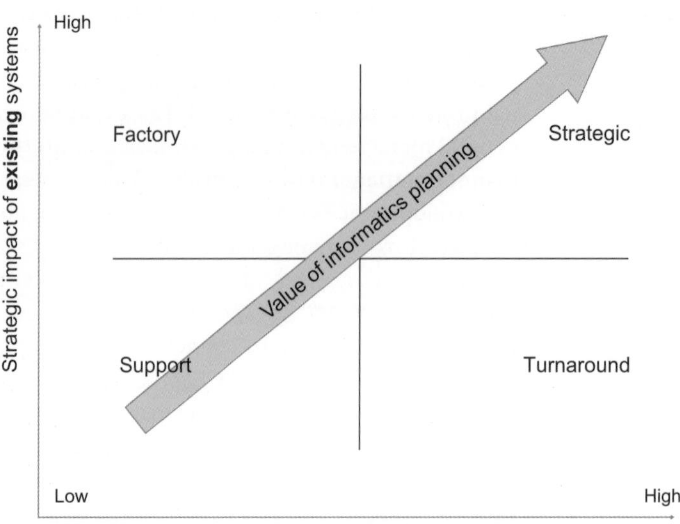

Figure 10.2: *Cash's taxonomy*

Many organisations in the retail industry come into this category. Food retail for instance used not to be a heavy user of ICT, but in the 2000s ICT innovation and the development of applications have become critical to competitive success, at least for the large supermarket chains.

For smooth operation, a **factory organisation** is heavily dependent on a cost-effective, reliable informatics infrastructure. However its system development portfolio is likely to be heavily dominated by maintenance work, and the applications under development, though important, are not fundamental to its ability to compete. So for organisations in this category, mass effort in informatics planning is probably not needed, although year-by-year operational planning is still essential.

The manufacturing sector has implemented many systems, such as just-in-time manufacturing systems, that are heavily reliant on good informatics infrastructure. However, it is currently unclear in many organisations how ICT will be able to stimulate further improvements in internal manufacturing processes.

Reflect
What sort of measurements might be used to place an organisation accurately in one of Cash's sectors? In other words, how would you assess which quadrant is most appropriate for all or a part of an organisation?

Some organisations are not particularly dependent on the smooth functioning of ICT, nor are their applications portfolios critical to future effectiveness. In **support organisations** there is a tendency to assume that little if any informatics planning is needed. The danger, however, is that there might be opportunities opening up as a result of evolving technology that they will miss.

For instance, organisations in the agricultural sector have historically not been heavy investors in ICT, and look relatively unlikely to be large investors in the future.

This taxonomy can be applied to parts of organisations as well as the whole organisation. Different divisions, departments or business units may be in different quadrants of the innovation matrix at different times. For instance, a company's manufacturing operations might be in the factory or support segment, whereas the marketing division is in the strategic or turnaround quadrant. Organisations can also move around the quadrants over time, starting in the support quadrant, then moving through turnaround and strategic quadrants into the factory quadrant.

Sensing the environment

Planning is not a one-off process. Organisations must continually sense their environment and adapt to environmental change (see Chapter 2). Typically, three main types of sensing activity provide input to the informatics planning process (see Figure 10.3):

Organisational analysis: The process of analysing and redesigning key business processes or human activity systems.

- ORGANISATIONAL ANALYSIS feeds in information concerning the shape of current organisational processes/activities and plans for changes to them. Part of this activity will be an assessment of infrastructure (see below).
- **Environmental analysis** inputs information concerning current and future trends in the immediate environment of the organisation – economic, social, political and ecological trends affecting the organisation. It particularly involves assessment of its current and potential place in its value network (see Chapter 7).
- **Technology analysis** provides information on trends in ICT that are likely to affect the organisation in the short to medium term, and that are likely to stimulate a need for change in its ICT infrastructure.

For example, in the financial services sector an environmental analysis might highlight opportunities and threats posed by the deregulation of key areas (see Chapter 5). A technology analysis might highlight the potential of critical technologies such as CRM systems (see Chapter 6) for customer acquisition and retention. An organisational analysis might identify key problems with business processes, such as response time to customer enquiries (see Chapter 2).

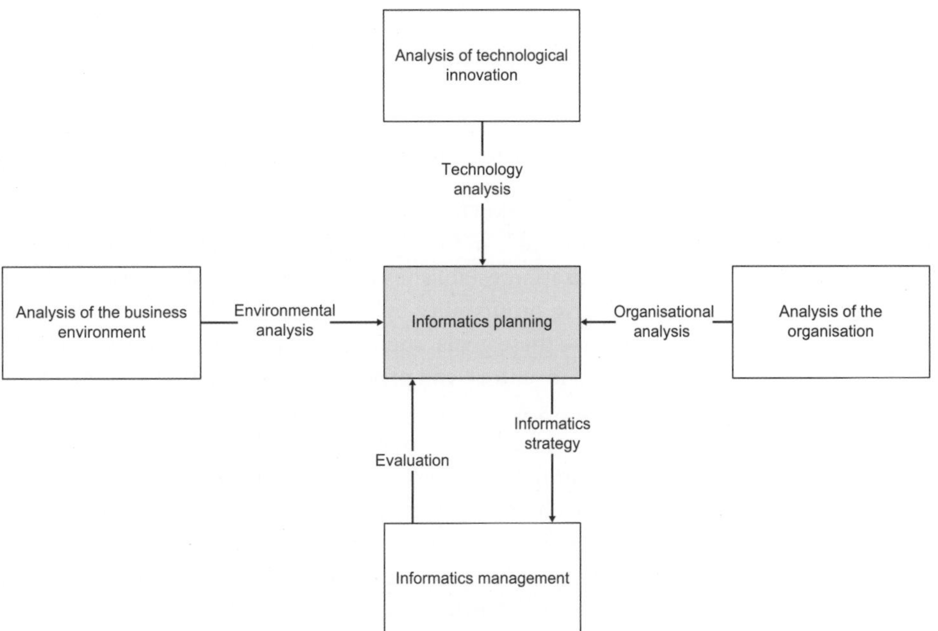

Figure 10.3: *Inputs into the informatics planning process*

The objective of informatics planning is to develop an effective informatics strategy. The practical output of informatics planning is a document or set of documents that describes strategy in this area. Informatics planning will also receive feedback from management activities, in the form of various types of evaluation of the performance of the organisation and its information systems (see Chapter 9).

Planning approaches

There are three major approaches to the planning of informatics strategy (Ward and Peppard, 2002) (see Figure 10.4):

- **Target-driven** is a top-down approach to the planning of strategy. Here strategy is directed through goals or targets set. Consideration is then given to ways of achieving targets and resources needed to conduct activities.
- **Resource-driven** planning is a bottom-up approach to strategy. Here strategy begins with available resources. Activities are specified in terms of these resources and goals achieved in relation to activities.

PART 4

- **Implementation-driven** planning is a middle-out approach to strategy. Here means and ends are continually assessed and adjusted over time in the shaping of activities.

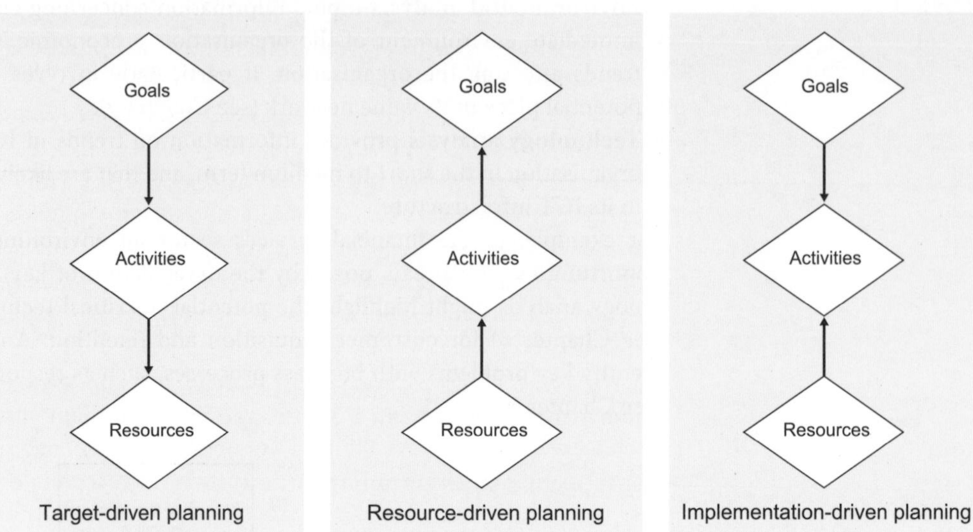

Figure 10.4: *Three approaches to planning of strategy*

The top-down or target-driven approach to informatics planning is certainly the best documented, and it receives the most attention in this chapter. In target-driven planning the organisation establishes a mission, consisting of a series of measurable objectives such as to improve profitability by 5 per cent in three years. A series of activities are then planned to achieve these goals, such as to decrease inventory levels through the introduction of an integrated inventory and production information system. Development and project management resources such as programmers, hardware and software then have to be provided to support the planned development activities.

Among the generic activities for the informatics planning process using a target-driven approach are setting up a planning unit and approach, assessment of the current informatics infrastructure, establishing a vision for informatics, specifying the informatics strategy, developing strategic plans for the informatics service and developing operational plans for the informatics service. These phases can be adapted to resource-driven and implementation-driven approaches.

The American general and president Dwight D. Eisenhower once said that in preparing for battle he found plans useless but planning indispensable.

Setting up a planning unit and approach

Most organisations start to develop an informatics strategy by evaluating various existing planning methods and choosing one, or customising one (for instance, Business motivation modelling, discussed below). The organisation then sets up an informatics planning unit. If it is using a proprietary planning method, its supplier is likely to provide training which will help guide the planning study. Next the unit carries out the multiple phases of the study, which generally last several months. Its staff first look to define current business processes, drawing on existing documentation and other techniques such as interviewing other stakeholders (see Chapter 2). They will also study how the current information systems support these processes. Using its documented understanding, the unit then identifies and prioritises key information systems for the future infrastructure, and draws up an implementation schedule. It prepares a report that includes a plan with recommendations for hardware, software, data, communication technology and personnel support.

Assessment of the current informatics infrastructure

Any planning process must begin with an assessment of the current situation. Current performance is compared with a set of objectives. For informatics planning these normally include both business and informatics objectives, because it is a sociotechnical exercise in which all four layers of organisational infrastructure need to be examined: activity, information, information systems and ICT. Once the team has established the current performance of these layers, it can start to define what future performance should be, and determine the shape of associated performance management systems (see Chapter 7).

The informatics planning process typically begins with an assessment of the use of information, information systems and ICT in the entire organisation, as well as an assessment of the work of the informatics service (see Chapter 11). This assessment might be conducted by a group of both informatics professionals and user-managers. Outsiders, particularly from informatics consultancies, are also frequently used to provide a cross-organisational view of the situation.

An informatics assessment will probably document current levels of information, information systems and ICT use, and compare them against a set of standards, perhaps produced as benchmarks of past performance or by analysing industry norms. A technical assessment of current information systems and technology infrastructure will also form part of the picture, as will an assessment of current attitudes to information systems and ICT in the organisation.

Another important part of the assessment is a review of the mission of the informatics service (see Chapter 11). This should address the important issue of the business rationale for having an informatics service, looking at the three issues of efficiency, effectiveness and competitiveness. In efficiency terms, a key question is whether the informatics service helps the organisation remain active with the minimum use of resources. In terms of effectiveness, the key question is whether the informatics service helps the organisation spend its time doing the right things. Finally, in terms of competitiveness, the key question is whether the informatics service is engaged in projects that will improve the position of the organisation in its environment.

Many organisations have clearly answered 'no' to questions such as these, and considered alternatives to an internal informatics service, such as facilities management and outsourcing. Outsourcing means transferring the whole or part of the informatics service, particularly support activities, to outside suppliers. In facilities management the management of the informatics infrastructure is also transferred to outside contractors (see Chapter 11).

Establishing a vision for informatics

Establishing a vision for informatics normally involves assessing the **competitive advantage** that information systems can deliver. Among the frameworks that have been proposed for doing this are critical success factors, the five forces model, the customer resource lifecycle and the value chain. The value chain was discussed in Chapter 7, along with the idea of the value network and value network analysis, so this section focuses on the other three approaches.

Critical success factors

Critical success factor: A factor that is deemed crucial to the success of a business.

Any organisation needs to identify areas in which it has relative superiority, and to use that superiority both to create barriers to entry and to launch strategic offensives. The CRITICAL SUCCESS FACTOR (CSF) concept is a popular way of doing this. A CSF is a factor that is considered core to the success of a business, so it is an area that must be given special attention by management. CSFs are also critical points of leverage for achieving competitive advantage. Each organisation normally has only a few CSFs – perhaps between three and eight – so CSFs are said to follow a Pareto or 80/20 rule: only a few issues really count in levering improvements in organisational effectiveness.

CSFs are usually contrasted with CFFs, or critical failure factors. The poor management of a CFF is likely to precipitate organisational failure. A CSF for a chain of high street jewellers might be location of its outlets; for a health authority, it will be the quality of service it gives to patients. A CFF for the high street jeweller chain could a high amount of shrinkage in consumer demand, while the health authority's might be poor coordination of staff, particularly subcontractors.

CSFs and CFFs are useful ways of identifying areas for the maximal application of information systems and ICT. For instance, the jeweller chain would benefit from an information system that enabled managers to select optimal locations for stores based on factors such as population density and the state of local economy. A health authority would benefit from an information system that ensured the efficient work scheduling of nursing staff.

Five forces model: A strategic planning framework attributed to Porter and Millar.

The five forces model

Another framework for assessing competitive advantage is based on the work of Porter and Millar (1985) (see Chapter 5). They argue that a successful firm shapes the structure of competition by influencing five primary forces (see Figure 10.5), discussed below with a brief analysis of the effects of informatics on them (Porter, 2001).

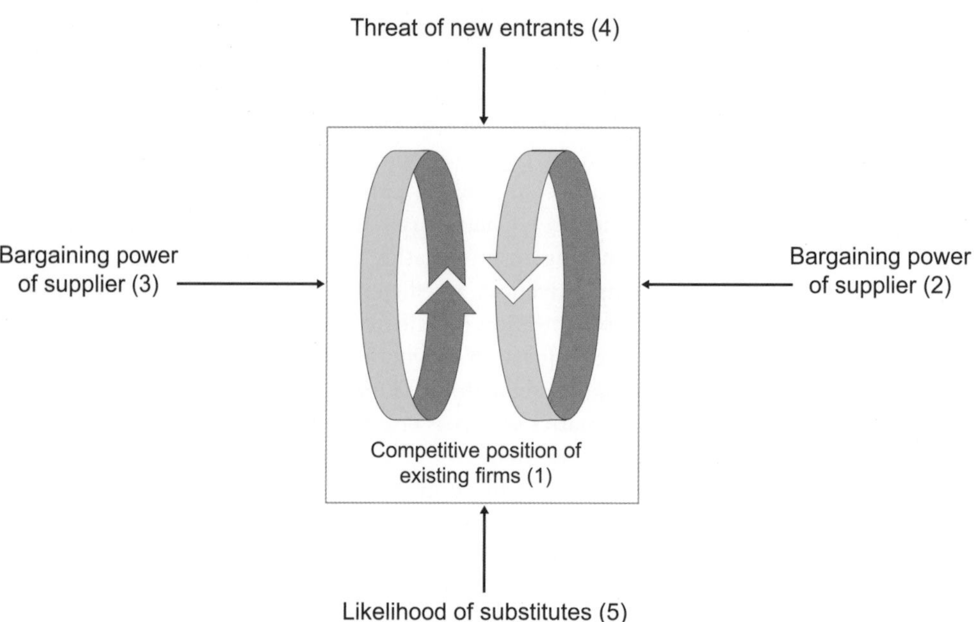

Figure 10.5: *The five forces model*

- **Industrial rivalry**, the competitive position of rival organisations. Bricks and mortar companies in certain sectors such as banking, travel and insurance have already experienced increasing competition with the rise of clicks-only organisations such as online banks. In many sectors there has also been increased disintermediation, in others significant amounts of reintermediation through electronic delivery channels.
- **Customer bargaining power.** Electronic trading has increased the bargaining power of customers in the sense that they are able to search for and examine a wider array of goods and services. This appears to have a collective effect of driving down prices.
- **Supplier bargaining power** might decrease with the increasing adoption of B2B eCommerce. Companies might insist that their established suppliers use electronic communication to improve supply-chain efficiency. Also, the cost of switching to alternative suppliers might be reduced with the rise of B2B hubs.
- **Barriers to entry** and the threat of new entrants. Arguably there are lower start-up costs for entering digital rather than conventional markets, so the barriers to entry are lower and the threat of new entrants is higher. However, as the dot com crash demonstrated, it seems to be just as difficult, if not more so, to maintain a sustainable online presence as to keep up a conventional physical market presence.
- **Threat of substitutes.** In the eBusiness arena the rise of digital products (such as digital

music) and the increasing degree of digital convergence pose major threats to companies whose products are primarily intangible. For services, new business models for electronic service delivery threaten existing delivery channels.

Many combinations of these factors, such as low industrial rivalry, high barriers to entry and low buyer bargaining power, can lead to sustainable, above-average long-term profits. EBusiness can be used to achieve these goals by changing the basis of competition, strengthening customer relationships, overcoming supplier problems, building barriers against new entrants and generating new products or services.

For example, customer information systems for marketing and sales can have a strategic impact by winning customers from the competition. They could do this by using a large customer database, market research databases to target customer 'need', and eMarketing and direct mailing to improve sales. The cost of setting up and maintaining an accurate customer database is itself a considerable barrier to entry in certain sectors.

The customer resource life-cycle

Ives and Learmonth (1984) define an information system as strategic if it changes a company's product or the way it competes in its industry. They use the idea of a customer resource life-cycle to identify potential strategic information systems. This model considers a firm's relationship with its customers (the customer chain) and how this relationship can be changed or enhanced by the strategic application of ICT.

Customer resource life-cycle: A strategic planning framework developed by Ives and Learmonth. Also useful in defining elements of the customer chain.

The CUSTOMER RESOURCE LIFE-CYCLE is a sequence of 13 stages based around the customer's interaction with a 'resource'. A resource in this sense is a product and/or service delivered by an organisation:

1. The customer establishes requirements, in the sense of how much of a resource is required.
2. The customer specifies its requirements, detailing the attributes of the required resource.
3. An appropriate supplier for the resource is selected.
4. A quantity of the resource is ordered from the supplier.
5. The customer authorises and pays for the resource; authority for the expenditure must be obtained and payment made.
6. The customer acquires or takes possession of the resource.
7. The customer verifies the acceptability of the resource before putting it to use.
8. The resource is added to an existing inventory.
9. The customer monitors to ensure that the resource remains acceptable while in inventory.
10. If requirements change, it may be necessary to upgrade resources.
11. It may prove necessary to maintain or repair a resource.
12. The customer may transfer or dispose of a resource.
13. The customer accounts for the resource in the sense of monitoring where and how money is spent on resources.

The idea of a customer resource life-cycle is relevant to both private sector and public sector organisations, such as the UK National Health Service (NHS). In this setting, the patient is the primary health service customer and can be considered as consuming a health service resource. The customer resource life-cycle might then be:

- **Requirements specification.** ICT can be used as a means to aid a general practitioner (GP) and the patient in establishing what health resource is required, in what quantity.
- **Selection.** A series of options are presented to the patient: for instance, a number of hospitals able to offer the chosen treatment.
- **Order.** The GP queries a hospitals' elective admission system to find out whether it can schedule the treatment. If what is available suits the patient, a provisional booking is made.
- **Authorise and payment.** Appropriate routines update the treatment accounts of the hospital and the budget of the general practice.
- **Acquire.** When the patient arrives for their stay in hospital, their details are transferred from the GP's system to its patient administration system.

PART 4

- **Test.** The patient is given details of the proposed treatment and requested to sign an agreement.
- **Integrate.** The consumption of the health care resource is added to the patient's history record in a regional data register.
- **Monitor and upgrade.** Preliminary investigation might change the initial prognosis, leading to modification of the original health care plan. Any changes or additions to the plan are recorded by hospital systems.
- **Maintain.** The patient is given regular checkups to make sure they are recovering from the treatment. Details are notified to patients by the GP system, and the results recorded by the system.
- **Accountability.** The patient receives a report of every treatment given, with the cost to the health service budget.

Strategic and operational plans for the informatics service

An informatics services strategic plan sets goals for this organisational function over an agreed timeframe. It normally includes:

- A statement on the organisation of the informatics services function. Prior planning processes should already have established the basis for financial control. There are two main options: an unallocated cost centre, in which the service is given a budget and user departments do not pay directly for informatics work, or an allocated cost centre and charge-out, in which user departments have informatics budgets and the service charges them when they use it (Chapter 11).
- Details of how the informatics strategy is aligned with the business strategy. Cash and colleagues (1992) discuss one significant difficulty here: business strategy is generally set within a one-year frame of reference, whereas informatics strategy must consider a three to five-year frame of reference. They suggest that one way of improving the coupling between business and informatics is for a chief information officer (CIO) to be a member of the main board.
- Portfolios of development plans for new information systems and maintenance plans for existing information systems.
- A portfolio of operational and support plans for the informatics infrastructure, including training and helpdesks (see Chapter 11). Operational plans relate the activity of the informatics service to goals and budgets. They normally include descriptions of development projects, maintenance activity, operational effort and planning and management activity, all with associated resource implications and costing.

Recap 

Informatics planning is the process of deciding on the optimal informatics infrastructure for an organisation. It uses as input three major forms of STRATEGIC ANALYSIS: organisational analysis, environmental analysis and technological analysis. There are three major approaches to the planning of informatics strategy: target-driven, resource-driven and implementation-driven. In target-driven strategy, informatics planning involves setting up a planning unit and approach, assessing the current informatics infrastructure, establishing a vision and specifying an informatics strategy. Establishing a vision for informatics normally involves assessing the competitive advantage that information systems could deliver. Among the frameworks proposed for this purpose are critical success factors, the five forces model, the customer resource life-cycle and value-chain or value-network analysis.

Strategic analysis: The process of determining the organisation's mission and goals.

Strategy

Strategy: The art of a commander-in-chief; the art of projecting and directing the larger military movements and operations in a campaign.

Tactics: Tactics belongs only to the mechnical movement of bodies set in motion by strategy.

The term STRATEGY has historical roots in military operations. According to the *Oxford English Dictionary*, strategy is the art of a commander-in-chief; the art of projecting and directing larger military movements and operations in a campaign. It is not the same as TACTICS, which concerns the mechanical movement of bodies set in motion by strategy. Strategy is now used in much the same sense in a business context.

Ansoff (1965) defines strategic decisions as primarily concerned with external rather than internal problems of the firm, and specifically with selection of the product mix (what the firm will produce) and the market to which it will sell. Strategic decisions are concerned with establishing an 'impedance match' between the firm and its environment. In other words, they focus on deciding what business the firm is in and what kinds of business it will seek to do. In systems terms, strategy concerns issues surrounding both the viability and sustainability of organisations (see Chapter 2).

Organisational strategy

Over the last 20 to 30 years the trend has been for the manager's job to be seen as developing an explicit organisation strategy and creating effective ways of planning and implementing it (Porter, 1996). In the informatics field, the manager's concern is with how strategies for information, information systems and ICT can be developed and aligned with organisation strategy. This is the notion of **informatics strategy.** More recently there has been a lot of interest in the strategic implications of closely linking changes to activity infrastructure and technological change. This comprises **eBusiness strategy.**

Porter has argued that there are three major ways in which organisations can gain competitive advantage (Chapter 7): cost advantage, differentiation and location. These can be seen as particular types of organisational strategy:

Cost advantage: This essentially aims to establish the organisation as a low-cost leader in the market.

Differentiation strategy: A strategy undertaken by an organisation to differentiate its product or service from its competitors.

Location strategy: A strategy that involves the organisation attempting to find a niche market to service.

- **Cost advantage.** A commercial organisation can gain competitive advantage or leadership by establishing itself as a low-cost leader in the market. Cost advantage is usually achieved by doing things more efficiently.
- **Differentiation.** It can gain competitive advantage by differentiating its product in the marketplace. This generally involves persuading consumers that it offers something special in the way of a product or service. There are two parts to this, of course: having an unique and desirable offering to sell, and persuading consumers that this is so.
- **Location.** Finally, a commercial organisation can gain competitive advantage by finding a niche in the marketplace for its product or service. This can be achieved in a number of ways. It might offer an entirely new product or service, for example, or offer its product or service to a previously untapped group of customers, perhaps through an innovative access channel (see below).

Did you know?

One of the earliest texts on strategy is thought to have been written by the Chinese general Sun Tzu (544–496 BC) : *The Art of War*. He stated that it was always desirable to conquer the enemy without resorting to war, through the application of strategy.

Formulation of business strategy

According to Johnson and Scholes (Johnson, Scholes and Whittington, 2007), the formulation of business strategy involves three interdependent activities:

Strategic choice: The process of generating strategic options, evaluating them and selecting a suitable strategy to achieve the selected option.

Strategic implementation: Determining policies, making decisions and taking action.

- **Strategic analysis:** of the environment, expectations, objectives, power and culture in the organisation and organisational resources. Strategic analysis involves determining the organisation's mission and goals, and answering the questions, what should we be doing and where are we going?
- **Strategic choice:** generating strategic options, evaluating them and selecting both an option and a suitable strategy to achieve it. Strategic choice involves answering the question, what routes have we selected?
- **Strategic implementation:** organising resources, restructuring elements of the organisation, and providing suitable people and systems. Strategic implementation comprises determining policies, making decisions and taking action. It aims to answer the questions, how do we guide our collective decisions to get there, what choices do we have and how shall we do it?

Strategic thinking is normally documented in an organisation's **mission statement.** This comprises a short list of statements of future intention, for each of which a number of goals may be formulated. In turn, for each goal a number of strategies or routes forward may be planned. Each strategy has to be made operational in a series of plans. Plans in their turn are collections of decisions which involve a series of actions, so strategic planning involves constructing a hierarchy of goals, strategies, policies, decisions and actions. For example:

- **Mission**: to be the industry cost leader.
- **Goal**: achieve staff productivity gain of 5 per cent within three years.
- **Strategy**: reduce the time to process a customer transaction.
- **Policy**: improve customer-facing information systems and integration.
- **Decision**: introduce a corporate-wide CRM information system.
- **Action**: set up and resource an implementation project.

An organisation's mission statement at various levels of the hierarchy consists of a limited number of objectives, which act as a guide to future intention. These should be SMART objectives:

- **Specific**: each objective should be clear and focused.
- **Measurable**: it should be clear how achieving the objective can be measured.
- **Achievable**: the objective should be achievable with organisational resources.
- **Realistic**: the objective should be realistic in terms of organisational constraints
- **Timely**: the objective should specify a duration by which it will be achieved.

EBusiness strategy

There are at least three different viewpoints on what eBusiness strategy is (Lord, 2000). None of them is the sole correct view, since the appropriate viewpoint is defined by organisational context. In other words, eBusiness strategy will depend on the context of an appropriate business model for eBusiness in the general context of the business. Options include a complete overlap between organisation and eBusiness strategy, eBusiness strategy as a business unit strategy, and eBusiness strategy as a process strategy.

In the most extreme form there is little or no distinction between organisation strategy and eBusiness strategy. This definition is appropriate if the eBusiness is effectively the entire corporation. In practice it may only be applicable if a traditional bricks and mortar company sets out to completely re-engineer its processes around ICT, or a new greenfield eBusiness is established – a clicks-only strategy.

In many companies the eBusiness strategy applies only to a particular part of the business: a division, department or unit. In one approach a firm packages its eBusiness activities as a separate organisation isolated from the parent firm. This organisation is expected to innovate with new products and services. At the other extreme, the eBusiness activity is fully integrated with the parent organisation but under the control of specific business units: a clicks and mortar strategy. In a middle path, companies run their eBusinesses as separate but parallel operations, implying a certain level of integration between the parent organisation and the eBusiness but also a certain degree of autonomy for the eBusiness.

Reflect
As more and more companies embrace eBusiness, which form of eBusiness strategy will become the most prevalent? Will the type of eBusiness strategy vary by industry? In other words, will companies in the financial services sector have a different profile of eBusiness strategies from those in retail or manufacturing?

The company might choose a key organisational process or activity system, or perhaps an integrated set of processes, for radical redesign with ICT innovation. For example, it could concentrate on redesigning its supply chain or customer chain processes. This is probably the most common current form of eBusiness strategy.

So Amazon.com's eBusiness strategy will equate to its organisation strategy, because it is an eBusiness-oriented company. Other companies might develop supply chain management or customer relationship management as an eBusiness strategy, or pick an area of eCommerce such as B2C or B2B eCommerce (see Chapter 8). These might be either business unit or process strategies depending on the structure of the organisation.

Competitive advantage and information systems

Information systems can be used in two ways in organisations. First, they can be used to support current activity systems, which form part of the current informatics infrastructure. Second, they can be developed to support new activity systems. These information systems directly assist an organisation in achieving its strategy, and are designed to have a direct impact on its competitive advantage For this reason, they are sometimes referred to as STRATEGIC INFORMATION SYSTEMS.

Strategic information system: An information system that delivers competitive advantage.

Strategic information systems contribute to one or more of the generic organisational strategies discussed above. For instance, banks worldwide have set up online banking facilities. There are a number of reasons that this can lead to performance improvements, not least the low cost of banking transactions online compared with traditional banking services, so online banking could at one time be seen as a form of strategic information system. Internet-based retailing is an obvious area for establishing new ways of delivering products and services. Amazon.com was one of the first to sell books and CDs online, and has established a relative dominance in this segment of eTailing.

An analysis of cases like this produces a list of common characteristics of strategic information systems:

Reflect
Consider a university as an organisation to which ICT transformation might be applied. What would be appropriate strategic information systems and why?

- Many strategic information systems are built from an established informatics infrastructure.
- Organisational leverage is frequently achieved simply by integrating systems and creating more effective information flows in support of business processes.
- Many strategic information systems link the organisation more efficiently or effectively with its customers and suppliers. To be of benefit, strategic information systems must offer real value to the customer or supplier.
- A strategic information system must not be too easy to copy by competitors. It must be able to offer a medium to long-term impact on organisational performance to justify the investment in its development.
- A strategic information system must be capable of changing the marketplace's perception of the firm, for example by enabling it to offer new products or services, or offer its existing ones in different ways.
- Many strategic information systems are strategic in the sense that they provide high-level management with better information about internal operations and/or the organisation environment, enabling them to plan strategically far more effectively.

Reflect
How are mergers between companies or public sector organisations likely to affect informatics strategy, and why?

An information system is only likely to remain strategic for a limited period of time. Usually the competitive advantage it provides will be eroded in time because of emulation by competitors, but the first entrant into an area frequently determines standards in terms of technology and its use. This often means that customers face a switching cost if they abandon it for a later rival. A strategic information system will therefore offer a strategic advantage to an organisation in intangible as well as tangible ways.

PART 4

Case check: Case 10, Inland Revenue, UK

The Inland Revenue was until recently the UK government department responsible for collecting and administering taxation. It has attempted to be at the forefront of eGovernment in the United Kingdom by transforming its performance using ICT. The department set out its first eBusiness strategy in 2000. The key feature was the development of a number of electronic channels for different customer groups, with clear incentives to encourage their use.

Informatics strategy

Information systems strategy: That part of an informatics strategy concerned with specifying the future control of an information systems infrastructure and implementation of new elements of this infrastructure.

ICT strategy: The process of managing the current ICT infrastructure and implementing a new ICT infrastructure.

EBusiness strategy, as we have seen, is subtly different from but interdependent with informatics strategy. An informatics strategy defines the structure within which information, information systems and ICT are to be applied in an organisation over a future timeframe. It therefore has three major layers:

- An information strategy details the information needs of the organisation, and processes necessary to collect, produce, store and disseminate information.
- An INFORMATION SYSTEMS STRATEGY consists of a specification of the information systems needed to support organisational activity in the areas of collection, storage, dissemination and use of information.
- An ICT STRATEGY is a specification of the hardware, software, data, communication facilities and ICT knowledge and skills needed by the organisation to support its information systems.

Classic models of informatics strategy formulation try to achieve the ideal of alignment between organisation strategy and informatics strategy. Ideally, four layers of strategy support each other: a strategy for activity systems in the organisation (organisation strategy) is supported by the three layers of informatics strategy. The information needed by the organisation will determine the information systems it requires. In turn, the information systems needed determine the ICT infrastructure required.

Organisation planning: The process of formulating an organisation strategy.
Organisation strategy: The general direction or mission of an organisation.

The notion of alignment suggests that business strategy formulation should ideally come before informatics strategy formulation, as is illustrated in Figure 10.6. ORGANISATION PLANNING is the process of formulating an organisation strategy. **Informatics planning** is the process of formulating an informatics strategy. An ORGANISATION STRATEGY will critically affect the direction of an **informatics strategy**. However, in the modern business world organisational and informatics strategy are typically related in a mutual cycle of reinforcement. The formulation of an informatics strategy is likely to have a major influence on the formulation of future business strategy.

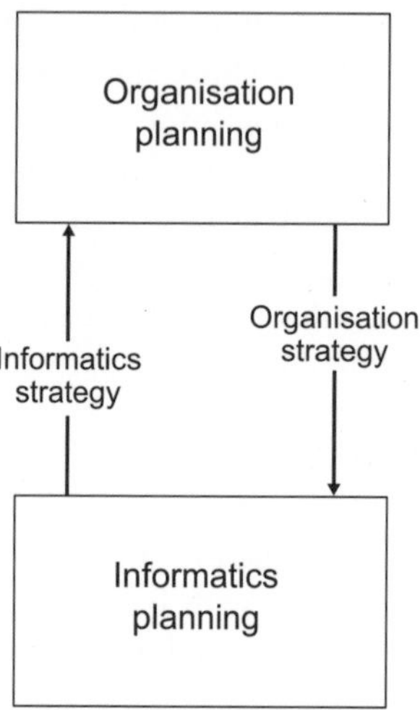

Figure 10.6: *The relationship between organisation and informatics planning*

The objective of informatics planning is to develop strategy in each of the three areas outlined above. The practical output of informatics planning is a set of documents which describe strategy in these three areas. An informatics strategy can be described as the structure within which information, information systems and ICT are intended to be applied in the organisation. It should establish a long-term infrastructure which will allow information systems to be designed and implemented efficiently and effectively. An informatics strategy is particularly directed at avoiding fragmentation, redundancy and inconsistency amongst information systems (see Chapter 6), and increasing their interoperability.

An informatics strategy will be constrained by an existing informatics infrastructure (Chapter 4). Very few organisations are able to build a 'clean-slate' or a 'greenfield' strategy in this area. Usually existing information needs, information systems and ICT have to be taken into account in formulating strategy.

Channel strategies

The relationship between general business strategy and eBusiness strategy is easily demonstrated in channel strategy. An access channel is a means for an organisation to deliver goods and/or services to its customers (see Chapter 8). Traditional access channels include voice and face-to-face contact. There are also a range of remote access channels, of which telephone contact and more recently Internet access are the most familiar (Chapter 8). Goods and services can either be delivered directly by an organisation or indirectly using intermediaries (Chapter 6).

A **channel strategy** is a set of choices for the organisation about how, and through what means, services and goods will be delivered. This typically means deciding which access channels will be made available to which customer segments (see Chapter 9). Different levels of interactivity and content may be required to meet the needs of differing customer segments. The capability of a particular access channel to cope with demand is a critical part of any channel strategy, and so is integration between different access channels.

For example, a local authority's channel strategy will involve deciding what proportion of services (if any) it will deliver remotely to PCs or through digital TV. It will also involve deciding to what extent it will use contact centres to manage the delivery of its services, and ensuring that it can deliver them seamlessly across multiple access channels.

Reflect
Are call centres run by major companies the same as contact centres? How important is effective integration of information systems to the performance of contact centres?

Channel strategies typically involve tiered access to products and services. Most large-scale private and public sector organisations offer at least three tiers, each of which has different cost and availability implications. The first tier is remote direct access through a subset of the access devices discussed in Chapter 6. The second tier is through a multichannel access centre. Here, contact centre staff manage delivery through computer integrated telephony. The third tier involves direct contact with employees through face-to-face communication or letter. This is illustrated in Figure 10.7.

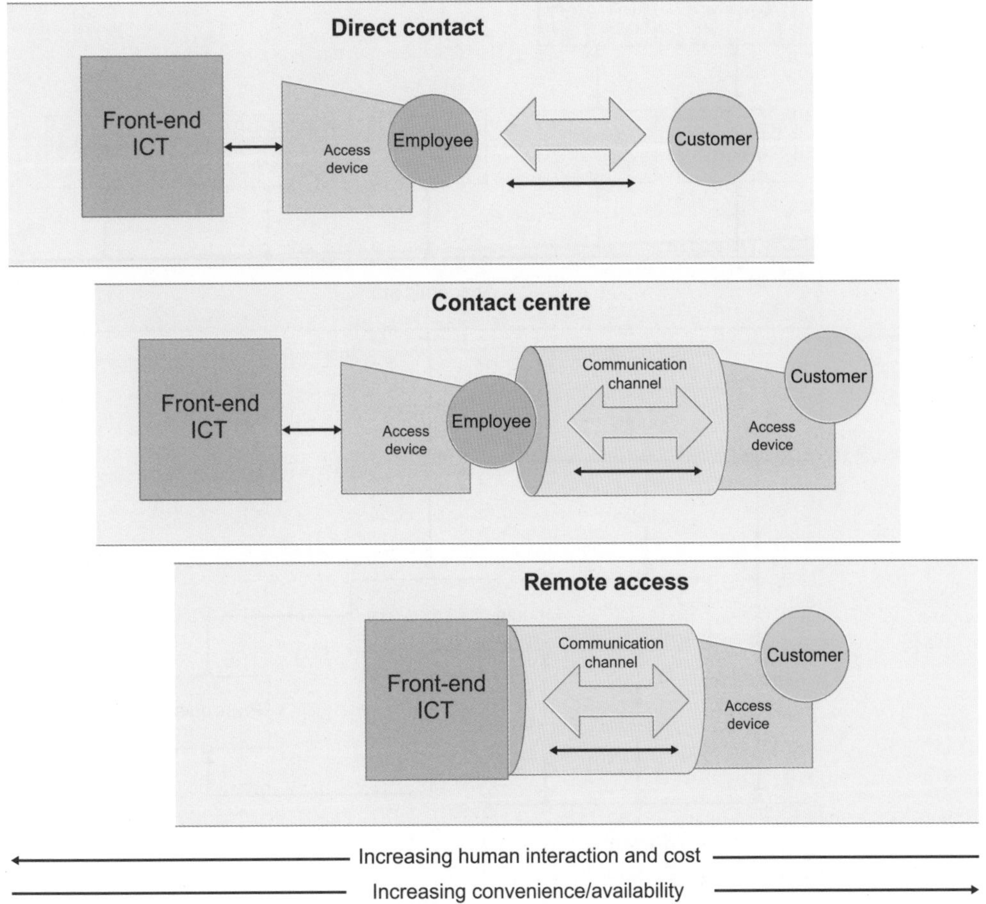

Figure 10.7: *Tiered access*

The channel strategy chosen will have a major impact on informatics strategy. For instance, if an organisation provides tiered access, it needs to ensure that it can deal in a uniform way with customer information acquired through the different access channels, which is likely to mean setting up a customer relationship management system (see Chapter 4). It might either buy a packaged system or build one in-house, perhaps using existing ICT infrastructure such as customer databases as a platform.

Developing information strategy

An information strategy details the information needs of the organisation and the processes necessary to collect, produce, store and disseminate information. There is no rule about the form of one, but it usually has three core elements:

Organisation process: A set of activities cutting across the major functional divisions in organisations, by which organisations accomplish their mission.

Organisation process model: A high-level map of organisational processes.

Process/information matrix: A matrix which relates classes on an organisation information model against processes on an organisation process model.

- An organisation information model which details the structure of the major information classes used by the organisation, and the relationships between them (see Chapter 3). For medium to large-scale organisations this will be described at a high level of abstraction.
- An ORGANISATION PROCESS MODEL which details the necessary information collection, storage, dissemination and use activities, again at a suitably high level of generality.
- A PROCESS/INFORMATION MATRIX which documents which information classes are used by which processes. It allows managers and developers to identify key clusters of common applications and databases around which new information systems should be built. It is also of particular use for managers in considering issues of integration or fragmentation in the informatics infrastructure.

Figure 10.8 is a simplified example of an organisation information model for a UK university.

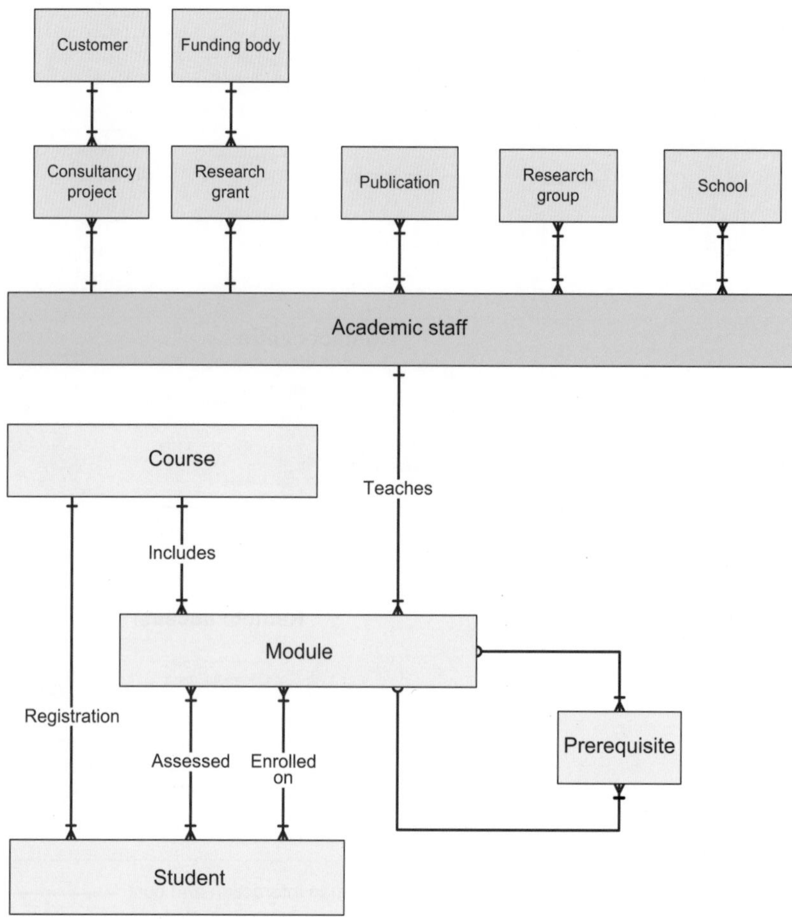

Figure 10.8: *University information model*

Figure 10.9 is an example of the related organisation process model. There are three main activities in any university: teaching, research and consultancy. Each activity system consists of a number of processes. For instance, teaching as an activity system involves handling student applications, enrolling students, delivering modules, assessing students, progressing students and creating new courses and modules. One other activity system is included for administering the information needed to manage learning resources such as books, journals, CD-ROMs, DVDs, as well as other resources such as buildings and staff.

Figure 10.10 is a simplified process/information matrix. The shaded boxes indicate which information class on the organisation information model is used by which major organisational process.

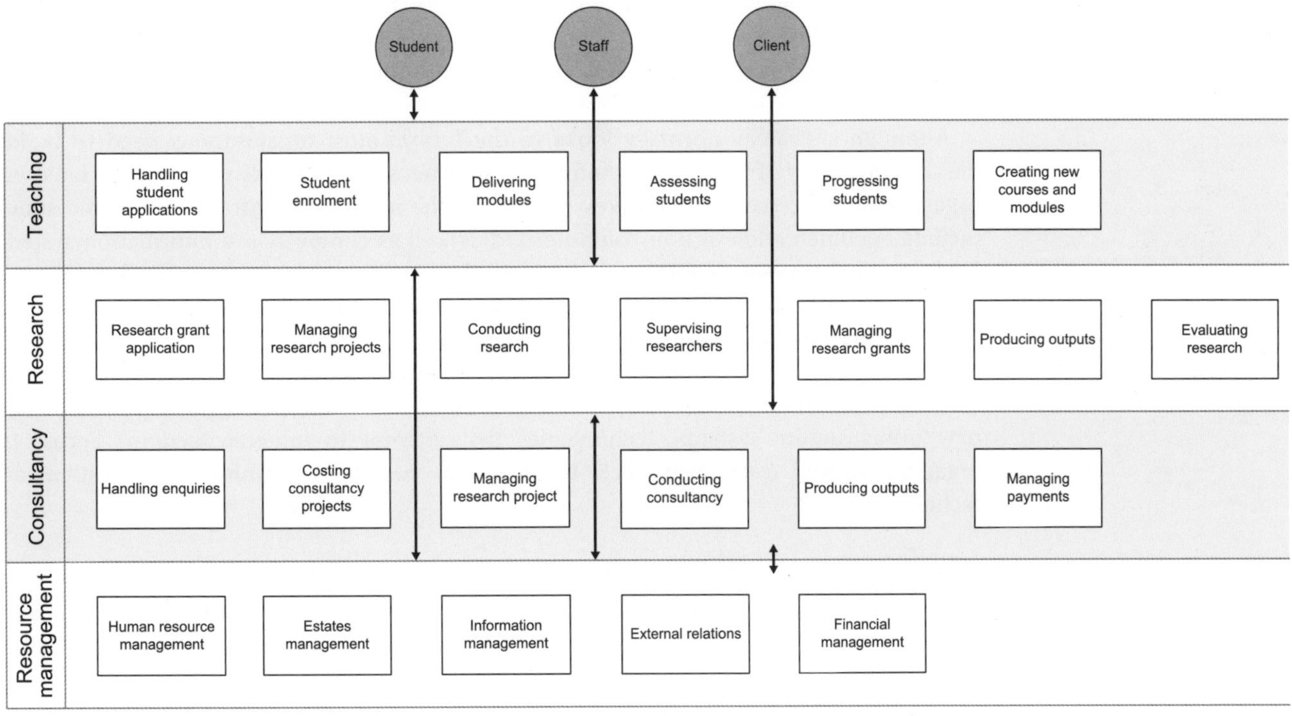

Figure 10.9: *University process model*

Developing information systems strategy

Information systems planning: information systems architecture.

An information systems strategy consists of a specification of the information systems needed to support organisational activity in the areas of collection, storage, dissemination and use of information. Informatics PLANNING will collate and prioritise requests for new information systems. An information systems strategy should include details of the current and future information systems portfolio.

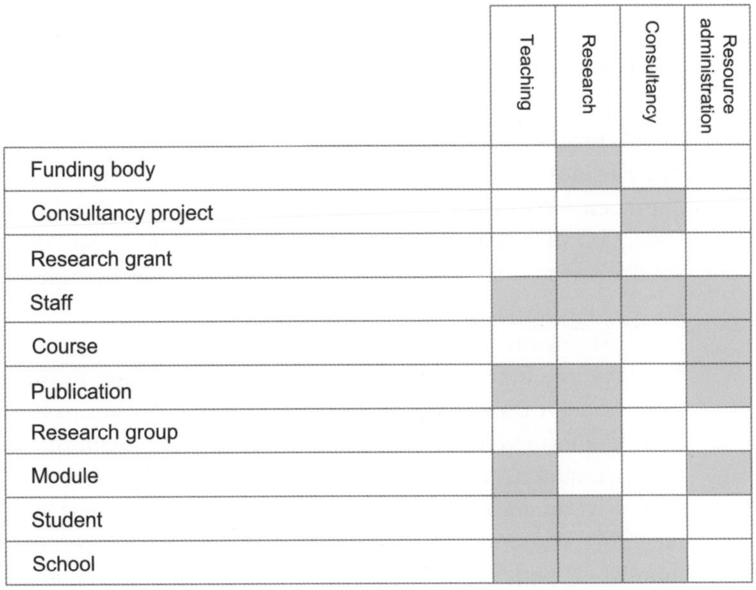

	Teaching	Research	Consultancy	Resource administration
Funding body		■		
Consultancy project			■	
Research grant		■		
Staff	■	■	■	■
Course				■
Publication	■	■		■
Research group		■		
Module	■			■
Student	■	■		
School	■	■	■	

Figure 10.10: *A process/information matrix for a university*

An information systems strategy should also clearly state how information systems link to supporting current and future organisation processes. To achieve this, there need to be effective organisational analysis, and an awareness of the core competencies/critical success factors.

Although a strategy normally looks to the future, most organisations need to build a detailed inventory of their current information systems and the links such systems have with organisation processes. This is a key element of the informatics infrastructure, and should include documentation of non-computerised as well as computerised information systems. High-level information system models as described in Chapter 4 are useful for this.

A future information systems portfolio should detail the planned information systems projects for the organisation over a time frame of perhaps three to five years. It will include projects such as corrections to existing information systems, enhancements to existing information systems, major new information systems development projects, major new infrastructure systems, technologies that attempt to integrate systems across the organisation, and research projects to investigate new possible information systems and technologies.

Developing ICT strategy

An ICT strategy consists of a specification of the hardware, software, data, communication facilities and ICT knowledge and skills needed by the organisation to support its information systems. The five major elements of an ICT strategy are:

- An **ICT systems model**: a detailed inventory of both current and future ICT systems.
- **Hardware standards**: a list of the standards to be adopted in connection with computers and peripheral devices.
- **Software standards**: a list of the standard system, communication and application software to be adopted throughout the organisation.
- **Communication standards**: details of appropriate properties for communication technology and networks.
- **Data standards**, documenting agreements about data representation and formats.

Reflect
Consider an organisation such as Tesco. In running its supermarket network, what sort of concerns might feed into its ICT strategy?

The major objectives of an ICT strategy are to reduce fragmentation, inconsistency and redundancy amongst ICT systems, and improve levels of interoperability. This might be achieved by buying new software packages (such as ERP as discussed in Chapter 6) or developing new bespoke information systems. Part of the ICT strategy must also consider the operational support (see Chapter 11) and maintenance needed for both current and planned ICT systems (see Chapter 12).

Business motivation modelling

The **Business Motivation Model** (BMM) (OMG, 2007) is explicitly designed as a modelling approach for strategic planning. This framework is produced by the Object Management Group (OMG), a body attempting to standardise aspects of systems development practice, particularly notations for modelling systems of various kinds. Version 1.0 of the BMM standard was released in 2008.

BMM essentially consists of a standardised vocabulary for business plans, which are specifications for business models (see Chapter 7). The aims are to allow clear tracking of the motivation or reasons for the design of a particular business model, and enable better alignment of business plans/models to ICT systems through the mediating concepts of business processes and rules.

The 'vocabulary' underlying BMM consists of a number of high-level concepts/terms including ends, means and influencers. A business model is expressed in terms of a number of **ends** to be achieved through a number of **means**. The achievement of ends through means will be affected by a number of **influencers**. Each of these terms is further elaborated using subconcepts/terms (see Figure 10.11). This vocabulary can be used to build an organised set of statements which indicate clear relationships between business and informatics strategy.

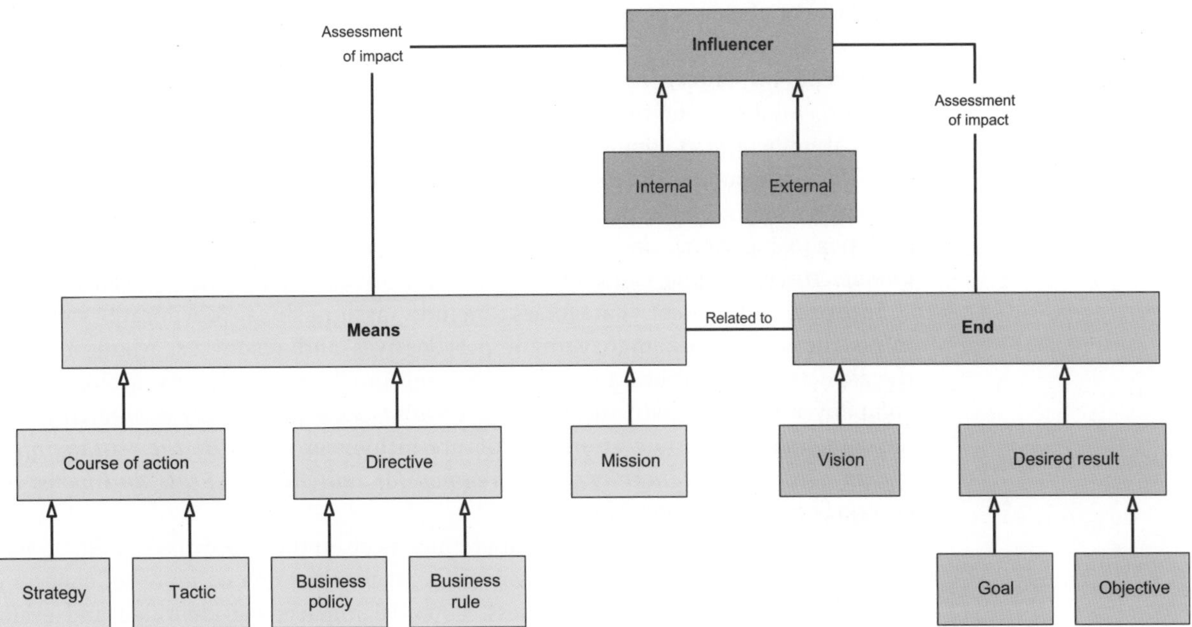

Figure 10.11: *Elements of the BMM*

Ends are expressed as a vision and desired results. A **vision** is an overall image of what the organisation wants to be or to become. For instance, a car rental company's vision statement might be *to be the car rental brand of choice for business users in the countries in which we operate.*

Desired results are goals or objectives. **Goals** are specific, long-term desired results. **Objectives** are steps towards achieving goals. Examples of goals for a car rental company are *to provide industry-leading customer service* and *to provide well-maintained cars.* Examples of objectives are *by end of current year to be rated in the top six car rental companies in each operating country in the European Union* and *during the fourth quarter of the current year, no more than 1% of rentals need the car to be replaced because of mechanical breakdown (excluding accidents).*

Means are what the organisation has decided to do in order to become what it wants to be. They are organised as a mission, courses of action and directives.

A **mission** specifies the ongoing operational activities as a set of core competencies. For the car rental company, it might be *to provide a car rental service across Europe and North America to business and personal customers.*

Courses of action are what the organisation has decided to do; a way of configuring some aspect of the enterprise to channel efforts towards desired results. They are specified as strategies or tactics. **Strategies** are long-term courses of action with wide scope; **tactics** are short-term courses of action of narrow scope. An example of a strategy statement for a car rental company is *to operate nation-wide at major airports in each country within the European Union and compete effectively with other premium car rental companies.* An example of a tactical statement is *to issue each member of the sales force with a digital assistant able to access central pricing and booking systems.*

Directives are business policies or business rules. **Business policies** exist to govern strategy and tactics. A **business rule** is an actionable element of business policy. Chapter 3 gave a series of business rules that might implement the policy established for a car rental company that customers who make early bookings or have a club card get a discount. **Business processes** realise courses of action, so it should be possible to specify the activities of a particular business process using process modelling techniques as discussed in Chapter 2 in support of a particular set of courses of action.

An **influencer** is something that can cause changes that affect the enterprise in its employment of means or achievement of ends. Influencers can be either internal or external to the enterprise.

External influencers are similar to the idea of external stakeholders or external agencies in an organisation's environment (see Chapter 7). The BMM standard lists the categories of external influencer as competitors, customers, partners, regulators, suppliers and technology. There is also an aggregate category, environment. For a car rental company, external influencers might be *the presence of 'premium-brand' car rental companies such as Hertz and Avis* (competitor), *car models, prices and contract terms and conditions offered by car manufacturers* (supplier) and *vehicle identification and tracking systems* (technology).

Internal influencer categories include assumptions, corporate values, habits, infrastructure, issues, management prerogatives and resources. Many are similar to the aspects of organisation culture discussed in Chapter 2. For example, the car rental company might maintain the habit that *managers are generally promoted from within the company*. In contrast an infrastructure influencer might be *the rentals information system used by the company was developed for individual rentals and hence it cannot currently support corporate rentals.*

Assessments are judgements about an influencer on the enterprise's ability to employ its means or achieve its ends. An assessment is made when one or more influencers indicate changes that could affect the business. Potential impacts are identified and evaluated in terms of risk and potential reward, and what effects they would have on achievement of ends (vision, goals and objectives) and employment of means (mission, strategies, tactics, business policies and business rules). SWOT (strengths/weaknesses/opportunities/threats) analyses are suggested for assessments.

Reflect
What do your think are the key advantages of using BMM for the specification of business models?

An organisation has to decide how to react to influencers. This often requires changes to some ends and/or means, which must be carried forward into operations. The BMM includes 'placeholders' which reference where in the operational business the changes have been, or will be, made. It provides placeholders for referencing business processes, business rules, organization units, fixed assets, resources, and offerings (products and services).

Recap

An informatics strategy defines the structure within which information, information systems and ICT are to be applied in an organisation. It should establish an organisation's long-term informatics infrastructure, which will allow information systems to be designed and implemented efficiently and effectively. It is particularly directed at avoiding fragmentation, redundancy and inconsistency between information systems. It is also a key vehicle in promoting the interoperability of systems. So an informatics strategy should be directed at ensuring an optimal 'fit' between an organisation and its information systems. It typically comprises three levels, an information strategy, information systems strategy and ICT strategy. It can be specified using an organisation information model, an organisation process model and an associated information/process matrix. It should document the current information system portfolio and a future information system portfolio. It should include an ICT systems model and standards for hardware, software, communication technology and data management technology.

Informatics management

Informatics management is the process of implementing plans produced by informatics planning and monitoring their results. It is a key control process for effective project management, and in turn, informatics planning forms a control for informatics management. Therefore, informatics management is one of the critical activities of the informatics service (see Chapter 11).

Information, information systems and ICT management

Michael Earl (1989) has distinguished between three forms of management relevant to informatics, on the criteria of their primary objective, the basis of management and the primary focus and responsibility:

Information management: That part of informatics management concerned with the management of information.

Information systems management: The process of managing the current information systems architecture and implementing the information systems strategy.

- INFORMATION MANAGEMENT is concerned with the general planning, regulation and coordination of information policies in the organisation. It determines the overall strategic direction of the organisation in terms of its information. Earl suggests that it needs to be a role of senior management.
- INFORMATION SYSTEMS MANAGEMENT is concerned with the management of information-handling applications in the organisation. It deals with the planning, execution and operation of information systems to support organisational activities. As such, Earl suggests that it is a role for managers of business units.
- **ICT management** is concerned with the maintenance of the ICT infrastructure, developing new applications and maintaining existing ICT applications. It is the concern of technical specialists.

This framework is interesting in that it suggests that a range of competencies are required in the management of information, information systems and ICT, and that the forms of management should logically be sited at various levels within organisations. It also presumes that business managers are given informatics knowledge, experience and responsibilities through some form of training. As discussed in an earlier section, it suggests that organisations need to have three levels of planning in place, and three corresponding levels of informatics strategy.

Management, strategy and infrastructure

An informatics strategy is the major output of informatics planning. This acts as the major control input into the informatics management process. Informatics management is also constrained by the current informatics infrastructure. Hence, this is also a key control input into the management process. Each element of informatics management takes responsibility for different aspects of both strategy and infrastructure.

There are two major aspects to informatics management, controlling the informatics infrastructure and implementing the informatics strategy. Control means essentially managing the current information, information systems and ICT; this is a regulatory process. Implementation consists essentially of managing the development of the future information, information systems and ICT; this is an adaptive process.

Ideally, information management should drive information systems management, which in turn drives ICT management. An organisation needs to identify its information needs, then decide on the information systems that will supply those needs, and finally decide on appropriate ICT for supporting its information systems.

Information management activities

In recent years many organisations have recognised the importance of information, and of effective management of this critical resource. The rise of information management is a result of the recognition that information is critical to the effective operation of activity systems, and particularly to measuring their performance. It should be managed in a similar manner to other organisational resources such as human resources (staff) and material resources (plant and machinery).

In essence, information management activities consist of the two major processes of managing the current information infrastructure and implementing the future information strategy. Managing an information infrastructure includes activities such as continuously evaluating organisation information needs, identifying integration and interoperability opportunities, maintaining the organisation information model and process model, and maintaining organisational standards for information and process representation. Implementing an information strategy includes activities such as enforcing information, data and process standards, re-engineering aspects of the information and process model, and checking the conformance of new information systems with the information infrastructure.

A number of terms are used to describe various approaches to what is here called information management. This section considers three: data management or administration (the administration of the data resource), knowledge management (the management of organisational memory) and records management. The related issue of content management (the management of web-based material) was considered in Chapter 6. All four are fundamentally forms of information management, and all are concerned with the administration of various aspects of the information resource. This might be in traditional paper-based form, or stored in a range of ICT including databases, data warehouses and web material.

It is easy to confuse data management as an organisational function (what used to be referred to as data administration) with data management as a technical role (particularly focused around issues of database administration). DATA ADMINISTRATION involves the planning, management, documentation and operation of an organisation's data resource (Gillenson, 1982). It is concerned with the management of an organisation's metadata: that is, data about data, and is a function that deals with the conceptual or business view of an organisation's data resource. In contrast, **database administration** involves the technical implementation of database systems, managing the database systems currently in use and setting and enforcing policies for their use.

Data administration: The function concerned with the management, planning and documentation of the data resource of an organisation.

Why is data such a critical resource for organisations? Consider a university. Without data on for instance what students are enrolled, what students are taking which modules and what grades students have achieved, a university would be unable to operate effectively. Now imagine that the different university departments or schools maintain their own distinctive collections of data, with their own distinctive definitions for data items. As a consequence, data are frequently missing or incomplete, are frequently out of date, and staff have incomplete knowledge on what data are collected, and where they are kept.

In the larger sense, data management encompasses all of the issues of data storage, integration, sharing and security discussed in Chapter 6, as well as others important for effective management of the data resource such as data definition, data integrity and data control. In this sense effective data administration inherently assumes an interest in both the physical and electronic records of organisations, so it includes records management (DAMA, 2007). **Records management** is defined by the International Standards Organisation as 'the field of management responsible for the efficient and systematic control of the creation, receipt, maintenance, use and disposition of records, including the processes for capturing and maintaining evidence of and information about business activities and transactions in the form of records' (ISO 15489, 2001).

Data management is important not only for internal processes, but for effective data sharing between organisations, so it is particularly important to effective B2B eCommerce (see Chapter 8). Key innovations such as eProcurement in both the private and public sectors could not occur without interorganisational standards for data storage and transfer.

Recently it has been argued that knowledge is a significant resource for organisations (Alavi and Leidner, 2001), because increased knowledge leads to an increased ability to perform effectively. Knowledge is also complex and usually difficult to imitate, so it has the potential to generate long-term and sustainable competitive advantage. When organisations lose personnel with significant amounts of knowledge (when they retire, quit, or are made redundant through downsizing) it is a significant loss. It is less so if their knowledge remains in the organisation, so there has been much emphasis on capturing, storing and sharing knowledge.

People clearly acquire knowledge that improves their performance in specific fields, but to what degree is it appropriate to speak of groups and organisations as having knowledge? One useful concept is **organisational memory**. This is what an organisation knows about its processes and its environment. The knowledge in an organisation's memory is a critical resource for organisations in that it enables them to act effectively in economic markets.

If knowledge is networked information (see Chapter 3), then information is clearly a prerequisite to effective knowledge. KNOWLEDGE MANAGEMENT can be seen as the topmost layer of management processes in organisations that are reliant on effective information management. It consists of three key processes (Davenport and Prusak, 2000):

- KNOWLEDGE CREATION involves the acquisition of knowledge from organisational members and the creation of new organisational knowledge.
- KNOWLEDGE CODIFICATION and storage consists of the representation of knowledge for ease of retrieval.

Knowledge management: Consists of knowledge creation, knowledge codification and knowledge transfer.

Knowledge codification: The representation of knowledge for ease of retrieval.

Knowledge creation: The acquisition of knowledge from organisational members and the creation of new organisational knowledge.

Knowledge transfer: The communication and sharing of knowledge among organisational members.

▸ KNOWLEDGE TRANSFER involves the communication and sharing of knowledge between organisational members.

Information systems management activities

Information systems management is concerned with the management of information-handling applications, both computerised and non-computerised. Its activities include management of the current information systems infrastructure, which involves maintaining an inventory of it, and ensuring its effective operation and maintenance. It also includes managing the development of information systems planned in the information systems strategy. This involves monitoring and controlling the range of development projects both under way and planned. As a consequence, controlling budgets for information systems investment is important. This involves strategically monitoring planned against occurred expenditure. Finally, completed information systems need to be evaluated. This involves conducting rigorous summative evaluations to determine how successful they are. For abandoned projects it also involves conducting a post-mortem analysis to ensure that the organisation learns from its mistakes (see Chapter 9).

Did you know? The idea and importance of information management arose initially out of the information processing metaphor of the organisation (Chapter 2) and particularly Herbert Simon's work on decision making.

ICT management activities

Reflect
It has been suggested that a chief information officer (CIO) role should be created in organisations, to oversee all their informatics management. In what way do you think this role might be important to effective informatics management?

ICT management is concerned with the maintenance of the ICT infrastructure, developing new applications and maintaining existing ICT applications. Its activities are the two major processes of managing the current ICT architecture and implementing the future ICT strategy.

Managing ICT infrastructure involves activities such as maintaining ICT system standards, hardware standards, software standards, data standards and communication standards. It also involves operational activity such as monitoring the total cost of ownership of the ICT infrastructure and providing helpdesk facilities. These issues are considered in Chapter 11.

Implementing the ICT strategy involves managing the development of bespoke and packaged ICT systems, the maintenance of existing ICT systems, the purchase of hardware, software, data and communication technology. It also involves making sure ICT systems match with corporate objectives established in the organisation strategy.

Key skill 

ICT governance

IT or **ICT governance** is a subset of the discipline of corporate governance, focused on ICT systems and their performance. Its primary goals are to ensure that ICT investments generate business value and to mitigate the risks associated with ICT (Weill and Ross, 2004). This is achieved by implementing organisational structures and processes with well-defined roles and clear lines of responsibility for, or decision rights over, various aspects of informatics infrastructure.

There are three reasons for the contemporary interest in ICT governance:

- ▸ A growing acknowledgement that ICT is critical to the modern organisation and that therefore key decision making in this area must be a responsibility at board level.
- ▸ An acknowledgment that ICT system projects easily get out of control and this can profoundly affect the performance of an organisation.
- ▸ The fact that certain organisations, particularly in the public sector, have to follow compliance rules such as the Sarbanes–Oxley Act in the United States and Basel II in Europe.

There are a number of frameworks for ICT governance. One of the most prominent is Control Objectives for Information and related Technology (COBIT). This is a framework of measures, indicators, processes and best practices for ICT management created by the

Information Systems Audit and Control Association (ISACA), and the IT Governance Institute (ITGI). Originally created in 1992, COBIT assists managers, auditors and ICT users in achieving benefits through the use of ICT and developing appropriate control of the ICT infrastructure.

COBIT 4.1, the latest version of the framework, has 34 high-level processes which cover 210 control objectives categorised in four domains: Planning and Organization, Acquisition and Implementation, Delivery and Support, and Monitoring (see Figure 10.12) These domains overlap with both the planning and management processes considered in this chapter and the operational activities discussed in Chapter 11.

- **Planning and organization** focuses on the use of ICT to achieve business goals. High-level control objectives for this domain include defining an ICT strategy and ICT infrastructure, managing ICT human resources and managing ICT projects.
- **Acquire and implement** focuses on identifying ICT requirements, acquiring technology and implementing ICT systems aligned with business processes. High-level control objectives for the domain include acquiring and maintaining application software, enabling operation and use, and managing change.
- **Delivery and support** focuses on ensuring the effective operation of ICT systems and support processes. High-level control objectives for the domain include defining and managing service levels, educating and training users, and managing operations.
- **Monitoring and evaluation** focuses on continually assessing needs and whether ICT infrastructure meets them. High-level control objectives for the domain include monitoring and evaluating ICT processes and ensuring regulatory compliance.

Reflect
Some people argue that the discipline of ICT governance and frameworks such as COBIT might constrain ICT innovation in organisations. Why do you think this might be the case?

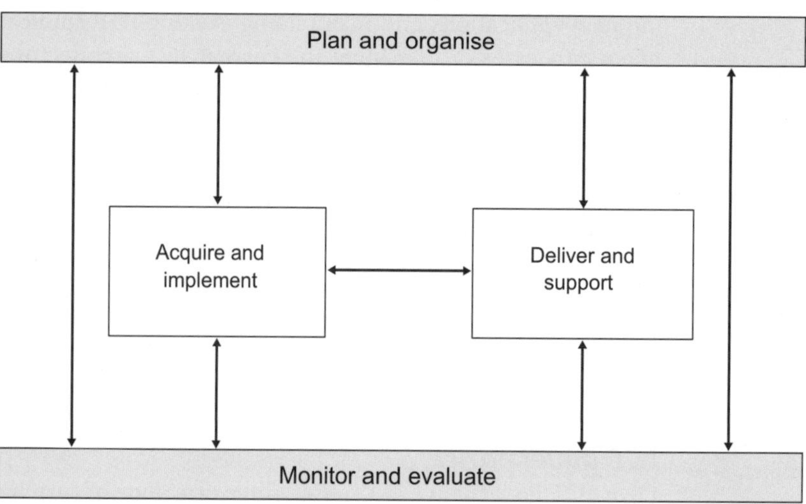

Figure 10.12: *COBIT domains*

Summary

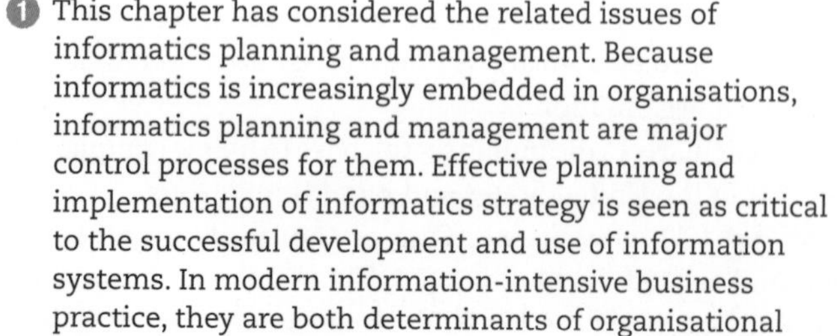
1. This chapter has considered the related issues of informatics planning and management. Because informatics is increasingly embedded in organisations, informatics planning and management are major control processes for them. Effective planning and implementation of informatics strategy is seen as critical to the successful development and use of information systems. In modern information-intensive business practice, they are both determinants of organisational success (see Chapter 9).

2. Informatics planning is the process of deciding on the optimal informatics infrastructure. It uses as input three major forms of strategic analysis: organisational analysis, environmental analysis and technological analysis. There are three major approaches to planning an informatics strategy: target-driven, resource-driven and implementation-driven. In the target-driven form, informatics planning involves setting up a planning unit and approach, assessing the current informatics infrastructure, establishing a vision and specifying an informatics strategy.

3 Establishing a vision for informatics normally involves assessing the competitive advantage that information systems can deliver. Among the frameworks for this are critical success factors, the five forces model, the customer resource life-cycle, and value-chain or value-network analysis.

4 An informatics strategy defines the structure within which information, information systems and ICT is to be applied within an organisation. An informatics strategy should establish an organisation's long-term informatics infrastructure, which will allow information systems to be designed and implemented efficiently and effectively. It is particularly directed at avoiding fragmentation, redundancy and inconsistency, and is also a key vehicle in promoting the interoperability of systems. Hence, an informatics strategy should be directed at ensuring an optimal 'fit' between an organisation and its information systems.

5 There are three levels to an informatics strategy: an information strategy, an information systems strategy and an ICT strategy. An information strategy is specified through an organisation information model, an organisation process model and an associated information/process matrix. An information systems strategy consists of documentation of the current and future information system portfolios. An ICT strategy includes an ICT systems model and standards for hardware, software, communication technology and data technology.

6 There are three forms of informatics management: information management, information systems management and ICT management, which correspond both to the three levels of informatics strategy and to the three levels of informatics infrastructure discussed in Chapter 3. One side of informatics management involves implementing strategy in each of these three areas: that is, implementing future information systems that deliver new forms of information to support new forms of activity The other side of informatics management involves managing the existing informatics infrastructure: ensuring that current information systems work efficiently and effectively in support of current activity.

Chapter 11 considers the management of existing infrastructure and operations in more detail. The operation of the current informatics infrastructure is a neglected but critical part of the provision of informatics, and is often run as a service partnership in organisations.

Focus on Value

Most modern organisations could not perform effectively without information, information systems and ICT. Hence, there is key value for organisations in controlling their informatics infrastructure. The planning of informatics strategy should be aligned with general business strategy. Following from this there is key value in managing informatics infrastructure appropriately. This means controlling current informatics infrastructure as well as implementing new informatics infrastructure.

Review test

1	Put the classic phases for informatics planning into the correct order. Label the first phase 1 and so on. ☐ Developing the information systems architecture ☐ Assessing the informatics infrastructure ☐ Setting up a planning organisation ☐ Developing the informatics services strategic plan ☐ Developing information services operational plans and budgets ☐ Establishing a vision of how the organisation should use information systems
2	A CSF is a factor that is deemed crucial to the success of a business. True or false? ☐ True ☐ False
3	Identify Porter's five forces that influence the competitive position of a company. Select all that apply. ☐ Customer bargaining power ☐ Industrial rivalry, the competitive position of rival organisations ☐ Competitive advantage ☐ Supplier bargaining power ☐ Threat of substitutes ☐ Company size ☐ Barriers to entry, threat of new entrants
4	The ____________ considers a firm's relationship with its customers (the customer chain) and how this relationship can be changed or enhanced by the strategic application of ICT. Fill in the blank.
5	Distinguish strategy from tactics. Write two sentences.
6	An informatics ____________ is the major output of informatics planning. Fill in the blank.
7	An informatics strategy comprises three levels – what are they? Select all that apply. ☐ ICT strategy ☐ Information strategy ☐ Computing strategy ☐ Information systems strategy
8	What makes an information system strategic? Write two sentences.
9	What is the purpose of Business Motivation Modelling? Write two sentences.
10	How do strategic plans differ from operational plans? Write two sentences.

PART 4

11	As a minimum there are three major elements of an information strategy – what are they? Select all that apply. ☐ Process/information matrix ☐ Organisation information model ☐ Organisation process model ☐ Object model
12	A channel strategy is a set of choices about how, and through what means, goods and services are delivered to customers. True or false? ☐ True ☐ False
13	Information management is concerned with the maintenance of the ICT infrastructure, developing new applications and maintaining existing ICT applications. True or false? ☐ True ☐ False
14	Why is ICT governance important to informatics management? Write two sentences.

Exercises

1. Write a brief description of what you feel should be included in any organisational analysis. Do the same for an environmental and technology analysis.
2. Determine how planning is best described in an organisation known to you – target, resource or implementation-driven.
3. Determine whether there is a specific unit devoted to informatics planning in an organisation known to you. Determine the way it is organised.
4. Attempt to apply one of the approaches to establishing an informatics vision to a public sector organisation such as a university.
5. Determine whether an organisation known to you has an organisation information model and process model.
6. Provide an example of each of the activities listed under managing the information, information systems or ICT infrastructure.
7. Develop a small analysis of how information systems might be used to improve the strategic position of an organisation using one or more of the frameworks discussed in the chapter.
8. List two critical success factors for an organisation known to you.
9. Produce one example of how information systems might affect Porter's five forces model.
10. From the planning frameworks discussed, choose what you feel to be the most effective framework and briefly justify your choice.
11. Consider an information system known to you. In what respect would you define it as strategic, and why?
12. Find one example of a modern strategic information system in the cost leadership, differentiation or niche strategy.
13. Find one example of a system which can be regarded as strategic but which is built on existing informatics infrastructure.

Projects

1. Informatics planning is important but do organisations engage in it? Investigate the degree to which a small sample of organisations conduct systematic informatics planning. Determine the forms of informatics planning undertaken.
2. Find an organisation that conducts informatics planning. Determine the key benefits experienced by this organisation. Also, attempt to determine the costs associated with conducting informatics planning. In other words, what sort of business case does the organisation have for conducting continuous informatics planning?
3. Assess the current state of the information systems in an organisation known to you. Attempt to measure the degree to which the information systems are integrated. How has the infrastructure been built over time?
4. The customer resource life-cycle can be seen as a model of the customer chain. Determine its applicability for considering B2C eCommerce. In other words, assess how useful it is for considering ways in which an organisation may use B2C eCommerce to improve its performance.
5. Analyse either B2B or B2C eCommerce in terms of Porter's five forces model. In other words, what effect does B2B eCommerce have on issues such as supplier bargaining power?
6. Collect data on a given organisation's informatics strategy. Does it distinguish between an information, information systems and ICT strategy? How was strategy formulated? How is it used and maintained?
7. Develop a high-level organisation information model, organisation process model and information/process matrix for some organisation. How useful are such models practically to help decide where information systems are important? Develop a high-level information systems strategy based on your information strategy.
8. Use business motivation modelling to produce a specification of a new business plan for a particular company. How successful is such modelling for linking strategy, processes and technology?
9. Consider outsourcing as part of an informatics strategy. Examine some of the literature on this topic, and determine the critical success factors for successful outsourcing of informatics.
10. Develop a case study of a strategic information system in the area of eCommerce. What made the information system strategic? How long did the system remain strategic?

11 The management of informatics is likely to be organised differently in different organisations. Try to investigate some differences in a small range of organisations. For instance, how closely do organisations distinguish between information, information systems and ICT management?

12 ICT governance is an important part of corporate governance, and organisations are increasingly required to implement controls in these areas. Investigate the application of ICT governance in a range of organisations. Identify the approaches used and the costs and benefits of applying ICT governance.

13 Earl argues that informatics management demands different competencies. Take an organisation and try to examine the extent to which the management of informatics is distributed through the technical and business sides.

Further reading

Robson (1997), although somewhat dated, still provides one of the most accessible accounts of informatics planning and strategy. Applegate, Austin and McFarlan (2002) build on the classic work by Cash, McFarlan and McKeney (1992) on Informatics management. However, Ward and Peppard (2002) provide one of the most cited texts on planning issues as it affects informatics. Galliers and Leidner (2002) also provide a good overview of issues relating to the management of informatics.

References

Alavi, M. and Leidner, D. (2001) 'Knowledge management and knowledge management systems', *Management Information Systems Quarterly* **25**(1): 107–36.

Ansoff, H. I. (1965) *Corporate Strategy*. New York, McGraw-Hill.

Applegate, L. M., Austin, R. D. and McFarlan, W. (2002) *Corporate Information Strategy and Management: Text and Cases*. New York, McGraw-Hill.

Cash, J. I., McFarlan, F. W. and McKeney, J. L. (1992) *Corporate Information Systems Management*. Homewood, Ill., Richard Irvin.

DAMA (2007) DAMA-DMBOK Functional Framework, Data Management Association.

Davenport, T. H. and Prusak, L. (2000) *Working Knowledge: How organisations manage what they know*. Boston, Mass., Harvard Business School Press.

Earl, M. J. (1989) *Management Strategies for Information Technology*. Hemel Hempstead, Prentice Hall.

Galliers, B. and Leidner, D. (2002) *Strategic Information Management: Challenges and Strategies in Managing Information Systems*. New York, Butterworth-Heinemann.

Gillenson, M. L. (1982) 'The state of practice of data administration', *Communications of the ACM* **25**(10): 699–706.

Gray, I. (1984) *General and Industrial Management*. New York, IEEE Press.

Ives, B. and Learmonth, G. P. (1984) 'The information system as a competitive weapon', *Communications of the ACM* **27**(12): 1193–201.

Johnson, G., Scholes, K. and Whittington, R. (2007) *Exploring Corporate Strategy: Text and cases*. Englewood-Cliffs, N.J., Prentice-Hall.

Lord, C. (2000) 'The practicalities of developing a successful e-Business strategy', *Journal of Business Strategy* **21**(2): 40–47.

OMG (2007) *Business Motivation Model (BMM) Specification*. Object Management Group.

Porter, M. E. (1996) 'What is strategy?' *Harvard Business Review* Nov–Dec: 59–78.

Porter, M. E. (2001) 'Strategy and the Internet', *Harvard Business Review* **79**(3): 63–78.

Porter, M. E. and Millar, V. E. (1985) 'How information gives you competitive advantage', *Harvard Business Review* **63**(4): 149–60.

Robson, W. (1997) *Strategic Management and Information Systems: An integrated approach*. London, Prentice-Hall.

Ward, J. and Peppard, J. (2002) *Strategic Planning for Information Systems*. Chichester, John Wiley.

Weill, P. and Ross, J. (2004) *IT Governance: How top performers manage IT decision rights for superior results*. Boston, Mass., Harvard Business School Press.

CHAPTER 11

Services, projects and operations

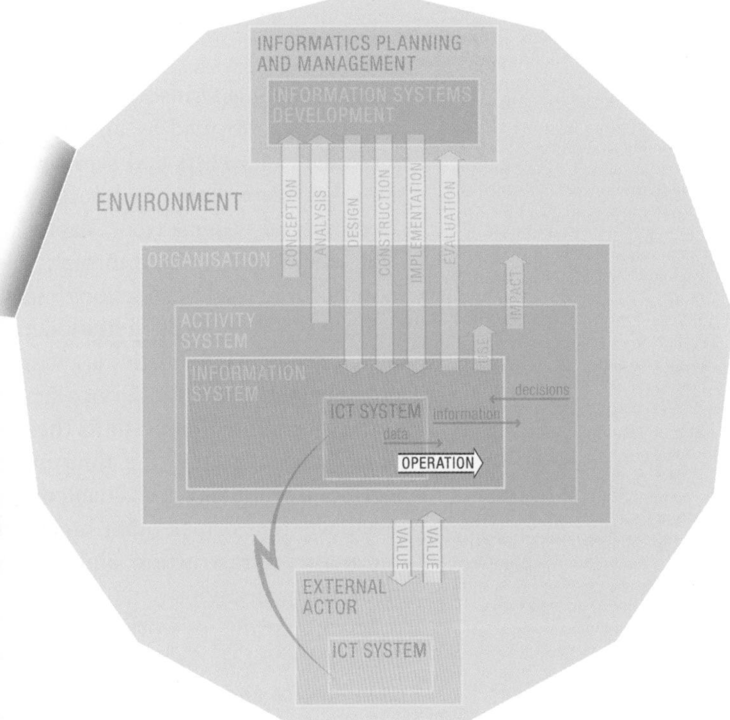

Great services are not cancelled by one act or by one single error.

Benjamin Disraeli (1804–1881)

Civilisation advances by extending the number of important operations which we can perform without thinking about them.

Alfred North Whitehead (1867–1947)

LEARNING OUTCOMES	PRINCIPLES
Explain the structure of the informatics industry in terms of the distinction between producers and consumers.	The informatics industry is a significant element of the service sector of the economy. Actors in this sector can be distinguished as either informatics producers or informatics consumers.
Describe what is meant by the informatics service and define various ways it can be organised, including outsourcing.	In consuming organisations with a significant informatics infrastructure it is important to establish the form and management of an important function: the informatics service. Many organisations have decided that the whole or part of this function should be outsourced to external vendors.
Distinguish between informatics management and project management, and explain the distinction between project planning, project control and project organisation.	The process of informatics management was described in Chapter 10. Since much informatics work is organised as projects, good project management practice is important. Project management involves the interrelated processes of planning a project, establishing a project organisation and controlling a project.
Define what is meant by informatics operations in terms of the philosophy of ICT services management, and outline some of the major processes involved in managing ICT services.	Ensuring the effective operation of informatics infrastructure is an important part of informatics management. Operations is now generally considered as a set of interrelated service processes including service strategy, service delivery, service support and service improvement.

CHAPTER OUTLINE

Introduction

In organisational terms a service is the non-material equivalent of a good. It typically involves an activity performed by an organisation for an external stakeholder (see Chapter 7). The vocabulary of servers and services is familiar in the informatics infrastructure of organisations. Service-oriented architecture, for instance, is seen as a means of improving the interoperability of systems (see Chapter 6). This chapter considers the term **services** in another light: the ways in which informatics as an organisational function is delivered as a service, or more accurately as a collection of services.

Since ICT is embedded in modern organisational life as well as in the wider environment, not surprisingly informatics is a vast industry of both producers and consumers, which forms an important part of the service sector in an economy.

In consuming organisations there is normally a function charged with developing, maintaining and operating the informatics infrastructure, which is known as the **informatics service.** Technology has enabled organisations to transform their informatics service as they have transformed other organisational functions. The outsourcing of various aspects of informatics infrastructure, and how to manage this effectively, are therefore critical issues for modern organisations.

Much informatics work is organised in projects, so the effective management of projects is critical not only to the successful development of information systems, but also to their maintenance and operation. The servicing of informatics operations is frequently taken for granted and unexplored in texts on business information systems. Because of its increasing importance to modern-day organisations, this chapter considers a number of issues of concern, including ensuring the availability and continuity of informatics infrastructure. To help organise this topic, recent approaches in the area of **ICT services management** are discussed.

The informatics industry

Information systems and their associated technologies are essential for the effective working of modern economies, societies and polities. Therefore, not surprisingly, a vast industry has developed worldwide to service the informatics needs of organisations, groups and individuals. Many people are now employed in information-rich industries, and these are heavily reliant on efficient and effective information systems.

Informatics practice: The practical application of informatics knowledge and skill in organisations.
Informatics profession: The bodies exercising control over informatics practice.

Informatics is primarily part of the service sector of the economy. One of the notable facets of the change in employment patterns in Western countries over the last 40 years has been the rise in the service sector. The most rapid growth in employment has been in office-based private services such as financial, business and professional services.

Informatics personnel work either for a producer of information systems and ICT, or for an established user of information systems and technology; what we might call informatics consumers. Providers produce elements of information systems, and consumers use them for organisational purposes.

Producers

Informatics providers can be divided into:

- **Hardware providers**, organisations that produce computing devices, input devices, output devices, storage devices and communication devices (see Chapter 6). Representative organisations are Dell, Intel and Apple.
- **Software providers**, organisations that produce software such as office software and enterprise software. Representative organisations are Oracle and Microsoft.
- **Application providers**, a special type of software provider offering integrated package solutions to informatics infrastructure problems. A representative company is SAP AG.
- **Communication infrastructure providers**, companies that build, maintain and support the physical telecommunication infrastructure of organisations, regions and countries. Representative companies are BT (British Telecom) and Deutsche Telefon.

- **Internet service providers**, companies that provide access to the Internet for individuals, groups and organisations. Representative companies are America Online (AOL) and BTInternet.
- **Application service providers** (see below), companies that operate and maintain aspects of an organisation's informatics infrastructure. They are similar to what used to be known as service bureaux. A representative company is Storagetek (Sun).
- **Informatics consultancies**, companies that provide informatics services particularly in the areas of planning, management and development. A representative company is PriceWaterhouseCoopers.
- **Outsourcing vendors**, companies that offer informatics outsourcing solutions either in whole or in part to companies. Representative companies are EDS and CapGemini.

Reflect
How much of a typical Western economy do you think the informatics industry makes up? How much does it contribute to the gross domestic product?

Case check:
Case 11, Microsoft

Microsoft was founded to develop and sell interpreters for the programming language BASIC, which ran on an early microcomputer, the Altair 8800. It rose to dominate the personal computer market with its sales of the operating system MS-DOS, produced in the mid-1980s.

Microsoft is organised as three core divisions: the Microsoft Platform Products and Services Division, the Microsoft Business Division and the Microsoft Entertainment and Devices Division.

The Platform Products and Services Division produces the Windows operating system, Microsoft Visual Studio (a set of development tools) and enterprise software such as Microsoft SQL Server (a relational DBMS).

The Microsoft Business Division produces Microsoft Office, which includes Word (a word processor), Access (a personal relational database application), Excel (a spreadsheet program), Outlook (Windows-only groupware), PowerPoint (presentation software), and Publisher (desktop publishing software).

The Entertainment and Devices Division produces software for mobile devices such as Windows CE for PDAs and gaming software for its own gaming console the Xbox, and computer games that run on Windows PCs, including titles such as *Age of Empires*, *Halo* and the *Microsoft Flight Simulator* series. It also produces a line of reference works which includes encyclopaedias and atlases, under the name Encarta.

Consumers

There are informatics consumers in almost all industrial sectors, such as manufacturing, agriculture, process industries such as petrochemicals, transport, financial services, retail, and local and central government. Some sectors are much more advanced in ICT use than others. For instance, the financial services sector continues to invest heavily in ICT, but the agriculture sector continues to be a poor investor.

Informatics consumers can also be divided into large, medium, small and micro enterprises. In recent years in the European Union there has been a particular focus on small and medium-sized enterprises (SMEs), companies with less than 250 employees. They are seen as the major seedbed for innovation in industrial economies. There have been several major initiatives to stimulate their adoption of ICT and eBusiness.

Informatics careers

Informatics professionals work for either informatics providers or informatics consumers, and have become an increasing part of the workforce of developed countries. This is clearly an indicator of the growth in the information society (Chapter 3).

Informatics is a relatively young area of industrial practice, and one that is subject to rapid change. Recruitment patterns tend to be driven by requirements for short-term technological skills, such as the ability to program in the Java language, rather than longer-term transferable skills such as the ability to design effective and efficient programs. This has made it difficult to establish coherent and consistent career patterns across the industry.

Professional bodies such as the British Computer Society (BCS) have attempted to address some of these difficulties. For instance, the BCS has developed an **industry structure model** which tries to specify career paths for informatics professionals. It classifies some 200 roles in the informatics domain into nine broad functional areas: (1) management, (2) policy, (3) planning and research, (4) systems development and maintenance, (5) service delivery, (6) technical advice and consultancy, (7) quality, (8) customer relations, education and training, and (9) support and administration.

Ten levels of autonomy, accountability and responsibility are defined across these nine functional areas, ranging from unskilled entry through experienced practitioner to senior manager/director/consultant. Not all functions are performed across all levels of responsibility. Programming as a role, for instance, only involves the lower levels, whereas management involves the higher levels. For each role the BCS has specified the ideal background for the person to fill it, as well as the range of activities they are likely to undertake. The emphasis is on generic skills such as an ability to design and build databases, rather than specific vendor-related skills such as abilities in the Oracle tool-set.

Reflect
There is a gender imbalance in people opting for a career in informatics: more boys rather than girls take secondary, tertiary and higher-level courses with an ICT component. Why do you think this is, and how would you begin to address this imbalance?

Because informatics is now central to most organisations, the demand for skilled informatics staff has remained steady, and in some sectors has grown significantly over the last decade, fuelled by growth in eBusiness and eCommerce strategies in both the private and public sectors. Because there is a shortage of skilled informatics professionals in many countries, many Western economies have looked to other countries worldwide to supply workers. Many US companies, for instance have outsourced informatics activities such as development and maintenance to the Indian subcontinent, particularly the Bangalore region. Countries such as the United Kingdom have included informatics workers in their list of preferred occupations, so that those who offer these skills get priority in immigration procedures.

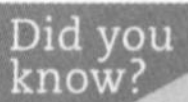

The UK bank Lloyds TSB claimed in 2008 that the move of two-thirds of its ICT staff to India was not to save money. It was because it could not source enough skilled ICT people from the UK higher education system.

The informatics service

As 'consumers' in the informatics industry, most medium to large-scale organisations have people specifically employed in informatics work. This section considers a number of important issues relating to the organisation of business units that do this work. Some organisations called this the ICT or IS department, or the DP (data processing) department. This chapter refers to it generically as the **informatics service**, to emphasise that in most organisations information systems and technology are a critical strategic service supplied to the organisation in support of other activity.

Structure

Some organisations, particularly small organisations, do not have a specific section or department specialising in informatics, but there is a specialist function in most medium to large-scale organisations, in both the private and public sectors. It can be structured in several different ways. This section discusses its structuring by division of labour and location.

Division of labour: The way in which tasks and responsibilities are assigned to members of an organisation.

DIVISION OF LABOUR refers to the way in which various jobs or roles are defined and structured in the informatics service (see Chapter 2). It used to involve rigid job specifications based around a hierarchy of control. Over the last 20 years or so a number of pressures for change have caused the gradual fragmentation of this structure, and newer, more flexible structures for the informatics service have emerged.

Figure 11.1 shows the old structure, which derived from the day-to-day demands of building and running informatics on large, centralised mainframes. It had a hierarchy of clearly delineated jobs. At the bottom were operating staff, tasked with maintaining the operation of the centralised mainframe and the systems that ran on it. Next came programmers, organised typically into groups such as maintenance programmers and development programmers. Development programmers built new applications while maintenance programmers repaired and extended existing applications. Systems analysts were the next rung in the hierarchy. These were professionals primarily involved in the analysis and design of information systems, who made contact with business users. Many organisations segmented staff further into project teams of analysts, programmers and sometimes operators, each headed by a project manager. The head of department was often called the data processing (DP) manager. In a large organisation there were frequently a number of middle-level managers such as operations managers, development managers and maintenance managers, each coordinating a particular aspect of informatics work.

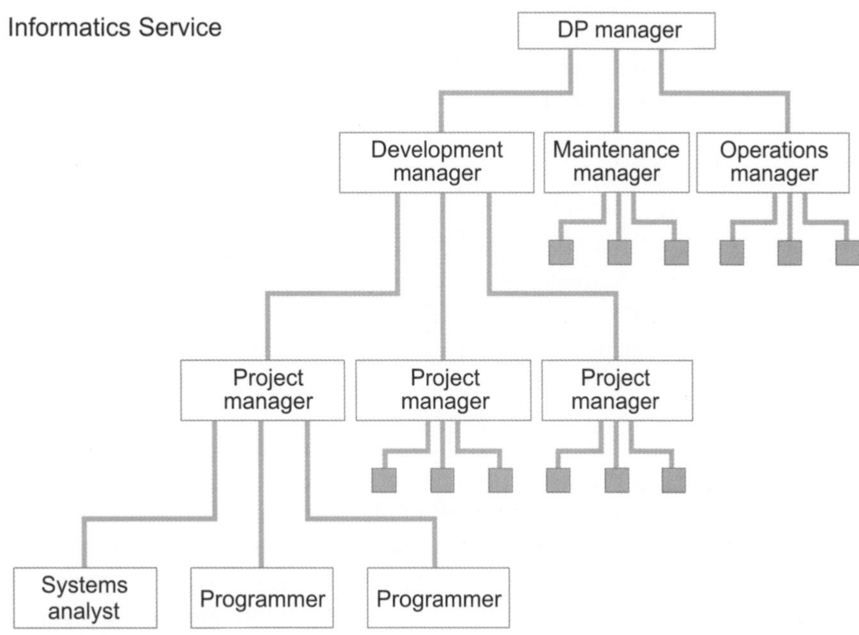

Figure 11.1: *Traditional structure of the informatics service*

The technical changes in the 1970s and 1980s which led to changes in this structure accelerated during the 1990s:

- Desktop computers came to be used more and more, which meant that computing power could be sited wherever it was required. Desktop packages such as word-processing software and spreadsheets were specifically written for end-users rather than ICT professionals, so they gained much more experience of computing and became much more confident in expressing their requirements, sometimes even building applications themselves.
- The developing use of databases and in particular the database approach meant that organisations began to plan for and manage data at the corporate level. Organisations saw key added value from integrating information systems across sectors.
- More and cheaper processing power and storage capacity meant that these resources no longer needed to be centralised (see Chapter 6). Processing and storage could be distributed around the organisation on diverse sets of hardware platforms and diverse software-enabled applications to cooperate across local and wide area networks.

Information centre: A structure for the informatics service in which the service acts as a centre of expertise for other business units.

In response to these pressures and others, the informatics service recast itself in various different forms. One was the INFORMATION CENTRE, a body of informatics expertise whose role was to service other departments, which handled a large proportion of their informatics work themselves. So unlike the traditional ICT department, the information centre no longer had a monopoly over organisational informatics.

This in turn led to a greater diversification of informatics staff. Roles such as hybrid managers, analyst/programmers, database administrators, data analysts, business analysts and systems integrators took shape. One particularly notable trend was the growth in support or operations staff (see below): staff tasked not directly with developing new information systems, but with installing and integrating existing ICT, operating corporate information systems and helping end-users in the use of technology and systems.

In recent years the increasing importance of the ICT infrastructure to organisations, coupled with its increasing complexity, has led to changes in the conception of the informatics service. Over the last decade particularly, service management practices have been applied to ICT. In this philosophy the informatics service is seen as a strategic business partner rather than a purely technology function.

Chief information officer: A term for the executive-level manager in the organisation responsible for informatics.

Wedded to this change, organisations started to create a senior management role with responsibility for informatics infrastructure, often designated CHIEF INFORMATION OFFICER (CIO), following the US terminology of chief executive officer (CEO). Because of the importance of informatics to organisational performance, and the need to integrate informatics strategy with business strategy (see Chapter 10), many have argued that the CIO should be a main board member.

Location

The rise of new organisational forms such as the information centre is partly the result of an increased number of **location** options:

- A **centralised** service is the traditional model in which informatics provides one service with single access. The informatics service is located in one large office, with all other organisational units relying on it for their informatics provision.
- In a **decentralised** model the informatics service is structured around a number of smaller units, each providing single access. Under this model the informatics service still forms a logical whole, but the various functions it provides such as planning, management, development, maintenance and operations are segmented off into separate organisational units.
- Within a **distributed** model the informatics service is made up of a set of connected functions each providing multiple services. This is because in large-scale organisations such as multinationals it may prove impossible to provide any one function on a centralised basis. Each country might have its own informatics services function, providing all the activities to their national units.
- A **devolved** model also has a distributed framework but each informatics unit is not independent. Instead, the informatics service is made up of a matrix of units each sited close to the point of need and falling under direct business unit control.
- Because many organisations were not satisfied with the informatics service provided in any of these ways, many have recently pursued an **outsourcing** strategy. Here, the informatics service is provided in whole or in part by external contractors. This issue is discussed in more detail below.

Each of these forms of location has advantages and disadvantages, which can be illustrated by comparing a centralised and a decentralised service.

The advantages of a centralised informatics service revolve around the issue of control. Fundamentally, centralisation makes it possible to exercise greater control over the management and operation of informatics resources. For instance, recruiting and maintaining informatics skills becomes easier, and there can be economies of scale in procuring hardware and software. Duplication of effort is more easily avoided and greater standardisation and compatibility of systems can be achieved. Overall, speedier and more consistent strategic decision making is possible, particularly for issues such as integration of systems and the development of large infrastructure projects.

Reflect
What advantages might a distributed or devolved model offer?

Disadvantages tend to centre on the fact that a centralised informatics service is more likely to be divorced from the 'coal face' of the business. It can prove less able to adapt quickly to changes in the business environment and technology. Business units sometimes become dissatisfied with the level of personal attention they are given and the speed of response to their needs. Some diseconomies may also be evident such as high back-up costs.

Case check:
Case 20, Tesco

In 2008 Tesco announced its intention to overhaul its ICT infrastructure. It planned to replace a number of separate voice and data networks with a single communication network, which was eventually outsourced to Cable & Wireless. It intends to use this network to standardise its key ICT systems in areas such as finance, human resources, payroll, in-store management, distribution and sales.

The intention is to manage these ICT systems centrally across the entire network from its

ICT services centre in Bangalore, India. Informatics professionals based in other countries of operation will supply only front-line support. This standardisation is built on an effort the company initiated in 2005, known as 'Tesco in a box'. It was a programme of standardisation based on an Oracle ERP system which was implemented in all countries of operation.

The rollout of these standard ICT systems is seen as a key enabler for standard business processes and standard management information across the Tesco group. This allows stores newly opened in Malaysia and Japan to operate and be managed in exactly the same way as a store in the United Kingdom.

Key processes

Depending on the size of the function, the informatics service may engage in a vast range of activities. Essentially however every informatics service has six major roles: (1) informatics planning, (2) informatics management, (3) project management, (4) development, (5) maintenance and (6) operations (see Figure 11.2).

As discussed in Chapter 10, **planning** involves formulating strategy for information, information systems and ICT in an organisation. The strategy includes plans for changing aspects of the informatics infrastructure, so it produces a portfolio of system development work.

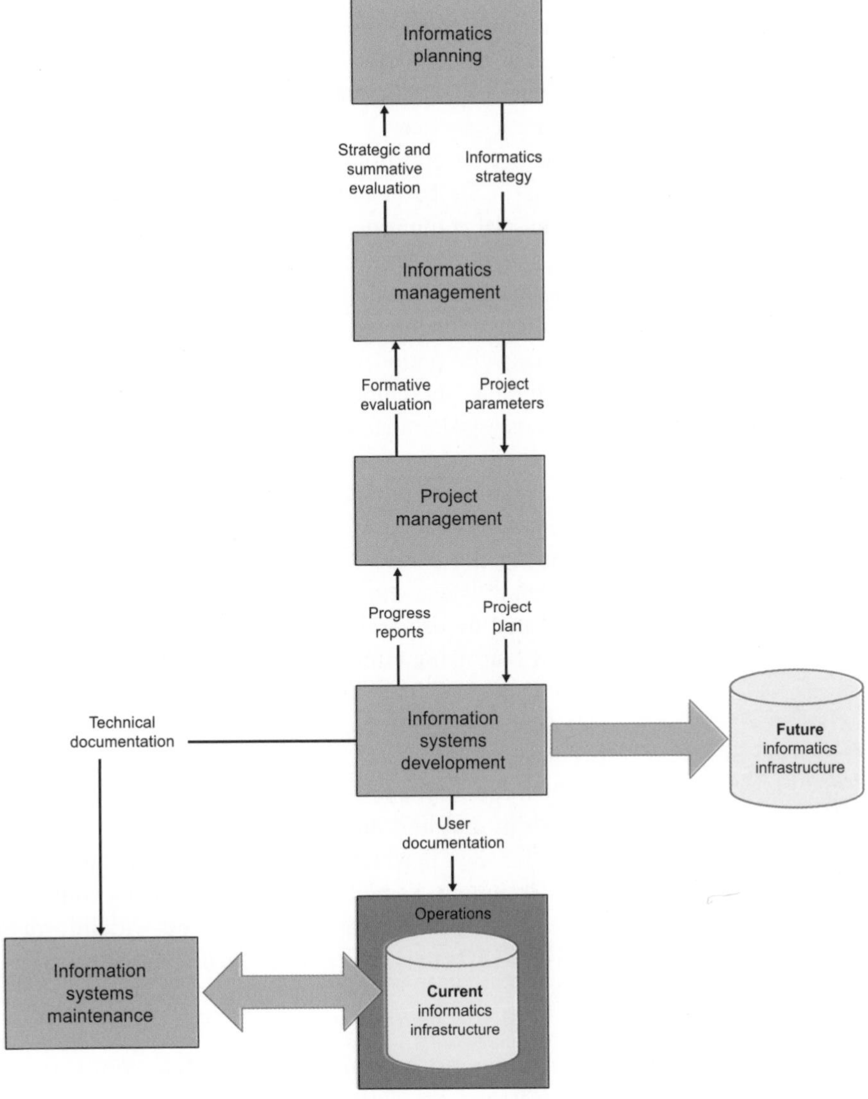

Figure 11.2: *Processes of the informatics service*

Management involves both implementing plans for future infrastructure and controlling existing informatics infrastructure. As such it involves continual evaluation of the investment in information systems, and monitoring the success of development, maintenance and operations projects as well as the service itself. Other management roles are recruiting and organising informatics personnel, and maintaining staff development programmes.

Project management: The process of planning for, organising and controlling projects.

Concrete work in informatics is likely to be organised as projects of development, maintenance or operations activity, so effective PROJECT MANAGEMENT is a critical aspect of the informatics service. **Development** is the activity of constructing and delivering new application systems: analysing, designing, producing, testing and implementing them. **Maintenance** is the activity devoted to fine-tuning aspects of the informatics infrastructure to make sure it works effectively. **Operations** is an area of the informatics service that runs and supports the use of information systems throughout the organisation (see below).

Strategy of the informatics service

An important part of any informatics strategy (Chapter 10) is a strategy for the informatics service itself. This will consider issues such as the size and location of the service and which informatics processes to outsource (see below) or maintain in-house.

Each of the different possibilities for the structure of the informatics service reflects historical features of the environment of commercial computing. In his global, historical study of the commercial information systems industry, Friedman (Friedman and Cornford, 1989) identified three phases in the history of commercial computing up to the late 1990s, each dominated by a different set of constraints and so determining a different strategy for the informatics service.

The period up to the mid-1960s was subject to **hardware constraints**, in the sense that high hardware costs and limitations in the capacity and reliability of equipment dominated commercial computing. Not surprisingly, the shape of the informatics service reflected the need to maintain large corporate data centres. Much of the strategy for the informatics service in this phase was dominated by a concern with controlling costs and maintaining effective allocation of the limited computing resource.

During the period between the mid-1960s and the mid-1980s hardware costs declined substantially. Therefore, this phase was dominated by **software constraints** in the sense that the focus was dominated by the productivity of systems developers and difficulties of delivering systems on time and within budget. Here the emphasis shifted from strategies focused around hardware to strategies focused around the need to manage the information systems development process more effectively.

During the period between the mid-1980s and early 1990s software concerns moved from centre stage with the increasing availability of packaged software. This phase became dominated by **user relations constraints** focused around system quality problems. It was argued that many informatics services had an inadequate perception of user demands and were inadequate in servicing user needs. In this phase the information centre was born as a way of attempting to satisfy concerns over the benefit the informatics service was providing to companies.

Since the early 1990s commercial computing has entered a fourth phase dominated by **organisational and environmental constraints**. The particular focus of this phase is the search for ways in which information systems can improve the position of the organisation in its environment. Some have argued that a key emphasis of this phase, which still continues, is the need for close alignment of business with informatics strategy. One way of encouraging this is for CIOs to sit on company main boards.

Funding the informatics service

Since informatics is normally a service function, a crucial feature of any strategy for the informatics service is a clear specification of how it is funded. The options include free service, profit centre, separate company and outsourced arrangements.

Traditionally an internal informatics service was farmed out **free** of charge to other departments or functions. Each business unit had its budget top-sliced in some way to finance informatics work.

In the **profit centre** model the informatics service bills other departments for its work using service level agreements (SLAs), which specify a fixed fee for a specified number of services for a given contract duration. An excess fee is usually negotiated for additional services. This is the philosophy underlying the move to **ICT service management**, described below.

One step removed from the profit centre is the concept of the informatics service run as a **separate company**, a subsidiary which contracts its services to the parent company and potentially to external customers as well. Finally, in **outsourcing** the service, informatics is given over either in whole or part to a unrelated specialist company.

Outsourcing the informatics service

Although information systems and ICT are now seen to be central to the performance of most organisations, the informatics service has traditionally experienced great difficulty in quantifying its benefits to the organisation (see Chapter 9). For this reason many organisations have decided over the last decade to outsource their informatics service. **Outsourcing** is the use of external agents to perform one or more organisational activities. A contract is negotiated with an external supplier, normally in the form of a service-level agreement.

There are a number of types of informatics outsourcing:

- **body shop outsourcing**, where contract programmers are brought in to supplement in-house informatics personnel, particularly for development or maintenance work
- **project outsourcing**, where outside vendors are used to develop new systems
- **support outsourcing**, in which vendors are contracted to maintain and support a particular application system
- **hardware outsourcing**, where organisations outsource hardware operations, disaster recovery, and management of the communication network
- **'keys to the kingdom'**, the most radical form: outsourcing the entire informatics service including the development, operation, management and control.

There are a number of claimed benefits for outsourcing. For instance, scale and specialisation enable vendors to deliver the same value for less money than insourcing. More effective control of vendors is also claimed to lead to a better quality of service, and fixed-price contracts and service-level guarantees eliminate uncertainty for the business. Business growth can be accommodated without quantum changes in infrastructure, and scarce and costly informatics talent can be refocused on higher-value activity.

During the 1990s Lacity and Hirschheim (1993) conducted a major research of outsourcing strategies in the United States. Their results questioned many of these benefits, and in particular three dominant assumptions:

- That organisations initiate outsourcing for reasons of efficiency. Lacity and Hirschheim argued that organisations may initiate outsourcing for a variety of other reasons, such as to acquire or justify additional resources, to react to positive media reports of outsourcing, to reduce personal risk to management associated with uncertainty, and to enhance the personal credibility of CIOs.
- That an outsourcing vendor is inherently more efficient than an internal informatics service through economies of scale. They found that an internal informatics service can frequently supply a service as efficiently as an external vendor.
- That vendors are partners. If a company decides to outsource, the contract is the only mechanism to ensure that expectations are realised, so 'partnership' in this area needs to be heavily controlled.

Case check: Case 7, Electronic Data Systems

Electronic Data Systems (EDS) is a global business and technology services company which classifies its services into three portfolios: infrastructure, applications and business process outsourcing. The infrastructure services portfolio involves operating of all or part of a client's computer and communication infrastructure, such as networks, mainframes, Web servers, desktops and laptops, and printers. The applications services portfolio involves the development, integration and possible maintenance of applications software for clients. The business process outsourcing portfolio includes performing a specific business function for a client such as payroll processing, processing of insurance claims or operation of call centres.

PART 4

Project management

A project is any concerted effort to achieve a set of objectives. All projects comprise teams of people engaged in the achievement of explicit objectives, usually with a set timescale. Most informatics work in organisations is structured as projects, so planning, management and even organisational analysis (Chapter 2) are conducted as projects. This section focuses on development projects: concerted efforts to develop an information system.

Initiating development projects is part of an organisation's informatics planning and informatics management process (see Chapter 10). Project management interacts with the development process (see Chapter 12) in the sense that it acts as the major control process for development. These connections are illustrated in Figure 11.3.

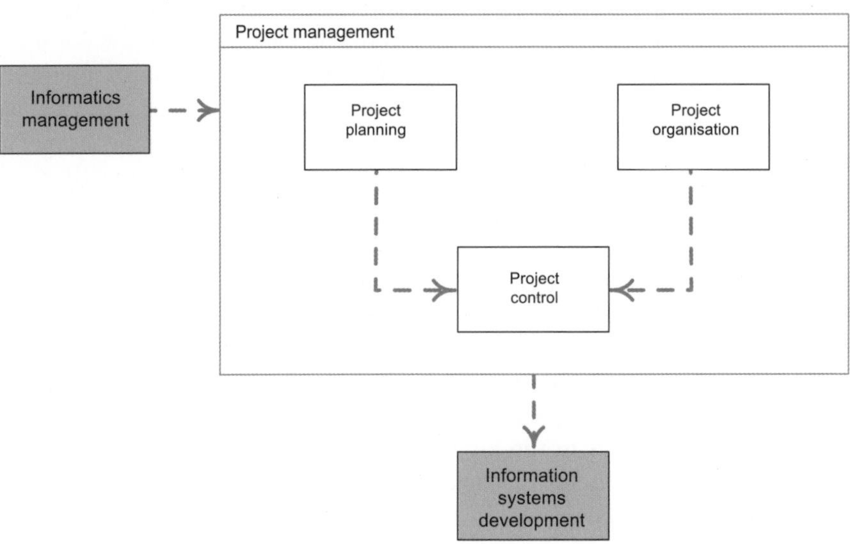

Figure 11.3: *The process of project management*

The process of project management can be divided into three interrelated activities (O'Connell, 1996):

Project planning: Determining as clearly as possible the likely parameters associated with a particular project.

Project control: The process of ensuring that a project remains on schedule, within budget and produces the desired output.

- PROJECT PLANNING involves determining as clearly as possible the likely parameters associated with a particular project.
- **Project organisation** concerns how to structure staff activities to ensure maximum effectiveness.
- PROJECT CONTROL involves ensuring that a project remains on schedule, within budget and produces the desired output.

Project planning

The classic questions of project planning are what, who, when, how, and progress?

In terms of **what**, the product or output of the project must be defined and the project must be broken down into a series of activities or tasks. Keeping to a standard model of information systems development (see Chapter 12) clearly aids this process. It is important also to identify standards to be used in the project, such as in the case of a development project, appropriate notations for specifying requirements.

In terms of **who**, staff must be assigned to the project and responsibilities identified. The most popular method of estimating the number of staff needed for a project is to use experienced people who have conducted similar projects in the past. Another approach is to estimate the size of the proposed product and derive a staff estimate from this figure by applying an appropriate formula.

In this latter approach software metrics have a place. A **software metric** is a number extracted from a software product. Metrics are used in a number of ways: to provide feedback to staff on the quality of their work, to monitor the structural degradation of a system during systems maintenance (Chapter 12), and to aid in costing and estimating software projects.

The class of metrics used for project estimation is known as function-based metrics, and they are associated with an estimating technique known as **function-point analysis.** Project managers conduct this by counting the features of a functional specification (Chapter 12), such as the number of information classes or processes in a system. These numbers are then inserted into an algebraic expression that produces a function point count. Function point counts and actual costs of projects are stored in a historical database. These figures are used to produce a statistical estimate of resources required for the current project.

In terms of **when**, it is important for milestones to be identified and schedules established. Many experienced project managers recommend that a software project is divided into sequential phases, and a milestone or control point is established at the end of each phase.

In terms of **how**, a budget for the project must be constructed and resources must be allocated to it. The likely cost of the project must be calculated and a case made for a budget. This is a critical aspect of the systems conception (see Chapter 12) phase of a development project.

In terms of **progress**, an effective mechanism for monitoring the progress of projects must be established. Milestones can be used as points of audit to ensure that standards are being adhered to and the project is on schedule.

Since a project is effectively an activity system, the conventional way of planning a project is to segment it into a number of activities, each of which can be managed independently. Each of these activities may be broken down further into a series of tasks.

One popular method of representation is to lay out a project in diagrammatic form as a network (see Figure 11.4). This can use a notation slightly modified from the one used for process modelling (see Chapter 2). Boxes are used to represent project activities and dotted lines to indicate their precedence. The planner then estimates the resources required to achieve each activity, usually expressed as a number of person-days. The sum of these person-days, plus a contingency factor for emergencies, is the estimated time required for each activity. Doing this calculation for each activity in a project will give the project manager an idea of the overall person-days required for the project. Since person-time is also the most significant cost factor, this gives an idea of total approximate cost.

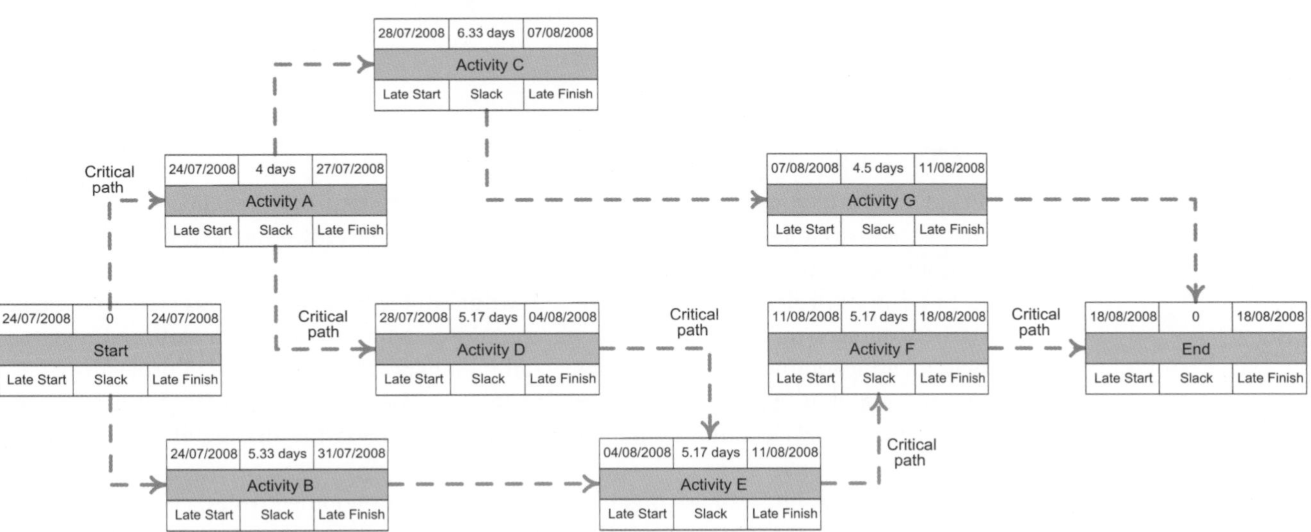

Figure 11.4: *An activity-based plan*

For each activity the earliest possible start date is calculated on the basis of a schedule assigned to predecessor activities. A latest completion date is also calculated for each activity on the basis of the scheduled start dates for each of the activity's successors and the target completion date for the overall project. The difference between the calculated time available to complete an activity and the estimated time required to complete it is known as an activity's **float**. If the float is zero, the activity is said to be critical, since any delay in completing it will cause a delay in completing the final project.

A related concept is the **critical path.** This is the longest possible continuous path between the start activity for a project and the end or terminating activity. Since the critical path determines the total calendar time required for a project, any time delay along the critical path will delay the project as a whole by an equivalent amount.

This estimating approach is usually complicated by the fact that since no two information systems projects are ever the same, there is uncertainty about the time required for each activity. Brooks (1997) has also discussed how using person-days, person-weeks or person-months as the central unit of estimating and scheduling can be misleading. It is tempting to infer from this that the progress of a project improves with the number of people assigned to it, but Brooks argues that 'adding manpower to a late software project makes it later'. There are many reasons: people take time to settle into a project, new personnel need to be trained, the amount of communication between team members increases the greater the size of the group, and so on.

This process of project planning described above is focused around activities, so it is known as **activity-based project planning**. More recently there has been an emphasis on a form of project planning based around products rather than activities. **Product-based planning** is particularly popular in agile approaches to development work (see Chapter 12).

Fundamentally, product-based planning works with two concepts: deliverables and timeboxes. A **deliverable** is a part of an information system that the development team agree to demonstrate to representatives of relevant stakeholder groups at a review session. A deliverable is normally expressed in terms of what the information system module will be able to do. A **timebox** is an agreed period of time for the production of a deliverable, and is normally expressed as a fixed deadline. The timebox is never changed once established. However, the functionality of a deliverable may be renegotiated to fit the timebox.

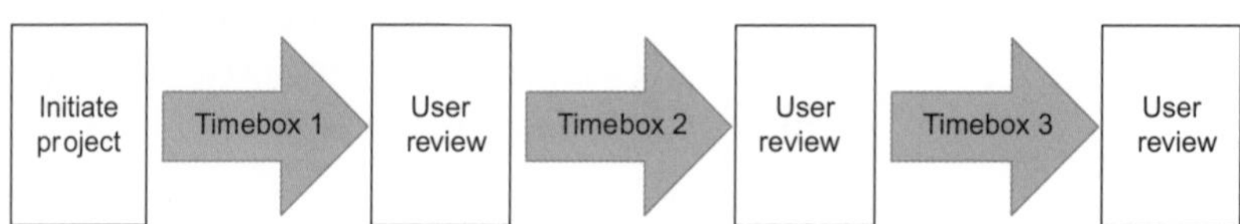

Figure 11.5: *Product-based planning*

Project organisation

Project organisation concerns how to organise staff so that they produce the desired output. Essentially there are three alternatives in organising staff: around projects, roles or a combination of the two (see Figure 11.6).

In terms of **projects**, staff are organised within project boundaries. This form of organisation encourages quick decision making, minimises interfaces between staff and generates high identification with projects among staff members. This is the style of project organisation promoted in agile approaches (see Chapter 12). The disadvantages are that it works well only for small projects, the economies of scale are low, and the sharing of expertise across projects is minimal.

In terms of **roles**, staff are organised according to development roles, each role supporting a number of different projects. This form of organisation generates economies of scale, promotes the growth of specialists, and reduces the effects of staff turnover. It is probably the most common type of project organisation in large development centres. The disadvantages are that it generates lots of communication across projects, decreases the number of people with a general feel for a project and reduces the cohesion of projects.

In a **matrix** organisation, staff are mixed across projects and roles. The basic organisation is based around development roles, but a project organisation is imposed under a series of project managers. The advantages of this approach are that short-term objectives (the success of a project) are maximised via the project organisation whereas long-term objectives (such as promoting specialism amongst developers) are maximised via division around roles. The major disadvantage is that the needs of a project and of the developer roles might conflict.

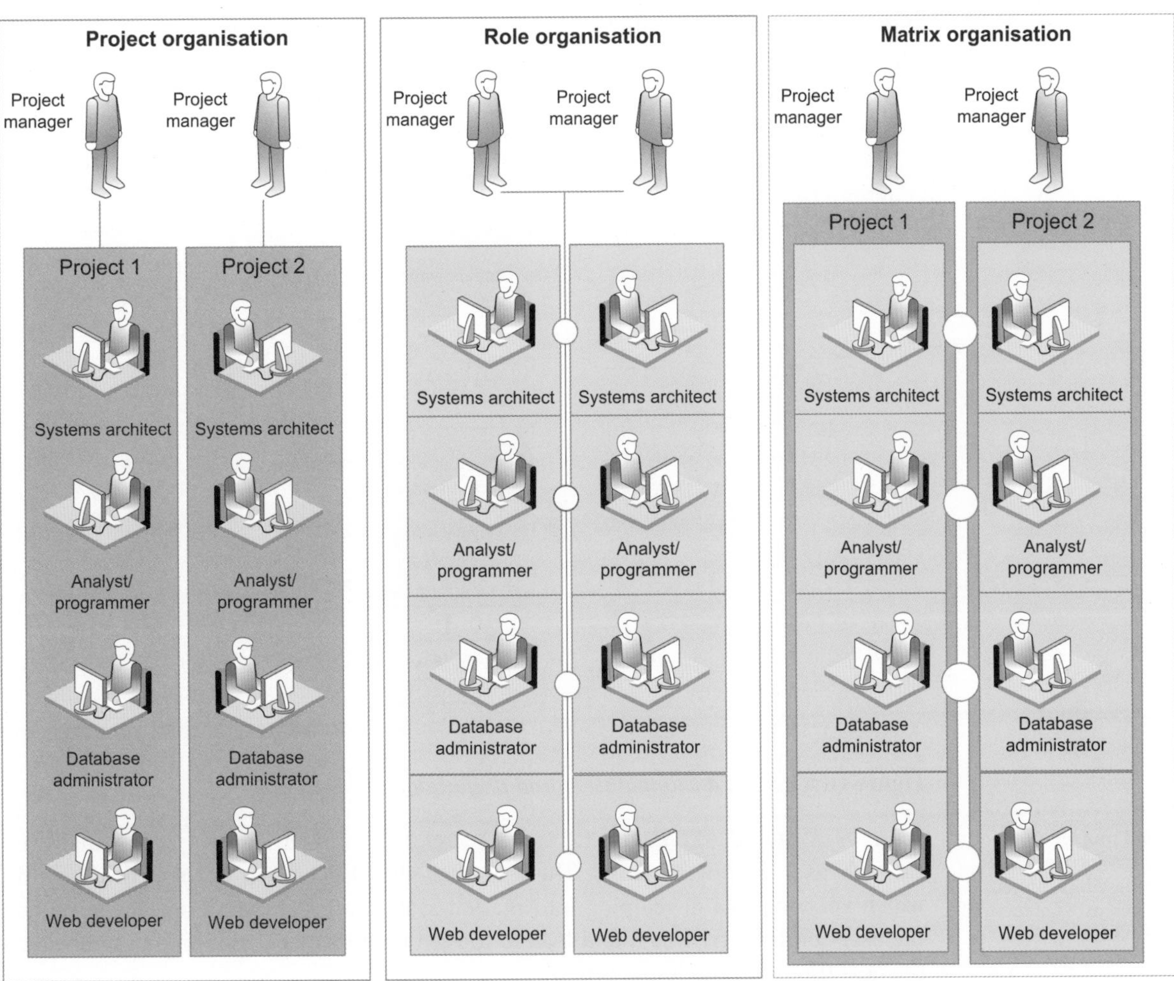

Figure 11.6: *Forms of project organisation*

Project control

Project control is a type of formative evaluation (see Chapter 9). Its aim is to ensure that schedules are met, that the project stays within budget and appropriate standards are maintained. The most important objective of project control is to focus attention on problems in sufficient time for something to be done about them. This calls for continual monitoring of progress.

Figure 11.7 illustrates the need for two major forms of information system in support of the development process. The actual process of development needs documentary support to enable collaboration between the development team (Chapter 12). The process of managing a project also needs its associated information system. This will store not only project plans but data concerning progress against plans.

Activity-based project management: A form of project management in which planning and control is conducted in terms of project activities.

In ACTIVITY-BASED PROJECT MANAGEMENT the primary document used for the evaluation of progress is a progress report (Figure 11.8). This contains information on time estimated for each activity plotted against actual time spent. Another useful measure is an estimate of the percentage of completeness.

Time actually spent on a project is usually collected via weekly time-sheets, which indicate the tasks performed by development staff and their duration. They are also useful in highlighting time spent on unplanned work.

Progress reports can be used by either management reviews or project audits. **Management reviews** are scheduled opportunities for project managers to consider the accomplishments and problems associated with a project. **Project audits** are formal events scheduled into the life-cycle of a project, in which an independent audit team examines the documentation and interviews key team members. The process of activity-based project control is illustrated in Figure 10.8.

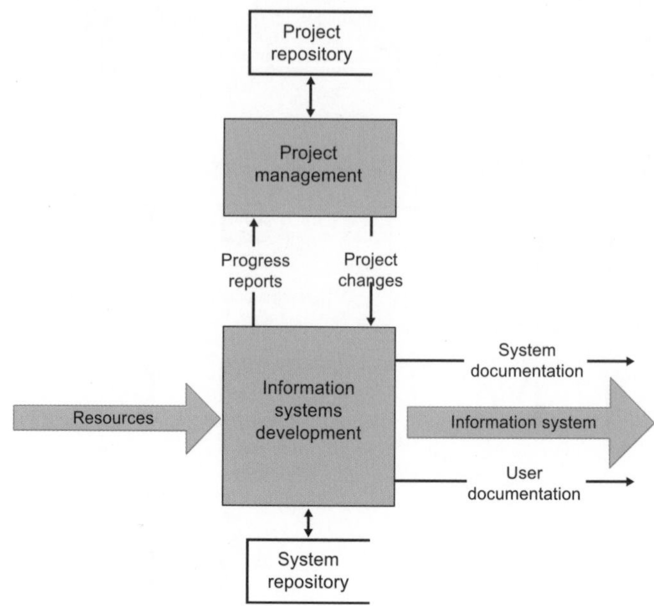

Figure 11.7: *System documentation and project documentation*

Product-based project management: A form of project management in which project planning and control are focused around information systems products.

In PRODUCT-BASED PROJECT MANAGEMENT, project control is normally exercised through **user review sessions**. These are scheduled events at the end of each timebox at which versions of a developing information system are demonstrated to representatives of the user community. This might lead to the parameters of the system being renegotiated for the next timebox (Stapleton, 1997).

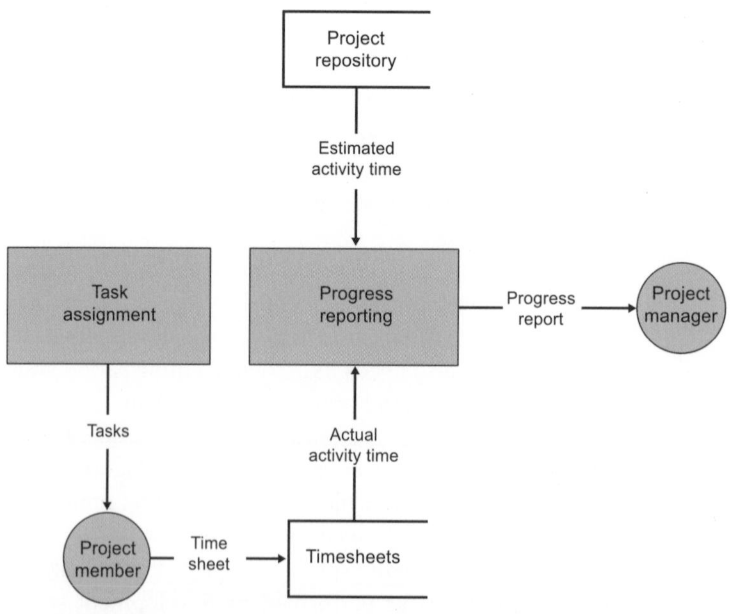

Figure 11.8: *Activity-based project control*

Information system projects may also use a change control mechanism. This involves setting up a systematic mechanism (sometimes known as configuration management: see

Chapter 12) for handling all changes to a developing piece of software. Normally a change management committee is instituted for decision making and a change management procedure is established. The essence of this procedure is to ensure that each version of a product associated with a project can be uniquely identified, and that time and money is not wasted on unimportant work such as searching for an appropriate version of software to work on.

Methods, techniques and tools

There are a number of different methods, techniques and tools for project management. For instance, PRINCE (PRojects IN Controlled Environments) is a structured method for project management, originally developed from a UK government-sponsored initiative in the 1970s (see below). PERT (Programme Evaluation Review Technique) was developed in the late 1950s and is also known as the critical path technique. It is frequently used as an aid to activity-based planning, and is similar to the approach discussed under project planning. Many automated tools such as Microsoft Project are now available to aid project managers. They use a graphical approach to show plans and estimates associated with each activity. Time-sheet data can be fed into the system and progress reports automatically generated. Some software packages for project management even allow the manager to perform 'what-if' reasoning on the project model.

Programme management

Reflect
How much of working life in an organisation known to you is taken up with project work of any form?

Recently organisations have started to distinguish between **programme management** and project management. Whereas a project is a coherent piece of usually one-off work of definite duration, a programme is an ongoing or continuous piece of work implemented in a business to consistently achieve certain results. In this sense, informatics planning, management and operations are all examples of coherent programmes of work associated with informatics infrastructure.

Programme and project management are related in that a programme is frequently organised as a set of interdependent projects for the purposes of effective organisational control, so programme management can be seen as a higher-level layer above project management. This is the position taken in the PRINCE2 method.

Key skill 

PRINCE2

The acronym **PRINCE** stands for PRojects IN Controlled Environments. PRINCE is a structured method for project management, originally developed from a UK government-sponsored initiative in the 1970s which resulted in the method known as PROMPT. PRINCE2 was introduced in 1996, and the most recent version at the time of writing was released in 2005. PRINCE2 is now used in more than 50 countries around the world (Bentley, 2005).

PRINCE2 assumes that a customer and supplier will work together to complete a project. These two groups will frequently come from separately managed areas and often from separate organisations. Customers specify the desired outcomes, make use of the final product and in most cases fund the project. Suppliers provide resources to create the intended outcome.

PRINCE2 includes a method for defining the organisation structure for a project as well as a definition of the host company. This ensures that both business interests and technical concerns are covered. It defines the structure and content of project planning, and defines a set of controls and reports that can be used to monitor whether a project is proceeding to plan. It also defines procedures for dealing with exceptions to the plan. As such it actively encourages the monitoring of quality.

PRINCE2 considers a project as a system or process consisting of a number of generic subprocesses or activities: starting up a project, initiating a project, planning, directing a project, controlling a stage, managing product delivery, managing stage boundaries, and closing a project (see Figure 11.9). The arrows on Figure 10.9 indicate necessary information flows between subprocesses.

In **starting a project**, a project board and project management team are appointed. The project board is given overall responsibility for project governance. The project manager and project management team are given overall responsibility for implementing the project. The main objective of this subprocess is to produce a **project brief.** This describes, in outline, what the project is attempting to achieve and the business justification. In addition, the overall approach to be taken is decided and the next stage of the project is planned. A decision point is then reached in which the project board is asked to authorise the next stage, initiating the project.

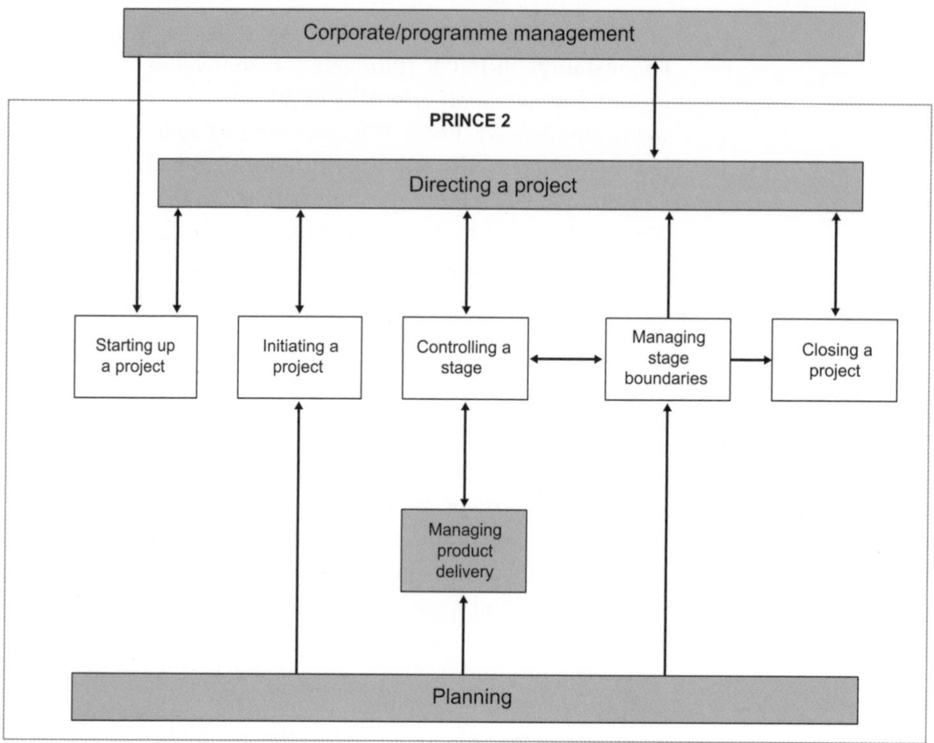

Figure 11.9: *The PRINCE2 process*

Planning is an overarching and repeatable subprocess which plays an important role in other processes. The application of PRINCE2 revolves around identifying the products that are to be created by a project, rather than the more usual concentration on the tasks to be completed. Identifying products leads to identifying the activities needed to produce them, as well as the dependencies between activities. Once the activities have been identified it is possible to estimate the effort required for each activity, and schedule activities into a plan. The risk associated with completion of activities is analysed. Finally, a process for completing a project is agreed.

Initiating a project builds on start-up activity in that the project brief is augmented to form a business case. The approach taken to ensure quality on the project is agreed together with the overall approach to controlling the project itself. Project files are also created, as is an overall plan for the project and a plan for the next stage of the project. This information can be put before the project board for them to authorise the project.

PRINCE2 suggests that projects should be broken down into stages. **Controlling a stage** is therefore a subprocess that dictates how each individual stage should be controlled. This includes the way in which work packages are authorised and received for each stage. It also specifies the way in which progress should be monitored and how summaries of progress should be reported to the project board. The method suggests means for capturing and assessing project issues together with the way in which corrective action should be taken. It also lays down the approach by which project issues should be referred to the project board when necessary.

Managing project delivery specifies how a work package should be accepted, executed and delivered. **Managing stage boundaries** dictates what should be done towards the end of a stage. In particular, the next stage should be planned and the overall project plan, risk log and business case amended as necessary. The subprocess also details what should be done in the case of a stage that has gone outside its tolerance levels. Finally, the process dictates how the end of the stage should be reported.

Directing a project is an overarching subprocess which enables the project board to control the overall project. It runs from project start-up to project close-down. The project board uses reports generated from other subprocesses at a number of decision points. It authorises project initiation and close-down as well as the plans for each stage of a project. It can also authorise additional resource for a stage following slippage or other unforeseen circumstances.

The subprocess **closing a project** details activities that should be done at the end of a project. The project should be formally decommissioned and resources freed up for allocation to other activities, A series of follow-on actions should be identified and the project itself needs to be formally evaluated.

Operations

Of the various processes illustrated in Figure 11.2, informatics planning and informatics management are covered in Chapter 10. Project management is covered in this chapter, and information systems development and maintenance are covered in Chapter 12.

This section devotes its attention to the process of ***operations***. This is an area of the informatics service that is frequently forgotten and left unexplored in many accounts of ICT and organisations. However, an increasing range of informatics professionals are now involved in operations work rather than planning, management, development and maintenance work. This is not surprising in that once an organisation has invested in informatics infrastructure it needs a continuing commitment to ensuring it operates properly.

We can frame operation of the ICT infrastructure using the philosophy of **ICT service management.** This means that the ICT infrastructure is considered as a set of defined services delivered to users in the organisation. Considering ICT infrastructure as a portfolio of services in this way encourages organisations to think of those services they need to provide internally and those that can be sourced externally.

Take email as a service provided by the ICT infrastructure. It is now a major communication medium, both inside and outside organisations, so its effective management has become a significant issue. Email management involves developing and operating procedures for ensuring that inbound and outbound email is stored and processed efficiently.

For emails from outside the organisation, procedures and technologies need to ensure they reach the appropriate person promptly, and responses are sent within a specified timeframe. Frequently, auto-responders or mail-bots are used to notify the sender that their email is being processed. Various workflow technologies are used to aid processing by back-office staff. Outbound email may be a significant aspect of eMarketing strategy (Chapter 8). For instance, outbound emails to customers might be sent as part of a marketing campaign, or on a more regular basis, such as an electronic newsletter.

Many organisations now impose constraints on employees' use of email, because of concern with the volume of internal emails generated and the dangers of their inappropriate use. For example, in **flaming attacks** emails are used to abuse or bully fellow employees. Many companies have trained staff in **email etiquette**, and some have even barred the use of email for certain corporate communications.

Did you know?

The estimated volume of spam emails worldwide was 100 billion per day in 2008.

Approaches to ICT services management

A number of related approaches have been published for ICT service management, all based around an integrated process model. This section concentrates on an approach based on ITIL.

The *Information Technology Infrastructure Library* (ITIL) was established in 1989 by the former UK Central Computer and Telecommunications Agency (CCTA), and is now managed by the UK Office of Government Commerce (OGC). In November 2000 the British Standards Institute published a new standard for IT service management, BS15000. This has been largely adopted as the ISO 20000 standard for IT service management. Both standards extend the original ITIL specification.

The description of ICT service management here is based on these standards but has been adapted in part to fit with the description of other key processes of the informatics service in this chapter and Chapters 10 and 12.

This type of approach generally sees ICT service management as a number of high-level processes such as service strategy, service support, service improvement and service delivery (see Figure 11.10).

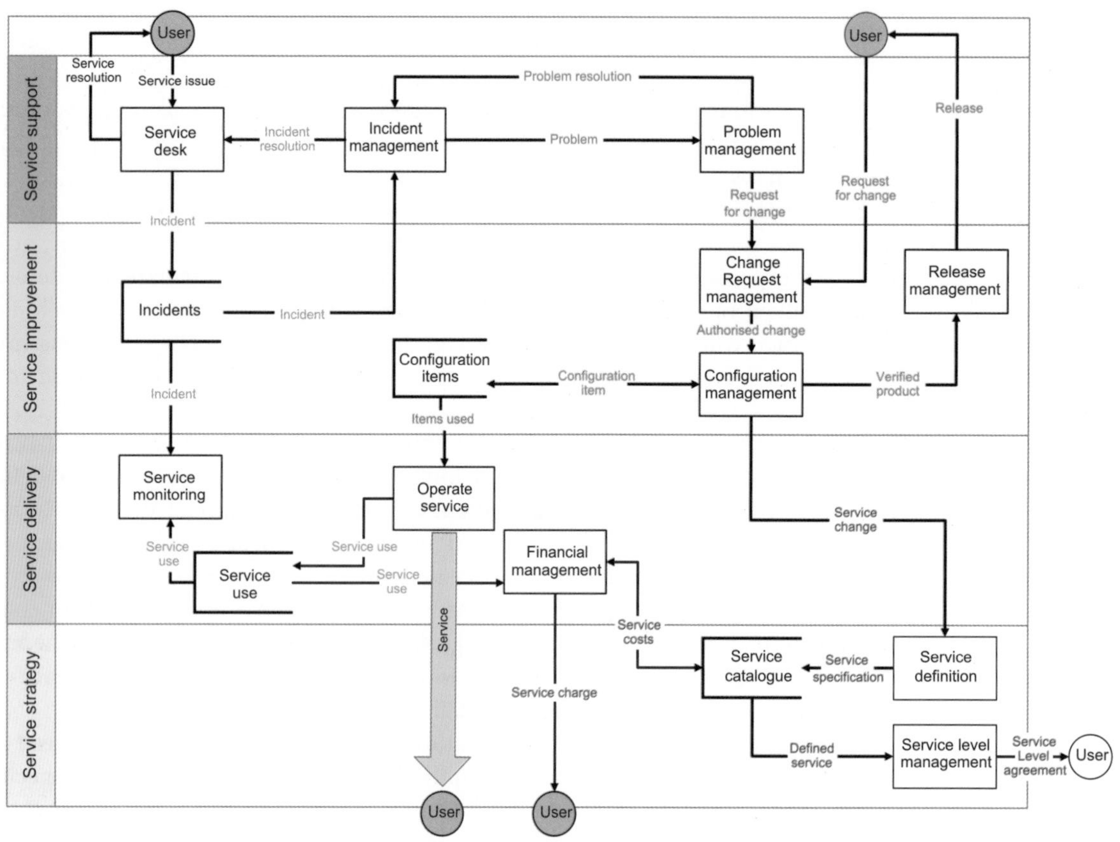

Figure 11.10: *ICT services management*

Service strategy

Functional requirements: Expected features of an information system.

Non-functional requirements: Constraints set on the development of an information system.

In the philosophy of ICT services management, an organisation must first define services relevant to its ICT infrastructure. The definitions can be based on FUNCTIONAL REQUIREMENTS such as *producing a service report* or *generating an invoice* or NON-FUNCTIONAL REQUIREMENTS (see Chapter 12) such as *providing service availability* and *information security*. Service definitions then need to be published in a **service catalogue,** preferably as one central catalogue available to all potential users of ICT services.

Service strategy also involves specifying an **end-user request model** or subscription model for services. The request model enables the user to select services from the service catalogue. The subscription model automatically delivers a standard set of services according to a prearranged service level agreement. For example, one service might be *create a new* *email account*, and automatically create a request to subscribe a particular user to the email service.

Effective planning for ICT services relies on an effective grip on the significant investment made in ICT infrastructure. This investment is not solely associated with the acquisition of hardware (such as computers, printers and storage) and software (such as operating systems and enterprise software). Other costs include installation costs, environmental costs (wiring, furniture, air conditioning and so on), running costs (electricity, communication costs and so on), maintenance costs (on hardware and software), security costs (risk management and disaster recovery mechanisms), networking costs (network hardware, software and maintenance), training costs and wider organisational costs (new salary structures, management and the like).

The cost of running the informatics infrastructure is also not a one-off cost; it is an ongoing cost of ownership. Hardware, software and the skills of personnel, for instance, have to be upgraded regularly. **Total cost of ownership** (TCO) is a financial estimate designed to help informatics managers assess direct and indirect costs associated with operation of the informatics infrastructure. It is perhaps better called the total cost of operation. A TCO estimate ideally reflects not only the purchase costs of hardware, software, data and communication technology, but all costs involved in the use and maintenance of the equipment, devices or systems considered part of the infrastructure. This includes the costs of training support personnel and the users, costs associated with failure or outage, diminished performance, costs of security breaches, costs of disaster preparedness and recovery, floor space, electricity, development expenses, testing infrastructure and expenses, quality assurance, decommissioning equipment and eWaste handling.

Did you know?

It has been estimated the cost of purchasing a personal computer for a large company is around US$1,200. If this machine is kept for four years the total cost of ownership for it could rise to close to US$6,000 a year.

PART 4

Strategies for reducing TCO include the use of a thin client model of distributed computing (see Chapter 9), the adoption of open source software (see Chapter 12) and the outsourcing of informatics operations (considered above).

Service support

Service support can be considered as consisting of a number of interrelated subprocesses: running a service desk, incident management and problem management, change request management, configuration management and release management.

A **service desk** provides a single and first point of contact for the customer/user of defined services. It helps users with difficulties or queries, handles requests for changes and communicates with the user community, particularly releasing new versions of infrastructure to users.

End-users require support in the operation of their ICT environment. This environment will differ depending on the hardware, software and communication facilities the user has access to, as well as the degree of sophistication needed to use them. The **help desk** helps solve problems end-users face with their ICT environment. This can range from replacing a printer cartridge to producing reports from a corporate database. Because of the high degree to which ICT is embedded in modern organisations, the help desk is now a significant organisational function. Satisfaction with the help-desk service frequently reflects on the overall satisfaction with the informatics service.

A key part of the help desk is ensuring that care is taken in managing user requests and solving them promptly. A common approach has a front-line interface to the help desk in which junior staff log problems and consult a knowledge base of common solutions. If they cannot solve the problem it is passed on to appropriate technical experts. Not surprisingly, the help desk in a large organisation frequently overlaps with a training facility, because metrics generated from problem logging are a useful means of identifying user training needs.

Service desk operation relies on effective incident and problem management. An **incident** is any deviation from the expected and defined operation of a service. **Incident management** is the process that restores normal service operation as quickly as possible by whatever means possible. A **problem** is a condition that has been identified and defined from incidents exhibiting common characteristics that have no known cause. The objective of **problem management** is to ensure the stability of ICT services by identifying and resolving known errors in the ICT infrastructure.

Service improvement

Configuration management: The process of controlling the changes made to an information system over time.

Incidents and problems are resolved through the operation of three interrelated processes of service improvement: change request management, configuration management and release management. A **configuration item** is a component of the ICT infrastructure. CONFIGURATION MANAGEMENT is the process involved in managing the ICT infrastructure by identifying, recording and controlling configuration items. A **change** is an action triggered by a request that results in a change of state for a configuration item. The objective of **change request management** is to effectively handle the recording, authorisation and control of all changes requested to ICT infrastructure. The objective of **release management** is to ensure that only authorised versions of ICT infrastructure such as software and hardware are made available to users.

Service delivery

The **service delivery** process consists of the subprocesses service monitoring, service operation and financial management:

- **Service monitoring** ensures the continual review of agreed levels of services as required by the business.
- **Service operation** involves ensuring the effective delivery of services through capacity, availability and continuity management. **Capacity management** involves matching ICT resources to business demand. **Availability management** means ensuring ICT availability in order to support the business at a justifiable cost. **Continuity management** is concerned with the rapid restoration of ICT services in the event of disaster.
- **Financial management** involves costing the delivery of services and charging users for them.

Disaster recovery is a critical aspect of continuity management: restoring operations critical to the resumption of business after a disaster, either natural or human. For informatics this particularly involves regaining access to aspects of ICT infrastructure, particularly data and communication networks that support key business processes.

To achieve effective recovery a well-established and thoroughly tested **data recovery plan** needs to be developed. It should include procedures for coping with the unexpected or sudden loss of communications and/or key personnel, but the focus here is on the recovery of data. This typically involves backing up data to peripheral storage such as tape and sending it offsite at regular intervals (preferably daily). It also includes back-ups to disks onsite and automatically copied to offsite disks, or made directly to offsite disks.

A more sophisticated approach is replication of data at an offsite location. Organisations such as online banks which demand high-availability systems might replicate both data and processing offsite, enabling continuous access if there is an onsite disaster. Many organisations outsource disaster recovery, using an external provider of a stand-by site and systems rather than their own remote facilities.

In addition to making plans to recover systems, organisations need to take precautionary measures to reduce the likelihood of disasters occurring. These include mirroring of systems and data, surge protectors to minimize the effect of power surges on delicate electronic equipment, uninterruptible power supplies to keep systems going in the event of a power failure, and anti-virus software and other security measures such as firewalls (see Chapter 6) to prevent data corruption and loss.

Infrastructure provision and administration

One of the key objectives of informatics operations is to ensure the effective running of large multi-user back-end and front-end information systems (see Chapter 4). To do this it not only needs to operate and maintain the systems themselves, it also needs to provide and administer associated technology such as database systems.

Chapter 10 distinguished between data administration and database administration. The **database administrator** (DBA) is responsible for the technical implementation of database systems, managing the systems currently in use and setting and enforcing policies. Whether a specialist database administration function is needed depends mostly on the size of the database system. The main user of a small desktop database system will probably perform administration tasks such as regularly backing up data themselves. However, when a database is being used by many users and the volume of data is significant, there needs to be a designated person to do this. The database administrator's core responsibilities are administration of the database, administration of the DBMS and administration of the database environment.

Database administrators normally also get involved in the design and implementation of databases, so they are part of development teams (see Chapter 12). They also ensure that the data is documented in a standard way so that multiple applications and end-users can access it effectively. Database administration involves monitoring live running against a database and modifying the structure of the database system to increase its performance. Finally, the database administrator will establish a strategy for archiving 'dead' data and a procedure for backing up data and recovering it in the event of hardware or software failure.

Administering a DBMS also involves a range of activities. For instance, it includes taking key responsibility for installing a DBMS or DBMS components, and enforcing policies and procedures for managing updates and changes to the software of the database system. It also involves monitoring live running of the DBMS and tailoring elements of the DBMS structure to ensure its effective performance.

Administering the database environment means monitoring and controlling access to the database and DBMS by users and application systems. Activities in this area include establishing user groups and assigning passwords to users and groups. Users are assigned various levels of access privileges both to DBMS facilities and to parts of databases. The database administrator will also ensure that strategies laid down by data administration for data integrity, security and privacy are adhered to at the technical level.

Increasing connectivity and performance of communication networks has enabled applications to be provided remotely. **Application service provision** (ASP) is the process by which a business provides informatics services to customers over a network. Software services offered using ASP are also known as on-demand software and software as a service. ASP has been proposed as part of a solution to the TCO problem, in the sense that an ASP might be able to able to provide the latest software at lower cost to customers over computer networks. ASP can also be considered as a type of informatics outsourcing in that a provider typically provides 24 x 7 technical support and physical and electronic security as well as the service itself.

There are several types of provider. A **functional ASP** delivers a single application, such as credit card payment processing or timesheet services. A **vertical market ASP** delivers a solution package for a specific customer type, such as a dental practice. An **enterprise ASP** is likely to deliver a broad spectrum of applications to organisations, while a **local ASP** will deliver services within a limited area.

ASP relies on a distributed processing model (see Chapter 6). The application software resides on the vendor system and is accessed by users through a web browser using HTML or special-purpose client software provided by the vendor. Custom client software can also interface to such systems through XML (Chapter 5) and application programming interfaces. So the provider fully owns and operates the software application(s) and owns, operates and maintains the servers that support them, and makes information available to customers via the Internet or a thin client (see Chapter 6). The provider bills the customer either on a per-use basis or via a monthly/annual fee.

Reflect
In what ways can the effective operation of ICT infrastructure contribute to the green credentials of a company or public sector agency?

PART 4

Summary

1. Chapter 10 established that informatics planning and management are critical activities for modern organisations. Organisations used to do these in-house, but more recently there has been a trend to outsource them.

2. Informatics is primarily part of the service sector, and is an increasingly prominent part of most Western economies. The informatics industry can be divided into producers of informatics products and services, and their consumers. Informatics in both producing and consuming organisations suffers from a lack of defined career paths. Professional bodies such as the British Computer Society are attempting to address this problem through the introduction of clear skills profiles for various forms of informatics work.

3. The informatics service is the part of the organisation tasked with supporting information, information systems and ICT. It can be structured in various ways including outsourcing in whole or part. Its four main processes are planning, management, development and operations. It delivers services in support of the current informatics infrastructure, and project management and development services in support of the future informatics infrastructure.

4. In the informatics service, planning, management, development and even operations activity is typically organised as projects. Project management can be divided into project planning, project organisation and project control. Project planning involves determining as clearly as possible the likely parameters associated with a particular project. Project organisation concerns how to structure staff activities to ensure maximum effectiveness. Project control involves ensuring that a project remains on schedule, within budget and produces the desired output.

5. Informatics operations are frequently forgotten in accounts of ICT and organisations, but an increasing range of informatics professionals work in operations, which is now typically packaged as ICT services management. There are a number of approaches to it, and it can be seen to consist of four high-level processes: service strategy, service delivery, service support and service improvement.

This chapter and Chapter 10 have gradually travelled down the hierarchy of control relevant to informatics, from informatics planning and management to operations and project management. Chapter 12 considers the last level in this hierarchy: the process of developing new information systems and maintaining existing ones.

Focus on Value

An organisation with an informatics infrastructure must establish ways of operating and servicing it. A key decision is whether to do this internally or outsource it. Organisations need to make significant investment not only in planning and management work but also in providing the informatics service. Also, since much informatics work is project-based there is key value in good project management.

Review test

1	How would you distinguish between informatics producers and consumers? Write two sentences.
2	A model in which informatics provides one single service with single access provision. Select the most appropriate type of location. ☐ Distributed ☐ Decentralised ☐ Centralised
3	The informatics service includes four main processes. What are they? Select all that apply. ☐ Planning ☐ Management ☐ Development ☐ Business Strategy ☐ Operations
4	CIO stands for: Select the most appropriate description. ☐ Central information officer ☐ Chief intelligence officer ☐ Chief information officer
5	SLA stands for: Select the most appropriate description. ☐ Service level agreement ☐ Serious licensing agreement ☐ Service legal agreement
6	____________ might be defined as the use of external agents to perform one or more organisational activities. Fill in the blank.
7	A ____________ is any concerted effort to achieve a set of objectives. Fill in the blank.

8	Project management involves three high-level activities. What are they? Select all that apply. ☐ Project planning ☐ Project estimation ☐ Project organisation ☐ Project control
9	There are two major project planning approaches based on focus. Select all that apply. ☐ Product-based planning ☐ Technology-based planning ☐ Activity-based planning ☐ Information-based planning
10	Project control is a type of ____________ evaluation. Fill in the blank.
11	PRINCE stands for: Select the most appropriate description. ☐ Project in Computer Environments ☐ Projects in Controlled Environments ☐ Projects in Controllable Environments
12	A ____________ provides a single and first point of contact for the customer/user of defined services. Fill in the blank.
13	The operation of an organisation's ICT infrastructure is now framed in terms of the philosophy of ICT ____________ management. Fill in the blank.
14	TCO stands for: Select the most appropriate description. ☐ Total control of ownership ☐ Total cost of ownership ☐ Total conception of ownership

Exercises

1. Search the Internet for companies in each of the informatics producer areas identified in this chapter.
2. Look through job advertisements in various informatics magazines and try to develop precise job descriptions for the roles described in this chapter.
3. Discuss the importance of regulation to the development of clear career paths for informatics professionals.
3. Develop a brief policy statement indicating possible strategies for addressing the skills crisis in informatics.
5. Take an organisation known to you and find out whether it has an informatics service function. In what way is the informatics service organised? Use the distinctions made in this chapter to help describe it. Is the department seen purely as a service function or in a more strategic sense? Is the service centralised, devolved or distributed? How is the service funded?
6. At what point do you think a critical mass is reached in project group size?
7. Discuss three of the main problems arising in the management of large project groups.
8. Which form of organisation do you think is most prevalent in the informatics service: project organisation, functional organisation or matrix organisation?
9. What sort of timings, effort and resource information should be kept in an organisation's project experience base?
10. Even the most carefully planned of projects fail. Suggest some reasons.
11. Try to identify the costs of maintaining a small network of personal computers.
12. Does an organisation known to you have a help-desk? Who staffs the help-desk? How would you rate satisfaction with it?
13. How do your back up your own personal data? How regularly? Do you store it off-site?

Projects

1. A number of different forms have been considered for the informatics service. Investigate two or more organisations. Consider differences in structure and function between their informatics services and why these differences have occurred.
2. ICT, information systems and information are increasingly important to successful organisational performance. Does this mean that the informatics service has more power in organisations? Investigate the power that the informatics service has in modern organisations. For instance, how prevalent is the practice of placing CIOs on the board?
3. Determine the precise make-up of informatics in a nation. For instance, try to determine whether it is possible to state the percentage in each producer area and the major consumers of informatics.
4. How commonplace are professional development schemes for informatics in organisations and how seriously are they treated? Investigate the use of the professional development schemes in the area of informatics in an organisation known to you.
5. Is there a skills shortage in the informatics area in your nation? If so, are there any attempts to address this shortage? If the shortage is not addressed, what effect is likely on the economy?
6. Good project management practices have been around for many years but information systems projects still fail frequently. Investigate the limitations of project management with respect to this problem.
7. Investigate the range of project planning techniques and how frequently they are applied in information system

projects in one large organisation or across a small number of organisations. Would you describe their project management practices to planning as activity-based or product-based?

8. Determine the prevalence of use of the PRINCE project management method in a specific area of the private sector. Is PRINCE used specifically for information systems projects or more generally?

9. Investigate the benefit provided by project management tools such as Microsoft Project to effective project management. What facilities do these tools provide and how do they aid the project manager?

10. How important is the successful operation of a helpdesk to the general rating of user satisfaction with informatics? Investigate the activities of the helpdesk in two or more organisations. Are there effective ways of measuring satisfaction with the helpdesk itself and more generally with the informatics service?

11. Attempt to calculate the total cost of ownership associated with desktop computing in an organisation known to you. How does the organisation attempt to control such costs? For instance, does the use of open source software have any part to play?

Further reading

Bott (2005) contains an overview of informatics as a profession. A recent edited book by Lacity and Wilcocks (2006) brings together much published material on informatics outsourcing. Oshri, Kotlarsky and Wilcocks (2008) consider business process outsourcing as well as ICT outsourcing. Bentley (2005) provides a classic account of the PRINCE2 project management method. The Information Technology Infrastructure Library is introduced in a text from the UK Office of Government Commerce (OGC, 2005).

References

Bentley, G. (2005) *Practical PRINCE2*. London, Stationery Office Books.

Bott, F. (2005) *Professional Issues in Information Technology*. London, British Computer Society Publications.

Brooks, F. P. (1997) *The Mythical Man-Month*. Reading, Mass., Addison-Wesley.

Friedman, A. L. and Cornford, D. S. (1989) *Computer Systems Development: History, organisation and implementation*. Chichester, John Wiley.

Lacity, M. and Hirschheim, R. (1993) *Information Systems Outsourcing: Myths, metaphors and realities*. Chichester, John Wiley.

Lacity, M. and Wilcocks, L. (eds) (2006) *Information Systems and Outsourcing*. Basingstoke, UK, Palgrave.

O'Connell, F. (1996) *How to Run Successful Projects II: The silver bullet*. Hemel Hempstead, Prentice Hall.

OGC (2005) *Introduction to ITIL*. London, Stationery Office Publications.

Oshri, I., Kotlarsky, J. and Wilcocks, L. (2008). *Outsourcing Global Services: Knowledge, innovation and social capital*. Basingstoke, Palgrave.

Stapleton, J. (1997). *DSDM – Dynamic Systems Development Method: The method in practice*. Harlow, Addison-Wesley.

CHAPTER 12
Development

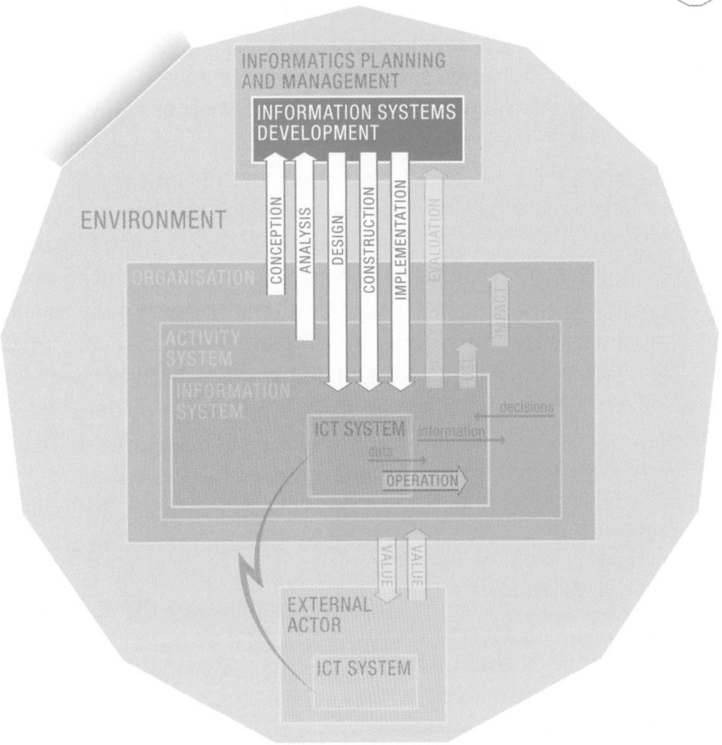

I must create a system, or be enslaved by another man's. I will not reason and compare: my business is to create.

William Blake (1757–1827). Jerusalem (1815), Chapter 1.

CHAPTER OUTLINE

LEARNING OUTCOMES	PRINCIPLES
Define the key stages of the information system development process and identify differences between major approaches to information system development.	The development of new information systems is a significant investment for organisations. Since information systems are sociotechnical systems, development involves the joint design of activity systems and ICT systems.
Describe the key front-end activities of the development process: conception, analysis and design.	The information systems development process consists of six major activities. The three front-end activities establish a business case for a development effort (conception), elicit and document the requirements for the information system (analysis) and express the shape of the proposed information system (design).
Describe the key back-end activities of the development process: construction, implementation and maintenance.	The back-end activities of the development process include the actual build of the information system (construction), the introduction of the information system into its context of use (implementation) and the ongoing repair and adaptation of the information system over time (maintenance).

Introduction

In a recent editorial in a computing magazine (*Personal Computer World*, April 2008) a technology journalist lamented the death of the term *programmer* and its replacement with what he thought was the poorer and more vague term *developer*. In a sense he was right. Developer is much less specific than programmer, and deliberately so. This is because modern development as an activity is much larger than simply programming. Indeed, as we shall see, much of the activity of modern information systems development in organisations does not produce any traditional program code whatsoever.

In Chapter 10 the case was made for the importance of informatics planning, management and strategy. Each of these areas is concerned with the issue of informatics infrastructure. The importance of these issues lies in the continuous need to adapt both informatics infrastructure and the infrastructure of activity in organisations to changing environmental circumstances.

This chapter considers the issue of development, a term which has traditionally been associated solely with the building of ICT systems. However, here information systems development is seen as one of the key organisational processes for modern-day organisations. This means that, following the definition of an information system as a sociotechnical system, this process must necessarily consider the joint development of both ICT systems and activity systems within and between organisations.

Tool: Software used to aid the development process.

Since it is a process, information system development can be considered as a system in itself. The key inputs to the development process are ICT resources and developer resources. A critical part of developer resources is the toolkit of methods, techniques and TOOLS available to the developer. The key output is an ICT system designed to support an information system as well as an associated human activity system. A number of key activities are involved in the development process: conception, analysis, design, construction, implementation and maintenance.

Development information system: An information system designed to support the development process.

The development process needs an information system itself. A DEVELOPMENT INFORMATION SYSTEM is essential to ensure the effective and efficient operation of the activity system which is the development process. Such an information system consists of both systems documentation and project documentation.

The development process is normally organised in projects and is managed through these units of activity. It is also normally undertaken by a specialist organisation, which was referred to in Chapter 11 as the informatics service. This is typically either part of the organisation in question or a vendor organisation which services its needs.

The development process

Information system development: The process of developing an information system.

INFORMATION SYSTEM DEVELOPMENT is the sociotechnical system concerned with the design, construction, implementation and maintenance of key aspects of an organisation's informatics infrastructure. This critical activity system for modern business is represented in Figure 12.1. The key inputs into the system are ICT resources and developer resources. **ICT resources** can be hardware and communication technology as well as construction tools or software packages. **Developer resources** include not only people but also a toolkit of methods, techniques and tools available to the development team.

The key outputs from this process are an ICT system and its associated activity system. **Information system** is used here as the anchor term for both these constructs. Information systems in themselves are sociotechnical systems since they include both an ICT system and a system of use. Hence, ideally the activity system and the ICT system should be designed in parallel. The ICT system might be a bespoke system or a configured/tailored software package.

Three key types of organisational stakeholder are critical to the development process: clients, end-users and developers. **Clients** are typically managerial groups involved in setting the major parameters for an information system development project. This stakeholder group provides budgets for projects, used for funding ICT and developer resources. They also typically define expected benefits and set constraints on the degree of organisational change.

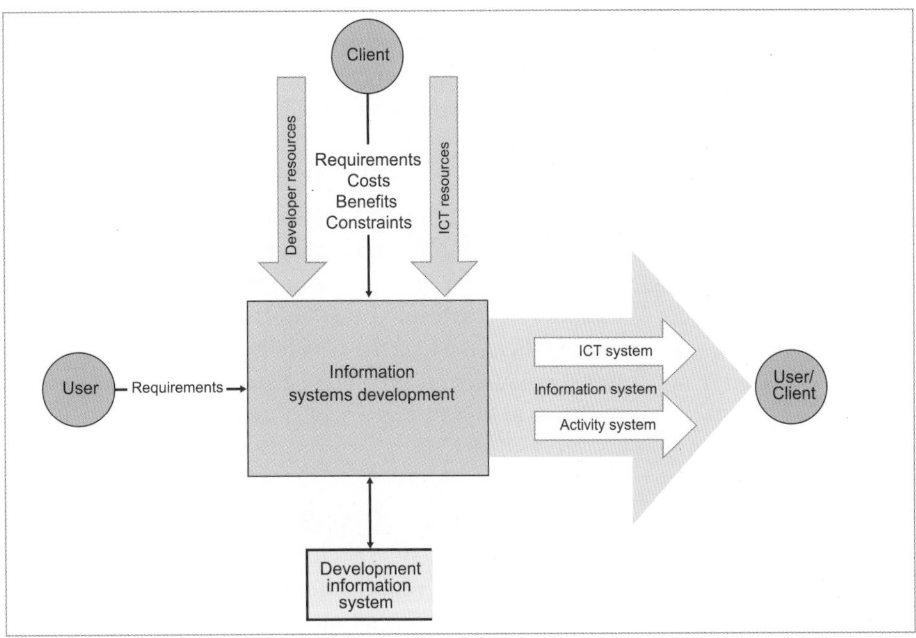

Figure 12.1: *The development process*

The eventual **users** (end-users) of an information system are also likely to be involved in the development process. They will typically be involved in analysis and design work, and provide important detailed requirements for the functionality and usability of the intended system. **Developers** are the persons tasked with analysing, designing, constructing and implementing the information system. They may also have a key part to play in delivering the information system into its context of use.

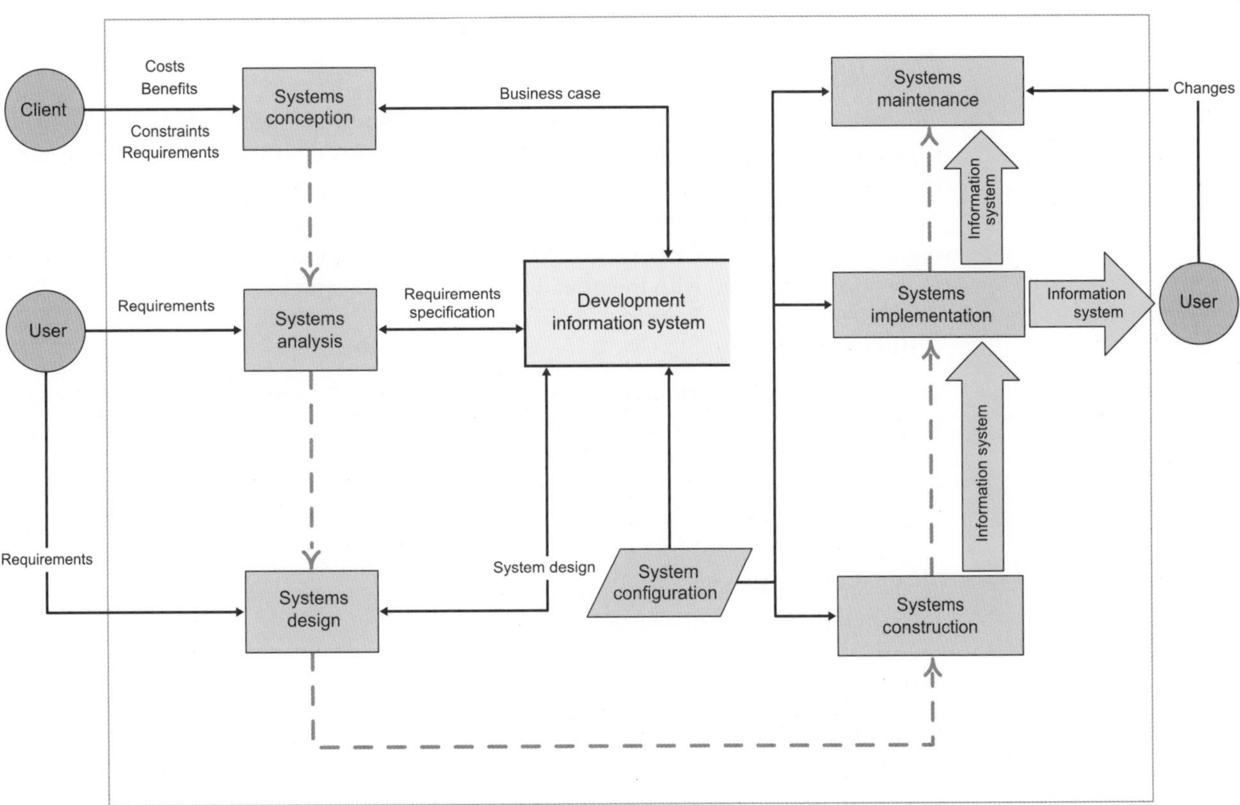

Figure 12.2: *Activities of information system development*

The process of information systems development involves a number of activities arranged in what is frequently referred to as a life-cycle of development (see Figure 12.2). The activities in a typical information system development project provide project managers (see Chapter 11) with a blueprint for controlling the project.

Conception

System conception: The part of the development process devoted to assessing the investment potential and feasibility of systems.

CONCEPTION is the first phase in the development process and typically follows on from informatics planning and management. In this phase the development team produce the key business case for an information system, an evaluation of the system in strategic terms (see Chapter 7). The team also attempt to estimate the degree of risk associated with the project. Finally, they consider the feasibility of the information system project in terms of organisational resources. A project that passes the strategic evaluation, risk analysis and feasibility tests passes on to a process of systems analysis.

Analysis

Requirements analysis: The stage in the database development process that involves finding out data requirements.

Information systems ANALYSIS involves two interrelated activities: requirements elicitation and requirements specification. **Requirements elicitation** is the process of identifying requirements, and **requirements specification** is the process of representing them in various ways. Generally, information systems analysis benefits from forms of stakeholder participation (see Chapter 7), especially in the process of elicitation.

Design

Systems analysis provides the major input into systems **design**. Design is the process of planning a technical artefact to meet requirements established by analysis as well as the use context into which it will be placed. It involves consideration of requirements and constraints, and selection from among design alternatives. The sociotechnical design of ICT systems and associated activity systems benefits from the participation of system stakeholders. A design or system specification acts as a blueprint for systems construction.

Construction

This phase involves building the information system to its specification. Traditionally ICT system **construction** involves the three related processes of programming, testing and documentation. This is done either by an internal team or by an outside or outsourced contractor. Many information systems are now bought in as a package and tailored to organisational requirements. Construction also involves the introduction of new job specifications and procedures associated with the intended use of the ICT system.

Implementation

The process of systems **implementation** (sometimes called systems delivery) follows on from systems construction. Systems implementation involves delivering an information system into its context of use. Since an information system is a sociotechnical system, its implementation involves the parallel implementation of both an information system and an associated activity system. Once a system is delivered into its context of use it will be subject to the processes of operation and systems maintenance. Operation (see Chapter 11) is not included in the development life-cycle since it is an issue of use and management rather than a direct concern for the development team.

Maintenance

Systems maintenance: The part of the development process devoted to maintaining systems.

SYSTEMS MAINTENANCE follows on from systems implementation. Maintenance is the process of making necessary changes to the functionality and/or usability of an information system (Burton Swanson, 1992). Information systems rarely stand still. They may change for a number of reasons. In the process of use, errors might be found or changes proposed. At some point in time a system might be abandoned or need to be re-engineered to fit new organisational circumstances. Changes also occur over time in adjustments made to the way both the information system and its context of use work. Maintenance activity may also stimulate suggestions for new systems. Hence, it may act as a key input into the process of systems conception and thus provides a form of feedback (Chapter 2) within the process of information system development.

Let's suppose a company wishes to set up an eCommerce website. We can map some of the actual activities in the plan for the development of this system against the phases of the development process described above:

- **Conception** is likely to involve building the business case for the new eCommerce site, registering the domain name for the site, producing a tender document, issuing the tender, reviewing submissions and awarding the contract.
- **Analysis** involves eliciting key requirements for the site from clients and users and producing key content and presentational requirements for the website.
- **Design** is the phase of producing key prototypes of content and presentation, considering changes to work practices and reviewing them with users.
- **Construction** involves producing the final content (HTML pages and graphics), programming any integration with back-end systems such as databases, testing the pages individually and as an integrated set, and setting up new organisational structures and processes to ensure that content in the website remains current.
- **Implementation** consists of producing a marketing campaign to accompany release of the website, updating stationery and registering the site, as well as publishing the site on its appropriate server and putting new organisational processes into action.
- **Maintenance** involves measuring the performance of the site, managing the content on the site over time and reviewing organisational structures and processes where necessary.

Approaches to information systems development

There are a number of distinct approaches to information system development. This section considers two major dimensions, the type of information system product and the form of sequencing of activities (Figure 12.3).

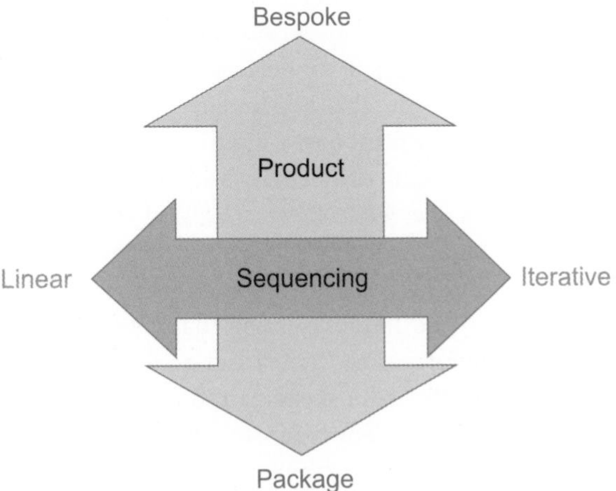

Figure 12.3: *Approaches to information systems development*

Type of information systems product

The product dimension contains two main types of development activity, bespoke development and package development.

Bespoke development: The development style in which an organisation produces a new information system to directly match its requirements.

In BESPOKE DEVELOPMENT an organisation builds an information system to directly match its requirements. This might involve programming the entire system, or building a system out of pre-established components. Bespoke development normally offers the organisation the opportunity to match closely the design of the information system to organisational processes. The main disadvantage is that the organisation must make a considerable investment in developing the information system. In particular it has to maintain a suitably skilled internal informatics service (Chapter 11) or put the work out to tender and manage an external supplier.

Package development: Process in which an organisation purchases a piece of software from a vendor and tailors it to a greater or lesser extent to meet its own demands.

In PACKAGE DEVELOPMENT an organisation obtains an existing piece of software and tailors the package to a greater or lesser extent to meet its own demands. The packaged software might either be purchased from a software vendor, run under application service provision (see Chapter 11) or obtained under some form of open source software licensing agreement (Fitzgerald, 2006).

A **software package** is a software application designed to provide the functionality needed to support activity in a generic business area. It might be customisable to a specific organisation's needs. In package development the usual relationship between system development and organisational processes is reversed. Traditionally, the ICT system is designed to meet the requirements of established or intended organisational processes. In package development, generally speaking, organisational processes have to be adapted to the package requirements.

Reflect
Reflect on an organisation known to you. How many of the information systems do you think have been developed in a bespoke and how many in a package manner?

It is not normally feasible for small to medium-sized organisations to develop bespoke systems because this is so expensive, so they normally obtain a package or hire an external contractor to produce a system. Even for these alternative approaches to development, the key phases above have to be followed. For instance, it is critical that organisations make a business case for the use of a package just as they would if they were proposing to construct the system themselves.

Form of sequencing

Sequencing is the way the various phases of the development process are organised. There are two broad forms, linear and iterative sequencing.

Linear development: The phases of development are strung out in a linear sequence with outputs from each phase triggering the start of the next phase..

The LINEAR MODEL of the development process is shown in Figure 12.4. Here the phases are strung out in order, with outputs from each phase triggering the start of the next phase. In the first three phases the key outputs are forms of system documentation. In the last three phases the outputs are elements of an information system.

The linear model has been particularly popular as a framework for large-scale development projects. This is mainly because a clear linear sequence makes for easier project planning and control (see Chapter 11). The major disadvantages lie in the difficulties associated with changing early analysis and design decisions late into a project.

Iterative development: In this model systems conception triggers an iterative cycle in which various versions of a system (prototypes) are analysed, designed, constructed and possibly implemented.
Prototyping: The development approach in which prototypes are produced.

The ITERATIVE MODEL of the development process is illustrated in Figure 12.5. In this model systems conception triggers a cycle in which various versions of a system known as PROTOTYPES are analysed, designed, constructed and possibly implemented.

The iterative model has been particularly popular for small to medium-scale projects. Iteration, the construction of prototypes (prototyping) and significant amounts of user involvement seems to reduce the risk associated with ICT innovations and generate stronger commitment from stakeholders. However, because it is frequently uncertain in an iterative approach how much resource will need to be devoted to the project, this approach can lead to more difficult project planning and management.

No one approach to development is applicable to all circumstances. Development projects are likely to use a range of approaches depending on development resources, the scale of the project and whether the systems work affects the front-end or back-end ICT infrastructure (see Chapter 6).

Generally speaking large-scale, back-end information system projects, which often involve implementing a large corporate database system, are likely to use a linear, bespoke model of development. Major modules in an ERP system (see Chapter 6) are also likely to be tailored using a linear, package approach. In contrast, front-end ICT systems, particularly those that are

Reflect
Besides those mentioned, what other advantages do you think there might be to using a linear as opposed to an iterative approach to information systems development?

Web-based, are likely to adopt iterative approaches because of the time pressures associated with them, and the high levels of interactivity and hence user involvement required.

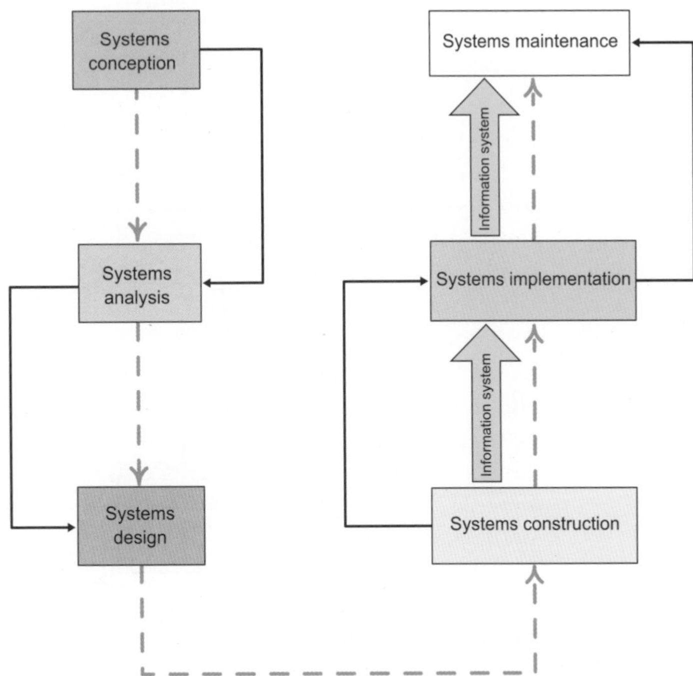

Figure 12.4: *The linear model of development*

Development organisation and information system

Development is normally organised in projects. All projects comprise teams of people engaging in the achievement of explicit objectives (Chapter 2), usually with a set duration. Most informatics work in organisations is structured as projects, so planning, management and development activities are all normally conducted on a project basis. This chapter focuses on development projects, concerted efforts to develop information systems.

Initiating development projects is normally part of an organisation's informatics planning and management processes (see Chapter 10). Project management (O'Connell, 1996) interacts with the development process in the sense that it acts as the major control process for development (see Figure 12.6).

Figure 12.6 illustrates the need for two major forms of information in support of development. The actual process of development needs documentary support to enable collaboration between the development team. The process of managing a project also needs an associated information system. This will store both project plans and data on progress against them.

Before the development process starts a development team is normally assembled. A number of development roles are critical to particular phases of the development process:

- A **business analyst** undertakes organisational analysis (see Chapter 2) and systems conception activities such as cost/benefit analyses and risk analysis.
- A **systems analyst** undertakes feasibility study, analysis and design activities.
- A **project manager** is concerned with managing the development process as a unit.
- A **programmer** undertakes construction and maintenance activities.
- A **change manager** is particularly concerned with the successful execution of implementation activities.

Representatives of other stakeholder groups, particularly clients and end-users, are also likely to form part of the development team, either throughout the development process or at key points in the development of the information system, such as in analysis and design.

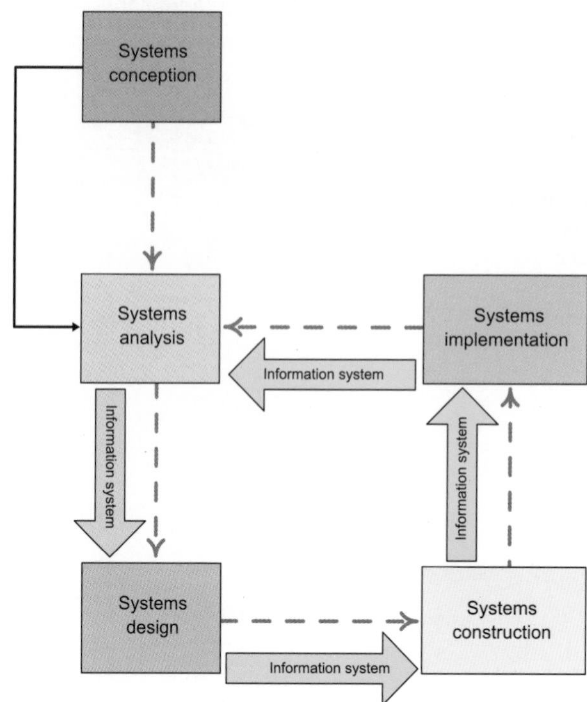

Figure 12.5: *The iterative model of development*

A development information system is essential to ensure the effective operation of the activity system that is the development process. Any reasonable-sized development project will need an information system to support communication between teams of developers, feed into a project management and an informatics management process, and communicate with other stakeholder groups such as users and business managers. It consists of both system documentation and project documentation. System documentation acts as a model of the developing system; **project documentation** acts as a model of the development process. The key point here is that all information systems in a sense model elements (artefacts or organisational activities) of other systems.

Development toolkit

Development toolkit: The methods, techniques and tools available to the development organisation.

The human species has been described as *homo habilis* – man the toolmaker. We make tools to extend our physical and mental grasp and so to help us to change our world. To undertake any development effort the information systems developer needs a toolkit. It consists of methods, techniques and tools which support the activities of the development process – conception, analysis, design, implementation and maintenance. Methods, techniques and tools are the supporting 'technology' for information systems development (Beynon-Davies, 1998). The term *technology* is used here in its broadest sense to refer to any form of device, conceptual or physical, that aids the work of a person or group of people.

Did you know?

The noted American psychologist Abraham Maslow once noted the effect that tools can have on both the problem-setting and problem-solving mindset of the tool user. If the only tool you have is a hammer, he said, you tend to see every problem as a nail.

Development method: A specified approach for producing information systems. Information system development method: A defined approach to developing information systems.

Information system development methods

DEVELOPMENT METHODS are frameworks that prescribe how to go about development activity. An information systems development method has these main components:

- a model of the information systems development process
- a set of techniques

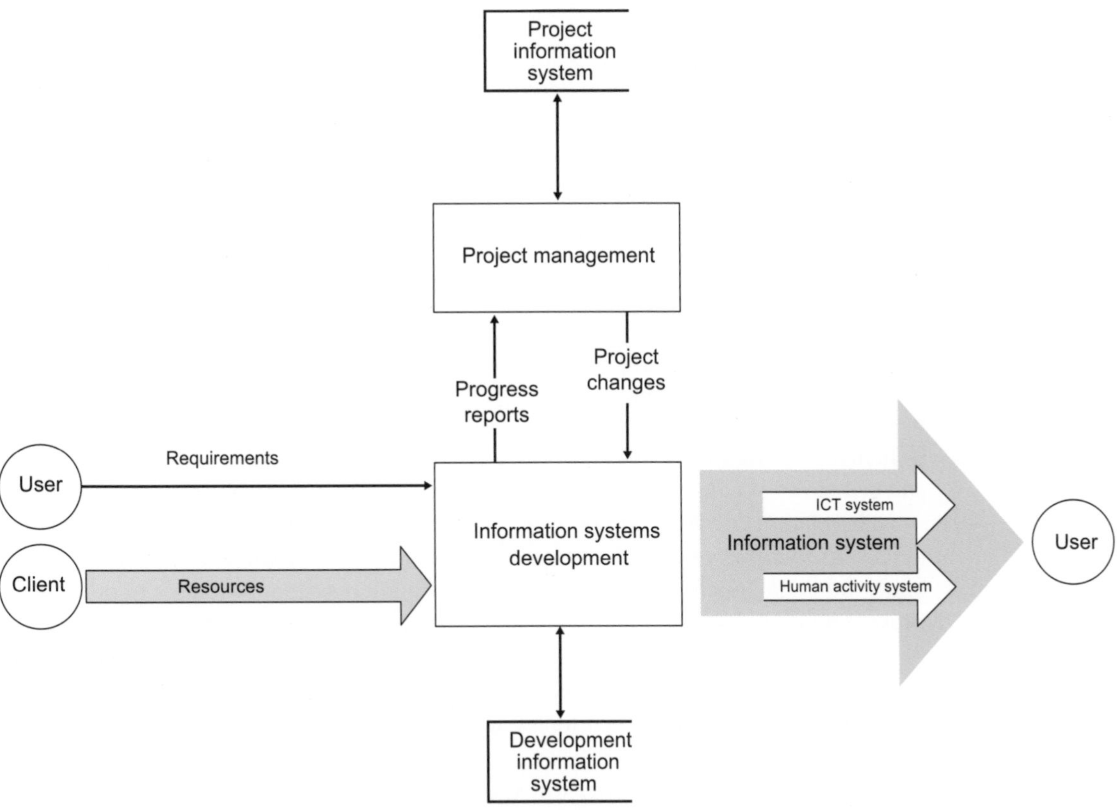

Figure 12.6: *The relationship between project management and information systems development*

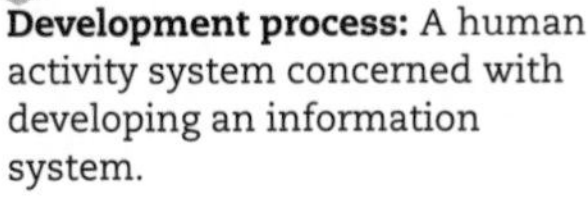

Development process: A human activity system concerned with developing an information system.

- a documentation method associated with these techniques
- some indication of how the techniques chosen along with the documentation method fit into the model of the DEVELOPMENT PROCESS.

There are three major types of development method: structured methods, agile development methods and object-oriented methods.

Structured methods developed during the 1980s and initially used a linear model of the development process. Here clear phases are identified, with clear inputs to and outputs from each phase. Techniques in areas such as information modelling (see Chapter 3) and information systems modelling (see Chapter 4) were initially developed within structured frameworks, so structured methods propose a standard notation for this kind of modelling. For example, Structured Systems Analysis and Design Method (SSADM) is a structured development method which was developed initially in the early 1980s as a public domain standard development method. It has been used extensively in both the public and private sectors, and has been substantially revised several times.

Reflect

It is often suggested that using a standard development method is a good way of managing developers, particularly new developers. Why do you think this might be?

Agile methods such as rapid application development (RAD) or extreme programming (XP) (Stapleton, 1997) use an iterative model of the development process and generally specify high-level phases based around a form of prototyping. They are frequently referred to as 'lightweight' methods in contrast to the 'heavyweight' methods available in the structured and object-oriented domains. This is because agile methods are generally contingent: they do not prescribe in detail the techniques (see below) to be used. A variety of techniques can be adapted to the needs of a particular project. As an example, Dynamic Systems Development Method (DSDM) is a non-proprietary RAD method. It is produced by the DSDM consortium, a non-profit-making organisation of vendors, users and individual supporters of RAD (Stapleton, 1997).

Object-oriented: A term applied to programming languages, design methods and database systems to mean providing support for constructs such as objects, classes and generalisation aggregation.

Most OBJECT-ORIENTED (OO) methods use a contingent model – sometimes a linear model, sometimes iterative – for the development process. OO methods tend to focus on objects and modelling, as discussed in Chapter 3. Unified modelling language (UML) and the rational development process is a popular OO development method. UML is a standard notation for object modelling developed as a hybrid of earlier OO specification methods. Rational development process is a method which specifies how UML can be used in a model of the development process based in OO development.

These three method types focus on the development of ICT systems. A number of other methods focus more on the development of human activity systems, such as those in the area of participatory design (see below).

Development techniques

Development technique: A technique used to guide activity in a phase of the development process.

Techniques guide activity within one phase of the development process. They are particular approaches to supporting the processes of systems analysis, systems design and systems construction. The modelling approaches discussed in previous chapters are all examples of techniques primarily for supporting the process of analysis. A technique consists of the three elements discussed in Chapter 2: a set of constructs, a notation for representing constructs, and principles of constructing models in the chosen technique.

A distinction can be made between developer-centric techniques and user-centric techniques. **Developer-centric techniques** are designed particularly for enabling developers to understand, document and communicate information system problems to other developers. Most of these techniques are primarily directed at specification, and they provide major input to the development information system. They include information modelling, information systems modelling and object modelling.

Information modelling techniques are typically directed at specifying the *data structures* of an information system. A key example is **entity-relationship-attribute diagramming**, described in Chapter 3. **Information systems modelling** techniques are directed at specifying the *behaviour* of an information system. An example is *data flow diagramming*, discussed in Chapter 4. **Object analysis** techniques are directed at specifying the object-space of an information system. They are in some ways similar to the ways of representing business knowledge discussed on page 000.

User-centric techniques are directed at supporting and developing an understanding of a work environment, and the potential ICT has in such settings. So they are primarily directed at elicitation and negotiation, and drift into the realm of activity systems. They include prototyping, scenarios and use cases. **Prototyping** involves building various representations or early versions of an information system, which are shown to clients and end-users in order to get feedback. **Scenarios** are informal descriptions of the use of ICT systems in a particular situation. **Use cases** are representations of the major actors and interactions with an information system. These techniques are discussed on page 350.

Development tools

Development tools are the hardware, software, data management and communication technology used to construct information systems and to support the development process. They can be categorised using the layered model of an ICT system discussed in Chapter 6.

Third-generation programming language: Also known as high-level language. A programming language two steps removed from assembly language.

Fourth-generation language: A high-level programming language used to develop an information system.

The four parts of a conventional ICT application used to be constructed using one tool, a high-level or THIRD-GENERATION PROGRAMMING LANGUAGE (3GL). A language such as COBOL was used to declare appropriate file structures (data subsystem), encode the necessary operations on files (transaction subsystem), validate data processed (rules subsystem) and manage the display screen for data entry and retrieval (interface subsystem). However, over the last couple of decades there has been a tendency to use a different, specialised tool for one or more of these layers. For instance, **graphical user interface** tools have developed as a means of constructing sophisticated user interfaces. FOURTH-GENERATION LANGUAGES have developed as a means of coding business rules and application logic. **Transaction processing systems** have developed to enable high throughput of transactions. **Database management systems** have developed as sophisticated tools for managing multi-user access to stored data. Communications are enabled by a vast range of software supporting local area and wide area communications.

An application server provides most of the functionality detailed in the definition of an ICT system in Chapter 6. Since application servers are a major part of the ICT infrastructure of organizations, interest has grown in the use of open source development tools to construct and maintain them (Fitzgerald, 2006). **Open-source software** is software for which the source code is available under a licence or some other arrangement whereby users are permitted to use, change, and improve the software, and redistribute it in modified or unmodified form. It is often developed in a public, collaborative manner. The main advantages of using open source software for development purposes are its low cost and the high degree of control it provides to the developer.

The acronym **LAMP** is used for a commonly available and much-used stack of open source software, which together offers most of the functionality required to build and maintain application servers. It consists of:

- the operating system **Linux**
- the Web server software **Apache**
- the **MySQL** DBMS
- the **PHP, Perl** or **Python** programming languages.

Systems engineering: A systems discipline concerned with the production of large, complex physical artefacts.

Computer aided information systems engineering (CAISE): ICT that is used to aid automation of aspects of the development process.

Information systems development is an activity system. Most activity systems need information systems to support them, and the development process is no different. Also, ICT has been used to help automate aspects of the development process. This area is frequently known as **computer-aided software engineering** (CASE) or COMPUTER AIDED INFORMATION SYSTEMS ENGINEERING (CAISE). CAISE is a logical consequence of a recursive or incestuous view of information systems development. It has stimulated the view that information systems development, considered as an activity system with its associated information system, should be subject to and benefit from the same sorts of automation as everyday information systems.

CAISE is therefore based on a particular model of the information systems development process. In this model, the development process is seen as a set of activities operating on objects to produce other objects. The objects manipulated by these activities can be documents, diagrams, file structures or even programs. Similarly, the activities involved may be relatively formal (for instance, compile a program) or informal (for example, obtain a user's requirements). It is not surprising therefore that the linear model of information systems development and the development methods associated with it are particularly suited to the application of CAISE. However, in recent times many CAISE tools have been adapted to handle object-oriented methods as well as agile development approaches.

Reflect
What do you think are the advantages for developers of using open source development tools for development work? What are likely disadvantages?

A distinction is normally made between back-end CAISE tools, front-end CAISE tools and integrated CAISE tools. **Front-end CAISE tools** are generally directed at the analysis and design stages of information systems development. **Back-end CAISE tools** are directed at the construction, implementation, testing and maintenance stages of information systems development. **Integrated CAISE tools,** sometimes known as integrated development environments, offer assistance at all the stages of information systems development, and normally work in association with an integrated data repository which models the developing information system at various stages of development.

Recap

The process of information systems development consists of the generic phases of conception, analysis, design, construction, implementation and maintenance. A development information system is essential to ensure the effective and efficient operation of the activity system that is the development process. Development is normally organised in projects. A development project is any concerted effort to develop an information system. To undertake any development effort the information systems developer needs a toolkit. This consists of methods, techniques and tools for supporting the activities of the development process.

Case check: Case 16, The open source software movement

Open source software is computer software for which the source code is made available under a copyright licence (or arrangement such as the public domain) and that meets the open source definition. The aim of the open source movement is to make software easier to understand, modify and duplicate. An open source licence permits users to use and change software, and to redistribute it in modified or unmodified form. Open source software can be developed in traditional ways. However, it has become associated with a particular model of software development which is seen as substantially different from traditional approaches.

Conception

Conception is the first phase in the development process. It involves four major sets of activities: producing the key business case for an information system (strategic evaluation); estimating the degree of risk associated with an information systems project; considering the feasibility of the information system project in terms of organisational resources; and identifying stakeholders and their likely impact on the project. A project that passes the strategic evaluation, risk analysis, feasibility and stakeholder exercises moves on to the process of systems analysis. This is illustrated in Figure 12.7.

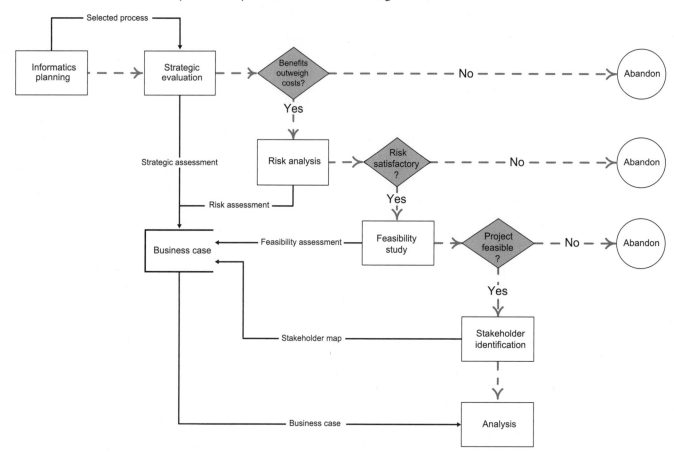

Figure 12.7: *The process of systems conception*

Key skill

Developing a business case

Developing a **business case** for a proposed information system is a part of strategic evaluation (see Chapter 9). This form of evaluation involves assessing or appraising an information system investment in terms of its potential for delivering benefit against estimated costs (see Table 12.1).

Information system projects that do not offer an appropriate level of benefits for the organisation are normally rejected. Those projects that have a reasonably substantial business case are subjected to some form of risk assessment and feasibility study.

There are two types of costs associated with information system projects: tangible or visible costs, and intangible or invisible costs. **Tangible costs** are frequently referred to as visible costs because they are reasonably straightforward to measure. **Intangible costs** are frequently referred to as invisible costs because most organisations experience difficulty in measuring them.

Table 12.1: *Types of costs and benefits associated with information systems*

	Costs	Benefits
Tangible	Hardware costs	Staff savings
Intangible	Wider organisational costs	Increased customer satisfaction

Information system projects normally incur hardware costs, software costs, installation costs, environmental costs, running costs, maintenance costs, security costs, networking costs, training costs and wider organisational costs (see Chapter 11). These must be taken into account over the entire useful life of an information system, not just its development. Organisations often forget that to decide to introduce an information system means a long-term commitment to pay for its operation and maintenance.

Information system benefits consist of the value that an organisation gains from having an information system. These too are both tangible and intangible. Often the project objective is to gain **tangible benefits** such as reducing staff count or increasing productivity (see Chapter 9). Tangible benefits are generally associated with issues of organisational efficiency. More recently, people have started to argue that **intangible benefits** such as increasing customer satisfaction or building better links with suppliers are just as relevant in investment decisions. Intangible benefits are generally concerned with issues of organisational effectiveness.

The classic direct benefits associated with information systems include the ability to handle a greater volume of information, getting information more quickly, increased accuracy of information, better quality information, more useful information, more relevant information, more secure information, the ability to use more information and use it more flexibly (see Chapter 4). Indirectly or intangibly, information systems influence features of the activity system they serve, with benefits that can include increased levels of work and productivity, increased work satisfaction, more effective working and providing a more reliable service to customers (see Chapter 9).

Cost–benefit analysis: The process of assessing whether or not the process of developing an information system (or any other project) is a worthwhile investment.

COST–BENEFIT ANALYSIS is critical to assessing whether an information system is likely to be a worthwhile investment. The investment can be justified in terms of efficiency gains such as cost savings, effectiveness gains such as better customer relations, or obtaining strategic advantage such as business growth. Most of these benefits are concerned with the *utility* of the system: that is, its impact on organisational activity (see Chapter 9).

Most of the established techniques for evaluating information system investments focus on tangible costs and benefits, and are directed primarily at assessing efficiency gains. Two of the most popular are return on investment and payback period. Most practitioners still seem to rely mainly on one or the other of these 'hard' evaluation techniques.

The **return on investment (RoI)** associated with a project is calculated using the equation RoI = average (annual net income/annual investment amount). So the calculation needs an estimate of the income (that is, the tangible benefit) likely to come from the introduction of the system, and the costs associated with it, over a defined future period.

Table 12.2 shows an example. It assumes it will take two years to get the system up and running, and that the development costs will be £300,000. It takes the life of the project to be ten years.

The **payback period** method also requires the user to estimate likely benefits and costs over a number of years. Benefit is measured as the cash inflow resulting from the information system. Payback is then calculated on the basis of payback = investment – cumulative benefit (cash inflow). The payback period is equal to the number of months or years for this payback figure to reach zero. Clearly the assumption here is that systems that provide the fastest and biggest financial benefits are the most successful. To use the Table 12.2 example again, if it is assumed that the cumulative benefit is the same as the income generated (which may not always be the case), the payback period is four years.

Table 12.2: *An example of a RoI calculation*

Year	Income	Investment	Income/Investment
1	£0	£200,000	0
2	£0	£100,000	0
3	£50,000	£10,000	5
4	£300,000	£10,000	30
5	£500,000	£10,000	50
6	£600,000	£11,000	55
7	£600,000	£11,000	55
8	£600,000	£12,000	50
9	£600,000	£12,000	50
10	£500,000	£13,000	38
11	£400,000	£13,000	31
12	£300,000	£14,000	21
RoI = average (annual net income / annual investment amount) = 32			

Did you know?

A typical investment in ICT costs from 5 to 10 per cent of the yearly turnover of a company.

Information economics: An approach to information systems evaluation that attempts to include the evaluation of intangible as well as tangible benefits.

INFORMATION ECONOMICS (Parker, Benson and Trainor, 1988) tries to improve on these standard methods by allowing for intangible as well as tangible benefits. It does this by assessing feasibility in the business domain and viability in the technological domain. It uses an extended form of RoI which includes both traditional cost–benefit analysis and a number of value assessments: value linking, value accelerating, value restructuring and innovation valuation.

Value linking and **value accelerating** are attempts to estimate the ripple effect of technology change on the organisation. **Value restructuring** is an attempt to assess the increases in productivity that arise from the introduction of information systems. At a practical level information economics involves completing a scorecard for each information system and computing the weighted score as an indication of the value of the system to the organisation. Table 12.3 shows an example.

Reflect

Many organisations now use **portfolio management** in considering the business case for information systems development. In other words, a range of possible projects are considered together and evaluated for their overall impact on the information systems infrastructure. Why do you think this approach is important?

Table 12.3: *An example of information economics*

Evaluator	Business domain						Technology domain				
	RoI (+)	SM (+)	CA (+)	MI (+)	CR (+)	OR (–)	SA (+)	DU (–)	TU (–)	IR (–)	
Business domain											
Technology domain											Weighted score
Weighted value											

Information systems portfolio: A list of current systems in the information systems architecture or future systems in the information systems strategy.

On this scorecard, RoI is a traditional return on investment calculation. SM stands for *strategic match*: that is, the degree to which the system matches the strategy of the organisation. CA is *competitive advantage*: the degree to which the system is expected to deliver competitive advantage for the company. MI stands for *management information support*. CR stands for *competitive response*: the degree to which the system will enable the organisation to react quickly to its environment, and OR for *organisational risk* associated with developing the information system. SA is *strategic information systems architecture*, and is an assessment of the degree to which the system matches the architecture (that is, the infrastructure) for information systems in the organisation. DU stands for definitional or *domain uncertainty* – the degree to which requirements for the information system remain uncertain – while TU is *technical uncertainty*, the number of technical imponderables in the project. Finally, IR stands for *information systems infrastructure risk*: the degree to which the system might adversely affect the INFORMATION SYSTEMS INFRASTRUCTURE.

Information systems infrastructure: The entire set of information systems used by an organisation.

Some columns are labelled as '+': these items positively contribute to value so their scores are positive. Other columns are labelled '-', representing items that will negatively contribute to value and which should be subtracted from the score. Note also that each of the factors on the scorecard can be weighted. This allows the evaluator to indicate the importance of each factor to a particular project. In one project, strategic match might be critically important and weighted as 10, but for another project, perhaps to produce a more operationally based or support information system, this factor may be judged to be of low importance and perhaps weighted as 4.

Risk analysis

Risk analysis: The identification, estimation and assessment of risk.

Information economics includes specific reference to the concept of risk. Perhaps because information systems failure appears commonplace (see Chapter 9), risk and risk assessment play a large part in research and discussion on software engineering and information systems development (Boehm, 1989).

Risk is clearly involved in all information system projects. It can be defined as a negative outcome that has a known or estimated probability of occurring, based on experience or a theory. Most people think of information system failure as the big risk, but as we have seen, this is a relative and not absolute concept. Emphasising the relationship between stakeholders and risk, Wilcocks and Margetts (1994) maintain that 'risk of a negative outcome only becomes a salient problem when the outcome is relevant to stakeholder concerns and interests. Different settings and stakeholders will see different outcomes as salient.'

RISK ANALYSIS involves:

- **risk identification**: generating a checklist of risks for a particular project
- **risk estimation**: assessing the likelihood or probability of a risk occurring, and determining its likely impact
- **risk assessment**: prioritising risks and planning how to avoid or monitor them.

Researchers have developed several frameworks which can be used to analyse risks. For instance, Cash, McFarlan and McKeney (1992) suggest that at least three important dimensions influence the risk of a project: project size, experience with the technology and project structure. In general, the smaller the project, the more experienced staff are and the more structured a project is, the less risk associated with it:

- **Project size** can be defined in a number of ways such as the level of investment needed. It is just as important to assess how many stakeholders will be affected by a project (see below).
- In general, the more **experience** the organisation has with the proposed technology, the less risk there is. This clearly relates to the skill and experience of developers. It also applies to the prior experience of various stakeholder groups in using or being aware of particular technologies.
- Generally, the more highly **structured** the project, the less risk is likely to be associated with it. If the project has clearly established and uncontroversial goals, it is likely to succeed. If stakeholder groups have not agreed on its goals, it is likely to fail.

Feasibility study

Feasibility study: That part of systems conception concerned with assessing the feasibility of developing an information system.

A FEASIBILITY STUDY can be considered as part of systems conception, or the first activity in the systems analysis process. This is an attempt to determine whether an information system is achievable given organisational resources and constraints. In order to assess the feasibility of an information system project, the assessor needs an initial idea of its functionality, usability and utility. An initial scope for the information system is then compared with the existing informatics infrastructure, to see whether the available hardware, software, data storage and communication infrastructure could handle it. Another aspect of feasibility is the development demand: the assessor needs to consider what resources will be needed in development, and whether they will be available. Ideally the feasibility study will assess a number of alternative solutions to the development problem, such as whether bespoke or package development is preferable.

Stakeholder identification

Stakeholder analysis: Analysing the types of and impact of stakeholders on information systems.

Chapter 2 defined a STAKEHOLDER as any group in or outside an organisation that has a vested interest in an organisational system. Stakeholder groups are likely to affect the trajectory and consequent success or failure of an information system (see Chapter 9). It is therefore important to identify them at the start of a project and make sure they are suitably involved.

One useful technique is to take the major types of stakeholder group defined in Chapter 9 and use a **responsibility assignment (RACI) matrix.** This considers the responsibilities of various roles or resources in delivering activities in a project, or operating a process. It is particularly useful when projects and/or processes cross functional or departmental boundaries. Usually between four and seven responsibilities are assessed. These ones are normally important to an information system project:

Role: A package of behaviour associated with a particular social situation.

- A ROLE is **responsible** (R) for the performance of an activity if the role-holder has to engage in work to complete the activity.
- A role is **accountable** (A) if the person is ultimately answerable for the correct and thorough completion of an activity. Someone in this role is therefore normally expected to sign off the activity before it becomes effective.
- A role is **consulted** (C) if it is necessary to seek its opinion on the exercise of some activity. In other words, there needs to be two-way communication with people fulfilling this type of role.
- A role is **informed** (I) if it needs to be kept informed of the progress or performance of some activity. In other words, there needs to be one-way communication with people fulfilling this type of role.

Clearly responsibilities will vary depending on the shape of a particular project. Generally however, producers tend to have responsibility for the various activities of development work, clients are accountable for such work and representatives of end-users should be consulted on the shape of an information system, as illustrated in Table 12.4.

Table 12.4: *A high-level template for stakeholder identification and involvement*

	Producer	Client	End-user	Partner	Customer	Supplier
Conception	R	A	C	I	I	I
Analysis	R	A	C	I	I	I
Design	R	A	C	I	I	I
Construction	R	A	C	I	I	I
Implementation	R	A	C	I	I	I
Maintenance	R	A	C	I	I	I

Analysis

Any system can be analysed. Here the term **systems analysis** is used to apply to the analysis of two types of system, ICT systems and activity systems. They should ideally be analysed in parallel. Systems analysis in information systems development is a form of sociotechnical analysis, and is normally conducted by specialists known as systems analysts.

Analysis can start by documenting current ICT systems and current activity systems, and will probably also involve the analysis of requirements for new ICT systems and new activity systems.

The analysis of activity systems will receive inputs from the process of organisational analysis (see Chapter 2) in the sense that a process suitable for redesign is likely to have been identified. The analysis of ICT systems will receive inputs from the process of systems conception. The entire process of analysis provides outputs to the process of systems design, and is illustrated in Figure 12.8.

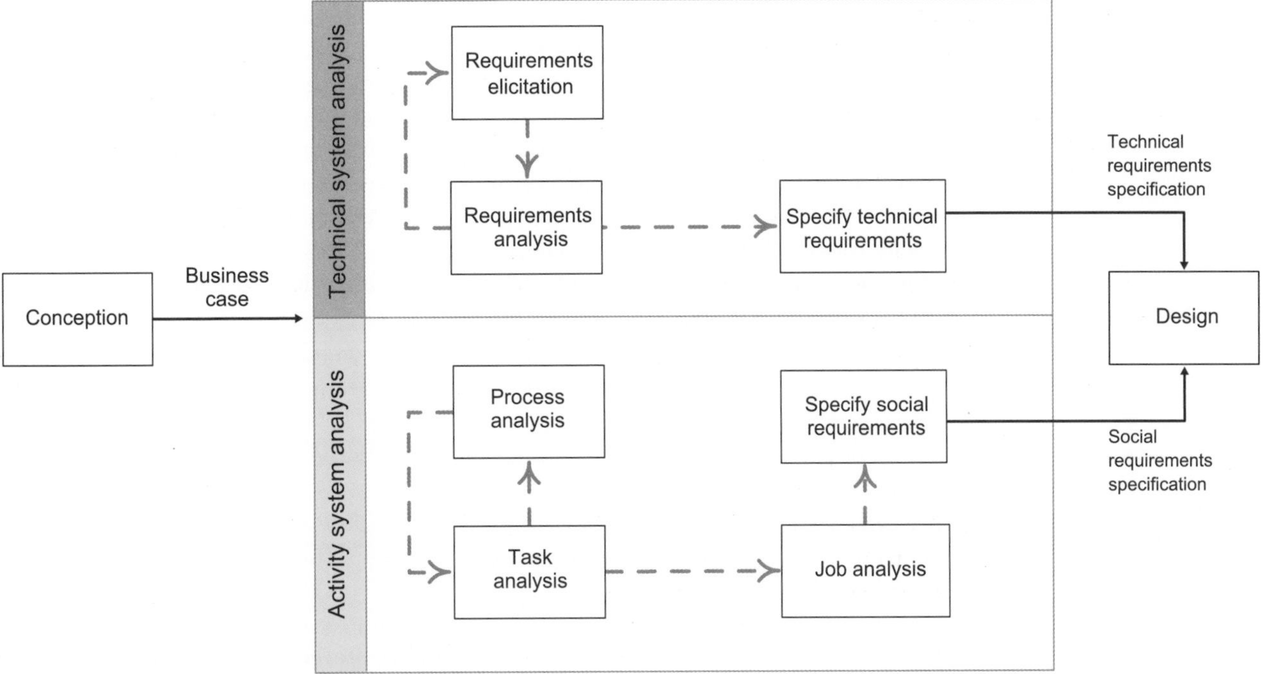

Figure 12.8: *The process of systems analysis*

Did you know?

Much of the impetus for systems analysis as a general approach to defining problems emerged from the work of the RAND Corporation (Research ANd Development). RAND was created in 1948 as a not-for-profit global policy think tank, initially to offer research and analysis to the US armed forces.

ICT systems analysis

ICT systems analysis involves three primary and interrelated activities:

- **Requirements elicitation** is the process of identifying requirements for the system from stakeholder groups.
- **Requirements analysis** involves negotiating and agreeing requirements with the various stakeholders.
- **Requirements specification** involves representing requirements using various modelling approaches.

One of the first things that must be done in any information systems project is to identify the relevant stakeholders (see above). For developing effective requirements, three types of stakeholder are important . First, **clients** normally set the key organisation objectives for the ICT system, particularly in terms of utility. Second, **end-users** are particularly important for setting the key functionality and usability requirements for an information system. Third, external stakeholders such as **customers** may be important in setting objectives for assessing the worth of the activity supported by the ICT system.

A **requirement** is any desired feature of an information system. It is sometimes thought that these are unproblematic, in the sense that it is not that difficult to find out from the stakeholder community what they want. However, as was argued in Chapter 9, requirements can vary depending on the stakeholder group. They are not objective in the sense that they will be the same for everyone; they are relative to a particular stakeholder's perspective or worldview (see Chapter 2). Different stakeholders' requirements might conflict. Requirements analysis therefore involves attempting to achieve an intersubjective agreement between stakeholder groups on their requirements. Requirements must be frozen at some point in order to construct an ICT system – an artefact – but they are likely to change over time. Part of the reason for the maintenance of systems is that requirements change, and organisations should plan for this.

Software engineering makes a distinction between functional and non-functional requirements. **Functional requirements** are expected features of an information system. **Non-functional requirements** are constraints set on the systems development project. The set of functional and non-functional requirements establishes the scope of the information system.

Requirements elicitation is the process of identifying requirements. It is sometimes called requirements capture, but this term does not really reflect the issues just outlined. Requirements cannot be captured, since they are intersubjective constructs; they have to be established via a process of negotiation.

The techniques for requirements elicitation include interviews, observation, documentary analysis, workshops, prototyping and ethnography.

- **Interviews** are the most commonly used technique. These are either formal or informal discussions with representatives of key stakeholder groups. Formal interviews are structured conversations in which questions are determined beforehand. Informal interviews are a form of discussion in which the questions are formulated within the flow of the interview itself.
- Interviews are often used together with other elicitation techniques such as observation. **Observation** usually involves being present in work settings and recording the detailed work behaviour of people.
- Documents are a valuable resource in most organisations. They are particularly important, for instance, in indicating data that needs to be stored in an information system and the type of reports that need to be generated from it. This suggests the importance of **documentary analysis** to requirements elicitation.
- **Workshops** are sessions in which developers and representatives of stakeholder groups get together in a structured situation. They provide controlled environments for the negotiation of requirements, so are often known as joint requirements planning workshops.
- Stakeholder groups might not be able to formulate what they require until they see a representation of what is planned. **Prototyping** involves building early versions of particular parts of a system to demonstrate to stakeholder representatives, in order to obtain their feedback.

Reflect
Of the range of requirements elicitation techniques, which do you think is the most commonly used in practice, and why?

Any one elicitation technique gives only a partial picture of the requirements space. Frequently what people describe in interviews, for instance, only partly reveals how they go about their everyday work. So it is important to 'triangulate', using a number of techniques in combination. The analyst might for example use interviews together with an elicitation technique such as observation, to check that what people say they do, they actually do in practice.

Requirements specification is representing the requirements established in the requirements elicitation process. It conventionally involves a form of **intermediate representation** – some notation for representing requirements, which is frequently graphical, sometimes textual, and occasionally mathematical.

Two user-centric requirements elicitation techniques, use cases and scenarios, are particularly relevant to specifying the high-level scope of the use context of an information system. Often these are used in a development workshop for negotiating requirements. The requirements are then specified in more detail using developer-centric techniques.

Use case model: A use case model provides a high-level description of major user interactions with an information system.

A USE CASE MODEL provides a high-level description of major user interactions with an information system. It uses two constructs, actors and use cases. An **actor** is any person, organisation or system that interacts with an information system. A **use case** is a delimited set of activities that collectively form an important element of the functionality of the system.

Figure 12.9 is a simple use case model for an automatic teller machine (ATM) system. There are three main actors: bank customers, ATM operators and back-end banking systems. Four main use cases are defined: withdrawing cash from the ATM (*cash withdrawal*), transferring funds between bank accounts (*transfer funds*), depositing funds in bank accounts (*deposit funds*), and administering the ATM (*administration*). The first three use cases are generic interactions between customers and banking systems. The last use case is a specialised function provided for technicians given the task of maintaining the operation of the machine.

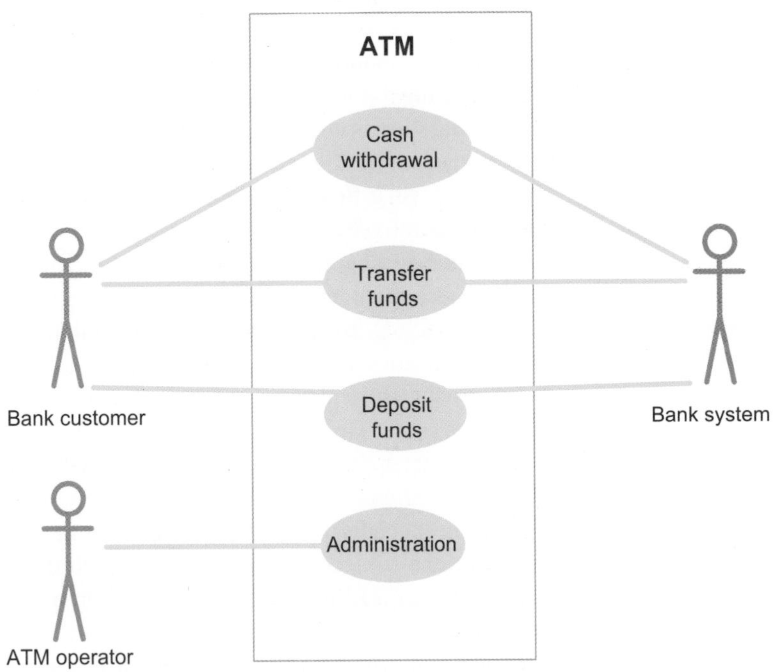

Figure 12.9: *A use case model*

Scenario: A narrative description of what people do and experience as they try to make use of computer systems and applications.

Each use case in a use case model can be specified in more detail as a SCENARIO. Scenarios are described by Carroll (1995) as 'a narrative description of what people do and experience as they try to make use of computer systems and applications'. Other definitions differ from this, but there are some common elements. Scenarios normally consist of key situations or episodes in the activity of people working with computers. The emphasis in a scenario is on concrete representation of use rather than abstraction of use. The focus is on specific instances of use in a work context. Scenarios are therefore a middle-level abstraction between the formality of an ICT system specification and the informality of everyday discussions between developers and users, so they tend to provide more of a user-centric than a developer-centric representation.

This is a short scenario describing the use of a company database for marketing purposes:

> An advert is placed in the local newspaper for short courses. A person phones up with an enquiry but is not in the company database. Operator needs to record his details while on the phone. Enter company details including interests as tags. Company details copied across to contact form. Enter contact details. Tag with interest in courses on personal computing. Place memo against contact – posting a letter. Back to to-do list. Removing items from to-do list.

This brings out the key elements of interaction with the data entry screens of this company's intended information system.

Activity systems analysis

In most information systems projects it is important to analyse the larger context of activity surrounding an ICT system. At the macro level this may involve some form of

Task analysis: Specifying the precise organisation of tasks associated with the use of a computer system.

organisational analysis (see Chapter 2). At the micro level it focuses on issues such as process analysis, TASK ANALYSIS and job analysis.

An activity system or organisational process can be decomposed into a set of activities. Each activity, in turn, can be decomposed into a set of tasks and subtasks. So there is a hierarchy of processes, activities and tasks which can in principle be specified for a given activity system.

Let's look again at the very simple example of an ATM again. Using the ATM is a major element of the activity system of a high-street bank. The process of using an ATM can be considered as a set of activities or use cases, as in the scenario above. Each activity can in turn be decomposed into tasks, which in this example might be inserting a debit or credit card, entering a personal identifier number (PIN), selecting/entering an amount, selecting a withdrawal slip, receiving cash, receiving the returned card, and receiving the withdrawal slip.

A variant of task analysis, particularly relevant to collaboration amongst teams, is the analysis of **work flow.** This involves determining ways in which ICT can be used to support collaborative work and improve the effectiveness of collaboration. A key feature of this activity is mapping existing work flow. This has many similarities with the idea of process modelling as considered in Chapter 2.

Job analysis: The analysis of the content and relationships of current jobs in terms of both organisational and individual objectives.

JOB ANALYSIS involves analysing the content and relationships of current jobs in terms of both organisational and individual objectives. Organisations generally have objectives such as improving the efficiency and/or effectiveness of work. Individuals also generally have objectives such as increasing their levels of fulfilment and job satisfaction.

Traditional approaches to analysing activity systems break them down into various levels of activities and tasks, which are then closely studied using tangible performance measures. Increasing specialisation and segmentation of tasks is seen as the primary way of achieving organisational objectives, but this often conflicts with individual objectives. Heavy specialisation can lead to substantial deskilling of the workforce, and people tend to find this unfulfilling and demotivating. It also leads to a decreasing level of flexibility.

Ideally, requirements are generated for new work systems as well as new technical systems. The aim is to achieve an optimal balance between social and technical objectives.

Many researchers have looked at issues of job satisfaction, and it is fairly clear what features characterise jobs that give workers satisfaction. People like jobs that allow ample opportunity for them to exercise their skills and extend them through learning. They like it if it is easy to understand how their work fits into the organisation, and if their work is explicitly valued. Also, the more people can control their own work, the higher their levels of satisfaction. Jobs supply satisfaction if they include collaboration and communication with others, and include a mix of routine and new demands. People also appreciate control over which new demands to accept, and jobs that do not interfere with their ability to participate in family and community life.

Did you know?

Many ICTs are not appropriate for particular activity systems. For example, a few years ago a major investment bank planned to introduce voice recognition software on its trading floor. It reasoned that the activities of buying and selling stocks and shares on the trading floor seemed to consist of primarily verbal communication between traders, so a trading information system should be able to automatically track trades using voice recognition software. However, when the analysts probed deeper, they realised that traders tended to communicate in single words (such as yes or no) or even single syllables (such as uh!). These terse verbal communications were accompanied by non-verbal cues such as holding up a number of fingers to signal the volume of a trade. Not surprisingly, the analysts decided that the voice recognition system would not work in this situation.

Design

Design can be conducted on any system, but **systems design** is used here to refer to the design of ICT systems and activity systems. As with analysis, such systems should ideally be designed in parallel, so information systems design is a form of sociotechnical design.

Design is planning the shape of something to meet requirements established by analysis. It involves a reflective conversation with the situation – considering requirements and constraints, and the selection from among design alternatives. Design benefits from the participation of system stakeholders (see Chapter 9).

Information system design produces a system specification that is the major input into systems construction. This system specification acts as a blueprint for construction work. This is illustrated in Figure 12.10.

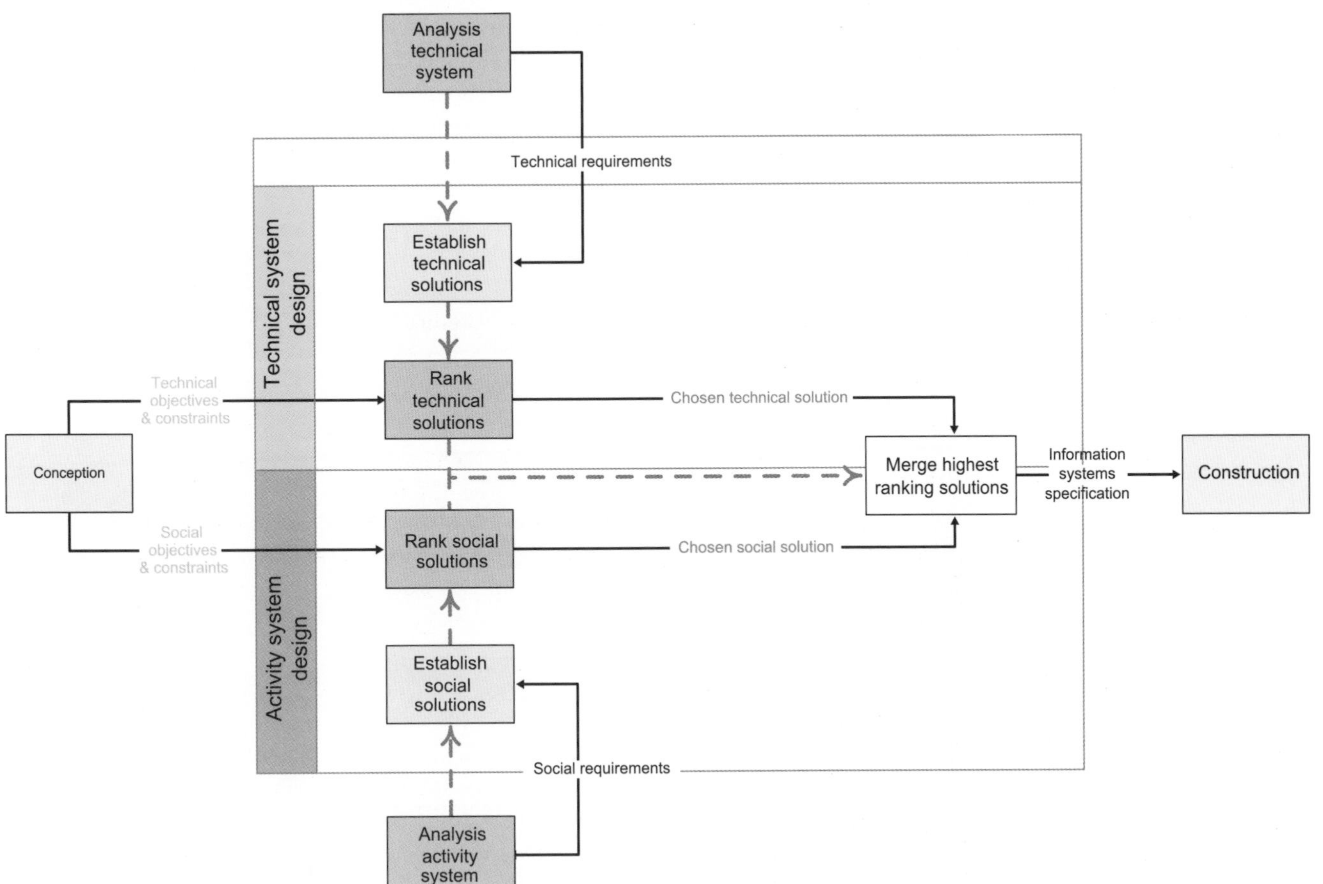

Figure 12.10: *The systems design process*

The design of information systems and the activity systems within which they exist is cyclically related. Information systems are normally built as a reflection of organisational work, since designing an information system involves investigating and defining organisational work. Introducing and using an information system may cause changes to organisational work. The introduction of ICT is normally an attempt to improve organisational work in some way, but it can decrease organisational effectiveness if not handled carefully (see Chapter 9).

An example of nursing in general hospitals should help show the interdependence of activity systems and information systems. There are three basic models of activity systems appropriate for organising nursing on a hospital ward: round nursing, primary care nursing and group nursing:

- **Round nursing** is very much task oriented. Each nurse has responsibility for one task on the ward. For example, one nurse is responsible for giving all patients their prescribed medicines.
- **Primary care** is patient oriented. One nurse has the responsibility for carrying out all the tasks associated with one patient. Usually each nurse is responsible for a small group of patients. In primary care, for instance, one nurse is likely to be responsible for giving all medicines to their group of patients.

- **Group nursing** is a mixture of the above. A group of nurses have the responsibility for carrying out several tasks, but only for one group of patients. In group nursing, for instance, one nurse may be given the responsibility for distributing regular medicines while all nurses give out additional medicines according to patients' needs.

Each of these nursing activity systems demands a substantially different information system. Figure 12.11 shows this. In round nursing there is a need to exchange medical information, such as which medicines have been given to which patients, but there is little need for information to coordinate tasks between nurses. In contrast, within primary care there is very little exchange of medical information between nurses, but there is a need to know which nurses care for which patients. In group nursing there is need both to exchange medical information and for much information necessary to the effective coordination of nursing tasks. This last form of activity system therefore demands the most complex information system to support its work.

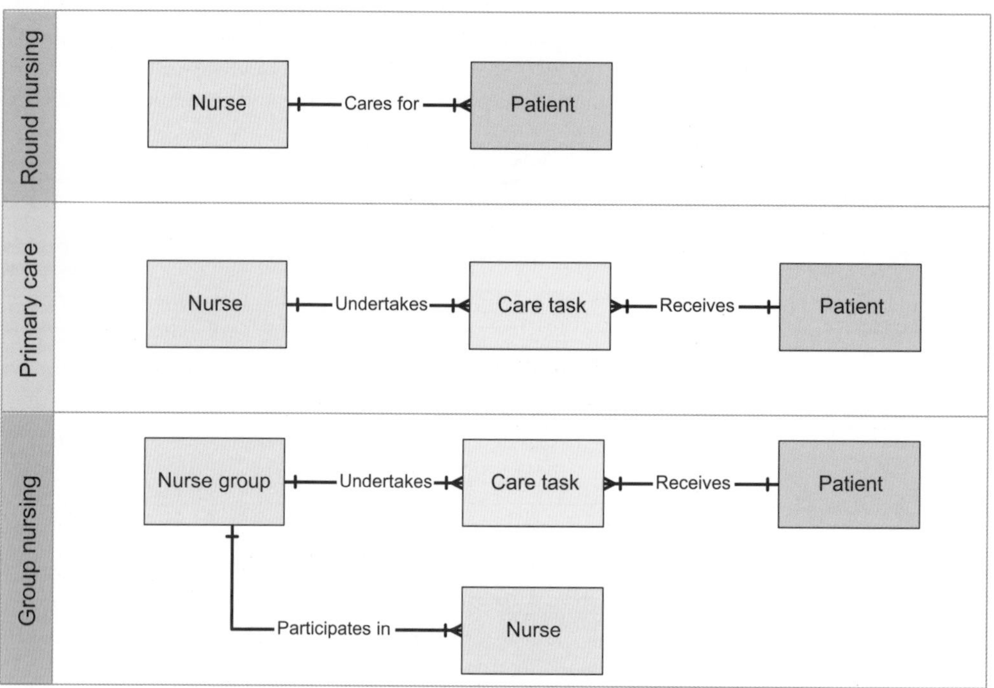

Figure 12.11: *Information models corresponding to distinct human activity systems for nursing*

Sociotechnical design

Sociotechnical design: The parallel design of both technical and social systems.

ETHICS: Mumford's sociotechnical design method.

Figure 12.10 (on page 365) is an attempt to represent the essence of sociotechnical design in the context of informatics work. It is based on three major approaches in this area.

The work of the late Enid Mumford (1983) provides one of the most coherent accounts of how to do sociotechnical design in an informatics context. She developed a method for it from her decades of work on the effective design of sociotechnical systems called ETHICS (Effective Technical and Human Implementation of Computer Systems). The objective of ETHICS is to design a new form of work organisation with the dual objectives of improving job satisfaction (the social system) and work efficiency (the technical system) (Mumford, 2006). Other approaches in the same vein include the Multiview method (Avison et al., 1998) and soft systems methodology (Checkland, 1999).

Analysis involves establishing both technical requirements (the shape of the intended ICT system) and social requirements (the shape of the intended activity system). These requirements should make a number of design solutions feasible in both the technical and social areas. These can then be assessed and ranked using the objectives and constraints established in the systems conception process. The highest-ranking technical solution is merged with the highest-ranking social solution, and this is then developed into a full specification for the information system.

Mumford provides a case study of a customer orders and accounts system which was analysed by the ETHICS approach, leading to the introduction of a new social and technical system. Although this case was conducted in the 1980s, it still illustrates the essential principles of the sociotechnical approach.

The basic technical system involved orders clerks filling out order forms, accounts clerks updating customer ledgers and any problems being resolved by passing around lots of paper. In the social system there was a clear distinction between orders clerks and accounts clerks, with each accounts clerk working across a number of different customer accounts. Problems were resolved by two senior clerks.

The motivations for change were both technical and social. Examples of technical problems were orders incorrectly filled out, customer ledgers incorrectly updated and slow methods of resolving problems. Examples of social problems were high absenteeism, high staff turnover and some 'industrial vandalism'.

Workers were asked to fill in a job satisfaction questionnaire, and this showed that they had low job satisfaction as a result of piecework, lack of overall picture, individual isolation, low status and poor prospects for advancement. What they wanted from the redesign was more responsibility, group working, more important work and better opportunities for advancement.

After the study was complete a new work and technical system was put in place. The technical system involved online input of orders, batch update of a central database and regular reports output from the ICT system. The social system was changed to small work groups of five clerks, with each work group handling orders and accounts for a group of customers. The group handled customer problems thrown up by printouts. When the new system was later evaluated, the assessors found increased rates of job satisfaction and increased productivity.

Stakeholder participation

Stakeholder participation: Involvement of stakeholders both in the development of the ICT system and the work surrounding its use.

As this example demonstrates, systems design benefits from forms of STAKEHOLDER PARTICIPATION. End-users are probably the most significant stakeholder group to involve in a development project. Some benefits of participation include a closer match between the information system and the requirements of stakeholders, a closer match between the information system and the activity system, and a greater commitment of stakeholders to the new sociotechnical system.

However, Hirschheim (1983) maintains that participation is not the same as involvement. All information system projects have some degree of stakeholder involvement, if only at the implementation phase, but only some are participatively developed. The major differences between user involvement and user participation relate to decision-making power. In user involvement the users are normally given a degree of power over decisions on the shape of the information system. In user participation that power is extended to decisions about social and job considerations.

Consultative participation: Decision making is still in the hands of systems analysts and systems designers, but a great deal of staff at every level are consulted before decisions are made.

Representative participation: A design group is formed made up of representatives of all grades of staff with systems analysts. The representatives however are selected by management.

Consensus participation: A design group is formed as in representative participation, but representatives are elected by staff and given the responsibility to communicate group decisions back to staff.

The forms of participation can be categorised using the dimensions of level of participation and type of participation. Mumford distinguished between three different levels of user participation in systems design. In CONSULTATIVE PARTICIPATION, decision making is still in the hands of systems analysts and systems designers, but staff at every level are consulted. With REPRESENTATIVE PARTICIPATION, a design group is formed made up of representatives of all grades of staff plus systems analysts. The representatives are selected by management. In CONSENSUS PARTICIPATION, a design group is formed as in representative participation, but representatives are elected by staff and given the responsibility to communicate group decisions back to staff.

There is also a distinction between intensive and phased modes of participation. In **intensive mode** stakeholder representatives are assigned for the entire duration of the project, so they form a permanent part of the development team. In **phased participation** stakeholders are invited to review the development effort at regular intervals. Intensive participation tends to be used more frequently on iterative development projects, whereas phased participation is typically characteristic of linear development projects (see page 350).

The components of design

Physical design: The process of detailing the major elements of how a system will work on a computer system.

Another useful distinction is between two levels of ICT systems design. **Logical design** is the attempt to specify the design of an ICT system independent of any implementation detail. PHYSICAL DESIGN is the design of the implementation of a system – a blueprint for its construction.

Logical design involves activities such as input design, output design, processing design, the design of key data structures, the design of a communication framework and the design of disaster recovery and security management. Physical design involves activities such as detailing hardware devices needed, describing the shape of programs, detailing the forms of communication hardware and software, designing database systems and designing the user interface.

Reflect
It is probably true that most development projects in commercial organisations involve stakeholders but few allow participation as described above. Why do you think this is?

Activity systems consist of people and the activities or procedures they perform. Three interrelated activities are part of activity systems design. **Job design** has the aim of balancing the needs of job satisfaction with work efficiency. **Team design** has the aim of establishing teams with clear structures of authority and control. **Procedure design** involves detailing established patterns of work.

In most commercial organisations, managerial groups usually determine the shape of designed activity systems. McGregor (1960) identified two distinct worldviews (Chapter 2) which influence the way in which managers think about workers, and so influence the design of activity systems. He called them theory X and theory Y. According to THEORY X, the average person dislikes work and avoids it wherever possible. They avoid responsibility and have little ambition. According to THEORY Y, physical and mental effort are important and natural human functions. If humans are committed to objectives they will exercise self-direction and self-control. The capacity to exercise imagination, ingenuity and creativity is widely distributed in the population.

Theory X: According to this theory the average human being is perceived as disliking work and hence avoiding it wherever possible. The average human being avoids responsibility and has little ambition.

Theory Y: According to this theory physical and mental effort are important and natural human functions. If humans are committed to certain objectives they will exercise self-direction and self-control. The capacity to exercise imagination, ingenuity and creativity are widely distributed in the population.

Using theory X, activity systems are designed with the clear intention of monitoring the workforce and controlling their behaviour through coercion. The objective is to provide sufficient information to management to enable them to exercise close control. Using theory Y, activity systems are designed to encourage ingenuity and creativity. Information systems are there to encourage cooperation and collaboration amongst the workforce in the achievement of objectives.

Adopting a theory Y perspective, a number of strategies can be used in the design of activity systems to increase levels of job satisfaction:

- **Job rotation** involves increasing variety and learning opportunities for the workforce. It also has substantial benefits in improving organisational flexibility.
- **Job enlargement** involves combining a number of tasks, and offers the potential of creating more complete and hence more meaningful jobs.
- **Job enrichment i**nvolves increasing the scope of a job and giving workers more responsibility for making decisions about their own work. The key aim is to improve the motivational aspect of work.
- **Group working** acts as an important source of support, encouragement and security for individual workers.

Recap 

The three front-end phases of the development life-cycle are conception, analysis and design. Conception is the phase involved with the production of the key business case, the analysis of risk and an assessment of the feasibility of an information system project. Analysis involves two interrelated activities related to requirements for the new system, elicitation and specification. Design involves planning the shape of an information system to meet the requirements established in systems analysis. It also involves designing the activity system into which the technical artefact will be placed.

Construction

Systems construction is the actual process of building the information system. It follows on from systems design and is followed by systems implementation. This sequence is illustrated in Figure 12.12. Since an information system is a sociotechnical system, two parallel construction activities must take place: constructing the ICT system and constructing the activity system.

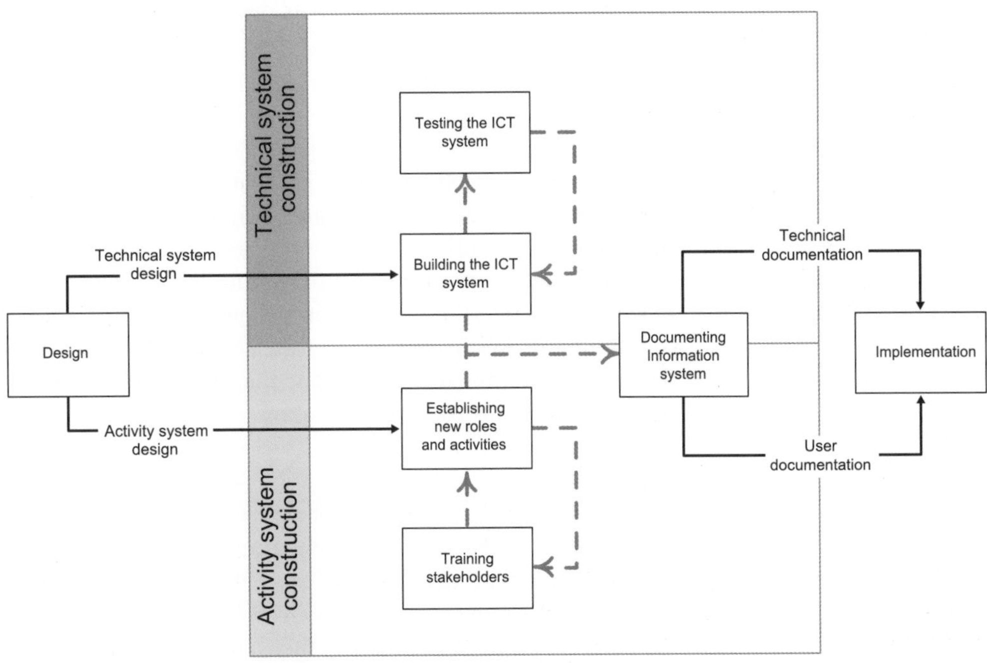

Figure 12.12: *Systems construction*

Traditionally ICT system construction involves the three related processes of programming, testing and documentation. These activities differ depending on whether the development is based on bought packages or is bespoke.

ICT system construction

Building ICT systems normally involves constructing the four layers of the ICT systems model and its associated communication facilities. This means building the user interface (constructing data entry forms, menus and reports), building the business rules and application logic (specifying integrity constraints and elements of processing), building the transaction layer (specifying the major update functions for the system) and building the data management layer (creating the data structures for storing data).

Although historically the four parts of a conventional ICT application were built using one tool, a high-level or third-generation programming language (3GL), over the last couple of decades there has been a tendency to use a different, specialised tool for one or more layers.

There are variants to this tool-based approach to building ICT systems. Package development using software packages involves the interrelated activities of package selection and package tailoring (see below). Building using software components involves using pre-built software components to construct either the whole or the part of an ICT system.

In the process of constructing the system various tests must be conducted to ensure that it is working effectively. Effectiveness is defined by specified functional requirements and non-functional requirements such as performance.

There are a number of distinct types of testing. UNIT TESTING is testing individual programs or software modules. SYSTEM TESTING tests an entire system as a unit. VOLUME TESTING involves testing the application with large amounts of data and use. At some point the system has to be assembled as a complete unit and testing conducted of all related systems together. This is known as INTEGRATION TESTING. Finally, ACCEPTANCE TESTING consists of conducting any tests required

Testing: Part of systems construction. Ensuring that an information system is working effectively.

Unit testing: Testing of individual programs or software modules.

System testing: Testing of an entire system as a unit.

Volume testing: Testing the application with large amounts of data and use.

Integration testing: Testing of all related systems together once a complex system has been assembled as a complete unit.

Acceptance testing: Conducting any tests required by the user to ensure that the user community is satisfied with the system.

PART 4

User documentation: A source of reference for users to turn to when puzzled about aspects of use.

Reflect
Why is system documentation so important to maintenance?

by the users, to ensure that the user community is satisfied with the system. Generally these forms of testing are performed in sequence, and some of the testing may pass over into the implementation phase.

An ICT system needs to be documented to ensure that it can be used and that adequate information is provided to ensure effective maintenance of the system. Two major types of documentation are required. USER DOCUMENTATION is a source of reference for users to turn to when puzzled about aspects of use. Systems or **technical documentation** describes the structure and behaviour of the ICT system for developers, particularly for use in maintenance (see below).

Package construction

Package construction involves a 'buy not build' strategy, and blurs the traditional boundaries of systems construction and systems implementation. Typically standard software modules for core business processes are combined with bespoke customisation to help the organisation differentiate itself and gain competitive advantage. Package implementation normally involves selecting software modules then deciding on the profile of adoption throughout the company. At one end of the scale an organisation might choose to standardise modules across organisational functions; at the other end, it varies module adoption. Customisation normally involves 'programming' configuration (tables) associated with each software module.

Mega-package construction is subtly different from traditional package construction. In a traditional model, companies decide what they want in terms of functionality, usability and utility, choose a package to closely meet those needs and then rewrite large portions of the software to ensure that there is a close fit with organisational imperatives. The mega-package model of development involves a change of emphasis. The organisation selects an enterprise resource planning (ERP) system, then adapts the enterprise to fit it. Some degree of customisation is possible, but the complexity of the system makes major modifications impractical. In this sense, mega-package procurement can be considered as another form of outsourcing information system development (see Chapter 10).

Activity system construction

Human activity system design: Design which includes job design, team design and procedure design.

Change management is the term for a structured approach to moving an organisation from a current state to a desired future state. How much change is involved will reflect the degree to which ICT is used to transform organisational processes. If the ICT system is to be used in an existing activity system, to *support* existing ways of doing things, change management will be restricted to training users thoroughly to use it. If it is used to *supplant* or automate existing human activities, or it *transforms* the activity system in a major way, the change management process will involve establishing new jobs and roles, organising any teams and establishing new work procedures.

Implementation

The process of **systems implementation** (sometimes called systems delivery) follows on from systems construction. This involves delivering an information system into its context of use (see Chapter 9). Since an information system is a sociotechnical system, an ICT system and some form of activity system are implemented in parallel. Once a system is delivered into its context of use it will be subject to the processes of operation (see Chapter 11) and systems maintenance (see page 371).

Types of systems implementation

Systems implementation involves both technical and social systems. **Technical systems implementation** means ensuring that the appropriate hardware, communications, software and data are in place. **Social systems implementation** involves ensuring that the appropriate users are identified, trained and supported in the use of the technology.

Systems implementation can take place in three major ways: direct conversion, parallel implementation and hybrid implementation:

- DIRECT CONVERSION is sometimes called 'Big Bang' implementation. This is a confident approach, in which the new system directly replaces the old system. There is no temporal overlap between the implementation of the new system and the system it replaces.
- In PARALLEL IMPLEMENTATION two information systems, the old and the new system, run in parallel for a while. This is a cautious approach in that if there are problems with the new system, the organisation can revert to the old system until they are resolved. Eventually the organisation should be happy enough with the new system for the old system to be terminated.
- HYBRID IMPLEMENTATION introduces particular components in a phased manner as replacements, or pilots major modules of the system. It is an evolutionary approach in the sense that the impact of implementation is distributed more evenly over time than in direct conversion.

Direct conversion: An implementation approach in which the new system directly replaces the old system.

Hybrid implementation: Implementation that phases in particular components as replacements or pilots major modules of the system.

Parallel implementation: An implementation approach in which two systems, the old and the new system, run in parallel..

Technical systems implementation

Technical systems implementation involves the following activities, generally in some form of sequence.

- **Software acquisition** is the acquisition of operating systems, DBMS, and possibly packaged software.
- **Hardware acquisition** is the purchase of computers, peripheral devices and communication networks.
- If a new system replaces an old system, there needs to be a form of **data transfer** between the systems. Data may have to be prepared for the transfer. For 'greenfield' systems certain data elements such as reference data will probably need to be prepared for entry into the system.
- Implementation involves the **installation** of hardware, software and entering data into the system.
- It also involves **testing** that the system works effectively as a complete configuration. Acceptance testing normally leads to a formal or informal **sign-off** of the system. This indicates some level of acceptance with the levels of performance the system provides.
- Finally there is introduction or **delivery**, and going 'live' with the system in its context of use.

PART 4

Social systems implementation

As a minimum, social systems implementation involves activities such as team formation, training and user acceptance. **User group formation** involves forming the appropriate user groups for using the system. There will need to be user and operator **training** in work practices and procedures for use of the system. This can be done by the developers of the system or by a user representative who becomes expert in the use of the system, then passes on this knowledge to other users. Finally, the system needs to be formally **accepted** by user groups. This involves some acceptance testing.

As part of any implementation a user document or manual is normally produced. This should act as a source of reference for the use of the system (see Chapter 9). Support is also usually provided in the form of a helpdesk or support service (see Chapter 11). This is a specialised service designed to answer any questions users may pose on the use of the system.

A system is not always unconditionally accepted by its user community. There is a lot of evidence of systems being resisted (see Chapter 9), so strategies for stakeholder management must be included not just in the implementation process, but across all phases of development.

Reflect
Implementation is probably one of the most critical stages at which an information system can fail. Why do you think this might be?

Maintenance

Systems maintenance follows on from systems implementation. **Maintenance** is the process of making necessary changes to the structure of an information system. Maintenance activity can stimulate suggestions for new systems, so it can act as a key input into the process of systems conception and thus provide closure to the process of information systems development.

An organisation might decide to make changes to an information system for several reasons:

- **Bugs** may be present: errors which need to be corrected.
- **Changes in processes.** An organisation rarely stays still. It continually needs to make changes to its organisational processes to compete in its environment, so changes are likely to be required in the information systems supporting these processes.
- **Requests** for new functionality may come from organisational stakeholders. However closely they have been involved in the development process, when people start to use a system they will produce a whole range of requests for changes in the way it works.
- **Technical problems** may be experienced with current hardware and software. For instance, the hardware and software might be faulty, or fail to perform effectively on criteria such as response time. It will then need to be replaced or perhaps upgraded.
- **Changes in the environment** may be a cause of maintenance. An example is a change in government regulation, obliging the organisation to do something that the system design has not allowed for.

Maintenance activity is a core part of the work of most informatics departments. This is primarily because information systems are domain-dependent systems, in the sense that there is a necessary interdependence between the system and its universe of discourse (that is, the organisation that sponsors the development). These systems are characterised by an intrinsic uncertainty about the universe of discourse. In other words, when a system is introduced it might change the nature of the universe of discourse and so the nature of the problem being solved. Just as the organisation adapts to it, it might need to adapt to changes in the organisation.

Perfective maintenance: Changes made to an information system which make improvements but without affecting its functionality.

Adaptive maintenance: Changes made to the information system to provide a closer fit between an information system and its environment, the human activity system.

Corrective maintenance: Changes made to correct previously unidentified system errors.

Preventive maintenance: Changes aimed at improving a system's maintainability such as documentation or improving the flexibility of an information technology system.

There are four major types of maintenance activity:

- PERFECTIVE MAINTENANCE involves changes to the information system which improve it but without affecting its functionality.
- ADAPTIVE MAINTENANCE consists of changes to the information system to provide a closer fit between it and its environment, the activity system.
- CORRECTIVE MAINTENANCE involves corrections of previously unidentified system errors.
- PREVENTIVE MAINTENANCE consists of changes aimed at improving a system's maintainability, such as documentation or improving flexibility.

Surveys of the cost of maintenance suggest that for old ICT systems (legacy systems), it can be as much as five times greater than the cost of development. Not surprisingly, maintenance costs are often a heavy component of the costs of supporting the informatics infrastructure, so an explicit plan and process for maintenance needs to be an inherent part of any informatics strategy (see Chapter 10).

Did you know?

Over 50 per cent of the activity of informatics departments can be involved with maintenance.

Reflect
Why do you think maintenance activity is not typically seen as a desirable form of development work?

The process of systems maintenance

Systems maintenance is a stage of both the bespoke and package development life-cycle. It could be argued that tailoring a software package to the specific requirements of an organisation is a form of maintenance. Unfortunately in many organisations systems maintenance is not seen as a valued activity by either developers or the organisation at large. Nor has it had much attention from academics and researchers (Burton Swanson, 1992).

Since maintenance is a significant activity for many organisations, it should be managed as a process. There are various ways in which this may be achieved. One strategy is to initiate specialist maintenance teams responsible for modifying, fixing and updating ICT systems. Reward structures can be created which reward good maintenance activity.

Systems can be designed with maintenance in mind. Systems can also be designed to be as flexible as possible in terms of likely future changes. This is termed **flexibility analysis** (Fitzgerald, 2000). Organisations can plan for the upgrade of ageing systems onto new software, hardware and communication environments. This should be an essential part of any ICT strategy (see Chapter 10). Finally, effective configuration management is a necessary condition for effective maintenance. Every ICT system configuration in the organisation must be documented as fully as possible.

Configuration management

Configuration management is a key umbrella activity applied throughout the development process by the informatics service. It involves identifying changes to products of the development process, controlling the changes made to products, ensuring that the changes are properly made, and reporting the changes to others. The conception of configuration management in this section is thus a small part of the way in which configuration management is treated in ICT services management (see Chapter 11).

Products of the development process include programs, data structures and documentation. Each type of product may be subject to change at various points during the development process. For instance, changes might be made to requirements specifications during analysis or testing, and they need to be echoed in the development information system. This documentation forms the **project repository** – an organised collection of all output from the development process.

Configuration management overlaps with systems maintenance but is also distinct from it. Systems maintenance occurs after the system is delivered to the customer. Configuration management is a set of monitoring and control activities that begin with the start of a development project and terminate only when the system is taken out of operation. There is a clear overlap with the ICT services management discussed in Chapter 11.

Configuration management is an important element of **quality assurance**. This is a planned and systematic pattern of all the actions necessary to provide adequate confidence that a system conforms to established requirements. Quality assurance is a form of evaluation activity (see Chapter 9).

A configuration management process works with baselines established in the project repository. A baseline is a version of a development product that is formally reviewed and agreed upon. Any changes to a baseline involve formal **change control** procedures.

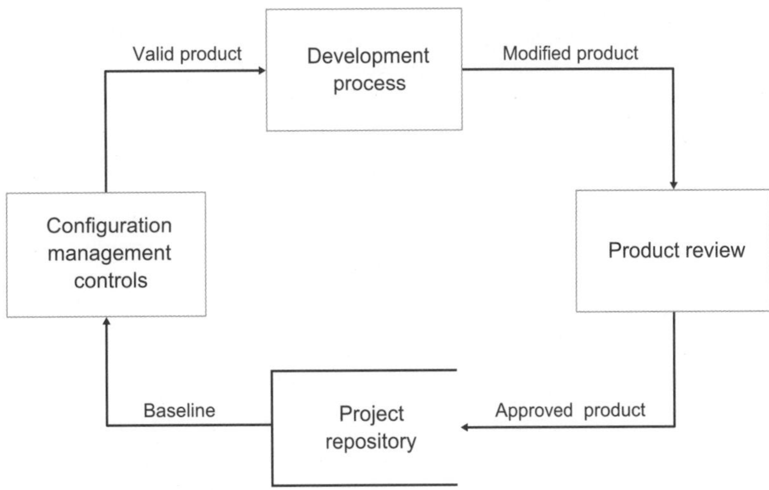

Figure 12.13: *The configuration management process*

A simplified configuration management process is illustrated in Figure 12.13. Any person wishing to make a change to a baseline accesses the product in the project repository. There should be controls in place to ensure that only authorised persons are allowed access to certain development products. Once changes have been made, the modified product is subject to a formal review. This considers such issues as the impact of the change on other aspects of the repository, and the suitability and validity of releasing the change into the project repository. If the change is sanctioned, the approved product is released into the project repository and forms the next baseline for development work.

Case check: Case 18, Research information system

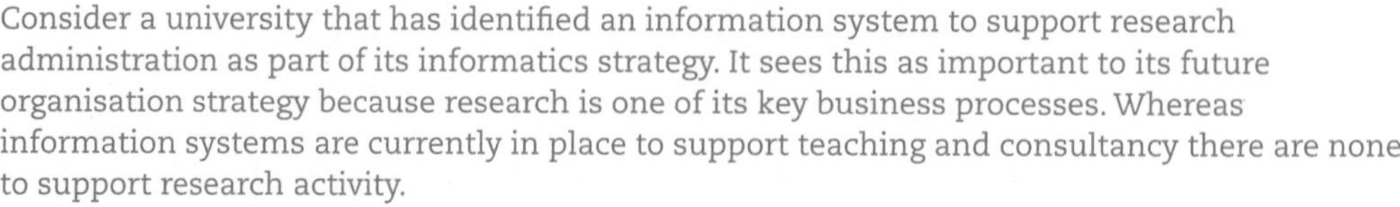

Consider a university that has identified an information system to support research administration as part of its informatics strategy. It sees this as important to its future organisation strategy because research is one of its key business processes. Whereas information systems are currently in place to support teaching and consultancy there are none to support research activity.

The pragmatic objective for the system is to gather data needed to produce a research assessment submission to central government agencies. The system needs to collect store and analyse data on key research outputs. Key research outputs are publications (journal and conference), grant income, research students and completions of postgraduate research degrees.

Summary

1. As has been emphasised throughout this book, business organisations need to continually refresh their informatics infrastructure to remain competitive. They do this through the organisational process of information system development, whose activities include conception, analysis, design, construction, implementation and maintenance. A development information system is essential to ensure the effective and efficient operation of the activity system that is the development process.

2. Development is normally organised in projects. A development project is any concerted effort to develop an information system. The information systems developer needs a toolkit to carry out the development work, which consist of methods, techniques and tools for supporting the activities of the development process.

3. Conception follows on from informatics planning, and involves producing the key business case, analysing risk and assessing the feasibility of an information system project. Any business case or strategic evaluation of an information system considers information system costs and benefits, both tangible and intangible. Appraisal techniques such as payback period primarily assess tangible benefits. Risk analysis is the process of identifying risks, estimating the likelihood of risks and planning for avoiding risks. A feasibility study is an attempt to determine whether an information system is achievable given organisational resources and constraints.

4. Information system analysis involves two primary and interrelated activities, requirements elicitation and requirements representation. A requirement is any desired feature of an information system. Requirements are not objective phenomena since they may vary depending on the stakeholder group. Requirements elicitation is the process of identifying requirements, and requirements specification is concerned with their representation. Requirements elicitation involves working to find an intersubjective agreement on stakeholder groups' requirements. Ideally, requirements are generated for new work systems as well as new technical systems. The aim is to achieve an optimal balance between social and technical objectives.

5. Information system design involves planning the shape of an ICT system to meet the requirements established in systems analysis. It also involves designing the activity system into which this technical artefact will be placed, so it is a form of sociotechnical systems design.

6. Information system construction involves the actual process of building the information system. Since an information system is a sociotechnical system, two parallel construction activities must take place: constructing the ICT system and constructing the activity system. Traditionally ICT system construction involves the three related processes of programming, testing and documentation. In contrast, package development involves customising a package to meet the requirements of an organisation.

7. Information system implementation involves delivering an information system into its context of use, and includes both technical and social systems implementation. Technical systems implementation covers software acquisition, hardware acquisition, data conversion, installation, testing and delivery. Social systems implementation involves user group formation, user training and user acceptance.

8. Information system maintenance is the process of making changes that are needed to an information system, and is a significant activity for organisations which should be planned for and managed by the informatics service. There are several types of maintenance: corrective, perfective, adaptive and preventative. Configuration management is an umbrella activity applied throughout the development process, and involves identifying changes to products of the development process, controlling the changes made to products, ensuring that the changes are made properly, and reporting the changes to others.

This chapter concludes the coverage of the substantive content of organisational informatics. Chapter 13 considers this content in terms of a body of knowledge relating to best practice. To help understand the relevance of this body of knowledge, a case study is used. This is one of the most widely discussed of all cases of information systems application, the London Ambulance Computer Aided Dispatch System.

Focus on Value

Organisations continually need to adapt their informatics infrastructure in line with organisational change, so the development of new information systems is critical to organisational success. There needs to be an evaluation process before deciding which information systems to build. The business case for an information system is typically based on assessments of the weight of tangible and intangible benefits against tangible and intangible costs. Deciding on what requirements to include in the design of an information system also needs a form of evaluation amongst options. Since information systems are sociotechnical systems they are not value-neutral. Values are embedded in the process of systems design.

Review test

1	The development process can be seen as a ____________ system. Fill in the blank.
2	The development process relies on an ____________ for effective performance. Fill in the blank.
3	Distinguish between the linear and iterative models of the development life-cycle. Write two sentences.
4	Place the phases of the information systems development life-cycle in the correct sequence. Mark the first phase with a 1 and so on. ☐ Maintenance ☐ Design ☐ Analysis ☐ Construction ☐ Conception ☐ Implementation
5	Information systems are built either as bespoke products or tailored from software ____________. Fill in the blank.
6	A developer's toolkit consists of ____________, techniques and tools. Fill in the blank.
7	____________ are particular approaches to supporting the processes of systems analysis, systems design and systems construction. Fill in the blank.
8	Conception is the phase in which the key business case is developed risk analysed and the feasibility of an information system assessed. True or False? ☐ True ☐ False
9	Distinguish between information system costs and information system benefits. Write two sentences.
10	Intangible costs are frequently referred to as visible costs because they are reasonably straightforward to measure. True or False? ☐ True ☐ False
11	The return on investment (RoI) associated with an information systems project is calculated using which equation? Select the most appropriate one. ☐ average (annual gross income / annual investment amount) ☐ average (annual net income / annual investment amount) ☐ average (annual net income / annual expenditure)
12	Payback = Investment – cumulative benefit (cash inflow). True or False? ☐ True ☐ False
13	Requirements ____________ is that process devoted to the identification of requirements. Fill in the blank.
14	Requirements elicitation techniques include: Select all that are appropriate. ☐ Interviews ☐ Scenarios ☐ Observation ☐ Use cases ☐ Prototyping ☐ Workshops
15	Match the type of analysis technique with the appropriate definition. Developer-centric — Directed at supporting the development of understanding of a work environment and the potentialities of information technology in this setting. User-centric — Designed particularly for enabling developers to understand, document and communicate IS problems to other developers.
16	A use case model provides a high-level description of major user interactions with some information system. True or False? ☐ True ☐ False

PART 4

17	Distinguish between a theory X and theory Y perspective on human behaviour. Write two sentences.
18	What are the major benefits of stakeholder participation in analysis and design work? Write two sentences.
19	System construction involves the three related processes of programming, testing and documentation. True or False? ☐ True ☐ False
20	Match the type of testing to the correct definition. Unit testing — Testing an entire system as a unit. System testing — Testing individual programs or software modules. Integration testing — Testing individual programs or software modules. Acceptance testing — At some point the system has to be assembled as a complete unit and testing conducted of all related systems together.
21	Systems implementation can take place in three major ways – what are they? Select the three most appropriate. ☐ Hybrid implementation ☐ Direct conversion ☐ Parallel implementation ☐ Phased implementation
22	What type of maintenance consists of changes made to the information system which make improvements but without affecting its functionality? Select the one most relevant. ☐ Adaptive ☐ Perfective ☐ Corrective ☐ Preventative
23	Maintenance is all about correcting bugs. True or False? ☐ True ☐ False
24	Why is configuration management important to effective maintenance? Write two sentences.

Exercises

1. Produce a list of some other benefits and/or costs associated with some information system. Categorise the costs and benefits in terms of tangible costs/benefits and intangible costs/benefits.
2. Choose an intended information system. Try to assess its utility using one of the standard techniques such as return on investment.
3. Apply the three risk factors identified in this chapter to a project known to you.
4. Identify actual clients, end-users and customers for a project known to you.
5. What requirements elicitation techniques are most readily used in an organisation known to you and why?
6. List two actual requirements from a development project.
7. Perform a small use-case analysis of some information system known to you. Develop one scenario of use for the system.
8. Consider an information system known to you. Assess the degree to which the surrounding human activity system encourages job satisfaction.
9. Find one other example of the interdependence of information systems with human activity systems.
10. Assess the degree of stakeholder participation in an information systems project known to you.
11. Find one example of each of the forms of testing described in this chapter.
12. Find some user documentation and describe its key elements.
13. Consider a specific ICT system. How many tools were used in its construction and for what purpose?
14. Consider a specific information systems project. What approach to implementation was taken and why?
15. Determine a more complete analysis of the advantages and disadvantages of each form of implementation strategy.
16. Assess the relative importance of data preparation and conversion to two ICT system projects known to you.
17. How much of a specific organisation's informatics service activity is taken up in maintenance?
18. What strategies has an organisation taken to manage maintenance activity more effectively?
19. Develop a brief configuration management strategy for a small-scale development.
20. Find a completed information systems development project and describe the elements contained in the information system supporting the project.
21. Consider an organisation known to you. Investigate what percentage of development is bespoke and package.
22. Investigate whether development primarily occurs in a sequential or iterative manner in an organisation known to you.
23. Find a past information systems development project. Determine how closely the project undertook activities similar to the phases described in the life-cycle.
24. Apply the information economics scorecard to the project to develop a specific information system.
25. Assess the degree of stakeholder participation in an information systems project known to you. Determine whether such participation is consultative, representative or consensus. Determine whether the participation is intensive or phased.

Projects

1. A common information system for a project is considered important for enabling collaboration amongst members of a project team. Investigate the shape of this project information system amongst a range of development projects. What sort of information is held in this repository and how is it used?
2. There is no standard approach to organising a development team. Survey the structure of development teams across a range of information system development projects. For instance, determine the degree to which representatives of users are included within development teams.
3. In a limited range of organisations investigate how many new systems have been developed in a bespoke manner and how many systems have been package development projects. Try to identify why organisational members chose bespoke or package development.
4. Agile development is seen by many as a solution to development problems. Investigate the degree to which organisations use a linear or iterative development process. For what sorts of application are these different approaches used?
5. Build a business case for a small-scale information system. Try to include an assessment of intangible costs and benefits as well as tangible costs and benefits. What risks are involved in the project? How feasible is it for the organisation to develop the information system?
6. Establish empirically by collecting data on a small number of projects the breakdown of tangible and intangible costs on bespoke compared with package projects. In other words, is the profile of costs and benefits substantially different in these two types of project?
7. Investigate the range of approaches that include ways of assessing intangible benefits, such as information economics. How often are they used in organisations? How successful has such application proven?
8. Many people have proposed that informatics professionals need to have a wider range of skills than the purely technical. For instance, if requirements elicitation is a process of intersubjective negotiation, investigate the key skills needed by successful analysts.
9. Determine which are the most commonly used requirements elicitation techniques in an organisation known to you. Build a detailed analysis of the strengths and weaknesses of particular requirements elicitation techniques.
10. Gather some actual requirements specification documents. Investigate how long it took to produce them and how closely the resulting information systems matched them. Determine which are the most commonly used requirements specification approaches in the organisation chosen.
11. Determine the degree to which some specific information systems projects truly are examples of sociotechnical design. For instance, do job considerations such as job satisfaction play a part in analysis activities? Does design include the design of activity systems as well as ICT systems?
12. Documentation has tended to move from the printed page to being online and Web-based. Determine the degree to which user documentation is now offered online, and consider some of the disadvantages and advantages of this over the paper form.
13. Investigate which type of system implementation is the most popular amongst a group of organisations and why. Construct an implementation plan for a small-scale information system and justify your proposals.
14. Determine the relative occurrence of each of the reasons for maintenance described in this chapter in the maintenance portfolio of a specific organisation. In other words, for one operational information system, attempt to determine the levels of perfective, corrective adaptive and preventative maintenance that has been applied to it.

Further reading

Avison and Fitzgerald (2006) provide a comprehensive overview of most of the topics covered in this chapter. Vidgen and colleagues (2002) describe the application of the Multiview approach to modern information systems. Multiview as a sociotechnical development approach has informed much of the discussion in this chapter. Mumford's 2006 paper on sociotechnical design (2006) provides a good overview of the history and background to this approach.

PART 4

References

Avison, D. E. and Fitzgerald, B. (2006) *Information Systems Development: Methodologies, techniques and tools*. McGraw-Hill.

Avison, D. E., Wood-Harper, A. T., Vidgen, R. T. and Wood, J. R. G. (1998) 'A further exploration into information systems development: the evolution of Multiview2', *Information Technology and People* 11(2): 124–39.

Beynon-Davies, P. (1998) *Information Systems Development: An introduction to information systems engineering*. Basingstoke, Macmillan.

Boehm, B. W. (ed.) (1989) *Software Risk Management*. Washington, IEEE Computer Society Press.

Burton Swanson, E. (1992) *Maintaining Information Systems in Organisations*. Chichester, John Wiley.

Carroll, J. M. (ed.) (1995) *Scenario-Based Design: Envisioning work and technology in systems development*. New York, John Wiley.

Cash, J. I., McFarlan, F. W. and McKeney, J. L. (1992) *Corporate Information Systems Management*. Homewood, Ill., Richard Irwin.

Checkland, P. (1999) *Soft Systems Methodology: A thirty year retrospective*. Chichester, John Wiley.

Fitzgerald, B. (2006) 'The transformation of open source software', *Management Information Systems Quarterly* **30**(3): 587–98.

Fitzgerald, G. (2000) 'Adaptability and flexibility in IS development', in R. Hackney and D. Dunn (eds), *Business Information Technology Management: Alternative and adaptive futures*. Basingstoke, Macmillan: 13–24.

Hirschheim, R. A. (1983) 'Assessing participatory systems design: some conclusions from an exploratory study', *Information and Management* 6: 317–27.

McGregor, D. (1960) *The Human Side of the Enterprise*. New York, McGraw-Hill.

Mumford, E. (1983) *Designing Participatively*. Manchester, Manchester Business School Press.

Mumford, E. (2006) 'The story of socio-technical design: reflections on its successes, failures and potential', *Information Systems Journal* **16**(4): 317–42.

O'Connell, F. (1996) *How to Run Successful Projects II: The silver bullet*. Hemel Hempstead, Prentice Hall.

Parker, M., Benson, R. and Trainor, H. (1988) *Information Economics: Linking business performance to information technology*. New Jersey, Prentice-Hall.

Stapleton, J. (1997) *DSDM – Dynamic Systems Development Method: The method in practice*. Harlow, Addison-Wesley.

Vidgen, R. T., Avison, D. E., Wood, B. and Wood-Harper, A. T. (2002) *Developing Web Information Systems: From strategy to implementation*. London, Butterworth-Heinemann.

Wilcocks, L. and Margetts, H. (1994) 'Risk assessment and information systems', *European Journal of Information Systems* **3**(2): 127–38.

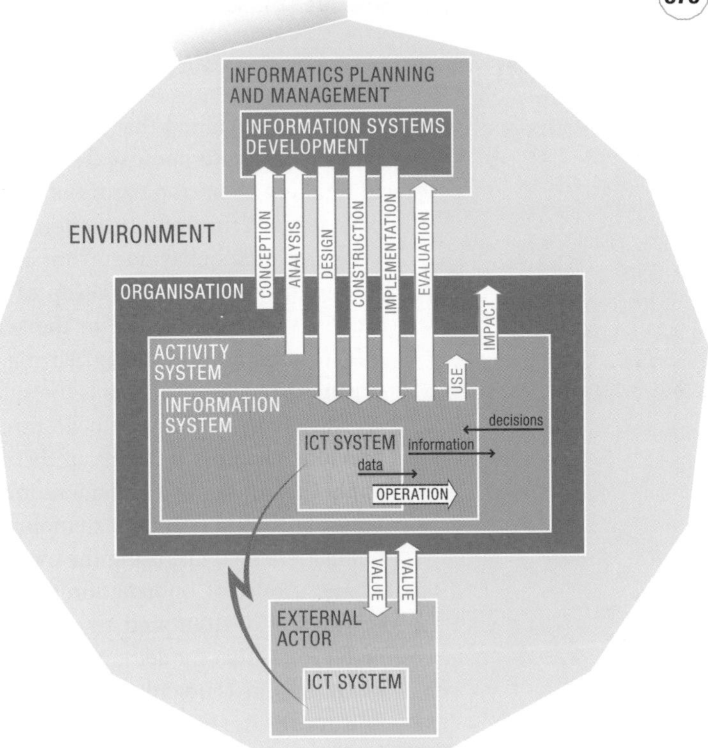

CHAPTER 13

Successful informatics practice

> Life can only be understood backwards; but it must be lived forwards.
>
> *Soren Kierkegaard (1813–1855)*

> Practise yourself what you preach.
>
> *Titus Maccius Plautus (254 BC–184 BC)*

CHAPTER OUTLINE

Introduction

Chapter 1 explained that the domain of organisational informatics is necessarily interdisciplinary in nature because its area of concern bridges the technical and social. Another way of thinking about the nature of organisational informatics is that it engages with three types of 'science'. From one direction it is inherently a *social science* because it is interested in organisational behaviour. From another direction it is inherently a *natural science* because it is interested in the make-up of physical artefacts such as electronic devices. In its third face it is a *design science* in the sense that it is interested in the productive application of ICT to organisations and their management (Hevner et al., 2004). This last perspective on organisational informatics is the subject of this final chapter.

This chapter attempts to do three things. The first is to synthesise the material from the previous chapters in terms of the domain model introduced in Chapter 1. The second is to apply this model to a consideration of one of the most prominent cases of information systems application. Third, it demonstrates some of the universals of best practice in the design of business systems, using the model of the domain that has structured the book.

The model of information systems and their interaction with organisations introduced in Chapter 1 attempted to capture the systemic nature of the organisational informatics endeavour. This model is used in this chapter to reflect on what constitutes the core body of knowledge (Hirschheim and Klein, 2003) on good practice in organisational informatics. This means the knowledge that is transferable from one organisation and one programme or project to another.

The case of the London Ambulance Services Computer Aided Dispatch (LASCAD) system is important for a number of reasons. It is one of the most discussed cases of information systems failure, so it has been much used in academic and professional teaching in various ways. It is perhaps surprising that there are still very few well-documented cases of information systems failure (Chapter 7), and there are even fewer well-documented cases of information systems failures that were turned into successes.

This book was written about 15 years after the original failure and a decade after the successful turnaround, and this provides a useful intellectual distance to reflect on the lessons for successful practice in organisational informatics. Obviously, the technology used in LASCAD is outdated now, and the functionality that was regarded as innovative in the 1992 system is now commonplace for command and control systems for ambulance services in the United Kingdom, as is described later in the chapter. However, the informatics planning, management and development issues highlighted in the case remain relevant today. The evidence from this longitudinal case study supports some well-established lessons of good informatics planning, management and development, and shows that ways are needed to formulate these in a defined body of knowledge for organisational informatics.

This historical case makes it clear that this body of knowledge is time-independent and universal. In the United Kingdom and elsewhere, there have been numerous examples of public sector information systems failing to deliver since LASCAD, and indeed before it too. These failures continue right up to the present day, and are probably continuing at the time of writing (Fortune and Peters, 2005). There have been inquiries into many of these information system failures whose findings have been made public, and they tend to identify the same reasons for failure, and recommend the same mechanisms and processes for avoiding it and achieving success.

The chapter concludes with a look at the likely near future environment for organisational informatics. Increased connectivity in the ICT infrastructure is likely to lead to changes to the exploitation and use of this technology within and between organisations. Substantial change is also likely to occur in the ways in which consumers or citizens interact with organisations. Both these trends are likely to affect the general economic environment, leading to greater global penetration of eBusiness and eCommerce, and increased potential for new organisational forms. This increased activity is likely to reinforce the continuing need for informatics professionals who engage in good informatics practice.

The LASCAD failure and its turnaround

On 27 October 1992 an information system made the lead story on the BBC's *Nine o' Clock News*. It was reported that a new computerised system at the headquarters of the London Ambulance Service (LAS) (the LAS Computer Aided Dispatch system, or the LASCAD system) had failed, and that as a direct result of this failure the lives of 20 to 30 people might have been lost (Beynon-Davies, 1995).

The key value produced by LAS was and still is the care it provides to patients. As is the case with any activity system, its performance can be judged in a number of ways. For many years the key performance indicator used by ambulance services in the United Kingdom has been the time taken between receiving an emergency call and the arrival of an ambulance at an incident.

In 1992 LAS was under pressure from government and the wider National Health Service to make changes, to address a number of perceived failings in performance. The argument was that LAS was clinging on to archaic practices and needed to update its activity systems if it was to perform effectively.

There had already been two attempts to introduce computerisation, but bad relations between stakeholder groups, a prior history of poor labour relations and a general distrust of management by the workforce made it difficult, and both projects were abandoned as a result. So there was considerable pressure on the 1992 developers to introduce a system that would make major changes, to bring the service up to date.

LAS at the time operated a largely unautomated activity system of ambulance dispatch, which consisted of three core processes: call-taking, resource identification and resource mobilisation.

Call taking was the process of emergency calls being received by ambulance control. Control assistants wrote down details of incidents on preprinted forms. They noted the location of each incident then recorded reference coordinates on the form. The forms were then placed on a conveyor belt which transported them to a central collection point.

The activity of **resource identification** involved other members of ambulance control collecting the forms, reviewing the details on them, and on the basis of the information provided, deciding which resource allocator should deal with each incident. Each resource allocator examined the forms passed to their sector, compared the details with information on each ambulance they controlled and its crew, and decided which ambulances should be sent where. The status information on the forms was updated regularly from information received via a radio operator. The resource allocated was recorded on the original form, which was passed on to a dispatcher.

In **resource mobilisation,** the dispatcher either telephoned the nearest ambulance station, or passed the mobilisation instructions to the radio operator if an ambulance was already out in the field. This triggered the dispatch of an ambulance to an incident. These activities are represented as a process model in Figure 13.1.

The essential functionality of the information system that was designed to replace this manual system is shown diagrammatically in Figure 13.2.

In the automated system, BT operators routed all 999 calls concerning medical emergencies as a matter of routine to LAS headquarters (HQ) in Waterloo, central London. 18 HQ 'receivers' were then expected to record on the system the name, telephone number and address of the caller, and the name, destination address and brief details of the patient. This information was then transmitted over a local area network to an 'allocator'. The system pinpointed the patient's location on a map display of areas of London. The system was expected to continuously monitor the location of every ambulance via radio messages transmitted by each vehicle every 13 seconds. This would enable it to determine the nearest ambulances to the patient.

Experienced ambulance dispatchers were organised into teams based on three zones (south, north-east and north-west). The system was designed to provide the dispatchers with details of the three nearest ambulances and the estimated time each would need to reach

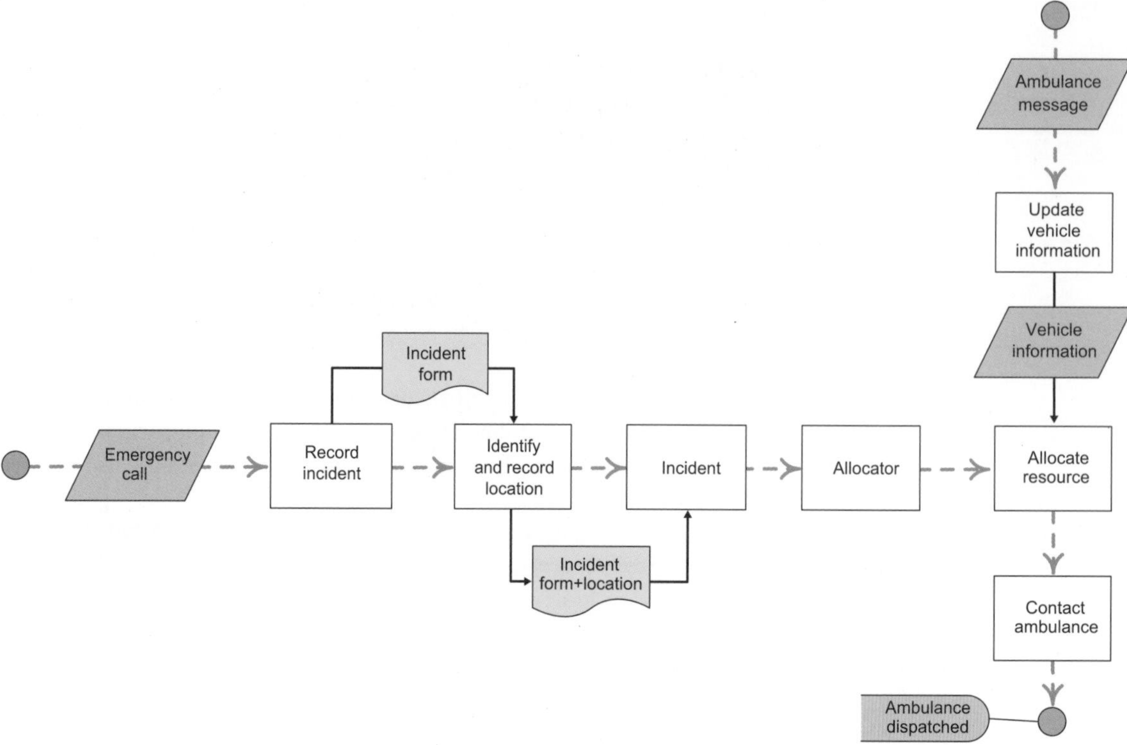

Figure 13.1: *The original activity system for ambulance dispatch*

the scene. The dispatcher then chose an ambulance and sent incident and patient details to a small terminal screen located on the dashboard of the ambulance. The crew were then expected to confirm to the system that they were on their way to the incident.

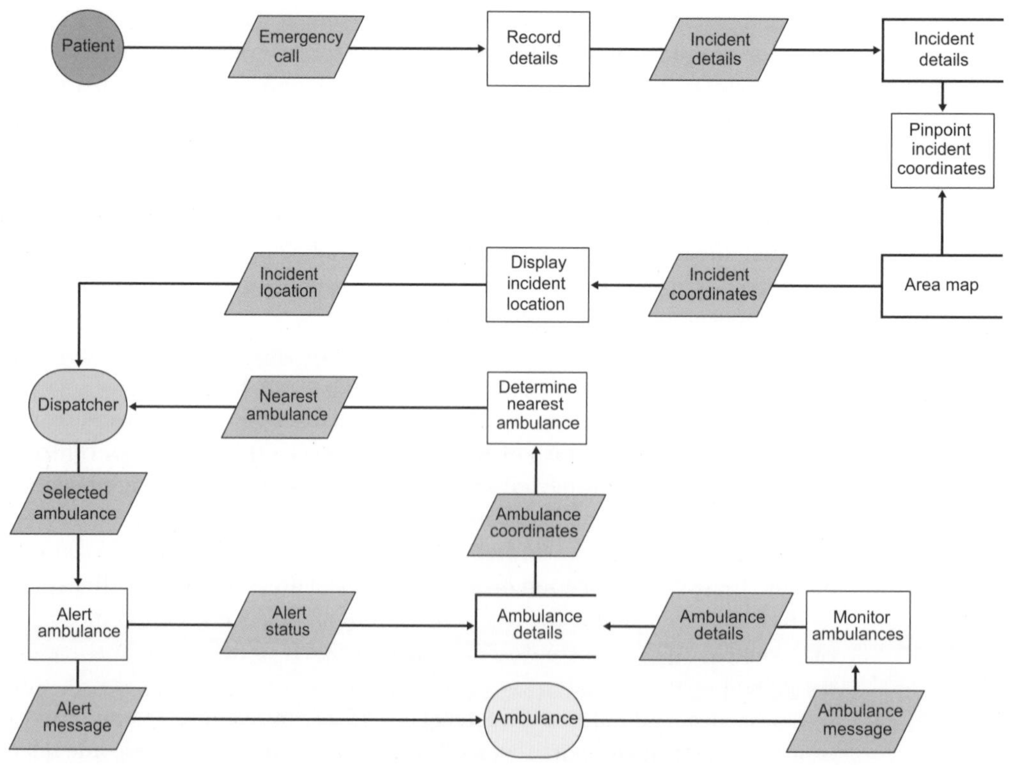

Figure 13.2: *The LASCAD information system*

If the selected ambulance was in an ambulance station, the dispatch message was received on the station printer. The ambulance crew were always expected to acknowledge a message, and the system automatically alerted LAS HQ if no acknowledgement was made. A follow-up message was then sent from HQ. The system could also detect from each vehicle's location messages if any ambulance was heading in the wrong direction, and alert controllers. Further messages told HQ when the ambulance crew had arrived with the patient, when it was on its way to a hospital and when it was free again.

Figure 13.3 shows an information model which would support this information system. The information classes on the diagram such as ambulances, incidents and patients indicate objects about which records need to be maintained in the system.

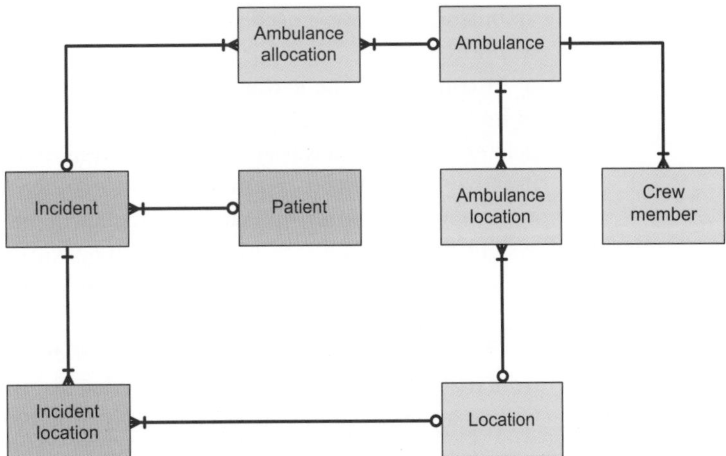

Figure 13.3: *An information model for the LASCAD system*

All this might appear perfectly reasonable, but unfortunately the system was a disaster when it went live. Instead of ambulances being dispatched more promptly to incidents, they were dispatched more slowly, or multiple ambulances turned up for the same patient. The chaos was headline news, as noted above, and the LAS chief executive resigned a couple of the days after the launch. He was quoted as saying he had done so because of the evident lack of confidence in the LAS.

A new chief executive was appointed the next day. Under pressure from a number of sources, the health secretary announced a public inquiry into the system, which was headed by the South Yorkshire ambulance chief. The findings of the inquiry were eventually published in an 80-page report in February 1993, which immediately became news in the UK computing and national press.

According to the report, the reason for the system's 'failure' was not that the ICT system crashed. The hardware and software worked reasonably well, but the communications and the sociotechnical system did not. Crews pressed the wrong buttons on their dashboard access devices, and no messages were received by HQ when ambulances were in radio black-spots. This led to a build-up in the amount of incorrect vehicle information. This had a knock-on effect because the ICT system then made incorrect allocations on the basis of the data it had. For example, multiple vehicles were sent to the same incident, or the closest vehicle was not chosen for dispatch. As a consequence, the ICT system was left with fewer ambulance resources to allocate.

The system also placed calls that had not gone through the appropriate protocol on a waiting list, and generated exception messages for incidents for which it had received incorrect status information. The number of exception messages appears to have increased to such an extent that staff were not able to clear the queue. It became increasingly difficult for staff to attend to messages that had scrolled off the screen. The increasing size of the queue slowed the system. All this meant that, with fewer resources to allocate, and the problems of dealing with the waiting and exception queues, it took longer to allocate resources to incidents. Eventually, a decision was made to switch off the system and return to a manual mode of operation.

Although the inquiry found evident problems with both the organisation and its ICT system, the report recommended that the LAS continue to seek to build an ICT system to support ambulance dispatch (Fitzgerald and Russo, 2005). However, it also recommended an extended timescale for development and implementation, and suggested that there should be effective stakeholder consultation, quality assurance, testing and training. As a result of this, the LASCAD project organisation was restructured and a new head of ICT appointed. This new head was reported at the time as having been given until August 1997, and a provisional budget of £13.5 million, to deliver an effective dispatch system for the LAS.

While the new system was being built the original manual system continued in operation but with greater staff resource. A series of 'warm-up' projects such as the construction of a new control room, the introduction of a digital phone system and the upgrading of the ambulance fleet were used to build a new level of trust between LAS management and the workforce.

In contrast to the earlier development project, it was decided to build the new system in-house using prototyping to help involve users in the development process. A slow and deliberate approach was adopted to provide time for the necessary user involvement and the iterative development required of prototyping. A new development platform was adopted built around the Informix database management system running under the UNIX operating system. This allowed access from around 60 workstations. A mirror system was implemented: a backup to which operations could immediately switch over in the event of a failure in the main operational system.

The first stage of the work involved building a system with much reduced functionality from that originally intended. This included features for call-logging, call transfer and address-finding against a computerised gazetteer. This system went live on 17 January 1996, and after a week of successful operation was moved into the new control room. Enhancements to this basic system were introduced gradually. For instance, additional functionality allowing early-call viewing was introduced in September 1996, followed by the implementation of an automatic vehicle location system.

The introduction of the new system into the LAS control room was seen by the new LAS management to be a core factor in operational performance improvements. For example, in the period 1996/97 the service faced an increase of 16 per cent in emergency calls. Nevertheless, the LAS managed to increase its proportion of ambulances dispatched within a three-minute activation period from 44 per cent in 1995/96 to 80 per cent in 1996/97. The number of complaints from users also fell from 100 per month to around 25 per month after the introduction of the new information system.

The domain model

Let us go back to the domain model presented in Chapter 1, Figure 13.4 attempts to represent the complex, systemic interaction between an information system and the organisation in which it exists. In a sense, it represents some of the core or critical elements of the domain of organisational informatics.

Central to the model is the **information system** (Chapter 4) acting as a sociotechnical system utilising ICT (Chapters 8 and 9) in support of human activity. The **operation** of ICT systems and their use (Chapter 7) take place within the larger information system, and foreshadow the **impact** of the information systems on the organisation. The **organisation** itself (Chapter 2) is considered as a series of interdependent activity systems, directed by strategy (Chapter 10). which interact with a wider environment (Chapter 5). Informatics **planning and management** form the context for development projects (Chapter 10). These projects are typically enacted as a process (Chapter 12), consisting of the activities of conception, analysis, design, construction, implementation and maintenance.

This book has used the term **informatics** rather than information systems throughout in order to keep the terminology as clear and consistent as possible. Informatics is the term for both an academic field and a practical discipline devoted to trying to improve the fit between information systems and organisations. All the component elements of the model have an effect, both separately and in their interaction, on the 'fitness for purpose' of an information system.

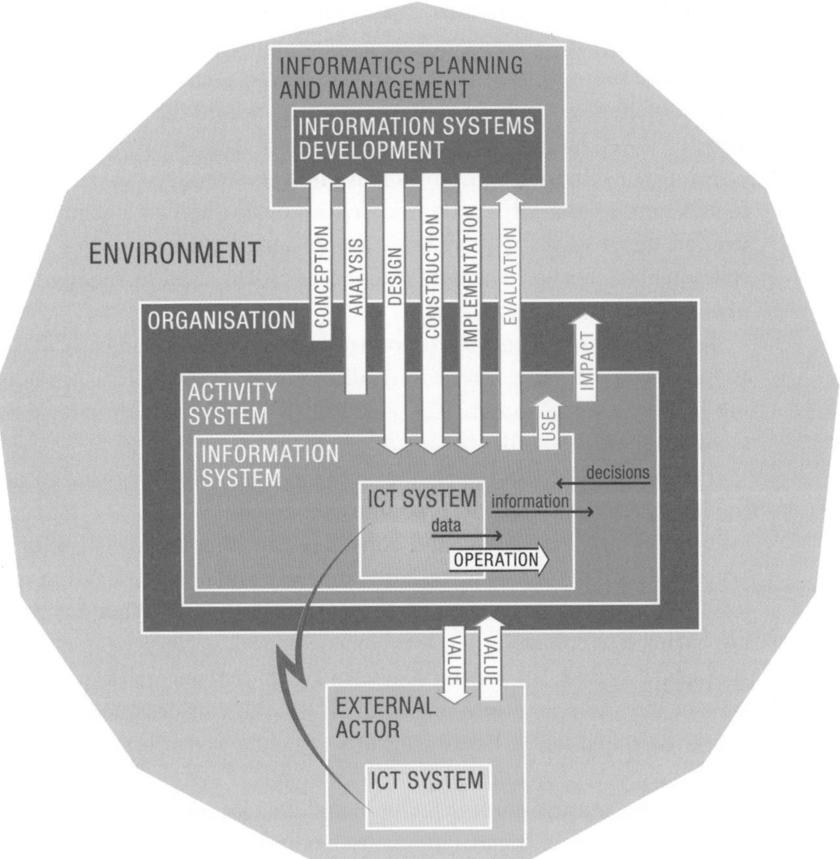

Figure 13.4: *The domain model*

To recap, informatics is the study of information, information systems and ICT applied to various phenomena. The term has been used repeatedly by various branches of the European Union to encompass the application of ICT in support of the information society. In Germany the term *informatik* and in France the term *informatique* are much used.

The term has also been extremely popular in the health and biological sciences fields, and *health informatics, medical informatics* and *bioinformatics* are now common terms. Some have used the term to elevate traditional information management (librarianship) concerns to a new plane founded in ICT. This book has used the term in the sense implied by Kling and Allen (1996), who use **organisational informatics** to encompass the application of information, information systems and ICT in organisations. This is similar to Kling and Scaachi's (1982) interest in what they called the 'web of computing'.

The information system

This rather dry discussion about the use of the term informatics is important, because it demonstrates that one problem lies in the language used to describe elements of concern in this general field. In much of popular, academic and professional literature the term *information system* is used to refer to a system of technology. This tends to focus vision and practice on the successful construction of technology. But technology is only part of the sociotechnical systems that are used in organisations, as this book has worked to show. It has argued for a clear distinction between three interdependent systems of concern: activity systems, information systems and ICT systems.

Organisational informatics is a systemic discipline. This means that the concept of **system** is central. A system is a coherent set of interdependent components that exists for some purpose, has some stability, and can usefully be viewed as a whole. Systems are generally portrayed in terms of an input–process–output model which locates them in a specific environment. The environment is anything outside the system that has an effect on the way it operates, and can be defined as the agents with which the system interacts. The inputs to the system are the resources it gains from agents in its environment. The outputs from the system are those things that it supplies back to agents in its environment. The process of the system is the set of activities that transform system inputs into system outputs. Systems can also be viewed hierarchically as a collection of subsystems and sub-subsystems.

A human activity system (or just **activity system**) is a social system – sometimes referred to as a 'soft' system. It is a set of activities performed by a group of people in fulfilment of a defined purpose. Activity systems are designed systems in the sense that sets of activities, roles, procedures and business rules are typically used to specify their workings. The output of an activity system is action.

Technology amounts to a set of artefacts for doing things. ICT is any technology used to support data gathering, processing, distribution and use. ICT provides a means of constructing ICT systems. Modern ICT consists of hardware, software, data and communications technology (see Part III).

It is important to recognise that information systems existed in organisations long before the invention of modern ICT, so information systems do not depend on modern ICT. However, in the modern, global and consequently complex organisational world, most information systems rely on hardware, software, data and communication technology to a greater or lesser degree. This is because of the performance gains that are made possible through the use of this technology.

An **ICT system** is a technical system. Such systems are frequently referred to as 'hard' systems in the sense that they consist of an assembly of designed artefacts. An ICT system is an organised collection of hardware, software, data and communication technology designed to support aspects of an information system. An ICT system takes data as input, manipulates such data as a process and outputs manipulated data for interpretation within an activity system.

Many systems in organisations are examples of sociotechnical systems. A sociotechnical system is a system of technology used within a system of activity. **Information systems** are primary examples of sociotechnical systems. Information systems consist of ICT used within an activity system. They therefore include both ICT and human activity. Part of the activity will involve the use of ICT systems. The input to an information system consists of data supplied from its associated ICT system. The output of an information system is information, and the information it provides drives decision making, leading to further action within the organisation.

In much media coverage of public-sector failures such as LASCAD, the blame is placed on the 'computer system' or 'ICT system', but that does not do much to show where the problem really lies. It particularly fails to separate out elements of technology from elements of communication and activity. And usually it is in the subtle interaction between activity systems, information systems and ICT systems that things work out in ways that lead to a judgement of success or failure.

The functionality of the 1992 ICT system at LAS was undoubtedly complex. It was in many ways groundbreaking for its day, and tried to automate most of the functions involved in dispatching ambulances to incidents. The new ICT system was dependent on bringing in a substantially different information system and activity system for the LAS command and control operations. It also called for significant changes to the activity of ambulance crews, because they had to get used to sending new types of information in new ways.

When a second new system was introduced in 1996, it was deliberately kept simple at first. Its functionality only covered call-taking. In a sense, this reduced functionality could be used to support most of the elements of the existing activity system. This clearly reduced risk, and enabled the project organisation to introduce both technical and organisational change in a much more controlled manner.

A number of lessons can be drawn from this. First, the use of clear terminology is important. A set of terms that make these differences apparent need to be adopted and used in practice. The term **information system** should be understood to mean a sociotechnical system which spans a social (activity system) and a technical (ICT system). This is important because it implies that undertaking an information systems development project calls for the parallel design and implementation of technology systems and corresponding social (activity) systems. Developing an ICT system independently of any concern with its encompassing information system and activity system is likely to lead to failure.

It is interesting that since the period described in the case, both the ICT and activity systems for UK ambulance command and control have changed substantially, and the systems are now similar to the one introduced in 1992. In other words, this organisational sector has seen substantial process and activity systems change as well as technology change.

The use and impact of information systems

The distinction between an ICT system, an information system and an activity system is useful in locating three distinct ways in which the quality of a development effort can be assessed.

Traditionally the 'quality' of an information system has been assessed in terms of its **functionality.** This is what an information system does, or should be able to do. Specifying the core functionality of a given information system is a critical aspect of the process of information systems development (see Chapter 12). Its functionality is normally determined by a close examination of organisational requirements. Assessments of functionality involve determining how closely an information system's constructed functionality matches the functionality that was specified in the early stages of the development project.

An ICT system is one major agent in the wider information system; the other major agent is human beings. The interaction between the two is typically judged in terms of the **usability** of the ICT system. Usability concerns how easy an ICT system is to use within its wider information system. Usability can also cover user satisfaction with the system. So usability is evident at the human–computer interface (see Chapter 9) – the place where the user interacts with the ICT system.

While functionality defines what an information system does and usability defines how an information system is used, **utility** defines how acceptable the information system is in terms of doing what is needed. Utility assesses the worth of an information system by the contribution it makes to its activity system and to the organisation as a whole. This is essentially a judgement of issues of information quality in decision making as a forerunner to action.

There is a clear relationship between the distinctions between functionality, usability and utility, and those between an ICT system, information system and activity system. Functionality is typically seen to be a property of the ICT system, whereas utility emerges as a property of the activity system. Usability is a mediating feature between the technical system (the ICT system) and the social system (the activity system), and is evident at the user interface.

As we move from the area of functionality into the areas of usability and utility, the issue of system stakeholders comes to the fore. This book has used the term **stakeholder** rather than user to emphasise that not just users, but many groups in organisations may have a 'stake' in an information system. For example, managerial groups typically support the development of an ICT system by allocating resources to the project, so they have a real interest and stake in it, even if they do not use the live system in any way. And the output from the ICT system may have a major effect on the performance of the workforce the manager is responsible for.

Ultimately, judgements about the success or failure of ICT systems are made by stakeholder groups, so issues of stakeholder satisfaction and possible stakeholder resistance emerge as key. Power differentials between stakeholder groups also have an impact on the trajectory of information systems development projects.

There were at least three stakeholder groups in the initial LASCAD project: management, control room staff and ambulance crews. Each of these groups was affected in different ways by the introduction of the ICT system. Staff in the control room were typical end-users of the system, and bringing in the new technology led to radical changes in their work system. The ambulance staff saw more minor changes in their work; they were required to use remote access devices (as we call them now: see Chapter 5) to input data to the central ICT system and get instructions via it. The managers were clients of the development effort, and had a definite stake in that they wanted the system to improve performance in LAS's overall activity systems. This was the main objective behind the introduction of the new information system: to improve organisational performance by for instance improving response times to incidents.

In 1992 some of the expected impacts of the new system were clearly not achieved. It actually caused deterioration in the activity system performance, and this was an especial problem because ambulances are such a time-critical service, and lives might well have been lost as a result.

Research has pointed to a number of ways in which stakeholder satisfaction with ICT systems can be improved and stakeholder resistance avoided. Stakeholder involvement in the design and development of ICT systems has a positive effect on satisfaction with them and commitment to their use. Comprehensive user training in the system prior to implementation is also critical to effective use, and so is continuous operational support post-implementation.

In 1992 control room staff and ambulance crews had little involvement in the development of the LASCAD system. The public inquiry also found that there had been poor and incomplete user training, and judged this to be a contributory factor in the project failure. There was also some evidence of stakeholder resistance: it was suggested that some ambulance crews were opposed to the new system, and rather than simply pressing the wrong buttons by mistake, they might have deliberately misused it in some ways.

In 1996, in contrast, the development team took great care to involve control room staff in the development of the new system. They were also given comprehensive user training, and not surprisingly, there was evidence of increased user satisfaction with, and commitment, to the system. The project organisation also deliberately built and introduced elements of the functionality of the system in a phased manner. This helped ensure that the system was introduced smoothly, and did much to help it meet its objective: that is, meeting the response time targets for the ambulance services set by its external regulators.

The key lesson from this is that the impact of ICT must be assessed on a number of levels. An ICT system cannot be assessed solely as a collection of hardware and software. Organisations are generally interested in the contribution it makes to the wider information system and in turn the wider activity system. This also means that the impact of the ICT system should be assessed or evaluated at a number of points in its life, and particularly after a period in use.

The organisation

Generally speaking the discipline of informatics is interested in human activity within organised groupings of individuals – that is, organisations. Organisations are collections of people in which formal procedures are used for coordinating the activities of members in the pursuit of joint objectives (see Chapter 2). We see an organisation as being something separate from the people who belong to it, but it needs to be borne in mind that because the organisation is made up of the changing actions of a large group of people, it is not fixed and static, but in a continual state of flux.

Business organisations in particular consist of complex chains of human activity concerned with the production and distribution of value. For commercial organisations this value resides in their **goods** or products, and for public sector organisations it is embodied in the **services** they provide. In the wider community, there is a form of value that is defined as **social capital** – networks of information, trust and reciprocity.

Control is the idea that any system, including a social system such as an organisation, needs to include a process that regulates it and enables it to adapt to changes in its environment. This is normally a feedback process, in which information is collected from a monitored process or subsystem and compared against defined levels of performance. The flow of information between a control process and its monitored process triggers actions designed to maintain the state of the system within given bounds. This is control as **regulation**. Control is also evident in the way in which a system monitors its environment and makes changes to its behaviour to **adapt** to this environment. From this perspective, information systems are essential for the effective strategic and operational management of modern organisations.

The immediate context for information systems is the activity systems infrastructure in an organisation. The key lesson here is that organisational features such as structure, culture and strategy have an influence on the success or otherwise of an information system – if only because organisational actors or stakeholders are the most important judges of success and failure.

Various stakeholder groups in organisations tend to 'frame' the technology in different ways, so it is essential for informatics professionals to identify who the stakeholders are and assess what their impact on the development is likely to be. It is also important to manage stakeholder groups' expectations about the benefits they will derive from a system.

We have seen that in spite of the pressure for change, the 1992 introduction of the LASCAD system was a disaster that had to be reversed. In 1996 there was still pressure to change. However, ironically the previous highly public failure had reopened the agenda for change amongst all stakeholder groups. External agencies such as the government and NHS could not countenance another failure in what had become a highly publicised area of healthcare. The new chief executive of LAS therefore exploited this new situation to obtain additional resources, and to open up discussions with the workforce and reassure them of the importance of their participation in the intended change effort.

The external environment

An organisation is affected by its environment. Organisations are not isolated entities but are open systems that build information systems to cope with environmental pressures and constraints. The success of any organisation depends on how well it integrates with aspects of its environment. Any organisation contributes value to this environment and receives value from it, so it is not surprising that changes and forces in the environment influence the direction of organisational change, and by implication the direction of information systems change.

The NHS is one of the largest organisations in Western Europe. The organisation and delivery of health care has always been a politically sensitive issue in the United Kingdom because it is publicly funded. All political parties have tended to suggest that management, administration and administrative systems are a burden on the health service, and in many senses a brake on the effective delivery of healthcare. Political fixes for the NHS have frequently been directed at improving the efficiency of its managerial and administrative systems, and as a consequence its information systems. However, paradoxically informatics management has never been given the prominence it deserves in the health service. Attempts to coordinate its informatics management have proven unsuccessful over a number of decades.

Over the period from 1992 to 1996 the environment of the UK health service did not change substantially. Although there were ongoing reforms which caused significant levels of structural change, little attempt was made to control ICT planning and strategy. Indeed planning and strategy was devolved even more to regions and hospitals, making central coordination of information, information systems and ICT management extremely difficult.

Fitzgerald and Russo (2005) argue that because the environment did not change substantially over the period, it cannot be seen as a key influence on the failure and subsequent success of LASCAD. However, the prominence of the failure in itself changed the environment for the LAS. The LAS became a special case within the NHS: it had to be turned around to demonstrate that computerising command and control in ambulance services was both desirable and feasible. So the new project organisation was given an unusual amount of staffing and time following the initial failure. Improvements to the general work environment were used to increase levels of trust between management and workforce.

The development process

The successful development of information systems relies in the end on good development practice. Oscar Wilde once said that the problem with common sense is that it is not widely distributed, and unfortunately much the same is true of good development practice. Although there are many good suggestions for development practice, they are ignored time and again in development projects.

For instance, it is important to use a systematic process for **development**. This book has outlined the process of information system development as a series of activities, and these provide a template for establishing good practice.

Conception is the phase in which an organisation develops a key business case for an information system. Before embarking on an investment, an organisation should evaluate an information system strategically and assess its feasibility. The organisation should also attempt to estimate the degree of risk associated. Only an information systems project that passes this strategic evaluation and feasibility assessment should pass on to a process of systems analysis.

Analysis consists of requirements elicitation, identifying the requirements for new information systems, and requirements specification, the process of documenting these identified requirements.

Design is the process of planning the shape of an information system to meet the requirements established by analysis. The design or system specification acts as a blueprint for systems construction.

The system can be **constructed** by either an internal team or an outside contractor. Many information systems are now also bought in as a package and tailored to organisational requirements.

Implementation involves the delivery of the system into its context of use. This can be done in a confident manner by immediately moving from the old to the new system. Alternatively, it can be approached in a cautious way in which the old and new systems are run in parallel for a period to ensure that there is a fallback position.

Maintenance can be considered as a feedback process that involves changes to information systems and to elements of the organisation. Information systems may need to be changed for a number of reasons, including systems errors and user requirements. At some point a system may need to be substantially re-engineered to fit new organisational circumstances.

Many parts of the development process, as well as the management of development projects, are frequently highlighted as deficiencies in public sector information systems projects. Examples of particular areas of concern are poor requirements management, poor configuration control and testing, inadequate user training and inadequate planning for changeover.

In the 1992 LAS effort, aspects of both project management and systems development were poor. The project management method PRINCE was mandated but not used. There was poor management of expectations by stakeholders because of low levels of involvement. A full 'waterfall' approach was used in a domain subject to high degrees of uncertainty. There was a direct changeover with little thought to a fallback position in the event of problems. This was compounded by a lack of thorough testing of the software.

In the 1996 project much effort was devoted to addressing failings in previous project management and development practices. Incremental development and implementation were used to manage the uncertainty in the setting. There was a lot of stakeholder involvement to improve design work, increased levels of user commitment and reduced levels of user resistance. PRINCE was used for effective project management and the system was tested thoroughly. Changeover was managed closely with the use of fallback systems in the event of difficulty. As a result, development remained on time and within budget.

Informatics planning and management

The introduction of information systems can have a number of negative effects. Some people have argued, for instance, that information systems have largely been used not to enhance effectiveness but to increase job loss and deskilling, so workers do not view them positively and they lead to a rapid loss of morale. Information systems have also been used as a way of monitoring and controlling staff more closely. Many information system projects have either been abandoned at great expense, or failed to deliver expected benefits in use.

So information systems do not always have the intended benefits, and sometimes have unintended drawbacks. How can we ensure that failure does not occur, that negative effects do not occur and that positive effects do occur? The main point is that we cannot do this by directing attention and resources solely at the information system itself. We must consider information systems in the context of an organisation, and the organisation in the context of its environment. Perhaps a better way of putting this is that an information system in some way contributes to the success of an organisation within its environment. But what makes a successful organisation?

Peter Drucker's *Theory of the Business* (1994) attributes organisational success to three factors:

- businesses understanding their external environments
- businesses undertaking missions (developing strategies) consistent with their external environments
- businesses developing core competencies needed to accomplish their missions.

Because information is so central to modern organisations, their success depends in large part on information systems success. Effective informatics planning and management are necessary conditions for ensuring information systems success. Planning and management are necessary to ensure that information systems are aligned with organisational strategy.

Informatics planning is the process of deciding on the optimal informatics strategy for an organisation. Its objective is to develop strategy in each of the areas of information, information systems and ICT. The practical output of the planning process is a set of documents that describe strategy in these three areas.

Planning is the process of determining what to do over a given time period. **Managing** is the process of executing, evaluating and adapting plans in the face of contingencies. There are three forms of management relevant to informatics, closely related to the three levels of informatics strategy and informatics infrastructure. **Information management** is concerned with the overall strategic direction of the organisation, and the planning, regulation and coordination of information in support of this direction. **Information systems management** is concerned with providing information handling to support organisational activities. **ICT management** is concerned with providing the necessary technical infrastructure for implementing this information handling.

The LASCAD case demonstrates the importance of a number of good practices in the area of planning and management:

- setting realistic budgets for development
- the importance of obtaining top-level management commitment to projects.
- the need to avoid naïve notions of technological determinism, particularly the idea of using ICT as a driver for activity change
- engaging in effective change management, such as parallel implementation of activity and technological change.

In 1992 unrealistic timescales were set for the project organisation, which also had a tight budget. There was clearly an attempt by the LAS management to introduce organisational change on the back of technological change. However, there was also poor change management in the attempt to achieve this.

In 1996 realistic timescales were set for the delivery of system elements and the project organisation was provided with a larger development budget. There was also evidence of good change management, in that ICT was carefully introduced in parallel with organisational change, albeit the change to organisational processes was not significant in the first instance.

Operations and service

Most medium to large-scale organisations employ people specifically in informatics work. The informatics service is the specialist function devoted to activities such as informatics planning, management, development and operation.

This service plans the strategy for changing aspects of the informatics infrastructure, and is also concerned with supporting, maintaining and evaluating the existing informatics infrastructure. Its activities include constructing and delivering new information systems: analysing, designing, producing, testing and implementing them. It also operates large, multi-user systems and/or supports the use of information systems throughout the organisation.

Although informatics is now seen to be central to most organisations, the informatics service has traditionally experienced great difficulty in quantifying its benefits to the organisation. For this reason many organisations have decided to outsource their informatics service. Outsourcing is the use of external agents to perform one or more organisational activities. Since the mid-1990s there has been a trend, particularly in large-scale companies, to hand over either the whole or part of the informatics function to external agents.

The LAS case highlights some of the difficulties in outsourcing aspects of the informatics service. It particularly highlights the importance of domain knowledge to successful development, because of the sociotechnical nature of information systems. This implies that any development organisation does not only need technical knowledge for the construction of an ICT system, it also needs social knowledge of the activity system within which the ICT will be placed. This domain knowledge frequently proves problematic when organisations outsource information systems development, so the effective planning and management of informatics becomes even more critical when ICT infrastructure operation, development and maintenance are outsourced.

Project escalation: The process in which decision makers become locked in an irrational course of action.

There is always a potential for PROJECT ESCALATION, particularly in development projects seen as critical for organisational viability, so projects need to be evaluated at a number of levels: prior to development itself (**strategic evaluation**), during the development process (**formative evaluation**) and after the system is in use (**summative evaluation**).

In 1992 there was evidence of a lack of domain knowledge in the contracted development organisation. It was its first experience of command and control systems in a health environment. There were also clear difficulties with the management of the contracted development, as is evident in the lack of thorough training and testing of the system. Since this was the third in a series of computerisation projects at LAS, there is evidence of a lack of good evaluation practice, and not surprisingly also evidence of project escalation.

In 1996 LAS deliberately decided to move development back in-house to provide more control. A new project organisation was established, with in-house developers recruited who had domain knowledge of command and control systems in the public sector (McGrath, 2002).

Modern ambulance command and control

In 1996 a review of ambulance service performance concluded that more clinically relevant performance measures were needed for the service. It suggested that the focus should be on the potential for saving lives, with shorter response times to patients suffering with life-threatening conditions. From 1996 to 2006, demand for emergency ambulance services in the United Kingdom increased by over 50 per cent while funding increased by only 17.5 per cent. The review recommended a long- term performance target of 90 per cent of life-threatening calls responded to within eight minutes. Subsequently, an interim target of 75 per cent of life-threatening calls to be responded to within eight minutes was introduced, and ambulance services were required to achieve this target by 2001.

Until 1997 the ambulance service in the United Kingdom worked using a first-come, first-served basis for responses to emergency calls. However, to achieve targets set by the performance review, most ambulance services have now instituted a process of 'triage' to prioritise the response to incidents.

Because most ambulance services in the United Kingdom are now formed as NHS trusts, they have the freedom and responsibility to establish their own business processes and technology. This means that there is variation between their activity systems, information systems and ICT systems. The description below is therefore based on a composite, and does not represent the systems for any specific trust. The composite information system for ambulance command and control is shown in Figure 13.5.

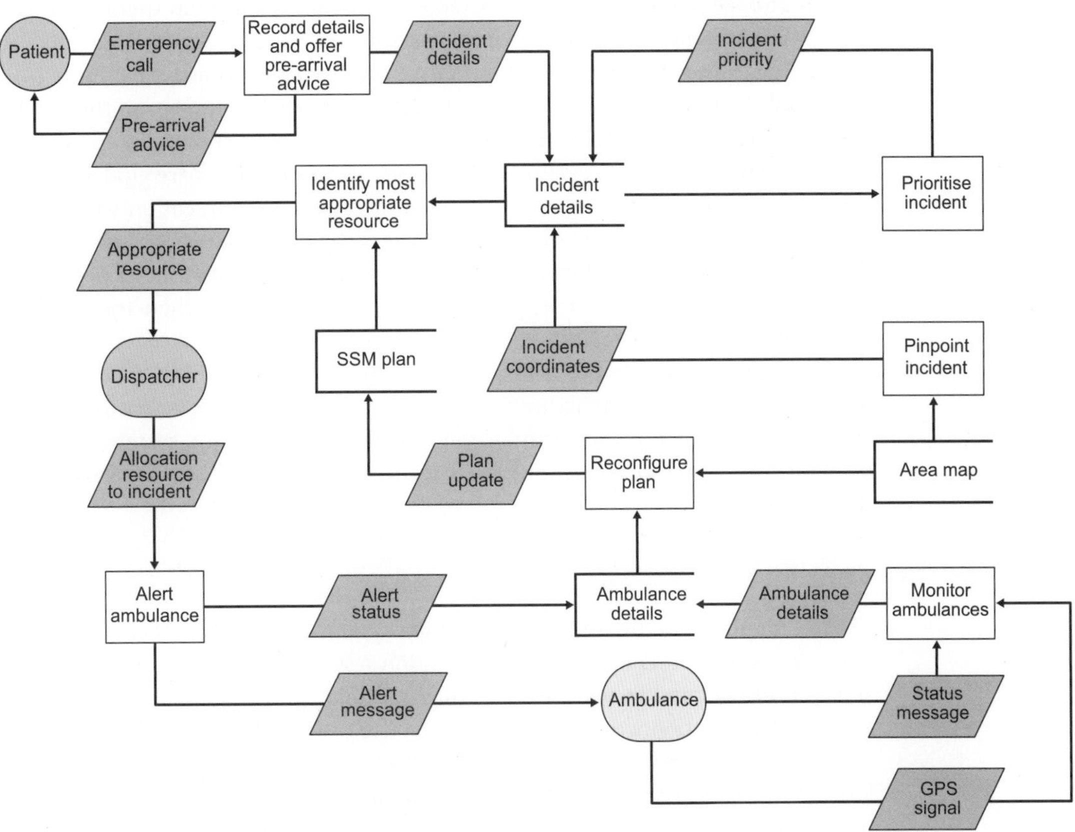

Figure 13.5: *An information system model for modern ambulance command and control*

In this system, BT operators take an emergency call and identify the caller's area code or closest mobile phone cell from the call. The call is then routed to the ambulance control call centre. A call-taker matches the number calling with an address using a computerised gazetteer, then asks a set series of questions prompted by a protocol embedded in the ICT system. On the basis of the answers, the system suggests appropriate action.

As soon as the location is identified, a dispatcher listens to the call. If it is rated as category A (life threatening) or category B (serious), a paramedic dispatcher might be asked to assist. Some ambulance services employ paramedics in the control room so they can be consulted if there is any doubt about the priority of the incident. The dispatcher assesses manually the nearest appropriate ambulance by using a number of screens: a screen indicating a plan designed to maximise the efficient use of resources (known as the system status management or SSM plan), a screen listing the status of all current resources, and a screen which plots the current location of ambulance resources against a computerised map and a touch-screen telephone. The SSM plan is an attempt to dynamically deploy vehicles around the area covered by the ambulance service, according to demand patterns established for day and time, geographical area and clinical urgency. As part of the ICT functionality the SSM plan is capable of prompting control room staff to shift resources such as ambulances on a continual basis to stay within plan.

Using this technology and their knowledge of the local area, the dispatcher assigns an ambulance to the incident. This means that the dispatcher does not always send the nearest ambulance: they can take into account issues such as the traffic flow in rush hour, to decide which ambulance is likely to get there soonest. Many ambulance services have a policy of recruiting control room staff from their pool of operational crews, because this kind of domain knowledge is so important to effective dispatch.

During this process the call-taker gives pre-arrival advice to the caller, relying on both the software and their own training. Meanwhile the dispatcher typically uses a radio message to tell the chosen ambulance crew to attend the incident, and send them the location (including a grid reference) and details of the patient's condition. Some ambulance services have communication systems that enable control staff to page ambulance crews.

Ambulances are fitted with a communication set, and a member of the crew signals when they go mobile. They are also fitted with global positioning system equipment which updates the dispatch system every 13 seconds with their location. Crews are guided by satellite navigation to the incident location, supplemented by radio communication with the control room. When the crew arrive at the incident they press the *arrive* button on the communication set. They press a *leave scene* button when leaving the incident and an *at hospital button* when they arrived at a hospital. Finally, they press a *clear* button when they are available to be allocated as a resource again.

The general conclusion to be drawn from the description of this case is that the informatics infrastructure and activity infrastructure in organisations is a continually changing landscape. Many of the features introduced in the failed information system at the LAS have now become commonplace for ambulance command and control activity systems in the United Kingdom.

Improving practice

The key argument in this book is that that the systemic interaction of all the elements described in the domain model contributes to information systems failure and success. Comparing the LAS situation in 1992 and in 1996 suggests that improving any one aspect of the LASCAD project trajectory in isolation would not have led to success in and of itself. For instance, say a new in-house project organisation decided to produce a new system to the original specification with little further consultation. Most likely it would not have worked very well, because it would not have addressed problems such as the mistrust between management and workforce.

The domain model is useful for understanding the theory of business information systems, and their good practice, but it also has a practical use as a vehicle for guiding and controlling practice. Success in organisational informatics comes first from an awareness of as many model elements as possible. Contracted, outsourced and off-shored information systems development has always proved difficult, and arguably this is because it is hard to acquire awareness of critical elements such as the prior history and culture of the organisation without intensive periods of immersion within it.

Moving from awareness to implementation, the project organisation and the wider organisation need to manage the interactions of the elements of the domain model as effectively as possible. Some aspects, such as subcultural differences between stakeholder groups, are likely to be outside the control of the project organisation. However, it needs to be aware of them and explicitly include them in risk assessments. Sometimes the imponderable nature of aspects such as these might cause an organisation to think twice about developing a new information system.

The future of informatics

Predicting the future is by its very nature prone to error, and never more so than in the area of technology and its impact. Four historical predictions relating to the future of ICT and its application make this very clear:

- In 1946, the head of 20th Century Fox predicted that people would get bored with watching television after six months.
- In 1949 ENIAC, an early computer, was equipped with 18,000 vacuum tubes and weighed 30 tons. It was predicted at the time that computers in the future might have only 1,000 vacuum tubes and perhaps weigh 2 tons.
- In 1957 the late Arthur C. Clarke predicted that in 50 years satellites would be positioned in space to provide television and microwave coverage for the whole planet.
- In 1977, the president of Digital Equipment Corporation predicted that no one would ever want to have a computer in their home.

Three of these predictions from well-respected people proved spectacularly wrong. One was treated with much scepticism at the time but proved spectacularly correct.

However, if we extrapolate from trends that are already apparent, there is more chance of success than with wild guesses. This enables us to provide a picture of some of the issues in the area of informatics that are likely to arise over the next ten years or so. They involve both individuals and organisations, and their use of the informatics infrastructure.

Communication infrastructure

Broadband communication channels are already in common use, and are likely to be used almost universally in future. An increasing range of social, economic and political activity will rely on an efficient and effective ICT infrastructure. Commercial organisations will depend heavily on it, and so will individuals, particularly in their interactions with organisations, obtaining entertainment and using electronically delivered private, public and voluntary sector services.

Convergence

The convergence of technologies around standards will become critical, making content accessible from a range of different devices and fostering easy coordination between devices. This will also foster an increasing range and sophistication of content, applications and services. The greater demands on communication channels will create a need for more bandwidth.

Access devices

The range and functionality of access devices will undoubtedly increase, so people will be able to access a host of new applications, services and content in public, home and work settings through high-bandwidth data communication infrastructure. Convergence of devices such as mobile phones, personal digital assistants (PDAs) and digital TV will be driven by increasing adoption of common technical standards. The role of the 'television' itself is likely to change from a passive receiver to a significant platform for accessing and delivering electronic content.

Consumer applications

Consumers will see continued growth in conventional applications such as Web surfing, email and music downloading. Alongside this, an increasing range of applications will develop, supporting an increasing range of content, much of it personalised. The key applications driving the increased provision of broadband to the home are likely to be voice over internet protocol (VOIP), video download, IPTV and HDTV. IPTV and HDTV will emerge as a major delivery platform for the delivery of broadcast content. As well as being used to deliver commercial content, this platform could be a significant channel for the introduction of public sector applications such as electronic medical monitoring and care.

Consumers and citizens

Floridi (2007) argues that the threshold between online and offline will break down in the near future. As a result, he claims we will all become *information organisms.* He means that the informatics infrastructure that penetrates everywhere will cause a fading between face-to-face and remote or mediated communication. The transition between the offline and the online worlds will therefore become almost invisible to the average citizen and consumer.

Content delivery

Much of the new generation of online content will be produced outside commercial and public sector organisations. Content delivery channels will multiply, leading to a continued increase in user-generated content. With this explosion new approaches to ensuring the quality control of content will develop. A new generation of content will be targeted at the person, not the place or the device. A mixed economy model of delivery of content is likely to develop in the future. Narrowcasting of content will become the norm, although a considerable proportion of content delivered will still be from broadcast organisations where the 'quality' of content is assured.

Changes to work

The near future should bring increasing demand for penetration of high-bandwidth broadband into the home to support multiple and sophisticated use by households for both leisure and work purposes. This is likely to be a critical driver for increased levels of home or remote working. There is predicted to be a growth in number of people working from home at least one day per week. This will probably be accompanied by a greater rise in the number of people who work on the move or nomadically. The growth in employee remote access channels and the convergence of access devices, coupled with the growth in nomadic working, will need to be supported by a reliable, efficient and widespread communication infrastructure (*Economist*, 2008). Much more communications traffic is likely to be loaded onto this network as traditional telephony moves onto the IP network. A growing range of collaborative applications supporting nomadic working will also rely on increasing connectivity of different access devices, and particularly mobile devices.

ICT infrastructure

The interoperability of components in the ICT infrastructure is likely to rely on the increased adoption of service-oriented architecture. The increasing migration of infrastructure to Web services should enable greater integration of ICT systems. This will act as continuing impetus to the distribution of data and processing around wide area networks through technologies such as cloud computing.

There should also continue to be a movement to the application of Web 2.0 technologies. Web 1.0 was characterised by static Web content; Web 2.0 has been typified by a range of technologies that encourage interactive content. The most prominent consequence of this has been the rise of social networking sites and systems.

Current predictions are that over the period to 2020 the major trend will be to provide greater control to the Web. What some people have called Web 3.0 will involve limits on the openness of the Web. Increasing fears over data privacy will lead to greater embedding of privacy-enhancing technologies in the architecture of the Web. Media companies are also likely to introduce greater restrictions on the distribution of content.

Economic growth

Chapter 1 claimed that in the early years of the twenty-first century, societies are moving from an industrial to an information basis. The provision of informatics infrastructure will have a significant impact on economic growth worldwide. Many new industries will rely on it, and competitive advantage will depend heavily on effective and efficient data communication infrastructures, as business activity is increasingly designed to be location-independent.

Electronic delivery

In the near future an increasing range of services in the private, public and voluntary sectors should be delivered electronically in an increasing number of areas of life. In the home, the integration of communication between domestic devices such as fridges and cookers, and access devices such as the mobile phone/PDA is forecast to lead to remote operation of devices. The growth of the use of ICT in schools will continue, with an increased range of educational content online and an increased use of eLearning as a delivery mechanism. In the public sector, there will be an increased range and penetration of government services available online, and of eHealth applications.

The sophistication of electronic delivery will demand intra-organisational data sharing between back-end and front-end information systems. Increasingly we should also expect increased inter-organisational sharing of data, particularly in the public sector. This is likely to occur not only between public sector organisations such as health bodies and social services, but also between a growing range of private and voluntary sector intermediaries. Data sharing in this context demands forms of inter-organisational records management.

Identity management

Information economy: An economy in which information is both important and essential to effective performance.

The key issue of identity management arises in forms of intra-organisational data sharing and particularly inter-organisational data sharing. The INFORMATION ECONOMY is likely to see an increasing need for identity registers of various forms, not only of persons but also of land, buildings, products and potentially services.

As levels of remote interaction between individuals and organisations increase, situations in which identifying people becomes important multiply, so the management of personal identity will assume increasing significance. This will act as an impetus to an increasing range of sociotechnical activity aimed at embedding personal identity management in and between organisations. Successful attempts at this are likely to further enable growth in levels of remote interaction.

Data privacy

As more and more activity moves online, securing data and systems is becoming increasingly critical for organisations in both the public and private sectors. Deviant activity associated with remote electronic delivery, such as identity fraud and theft, is likely to continue to be a problem. Ensuring the privacy of personal data and transactions will become critical to the trust invested in both public and private sector organisations. Protecting their identity and data will also become an increasing area of concern for individuals in everyday activities.

Organisational forms

Networking effects created by increased connectivity to informatics infrastructure are likely to create space for new organisational forms. 'Channel' applications may be key drivers of a 'network' effect in the private, public and voluntary sectors. A key aspect of organisational strategies will be finding spaces for organisational innovation in the wider value network through application of ICT.

Virtual organisation: An organisation built on an ICT infrastructure that enables collaborative eWorking amongst members. Also referred to as a network organisation. Characterised by a flat organisational hierarchy, formed around projects and linked by ICT.

Over the last few years interest has grown in VIRTUAL OR NETWORK ORGANISATIONS. These are organisations built on an informatics infrastructure that enables collaborative, remote and nomadic working. They are also characterised by flat organisational hierarchies, and workers are typically organised in teams working on transitory projects. Virtual organisations do not use traditional physical infrastructure such as office space. People work out of their homes or from wherever they can access communication infrastructure.

However, the inertia embedded within existing organisational structures and cultures will act as a brake on this kind of transformation through ICT. This means that traditional organisational forms will persist, and the conventional support and supplant strategies for the application of ICT will continue to be evident into the near future.

EBusiness

Information systems and ICT will continue to be embedded in organisational life. This will involve continued attempts to informate aspects of the value chain distributed over internal communication networks. It will also increasingly involve attempts to integrate the wider value network with the internal value chain.

ECommerce

A tipping point in B2C eCommerce has already been reached. There should be an increasing penetration of types of B2C eCommerce such as online retail, and also an increasing range of information-based corporations supplying content of various forms.

B2B eCommerce is also likely to merge with P2P eCommerce over the longer term. Some have referred to the development of a digital business ecosystem in which both competition and cooperation activity is supported through ICT. The Digital Business Ecosystem (DBE) is an Internet-based software environment in which business applications can be developed and used. The hope is that this will provide a common supporting infrastructure for the wider value network.

The community chain is likely to assume greater levels of significance. Companies are already interested in using Web 2.0 technologies to build communities of interest. The use of technologies such as wikis and blogs in the commercial context is therefore likely to increase.

Informatics practice

Informatics practice will have to adapt to technological change, but it is likely that most of the generic practices described in this book will continue to be relevant at least until 2020. In a sense they will assume greater significance as societies, economies and polities rely more and more on the successful development and maintenance of informatics infrastructure. In development, collaborative production models for software are likely to grow in importance, and experiments are likely in distribution and pricing models for software. However, the informatics industry is still likely to be dominated by major software and hardware producers using traditional business models.

Informatics professionals

The increased penetration of informatics infrastructure will mean a continued demand for people with informatics knowledge and skills. Informatics planning, management, operations and evaluation skills will become as important as traditional development skills over the longer term. This will reflect the need for organisations to develop informatics as a critical and embedded part of organisational planning, management and strategy.

Value of informatics

Let us return at the close of the book to the issue of value. The trends discussed above suggest that the value of informatics is likely to increase over the next decade for organisations of various forms. Informatics infrastructure will become embedded and universally available. Organisational, group and individual activity will as a consequence become more dependent on its effective and efficient provision. Hence, there will be an increasing need for individuals with an understanding of the multifaceted nature of informatics and its implications for organisations.

The first chapter raised three questions in relation to value and ICT:

- What is the value of ICT to business?
- How do we ensure the value of ICT to business?
- How do we improve the value of ICT to business?

This is the point at which to suggest a response:

- The value of ICT to business emerges from the systemic relationship between three forms of business systems: ICT systems, information systems and activity systems. ICT provides data which is interpreted as information in an information system; the information system provides information for deciding on appropriate action in an activity system.
- The value of ICT to business must be controlled in a systemic way. ICT has to be planned for, managed, developed and operated effectively. Its use has to be continually monitored and the impact on the organisation evaluated.
- Improvement in the value of ICT will arise from the adoption of the good practices in informatics described in the domain model. Adoption of the holistic approach implied in the model clearly demonstrates the value of organisational informatics as an important area of organisational practice.

Conclusion

In a book of classic science fiction the author Ursula Le Guin (1974) provides a quote which is very relevant to the issues considered in this book. A character says, 'The idea is like grass. It craves light, likes crowds, thrives on cross-breeding; grows better for being stepped upon.'

Organisational informatics is a practical discipline. Its growth relies on continues engagement with the application of information, information systems and ICT in and between organisations. Readers are encouraged to engage with the field-testing of the ideas described in this text, and contribute to the successful planning, management, development, operation and evaluation of information systems in organisations of many shades.

So give the ideas and approaches discussed in this book some light. Become part of the crowd engaged in good practice in organisational informatics. Don't be afraid of transporting new ideas into the mix and cross-breeding them with the ideas expressed here. Most importantly, don't be afraid of 'stepping on' the ideas. Please contact the author (beynon-daviesp@cardiff.ac.uk) and tell him when you have found the ideas useful, but more importantly, when you have not and why not.

References

Beynon-Davies, P. (1995) 'Information systems "failure": the case of the London Ambulance Service's Computer Aided Despatch System', *European Journal of Information Systems* 4: 171–84.

Economist (2008) 'Nomads at last: a special report on mobility.'

Fitzgerald, G. and Russo, N. L. (2005) 'The turnaround of the London Ambulance Service Computer-Aided Despatch System (LASCAD)', *European Journal of Information Systems* 14: 244–57.

Floridi, L. (2007) 'A look into the future impact of ICT on our lives', *The Information Society* **23**(1): 59–64.

Fortune, J. and Peters, G. (2005) *Information Systems: Achieving success by avoiding failure*. Chichester, John Wiley.

Hevner, A. R., March, S. T., Park, J. and Ram, S. (2004) 'Design science in information systems research'. *Management Information Systems Quarterly* **28**(1): 75–105.

Hirschheim, R. and Klein, H. (2003) 'Crisis in the IS field? A critical reflection on the state of the discipline', *Journal of the Association for Information Systems* **4**(5): 237–93.

Kling, R. and Allen, J.P. (1996) 'Can computer science solve organisational problems? The case for organisational informatics', in R. Kling (ed.), *Computerisation and Controversy: Value conflicts and social choices*. San Diego, Calif., Academic Press.

Kling, R. and Scaachi, W. (1982) 'The web of computing: computer technology as social organisation', *Advances in Computers* 21: 1–90.

Le Guin, U. (1974) *The Dispossessed*. New York, Harper and Row.

McGrath, K. (2002) 'The Golden Circle: a way of arguing and acting about technology in the London Ambulance Service', *European Journal of Information Systems* **11**(1): 251–6.

Case studies

This section contains case material of two forms: specially written case material and previously published teaching cases.

Thirty-three items of specially written case material for the book are included. Each of these case studies describes an organisation, project or technology of relevance to organisational informatics. Although the case studies are referenced in the main body of the book, they are deliberately written as independent but rich resources of educational content. This means they can be used as sources of consolidation and for discussion across a range of chapters and topic areas.

A common template is used to structure each case, consisting of a case description section, a commentary section, an issues section and a keywords section:

The case description is the main content for each case.

The commentary section briefly relates elements from the case to areas in the book.

The issues section discusses areas of concern arising from the case, mapped to key themes in organisational informatics which can be used to form the basis for discussion.

The keywords attached to each case provide some initial guidance on how the material might be used and give an indication of the hierarchical relationship between the terms used.

There are many other ways in which the cases can be used, and both students and lecturers are encouraged to experiment with the material.

The matrix that follows indicates the case material contained in the book (B) and on the website (W) at www.palgrave.com/business/beynon-daviesBIS. The content of each case is plotted against topic areas covered in chapters.

- Matrix 1 lists all the specially written cases. Twenty-three of these are included in the book and ten can be accessed from the website.
- Matrix 2 lists 12 teaching cases published in the *Journal of Information Technology*. Nine of these were published in a special issue in December 2007, and are based on original teaching cases presented at the International Conference of Information Systems, 2006. Three other cases are taken from other issues of the journal. To provide consistency, a common case template has been written which briefly introduces each case. Six of these case templates are included in the book while the remainder are on the website.

Access to the full teaching cases is available via the book's companion website. For further information on the *Journal of Information Technology* see www.palgrave-journals.com/jit/index.html.

Table C1: Specially written case material

Case study		Organisation Activity system	Information Information system	ICT Communication Technology Internet Web	ICT System websites Databases	Environment Value-chain Value-network	eBusiness eCommerce eGovernment	Use Impact Failure Evaluation	Planning Management Strategy	Informatics Industry Service Projects Operations	Development	Book or Web
Cases in the book												
1.	Amazon	■		■	■	■	■			■		B
2.	Cisco	■		■	■	■	■	■		■		B
3.	Dell	■		■	■	■	■	■		■		B
4.	Early Warning Network	■	■					■				B
5.	Easyjet	■		■	■	■	■	■		■		B
6.	eBay	■		■	■	■	■			■		B
7.	Electronic Data Systems	■							■	■	■	B
8.	Google	■		■	■	■	■			■		B
9.	IKEA*	■		■	■	■	■		■			B
10.	Inland Revenue	■	■			■	■	■	■			B
11.	Microsoft	■		■	■					■	■	B
12.	Movie industry			■		■	■	■				B
13.	MySpace			■	■	■	■			■		B
14.	MySQL				■						■	B
15.	OGC Gateway Process							■	■	■	■	B
16.	Open Source Software Movement			■	■					■	■	B
17.	Quipu	■	■									B
18.	Research Information System			■	■					■	■	B
19.	SAP			■	■		■		■			B
20.	Tesco	■	■	■	■	■	■	■		■		B
21.	UK National ID Card				■	■	■	■		■		B
22.	Wikipedia	■		■	■	■				■		B
23.	YouTube	■			■	■						B
Cases on the website												
24.	Beer distribution game	■	■		■							W
25.	Child Support Agency	■						■	■		■	W
26.	DotCym		■	■	■		■					W
27.	Herman Hollerith	■	■									W
28.	HiCar	■	■						■			W
29.	Linux				■						■	W
30.	Napster											W
31.	Passport Agency	■				■	■	■		■	■	W
32.	UK Electoral System	■	■				■					W
33.	UK Stock Market		■			■	■					W

* Written by Sharon Cox of Birmingham City University

Table C2: JIT teaching cases

Case Study		Organisation Activity system	Information Information system	ICT Communication Technology Internet Web	ICT system Websites Databases	Environment Value-chain Value-network	eBusiness eCommerce eGovernment	Use Impact Failure Evaluation	Planning Management Strategy	Informatics Industry Service Projects Operations	Development	Book or Web
Cases in the book												
JIT1.	Fixing the payment systems at Alvalade XXI: a case on IT project risk management. JIT 2007. *Ramon O'Callaghan*	■	■	■	■		■	■		■	■	B
JIT2.	Modernisation of the passenger reservation system: Indian railway's dilemma. JIT 2007. *Shirish C Srivastava, Sharat S Mathur and Thompson S H Teo*	■	■			■			■			B
JIT3.	Crafting and executing an offshore IT sourcing strategy: Globshop's experience. JIT 2007. *C Ranganathan, Poomima Krishnan and Ron Glickman*						■		■	■		B
JIT4.	Re-engineering at Leroy corporation: the move to component-based systems. JIT 2007. *Julian Kotlarsky*									■	■	B
JIT5.	The ultimate bluff: a case study of partygaming.com. JIT 2007. *Des Laffey*	■				■	■					B
JIT6.	Constructing the e-supply chain at the Eastman chemical company. JIT 2004. *Benjamin Yen, Ali Farhoomand, Pauline Ng*	■		■	■	■	■					B
Cases on the website												
JIT7.	Managing the Internet payment platform project. JIT 2007. *Janis L Cogan and Ulric J Gelinas Jr.*	■					■	■	■	■	■	W
JIT8.	Challenges in delivering cross-agency integrated e-services: the OBLS project. JIT 2007. *Kanapaty P Periasamy and Siew-Kien Sia*	■		■	■		■		■	■	■	W
JIT9.	Wireless technologies at Agriculture ITO. JIT 2007. *Eusebio Scornavacca*	■		■	■						■	W
JIT10.	Infosys technologies: improving organisational knowledge flows. JIT 2007. *Nikhil Mehta, Sharon Oswald and Anju Mehta*	■				■		■	■			W
JIT11.	E-business transformation at the crossroads: Sears' dilemma. JIT 2004. *C Ranganathan, Analini Shetty, Gayathri Muthukumaran*	■		■	■	■	■		■			W
JIT12.	DCXNET: e-transformation at DaimlerChrysler. JIT 2006. *Arnd Klein, Helmut Krcmar*	■				■	■		■			W

1 Amazon.com

Case description

Amazon.com is an American eCommerce company based in Seattle, Washington State, USA. It was one of the first major companies to sell goods over the Internet. It was also one of the most prominent traded securities of the late 1990s dot-com 'bubble'. When this bubble burst, many claimed that Amazon's business model was unsustainable. The company made its first annual profit in 2003, and Amazon.com is probably the most cited example of a company that has succeeded at B2C eCommerce (Saunders, 2001). The domain amazon.com attracts over 600 million visitors annually.

Amazon.com was launched on the Web in June 1995 by Jeff Bezos. Bezos obtained backing of venture capitalists in Silicon Valley to start the operation. He chose to name his site after the world's longest river because according to him, Amazon was set to become the world's largest bookstore. At the time of Amazon's entry into the market it had no significant rivals. Within a year the company was recognised as the Web's largest bookstore.

From the start Amazon offered a range of value-added services to its customers. A popular feature of the website is the ability for users to submit reviews for each product. As part of their review, users rate the product on a scale from one to five stars. These rating scales provide a basic measure of the popularity of a product. This reviewing facility has been seen by some as critical to the explosive growth of the company. Other added-value services include a personal notification service for customers requesting particular titles, a recommendations section where customers can recommend titles in various categories to other customers, an awards section which lists books that have won prizes and an associate programme where other booksellers can link to Amazon to sell their own selections.

At the start Bezos warned investors that they were unlikely to make a profit in the first five years of operation. However, Amazon has engaged in an aggressive expansion strategy since its inception. It has acquired a number of additional retail outlets such as toys and CDs, and has provided a facility for online auctions of small goods. It introduced zShops in 1999, a facility that allows any individual or business to sell through Amazon.com – a form of C2C trading. It has also invested in a number of dot-com companies such as Pets.com and Drugstore.com, and has opened a number of distribution centres and operations around the world.

Amazon has separate websites in Canada, the United Kingdom, Germany, France, China and Japan. However, it ships certain selected products globally. It also runs a number of fulfilment centres in North America, Europe and Asia.

The primary value stream for Amazon is therefore tangible products such as books and CDs. Recently it has attempted to broaden the range by offering products including computer software, video games, electronics, clothing, furniture, food and toys. It also provides added-value services such as a personalised notification service.

Currently the company is claimed to be the Internet's number one retailer. However, although Amazon is a retailer, its key business strategy is based on differentiation in technical infrastructure. For Amazon to keep this competitive differentiation it must continually be at the forefront of Internet technology. Bezos has indicated that he considers Amazon to be a technology company first and a retailer second. Hence, the key differentiating factor for Amazon over conventional retailers is the Internet and Web. Not surprisingly, the company has to innovate ceaselessly in technology terms, but it also needs to ensure that back-end systems managing its supply, sales and distribution processes work effectively.

Amazon primarily engages in B2C eCommerce but as described has recently started a C2C operation in support of its B2C site. Its back-end systems are more than likely to include a number of B2B systems. The company provides a number of levels of functionality through its website such as search features, additional content and personalisation. The site also provides searchable catalogues of books, CDs, DVDs, computer games and so on. Customers can search for titles using keyword, title, subject, author, artist, musical instrument, label, actor, director, publication date or ISBN.

In terms of added value, the company offers a vast range of additional content over and above its products: for example, cover art, synopses, annotations, reviews by editorial staff and other customers and interviews by authors and artists. The website attempts to personalise the customer experience by greeting customers by name, and providing instant personalised recommendations, bestseller listings, personal notification services and purchase pattern filtering.

Amazon also engages in P2P eCommerce. For instance, the websites of Borders (borders.com, borders.co.uk), Waldenbooks (waldenbooks.com), Virgin Megastores (virginmega.com), CDNOW (cdnow.com), and HMV (hmv.com) are all hosted by Amazon. The company also runs multi-channel access for a number of companies such as Marks & Spencer and Mothercare. These sites allow the customer to interact interchangeably with the retail website, standalone in-store terminals, and phone-based customer service agents.

Commentary

Amazon's service to customers relies on a close integration of its website to back-end information and activity systems. For instance, the company uses a streamlined ordering process which uses previous billing and shipment details captured from the customer. Amazon also utilises secure server software that encrypts payment information throughout its integrated fulfilment process. Most of the company's products are available for shipping within 24 hours.

It is possible to describe briefly some of the gains that Amazon experiences from its engagement with eBusiness, and in particular, the close integration of its ICT infrastructure with its activity infrastructure. In terms of **efficacy**, Amazon has been able to diversify into a vast range of products for retail. Since Amazon is primarily a B2C company it is able to run without any physical retail outlets and can pass on **efficiency** gains in lower costs to its customers. In terms of **effectiveness**, Amazon is able to sell its products across the world and relate to a large range of suppliers.

Issues

- Amazon obtained dominance in online book retail by being the first into a niche market. This raises the question of the importance of niche strategies in the online world.
- It took a considerable time for Amazon to make a profit. Many dot-com companies created in the same period now no longer exist. What caused Amazon to survive and other companies to go under?
- Dot-com companies such as Amazon rely on a critical mass of people with access to the Internet who are prepared to order and pay for goods and services online. What effect does the digital divide have on the customer base of these companies?
- Online retail of low-cost, packaged goods such as books, CDs and DVDs now outstrips physical retail of these items in many countries. How has online retail affected consumer behaviour generally?
- Amazon relies on effective management of a supply and distribution (customer) chain to make a profit. How effectively does Amazon engage in B2B eCommerce?
- Amazon.com does not publish a customer service number on its own website. Customers are instead asked to submit written service requests (which are answered by email) or to use a click-to-call service to be connected by phone to an available service representative. Despite the perceived difficulty in reaching customer service by phone, Amazon.com remains high in customer satisfaction surveys. Why do you think this might be?

Keywords

Private Sector Organisation		
Informatics Industry	Informatics Producer	
Internet	Hardware	
	Extranet	
eBusiness	Internal eBusiness	
	eCommerce	B2C eCommerce
		B2B eCommerce
		P2P eCommerce

References/Sources

Saunders, R. (2001) *Business the Amazon.com Way.* Oxford, John Wiley.

www.amazon.com

CASE-STUDY

2 Cisco

Case description

Cisco Systems was founded in 1984 at Stanford University by husband and wife team Leonard Bosack (who developed early router technology) and Sandra Lerner and three colleagues (Kraemer and Dedrick, 2002). Cisco is generally regarded as the leader in the market for inter-networking equipment. It is generally seen as the company which commercialised the router – a device which determines the optimal path along which packets of data should flow on a computer network. The growth of Cisco is also attributed to its setting of standards for networking equipment through its proprietary Internet Operating System (IOS). Both routers and IOS are key technologies supporting the Internet, which enables customers of the company to build large-scale, integrated computer networks.

Growth of the company has been driven by the surge in data traffic on the Internet. The company initially targeted universities, aerospace and government facilities, relying on word of mouth and contacts for sales. The market for routers opened up in the late 1980s, and Cisco became the first company to offer reasonably priced, high-performance routers. It went public in 1990 and soon afterwards initiated an acquisitions strategy to broaden the range of products offered. Originally focusing on corporate data networking, it began to target both internet service providers and the home networking market.

The primary value stream for Cisco is products, particularly routers. It has attempted to broaden the range of this value by offering a wider range of products. It also provides traditional added-value services such as after-sale service. However, Cisco also provides value by managing its wider value network with a range of partners. These include resellers that sell and support Cisco products, service specialists providing network integration and operations, and component manufacturers that provide most of the company's actual manufacturing capability.

Cisco engages in B2C and B2B eCommerce. For B2B eCommerce it has integrated its ERP systems with key suppliers through an extranet. For B2C eCommerce it has built a web portal which enables its customers to order and configure products online.

Cisco has implemented an eBusiness strategy to enable fast integration of its supply chain with key business processes. The supply chain is critical to the business as Cisco's manufacturing operation globally consists of 34 plants, only two of which are owned by the company. Suppliers make up to 90 per cent of the subassembly of Cisco products and 55 per cent of the final assembly. This means that suppliers regularly ship finished goods directly to Cisco customers.

A key component of Cisco's B2B eCommerce strategy is integration of its ERP systems with the information systems of its key suppliers. Suppliers use their ERP systems to run their Cisco production lines, allowing them to respond to demand from Cisco in real time. This is enhanced by the introduction of Cisco Manufacturing Online, an extranet portal that allows partners to access real-time manufacturing information including data on demand forecasts, inventory and purchase orders.

Such a technical infrastructure means that changes in parts of the supply chain are communicated almost instantaneously to the company. For instance, if one supplier is low on a component, Cisco can analyse its supply chain for excess supplies elsewhere. Changes in forecasted demand are also communicated in real time, enabling suppliers to respond immediately to requests for products or materials.

Payments to suppliers are triggered by a shop-floor transaction in the ERP system indicating that production is complete. The transaction initiates an analysis of inventory to determine the value of components sold by suppliers and triggers an electronic payment to suppliers. Annual savings from the use of this ERP system integration are estimated to total millions of dollars per year.

Cisco has also engaged in B2C eCommerce innovation. It has introduced a web portal known as Cisco Connection Online which consists of a dynamic online catalogue, a facility for ordering and configuring products online, a status agent which allows customers and retailers to track orders, a customer service section, a technical assistance section and a software library. The company currently estimates that it earns 75 per cent of its $20 billion sales through its portal. The portal is also indicated as contributing to a 20 per cent reduction in overall operating costs.

Commentary

Cisco's main transformation is the assembly of inter-networking equipment such as routers. The key inputs for Cisco consist of parts from a vast range of suppliers as well as a huge range of data associated with this supply. The key outputs from Cisco are completed products. The competitive environment for Cisco consists of companies producing comparable products in support of the infrastructure of the Internet. Control in the case of Cisco means ensuring that it has sufficient information abut its internal operations to ensure the efficient and effective delivery of goods to its customers (regulation). It also needs to ensure effective monitoring of its competitive environment to ensure that it develops new products for its marketplace (adaptation).

Interpreting this case, it is possible to describe briefly some of the gains that CISCO experiences from its engagement with eBusiness. In terms of **efficacy**, Cisco is able to relate to a large range of suppliers and assemble a vast range of parts to produce its technical products. In terms of **efficiency**, Cisco uses B2C and B2B eCommerce as well as intra-business eBusiness to lower its costs. In terms of **effectiveness**, Cisco maintains that eBusiness has allowed it to grow quickly and allows it to adapt more quickly to environmental changes. It is therefore better able to compete in its key markets.

Issues

- Cisco does have a general website. Could this be regarded as a form of B2C eCommerce? Who are the typical customers of Cisco?
- How much of Cisco business is P2P eBusiness? Does it maintain partnership networks and what role does ICT play?
- Cisco uses an ERP system to ensure integration of internal operations. Consider the benefits as well as costs of ERP in managing the internal value chain.
- Cisco uses an extranet to ensure integration of external relationships with suppliers. Consider the benefits as well as costs of extranets in managing the supply chain.

Keywords

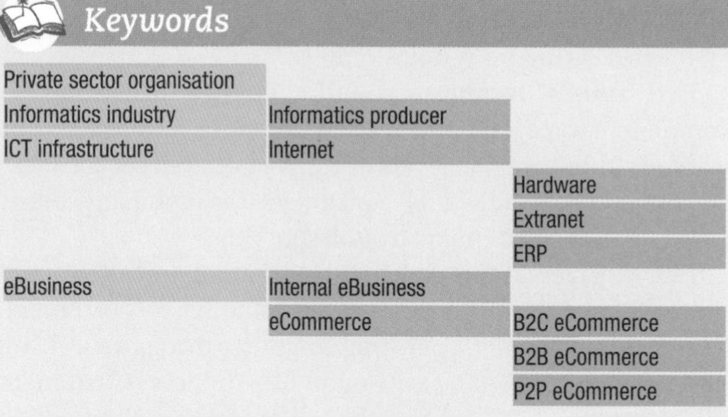

Private sector organisation		
Informatics industry	Informatics producer	
ICT infrastructure	Internet	
		Hardware
		Extranet
		ERP
eBusiness	Internal eBusiness	
	eCommerce	B2C eCommerce
		B2B eCommerce
		P2P eCommerce

References/Sources

Kraemer, K. L. and Dedrick, J. (2002) 'Strategic use of the Internet and e-Commerce: Cisco systems', *Journal of Strategic Information Systems* 11: 5–29.

www.cisco.com

3 Dell

Case description

The US-based technology company Dell Inc. has its headquarters in Round Rock, Texas. It develops, manufactures, markets, sells and supports personal computers, servers, data storage devices, network switches, software, televisions, computer peripherals and other technology-related products. As of 2008, the company employed more than 95,000 people worldwide.

Michael Dell, the founder of Dell Computer Corporation, is often credited with creating a revolution in the personal computer industry. Dell's business model, built around direct selling to the customer and managing its inventory and distribution processes effectively, is credited with a rapid growth in the business (Holzner, 2008).

The idea for the company originated in a business run from Michael Dell's parents' home when he was a teenager. From here he originally sold memory chips and disk drives for IBM PCs. He was able to sell his products through newspapers and magazines at 10–15 per cent below retail prices. He dropped out of college in 1984 and started assembling his own IBM clones, selling direct to customers at 40 per cent below retail price. In 1988 his company went public. Having experienced some problems in 1990 the company re-established its position through selling its PCs via mail order through soft warehouse/compUSA superstores. In 1994 the company abandoned superstores to return to its mail-order/direct retail roots. Dell is now a worldwide business based around integrated manufacturing and supply of hardware.

Dell originally started its Internet initiative in the late 1980s to attempt to increase its level of customer support. The company had formerly provided customer support using a call centre. At the call centre Dell customer care representatives normally advised customers to obtain software updates either sent on disks or as software downloads from a site run by Compuserve. By 1989 Dell began online distribution of software updates.

In 1996 the company launched www.dell.com to provide technical support online. Initially, the website was used to provide technical information to customers. Later, customers were able to order through a website that provided an online catalogue of products. Customers can now also enter details of specific configurations of hardware they require and hence configure systems online.

Dell routes technical support queries according to component type and the level of support purchased. For instance, there are five levels of support offered for business customers. For individual consumers the company offers 24/7 telephone and online troubleshooting.

Dell engages in supply-chain innovation including customisation of hardware and direct retailing to customers. Customers may order a personal computer through a website that provides an online catalogue of products. Customers can also enter details of specific configurations of hardware they require through this website. Such build-to-order retail requires assembly plants around the world (Austin, Texas; Limerick, Eire; Penang Malaysia) close to suppliers such as Intel (chips), Maxtor (hard drives) and Selectron (motherboards). Order forms follow each PC across the factory floor. As well as online customer support, the Dell site provides order and courier tracking, and pages of technical support related to the tagging of machines. Dell associates a Service Tag, a unique alphanumeric identifier, with most of its products.

Dell has sold all its products to both individual and business customers using a direct-sales model via online and telephone channels. The company receives payments for products before it has to pay for the materials and practises just-in-time (JIT) inventory management. This means that Dell builds computers only after customers place orders and by requesting materials from suppliers as needed.

Dell advertisements have used several channels including television, the Web, magazines, catalogues and newspapers. Marketing strategies include lowering prices at all times of the year, offering free bonus products (such as Dell printers), and offering free shipping.

Dell also runs its own online community site which members can access to contribute to fora and blogs on the use of latest technology.

Commentary

The primary value stream for Dell is tangible products such as computers and peripheral equipment. Some intangible items such as software are also provided to customers. It attempts to provide added-value services such as customisable configuration and online help and support.

Dell's main transformation is the assembly of computing equipment. The key inputs for Dell consist of parts from a vast range of suppliers as well as a huge range of data associated with this supply. The key outputs from Dell are completed products. The competitive environment for Dell consists of hardware companies producing comparable products. Control in the case of Dell means ensuring that it has sufficient information abut its internal operations to ensure the efficient and effective delivery of goods to its customers (regulation). It also needs to ensure effective monitoring of its competitive environment to develop new products as needed for its marketplace (adaptation).

Dell engages in both B2C and B2B eCommerce. It has also integrated its internal information systems to become an effective intra-business eBusiness. In terms of **efficacy**, Dell has been able to diversify into a vast range of hardware products for retail. In terms of **efficiency**, Dell has been successful at lowering its internal costs and is able to pass on these lower costs to its customers. In terms of **effectiveness**, Dell is able to sell its products across the world and to relate to a large range of suppliers.

Issues

- Would you describe Dell as engaging in customer relationship management through its website?
- Dell uses JIT inventory management and manufacturing. How important is ICT to this business philosophy?
- How important is tracking of products to the Dell business, for both the supply chain and the customer chain?

Keywords

Private sector organisation		
Informatics industry		
	Informatics producer	
eBusiness	Internal eBusiness	
	eCommerce	B2C eCommerce
ICT infrastructure	Hardware	B2B eCommerce
	Computers	
	Peripherals	

References/Sources

Holzner, S. (2008) *How Dell Does It.* New York, McGraw-Hill Professional.

www.dell.com

4 Early warning network

Case description

During the early 1930s accepted military strategy for air defence was to fly 'standing patrols' on flight paths likely to intercept bombing raids by an enemy. This was an extremely expensive strategy in that aircraft had to be kept permanently in the skies. Not surprisingly, this strategy was eventually replaced with the use of interceptor flights that could take off quickly and attack incoming bomber raids. However, the key question remained, how was an air force to determine the precise position of incoming enemy aircraft in sufficient time to enable effective interception?

The key solution to this problem involved the use of radio technology to detect aircraft – a technology that became known as radar. Both the Germans and British had access to this technology, and indeed German radar was technically superior to its British equivalent at the time. The crucial difference was that the British were better able to use the technology. They were able to gain competitive advantage as a result.

The first step in this process of achieving advantage was British Fighter Command constructing a chain of radar stations around the British coast. This was supplemented with a chain of posts manned by people who observed incoming aircraft, known as the Observer Corps.

The second step was the creation of an effective system in which the 'information technology' could be used. During the summers between 1936 and 1939, a series of teams formed from physicists, engineers and RAF personnel engaged in a series of practical exercises with the aim of solving the fundamental problem of turning raw data from radar and observer posts into information for pilots to fly to the precise point at which to intercept enemy raids. The eventual information system that was created allowed an initially under-strength RAF to compete successfully with a numerically greater force of enemy aircraft.

This system was not originally referred to as an information system. It was given a series of different names such as warning and control system, early warning network or the control and reporting system. Here it is called the early warning network (Holwell and Checkland, 1998a).

The early warning network was a system in the sense that it had inputs, processes and outputs. The key inputs to the system involved a continually changing stream of data from radar stations and Observer Corps posts. The key process of the system involved the timely collection, integration and evaluation of this data at a number of headquarter stations. The key outputs from the system were instructions to appropriate fighter squadrons to take off, be given directions by radio to meet incoming bombers and then fly back to base.

ICT was used in support of the information system, but not in the form we currently know it. There were actually two chains of radar station, one for detecting high-flying aircraft and one for detecting low-flying aircraft. Over 1000 observer posts and fighter airfields were also connected to headquarters by dedicated Post Office teleprinter and telephone lines.

The main headquarters of RAF Fighter Command at Bentley Priory, just north of London, had overall strategic control of operations. The organisation of Fighter Command was divided into four geographical groups covering major parts of the country. Each group was in turn divided into sectors with a sector HQ at each of the airfields. Group HQs had tactical control within their area and Sector HQs had control of pilots when airborne.

Data from the two chains of radar stations were telephoned to Fighter Command HQ. This data went first to a filter room, manned 24 hours a day, where members of the Women's Auxiliary Air Force (WAAF) turned such data into useful information. Filtered data was then passed on next door to the Fighter Command operations room. Filtered data and classified plots were recorded by members of the WAAF by moving wooden tokens across a large-scale map of the air-space. These tokens indicated the height, strength and direction of enemy raids. In addition a display called the 'tote' recorded enemy raids and the state of readiness of RAF squadrons – available in 30 minutes, five minutes, take-off readiness two minutes, or in the air – indicated by a series of lights. Changes to the positioning of tokens and updates to the tote were conducted simultaneously at headquarters, group and sector level.

The operations room at group level worked in the same way except that the maps used represented the group air-space. Group HQs also received data (aircraft sightings) from Observer Posts. This was first filtered at group level and then passed on to command and sector HQs.

The sector operations rooms were set up as two units. The first unit duplicated the picture at command and group level by copying the positioning of counters and updates to the HQ tote and plotting table at sector level. This allowed operations controllers at sector level to continually sense their sector's place in the larger operational picture. The second unit plotted at sector level on the map the exact location of their own planes from their radio transmissions. From here aircraft were assigned to a particular raid and their interception courses were continually plotted using compass, ruler, pencil and paper. The sector operations controller scrambled selected aircraft on command from the group HQ. Once in the air, command passed over to the flight leader until combat was over.

There were also links from the system to Anti-Aircraft command, the Observer Corps, the BBC and civil defence organisations such as those sounding air-raid warnings.

This information system proved its worth in action during the period from July to the end of October 1940. On Sunday 15 September 1940 the system was severely tested (Holwell and Checkland, 1998a). A hundred German bombers crossed the Kent coast at 11:30 that day. Seventeen squadrons from three groups of the RAF went to intercept them. At 14:00 the same day a second wave came in and was met by 31 squadrons (over 300 planes in all). At the end of the day RAF losses were 27 aircraft with 13 pilots killed. The Luftwaffe lost 57 aircraft.

Commentary

The warning network can clearly be seen as a system in that it is made up of a number of interdependent parts. It also had clearly identifiable inputs, processes and outputs, and the behaviour of the system was reliant on the effective performance of these parts.

Human activity systems are social systems. They consist of people engaging in coordinated and collaborative action. In the case of the warning network the human activity system consisted of the command and control of the fighter aircraft of the RAF.

Information systems are systems of communication. They involve people in producing, collecting, storing and disseminating information. The information system of the warning network involved collecting data from radar, organising this data for military decision making, and the dissemination of both decisions and data to airfields.

ICT is any collection of artefacts used to support aspects of an information system. The ICT described in the example was subtly different from modern ICT. ICT during the Second World War involved elements like radar, telephone communications and the use of maps, plotting tables and tote devices. However, the core of this system was not the technology, but the way in which it was used to support purposeful action. Its key benefit was its utility. Good information systems are critical to effective human action. The information system set up by the RAF enabled it to beat off the mass raids of the German Luftwaffe. Hence, the key utility of the system was established in relation to the effectiveness of action reliant on it.

An information system is a sociotechnical system which involves both ICT and human activity. In other words, information systems are communication systems designed to support human activity with the aid of technology.

The effective place of ICT in the larger information system has to be designed with the aid of system stakeholders. The identification of and participation of key stakeholders in the development of an information system is a key factor in its successful construction and use. The warning network was designed with the participation of a number of stakeholder groups including aircraft engineers, pilots and scientists.

Issues

- Besides anecdotally, how might it be possible to assess the value of this information system to its activity system? How much did the early warning network contribute to Allied success? Would the Battle of Britain have been won without the presence of this information system?
- The warning network is a classic example of an information system used for command and control, so it should be possible to consider the operation of this system in terms of the classic components of control. For instance, radar was one technology employed to sense the environment. What would comparators and effectors mean in the context of the warning network?
- The computer was created at the time of the Second World War. Investigate why it was created and to what purpose it was initially put.

Keywords

Historical case	
Information	
Activity system	
Information system	
Impact	
ICT	ICT system

References/Sources

Holwell, S. and Checkland, P. (1998a) 'An information system won the war', *IEE Proceedings Software* **145**(4): 95–9.

Holwell, S. and Checkland, P. (1998b) *Information, Systems and Information Systems.* Chichester, UK, John Wiley.

5 EasyJet

 Case description

In 1994 Stelios Haji-Ioannou launched easyJet as a low-cost air carrier, and in 1998 he created easyGroup as a holding company for a number of additional high-demand, low-margin businesses. EasyJet is one of the largest low-fare airlines in Europe, operating domestic and international scheduled services on over 300 routes between over 100 European and North African airports. It has seen rapid expansion since its creation, having grown through a combination of acquisitions and base openings fuelled by consumer demand for low-cost air travel (Jones, 2007).

It is reported that the company has a typical profit margin of only £1.50 per customer. Initially, in order to keep running costs low, the company used a single sales channel of the telephone. The group now uses the Internet as a low-cost sales channel, and this is also significant to the branding of the company as focused on eCommerce.

EasyJet offers high-frequency services on short and medium-haul routes within Europe. It sees itself as a 'no –frills' airline and has designed its business processes to avoid complexity. For example, it maintains single fares on flights, only offers fares one way, offers no in-flight refreshments, operates out of less heavily used and consequently less congested airports, and does not issue tickets but relies on booking numbers. To achieve this, the company relies heavily on close integration between its front-end sales systems and its back-end revenue management systems.

EasyJet's aircraft cabins are configured in a single-class, high-density layout. The airline's Boeing 737-700 aircraft carry 149 passengers plus three cabin crew, and its Airbus A319 aircraft carry 156 passengers plus four cabin crew. A typical Airbus A319 carries approximately 140 passengers in a single class configuration, but as easyJet does not serve meals the airline opted for smaller galleys and had a lavatory installed in unused space at the rear of the aircraft. The airline's 29-inch seat footprint allowed for the installation of 156 seats. Because of this high-density seating arrangement, easyJet's Airbus A319 aircraft have two pairs of overwing exits, instead of the standard one-pair configuration found on most Airbus A319 aircraft, to satisfy safety requirements.

EasyJet does not provide complimentary meals or beverages on board its flights. Instead, passengers can buy items such as sandwiches, toasted sandwiches, pizza slices, chocolate, snacks, hot drinks, soft drinks and alcoholic drinks. Onboard sales are an important part of the airline's ancillary revenue, so easyJet also sells gifts such as fragrances, cosmetics and easyJet branded items onboard, as well as tickets for airport transfer services.

EasyJet's early marketing strategy was initially based on 'making flying as affordable as a pair of jeans' and urged travellers to 'cut out the travel agent'. Its early advertising consisted of little more than the airline's telephone booking number painted in bright orange on the side of its aircraft. Initially booking was by telephone only since there is no incentive for travel agents to sell easyJet bookings because there is no commission, a standard practice for the low-cost carriers.

In December 1997, one of the company's adverting agencies suggested Haji-Ioannou should consider trialling a website for direct bookings. He originally said the Internet was for nerds, but the company's marketing director saw the potential and approved a website trial. This involved placing a different telephone reservations number on the website, to track success. Once Haji-Ioannou saw the results he changed his mind, and easyJet commissioned the development of an eCommerce website capable of offering real-time online booking from April 1998 – easyjet.com. EasyJet was the first low cost carrier to do so in Europe. Internet bookings were priced cheaper than booking over the phone, to reflect the reduced call-centre costs, and the aircraft were repainted with the web address.

By August 1999 the site accounted for 38 per cent of ticket sales. This meant that the company had exceeded its target of 30 per cent of sales online by 2000. Within a year of its launch over 50 per cent of bookings were made using the website. By April 2004 the figure had jumped to 98 per cent. Now, flights can only be booked over the Internet except during the two weeks immediately before the flight, when telephone booking is also available.

The transition to running the website proved relatively smooth. This was because easyJet was a 100 per cent direct phone sales company, and as such it was reasonably straightforward to integrate the website with its booking system. The savings the company makes through online booking have enabled the company to offer typical discounts of £1.00 to customers who book online.

The parent holding company of easyJet (easyGroup) has also launched easyEverything, a chain of 400-seat capacity Internet cafés. Although the cafés are run as a separate business the original intention was to give people with no Internet access the capability to buy online from easyJet.

EasyEverything customers can visit the easyJet website for free but pay a nominal charge for other Internet usage. This strategy of attempting to get its customers online meant that within two years of introducing its transactional website the company was selling two-thirds of its seats online.

EasyJet varies the mix of its promotional campaigns. It frequently runs Internet-only campaigns in newspapers designed to improve online sales. It ran the first of this type of promotional campaign in February 1999 with impressive results: 50,000 seats were offered to readers of *The Times* at discounted prices. Within the first day 20,000 of the seats had been sold, and 40,000 went within three days.

The website is also used as a public relations facility. For example, journalists wishing to learn about changes to company policy or strategy are referred to the website. This saves the company from employing a specialist PR company.

Commentary

Cost savings through use of online booking helped to establish the business model for low-cost airlines such as easyJet. Other re-engineering of processes associated with commercial airline travel has enabled further efficiency gains. For instance, the seating on easyJet aircrafts has been changed from the standard configuration and seats are not pre-allocated to customers before flights. Many airlines have also begun introducing forms of automatic check-in relying on ICT.

Issues

- EasyJet, just like most low-cost airlines, has introduced charging for certain added-value items such as priority boarding and baggage. Consider other ways in which low-cost airlines now make money from their online channels.
- The usability of websites is critical to the volume of bookings for companies such as easyJet. Assess the usability of easyJet's website compared with its major competitors.
- The easyJet website, like many others, gives customers the ability to create a profile of details which they can use to speed bookings. Consider this facility in relation to the security of personal data.
- Since easyJet relies so much on its website for bookings, the continuity and availability of the site is critical to its success. Consider the ways in which such continuity is assured.

Keywords

Private sector organisation		
Informatics industry		
	Informatics consumer	
Access channels		
eBusiness	eCommerce	B2C eCommerce
		eMarketing

References/Sources

Jones, L. (2007) *EasyJet: The story of Britain's biggest low-cost airline.* London, Aurum Press.

www.easyjet.com

6 eBay

Case description

EBay is probably the most significant contemporary example of C2C e-Commerce (Cohen, 2002). Pierre Omidyar created eBay in September 1995. Using a website hosted by Omidyar's internet service provider (ISP), he originally ran the company in his spare time from his apartment. In its early guise eBay was little more than a simple marketplace where buyers and sellers could bid for items. The company took no responsibility for the goods being traded and gave no undertaking to settle disputes between parties.

By February 1996 so many people had visited the site that Omidyar decided to introduce a 10 cent listing fee to recoup ISP costs. By the end of March 1996 eBay showed a profit. Eventually the volume of traffic to the site persuaded his ISP to ask him to move elsewhere. Omidyar decided to transfer the operation to a one-room office with his own web server, and hired a part-time employee. He also developed software capable of supporting a robust, scalable website as well as a transaction processing system to report on current auctions.

By August 1996 Omidyar had established one of his friends as the first president of eBay. In June 1997 the company approached venture capitalists for funding and secured $5 million. This enabled the company to establish a more extensive management structure for planned expansion. By the end of 1997 more than 3 million items (worth $94 million) had been sold on eBay, amounting to revenues of $5.7 million and an operating profit of $900,000. EBay had an operating staff of only 67 at the time.

In its early days eBay undertook only limited marketing and relied on the loyalty of its customer base and word-of-mouth referrals for its increased business growth. Eventually the company began to employ cross-promotional agreements including banner advertising on web portals such as Netscape and Yahoo! as well as providing an auction service for AOL's classified section. This evolved into a conventional marketing campaign through traditional print and broadcast media in 1998.

In 1999 the company expanded internationally by creating communities in Canada and the United Kingdom. This was followed by expansion into Germany, Australia, Japan and France. During this year and into 2000 the company successfully held its position against strong new entrants into the online auctions market such as Amazon.com. The company also moved into the bricks and mortar area with the purchase of a San Francisco-based auction house. Ebay used this acquisition to move into the higher-priced antiques sector of the market. By the end of June 1999 eBay had 5.6 million registered users and had conducted 29.4 million auctions during the previous three-month period. In the third quarter of 2000 $1.4 billion worth of goods were traded on eBay in 68.5 million auctions which generated $113.4 million in revenues.

At the time of writing approximately 1.5 million people are joining eBay each month from around the world. A survey by eBay in mid-2001 found that 10,000 people in the United States were full-time eBay traders. It is estimated that now 40,000 people around the globe earn a living in this way.

Essentially, eBay's business model is a simple one of providing C2C auctions online. Much activity relies on collectors trading small-priced items such as coins, stamps and militaria. Although the average item sold through these markets constitute no more than a few dollars, as a whole billions of dollars are traded every year in the United States in C2C trading of this nature.

The concept is to provide a website where anyone wishing to buy or sell must register by providing personal and financial details. Every user of eBay is given a unique identifier. EBay offers a virtual tour of its services but people can start buying and selling straight away.

Sellers list items for sale by completing an online form. They pay a small listing fee for this privilege. The size of the fee depends on where and how the listing is presented and whether a reserve price is required. Sellers also choose the timescale over which they wish buyers to bid for the item. At the end of an auction, eBay notifies the winning bidder and provides details of the successful bidder to the seller. The buyer and seller then make their own arrangements for payment and delivery of the goods, usually by exchanging emails. Payment can be made by cash, cheque and postal order or electronically through a payment service or financial intermediary such as Paypal (paypal.com), now a subsidiary of eBay. EBay charges a percentage of the final value of the transaction. For instance, suppose a British seller lists a collection of stamps for sale at £24.00. The seller might pay approximately 50p to eBay to make a standard listing on the website. If and when the collection is sold, the seller pays 5 per cent of the final sale price to the company.

Since buyers pay sellers before they receive items, the business model runs on trust. The eBay feedback system is used to indicate problems with particular users. Users can file feedback about any user on the feedback site. This discourages trade with rogue participants.

The only costs to eBay are therefore for the computing infrastructure and expenses associated with customer services. EBay keeps no inventory, has no distribution network and does not have to maintain a large staff.

Most of eBay's sellers are serious collectors and small traders who used it as their shop-front. EBay has enabled them to access a global marketplace for trading of collectibles. It has also set up the eBay café to service its sellers. This is a chat room where users of the site communicate and exchange information. It proved useful to the company as a way to monitor customer reaction to various initiatives. For instance, users often complained about changes in pricing. EBay has also used its customers to post answers to frequently answered questions (FAQs) on its bulletin boards, and even employed some active and knowledgeable users to provide email help to its new customers.

In an attempt to develop trust and loyalty amongst its customer community, eBay established SafeHarbour in February 1998. SafeHarbour offers verification and validation of customers, insurance associated with the selling and buying process and some regulation of sales activity. The company also created My eBay, a tool that customers can use to personalise their access to the site: keeping track of their favourite categories, viewing items they are selling or bidding on, or checking their account balance.

Following a number of outages, in 1999 the company decided to outsource its back-end infrastructure to an external supplier. It outsourced its web servers, database servers and routers to these companies with the expectation of having excess capacity for preserving its service. Periodic overhaul of the technical infrastructure is critical to its success.

Commentary

EBay is one of the foremost examples of C2C eCommerce. Its dominance is due to early entry into what was a niche market at the time. Its business model relies on that used in familiar exchange and mart catalogues that have existed for decades. The competitive edge for the business lies in the way in which eCommerce enables mass customers to trade low-cost items efficiently through an auction process across the world.

EBay uses a Dutch auction model for its business. In this

form of auction the seller places one or more identical items for sale at a minimum price for a set period. When the auction ends the highest bidder gains the item at their bid price.

EBay was recently successfully sued by a number of branded-goods companies for allowing traders to offer counterfeit versions of their products. Some commentators see this having many potential implications for C2C sites such as eBay.

Issues

- Consider the issue of trust in relation to eCommerce transactions and how eBay attempts to build trust with its customers.
- How are electronic payments managed by eBay?
- Examine the issue of auction types. Try to compare the model for electronic auctions applied in eBay with that of traditional cattle or antique auctions.
- Can eBay be considered a serious eProcurement hub?
- Investigate other ways of running auctions, and search for any sites that run alternative auction models.
- Will the recent problems with the trade in fake goods through eBay affect eBay's long-term business model?

Keywords

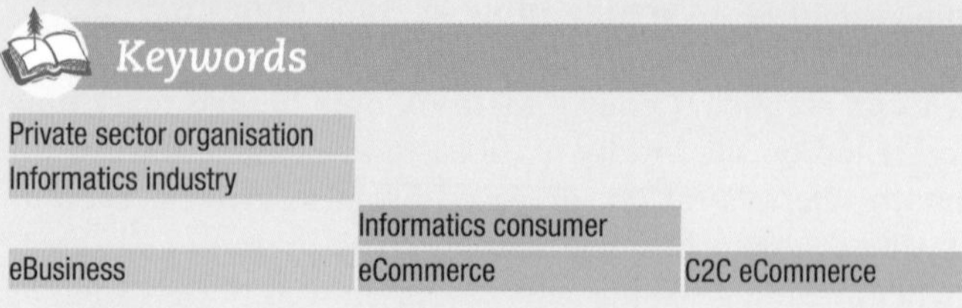

References/Sources

Cohen, A. (2002) *The Perfect Store: Inside eBay*. New York, Little, Brown.
www.ebay.com

7 Electronic Data Systems

Case description

Electronic Data Systems (EDS) is a global business and technology services company which has its headquarters in Plano, Texas. The company was established in 1962 by Ross Perot. General Motors (GM) acquired the company in 1984. However, in 1996 GM established the operation again as an independent company and became an EDS client itself. In 2006, EDS employed 117,000 people located in 58 countries, and reported revenues of $19.8 billion. It is ranked as one of the largest service companies on the Fortune 500 list.

EDS classifies its services into three portfolios: infrastructure, applications and business process outsourcing. The infrastructure services portfolio involves operating of all or part of a client's ICT infrastructure, such as networks, mainframes, web servers, desktops and laptops, and printers. The applications services portfolio involves the development, integration and possible maintenance of ICT systems for clients. The business process outsourcing portfolio includes performing a specific business function for a client such as payroll processing, processing of insurance claims or operation of call centres.

EDS has established a number of business alliances with other companies in its EDS Global Alliance programme. The alliances are grouped into three groups, agility alliances, solution alliances and technology alliances. Business alliance partners include Cisco Systems, Microsoft, Oracle Corporation, SAP, Sun Microsystems and Xerox.

Most of EDS's clients (in 65 countries worldwide) are very large companies and governments that need services from a company of the scale of EDS. EDS's largest clients include General Motors, KarstadtQuelle, Kraft, the US Navy and the UK Ministry of Defence.

When engaging in a large outsourcing contract EDS, like many informatics outsourcing companies, has a policy of basing its workforce at the workplace of the customer.

EDS has been prominent in large-scale ICT projects in the United Kingdom designed to provide infrastructure for government agencies. Some projects of this nature have experienced difficulty, as in the case of the ICT system created for the Child Support Agency.

Commentary

Outsourcing of informatics has been a successful strategy for many companies and public sector agencies. However, some have expressed concern over the centralisation of control of the ICT outsourcing market in the hands of a limited range of suppliers. In the United Kingdom there is a lot of concern about the use of ICT outsourcing under private finance initiative projects, and the long-term effectiveness of this as an informatics strategy for government.

Issues

- What advantages are there for a company in the use of informatics outsourcing suppliers such as EDS?
- When companies have outsourced to companies such as EDS the outsourcing vendor has taken over the ICT staff of the company. What implications does this strategy have for the future performance of the company?

Keywords

Private sector organisation	
Informatics industry	Informatics producer
	Informatics service
	Outsourcing

References/Sources

www.eds.com

8 Google

Case description

Google Inc. is probably one of the most well known of the recent American companies specialising in Internet search and online advertising (Vise, 2005). It is based in Mountain View, California, and had 13,748 full-time employees as of June 2007. Google's mission statement is 'to organize the world's information and make it universally accessible and useful'.

Google was co-founded by Larry Page and Sergey Brin while they were students at Stanford University, USA on the back of research they were conducting on improvement to the algorithms underlying search engines. Traditionally, search engines work by matching a series of search terms entered by the user against the terms found in web pages. They rank sites based on the number of times the terms searched for appear on their pages. Page and Brin produced an algorithm called PageRank which analyses the links from and to web documents, then assigns a numerical weighting to each element of a set of documents, with the purpose of measuring its relative importance in the set. In this sense, the PageRank algorithm treats links in a similar manner to academic citations. Generally, the larger the number of citations of an academic paper, the more important the paper is considered by the academic community.

Google uses web crawlers (also known as web spiders or web robots) to build and maintain its representation of the links between web documents. A web crawler is a type of software agent; a program or automated script which browses the World Wide Web in a methodical, automated manner. Web crawlers are mainly used to create a copy of all the pages visited for later processing by a search engine, which indexes the downloaded pages to provide fast searches for users.

Google is best known for its web search service, which as of December 2006 gave it a 50.8 per cent market share of the search engine market. Google indexes billions of web pages using the PageRank algorithm. Users search for content through the use of keywords and logical operators such as NOT and AND. The search engine ranks hits on the basis of the number of links a page receives as well as the importance of the web documents sourcing the links.

The company was first created in 1998 and went public in 2004. Through a series of new product developments, acquisitions and partnerships, it has expanded its initial search and advertising business into other areas, including web-based email, online mapping, office productivity and video sharing. Google has also employed its search technology in other search services, including Image Search, Google News, the price comparison site Google Product Search, the interactive Usenet archive Google Groups and Google Maps.

In 2004 Google launched its own free web-based email service, Gmail, which provides the capability to use Google technology to search email. The service generates revenue by displaying advertisements from the AdWords service that are tailored to the content of the email messages displayed on screen.

Google has also developed several applications for the desktop, The best known is Google Earth. This consists of an interactive mapping program powered by satellite and aerial imagery which provides precision images covering the vast majority of the planet.

Most of Google's revenue is derived from advertising. For the 2006 fiscal year, the company reported $10.492 billion in total advertising revenues and only $112 million in licensing and other revenues. The AdWords application allows clients to display advertisements alongside Google's search results and the Google Content Network, through either a cost-per-click or cost-per-view scheme. Google AdSense website owners are also able to display adverts on their own site, and earn money every time ads are clicked.

Commentary

In a sense although it developed merely as a search engine, Google, as a company is now the most prominent example of an information brokerage on the Web. To google is becoming established as a verb in the English language, synonymous with searching for information on any particular topic. As such, the company is in an unprecedented position as a gatekeeper to information on the global scale.

Issues

- Concern has been expressed over the dominance of Google in both the search engine market and the wider information brokerage market. As a reaction Microsoft proposed an alliance with the search engine Yahoo!, which came to nothing.
- For online businesses, it is crucial to optimise the chances of their website being retrieved early in the list of hits by search engines such as Google. This area of search engine optimisation is a specialist component of website design.
- Google has come under fire for allowing countries such as China to censor web content for users of the search engine. How healthy for individuals and organisations is the reliance on Google as a dominant gatekeeper to web content?

Keywords

Private sector organisation		
Informatics industry	Informatics producer	
eBusiness	eCommerce	Infomediary
ICT	Software	Search engine

References/Sources

Vise, D. A. (2005) *The Google Story.* New York, Random House.
www.google.com

9 IKEA*

* This case study was contributed by Sharon Cox of Birmingham City University, UK

Case description

IKEA was founded by Ingvar Kamprad in 1943. The name IKEA is formed by the founder's initials (IK) followed by the first letters of the village and farm in Sweden where he grew up, Elmtaryd (E) and Agunnaryd (A). This reflects the identity of IKEA, embedded in the characteristics and values of the Swedish farming community. Ingvar Kamprad sold a range of products door to door, and it was in 1948 that IKEA started selling furniture produced by local manufacturers. In 1951, the first IKEA catalogue was published enabling furniture to be sold on a larger scale, with the first retail furniture showroom opening in 1953 in Älmhult, Sweden. IKEA is reported to be the world's largest home furnishings retailer and currently has 231 retail stores in 24 countries.

IKEA's business strategy stems from a vision 'to create a better everyday life for the many people'. It has a clearly defined business idea; to offer a wide range of well designed, functional home furnishing products at prices so low that as many people as possible will be able to afford them'. This informs and directs all business processes, from product design and manufacture through to distribution and home assembly.

The IKEA range comprises 9500 products. The design process is rooted in the IKEA ethos and supports the business strategy by focusing on form, functionality and low price. Product design starts with an agreed selling price for the finished item. This influences the resources to be used in the product and requires consideration to be given to optimising manufacturing techniques. Consideration also has to be given to how the design and packaging of the product will affect its warehousing, distribution and final assembly. Product designers work closely with suppliers to find innovative cost-effective solutions to ensure that products are economical in their use of resources, recyclable and easy to transport.

IKEA has 45 trading officers in 31 countries which work with 1350 suppliers. Collection, processing and distribution of information are critical across the supply chain. Product information assistance (PIA) is one of IKEA's central ICT systems, introduced in 1998. It runs on a series of databases which support the management of product information, product range structures, technical specifications and drawings. PIA is a key resource for business units both within IKEA and for its suppliers. It supports the main milestones in the project management of product development, from requirements specification, through agreeing the technical specification with suppliers, to making the product available for IKEA retail stores to order.

Product designers, manufacturers and technical experts regularly engage in face-to-face meetings, working together to find ways of reducing costs. Meetings usually take place on the factory floor, reflecting IKEA's social values of respect, informality and equality. For example, a product developer was challenged to reduce the production costs of the LACK table, one of IKEA's best selling products. The table veneer accounted for one-third of the total production costs. The challenge was therefore to find a way of retaining the look and feel of the veneer while reducing production costs. This involved meetings with production managers and suppliers of different veneer and lacquering techniques. Working together, they developed a technique for creating an artificial veneer. Such innovative solutions have enabled the selling price of the LACK table to remain the same for over 20 years.

IKEA Components is a wholly owned division responsible for wholesale product distribution. It supplies raw materials for customers to build the furniture, the assembly kits needed for the flat-packed furniture and the packaging materials. Flat-packed products enable cost-effective product distribution to the retail stores. Reducing the air inside product packaging is an important factor in reducing distribution costs.

It is reported that analysis and redesign of distribution processes against key performance indicators (KPI) has resulted in a 30 per cent improvement of product availability, 85 per cent reduction in customer claims as a result of damaged, incomplete or incorrect components, and 30 per cent reduction in product handling costs (Green, 2008).

In 1990, IKEA developed its environmental policy to ensure that the company and its co-workers take environmental responsibility for all activities in the business. All suppliers are required to adhere to a code of conduct, the IKEA Way on Purchasing Home Furnishing Products (IWAY). This defines what suppliers can expect from IKEA and specifies what IKEA expects from its suppliers in terms of legal requirements, working conditions, active prevention of child labour, the external environment and forestry management.

IKEA's social responsibility is further demonstrated by its aim to reduce emissions of greenhouse gases generated through its operations by using renewable energy and by improving energy efficiency at its suppliers. It aims to improve the energy efficiency of all its stores by 25 per cent and develop sustainable customer transportation to and from its stores.

The website www.IKEA.com was launched in 1997. Three years later, customers in Sweden and Denmark were the first to be able to shop online with the store. The website seeks to convey the ethos underlying the IKEA experience. It includes a number of online planning tools to assist customers in improving their homes. The website also has an important role in cost reduction. Cost-effective customer support is provided by Anna, an automated customer service chat character driven by artificial intelligence. For example, if a customer finds that a part of the flat pack they are assembling is missing, Anna will arrange for the part to be sent to them, or for them to collect it from their local store. It is reported that in 2006, Anna provided support to UK customers generating cost savings of [e]10 million. The 'ask Anna' facility is being extended to the company's websites in other countries.

Commentary

IKEA is a low-cost retailer of home furnishings that seeks to provide quality products to its customers. It achieves this in three ways. First, it outsources costly processes such as production, as well as outsourcing final product assembly to the customer. This requires data relating to product specifications and assembly instructions to be carefully managed. Second, it engages in collaboration with suppliers to develop innovative design, production and distribution solutions. Third, it encourages the analysis and redesign of business processes throughout the value chain to meet not only efficiency objectives but also the company's declared strategy on corporate social responsibility. IKEA has a clearly defined business vision to which all its activities are aligned. It is founded on strong cultural values, and despite having stores worldwide, it makes minimal adaptation to local culture.

Issues

- IKEA is committed to addressing environmental issues and using sustainable resources. How can information systems and ICT contribute to improving the energy efficiency of its operations?
- information systems and ICT can be aligned with IKEA's business strategy. How can the strong cultural values be reflected in ICT?
- Effective collaboration with suppliers to support product development is a key factor in IKEA's success. Consider the extent to which information systems and ICT can support collaboration, beyond the transactional processes of eBusiness.
- Innovation in product design, manufacture and distribution enables IKEA to achieve its vision. What opportunities are there for information systems and ICT to contribute to innovation in IKEA's value chain?
- Consider the roles and interactions between technology and activity systems in product development projects at IKEA.

Keywords

Private sector organisation	Retail industry	
Business strategy	Informatics planning	Key performance indicators
Value chain		
Value network	Supply chain	
Organisational culture	Core values	Corporate social responsibility
B2C eCommerce		
B2B eCommerce	Supply chain management	

References/Sources

Baraldi, E. and Waluszewski, A. (2005) 'Information technology at IKEA: an "Open Sesame" solution or just another type of facility?' *Journal of Business Research* **58**(9): 125–60.

Green, C. (2008) 'IKEA self-assembles business process change', *ITPro Newsletter*, 19 March [online] www.itpro.co.uk/180309/IKEA-self-assembles-business-process-change

www.ikea.com

10 Inland Revenue (UK)

Case description

In April 2000 the UK e-Government Strategic Framework was published, requiring all central government departments to produce eBusiness strategies. These were intended to show how each department planned to implement eGovernment and to achieve electronic service delivery targets. The first draft was required in October 2000. From July 2001 departments were required to report progress against eBusiness strategies to the Office of the e-Envoy every six months (Beynon-Davies, 2005).

The Inland Revenue was until recently the UK government department responsible for collecting and administering taxation. It attempted to be at the forefront of eGovernment in the United Kingdom by transforming its performance using ICT. This is evident in much of the strategic thinking emanating from its leadership.

For instance, the organisation nominated four indicators to determine how well it had transformed itself. First, the receipt of clean data from customers would allow the Inland Revenue to remove work that added little value to the organisation and consequently release people to work at the front line of customer care. Second was increasing the organisation's capability to deliver services electronically and increasing the take-up of such services by customers. Third was increasing use of knowledge management so that its staff had better guidance, which in turn enhanced its customer service capabilities. Finally, information and data management would enable it to progress towards the 'joined-up government' vision: that is, to develop seamless, quality services and make best use of the data it received.

The department set out its first eBusiness strategy in 2000. The key feature of the strategy at this time was the development of a number of access channels for different customer groups, with clear incentives to encourage their use. As part of this strategy the organisation intended to offer improved eServices to the UK taxpayer, thus reducing the burden of compliance on individuals and organisations. It also planned to use intermediaries such as the National Association of Citizens Advice Bureaux, the Post Office and software suppliers to provide bespoke services to its customers. It planned to achieve all this through greater integration of its services with other departments and providing its services through commercial and government portals. It also required transformation of staff roles to focus around support for the customer through use of electronic tools.

In 2001 the Inland Revenue revised its strategy, keeping these fundamental principles but making two additions: a transformation of the organisation around a focus on the customer, and a philosophy based on customer relationship management, creating a technical framework that would deliver eServices in a modular but integrated fashion.

The Inland Revenue established three targets for its eBusiness strategy:

- 50 per cent of services would be available electronically by 31 December 2002. By this time the organisation aimed to offer basic secure eServices and have developed plans for organisational change based on them.
- 50 per cent take-up of its services by 2005. By 2004 the organisation aimed to have significantly increased take-up of its core services and have delivered significant benefits from this.
- All its services would be available electronically by 31 December 2005. By this date the Inland Revenue aimed to have achieved significant business transformation, with most customer transactions being conducted electronically.

Subsequent to publication of the strategy, the Inland Revenue merged with Customs and Excise in 2006 to form Her Majesty's Revenue and Customs (HMRC). This was part of a wider attempt at improving the efficiency of UK government departments, which was stimulated by a review of activity.

The newly formed HMRC soon came into the spotlight in

2007 for its failings in data management. In October 2007 a junior official based in Washington, Tyne and Wear sent two CDs containing government records to the National Audit Office (NAO) based in London. The NAO had requested the data so it could run an independent survey of child benefit payments. The disks were password-protected but the data was unencrypted. The package was sent unrecorded and unregistered using the courier company TNT. The records contained the names, addresses, birth dates and national insurance numbers of all the 25 million individuals the HMRC dealt with in relation to child benefits, plus details of partners, the names, sex and ages of children and bank/savings account details for each claimant. This meant that details of 7.25 million bank accounts associated with families were stored on the disks.

The disks failed to arrive at the NAO offices, and following notification of this a second package was sent by registered post and arrived safely. In November 2007 senior managers at HMRC were told that the first package had been lost. A week later the prime minister and other government ministers, most notably the chancellor of the Exchequer, were informed of the loss. Initially, government ministers were told that the CDs would probably be found, but when HMRC searches for the lost disks failed, the Metropolitan Police were called in to investigate.

This data loss led the chancellor to consult with the information commissioner, the person responsible for overseeing the implementation of data protection in the United Kingdom, and they agreed that consultation with UK banks and other financial institutions was required. At the request of the financial institutions the public were not informed of the data loss for some days in order to allow the institutions to monitor potential suspicious activity. The institutions tracked transactions back to the date at which the data was lost in an attempt to do this.

As a consequence of this data incident the HRMC chairman resigned and the chancellor made an announcement to the House of Commons. This claimed that the junior official had broken data security procedures in downloading the data to disks and sending them unrecorded through the post. The chancellor reassured the public that the police had no reason to suspect the data had got into the wrong hands. However, people were urged to keep a close eye on their bank accounts.

Many people suggested that criminals might gain access to the data and use it to engage in mass identity theft and fraud. They might not only gain access to existing bank accounts but also use the personal identity data to open new bank accounts or other financial products such as credit cards. The possibility of paedophile rings gaining access to the data on children and using it for 'grooming' activities was also raised.

A report into this incident was published in June 2008. The report identifies that the data loss was not the responsibility of a single person as originally reported in the popular press. Instead, more than 30 officials from various departments within the HMRC were identified as playing some part in the incident. The report concluded that the HMRC was woefully inadequate in its handling and managing of corporate data. It made a series of recommendations for tightening data security and improving data management practices across UK government.

Commentary

There has been a great deal of computerisation in large central government agencies such as the Inland Revenue, with many projects being financed by a mix of public and private sector investment. Some 4 million people work in local government, central government and public administrations such as the National Health Service in the United Kingdom. It is therefore not surprising that much of the rhetoric surrounding the expected benefits of eGovernment focuses on efficiency and effectiveness improvements associated with using integrated systems to reorganise departments and work, and cut down on staff. A key example here is the Gershon review at national level (Gershon, 2004), which led to the merger of the Inland Revenue with Customs and Excise. This was intended to be accompanied with technological change and lead to efficiency savings.

Issues

- Managing channels of access is a significant issue for eGovernment. How is this issue relevant to the current case?
- In what ways do you think strategy in this area for private sector organisations differs from that for public sector organisations?
- The case highlights the importance of good data security and data management for organisations. With increasing concern over identity theft and data privacy, the reputation of organisations increasingly depends on good practices in this area. Investigate what the private sector is doing to ensure this.

Keywords

Private sector organisation		
eGovernment	Electronic service delivery	Access channels
Informatics strategy		
Data management		
Data security	Personal identity management	
	Data privacy	Data protection

References/Sources

Beynon-Davies, P. (2005) 'Constructing electronic government: the case of the UK Inland Revenue', *International Journal of Information Management* **25**(1): 3–20.

Gershon, P. (2004) *Releasing Resources to the Front-Line: Independent review of public sector efficiency.* London, HMSO.

Poynter, K. (2008). *Review of Information Security at HM Revenue and Customs.* London, HM Treasury.

11 Microsoft

Case description

Microsoft Corporation is a multinational business with its headquarters in Redmond, Washington State, USA (Cusumano and Selby, 1995). It has approximately 79,000 employees based in 102 countries and global annual revenue of US $51.12 billion as of 2007. Microsoft develops, manufactures, licenses and supports a wide range of software products for computing devices. The best selling are the Microsoft Windows operating system and the Microsoft Office suite of software.

The company was founded by Bill Gates in 1979, originally to develop and sell BASIC interpreters for the Altair 8800, an early microcomputer. Microsoft rose to dominate the personal computer market with another software product, its operating system MS-DOS, which was a standard in the personal computer market by the mid-1980s. In 1985 Microsoft released its first retail version of Microsoft Windows, originally a graphical extension for MS-DOS. During the transition from MS-DOS to Windows, the success of the Microsoft Office suite allowed the company to gain ground on competitors of the time, such as WordPerfect and Lotus 1-2-3.

The company's official website is one of the most visited on the Internet. In the mid-1990s, Microsoft launched a major online service, MSN (Microsoft Network), as a direct competitor to America Online (AOL). MSN became an umbrella service for Microsoft's online services. The company also released its web browser, Internet Explorer, with the Windows 95 Plus! Pack in August 1995 and subsequent Windows versions.

Microsoft has a foothold in other markets besides operating systems and office suites, with assets such as the MSNBC cable television network, the MSN Internet portal, and the Microsoft Encarta multimedia encyclopedia. The company also markets computer hardware products such as the Microsoft mouse and home entertainment products such as the Xbox, Xbox 360, Zune and MSN TV.

Throughout its history Microsoft has been the target of criticism for various reasons, including alleged monopolistic business practices. Both the US Justice Department and the European Commission have brought Microsoft to court for antitrust violations associated with software bundling.

Microsoft is currently organised as three core divisions: the Microsoft Platform Products and Services Division, the Microsoft Business Division and the Microsoft Entertainment and Devices Division.

The Platform Products and Services division produces the Windows operating system, Microsoft Visual Studio (a set of development tools) and enterprise software such as Microsoft SQL Server (a relational DBMS).

The Microsoft Business Division produces Microsoft Office, which includes Word (a word processor), Access (a personal relational DBMS), Excel (a spreadsheet program), Outlook (Windows-only groupware), PowerPoint (presentation software), and Publisher (desktop publishing software).

The Entertainment and Devices division produces software for mobile devices such as Windows CE for PDAs, gaming software for its own gaming console the Xbox, and computer games that run on Windows PCs, including titles such as *Age of Empires, Halo* and the *Microsoft Flight Simulator* series. It also produces a line of reference works that include encyclopedias and atlases, under the name Encarta.

Microsoft is known for its developer-centric business culture. Large investment is made each year in recruiting young university-trained software developers and retaining their services. Key decision makers at every level in the company are either developers or former developers. In Microsoft the expression 'eating our own dog food' is used to describe the policy of using the latest Microsoft products inside the company in an effort to test them in 'real-world' situations.

Microsoft has historically given customer support to Usenet newsgroups and the Web. The company awards Microsoft Volunteer Partner status to volunteers who are deemed helpful in assisting the company's customers.

Technical reference for developers and articles for various Microsoft magazines such as *Microsoft Systems Journal* (*MSJ*) are available through the Microsoft Developer Network (MSDN). MSDN also offers subscriptions for companies and individuals, and the more expensive subscriptions usually offer access to pre-release beta versions of Microsoft software.

In June 2008 Bill Gates stepped down from the board of Microsoft to spend his time managing his charity, the Bill and Melinda Gates Foundation.

Commentary

Microsoft dominates the software industry, particularly in the areas of system and office software. In particular, its business tactics of 'embrace, extend and extinguish' have led to much controversy. Microsoft initially embraces a competing standard or product, then extends it to produce their own incompatible version of the software or standard, which in time extinguishes competition that does not or cannot use Microsoft's new version.

Many have recently questioned whether Microsoft can maintain its dominance in the software market given a number of emergent trends such as open source software, software as services and cloud computing. Microsoft is already developing strategy in light of these developments. For instance, it is investing in a network of data centres, and writing new software and adapting its existing software to run in the 'cloud'.

Issues

- Business tactics employed by Microsoft have led to various companies and governments filing lawsuits against the company. Consider whether this hinders the development of informatics.
- Concerns have been raised over the total cost of ownership associated with Microsoft products. Consider the implications of this for informatics infrastructure in organisations.
- Microsoft and the open source software movement have taken issue over digital rights management. Consider this issue in light of the software industry as a value network.

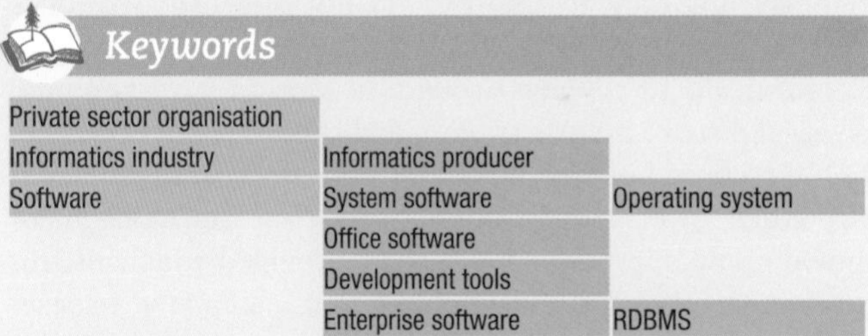

Keywords

Private sector organisation		
Informatics industry	Informatics producer	
Software	System software	Operating system
	Office software	
	Development tools	
	Enterprise software	RDBMS

References/Sources

Cusumano, M. A. and Selby, R. W. (1995) *Microsoft Secrets: How the world's most powerful software company creates technology, shapes markets and manages people.* New York, Free Press.

12 The movie industry

Case description

Some websites now offer thousands of the latest movies for download over the Internet for as little as a couple of dollars. This content can be downloaded onto personal computers and then burned to DVDs. It is also possible to download content to mobile devices such as iPods. The problem is that many are pirate sites (*Economist*, 2008). The growing presence of these sites is symptomatic of changes that are likely to affect the entire movie industry. It has been comparatively slow to react to the potential offered by the Web and the Internet. However, business analysts predict that it is likely to undergo fundamental change because of the way in which ICT changes fundamental business models in the sector.

Changes in the movie industry are all founded on the technological innovation of digital movie content. This is one example of the more encompassing phenomenon of digital convergence. The availability of technologies for managing movie content in digital form is leading to changes in the value network for this industry: the production, distribution and consumption of movies.

The conventional method of making a movie involves a sequence of three processes: pre-production, shooting and post-production. Pre-production involves activities such as establishing production schedules, establishing budgets, obtaining permits, hiring staff and purchasing equipment. Shooting involves the actual capture of pictures and sound, filming on and off sets. Post-production involves editing movie content, including adding effects, music and other audio.

Production is normally a costly exercise because production staff and particularly actors are expensive, studio space is expensive and the equipment used has been expensive. Filming action and stunt scenes in particular can prove very costly. For instance *Spider-Man 3*, the top box-office performer in 2007, cost $258 million to produce.

The cost of producing movies will potentially decrease with the move to digital format. The cost of the equipment required to capture and edit high-quality movie content has decreased substantially. The use of computer generated imagery (CGI) has particularly reduced the costs of action and stunt scenes. This could lower barriers to entry in this industry.

Conventional distribution involves making copies of the film, shipping and marketing it. These processes cost distribution companies many millions of dollars. The release of film content is tightly controlled in a windowing sequence of cinemas first, then DVD for rental and release to pay-per-view television channels, then DVD for purchase and finally release to broadcast television.

Digital projection equipment has been introduced in cinemas not only to improve quality but also to reduce distribution costs. Digital content can be transmitted electronically to cinemas around the world for a fraction of physical distribution costs. Potential supply-chain savings of $2 billion have been estimated for this. The cost of storage is also much lower than for film in reels. However, since major movie companies have themselves provided much of this investment, they are eager to recoup it via cinema releases before considering new access channels.

Successful films such as *Spider-Man 3* clearly allow the film industry to recoup its investment. Gross takings in the United States alone for this film reached $336 million, and the film was shown to nearly 49 million cinema goers. DVD sales reached 2.7 million in the United States by end of 2007 with a sales revenue of $116 million. However, this is the best performer: many other films made considerable losses.

The movement of movies onto digital format opened up new avenues for content distribution, particularly distribution via DVD. It is a short step to offering electronic delivery over the Internet. There is every reason to expect that consumers will want to access movie content online just as they access music, newspapers, television and radio. Some have argued that once people are able to buy or rent films easily on demand, the chances are they will pay for and watch more movies.

Currently, however the content available from legal download sites is very patchy. Hollywood has been slow to adopt new business models because of the risks and the lack of incentive to move on from a lucrative DVD market. However, some believe that DVD sales have reached their peak and the movie industry will need to investigate new ways of making revenue. One key advantage of online distribution is that movie producers and distributors can release their whole back catalogue of content.

Some have argued the importance of new access channels to movie content. These include direct to home/movies on demand via conventional satellite/cable; online content downloading (video on demand, P2P sharing, IP television); content download to video devices; and digital cinema. They also point to the potential that digital movie content has in providing an added-value service to consumers, such as increased interactivity and personalisation of content. It has been estimated, perhaps conservatively, that the online digital movie segment will constitute 3 per cent of all home movie entertainment revenues by 2011.

Others have raised the difficulties and dangers involved, and particularly the increasing potential for digital piracy. Silicon.com reckons that digital piracy cost the film industry $858.5 million in 2004, and this is estimated to rise to $1.7 billion by 2010. Currently, online piracy is thought to cost the industry less than the physical copying of DVDs, but the gap is diminishing. Some people have even suggested that it will be so difficult to keep content secure from piracy that it will lead to the end of the movie industry as we know it.

As well as new access channels, new technology is providing new ways of marketing movies. Movie companies have started experimenting with the release of clips on social networking sites such as YouTube. For instance, the movie *Iron Man* was heavily promoted on YouTube. Some producers have even experimented with using sites like this to involve viewers in the design of their product, such as asking for feedback on the attractiveness of plot lines. Not surprisingly, the big players in the movie value network are investing in these new marketing channels. For instance, News Corporation which owns the major movie company Fox Interactive Media has bought MySpace as the perfect vehicle for Fox to promote its movies.

However, there are a number of technological constraints holding back the electronic delivery of movies. First, movie files are large. The typical low-quality file is of the order of 750 Mb. This means that the typical download time on a 2Mb/sec Internet connection is 50 minutes; on a 8Mb/sec connection it is approximately 12 minutes. A DVD-quality movie file can be as large as 4 Gb, and this means a download time on a 2Mb/s connection of about four hours, or on a 8Mb/sec connection around an hour. Although the bandwidth in countries such as Korea and Japan has significantly improved beyond these typical UK bandwidths, there are major problems with rolling out higher bandwidth within countries such as the United Kingdom over the next few years.

Second, most people want to watch movies on televisions rather than personal computers because of the wide screens, better audio and potential for high definition. Products that connect PCs and televisions are currently available but difficult to install and use. The technology is not domestic enough for widespread adoption. However, digital convergence is likely to lead to devices such as Internet-enabled televisions in the near future.

Third, the lack of standards in the area of online digital movie content is preventing widespread uptake. For instance, each download site currently sells different usage rights. Attempts to develop common transportable standards are still ongoing.

Commentary

Movies are modern examples of digital content, and classic intangible goods. This makes it possible to transmit them over a number of distinct access channels and to a range of different access devices.

The case demonstrates the way in which ICT is starting to restructure a major industry. Any technology offers opportunities as well as threats. Technology adoption is likely to change business models because of the ways in which it affects the wider value network. The traditional value network in the movie industry consists of major film producers, major global distributors and mass consumers. The control of the content (value) along the network has typically been heavily controlled, with the phased release (cinemas, rental, purchase) described above. More recently online rental firms have emerged.

New channels of access include online downloading of movie content and video streaming. Online access to movie content is a form of disintermediation. Problems in upgrading the telecommunications infrastructure may hinder the rapid deployment and adoption of these access channels.

The high cost of DVDs has been explained by the high costs associated with film production and the high risk of failure. Technology such as low-cost camera equipment and PC-based editing reduces the costs of movie production, which means that barriers to entry to the production side of the industry are lowered.

Issues

- A key concern for the movie industry is to find ways of protecting against digital piracy. How might this be done?
- Digital rights management is a key issue affecting many forms of digital content. How do the producers of such content get a return on their creative investment?
- Investigate the business model underlying online DVD rental. Is this business model sustainable long-term?

Keywords

Value	Intangible goods	Content
Value network	Business model	
Access channels		
	Access devices	
Digital convergence		
Value network	Disintermediation	
Internet	Web	

References/Sources

Economist (2008) 'Coming soon', 23 February, 85–7.

13 MySpace

Case description

MySpace was founded in July 2003 by Tom Anderson, Chris DeWolfe and a small team of programmers. It was partially owned by Intermix Media, which was bought in July 2005 for $580 million by Rupert Murdoch's News Corporation. MySpace is thus now a commercial operation that employs 300 staff. It has its headquarters in Santa Monica, California, USA, while its parent company is headquartered in New York.

It describes itself as an 'online community that lets you meet your friends' friends'. It is pitched as a tool for creating or growing a private community or social network in which members can share content such as photos, journals and interests.

To use MySpace you create a profile then invite people to join your network. The profile can range from a simple list of preferences through to a comprehensive list of attributes, attitudes and opinions. The site also supports email and blogging, and enables users to browse other people's networks with the aim of inviting people to join their own network.

For instance, MySpace is home to various musicians, filmmakers, celebrities and comedians who upload songs, short films and other work directly onto their profile. These songs and films can also be embedded in other profiles, an interconnectedness which adds to MySpace's appeal.

MySpace profiles consist of three main elements:

- **Blurbs, blogs and multimedia.** Profiles contain two standard sections or 'blurbs': 'About me' and 'Who I'd like to meet'. Profiles also contain an 'Interests' section and a 'Details' section, but these sections are not displayed if members do not fill them in. They may contain a blog with standard fields for content, emotion and media. MySpace also supports uploading images. One of these images can be chosen to be the image that will be seen on the profile's main page. The site has also added the option to upload videos via the MySpace Videos service.
- **Friend space.** The user's friends space contains a count of a user's friends, a 'Top friends' area, and a link to view all the user's friends. Users can choose a certain number of friends to be displayed on their profile in the 'Top friends' area.
- **Comments.** By default a Comments section is placed below the User's friends space. Within this area, a user's friends may leave comments for all viewers to read. MySpace users have the option to delete any comment and/or require all comments to be approved before posting.

YouTube first appeared on the Web in early 2005, and it quickly gained popularity on MySpace thanks to MySpace members who embedded YouTube videos in their MySpace profiles. Realising the competitive threat to the new MySpace videos service, MySpace banned embedded YouTube videos from its user profiles. MySpace users widely protested against the ban, prompting MySpace to re-enable the feature shortly thereafter.

Commentary

MySpace is reputed to be one of the world's most popular English-language websites. It also has the largest proportion of visits to social networking websites. It has become an increasingly influential part of contemporary popular culture, especially in English-speaking countries.

MySpace relies on the strength of the network effect. For instance, professional content producers such as musicians load content onto MySpace with the aim of attracting a larger potential consumer base for their products. The attractiveness of MySpace lies in the size of its user network and the number of visits made to the site.

Companies have also started using the site to promote their goods and services. The revenue model is driven by advertisements via the site. However, concerns have been expressed over the viability of this business model long-term.

Issues

- Concerns have been expressed over data privacy issues involved with creating a user profile on MySpace. The personal details people post, such as images of themselves, their job, address and telephone number might contribute to identity fraud. Suggestions are that people's job prospects have also been compromised by material posted about themselves on MySpace.
- Concerns have been raised over the use of social networking sites for unacceptable behaviour. For instance, since users of MySpace can be as young as 14, concerns have been expressed over the use of the site by paedophiles wishing to 'groom' victims. Also, many schools and public libraries in the United States have restricted access to MySpace because they believe it has become a haven for malicious gossip, particularly about teachers.

Keywords

Private sector organisation	
Web 2.0	
Virtual community	Network effect
	Social networking

References/Sources

www.myspace.com

14 MySQL

Case description

First released in 1995, MySQL is a multi-user relational database management system (DBMS) which has more than 11 million installations worldwide. The applications software is considered one of the most prominent examples of open source software. MySQL is popular for web applications and acts as the DBMS component of the LAMP stack for application development. The DBMS has been used as part of the ICT infrastructure of organisations such as Wikipedia.

Commentary

Modern DBMSs such as MySQL are made up of three major parts: kernel, toolkit and interface. The DBMS kernel is the central engine which operates core data management functions such as most of those defined below. The DBMS toolkit is the vast range of tools that are now either packaged as part of a DBMS or are provided by third-party vendors. Between the kernel and toolkit is a defined interface. a standard database sublanguage which connects a tool such as a programming language with kernel functions.

A DBMS must enable users to create data structures, retrieve data from them, update data in them and delete data from them. These functions are known collectively as CRUD activities – Create, Read, Update and Delete. Kernel functions include these CRUD functions, a data dictionary, transaction management, concurrency control, recovery, authorisation, data communication, data integrity and data administration.

A DBMS must support a repository of metadata – data about data. This is known as a data dictionary or system catalogue. Typically it stores data about the structure of data, relationships between data items, integrity constraints expressed on data, the names and authorisation privileges associated with users.

A DBMS must offer support for the concept of a transaction and must manage the situation of multiple transactions impacting against a database. A transaction is a series of actions which access or cause changes to the data in a database.

A DBMS must enable many users to share data in a database – to access data concurrently. The DBMS must ensure that if two transactions are accessing the same data that they do not leave the database in an inconsistent state.

The DBMS must ensure that the database is able to recover from hardware or software failure which causes the database to be damaged in some way.

The DBMS must have facilities for the enforcement of data security. Generally, the DBMS must support the concept of an authorised user of a database and should be able to associate with each user privileges about access to data within the database and/or facilities of the DBMS.

A DBMS must be able to integrate with communication software running in the context of an ICT system. This is particularly important to enable the connection of toolkit software with the kernel of a DBMS.

Data integrity is the property of a database that ensures that it remains an accurate reflection of its universe of discourse. To enable this, the DBMS must provide support for the construction of an integrity constraint. The DBMS must be able to enforce such constraints in the context of CRUD activities.

The DBMS should ensure that there are sufficient facilities available for its administration. These include import and export facilities from and to other data sources, and facilities for monitoring usage and performance.

The DBMS interface will comprise a database sublanguage: a programming language designed specifically for initiating DBMS functions. This will contain one or more of a data definition language (DDL), data manipulation language (DML), data integrity language (DIL) and data control language.

The DDL is used to create structures for data, delete structures for data and amend existing data structures. It updates the metadata held in the data dictionary. The DML is used to specify commands which implement the CRUD activities against a database. It is the primary mechanism used for specifying transactions against a database. The DIL is used to specify integrity constraints. Constraints specified in a DIL are written to the data dictionary. The data control language is the part of the database sublanguage designed for use by the database administrator. It is particularly used to define authorised users of a database and the privileges associated with them.

The dominant database sublanguage is currently the structured query language or SQL. This is supported by MySQL.

Issues

- Why do companies need to have DBMSs such as MySQL in their ICT infrastructure?
- What does MySQL offer over other DBMSs supplied by traditional software vendors and products, such as Microsoft SQLServer?
- Why is MySQL preferred for use by companies such as Wikipedia?

Keywords

ICT	Development tool	DBMS
Open source software		
Data model Relational		

References/Sources

www.mysql.com

CASE-STUDY

15 OGC Gateway Process

Case description

Large-scale ICT in government agencies in the United Kingdom is now procured from external vendors rather than being built in-house. To manage this process effectively, acquisition programmes and procurement projects in UK central civil government are subject to Office of Government Commerce (OGC) Gateway Reviews. The OGC Gateway Process examines a project at critical stages in its life-cycle to provide assurance that it can progress successfully to the next stage.

In simple terms, a gateway review is a review of a procurement project carried out at a key decision point by a team of experienced people, independent of the project team. There are five OGC Gateway Reviews during the life-cycle of a project, three conducted before award of a contract and two looking at service implementation and confirmation of the operational benefits. A project is reviewed at the OGC Gateway Review appropriate to the point reached in its life-cycle.

Gate 0 establishes the business need for the programme or project. It asks how the proposed programme meets the business need, and assesses the capability of those who are responsible for the programme and the support of users and stakeholders.

Gate 1 develops the business case and asks whether the end project is feasible, affordable and likely to achieve value for money, and also whether the high-level plans for achieving it are clear and realistic.

Gate 2 develops the procurement strategy. It asks whether the tendering strategy sufficiently reflects business requirements, awareness of the market, good practice in procurement and changes to business need. It also establishes whether funding is available for the whole project and with adequate financial controls in place.

Gate 3 establishes the investment decision/competitive procurement. It asks whether the procurement process has met its objectives and followed good practice and whether the prospective contractor is likely to deliver on time, within budget and achieve value for money. It also assesses readiness of the business to implement the contract.

Gate 4 establishes readiness for service/award and implement contract. It assesses whether project plans are up to date and adapted to working successfully with the contractor and asks whether implementation of the project is going to plan with any lessons for the future being recorded.

Gate 5 establishes the realisation of benefits. It assesses whether expected benefits are being realised and what is being done to pursue continued improvements. It also asks what contingency plans there are for future changes.

The result of each gateway review is a signal of the assessed status of the project. If a review signals red then key actions are needed and to achieve success the project team should take action immediately. If a review signals amber, the project should go forward with actions on recommendations to be carried out before the next gateway review of the project. If the review signals green, the project is considered to be on target to proceed but may benefit from the uptake of recommendations.

Commentary

In recent decades the UK government has tended to procure ICT infrastructure from external suppliers using vehicles such as private-finance initiatives. The Gateway Process is designed for such work, and is an example of programme rather than project management. It focuses on high-level control issues and is particularly designed for managing programmes of large ICT and organisational change which involve substantial amounts of informatics outsourcing. The Gateway Process is similar to the model of information systems evaluation, and it is possible to embed approaches to strategic, formative and summative evaluation within it.

Issues

- The application of the OGC Gateway Process has not prevented public sector information system failures such as that experienced by the Child Support Agency. Why might this be?
- The gateway process is designed for high-level programme management rather than project management. Consider the differences between these two types of management.

Keywords

Evaluation	Strategic evaluation
	Formative evaluation
	Summative evaluation
Project management	Project control
Informatics outsourcing	

References/Sources

www.ogc.gov.uk

16 The open source software movement

 Case description

Open source software is computer software for which the source code is made available under a copyright licence (or arrangement such as the public domain) that meets the open source definition. The aim of the open source movement is to make software easier to understand, modify and duplicate. An open source licence permits users to use and change software, and to redistribute it in modified or unmodified form.

Open source software is the most prominent example of open source development, and often compared to user-generated content in that it is developed in a public, collaborative manner. Although it can be developed in traditional ways, the movement has become associated with a particular model of software development. Open source evangelist Eric S. Raymond (1999) maintains that open source development is substantially different from traditional development.

Raymond refers to the conventional model of software development promoted by people like Frederick P. Brooks in *The Mythical Man-Month* (1997) as the cathedral model. Here, development takes place in a centralised way. Roles are clearly defined and include people dedicated to designing (the architects), people responsible for managing the project, and people responsible for implementation. Raymond suggests that all software should instead be developed using a bazaar model. This he describes as 'a great babbling bazaar of differing agendas and approaches'. This has features such as:

- **Users as co-developers.** Users are encouraged to submit additions to the software, code fixes for the software, bug reports, documentation and so on. The general principle is that having more co-developers increases the rate at which the software evolves. One key claim is that the rate at which bugs are identified and fixed increases with open source production. Torvald Linus, the originator of Linux, states this as a law: 'Given enough eyeballs all bugs are shallow.'
- **Early releases.** Versions of software are released as early as possible so as to increase the chance of finding co-developers.
- **Frequent integration.** New code is integrated as often as possible so as to avoid the overhead of fixing a large number of bugs at the end of the project life-cycle. Some open source projects have nightly builds, where integration is done automatically on a daily basis.
- **Several versions.** Open source software tends to have at least two versions. A development version is for users who want immediate use of the latest features, and are willing to accept the risk of using code that is not yet thoroughly tested. The users can then act as co-developers, reporting bugs and providing bug fixes. The stable version offers the users fewer bugs but usually fewer features.
- **High modularisation.** Open source software tends to be highly modular to allow for parallel development by a larger network of programmers.
- **Dynamic decision-making structure.** A decision-making structure, either formal or informal, is needed to makes strategic decisions about the ongoing design of the software.

The Open Source Initiative is an organisation dedicated to promoting open-source software. The organisation was founded in February 1998 by Bruce Perens and Eric S. Raymond, when Netscape Communications Corporation published the source code for its flagship Netscape Communicator product (a web browser) as free software. This was because of the lowering profit margins and competition with Microsoft's Internet Explorer software.

 Commentary

The bazaar model of software development might be seen as an alternative to conventional approaches to information systems development. However, Fitzgerald (2006) maintains that the approaches promulgated by the open source movement are not suitable for bespoke information systems development for a number of reasons. Perhaps the most important difficulty is that the requirements for such systems rely on a great deal of business domain knowledge whereas open source production relies on a wide distribution of commonly accepted requirements for software.

 Issues

- Investigate the range of software produced using the open source model. For instance, is office software available as open source? Can you run an entire desktop computer using open source software?
- Investigate the similarities between open source software production and the collaborative production of web content.
- Some have argued that open source software lacks a

sufficiently robust revenue model to make it sustainable in a business sense. Is this a problem?

Keywords

Open source software
Collaborative production
Software development
Social networking

References/Sources

Brooks, F. P. (1997) *The Mythical Man-Month.* Reading, Mass., Addison-Wesley.

Fitzgerald, B. (2006) 'The transformation of open source software', *Management Information Systems Quarterly* **30**(3): 587–98.

Raymond, E. S. (1999). The Cathedral & the Bazaar. *Knowledge, Technology and Policy* 12(3): 23-49.

17 Quipu

Case description

The Inca people made up a sophisticated and wealthy society existing in a comparatively hostile environment – the high Andes in South America (Saunders, 2000). The civilisation was highly successful although it survived for a comparatively short time (*c.*1200–1475 AD). The success of Inca society is remarkable in that it operated effectively without the benefits of a written language or any mode of transportation based on the wheel.

The Incas were a highly regimented society with individuals occupying strictly defined roles. At the top of the society was the *sapa* Inca or 'emperor' who ruled by divine right as the son of the sun. Worshipped as a living god, the *sapa* Inca's official wife was his full-blooded sister. The *sapa* Inca also maintained a harem of concubines whose offspring held positions of power and influence in the Inca empire. These formed part of the upper class of the Inca nobility, a hereditary aristocracy occasionally supplemented by Incas assigned this privilege of rank through merit or exceptional service. Below this ruling class were the *curacas* who formed the lower echelons of Inca nobility. These individuals generally filled the administrative offices of government and supervised the large bureaucracy of the empire. Officials called the *cacique* were placed at the head of agricultural communities made up of a group of domestic units or *ayllu.* Land was redistributed amongst the *ayllu* every year according to the number of active people in each household. The land at the disposal of each *ayllu* was divided into three unequal parts. The largest part was given to the community to farm, and the other two were consecrated to the cult of the sun and to the state. Communities also paid a tribute of textiles to the state and a periodic tax of labour. This labour tax was used by the empire for collective works such as building roads, monuments and irrigation canals.

The success of the Inca empire is generally attributed to the ability of the bureaucracy to record details of the empire's activities and use this information efficiently to administer the far reaches of the empire. This control was also clearly reliant on effective information flow between parts of the empire, in that information storage and transmission was essential for maintaining the institutional structures such as agriculture and defence. This phenomenon was the Inca imperial 'information system'.

Because the Incas did not possess writing or the wheel, the 'information technology' they used was different from that found in the Western world at the time, and also from all known global bronze age civilisations (Beynon-Davies, 2007). In essence, the Inca imperial information system consisted of a large and efficient transport network, specialist information personnel – the *chasquis* and the *quipucamayuq* – and a method for recording data, the *quipu.*

The Inca transport network was composed of thousands of kilometres of purpose-built roads and rope bridges. It straddled the Andes, stretching across modern-day Peru and Ecuador, and reached the coast of modern-day Peru as well as extending into modern Colombia, Bolivia, Argentina and Chile. Most of the roads were stone-lined and in places extremely narrow, allowing only foot travel and transport using llamas. The roads could not be used by everyone. Only those on official business, the imperial runners and the emperor and his armies were permitted to use the transport network.

The *chasquis* were agile and highly trained runners employed purely in delivering messages throughout the empire. They were trained from birth to reproduce the messages they carried verbally and accurately. A long series of *chasqui* huts or posts (known as *tambos*, small shelters with food and water) were arranged along the transport network. Individual *chasqui* would transport messages by running between two posts, then pass them on to the next runner. A relay of *chasqui* could send a message up to 250 km in one day, and it is claimed that a message could be delivered from Cusco to Quito, a distance of over 1500 km, within a week.

Each *chasqui* carried a *pututu*, a trumpet made of a conch shell or of animal horn, and a *qipi* on his back to hold objects to be delivered such as royal delicacies. The Inca bureaucracy sent and received many messages daily as they were essential to maintaining the human activity of the empire. Typically they contained details of resources such as items required or available in store houses, taxes owed or collected, census data, the output of mines or the composition of particular workforces.

Messages had to be clear, compact and portable, and for this purpose the form of data storage known as the *quipu* was used (see Figure C.1).This was an assemblage of coloured, knotted cotton or camelid (llama or alpaca) cords (*quipu* means to knot). The *quipucamayuq* (the keeper of the *quipus*) were responsible for encoding and decoding messages contained in the *quipus.* Encoding or 'writing' a *quipu* involved tying together a complex network of strings of different materials and colours, and tying into them a series of different forms of knots. Decoding or 'reading' a *quipu* involved a *quipucamayaq* running his fingers rapidly over the knots, rather like a Braille reader. Some 600 or so examples of *quipu* survive. Some have only a few strands but the largest are over 3 metres long and have over 2000 strands.

The way in which data was encoded in a *quipu* is still very much a matter of debate and investigation. Leland Locke in the 1920s established that 100 or so of the remaining *quipu* were used to store the results of calculations and record keeping, possibly in support of the Inca imperial administration (Mann, 2003). Urton has recently shown how *quipu* acted as a complex accounting system which enabled census and tribute data collected in the empire to be synthesised, manipulated and transferred between different accounting levels in the Inca administration (Urton and Brezine, 2005). There is a binary form of coding evident in the manipulation of knots and strings, and Urton has suggested that although *quipu* undoubtedly developed originally as a form of accounting system, these three-dimensional devices could also have been used as mechanisms for conveying narrative; in other words, as a form of 'writing' (Urton, 2003).

If this proves correct, then *quipu* would be a unique form of writing system: the only example of the use of a binary coding system for ordinary communication. It would also be one of the few examples of semasiographic writing – texts that are not direct representations of spoken language. Although most existing systems for writing natural languages are based on a correspondence between the written sign and some element of the spoken word, a system of signs does not have to replicate speech to communicate narrative.

A number of significant units have been proposed within *quipu* for encoding the variety (Stamper, 1973) demanded of the construction of messages with a significant meaningful content:

- **Type of cord.** Strings on a *quipu* are either cotton or wool. Also, there is variation in the spin and ply direction of cords (slant of the threads).
- **Colour.** The colour of each cord might represent the object referred to, such as yellow for gold, red for soldiers or white for silver. It has been proposed that a black cord was used to indicate time, and formed the central cord from which all other cords were hung.
- **Connectivity.** The way cords were connected is likely to indicate linkages between component elements of a message, such as linking a specific province of the empire to a record of its harvest.
- **Relative placement of cords.** The relative placement of cords on other cords could signify meaning such as the passage of time.
- **Spacing of cords.** The spaces between cords could particularly be used to indicate the presence or absence of key elements of a message.
- **Form of knots**. The types of knots on individual cords, the size of knots and the way they were tied are likely to have been used to signify distinct meanings. Urton, for instance, recognises distinct differences in the direction of the knots attached to the main pendant cord. Also, the direction of the slant of the main axis of each knot itself varies. This leads him to propose that each knot represents a seven-bit binary array which would allow the storage of 1536 bits of information (Urton, 2003).
- **Relative placement of knots.** Locke proposed that the relative placement of knots on a cord could be used to represent units or multiples of ten: the closer the knot to the top of a string, the higher the number. At the very top a knot represented multiples of 10,000, then 1000, then 100, then 10, then units.

To indicate the complexity of the *quipu* as a data storage device, suppose an official wanted to encode the following message:

> Before the reign of the first Inca, Manco Capac, there was no king, chief or religion. In the fourth year of his reign Manco Capac conquered ten provinces and this cost him many of his warriors. In one of these provinces he had seized 1000 units of gold and 3000 units of silver. After conquering these provinces he held a feast of thanksgiving to celebrate his victory and to honour the Sun god.

The *quipucamayuq* might use a black cord to indicate time and to form the central cord of the *quipu*. From this he would suspend many uncoloured pendant cords with many little knots tied in them. When he reached the centre of the black cord he would make one large knot and run crimson thread through it. This assemblage would indicate that before the time of the first emperor (represented by the crimson thread) for a very long time (many uncoloured threads and knots) the people had no ruler (no scarlet threads), no chiefs (no deep purple threads) and no religion (no blue threads). Embedded within the crimson thread there would be four small knots to indicate that the events to be recounted took place in the fourth year of the reign of the current ruler Manco Capac. Into the middle of these four knots he would attach a grey thread with 10 small knots to indicate the number of subdued provinces. Each of the 10 knots on this grey thread would have fastened to it a green thread with appropriate knots to indicate the number of enemy killed in each province. In the same way he would add a red string to each of the 10 knots to describe the number of the imperial army killed from each province. To signify the nature and amount of treasure taken from each province a string of yellow for gold and white for silver would be suspended from the thread of the province from which it was taken. Finally, he would add a twist of threads with the colours blue, white and yellow to indicate that a celebration had been held in honour of the god who resided in the sky (blue) and made silver (white) and gold (yellow).

The main element of tribute paid to the Inca state was a labour tax in which each 'taxpayer' had to work a specified number of days each year on state projects such as road construction. Using the data recorded in *quipu*, 'accountants' in the Inca empire assessed the levels of this tribute and assigned tasks to local workers. At the lowest level of accounting, tributaries were grouped into five accounting units of 10 members each. One of each of the groups of 10 would serve as a *chuka kamayoq* or 'organiser of 10'. Five groupings of 10, making a group of 50 tribute payers, would be placed under the authority of a *pichqa-chunka-kuraca* or 'lord of the 50'. Two groups of 50 would be combined into a unit of 100 tributaries led by a *pachaka kuraca* or 'lord of 100'. This hierarchical system of tributary units would continue up to the head of one of the 80 provinces of the empire known as *t'oqrikoq*. These provincial lords or governors were in turn placed under the control of an appropriate lord of the four quarters, who served directly the Inca emperor based in Cusco (Urton and Brezine, 2005).

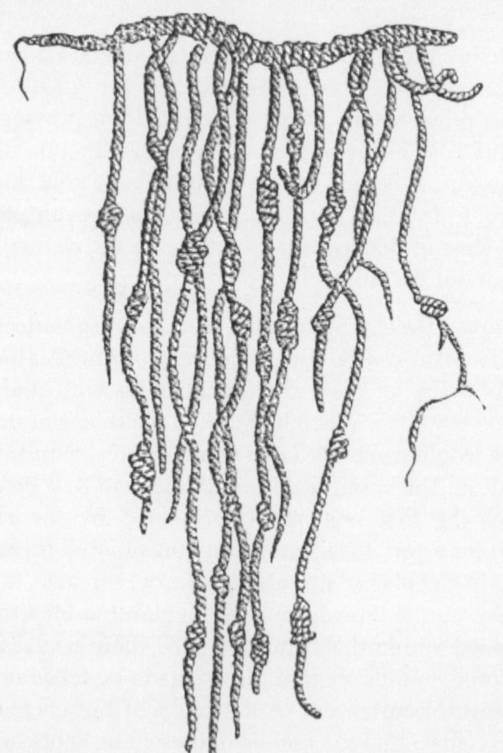

Figure C1: *Representation of a quipu*
Source: http://en.wikipedia.org/wiki/Image:Quipu.png

The governor of each province was required to keep a copy of *quipu* accounts so that 'no deception could be practised by either the Indian tribute payers or the official collectors' (Urton and Brezine, 2005). Historical accounts claim that even the smallest of Inca villages had as many as four *quipucamayaq*. Effectively these people acted as the record keepers or accountants in Inca society. Apparently, the records kept by each 'accountant' in a village were used as a verification check by the Inca administration.

Urton proposes two major information flows reliant on the use of *quipu*. Information flow concerning tribute flowed up the administrative hierarchy and decisions flowed down it. He further claims that information was partitioned based on the administrative units, so the local accountants would pass on data on completed tasks. Information at each administrative level would represent the summation of accounts from the level immediately below. This data would eventually be used by imperial accountants based in Cusco.

Urton analysed a series of *quipu* found in a house in the archaeological site of Puruchuco. Archaeologists believe this was the house of a *quipukamayuq* who served the lord of the local palace. He believed that seven of the 21 *quipu* discovered contained related accounts from three levels in the administrative hierarchy of the Inca. In particular, *quipu* on the same administrative level contain similar numerical sequences and colour matching. This suggests evidence of the checks and balances employed in the Inca administration. Values on the *quipu* sum upward and are subdivided downward. In other words, the numerical values of certain groupings of strings on *quipu* at the lowest level sum to numerical values tied onto the strings of *quipu* at the level above. Also, moving down the hierarchy, values tied to strings of higher levels are partitioned among groupings of strings on the level below.

Commentary

The human use of signs to convey information is universal in the sense that it is characteristic of all human time-periods and civilisations. The Inca system is an example of this universality. It can be seen to comprise activity systems, information systems and ICT systems. The organisation of activity evident in Inca administration was reliant on an efficient system of communication using a record-keeping system (a data structure) based in *quipu*.

A number of activity systems of the Inca Empire such as tax collection, the administration of workforces in the building of collective works and the distribution of goods relied on an effective system of information flow. The usefulness of the information system and the technology described can be judged in terms of the contribution made to the imperial activity systems of the Inca.

The essence of an information system lies not in the technology or the activity, but in the way in which technology is used in support of purposeful action. The use of *quipu* as a mechanism of data storage and transfer only makes sense in the context of the information specialists, the *quipucamayuq* and the *chasqui*, and their use of the Inca transport network.

It also is only significant in the context of the tributary systems of the Inca and their need to manage the distribution of labour throughout the empire.

Issues

- In what way can we consider the *quipu* as a sign-system? Try to use the levels of semiotics to help unpack the relationship of the *quipu* to the constructs of data and information. In other words, how are the pragmatics, syntactics, semantics and empirics worked out?
- Alternatively, consider a *quipu* as a data structure. What constitute data elements and data items in this data structure?

Keywords

Historical information system
Data
Information
Activity system
Information system
ICT

References/Sources

Beynon-Davies, P. (2007) 'Informatics and the Inca', *International Journal of Information Management* **27**(5): 306–18.

Mann, C. M. (2003) 'Cracking the Kipu code', *Science* **300** (13 June): 1650–2.

Saunders, N. J. (2000) *The Incas*. Gloucs, Sutton.

Stamper, R. K. (1973) *Information in Business and Administrative Systems*. London, Batsford.

Urton, G. (2003) *Signs of the Inka Kipu: Binary coding in the Andean knotted-string records*, University of Texas Press.

Urton, G. and Brezine, C. J. (2005) 'Khipu accounting in ancient Peru', *Science*, **309** (12 August): 1065–8.

18 A research information system

Case description

Consider a university that has identified a need for an information system to support research administration as part of its informatics strategy. It sees such a system as important to its future organisation strategy because research is one of its key activity systems. Although it has information systems to support teaching and consultancy, it has none to support research activity (Beynon-Davies et al., 1999).

The pragmatic objective for the system is to gather information needed to produce research assessment submissions, for the university to send to central government agencies. The system needs to collect, store and analyse information on key research outputs, which include publications (journal and conference), grant income, research students and completions of postgraduate research degrees.

Research outputs have been historically collected in academic schools and departments by research coordinators. However, there have been difficulties in collecting it within a reasonable time, and there are numerous errors in this manual process.

The longer-term aim is to use the information system to support the university's research strategy. The university has introduced the idea of research units and research centres to manage research. Research units are collections of research active staff working in the same area. Research centres are collections of research units, which may cross academic schools.

There are a number of constraints and non-functional requirements. An initial prototype needs to be built within six months in order to be able to perform a mini-research assessment. It is initially to be built for academic registry and used by six staff there. Eventually the system will be used by research coordinators within schools, research administrators in central support services and possibly active researchers within departments.

The university has an internal informatics service which has been downsized over the last few years, so no major information systems development takes place in-house. Although the development effort on this project is reasonably small-scale, the informatics service seems reluctant to take it on because, among other reasons, they feel the requirements have not been agreed by all stakeholders.

Two development staff are assigned the task of completing

the initial prototype system, which will act as a centralised resource for research information on, for example, publications, grants and research students. It is intended that the system should be used to monitor the research performance of schools, centres and units, and be a key input into the university's future research strategy.

An initial joint requirements planning (JRP) workshop is conducted with a limited number of stakeholder representatives. This enables scoping of the project within the six months available. From this workshop the following list of initial functional requirements are generated. The system must:

- capture information about all journal research papers by members of staff
- capture information about research student completions
- capture information about all research grants submitted to external research bodies
- provide information on research active staff in the university
- enable management to monitor the research performance of academic departments
- capture information about research income achieved by the university
- enable academic departments to monitor their research activity
- capture information about all research papers given by members of staff of the university at conferences
- be able to generate information for use in reports provided for external agencies: prospectuses, research reports, brochures and so on
- capture information about research student supervision
- capture information about all books or chapters in books produced by members of staff
- enable academic research coordinators to maintain records of research students, publications, grants etc.
- capture information about research student progression.

This leads to the development of an initial information and information systems model, part of which is shown as Figure C.2.

A development team is formed consisting of two developers and two user representatives. One developer acts as project manager/analyst, the other as a programmer. Three key phases for the project are planned, consisting of joint design workshops followed by a period of construction work. The last phase terminates in a user review which is open to all stakeholders in the university. After the third phase, three weeks are scheduled to be spent in consolidation work (documentation), testing and training.

The project takes six months, and between 10 and 20 stakeholders (other than the development team) are periodically involved. The team are skilled in the use of the development environment and knowledgeable about the business issues. All project activity takes place in an open-plan office situated at the users' site. One of the developers focuses completely on the project during the project period but the users interleave their project involvement with other work. The system produced is of medium background complexity and displays a high level of interactivity. Explicit use is made of incremental prototyping throughout the project.

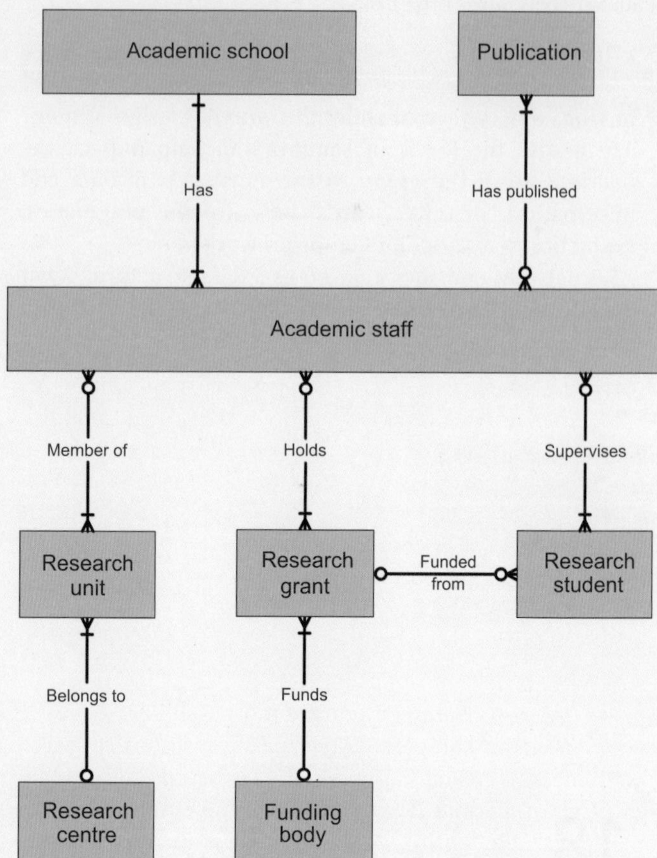

Figure C2: *Information model for the research information system*

The interface to this system is built using the forms generation facilities of Microsoft Access. The business rules and application logic are programmed in part using Access and Microsoft Visual Basic (a fourth-generation language). Visual Basic is also used to communicate through an application programming interface (transaction management) to a data management layer built using Microsoft SQL Server.

Commentary

The most interesting feature of this project is the large number of stakeholders affected by the system. Virtually every academic unit and the majority of administrative units either supply data to it or need to pull data off it. Therefore, user review sessions are as much a forum for informing and consulting with diverse stakeholders as opportunities for design.

Issues

- Why do you think information about the conduct of research is so critical to a university?
- Stakeholder participation is particularly critical to the successful development of this information system. Why do you think this is?

- This case describes a project that primarily uses an agile development approach. Besides prototyping what other features of an agile approach are adopted?

Keywords

Information systems development	Method	Agile
	Toolkit	
	Conception	
	Design	Requirements
	Analysis	
	Construction	
	Implementation	

References/Sources

Beynon-Davies, P., Carne, C., Mackay, H. and Tudhope, D. (1999) 'Rapid application development: an empirical review', *European Journal of Information Systems* **8**(2): 211–23.

19 SAP

Case description

SAP AG is the largest European software company. Known for its enterprise resource planning (ERP) software, it has its headquarters in Walldorf, Germany.

It was founded in 1972 in Mannheim, Baden-Württemberg as Systemanalyse und Programmentwicklung by five former IBM engineers. The acronym was later changed to stand for Systeme, Anwendungen und Produkte in der Datenverarbeitung (systems, applications and products in data processing). In 1976 SAP GmbH was founded, and the following year it moved headquarters to Walldorf. SAP AG became the company's official name after the 2005 annual general meeting (AG is short for Aktiengesellschaft, and is a type of German company).

The company's main product is the SAP ERP package. This is an integrated suite of ERP software targeted at supporting the requirements of medium to large-scale organisations in a number of industries and sectors.

Up until recently the SAP product was produced in three versions R/1, R/2 and R/3. The R stands for 'real-time', although it is not normally what many would consider true real-time software. The number refers to the number of layers in the software architecture: R/3 refers to a three-tier client–server architecture whereas R/2 ran on a traditional mainframe architecture.

SAP R/1 was launched in 1972, SAP R/2 in 1979 and SAP R/3 in 1992. A major overhaul of the package was undertaken culminating in the launch of SAP ERP in 2003.

SAP ERP includes four individual solutions that support key back-end functional areas:

- SAP ERP Financials
- SAP ERP Human Capital Management
- SAP ERP Operations
- SAP ERP Corporate Services

SAP ERP is one of five major enterprise applications in SAP's Business Suite. The other four applications, which support front-end functions, are:

- customer relationship management (CRM) – helps companies acquire and retain customers, gain deep marketing and customer insight, and align the organisation on customer-focused strategies
- product lifecycle management (PLM) – helps manufacturers with a single source of all product-related information necessary for collaborating with business partners and supporting product lines
- supply chain management (SCM) – helps companies enhance operational flexibility across global enterprises and provide real-time visibility for customers and suppliers
- supplier relationship management (SRM) – customers can collaborate closely with suppliers and integrate sourcing processes with applications throughout the enterprise to enhance transparency and lower costs.

SAP officials say there are over 100,600 SAP installations serving more than 41,200 companies in more than 25 industries in more than 120 countries.

Commentary

ERP software is an attempt to provide an integrated ICT

infrastructure for a company. The software can be tailored to a specific company's mode of operation but this normally involves considerable investment.

The architecture of products such as SAP tends to echo the distinctions made between core back-end information systems and front-end information systems discussed in Chapter 4.

A vast industry has arisen around the implementation of ERP packages such as SAP. Many informatics professionals and consultancies specialise in SAP work.

Issues

- ERP software is marketed as providing a complete solution for the business. However, numerous companies have experienced difficulties with their ERP implementation. Why do you think this is?
- Try to relate the description of ERP infrastructure to the information systems infrastructure described in chapter 4.

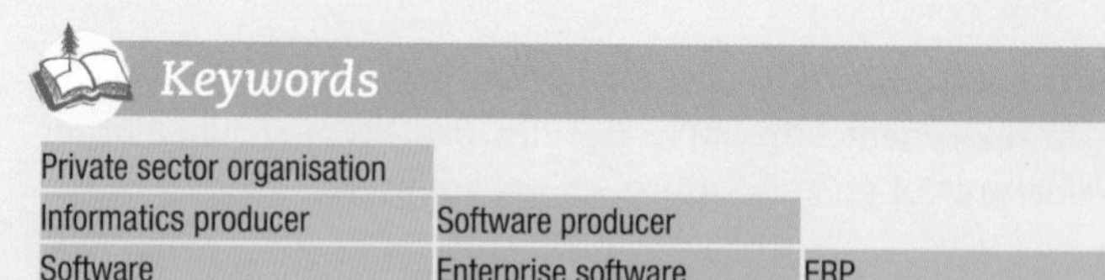

Keywords

Private sector organisation		
Informatics producer	Software producer	
Software	Enterprise software	ERP

References/Sources

www.sap.com

20 Tesco

Case description

History

Tesco plc is an international grocery and general merchandising retail chain. Founded in the United Kingdom, it is the largest British retailer and globally the third largest after Wal-Mart and Carrefour. Tesco now controls just over 30 per cent of the grocery market in the United Kingdom. In 2007 it announced profits of over £2.55 billion.

Its declared mission is to 'create value for customers to earn their lifetime loyalty', and its declared strategy is based on offering a range of different types of stores, understanding its customers and treating its employees well. The company originally specialised in food retail. It has now diversified into other retail areas such as discount clothes, consumer electronics, consumer financial services, selling and renting DVDs, compact discs and music downloads, Internet service provision, consumer telecoms, consumer health insurance, consumer dental plans and budget software.

The Tesco brand first appeared in 1924. Jack Cohen, its founder, bought a shipment of tea from T. E. Stockwell, and made new labels using the first three letters of the supplier's name (TES), and the first two letters of his surname (CO). The first Tesco store was opened in 1929 in Burnt Oak, Edgware, Middlesex. The company was floated on the London Stock Exchange in 1947 as Tesco Stores (Holdings) Ltd. The first self-service store opened in St Albans in 1947 and the first supermarket in Maldon in 1956. During the 1950s and the 1960s Tesco grew through opening new stores and also a series of acquisitions. By the end of this period, it owned more than 800 stores.

In 1973 Jack Cohen resigned and was replaced as chairman by his son-in-law Leslie Porter. Porter and managing director Ian MacLaurin changed the strategy of the company from a 'pile it high, sell it cheap' philosophy which had left the company stagnating and with a bad brand image. In 1977 Tesco abandoned a discount savings scheme, Green Shield stamps, and implemented price reductions and centralised buying for all its stores.

During the 1970s and 1980s the company continued its strategy of acquiring new stores through the takeover of existing food retail chains. During the 1990s it began to diversify its product range, its operating area and its delivery channels. Acquisition of Associated British Foods gave it a major presence in Northern Ireland and the Republic of Ireland. A business alliance with the Esso Petroleum Company allowed the leasing of petrol stations under the Tesco Express format. This period also saw the introduction of a loyalty card and an Internet shopping service. As of November 2006 Tesco was the only food retailer to make online shopping profitable.

This process of diversification and expansion continued during the early 2000s as Tesco started to become a major international food retailer. In October 2003 it launched a UK telecoms division, comprising mobile and home phone services, to complement its existing Internet service provider business.

Tesco's UK stores are currently divided into four major formats, differentiated by size and the range of products sold. Tesco Extra are the largest stores, located mainly out of town and offering the complete range of physical products. Tesco superstores are standard large supermarkets, stocking groceries and a much smaller range of non-food goods than Extra stores. Tesco Metro stores are sized between Tesco superstores and Tesco Express stores and are mainly located in city or town centres.

Informatics infrastructure

Tesco uses ICT and information systems more generally in a number of ways. The company chairman, Terry Leahy, claimed in 2007 that if the firm's ICT failed the firm would fail.

Tesco introduced its loyalty card for customers, the Clubcard, in the mid-1990s. Customers have to supply a range of personal details in order to get a card, which they can then use in all interactions with the company. There were 11 million loyalty card customers in the United Kingdom in 2007. When a Clubcard is swiped through the EFTPOS terminals at checkouts, purchased items are associated with the individual customer, who accrues points which can be redeemed via a discount voucher scheme. The data captured in this way has become critical to company operation. It is aggregated in data warehouses, and allows the company to identify purchasing patterns and plan product and store operations accordingly (Hunt, Humby and Phillips, 2006).

In common with most other large retailers, Tesco draws goods from suppliers into regional distribution centres, for preparation and onward delivery to stores. Radio frequency identification (RFID) technology plays an increasing role in the distribution process.

In the stores themselves the company's 'one in front' initiative', introduced in 1994, is heavily reliant on ICT. Thermal imaging technology is used to measure and predict customers' arrivals at checkouts. This enables store managers to ensure that the right number of checkouts are open for every customer to wait behind no more than one other person.

In 2008 Tesco announced its intention to overhaul its ICT infrastructure. It planned to replace a number of separate voice and data networks with a single communication network, which was eventually outsourced to Cable & Wireless. It intends to use this network to standardise its key ICT systems in areas such as finance, human resources, payroll, in-store management, distribution and sales.

The intention is to manage these ICT systems centrally across the entire network from its ICT services centre in Bangalore, India. Informatics professionals based in particular countries of operation will supply only front-line support. This standardisation is built on 'Tesco in a box', a programme of standardisation begun in 2005, based on an Oracle ERP system, which was implemented in all countries of operation.

The rollout of these standard ICT systems is seen as a key enabler for standard business processes and standard management information across the Tesco group. This allows stores newly opened in Malaysia and Japan to operate and be managed in exactly the same way as a store in the United Kingdom.

B2C eCommerce

Tesco.com is an eCommerce website operated by Tesco which was formally launched in 2000. The company claims to be the world's largest online grocery retailer, and also offers a wide range of other products, including electronic goods, books, broadband and financial services. The company uses a content management system to maintain its websites. Only 75 users are able to generate content for final approval. More recently, Tesco has introduced the option in a limited range of stores for customers to pick up in person groceries that they have ordered online, to avoid paying a delivery charge. In this system, each customer's order is hand-picked from the goods in each store, in contrast to other business models which pick items from warehouses. The pick from store model allows rapid expansion with limited investment, but can lead to a high level of substitutions when stock is unavailable.

Tesco claimed in its 2005 annual report to be able to serve 98 per cent of the UK population from its 300 participating stores. In 2006 Tesco was reported as having picked up two-thirds of all online grocery orders in the United Kingdom, and had over 750,000 regular users of its online grocery service, generating over 22,000 orders per week. This rose to 1 million active users in 2008 and a growth of 50 per cent in online sales over the previous year. Internet sales were reported as contributing 4.2 per cent of profits and 3.1 per cent of overall sales.

In July 2001 Tesco became involved in Internet grocery retailing in the United States when it obtained a 35 per cent stake in GroceryWorks. This was a joint venture with the American Safeway Inc. operating in the United States and Canada. GroceryWorks did not expand as fast as initially expected and Tesco sold its stake to Safeway Inc. in 2006.

Tesco launched its first home shopping catalogue in autumn 2006, as another channel for sales of its non-food ranges. This is integrated with the Internet operation, with both channels being branded as Tesco Direct. Tesco has also launched an advertising campaign for its VOIP product, marketing the service to customers by offering free calls to all other Tesco Internet phone customers.

Commentary

Organisation

From an institutional perspective Tesco is a large multinational producing goods and services and competing in a number of markets. Other aspects of interest are the strategy of the organisation and ways of designing its activities in areas such as its supermarket operations to improve its performance. This leads to an examination of the place of information in support of activities, such as deciding which products to stock where.

From an action perspective, issues include how employees of Tesco plc perform their work – for instance, the experience of working as a checkout person – and the established procedures for operating checkouts, stocking shelves, receiving goods into the supermarket store and so on. Some of the knowledge about this will be formalised in the sense of being written down. Many other aspects of everyday work will rely on tacit knowledge. Other issues are how this knowledge is communicated and how it is acquired.

System and environment

Tesco plc can be considered in systems terms. As a food retailer the inputs to the organisation are the foodstuffs it receives from its suppliers. Outputs consist of foodstuffs sold on to customers. Its key transformation consists of those activity systems that support the sale of foodstuffs, which can be considered hierarchically. The company will have systems of supply, supermarket operation and financial management which all contribute to its overall purpose: making a profit for its shareholders.

The environment of the organisation consists of the retail industry generally and specifically supermarket retail. In the United Kingdom the dominance of big supermarkets in food retailing means that they have enormous power in determining the prices they pay their suppliers for key foodstuffs. However, the food retail industry is subject to quite heavy degrees of regulation in such areas as environmental health. This sector is still growing in the United Kingdom. Over the 1990s and 2000s the major supermarkets dramatically increased their levels of technological deployment, and they have used their information systems in new areas such as financial services. The basis of competition used mostly to be price, although other bases such as quality (particularly organic foodstuffs) have recently come into play.

The value chain and value network

Tesco's value chain primarily involves the sale of foodstuffs to customers. Its declared mission is to 'create value for customers to earn their lifetime loyalty'. Value also includes the additional value services available to loyalty card customers, such as discounting of goods.

Tesco's performance can be considered using the three Es. **Efficacy** measures are likely to include sales for product groups across different supermarkets. **Efficiency** measures are likely to include profit margins against product lines or measures of stock fulfilment against orders in warehouses. **Effectiveness** measures might include the degree to which new customers are attracted to stores, old customers continue to come to the stores, and the levels of satisfaction customers show with the level of service.

Some of the key processes from the internal value chain can be mapped onto a supermarket chain. Inbound logistics involves managing the purchasing of foodstuffs and the distribution of foodstuffs to warehouses. The process of operations involves unpacking bulk deliveries and presenting products on supermarket shelves. Outbound logistics involves the distribution of bulk foodstuffs from warehouses to supermarket stores. Marketing and sales involves advertising product lines and the purchase of foodstuffs from stores. After-sales service involves handling customer enquiries and complaints.

Tesco operates a number of information systems which contribute to operational control through single-loop feedback and to strategic control through double-loop feedback. For instance, sales of products in stores are recorded at checkouts and update information about stock levels in the service area of the store. This information triggers a replenishment from stock held in the inventory area. This is an example of operational control. Sales to loyalty card holders provide valuable information to the company which is used for determining which products to sell at which stores at which times of the year. This is an example of strategic control.

eBusiness and eCommerce

Tesco is a clicks and mortar company: it is primarily a physical operation but it has an online service as well. It has made eCommerce work successfully and integrated it with its core business.

Tesco as a food retailer has relationships with its customers and suppliers. Revenue flows into its value chain from its customers and on to its suppliers. Customers are mainly attracted to supermarkets by a combination of low prices and a large variety of goods on offer. Supermarket chains typically sell large volumes, so their business strategy is typically based on low-cost/high-volume operations with low margins on each product. Costs are minimised by for example buying in bulk from suppliers and letting customers bear the costs of selecting products from shelves, packing them and transporting them home. The critical success factor for a supermarket chain is to attract sufficient customers to its store. This means that location of stores is crucial. They need to be within easy reach of a sufficient catchment area.

An eCommerce site such as Tesco.com (see Chapter 6) changes the business model of a supermarket chain. Relationships with customers and suppliers change, as do costs and revenue. For example, if a supermarket fulfils online orders by having a member of staff walk around the store picking goods then packing them, then transports them to customers' homes in delivery vans, its costs of the operation will increase substantially. Many supermarkets pass on this cost to the customer through a charge for delivery, as does Tesco.

An alternative business model is to do away with stores entirely. Goods are instead stored in and delivered from low-cost warehouses. Here the additional order fulfilment costs (picking, packing and transporting) can be balanced by lower operational costs (larger range, reduced inventory, larger volume, lower margins).

Technology has clearly had, and continues to have, an impact on organisational practices. The introduction of barcode scanners and electronic point of sale terminals at checkouts has improved customer throughput. Like many other large retail companies, Tesco has introduced automated self-service checkouts with the longer-term aim of reducing staffing costs. It is experimenting with the use of RFID tagging in its supply chain and intelligent trolleys in its stores.

Issues

- Supermarket chains such as Tesco have been criticised for the control they exercise over their customer chain and their supply chain. In food retailing in the United Kingdom, the dominance of big supermarkets means that they have enormous power in determining pricing levels. People have also criticised the way they have led to the decline in traditional smaller retail outlets on the high street.
- The food retail industry is subject to quite heavy degrees of regulation in such areas as environmental health. These create significant barriers to entry.
- The food retail sector is still growing in the United Kingdom. Over the 1990s and 2000s the major supermarkets dramatically increased their levels of technological deployment and used their information systems in new areas such as financial services.
- The basis of competition has traditionally been price although other bases such as quality (particularly organic foodstuffs) have recently come into play. The value network in food retail shows signs of changing subtly. For instance in the United Kingdom there has been significant growth in organic suppliers selling direct to customers through the Web – a form of disintermediation.
- Tesco has used information systems in a number of ways to help build customer loyalty and retention. Through use of its loyalty card scheme the company captures a lot of information about consumer behaviour. Concerns have been raised over the potential dangers of using this kind of transactional data, and the personal privacy questions it raises.

Keywords

Private sector organisation	Food retail	
Informatics consumer		
Informatics provider	Internet service provider	
eBusiness	Inventory management	
eCommerce	B2C eCommerce	
	B2B eCommerce	RFID
ICT	VOIP	
Informatics outsourcing		

References/Sources

Hunt, T., Humby, C. and Phillips, T. (2006) *Scoring Points: How Tesco continues to win customer loyalty.* London, Kogan Page.

www.tesco.com

21 The UK national identity card

 Case description

In the United Kingdom, the issue of personal identity management came to the fore in 2002 when home secretary David Blunkett resurrected the idea of introducing a national identity card, as had been done during the First and Second World Wars (Beynon-Davies, 2006).

For two years there was consultation on draft legislation for creating a national identity management infrastructure for the United Kingdom, consisting of a large central registry of personal identity data and the issuing of biometric tokens to all UK citizens by 2013.

In the original Home Office consultation document, the identity card was described as having a number of purposes. First, it would be a token through which people's identity was authenticated by public and private ICT systems. Second, the data held would be used to create integrated records for use in various government systems. Third, people's identity data would give them access to the rights of citizens, and in particular enable them to enrol in government activity systems (so they could, for example, use health and education services, be taxed and vote in elections).

Government ministers explicitly 'configured' the identity card as a weapon against identity fraud, which was seen as a growing threat to public and private sector activity systems. They also maintained that it would prove a significant weapon in the fight against illegal immigration. Arguably the fact that there is no requirement to hold an identity card in the United Kingdom acts as a magnet to illegal immigrants, who believe that they can work and access benefits with impunity. Many commentators suspected that the key rationale for the proposed introduction was to help in the attempt to combat terrorism post 9/11.

In short, much of the debate centred on issues of authentication, identification and enrolment. There was seen to be a clear relationship between citizenship, national identity and the possession of an identifier embodied in a national identity card. However, various groups expressed concerns about the consequences for data integration and data protection. This was fundamentally a debate over the purposes to which identity data would be put, both within and across government human activity systems.

An Identity Cards Bill was first introduced to Parliament in autumn 2004. It failed to reach its second reading before parliament was dissolved for the general election in April 2005. A slightly revised bill was reintroduced in autumn 2005. There was much debate in both houses of Parliament, and a number of amendments were incorporated in the Identity Cards Act which became law on 30 March 2006.

The Identity Cards Act provides the legal framework required to establish a National Identity Register (NIR) and to issue identity cards to those on it. Its main features include:

- **Defining the statutory purpose of the NIR**: 'the provision of a convenient method for individuals to prove their identity and to provide a secure and reliable means of identifying individuals where it is considered to be in the public interest'.
- **Indicating how the NIR is to be implemented**. A national identity management infrastructure is likely to involve establishing a population register with a definitive record for each for 67.5 million or so people resident in the United Kingdom aged 16 or over.
- **Establishing the powers to issue ID cards.** The ID cards scheme will involve issuing cards to every person registered as entitled to remain in the United Kingdom for longer than three months. Existing documents such as passports can be designated as documents with which the ID card will automatically be issued, so any person applying for a designated document will simultaneously need to apply for an ID card unless they already have one. People can choose to opt out of this arrangement until 1 January 2010. The Act includes powers to capture and record biometric data. ID cards will have a limited validity depending on the holder's category. For instance, elderly citizens might be issued with cards that are valid for the rest of their lives. Foreign nationals who have not resided in the United Kingdom for more than three months, but who regularly visit and work there, will be issued with cards with more limited validity.
- **Ensuring that biographical checks can be made**. Checks against other databases will confirm an applicant's identity and guard against fraud. These are also made in issuing British passports.
- **Setting out what information can be held on the individual in the NIR and establishing safeguards to protect individuals' data.** The NIR will hold core personal data such as name, residential address, date of birth, place of birth, sex, nationality and two or three forms of biometric identification. The Act does not permit the recording of Police National Computer reference numbers on the NIR, but other 'personal reference

numbers' such as driving licence and national insurance numbers can be held. Every person entered on the NIR will be assigned a unique number known as the National Identity Registration number. Other information such as emergency contact details may only be included at the request of the person applying to be included.

- **Enabling public and private sector organisations to verify someone's identity (with the person's consent) before providing services.**
- **Defining the circumstances in which public authorities such as the police can be provided with information (without the individual's consent).** This can be done if it is 'in the public interest', and reasons include national security, prevention and detection of crime, enforcement of immigration controls, enforcement of prohibitions on unauthorised working or employment, and efficient and effective provision of public services.
- **Providing for the creation of a National Identity Scheme commissioner**. This official will oversee the scheme, collaborate with the UK data protection (information) commissioner and report to the secretary of state and to Parliament on the operation of the scheme on a regular basis.
- **Creating new criminal offences relating to the misuse of ID cards and identity fraud**. This includes powers to link future access to specified public services to the production of an ID card and suitable checks against the NIR. This effectively establishes the possible use of the ID card as an authentication token to key public services.

Commentary

Identity management is a much larger issue than purely personal identity management. It involves systems for the identification of a variety of objects supporting societal behaviour: people, goods, places and so on. Personal identity management is however the most controversial and sensitive area because of its association with issues of personal privacy and individuality.

It is a critical issue in the information society because of the increasing use of remote interaction and electronic service delivery, which makes it impossible to identify people in the ways that used to be commonplace. Identifying people is important for service providers, but it also creates security risks. Personal identity management is therefore characterised by a movement from natural (such as personal names) to surrogate identifiers (such as identity numbers).

Personal identity management is also a larger issue than solely the authentication of individuals. Personal identification is distinct from, but a necessary precondition, of personal identity. In the information age identification involves using a person's common attributes or features to access a vast range of other data about them. This is distinct from authentication (validating the association between an identifier and the person it stands for) and enrolment (assigning an individual rights, responsibilities and actions in a human activity system).

Individuals might benefit from having an identity card and associated record because it will provide a simpler and more convenient token of identity for accessing government services. A good identification system would be universal, unique, permanent, indispensable and exclusive.

Benefits for government lie not only in the area of authentication but potentially in the areas of identification and enrolment. If implemented successfully, a national identity management infrastructure will facilitate clearer authentication protocols for service delivery and easier integration and interoperability of government information systems. These infrastructure benefits, it is claimed, will lead in turn to more efficient and effective human activity systems, particularly in law enforcement agencies .

There are also drawbacks and concerns. Many centre around the risk to people's personal privacy in general, and data privacy in particular. Opponents also argue that the identity management infrastructure would be very expensive, and the costs cannot be justified by the facilities it would provide to, for example, combat illegal immigration and terrorist activity.

Issues

- How important is personal identity management to effective eCommerce and eGovernment?
- Is a national identity card an appropriate mechanism for ensuring personal identity in the information age?
- Will data protection assume greater significance in the future, and will an identity card make data protection easier or more difficult?
- What relevance does the Data Protection Act have in this context?

Keywords

Information society	
Political environment	eGovernment
Personal identity management	
Transactional data	
Data security	Data protection
	Data privacy

References/Sources

Beynon-Davies, P. (2006) 'Personal identity management in the information polity: the case of the UK national identity card', *Information Polity* **11**(1): 3–20.

CASE-STUDY

22 Wikipedia

Case description

Wikipedia was created by Larry Sanger and Jimmy Wales and launched as an English-language project on 15 January 2001. It is now operated by the not-for-profit Wikimedia Foundation (Poe, 2008). It is a multi-lingual project which offers a free encyclopaedia on the World Wide Web. The name Wikipedia is a combination of the words wiki and encyclopedia. Wikipedia uses a type of software called a wiki which handles the construction of shared content which can be updated using easy-to-use tools through a web browser.

Only registered users of Wikipedia are able to create new articles. However, once an article is present on the site anyone with access to it can change its content, and changes made to pages are instantly displayed. The consequence of this is that Wikipedia does not declare any of its articles to be complete or finished.

This process of collaborative content production is built on the premise that collaboration among users will improve articles over time, in much the same way that open source software develops. Some of Wikipedia's editors have compared this process to Darwinian evolutionary processes where the 'fitness' of content improves over time.

However, the model also means that 'vandalism' and disagreements about content are common. Some take advantage of Wikipedia's openness to add nonsense to the encyclopedia. Collaboration also sometimes leads to 'edit wars': prolonged disputes when editors do not agree.

Currently Wikipedia has more than 5 million articles in many languages, including more than 1.4 million in the English-language version. There are 250 language editions of Wikipedia, and 17 of them have more than 50,000 articles each.

Wikipedia runs on a cluster of dedicated Linux servers located in Florida and four other locations around the world. It uses its own in-house created software, known as MediaWiki, which is an open source wiki system written in PHP and built on MySQL.

Commentary

Wikipedia has been called the pre-eminent example of the use of Web 2.0 technologies in collaborative production (Tapscott and Williams, 2006). The content is user-generated by a network of authors around the world for no financial gain. It thus has similarities with the production of open source software.

Issues

- Controversy has surrounded the project since its inception. Much criticism centres around the reliability and accuracy of the content, some of which has been criticised for uneven quality and inconsistency, systemic bias, and preference for consensus or popularity over credentials. Some articles contain unconfirmed and questionable information, and lack proper sources. Authors need not have any expertise or qualifications in the subjects of the articles they edit, and users are warned that their contributions may be edited mercilessly and redistributed at will by anyone who wishes to do so.
- In 2005 the science journal *Nature* compared sections of Wikipedia and the Encyclopædia Britannica, and found that for articles on the natural sciences, the two were close in terms of accuracy. However this study was challenged by Encyclopædia Britannica, which described it as fatally flawed.
- There is a battle for the future of Wikipedia. Inclusionists would like everybody to be able to provide content on whatever subject they choose. Their idea is to have as many articles on as many subjects as possible. Deletionists believe that Wikipedia is more likely to be successful if it maintains relevance and quality thresholds for its content. This implies a certain level of editorial control over content.
- Currently deletionists have the upper hand. Decisions on whether to keep or delete articles are made after deliberation by some 1000 or so of Wikipedia's most ardent contributors. If a member of this group believes an article fails to meet the 'notability criteria' it can be nominated for immediate deletion, or to be removed after five days if no one objects. Notability criteria consist of a host of ever-changing rules. For instance, articles in journals have a higher notability rating than an article in a newspaper, ten matches on Google are better than one match, and so on. Not surprisingly, debates about the merit of articles can drag on for weeks.
- Some believe that the governance bureaucracy surrounding collaborative production deters people from contributing to Wikipedia. This is because to ensure that an article survives, authors have to make sure it is deletion-proof. This raises the threshold for writing articles to a level which deters many.

Keywords

Private sector organisation	
Collaborative production	Content production
Web 2.0	Wikis

References/Sources

Poe, M. T. (2008) *Everyone Knows Everything: Wikipedia and the globalization of knowledge.* New York, Random House.

Tapscott, D. and Williams, A. D. (2006) *Wikinomics: How mass collaboration changes everything.* London, Atlantic Books.

23 YouTube

Case description

YouTube is a popular free video-sharing website which lets users upload, view, and share video clips (Tapscott and Williams, 2006). It was founded in February 2005, and the wide variety of site content includes movies, TV clips and music videos as well as amateur content such as videoblogging.

YouTube.com was founded by Chad Hurley, Steve Chen and Jawed Karim, who were all early employees of PayPal. The domain name YouTube.com was activated on 15 February 2005 and the website was developed over the following months. In August 2005 Macromedia released FlashPlayer 8, which provided a large increase in video quality over FlashPlayer 7 and has a very small download size, decreasing download time. For the first time ever, users did not have to use a separate video player such as Windows Media Player or Realplayer. It has been claimed that without the capabilities of Flashplayer 8, YouTube would not have grown so much, so fast.

YouTube is still one of the fastest-growing websites According to a July 2006 survey, 100 million clips are viewed daily, with an additional 65,000 new videos uploaded every 24 hours.

On 9 October 2006, it was announced that the company would be purchased by Google for US$1.65 billion in stock. YouTube will continue to operate independently, and the company's 67 employees and its co-founders will continue working for it.

Before being bought by Google, YouTube stated that its business model was advertising-based. Industry commentators have speculated that YouTube's running costs may be as high as US$1 million per-month. This fuelled criticisms that the company, like many Internet start-ups, did not have a viable business model. Advertisements were launched on the site beginning in March 2006. Given its traffic levels, video streams and pageviews, some have calculated that YouTube's potential revenues could be millions of dollars a month.

Commentary

YouTube has stimulated a number of controversies. For instance, its policy does not allow content to be uploaded by anyone not permitted by United States copyright law to do so. The company frequently removes uploaded content that infringes US legislation, but a large amount of copyright content continues to be uploaded. Generally, unless the copyright holder reports them, YouTube only discovers copyright infringements through self-policing in the YouTube community.

In June 2006, British media reported that YouTube and similar sites were encouraging violence and bullying amongst teenagers. Teenagers were filming 'happy-slapping' fights on their mobile phones then uploading them. While the site provides a function for reporting excessively violent videos, news reports stated that communication with the company about this can be difficult.

Issues

- YouTube is considered a pre-eminent example of a social networking site. It uses income from advertisements as its main revenue stream. How viable is this revenue model longer-term?
- What place does YouTube play in the eMarketing strategies of the major companies?
- How can sites like YouTube ensure that their content is ethical?

Keywords

Private sector organisation	
Social networking	
Web 2.0	
Content	User-generated content

References/Sources

Tapscott, D. and Williams, A. D. (2006) *Wikinomics: How mass collaboration changes everything.* London, Atlantic Books.

For cases 24–33 visit:
www.palgrave.com/business/beynon-daviesbis

JIT 1 Alvalade XXI

Case description

This case describes the implementation and subsequent failure of an innovative ICT system installed in the bars of Alvalade XXI, the recently built football stadium in Lisbon, Portugal. Casa XXI, the company running the bars, had entrusted the project to an ICT supplier which had limited experience with large systems. During the inauguration, the information system failed spectacularly, causing chaos for customers and employees. The failure meant not only a financial loss, but also a blow to the reputation of the company. The management blamed the ICT system supplier for the failure. The supplier, however, claimed that the problem was not technical but organisational, and was particularly caused by poor planning of operations. Subsequent tests were inconclusive and failed to restore trust. At the end of the case, the CEO at Casa XXI is considering the possibility of switching to an alternative ICT supplier. He also wonders what the company could have done to manage the project and the associated risks more effectively.

Commentary

The case highlights the importance of considering the joint development of activity systems with ICT systems, and the exercise of good practice. Activity systems must be designed and fully tested, and so must ICT systems. The causes of information systems failure frequently lie in the space between activity systems and ICT systems. The case demonstrates that it is frequently difficult to assign blame purely to technology in such failures.

The case also highlights some of the difficulties of outsourcing information systems development, and particularly the selection of an outsourcing vendor. This decision calls for risk assessment and cost–benefit analysis. Other relevant issues are the degree of innovation desired and the most appropriate architecture for the ICT system.

Issues

The case particularly raises governance questions in relation to the outsourcing of information systems development.

- Who is responsible for the success of an outsourced project?
- How should the roles and responsibilities be apportioned between the company and the ICT supplier(s)?
- What mechanisms should be used to plan and execute ICT outsourced projects, and control their risks?

Keywords

Private sector organisation		
Informatics industry	Informatics consumer	
Business systems	Activity system	
	Information system	ICT system
Information systems evaluation	Information systems failure	
Informatics management	Project management	Risk assessment

References/Sources

O'Callaghan, R. (2007) 'Fixing the payment systems at Alvalade XXI: a case on IT project risk management', *Journal of Information Technology* **22**(4): 399–409.

See www.palgrave.com/business/beynon-daviesbis and www.palgrave-journals.com/jit for further information and access to the original article.

JIT 2 Indian Railways

 Case description

This teaching case discusses the challenges faced by technology managers at Indian Railways (IR) in endeavouring to modernise its central passenger reservation system (PRS). The old PRS was a classic legacy information system. It had served the organisation for nearly two decades, was critical to the operation of the railway and had proved reliable. However, IR was facing increasing competition from road transport and from low-cost airlines, so it wanted to change its rules of operation. The design of the PRS was inflexible in the face of rapidly changing business requirements. The case describes the dilemma faced by the head of the Centre for Railway Information Systems (CRIS), the informatics service of IR. Should IR continue using the old PRS with its inherent shortcomings, or should it take the risk and build a wholesale replacement with new state-of-art technology which would make it easier to meet new changing business requirements through greater maintenance flexibility?

 Commentary

The case describes a dilemma familiar to anybody concerned with developing informatics strategy: whether, and how, an organisation should change core aspects of its informatics infrastructure. The case demonstrates the necessary interdependence of business activity and information systems. It highlights some of the dilemmas inherent in decision making in this area; examples of business decision making in general and risk assessment in particular.

 Issues

- The case describes a number of ways in which the PRS is critical to the operation of Indian Railways. How would you go about evaluating the benefits to the organisation?
- Organisations do not stand still and their information systems have to change along with them. In what way are information systems a brake on organisational change?
- IR runs a highly centralised informatics service. Outline some of the advantages this has for this project, as well as some of the disadvantages.
- If IR decides to build a new information system, how would you recommend it handle implementation of the system?

 Keywords

Public sector organisation		
Informatics industry	Informatics consumer	
Business systems	Activity system	
	Information system	ICT system
Legacy system		
Informatics management	Project management	Risk assessment

 References/Sources

Srivastava, S. C., Mathur, S. S. and Teo, T. S. H. (2007) 'Modernisation of the passenger reservation system: Indian railway's dilemma', *Journal of Information Technology* **22**(4): 432–9.

See www.palgrave.com/business/beynon-daviesbis and www.palgrave-journals.com/jit for further information and access to the original article.

JIT 3 GlobShop

Case description

This case discusses the decisions facing GlobShop, a global travel agent, in its efforts to offshore a significant portion of its ICT work. In response to the business challenges that arose as a result of the 11 September 2001 terrorist attacks, the company decided to outsource many of its ICT activities to the Indian subcontinent. This case traces the key decisions made by the CIO and the challenges that were encountered during the planning and execution of the offshore sourcing strategy. These decisions relate to the choice of tasks to be offshored, decisions about the vendor and the nature of sourcing arrangement, managing the vendor relationship, and change management issues. As GlobShop nears the completion of its three-year agreement with the offshore vendor, the CIO is faced with decisions regarding continuing offshore outsourcing, extending the contract and the implications this has for the future of the informatics service at GlobShop.

Commentary

The case describes a generally successful arrangement where over time a multinational retailer outsourced major elements of its informatics service to a vendor on the Indian subcontinent. Globshop initially considered outsourcing as part of its attempt to centralise and standardise business processes and ICT infrastructure across many separate countries. Events in the environment such as 9/11 caused a major reorientation of this informatics strategy to one of cost reduction.

The case also highlights the important effort required in managing the relationship between the company and a partner handling major parts of its informatics infrastructure. The issue of human resources and skills is particularly highlighted in the case.

Issues

In the latter part of the case study issues relating to the future use of informatics outsourcing by Globshop come to the fore. Like many companies, Globshop is attempting to balance the costs and benefits it gains from offshoring elements of its informatics provision against the need to control such provision long-term, particularly for future ICT developments. On the basis of your understanding of the case, how would you achieve such a balance?

Keywords

Private sector organisation	
Informatics industry	Informatics consumer
Informatics service	Centralisation
Informatics strategy	Outsourcing
Informatics infrastructure	ICT system infrastructure

References/Sources

Ranganathan, C., Krishnan, P. and Glickman, R. (2007) 'Crafting and executing an offshore IT sourcing strategy: Globshop's experience', *Journal of Information Technology* **22**(4): 440–50.

See www.palgrave.com/business/beynon-daviesbis and www.palgrave-journals.com/jit for further information and access to the original article.

JIT 4 LeCroy Corporation

Case description

Component-based (software) development (CBD) involves two processes: the development of software components and the building of software systems through the integration of pre-existing components. Software components may be developed in-house or procured from the component market. LeCroy Corporation was one of the early adopters of CBD, and chose this route to gain competitive advantage. The case describes several decisions, challenges and opportunities faced by the managers of a globally distributed software development team over the period of time during which they re-engineered a monolithic system into a component-based system.

Commentary

This case study illustrates two themes that are becoming increasingly important to modern software development practice. The first is the re-engineering of 'monolithic' ICT systems into systems based on software components; the second, the distribution of software development work around the globe.

Issues

- For companies involved in software development, CBD offers the promise of constructing ICT systems more efficiently. In turn, this promises shorter time to market for ICT systems and reduced development costs. However, the adoption of CBD requires companies not only to re-engineer their existing software systems (products) but also to develop new development and managerial practices. Consider some of the costs and benefits of CBD in these terms.
- CBD demands a new mind-set from developers. Consider what this means in this case.
- Consider the place of open source software in CBD.

Keywords

Private sector organisation	
Informatics industry	Informatics producer
Software development	Component-based development

References/Sources

Kotlarsky J. (2007) 'Re-engineering at LeCroy corporation: the move to component-based systems', *Journal of Information Technology* **22**(4): 465–78.

See www.palgrave.com/business/beynon-daviesbis and www.palgrave-journals.com/jit for further information and access to the original article.

CASE-STUDY

JIT 5 Partygaming.com

Case description

Partygaming is an online gambling operation formed in 1997. In June 2005 it was floated (made an initial public offering) on the London Stock Exchange, which valued the firm at £4.64 billion, giving it a larger market capitalisation than British Airways. Partygaming had become the dominant player in the booming online poker market, with its PartyPoker brand having over 50 per cent market share. However, this flotation was not without controversy. While Partygaming had an online gambling licence from the tax haven of Gibraltar, nearly 90 per cent of its revenue came from the United States, where the authorities viewed Internet gambling as illegal and threatened legal action. The complex operations of this truly global firm, with bases in London, India, Gibraltar and Canada, the background of its founder Ruth Parasol in Internet pornography, and the handling of its flotation, also raised concerns from an ethical perspective. Some commentators questioned whether the flotation should have been allowed at all. These concerns were proved justified when US legislation to curb online gambling was passed in September 2006. This led to PartyGaming's exit from the US market and an immediate fall of 58 per cent in its share price.

Commentary

This case analyses the entrepreneurs behind PartyGaming, the growth of this 'clicks-only' business, the challenges it has faced, the ethical issues it poses and its future prospects. In a sense, gambling is a classic information-intensive industry in the sense that it offers an intangible service. Not surprisingly, the case demonstrates the ways in which the gambling industry been much subject to recent technological innovation. This trend has brought the possibility of running gambling as global businesses up against ethical and legislative considerations specific to nation-states. So the case further demonstrates the ways in which an organisation, its technological infrastructure and the wider business environment interact.

Issues

- In what sense is online gambling a form of B2C eCommerce?
- Gambling can develop into an acknowledged addiction. Consider the rising levels of gambling addiction in certain countries. Does the presence of online gambling sites contribute to this process?
- Concerns have been raised over the ease with which children can gain access to online gambling sites. Consider some of the social consequences of this, and consider whether any technological fixes are possible to prevent it from happening.

Keywords

Private sector organisation	
Informatics industry	Informatics consumer
eCommerce	B2C eCommerce
Ethics	

References/Sources

Laffey D. (2007) 'The ultimate bluff: a case study of partygaming.com', *Journal of Information Technology* **22**(4): 479–88.

See www.palgrave.com/business/beynon-daviesbis and www.palgrave-journals.com/jit for further information and access to the original article.

JIT 6 Eastman

Case description

The Asia Pacific digital business and customer services manager of Eastman Chemical Company was given a mandate to sell Eastman's philosophy for an integrated electronic supply chain, otherwise known as the integrated system solution (ISS), to its business partners in the region, and to encourage adoption. Having invested in a state-of-the-art ICT infrastructure that would support interconnectivity with all parties along the supply chain, Eastman was keen to realise the full benefits to be gained from an integrated electronic supply chain on a global scale. Following numerous rounds of discussion with key business partners in the Asia Pacific region, some progress was made. One partner, Nagase & Co. Ltd of Japan, agreed to progress electronic connections with Eastman. However, it had some reservations regarding the extent of the integration proposed, particularly the implications for its established business processes and corporate strategy.

Commentary

The case describes the environment of the chemical industry and key elements of the value network for Eastman. It outlines the key motivations for eBusiness at Eastman and some of the developments undertaken in formulating its eBusiness strategy. In the early 1990s Eastman adopted a SAP ERP system as the core element of its informatics infrastructure. The case details how this software architecture enabled Eastman to integrate some of its key business processes. The case particularly focuses upon the attempt to extend core infrastructure into its supply chain using XML technology.

Issues

- At a number of points in the case an attempt is made to evaluate the impact of eBusiness changes on the performance improvement of the company. Consider what this case shows about the benefits of information integration to organisational performance in these terms.
- ERP is a significant backbone technology for Eastman. How important is this technology to the effective rollout of its eBusiness strategy?
- In terms of the case, describe why XML is an important technology for supply-chain operations.

Keywords

Private sector organisation	
Informatics industry	Informatics consumer
Value network	Chemical industry
Informatics planning	eBusiness strategy
eCommerce	B2B eCommerce
Communications infrastructure	XML
Information systems evaluation	

References/Sources

Yen, B., Farhoomand, A., and Ng, P. (2004) 'Constructing the e-supply chain at the Eastman chemical company', *Journal of Information Technology* **19**(2). 93–107.

See www.palgrave.com/business/beynon-daviesbis and www.palgrave-journals.com/jit for further information and access to the original article.

For cases JIT 7–12 visit:
www.palgrave.com/business/beynon-daviesbis

CASE-STUDY

Bibliography

Ackoff, R. L. (1967) 'Management misinformation systems', *Management Science* **14**(4): 147–56.

Alavi, M. and Leidner, D. (2001) 'Knowledge management and knowledge management systems', *Management Information Systems Quarterly* **25**(1): 107–36.

Angeles, R. (2005) 'RFID technologies: supply-chain applications and implementation issues', *Information Systems Management* **22**(1): 51–65.

Ansoff, H. I. (1965) *Corporate Strategy*. New York, McGraw-Hill.

Applegate, L. M., Austin, R. D. and McFarlan, W. (2002) *Corporate Information Strategy and Management: Text and cases*. New York, McGraw-Hill.

Argyris, C. and Schön, D. A. (1978) *Organizational Learning: A theory of action perspective*. Reading, Mass., Addison-Wesley.

Ashby, W. R. (1956) *An Introduction to Cybernetics*. London, Chapman Hall.

Avison, D. E. and Fitzgerald, B. (2006) *Information Systems Development: Methodologies, techniques and tools*, New York: McGraw-Hill.

Avison, D. E., Wood-Harper, A.T., Vidgen, R. T. and Wood, J. R. G. (1998) 'A further exploration into information systems development: the evolution of Multiview2', *Information Technology & People* **11**(2): 124–39.

Backhouse, J., Liebenau, J. and Land, F. (1991) 'On the discipline of information systems', *Journal of Information Systems* **1**(1): 19–27.

Bakos, J. Y. (1997) 'Reducing buyer search costs–implications for electronic marketplaces', *Management Science* **43**(12): 1676–92.

Barrette, S. and Konsynski, B. R. (1982) 'Inter-organisational information sharing systems', *MIS Quarterly*, **6**(4): 93–105.

Beer, S. (1966) *Decision and Control: The meaning of operational research and management cybernetics*. Chichester, John Wiley.

Beer, S. (1972) *Brain of the Firm: The managerial cybernetics of organisation*. London, Allen Lane.

Beer, S. (1985) *Diagnosing the System for Organisations*. Oxford, Oxford University Press.

Benbasat, I. and Zmud, R. (2003) 'The identity crisis within the IS discipline: defining and communicating the discipline's core properties', *MIS Quarterly* **27**(2): 183–94.

Bentley, G. (2005) *Practical PRINCE2*. London, Stationery Office Books.

Berners-Lee, T. (1999) *Weaving the Web: The past, present and future of the World Wide Web by its inventor*. London, Orion Business.

Berners-Lee, T., Hendler, J. and Lassilo, O. (2001) 'The semantic web', *Scientific American* **284**(5).

Bertalanffy, L. V. (1951) 'General Systems Theory: a new approach to the unity of science', *Human Biology* **23** (Dec.): 302–61.

Beynon-Davies, P. (1995) 'Information systems "failure": the case of the London Ambulance Service's Computer Aided Despatch System', *European Journal of Information Systems* **4**(1): 171–84.

Beynon-Davies, P. (1998) *Information Systems Development: An introduction to information systems engineering*. London, Macmillan.

Beynon-Davies, P. (2004a) *e-Business*. Houndmills, Basingstoke, Palgrave.

Beynon-Davies (2004b) *Database Systems*. Houndmills, Basingstoke, Palgrave.

Beynon-Davies, P. (2005) 'Constructing electronic government: the case of the UK Inland Revenue', *International Journal of Information Management* **25**(1): 3–20.

Beynon-Davies, P. (2006) 'Personal identity management in the information polity: the case of the UK National Identity Card" *Information Polity* **11**(1): 3–20.

Beynon-Davies, P. (2007) 'Informatics and the Inca', *International Journal of Information Management* **27**(5): 306–18.

Beynon-Davies, P., Carne, C., Mackay, H. and Tudhope, D. (1999) 'Rapid application development: an empirical review', *European Journal of Information Systems* **8**(2): 211–23.

Beynon-Davies, P., Mackay, H. and Tudhope, D. (2000) "'It's lots of bits of paper and ticks and post-it notes and things...": A case study of a rapid application development project', *Journal of Information Systems* (currently *Information Systems Journal*) **10**(8): 195–216.

Beynon-Davies, P., Owens, I. and Williams, M. D. (2004) 'IS failure, evaluation and organisational learning', *Journal of Enterprise Information Management* (formerly *Logistics and Information Management*) **17**(4): 276–82.

Biles, G. (1989) 'Herman Hollerith: inventor, manager, entrepreneur–a centennial remembrance', *Journal of Management* **15**(4): 603–15.

Black, E. (2002) *IBM and the Holocaust*, New York, Time Warner.

Blakey, G. (2008) *A History of the London Stock Market 1945–2007*. London, Harriman House.

Boehm, B. W. (ed.) (1989) *Software Risk Management*. Washington, IEEE Computer Society Press.

Bott, F. (2005) *Professional Issues in Information Technology*. London, British Computer Society.

Boulding, K. E. (1956) 'General Systems Theory: the skeleton of a science', *Management Science* 2(April): 197–208.

Bratton, J., Callinan, M., Forshaw, C. and Sawchuk, P. (2007) *Work and Organisational Behaviour*. Basingstoke, Palgrave.

Brooks, F. P. (1997) *The Mythical Man-Month*. Reading, Mass., Addison-Wesley.

Brynjolfson, E. (1993) 'The productivity paradox of information technology', *Communications of the ACM* **36**(12): 67–77.

Brynjolfson, E. and Hitt, L. (1998) 'Beyond the productivity paradox', *Communications of the ACM* **41**(8): 49–55.

Burns, T. and Stalker, G. M. (1961) *The Management of Innovation*. London, Tavistock.

Burton Swanson, E. (1992) *Maintaining Information Systems in Organisations*. Chichester, John Wiley.

Bush, V. (1945) 'As we may think', *Atlantic Monthly* **176**: 101–3.

Button, G. and R. H. R. Harper (1993) *Taking the Organisation into Accounts. Technology in Working Order: Studies of work, interaction and technology*. London, Routledge.

Capra, F. (1996) *The Web of Life: A new synthesis of mind and matter*. London, Flamingo.

Carroll, J. M. (ed.) (1995) *Scenario-Based Design: Envisioning work and technology in systems development*. New York, John Wiley.

Cash, J. I., McFarlan, F. W. and McKeney, J. L. (1992) *Corporate Information Systems Management*. Homewood, Ill., Richard Irvin.

Castells, M. (1996) *The Rise of the Network Society*. Mass., Blackwell.

Chaffey, D. (2006) *E-Business and E-Commerce Management*. Harlow, Essex, Pearson Education.

Chan, Y. E. and Reich, B. H. (2007) 'IT Alignment: what have we learned?', *Journal of Information Technology* **22**(4): 297–315.

Channel 4 (1999) *Station X*. UK, Channel 4 programmes.

Checkland, P. (1987) *Systems Thinking, Systems Practice*. Chichester, John Wiley.

Checkland, P. (1999) *Soft Systems Methodology: A thirty year retrospective*. Chichester, John Wiley.

Churchman, C. W. Ackoff, R. L. and Arnoff, E. l. (1957) *Introduction to Operations Research*. New York, Wiley.

Clemons, E. K. Croson, D. C. and Weber, B. W. (1996) 'Reengineering money: the Mondex stored value card and beyond', *International Journal of Electronic Commerce* **1**(2): 5–31.

Coase, R. H. (1937) 'The nature of the firm', *Economica* **4**(16): 386–405.

Cohen, A. (2002) *The Perfect Store: Inside eBay*. New York, Little, Brown.

Conklin, E. J. (1987) 'Hypertext: an introduction and survey', *IEEE Computer* **2**(9): 17–41.

Coopers (1996) *Managing Information and Systems Risks: Results of an international survey of large organisations*. Coopers & Lybrand, London.

Currie, W. (2000) *The Global Information Society*. Chichester, John Wiley.

Curtis, G. and Cobham, G. (2005) *Business Information Systems: Analysis, design and practice*. Harlow, Prentice-Hall.

Cusumano, M. A. and Selby, R. W. (1995) *Microsoft Secrets: How the world's most powerful software company creates technology, shapes markets and manages people*. New York, Free Press.

DAMA (2007) DAMA-DMBOK *Functional Framework*. Data Management Association.

Davenport, T. H. (1993) *Process Innovation: Re-engineering work through IT*. Cambridge, Mass., Harvard Business School Press.

Davenport, T. H. (1998) 'Putting the enterprise into the enterprise system', *Harvard Business Review* **76**(4): 121–31.

Davenport, T. H. (2000) 'Putting the I in IT', in D. A. Marchand, T. H. Davenport and T. Dickson (eds), *Mastering Information Management*. Harlow, Essex, Pearson.

Davenport, T. H. and Prusak, L. (2000) *Working Knowledge: How organisations manage what they know*. Boston, Mass., Harvard Business School Press.

Deise, M., Nowikow, C., King, P. and Wright, A. (2000) *Executive's Guide to E-Business: From tactics to strategy*. New York, John Wiley.

DeLone, W. H. and McLean, E. R. (1992) 'Information systems success: the quest for the dependent variable', *Information Systems Research* **3**(1): 60–95.

DeLone, W. H. and McLean, E. R. (2003) 'The DeLone and McLean Model of Information Systems Success: a ten year update', *Journal of Management Information Systems* **19**(4): 9–30.

Dreyfus, H. L. (2001) *On the Internet*. London, Routledge.

Drummond, H. (1994) 'Escalation in organisational decision-making: a case of recruiting an incompetent employee', *Journal of Behavioural Decision-Making* 7: 43–55.

Drucker, P. F. (1994) 'The theory of the business', *Harvard Business Review* **72**(5): 95–104.

Durkheim, E. (1936) *The Rules of Sociological Method*. Glencoe, Ill., Free Press.

DWP (2006) *Child Support Agency: Implementation of the child support reforms*. Department of Work and Pensions. London

Earl, M. J. (1989) *Management Strategies for Information Technology*. Hemel Hempstead, Prentice Hall.

Eason, K. D. (1988) *Information Technology and Organisational Change*. London, Taylor & Francis.

Economist (2008) 'Coming soon', *Economist*, 23 February, 85–7.

Economist (2008) 'Nomads at last: a special report on mobility', *Economist*,12 April, 75–6.

Ellis, W. D. (1938) *A Source Book of Gestalt Psychology*. London, Routledge & Kegan Paul.

Emery, F. E. and Trist, E. L. (1960) 'Socio-technical systems', in C. W. Churchman and M. Verhulst (eds), *Management Science, Models and Techniques*. New York, Pergamon: 2.

Ewusi-Mensah, K. and Przasnyski, Z. H. (1994) 'Factors contributing to the abandonment of information systems development projects', *Journal of Information Technology* **9**(3): 185–201.

Ewusi-Mensah, K. and Przasnyski, Z. H. (1995) 'Learning from abandoned information system development projects', *Journal of Information Technology* **10**(1): 3–14.

Farbey, B., Targett, D. and Land, F. (1998) *Hard Money Soft Outcomes*. London, Nelson Thornes.

Fitzgerald, B. (2006) 'The transformation of open source software', *Management Information Systems Quarterly* **30**(3): 587–98.

Fitzgerald, G. (2000) 'Adaptability and flexibility in IS development', in R. Hackney and D. Dunn (eds), *Business Information Technology Management: Alternative and adaptive futures*. London, Macmillan: 13–24.

Fitzgerald, G. and Russo, N. L. (2005) 'The turnaround of the London Ambulance Service Computer-Aided Despatch System (LASCAD)', *European Journal of Information Systems* **14**: 244–57.

Floridi, L. (2007) 'A look into the future impact of ICT on our lives', *The Information Society* **23**(1): 59–64.

Flowers, S. (1996) *Software Failure, Management Failure: Amazing stories and cautionary tales*. Chichester, John Wiley.

Fontaine, J. E. (2001) *Building the Virtual State: Information technology and instituional change*. New York, Brookings Institution.

Fortune, J. and Peters, G. (2005) *Information Systems: Achieving success by avoiding failure*. Chichester, John Wiley.

Freeman, R. E. (1984) *Strategic Management: A stakeholder approach*. Boston, Pitman.

Galliers, B. and Leidner, D. (2002) *Strategic Information Management: Challenges and strategies in managing information systems*. New York, Butterworth-Heinemann.

Gershon, P. (2004) *Releasing Resources to the Front-Line: Independent review of public sector efficiency*. London, H. M. Treasury/ HMSO.

Gillenson, M. L. (1991) 'Database administration at the crossroads: the era of end-user-oriented, decentralised data processing', *Journal of Database Administration* **2**(4): 1–11.

Gladden, G. R. (1982) 'Stop the lifecycle I want to get off', *Software Engineering Notes* **7** (April) (2): 35–9.

Glieick, J. (1997) *Chaos: The making of a new science*. London, Vintage.

Goffman, E. (1990) *Stigma: Notes on the management of spoiled identity*. Harmondsworth, Middlesex, Penguin.

Graham, I. (2006) *Business Rules Management and Service Oriented Architecture: A pattern language*. London, John Wiley.

Granovetter, M. (1973) 'The strength of weak ties', *American Journal of Sociology* **78**(6): 1360.

Gray, I. (1984) *General and Industrial Management*. New York, IEEE Press.

Gregor, S. (2006) 'The nature of theory in information systems', *Management Information Systems Quarterly* **30**(3): 611–42.

Gwillim, D., Dovey, K. and Wieder, B. (2005) 'The politics of post-implementation reviews', *Information Systems Journal* **15**(4): 307–20.

Hammer, M. (1990) 'Re-engineering work: don't automate, obliterate', *Harvard Business Review* July–August: 104–12.

Hammer, M. (1996) *Beyond Re-engineering: How the process-centred organisation is changing our lives*. London, Harper Collins.

Hammer, M. and Champy, J. (1993) *Reengineering the Corporation: A manifesto for business revolution*. London, Nicholas Brearley.

Hay, D. C. (1996) *Data Model Patterns: Conventions of thought*. New York, Dorset House.

Heeks, R. (ed) (1999) *Reinventing Government in the Information Age: International practice in IT-enabled public sector reform*. London, Routledge.

Heier, H. and Borgman, H. P. (2002) *Knowledge Management Systems Spanning Cultures: The case of Deutsche Bank's HRBase*. European Conference on Information Systems, Gdansk, Poland.

Heims, S. J. (1991) *The Cybernetics Group*. MIT Press, Boston, Mass.

Hevner, A. R., March, S. T., Park, J. and Ram, S. (2004) 'Design science in information systems research', *Management Information Systems Quarterly* **28**(1): 75–105.

Hirschheim, R. A. (1983) 'Assessing participatory systems design: some conclusions from an exploratory study', *Information and Management* **6**(4): 317–27.

Hirschheim, R. and Klein, H. (2003) 'Crisis in the IS field? a critical reflection on the state of the discipline', *Journal of the Association for Information Systems* **4**(5): 237–93.

Hirschheim, R. and Newman, M. (1988) 'Information systems and user resistance: theory and practice', *Computer Journal* **31**(5): 398–408.

HMSO (1993) *Wessex Regional Health Authority Regional Information Systems Plan: Report of the public accounts committee*. HMSO. London

Hofstede, G. (1991) *Cultures and Organisations*. New York, McGraw-Hill.

Holwell, S. and Checkland, P. (1998) 'An information system won the war', *IEE Proceedings Software* **145**(4): 95–9.

Holwell, S. and Checkland, P. (1998) *Information, Systems and Information Systems*. Chichester, John Wiley.

Holzner, S. (2008) *How Dell Does It*. New York, McGraw-Hill Professional.

Home Office (2002) *Entitlement Cards and Identity Fraud: A consultation paper*. London, HMSO.

Hoque, F. (2000) *E-enterprise: Business models, architecture and components*. Cambridge, Cambridge University Press.

Hunt, T., Humby, C. and Phillips, T. (2006) *Scoring Points: How Tesco continues to win customer loyalty*. London, Kogan Page.

Introna, L. (1997) *Management, Information and Power: A narrative of the involved manager*. Basingstoke, Macmillan.

Ives, B. and Learmonth, G. P. (1984) 'The information system as a competitive weapon', *Communications of the ACM* **27**(12): 1193–201.

Jackson, M. C. (2003) *Systems Thinking: Creative Holism for managers*. Chichester, John Wiley.

Johnson, G., Scholes, K. and Whittington, R. (2007) *Exploring Corporate Strategy: Text and cases*, 8th edn. Englewood-Cliffs, N.J., Prentice-Hall.

Johnson, S. (2002) *Emergence: The connected lives of ants, brains, cities and software*. London, Penguin.

Jones, L. (2007) *EasyJet: The story of Britain's biggest low-cost airline*. London, Aurum Press.

Kalakota, R. and Robinson, M. (1999) *E-Business: Roadmap for success*. Reading, Mass., Addison-Wesley.

Kalakota, R. and Whinston, A. B. (1997) *Electronic Commerce: A manager's guide*. Harlow, UK, Addison-Wesley.

Katz, D. and Kahn, R. L. (1966) *The Social Psychology of Organisations*. New York, Wiley.

Keen, P. (1981) 'Information systems and organisational change', *Communications of the ACM* **24**(1): 24–33.

Keen, P. G. W. (1980) *Reference Disciplines and a Cumulative IS Tradition*. International Conference on Information Systems, Philadelphia.

Klein, H. K. and Hirschheim, R. A. (1987) 'A comparative framework of data modelling paradigms and approaches', *Computer Journal* **30**(1): 8–14.

Kling, R. and Allen, J. P. (1996) 'Can computer science solve organisational problems? the case for organisational informatics', in R. Kling (ed.), *Computerisation and Controversy: Value conflicts and social choices*. San Diego, Calif., Academic Press.

Kling, R. and Iacono, S. (1984) 'The control of IS developments after implementation', *Communications of the ACM* **27**(12): 1218–26.

Kling, R. and Scaachi, W. (1982) 'The web of computing: computer technology as social organisation', *Advances in Computers* **21**(1): 1–90.

Koestler, A. (1967) *The Ghost in the Machine*. London, Hutchinson.

Kraemer, K. L. and Dedrick, J. (2002) 'Strategic use of the Internet and e-Commerce: Cisco systems', *Journal of Strategic Information Systems* **11**(1): 5–29.

Kumar, K. (1990) 'Post implementation evaluation of computer-based information systems: current practices', *Communications of the ACM* **33**(2): 236–52.

Lacity, M. and Hirschheim, R. (1993) *Information Systems Outsourcing: Myths, metaphors and realities*. Chichester, John Wiley.

Lacity, M. and Wilcocks, L. (2006) *Information Systems and Outsourcing*. Basingstoke, Palgrave.

Landauer, T. K. (1995) *The Trouble with Computers: Usefulness, usability and productivity*. Cambridge, Mass., MIT Press.

Le Guin, U. (1974) *The Dispossessed*. New York, Harper and Row.

Liebenau, J. and Backhouse, J. (1990) *Understanding Information: An introduction*. London, Macmillan.

Liebowitz, J. (ed) (1999) *Knowledge Management Handbook*. Boca Raton, Fl., CRC Press.

Linder, J. C. and Cantrell, S. (2000) *Changing Business Models: Surveying the landscape*. Working paper, Accenture Institute for Strategic Change.

Lovelock, J. (2000) *Gaia: A New Look at Life on Earth*. Oxford, Oxford University Press.

LSE (2005) *The Identity Project: An assessment of the UK Identity Cards Bill and its implications*. London School of Economics and Political Science.

Lucas, H. C. (1975) *Why Information Systems Fail*. New York, Columbia University Press.

Lyytinen, K. (1988) 'The expectation failure concept and systems analysts view of information systems failures: results of an exploratory study', *Information and Management* **14**(1): 45–55.

Lyytinen, K. and Hirschheim, R. (1987) 'Information systems failures: a survey and classification of the empirical literature', *Oxford Surveys in Information Technology* **4**(2): 257–309.

Malone, T. W., Crowston, K. G., Lee, J. and Pentland, B. (1999) 'Tools for inventing organisations: toward a handbook of organisational processes', *Management Science* **45**(3): 425–43.

Malone, T. W., Yates, J. and Benjamin, R. I. C. (1987) 'Electronic markets and electronic hierarchies', *Communications of the ACM* **30**(6): 484–97.

Marchand, D. A., Davenport, T. H. and Dickson, T. (eds) (2000) *Mastering Information Management*. Harlow, Essex, Pearson.

Marchand, D. A., Kettinger, W. J. and Rollins, J. D. (2000) 'Company performance and information management: the view from the top', in D. A. Marchand, T. H. Davenport and T. Dickson (eds), *Mastering Information Management*. Harlow, Essex, Pearson.

Martin, J. (1996) *Cybercorp*. New York, American Management Association.

Mason, R. O. (2004) 'The legacy of LEO: lessons learned from an English tea and cake company's pioneering efforts in information systems', *Journal of the Association for Information Systems* **5**(5): 183–219.

Mason, R. O. and Mitroff, I. I. (1981) *Challenging Strategic Planning Assumptions: Theory, cases and techniques*. New York, John Wiley.

Maurer, J. G. (1971) *Readings in Organisation Theory: Open systems approaches*. New York, Random House.

Mayo, E. M. (1933) *The Human Problems of an Industrial Civilisation*. New York, Macmillan.

McGrath, K. (2002) 'The golden circle: a way of arguing and acting about technology in the London Ambulance Service', *European Journal of Information Systems* **11**(1): 251–6.

McGregor, D. (1960) *The Human Side of the Enterprise*. New York, McGraw-Hill.

McKenzie, D. (1994) 'Computer-related accidental death: an empirical exploration', *Science and Public Policy* **21**(4): 233–48.

Menn, J. (2003) *All the Rave: The rise and fall of Shawn Fanning's Napster*. New York, Crown Business.

Morgan, G. (1986) *Images of Organisation*. London, Sage.

Morris, C. (1964) *Signification and Significance*. Cambridge, Mass., MIT Press.

Mumford, E. (1983) *Designing Participatively*. Manchester, Manchester Business School Press.

Mumford, E. (1996) *Systems Design: Ethical tools for ethical change*. London, Macmillan.

Mumford, E. (2006) 'The story of socio-technical design: reflections on its successes, failures and potential', *Information Systems Journal* **16**(4): 317–42.

NAO (1999) *The United Kingdom Passport Agency: The passport delays of Summer 1999*. National Audit Office.

Newman, M. and Sabherwal, R. (1996) 'Determinants of commitment to information systems development: a longitudinal investigation', *MIS Quarterly* **20**(3): 23–54.

Nielsen, J. (1993) *Usability Engineering*. Boston, Mass., Academic Press.

Nonaka, I. and Takeuchi, H. (1995) *The Knowledge-Creating Company*. New York, Oxford University Press.

Norris, M. and West, N. (2001) *eBusiness Essentials*. Chichester, UK, BT/John Wiley.

Office of Government Commerce (OGC) (2005) *Managing Successful Projects with PRINCE2*. London, The Stationery Office.

OGC (2005) *Introduction to ITIL*. London, Stationery Office Publications.

Ogden, C. K. and Richards, I. A. (1923) *The Meaning of Meaning*. London, Routledge & Kegan Paul.

OMG (2007) *Business Motivation Model (BMM) Specification*. Object Management Group.

Orlikowski, W. T. (1996) 'Realising the potential of new technologies: an improvisation model of change management.' Business Information Technology Conference, Manchester Metropolitan University, October.

Orlikowski, W. T. and Gash, T. C. (1994) 'Technological frames: making sense of information technology in organisations' *ACM Transactions on Information Systems* **12**(2): 17–207.

Oshri, I., Kotlarsky, J. and Wilcocks, L. (2008) *Outsourcing Global Services: Knowledge, innovation and social capital*. Basingstoke, Palgrave.

Osterwalder, A. and Pigneur, Y. (2002) *An Ebusiness Model Ontology for Modeling Ebusiness*. 15th eCommerce conference, Bled, Slovenia.

Oz, E. (1994) 'When professional standards are lax: the confirm failure and its lessons. *Communications of the Association for Computing Machinery* (ACM) **37**(10): 29–36.

Paolini, C. (1999) *The Value Net: A tool for competitive strategy*. Chichester, John Wiley.

Parker, M., Benson, R. and Trainor, H. (1988) *Information Economics: Linking business performance to information technology*. New Jersey, Prentice-Hall.

Peppard, J. (2000) 'Customer relationship management in financial services', *European Management Journal* **18**(3): 312–27.

Pinker, S. (2001) *The Language Gene*. Harmondsworth, Penguin.

Podolny, J. M. and Page, K. l. (1998) 'Network forms of organisation', *Annual Review of Sociology* **24**(1): 57-77..

Poe, M. T. (2008) *Everyone Knows Everything: Wikipedia and the globalization of knowledge*. New York, Random House.

Polanyi, M. (1962) *Personal Knowledge*. New York, Anchor Day.

Porter, M. E. (1985) *Competitive Advantage: Creating and sustaining superior performance*. New York, Free Press.

Porter, M. E. (2001) 'Strategy and the Internet', *Harvard Business Review* **79**(3): 63–78.

Porter, M. E. and Millar, V. E. (1985) 'How information gives you competitive advantage', *Harvard Business Review* **63**(4): 149–60.

Raymond, E. S. (1999) 'The cathedral and the bazaar', *Knowledge, Technology and Policy* **12**(3): 23–49.

Rayport, J. and Sviokla, J. (1996) 'Exploiting the virtual value-chain', *McKinsey Quarterly* **1**(20–37)

Robey, D. and Markus, M. L. (1984) 'Rituals in information systems design', *MIS Quarterly* **8**(1): 5–15.

Robson, W. (1997) *Strategic Management and Information Systems: An integrated approach*. London, Prentice-Hll.

Sardar, Z. and Ravetz, J. R. (eds) (1996) *Cyberfutures: Culture and politics on the information super-highway*. New York, New York University Press.

Sauer, C. (1993) *Why Information Systems Fail: A case study approach*. Henley-on-Thames, Alfred Waller.

Saunders, R. (2001) *Business the Amazon.com Way*. Oxford, John Wiley.

Sawhney, M. and Parikh, D. (2001) 'Where value lies in a networked world', *Harvard Business Review* **79**(1): 79–86.

Schneiderman, B. and Plaisant, C. (2004) *Designing the User Interface: Strategies for effective human-computer interaction*. New York, Pearson.

Scott-Morton, M. S. (ed.) (1991) *The Corporation of the 1990s: Information technology and organisational transformation*. New York, Oxford University Press.

Senge, P. M. (2006) *The Fifth Discipline: The art and practice of the learning organisation*. New York, Doubleday.

Senn, J. (1998) 'The challenge of relating IS research to practice', *Information Resources Management Journal* **11**(1): 23–8.

Shanks, G., Seddon, P. B. and Wilcocks, L. P. (2003) *Second-Wave Enterprise Resource Planning Systems: Implementing for effectiveness*. Cambridge, Cambridge University Press.

Shannon, C. E. (1949) *The Mathematical Theory of Communication*. Urbana, University of Illinois Press.

Silver, M. S., Markus, M. L. and Beath, C. M. (1995) 'The Information Technology Interaction Model: a foundation for the MBA core course', *MIS Quarterly* **19**(3): 361–90.

Silverman, D. (1982) *The Theory of Organisations*. London, Macmillan.

Simon, H. (1960) *The New Science of Management Decisions*. New York, Harper & Row.

Simon, H. A. (1976) *Administrative Behavior: A study of decision-making processes in administration*. New York, Free Press.

Sobel, D. (1996) *Longitude*. London, Fourth Estate.

Sowa, J. F. (1984) *Conceptual Structures: Information processing in mind and machine*. Reading, Mass., Addison-Wesley.

Stacey, R. D. (1991) *Chaos Frontier: Creative strategic control for business*. Oxford, Butterworth-Heinemann.

Stacey, R. D. (2003) *Strategic Managment and Organisational Dynamics: The challenge of complexity*. Harlow, Pearson Education.

Stamper, R. K. (1973) *Information in Business and Administrative Systems*. London, Batsford.

Stamper, R. K. (1985) 'Information: mystical fluid or a subject for scientific enquiry?', *Computer Journal* **28**(3).

Stamper, R. K. (2001) 'Organisational semiotics: informatics without the computer?', in L. Kecheng, R. J. Clarke, P. Bogh-Anderson and R. K. Stamper (eds), *Information, Organisation and Technology: Studies in organisational semiotics*. Dordrecht, Netherlands, Kluwer.

Stapleton, J. (1997) *DSDM – Dynamic Systems Development Method: The method in practice*. Harlow, England, Addison-Wesley.

Tapscott, D. (1996) *The Digital Economy: Promise and peril in the age of networked intelligence*. New York, McGraw-Hill.

Tapscott, D. and Williams, A. D. (2006) *Wikinomics: How mass collaboration changes everything*. London, Atlantic Books.

Taylor, F. W. (1911) *Principles of Scientific Management*. New York, Harper & Row.

Thomas, D., Ranganathan, C. and Desouza, K. C. (2005) 'Race to dot com and back:lessons from ebusiness spin-offs and reintegration', *Information Systems Management*, **22**(3): 23–80.

Timmers, P. (1999) *Electronic Commerce: Strategies and models for business to business trading*. Chichester, John Wiley.

Tsitchizris, D. C. and Lochovsky, F. H. (1982) *Data Models*. Englewood Cliffs, N.J., Prentice-Hall.

US (1985) 'US Government Accounting Office Report FGMSD-80-4', *ACM Sigsoft Software Engineering Notes* **10**(5).

Vickers, G. (1965) *The Art of Judgement*. London, Chapman & Hall.

Vidgen, R. T., Avison, D. E., Wood, B. and Wood-Harper, A. T. (2002) *Developing Web Information Systems: From strategy to implementation*. London, Butterworth-Heinemann.

Vise, D. A. (2005) *The Google Story*. New York, Random House.

Von Baeyer, H. C. (2003) *Information: The new language of science*. London, Weidenfeld & Nicolson.

Von Krogh, G. A. and Spaeth, S. (2007) 'The open source software phenomenon: characteristics that promote research', *Journal of Strategic Information Systems* **16**(3): 236–53.

W3C (2000) *XML 1.0* (2nd edition). World-Wide-Web Consortium.

Waddington, C. H. (1977) *Tools for Thought*. St Albans, Herts, Jonathan Cape.

Walsham, G. (1993) *Interpreting Information Systems in Organisations*. Chichester, John Wiley.

Walsham, G. and Han, C.-K. (1991) 'Structuration theory and information systems research', *Journal of Applied Systems Analysis* **18**(1): 77–85.

Ward, J. and Peppard, J. (2002) *Strategic Planning for Information Systems*. Chichester, John Wiley.

Ward, J., Taylor, P. and Bond, P. (1996) 'Evaluation and realisation of IS/IT benefits: an empirical study of current practice', *European Journal of Information Systems* **4**(1): 214–25.

Weber, M. (1946) *Essays in Sociology*. Oxford, Oxford University Press.

Weill, P. and Ross, J. (2004) *IT Governance: How top performers manage IT decision rights for superior results*. Boston, Mass., Harvard Business School Press.

Whiteley, D. (2000) *E-commerce: Strategy, technologies and applications*. Maidenhead, Berks, McGraw-Hill.

Whyte, W. S. (2001) *Enabling E-Business: Integrating technologies, architectures and applications*. Chichester, John Wiley.

Wiener, N. (1948) *Cybernetics*. New York, Wiley.

Wilcocks, L. and Margetts, H. (1994) 'Risk assessment and information systems', *European Journal of Information Systems* **3**(2): 127–38.

Wilson, B. (1990) *Systems: Concepts, methodologies and applications*. Chichester, UK, John Wiley.

Womack, J. P. and Jones, D. T. (2003) *Lean thinking: Banish waste and create wealth in your corporation*. London, Free Press Business.

Worthington, I. and Britton, C. (2005) *The Business Environment*. Englewood Cliffs, N.J., Prentice Hall.

Wright, J. V. (1992) *The UK Political System*. London, Pulse Publications.

Wright, R. (1989) *Systems Thinking: A guide to managing in a changing environment*. Dearborn, Mich., Society of Manufacturing Engineers.

Yeates, D., Paul, D., Jenkins, T., Hindle, K. and Rollason, C. (2007) *Business Analysis*. London, BCS Publications.

Zorkadis, V. and Donos, P. (2004) 'On biometric-based authentication and identification from a privacy-protection perspective: deriving privacy-enhancing requirements', *Information Management and Computer Security* **12**(1): 125–37.

Zuboff, S. (1988) *In the Age of the Smart Machine: The future of work and power*. London, Heinemann.

Glossary

Term	Definition
A	
Acceptance testing	Conducting any tests required by the user to ensure that the user community is satisfied with the system.
Access	A precondition for the electronic delivery of services and goods. Stakeholders must have access to remote access devices.
Access channel	An access device plus an associated communication channel.
Access device	A mechanism used to formulate, transmit, receive and display messages.
Accounting information system	The part of the information systems infrastructure devoted to managing information concerning the financial state of the organisation.
Action perspective	The perspective on organisations that focuses on the process of organising.
Activity-based project management	A form of project management in which planning and control is conducted in terms of project activities.
Adaptive maintenance	Changes made to the information system to provide a closer fit between an information system and its environment, the human activity system.
Adjunct community	An eCommunity fostered by a commercial operation.
ADSL	Asynchronous digital subscriber line. A broadband communication channel for the local loop.
After-sales service	A primary process in the internal value chain. These are services that maintain or enhance product value by attempting to promote a continuing relationship with customers. They involve such activities as the installation, testing, maintenance and repair of products.
Agent	Something (usually a person, group, department or organisation but possibly some other information system) that is a net originator or receiver of system data.
Aggregation	This type of relationship serves to collect a set of different classes into one unit or aggregate.
Analysis	See systems analysis.
Application	A term generally used as a synonym for an ICT system or another piece of software designed to perform a particular function.
Application service provider	A company supplying a software service as an application.
Application software	Software designed for a particular set of tasks in an organisation.
Association	An association relationship establishes a connection between the instances of classes and is defined by cardinality and optionality.
Auction	A form of commercial exchange involving bidding.

Term	Definition
Authentication	The process of identifying an actor to a system.
Authority	Legitimated power in that those over whom it is exercised accept it.
Authorisation	The facilities available for enforcing database security.
Awareness	A precondition of electronic delivery. Stakeholders must be aware of the potential benefits.
B	
B2B	Business to business. See supply chain.
B2B eCommerce	The use of e-Commerce in the supply chain.
B2B IOS	An interorganisational information system used to connect businesses.
B2C	Business to consumer. See customer chain.
B2C eCommerce	The use of eCommerce in the customer chain.
B2C IOS	An interorganisational information system used to connect businesses to customers.
Back-end ICT infrastructure	The ICT systems used to support the core information systems of the business.
Back-end ICT system	A core ICT system involved in manipulating the key data for the organisation.
Back-end information system	A core transaction processing information system concerned with supporting the internal processes of an organisation.
Back-end information systems infrastructure	The core set of transaction processing information systems in organisations.
Balanced scorecard	A popular form of organisational evaluation which benchmarks against an holistic measurement system.
Bandwidth	A measure of the amount of data that can be transmitted along a communication channel in a unit of time. Normally measured in bits per second.
Benchmarking	Sometimes called competitive practices benchmarking. The process of comparing performance against other comparable organisations or processes.
Bespoke development	The development style in which an organisation produces a new information system to directly match its requirements.
Bit	An abbreviation of binary digit – one of the two digits (0 and 1) used in binary notation.
Branding	The process of using some form of sign to identify a product or service.
Bricks and mortar businesses	Businesses in the sense that they have a physical presence, usually buildings where they can be located.

Term	Definition
Broadband	A term generally used to describe a high-bandwidth communication channel.
Browser	A program that allows users to access and read Web documents.
Bulletin board	Web facilities that permit users to post items to a central access area.
Business case	The case made for the utility of an information system.
Business model	Specifies the structure and dynamics of a particular enterprise, particularly the relationship between different stakeholders, benefits and costs to each, and key revenue flows.
Business process	See organisational process.
Business process re-engineering	An organisational analysis approach to redesigning business processes.
Business strategy	See organisation strategy.
Buyer-oriented B2B	The consumer opens an electronic market on its own server and requests bids.
Byte	A set of eight binary digits/bits.
C	
C2C eCommerce	Consumer to consumer eCommerce. ICT enablement of aspects of the community chain.
Capacity	See bandwidth.
CAISE	See computer aided information systems engineering.
Cardinality	Establishes how many instances of one entity are related to how many instances of another entity.
Cash commerce	Occurs when irregular transactions of a one-off nature are conducted between economic actors. In cash commerce the processes of execution and settlement are typically combined.
Chain of command and control	Refers to the relationships of power and authority established in the organisation between its members.
Character set	A scheme for representing symbols in binary notation.
Chat	Technology enabling near-synchronous many-to-many communication over the Internet.
Chief information officer	A term for the executive-level manager in the organisation responsible for informatics.
CIO	See chief information officer.
Cisco	A leading firm in the market for inter-networking equipment.
Class	See object class.
Clicks and mortar businesses	Businesses that still maintain a physical presence but also offer services and products that are accessible online.
Clicks-only businesses	Businesses that have emerged entirely in the online environment.
Client	A key type of organisational stakeholder. Clients sponsor and provide resources for the construction and continuing use of an information system.
Client–server	An applications architecture in which the processing is distributed between machines acting as clients and machines acting as servers.
Closed system	A system that does not interact with its environment.

Term	Definition
Commerce	A process consisting of pre-sale, sale execution, sale settlement and after-sale activities.
Communication channel	The medium along which messages travel.
Communication software	Software enabling the interconnection of computer systems.
Communication subsystem	That part of an ICT system enabling distribution of the processing around a network
Communication technology	Technology used for communications.
Communications subsystem	Layer of an ICT system concerned with communications.
Community chain	Based on informal social networks of individuals, a major force underlying C2C eCommerce.
Comparator	A mechanism that compares signals from sensors with control inputs.
Competitive position	An organisation takes up a particular position in a market defined by its activities and relationships with its competitors, suppliers, customers and regulators.
Competitor	A key type of organisational stakeholder. Key organisations in the same industrial sector or market that compete with an organisation.
Computer aided information systems engineering (CAISE)	ICT that is used to aid automation of aspects of the development process.
Concept	The idea of significance. The collection of properties that in some way characterise a phenomenon.
Conception	See systems conception.
Conceptual model	A model that represents a universe of discourse at a high-level. Used within soft systems approaches to refer to a high-level model of key activities.
Configuration management	The process of controlling the changes made to an information system over time.
Consensus participation	A design group is formed as in representative participation, but representatives are elected by staff and given the responsibility to communicate group decisions back to staff.
Construction	See systems construction.
Consultative participation	Decision making is still in the hands of systems analysts and systems designers, but a great deal of staff at every level are consulted before decisions are made.
Consumer	An actor (individual, group, organisation) which consumes a good or service. See customer.
Consumer behaviour	The behaviour of consumers, and particularly their decision making, in the commercial process.
Content management	The organisational process that manages the maintenance of Web-based material.
Contract	An agreement between actors which is enforceable in law.
Control	The mechanism that implements regulation and adaptation in most systems.
Control inputs	Special types of input to a control process that define levels of performance for a system.

Term	Definition
Control subsystem	The subsystem that regulates the behaviour of a system it is monitoring. Also known as a control process or mechanism.
Cookie	A data file placed on a user's machine by a Web browser. Used by an organisation's ICT system to monitor interaction.
Corrective maintenance	Changes made to correct previously unidentified system errors.
Correspondence failure	Lack of correspondence between objectives and evaluation.
Cost advantage	This essentially aims to establish the organisation as a low-cost leader in the market.
Cost–benefit analysis	The process of assessing whether or not the process of developing an information system (or any other project) is a worthwhile investment.
Credit-based payment systems	Systems modelled on conventional payment mechanisms such as cheques and credit cards except that signatures are digital rather than physical.
Credit commerce	Irregular transactions occur between trading partners and the processes of settlement and execution are separated.
Critical success factor	A factor that is deemed crucial to the success of a business.
CRM	See customer relationship management.
Culture	The set of behaviours expected in a social group.
Customer	A key type of organisational stakeholder. Consumers of an organisation's products or services.
Customer chain	The chain of activities that an organisation performs in the service of its customers.
Customer profiling and preferencing	A mechanism of customising online products and services for the customer based on detailed information captured about the customer.
Customer relationship management	The set of activities devoted to managing the customer chain.
Customer relationship management system	An information system devoted to managing all interactions of a customer with an organisation.
Customer resource life-cycle	A strategic planning framework developed by Ives and Learmonth. Also useful in defining elements of the customer chain.
Customer-facing TPS	Transaction processing systems that interface with customers.
D	
Data	Sets of symbols.
Data administration	The function concerned with the management, planning and documentation of the data resource of an organisation.
Data flow	A pipeline through which packets of data of known composition flow.
Data management	The set of facilities needed to manage data.
Data management layer	That part of an ICT system concerned with data management.
Data mining	The process of extracting previously unknown data from large databases and using it to make organisational decisions.
Data model	An architecture for data or a blueprint of data requirements for an application.

Term	Definition
Data privacy	Ensuring the privacy of personal data.
Data protection	The activity of ensuring data privacy.
Data security	The process and technologies associated with ensuring the security of data.
Data store	A repository of data.
Data subsystem	That part of an ICT system concerned with managing the data needed by an application.
Data type	A categorisation of data defining the format and operations for it.
Data warehouse	A type of contemporary database system designed to fulfil decision-support needs. It uses large amounts of data from diverse sources to fulfil multidimensional queries.
Database	An organised pool of logically related data.
Database management system	A suite of computer software providing the interface between users and a database or databases.
Database system	A term used to encapsulate the constructs of a data model, DBMS and database.
Database/website integration	The technologies associated with integrating database systems with websites.
Datum	A unit of data.
DBMS	See database management system.
Decision making	The activity of deciding on appropriate action in particular situations.
Decision support database	Databases used to support organisational decision making.
Decision support system (DSS)	See executive information system.
Demand chain	See customer chain.
Design	See systems design.
Designation	See symbol.
Developer	See producer.
Development failure	Failure of an information system project while in development.
Development information system	An information system designed to support the development process.
Development method	A specified approach for producing information systems.
Development organisation	That specialist form of organisation charged with producing an information system.
Development process	A human activity system concerned with developing an information system.
Development technique	A technique used to guide activity in a phase of the development process.
Development toolkit	The methods, techniques and tools available to the development organisation.
Differentiation strategy	A strategy undertaken by an organisation to differentiate its product or service from its competitors.
Digital cash	A type of non-credit-based payment system.
Digital certificate	Sometimes referred to as digital signature, used to authenticate parties in an eCommerce transaction.
Digital convergence	The convergence around digital standards allowing interoperability of digital technologies on a global scale.

Term	Definition
Digital divide	The phenomenon of differential rates of awareness, interest, access, skills and use of ICT by different groups in society.
Direct conversion	An implementation approach in which the new system directly replaces the old system.
Direction	A property of a communication which refers to the direction of the data flow between sender and receiver.
Disintermediation	The process available though electronic markets of enabling companies to sell directly to customers.
Division of labour	The way in which tasks and responsibilities are assigned to members of an organisation.
Domain name	A hierarchical naming convention for identifying host computers on the Internet.
Double-loop feedback	A system in which monitoring of single-loop feedback systems and the environment triggers examination and possible revision of the principles upon which a control system is established.
E	
EBusiness	Electronic business, the conduct of business using information and communication technology. A superset of eCommerce.
ECommerce	Electronic commerce. The conduct of business commerce using ICT such as that supporting the Internet.
ECommunity	Electronic community, either a traditional community enabled with ICT or a virtual community.
Economic actor	An agency that engages in economic exchange.
Economic environment	The markets within which an organisation competes. An economic system is the way in which a group of humans arrange their material provisioning.
Economic relationship	The relationships of exchange between economic actors.
Economic system	See economic environment.
EDI	Electronic data interchange. A set of standards for the transfer of electronic documentation between organisations.
Effectiveness	A measure of the extent to which the system contributes to the purposes of a higher-level system.
Effector	Components of a control process that cause changes to a system's state.
Efficacy	A measure of the extent to which a system achieves its intended transformation. See also utility.
Efficiency	A measure of the extent to which a system achieves its intended transformation with the minimum use of resources.
EFT	Electronic funds transfer, a means for transferring money between financial repositories such as banks or bank accounts.
EFTPOS	Electronic funds transfer at point of sale, a form of EFT where the purchaser is physically at the point of sale.
EIS	See executive information system.
Electronic delivery	The delivery of services and intangible products over communication networks.

Term	Definition
Electronic government	The use of ICT to enable government administrative processes.
Electronic hierarchy	A hierarchy in which exchanges on a one-to-many basis are conducted using ICT.
Electronic payment system	A system for the electronic transfer of monetary data.
Email	Electronic mail. The transmission and receipt of electronic text messages using communication networks.
Email protocol	A communication protocol for the transfer of electronic mail.
EMall	Electronic mall, a collection of eShops.
EMarket	Electronic market, a market in which economic exchanges are conducted using information technology and computer networks.
EMarketing	Electronic marketing, the process of planning and executing the conception, pricing, promotion and distribution of ideas, goods and services using electronic channels.
Empirics	Branch of semiotics concerned with the physical characteristics of a communication channel.
Employee-facing information systems	Transaction processing systems that interact with employees of an organisation.
ENabled community	A traditional community supported by ICT.
Encryption	The process of encoding and decoding messages to ensure their security in transmission.
End-user	That stakeholder group that uses an information system to conduct work.
Enterprise resource planning system	A software package consisting of a set of IT systems which are integrated to form an infrastructure for an organisation.
Environment	Anything outside the organisation from which it receives inputs and to which it passes outputs.
EProcurement	Electronic procurement. A term used to refer to ICT-enablement of key supply chain activities.
ETHICS	Mumford's sociotechnical design method.
Executive information system (EIS)	An information system designed to support high-level, strategic decision making in organisations
Expectation failure	The inability of an information system to meet a specific stakeholder group's expectations.
Explicit knowledge	Readily accessible, documented and organised knowledge.
Extension	See referent.
Extranet	Allowing access to aspects of an organisation's intranet to accredited users.
F	
Feasibility study	That part of systems conception concerned with assessing the feasibility of developing an information system.
Feedback	The way in which a control process adjusts the state of a system being monitored to keep it within specified limits.
File	A physical data structure.
Firewall	A collection of hardware and software placed between an organisation's internal network and an external network such as the Internet.

Term	Definition
Five forces model	A strategic planning framework attributed to Porter and Millar.
Formalism	See representation formalism.
Formative evaluation	A form of information systems evaluation concerned with monitoring the developing functionality and usability of a product.
Fourth-generation language	A high-level programming language used to develop an information system.
Fragmentation	A measure of the degree to which data and processing are fragmented amongst information systems.
Front-end ICT infrastructure	The organised collection of ICT systems interacting with key stakeholders.
Front-end ICT system	An ICT system that supports a front-end information system.
Front-end information system	An information system which interacts with internal or external stakeholders of the organisation.
Front-end information systems infrastructure	That part of the information systems infrastructure concerned with the core front-end information systems of the organisation.
FTP	File transfer protocol, a protocol for transferring files over communication networks.
Functional requirements	Expected features of an information system.
Functionality	What a system does or should be able to do.
G	
General systems theory	An endeavour which attempted to study the properties and behaviour of all systems.
Generalisation	This type of relationship establishes levels of abstraction between object classes.
Gigabytes	1,000,000,000 bytes (billion).
Global information system	An information system that operates across the globe.
Globalisation	The process by which organisations are operating across the globe.
Goods	Tangible or intangible objects produced by organisations.
Grammar	Rules that control the correct use of a language.
H	
Hardware	The physical (hard) aspects of ICT consisting of processors, input devices and output devices.
Hierarchy	An important systems concept in which a system can be decomposed to various levels of detail.
Holistic thinking	Thinking about the properties of whole systems rather than their parts.
Homeostasis	The process of ensuring that a system remains regulated within defined limits.
Homeostat	A mechanism for ensuring homeostasis.
Horizontal portal	Portal that attempts to serve the entire Internet community, typically by offering search functions and classification for the whole of Web content.
HTML	Hypertext markup language, a standard for marking up documents to be published on the WWW.
HTTP	Hypertext transfer protocol, an object-oriented, stateless protocol that defines how information can be transmitted between client and server.

Term	Definition
Human activity system	A logical collection of activities performed by a group of people.
Human activity system design	Design which includes job design, team design and procedure design.
Human resource management	A secondary process in the internal value chain, involving the recruiting, hiring, training and development of employees.
Hybrid implementation	Information systems implementation that phases in particular components as replacements or pilots major modules of the system.
Hypermedia	The approach to building information systems made up of nodes of various media (such as text, audio data and video data) connected by a collection of associative links.
Hypertext	A subset of hypermedia concentrating on the construction of loosely connected textual systems.
I	
ICommerce	Internet commerce, the use of Internet technologies in support of eCommerce.
ICT	See information and communication technology.
ICT infrastructure	The set of interrelated ICT systems used by an organisation.
ICT strategy	The process of managing the current ICT infrastructure and implementing a new ICT infrastructure.
ICT system	A technical system, sometimes referred to as a 'hard' system. An organised collection of hardware, software and communications technology designed to support aspects of an information system.
Impact	A precondition of electronic delivery. Use of remote access mechanisms must reach a critical threshold driving a virtuous cycle.
Implementation	See systems implementation.
Implicit knowledge	Knowledge accessible through querying and discussion but needing communication.
Inbound logistics	A primary process in the internal value chain involving the receipt and storage of raw materials and the distribution of them to manufacturing units.
Inconsistency	A measure of the degree to which data is held or processed differently across information systems.
Informatics	The study of information, information systems and ICT as applied to various phenomena.
Informatics field	The academic study of informatics issues and problems.
Informatics infrastructure	The sum total of information, information systems and ICT resources available to the organisation at any one time.
Informatics management	The process of putting information, information systems and ICT plans into action.
Informatics planning	The process of defining the optimal informatics architecture for an organisation.
Informatics practice	The practical application of informatics knowledge and skill in organisations.
Informatics profession	The bodies exercising control over informatics practice.
Informatics service	The organisational function devoted to the delivery of informatics services.

Term	Definition
Informatics strategy	A definition of the structure within which information, information systems and information technology are to be applied in an organisation.
Information	Data interpreted in a meaningful context.
Information centre	A structure for the informatics service in which the service acts as a centre of expertise for other business units.
Information and communication technology (ICT)	Any technology used to support information gathering, processing, distribution and use. ICT consists of hardware, software, data management technology and communication technology.
Information and communication technology infrastructure	See ICT infrastructure.
Information and communication technology strategy	See ICT strategy.
Information and communication technology system	See ICT system.
Information economics	An approach to information systems evaluation that attempts to include the evaluation of intangible as well as tangible benefits.
Information economy	An economy in which information is both important and essential to effective performance.
Information infrastructure	Definitions of information need and activities involved in the collection, storage, dissemination and use of information in an organisation.
Information management	That part of informatics management concerned with the management of information.
Information security	The process of protecting information systems from criminal or unwanted activity.
Information society	A term very loosely used to refer to the effect of ICT, information systems and information generally on modern society.
Information strategy	That part of an informatics strategy concerned with specifying the information need for the future in an organisation.
Information system	A system of communication between people. A system involved in the gathering, processing, distribution and use of information.
Information system development	The process of developing an information system.
Information system development method	A defined approach to developing information systems.
Information system model	A representation of an information system.
Information systems infrastructure	The entire set of information systems used by an organisation.
Information systems management	The process of managing the current information systems infrastructure and implementing the information systems strategy.
Information systems planning	The process of defining an information systems architecture.
Information systems portfolio	A list of current systems in the information systems architecture or future systems in the information systems strategy.

Term	Definition
Information systems strategy	That part of an informatics strategy concerned with specifying the future control of an information systems infrastructure and implementation of new elements of this infrastructure.
Input	The elements that a system takes from its environment.
Input device	A device concerned with the input of data.
Input subsystem	The part of a computer system concerned with the input of data.
Institutional perspective	The perspective on organisations that treats them as wholes or units.
Intangible goods	Goods that fundamentally can be represented as data and hence can be delivered to the customer electronically.
Intangible services	Services that fundamentally comprise information and hence can be delivered to the customer electronically.
Integration testing	Testing of all related systems together once a complex system has been assembled as a complete unit.
Intension	See concept.
Interaction failure	The argument that if a system is heavily used it constitutes a success; if it is hardly ever used, or there are major problems involved in using it, it constitutes a failure.
Interactive digital television	A remote access device. A combination of digital television and an up-channel using conventional telephony.
Interest	A precondition of electronic delivery. Stakeholders must be interested in using remote access channels for electronic delivery.
Interface subsystem	The part of an ICT system concerned with managing the user interface.
Intermediary	Sometimes known as a channel organisation. An organisation that mediates between other organisations in the value network.
Intermediary-oriented B2B	A process in which an intermediary runs an electronic market for buyers and sellers in a specific area.
Intermediation	The process of introducing intermediaries or channel organisations into the supply or customer chain.
Internet	A set of interconnected computer networks distributed around the globe.
Internet auction	An auction conducted over the Internet.
Internet service provider (ISP)	A company supplying connections to the Internet.
Interoperability	A measure of the degree to which information systems can be coordinate and collaborate.
Inter-organisational information system	A form of information system that is developed and maintained by a consortium of companies in an area of business for mutual benefit.
Intra-business eBusiness	The use of ICT to enable internal business processes.
Intranet	The use of Internet technology in a single organisation.
IP address	Internet protocol address, a unique identifier for the computers on a communications network using TCP/IP.

Term	Definition
ISDN	Integrated service digital network, a broadband communication channel for the local loop.
Iterative development	In this model systems conception triggers an iterative cycle in which various versions of a system (prototypes) are analysed, designed, constructed and possibly implemented.
J	
Job analysis	The analysis of the content and relationships of current jobs in terms of both organisational and individual objectives.
K	
Kilobyte	1000 bytes.
Knowledge	Knowledge is derived from information by integrating information with existing knowledge.
Knowledge codification	The representation of knowledge for ease of retrieval.
Knowledge creation	The acquisition of knowledge from organisational members and the creation of new organisational knowledge.
Knowledge management	Consists of knowledge creation, knowledge codification and knowledge transfer.
Knowledge transfer	The communication and sharing of knowledge among organisational members.
L	
Law of requisite variety	See requisite variety.
Linear development	The phases of development are strung out in a linear sequence with outputs from each phase triggering the start of the next phase.
Local area network (LAN)	A type of communication network in which the nodes of the network are situated relatively close together.
Local loop	The communication channels between the local telephone exchange and the customer.
Location strategy	A strategy that involves the organisation attempting to find a niche market to service.
M	
Main memory	See primary storage.
Maintenance	See systems maintenance.
Management	A key control process for organisations.
Management-facing information systems	Front-end information systems used by management. See management information system, executive information system.
Management information system (MIS)	A type of information system supporting the tactical decision making of managers.
Market	A medium for exchanges between buyers and sellers.
Marketing and sales	A primary process in the internal value chain. Marketing is the process of planning and executing the conception, pricing, promotion and distribution of ideas, goods and services to create exchanges that satisfy individual and organisational goals. Sales is the associated activity involved in the management of purchasing activities of the customer.
Marketing channel	A channel for the communication of marketing messages.
Megabyte	1,000,000 bytes (million).
Mega-package	See enterprise resource planning system.

Term	Definition
Message	A stream of symbols that is coded as signal.
Method	See information system development method.
MIS	See management information system.
Modelling approach	Constructs, notation and principles of use for modelling.
Modulation	The process by which variety is introduced into a signal.
MP3	Motion Picture Experts Group-1 Level 3. A format that employs an algorithm to compress a music file, achieving a significant reduction of data while retaining near CD-quality sound.
Multichannel access centre	A organisational hub for various access mechanisms.
Multimedia kiosk	A remote access device. Specialist access points to services provided on the Internet.
N	
Napster	A software application that enables users to locate and share digital music in MP3 format.
Negative feedback	Process in which a monitoring subsystem monitors the outputs from a system and detects variations from defined levels of performance. If the outputs vary from established levels, the monitoring subsystem initiates actions to reduce the variation.
Newsgroup	Technology for enabling threaded discussions between many-to-many users.
Non-credit based payment systems	Systems designed to encourage the exchange of micro-payments electronically.
Non-functional requirements	Constraints set on the development of an information system.
Non-repudiability	A user of an ICT system should not be able to deny that they have used the system for a commercial transaction.
Norm	An expectation of human behaviour.
O	
Object	A real world thing which can be uniquely identified. A package of data and procedures.
Object class	A grouping of similar objects.
Object-oriented	A term applied to programming languages, design methods and database systems to mean providing support for constructs such as objects, classes and abstraction relations such as generalisation and aggregation.
Ontology	That branch of philosophy concerned with theories of reality. Also used as a specification for a domain or universe of discourse.
Open system	A system that interacts with its environment.
Operating system	A piece of system software concerned with the management of all other applications on a computer system.
Operational management	The lowest level of management, involved with making structured decisions with detailed data.
Operational research	A discipline devoted to applying scientific methods to the problems of management.
Operations	A primary process in the internal value chain involving the transformation of raw materials into finished products.
Optionality	Establishes whether all instances of an entity must participate in a relationship or not.

Term	Definition
Organisation	A social collective in which formal procedures are used for coordinating the activities of members in the pursuit of joint objectives.
Organisation culture	The set of behavioural expectations associated with an organisation.
Organisation information model	A high-level map of the information requirements for an organisation.
Organisation planning	The process of formulating an organisation strategy.
Organisation process	A set of activities cutting across the major functional divisions in organisations, by which organisations accomplish their mission.
Organisation process model	A high-level map of organisational processes
Organisation strategy	The general direction or mission of an organisation.
Organisation structure	The set of objects of relevance to an organisation plus the relationships between these objects.
Organisation theory	That body of knowledge concerned with defining the key features of organisations.
Organisational analysis	The process of analysing and redesigning key business processes or human activity systems.
Organisational culture	The set of behavioural expectations associated with an organisation.
Outbound logistics	A primary process in the internal value chain involving the storage of finished products in warehouses and the distribution of finished products to customers.
Output	The elements that a system passes back to its environment.
Output device	A device that outputs data.
Output subsystem	The part of a computer system that outputs data to the user or to another device.
Outsourcing	The strategy in which the whole or part of the informatics service is handed over to an external vendor.
P	
Package development	Process in which an organisation purchases a piece of software from a vendor and tailors it to a greater or lesser extent to meet its own demands.
Packet-switched network	A communications network which employs packet-switching protocols and technologies. Data is broken into individual packets which are disseminated over a communications network through the application of routers.
Parallel implementation	An implementation approach in which two systems, the old and the new system, run in parallel.
Partner	A key type of organisational stakeholder. Key organisations in the same industrial sector or market that participate in a partnership arrangement with an organisation.
Payback period	Payback is calculated on the basis of Payback = Investment – cumulative benefit (cash inflow)
Payroll information system	The back-end information system dealing with the payment of employees.
Perfective maintenance	Changes made to an information system which make improvements but without affecting its functionality.
Performance	The degree to which a system reaches specified levels.

Term	Definition
Personal computer	A computer used on the desktop and normally devoted to individual computing use. Also used as a remote access device.
Physical design	The process of detailing the major elements of how a system will work on a computer system.
Physical flow	This represents the flow of tangible or physical goods and services such as foodstuffs and automobiles.
Political environment	The external environment of the organisation concerned with power and its exercise.
Portal	An entry point for users into the WWW.
Positive feedback	The process in a which a monitoring subsystem increasing the discrepancy between desired and actual levels of performance.
Post-mortem evaluation	A variant of summative evaluation concerned with assessing the reasons for and lessons from information systems failures.
Power	The ability of a person or social group to control the behaviour of some other person or social group
Pragmatics	The study of the general context and culture of communication.
Preconditions for electronic service delivery	A range of social factors, expressed in a sequence, which affect the likely take-up of the electronic delivery of goods and services.
Preventive maintenance	Changes aimed at improving a system's maintainability such as documentation or improving the flexibility of an information technology system.
Primary storage	Storage of data in media that can be directly acted upon by the central processing unit (CPU) of the computer, such as main memory or cache memory. Primary storage usually provides fast access to relatively low volumes of data.
Privacy	See data privacy.
Process	A transformation of input into output. In information systems modelling a process is a transformation of incoming data flow(s) into outgoing data flow(s).
Process failure	This type of failure is characterised by unsatisfactory development performance.
Process/ information matrix	A matrix which relates classes on an organisation information model against processes on an organisation process model.
Process map	See organisation process model.
Process mapping	See process modelling.
Process modelling	The activity of analysing and specifying major organisational processes.
Process redesign	See process re-engineering.
Process re-engineering	The process of analysing, redesigning and implementing organisational processes.
Procurement	A secondary activity in the internal value chain. The process of purchasing goods and services from suppliers at an acceptable quality and price and with reliable delivery.
Producer	A key type of organisational stakeholder. Teams of developers that have to design, construct and maintain information systems for organisations.
Product-based project management	A form of project management in which project planning and control are focused around information systems products.

Term	Definition
Production	The set of activities concerned with the creation of goods and services for human existence.
Productivity paradox	The paradox that organisations that have invested significantly in ICT do not appear to have experienced significant improvements in productivity.
Programming language	A language for instructing a computer system.
Project control	The process of ensuring that a project remains on schedule, within budget and produces the desired output.
Project escalation	The process in which decision makers become locked in an irrational course of action.
Project management	The process of planning for, organising and controlling projects.
Project organisation	The structuring of staff activities in projects to ensure maximum effectiveness.
Project planning	Determining as clearly as possible the likely parameters associated with a particular project.
Prototyping	The development approach in which prototypes are produced.
Public key infrastructure	An infrastructure for ensuring the security of electronic transactions which includes procedures for managing the assignment and storage of digital keys, and ensuring they are used only by legitimate holders.
Purchase-order processing information system	The information system that records details of purchase orders to suppliers.
R	
Record	A physical data element composed of fields.
Redundancy	A measure of the degree to which data is unnecessarily replicated across information systems.
Referent	That which is being signified. The range of phenomena referred to.
Regulator	A key type of organisational stakeholder. Groups or agencies that set environmental constraints for an information system.
Reintermediation	The process in electronic markets of new intermediaries developing between buyers and sellers.
Relationship	An association between entities or classes.
Repeat commerce	The pattern in which regular, repeat transactions occur between trading partners.
Representative participation	A design group is formed made up of representatives of all grades of staff with systems analysts. The representatives however are selected by management.
Requirements analysis	The stage in the database development process that involves finding out data requirements.
Requirements elicitation	See requirements analysis.
Requisite variety	Only variety can absorb variety. For full control of the system it is monitoring a control subsystem should contain variety – a number of states – at least equal to the system under control.
Return on investment (RoI)	The benefit gained from investment in a project. It is calculated using the equation: RoI = average (annual net income/annual investment amount).

Term	Definition
Ring network	A network topology in which network devices are connected in a loop.
Risk analysis	The identification, estimation and assessment of risk.
Role	A package of behaviour associated with a particular social situation.
Root definition	A way of specifying organisational processes in the soft systems method.
Routers	Hardware and software technology that directs packets to their indicated destination along a communications network.
Rules subsystem	The part of an ICT system concerned with application logic.
S	
Sales-order processing information system	The information system that records details of customer orders.
Satisficing	The term used by Herbert Simon to describe the characteristics of human decision making that is adequate rather than idealised.
Scenario	A narrative description of what people do and experience as they try to make use of computer systems and applications.
Scientific management	An approach to management thinking created by Frederick Taylor.
Search engine	A system that allows users to locate websites by matching keywords.
Secondary storage	Storage of data that cannot be processed directly by the CPU. It provides slower access than primary storage but can handle much larger volumes of data. Two of the most popular forms of secondary storage are magnetic disk and magnetic tape.
Secure socket layer (SSL)	Netscape's attempt to offer a secure channel of communication. It is a framework for transmitting sensitive information such as credit card details over the Internet.
Security	See data security.
Semantics	The study of the meaning of signs.
Semiosis	The process of using signs.
Semiotics	The study of signs and sign-systems.
Sense and respond	A systems view of the organisation which emphasises adaptation to environmental change.
Sensor	A mechanism that monitors the changes in the environment of a system.
Service	An activity delivered to a stakeholder.
SGML	Standard generalised markup language, a generalised markup language for describing the formatting of electronic documents.
Sign	Anything that is significant. Normally made up of symbol, concept and referent.
Single-loop feedback	A simple feedback process in which the performance plans for a system remain unchanged.
Social capital	The productive value of people engaged in a dense network of social relations. Social capital consists of those features of social organisation – networks of secondary associations, high levels of interpersonal trust, reciprocity – that act as resources for individuals and facilitate collective action.

Term	Definition
Social environment	The external environment of the organisation concerned with society.
Social infrastructure	The social infrastructure for eBusiness consists of those human activity systems central to supporting the conduct of eBusiness. These include competencies in planning, management, development and evaluation.
Social network	A network of people and social relations.
Sociotechnical design	The parallel design of both technical and social systems.
Sociotechnical system	A system of technology used within a system of activity.
Soft system	Collections of people undertaking activities to achieve a purpose.
Soft systems methodology	The approach to organisational analysis created by Peter Checkland.
Software	The non-physical (soft) aspects of information technology. Software is essentially programs – sets of instructions for controlling computer hardware.
Spamming	The process of sending unsolicited emails to large numbers of people.
SQL	See structured query language.
Stakeholder	The group of people to whom an information system is relevant.
Stakeholder analysis	Analysing the types of and impact of stakeholders on information systems.
Stakeholder involvement	Involvement of stakeholder representatives in the development of an ICT system.
Stakeholder participation	Involvement of stakeholders both in the development of the ICT system and the work surrounding its use.
Stakeholder resistance	The resistance of stakeholder groups to the introduction of an information system.
Stakeholder satisfaction	The state of satisfaction expressed by a stakeholder group in an information system.
Star network	A network topology in which network devices are connected to a central computer.
State	The state of a system is defined by the values appropriate to the systems' attributes or state variables.
Stock control information system	An information system for recording details of inventory.
Storage	The part of a system concerned with the representation of data.
Storage device	A device that persistently represents data.
Storage subsystem	The part of a computer system concerned with the persistent representation of data.
Strategic analysis	The process of determining the organisation's mission and goals.
Strategic choice	The process of generating strategic options, evaluating them and selecting a suitable strategy to achieve the selected option.
Strategic evaluation	The form of information system evaluation concerned with assessing the utility of an information system prior to development.
Strategic implementation	Determining policies, making decisions and taking action.
Strategic information system	An information system that delivers competitive advantage.

Term	Definition
Strategic management	The top level of management, concerned with making unstructured decisions based on heavily summarised data.
Strategy	The art of a commander-in-chief; the art of projecting and directing the larger military movements and operations in a campaign.
Structuration	The process by which human action both produces and reproduces social structure, and also how social structure both informs and constrains human action.
Structured query language (SQL)	A database sub-language. A standard for performing data manipulation, data retrieval and data control work with relational DBMS.
Subculture	The set of behavioural expectations associated with a part of a larger social grouping.
Suboptimisation	Optimising the performance of a component subsystem independently will not necessarily optimise the performance of the system as a whole.
Subsystem	A coherent part of a system.
Summative evaluation	The form of information system evaluation that assesses the worth of a system after implementation.
Supplier	A key type of organisational stakeholder. Organisations that supply goods and services to an organisation.
Supplier-facing information systems	Transaction processing systems that interface with suppliers.
Supplier-oriented B2B	Producers and consumers use the same electronic marketplace. Essentially the same as B2C eCommerce,
Supplier relationship management	The management of supply-chain activities. Sometimes referred to as supply chain management.
Supplier relationship management system	An information system devoted to managing all interactions of a supplier with an organisation.
Supply chain	The chain of activities that an organisation performs in relation to its suppliers.
Supply chain management	The collection of an organisation's activities devoted to management of the supply chain.
Symbol	That which is signifying something.
Synchronisation	A property of a communication channel. The degree to which the sender and receiver of messages participate in the process at the same time.
Syntactics	The part of semiotics devoted to the study of the structure of signs and sign-systems.
Syntax	The operational rules for the correct representation of terms and their use in the construction of sentences of a language.
System	A coherent set of interdependent components which exists for some purpose, has some stability, and can usefully be viewed as a whole.
System documentation	A description of the structure and behaviour of the ICT system for developers.
System lag	A delay between the issuing of a control signal and the adjustment of the system process to it.

Term	Definition
System software	The collection of programs that coordinate the activities of hardware and all programs running on a computer system.
System testing	Testing of an entire system as a unit.
Systems analysis	The part of the development process devoted to eliciting and representing the requirements for systems.
Systems conception	The part of the development process devoted to assessing the investment potential and feasibility of systems.
Systems construction	The part of the development process devoted to constructing systems.
Systems design	The part of the development process devoted to designing the functionality of systems.
Systems engineering	A systems discipline concerned with the production of large, complex physical artefacts.
Systems implementation	The part of the development process devoted to delivering the system into its context of use.
Systems maintenance	The part of the development process devoted to maintaining systems.
Systems thinking	See general systems theory.
T	
Table	The major data structure in the relational data model.
Tacit knowledge	Knowledge accessible only with difficulty through elicitation techniques.
Tactical management	Middle management which interfaces between strategic and operational management.
Tactics	Tactics belongs only to the mechanical movement of bodies set in motion by strategy.
Tangible goods	Goods that have a physical form and cannot be delivered to customers electronically.
Tangible services	Services that have a physical form and cannot be delivered to customers electronically.
Task analysis	Specifying the precise organisation of tasks associated with the use of a computer system.
TCP/IP	Transmission control protocol/Internet protocol is the communications model underlying the Internet.
Technical infrastructure	The supporting infrastructure of ICTs for eBusiness.
Technique	A systematic activity within the development process.
Technological frame	A collection of underlying assumptions, expectations and knowledge that people have about technology and its use.
Telecommunication carrier	An organisation that provides the telecommunication infrastructure for communications.
Telecommunication device	A piece of hardware that permits electronic communication to occur.
Telecommunication media	Media used for the transmission of data in communication networks.
Telecommunication service	See telecommunication carrier.
Telephony	A category of access device which includes fixed audio and video telephones as well as mobile telephones and fax machines.
Terabyte	1,000,000,000,000 (trillion) bytes.

Term	Definition
Testing	Part of systems construction. Ensuring that an information system is working effectively.
Theory X	According to this theory the average human being is perceived as disliking work and hence avoiding it wherever possible. The average human being avoids responsibility and has little ambition.
Theory Y	According to this theory physical and mental effort are important and natural human functions. If humans are committed to certain objectives they will exercise self-direction and self-control. The capacity to exercise imagination, ingenuity and creativity are widely distributed in the population.
Third-generation programming language	Also known as high-level language. A programming language two steps removed from assembly language.
Three-tier architecture	A client–server architecture divided into three layers: interface, business and data.
Tool	Software used to aid the development process.
TPS	See transaction processing system.
Transaction	A logical unit of work. A transaction transforms a database from one consistent state to another consistent state. Transactions are major ways of recording service delivery.
Transaction processing system (TPS)	A type of information system supporting the operational activities of an organisation.
Transaction subsystem	The part of an ICT system concerned with communicating between the interface and rules subsystem and the data subsystem.
Transactional data	Data that records events taking place between individuals, groups and organisations.
Tunnelling technology	Technology that involves the transmission of data over the Internet using leased lines to the local ISP. With the use of encryption, authentication and other security technologies such an approach can be used to produce a virtual private network (VPN) over a wide area network.
U	
Unit testing	Testing of individual programs or software modules.
Universal resource locator (URL)	A unique identifier for a document placed on the Web.
Usability	An information system's usability is how easy a system is to use for the purpose for which it was constructed.
Usability engineering	An approach that focuses on assessing, evaluating and testing the usability of ICT systems, with the aim of improving the design of the user interface.
Use	A precondition of electronic delivery. Stakeholders must regularly use remote access mechanisms in core areas of life.
Use case model	A use case model provides a high-level description of major user interactions with an information system.
Use failure	Failure of an information system after a period of use.
Use setting	A concept that includes the information-handling behaviours of stakeholders using a particular access device in a particular place.

Term	Definition
User documentation	A source of reference for users to turn to when puzzled about aspects of the use of an ICT system.
User interface	The part of an ICT system that allows the end-user to use the system.
Utility	The worth of an information system in terms of the contribution it makes to its human activity system and to the organisation as a whole.
V	
Value	A general term used to describe the outputs from an organisation.
Value added network (VAN)	A type of communication network in which a third party creates and maintains a network for other organisations.
Value chain	A series of interdependent activities that deliver a product or service to a customer.
Variety	A measure of the complexity of a system; the number of states a system can assume.
Vertical portal	An entry point to the WWW, that provides the same functionality as a horizontal portal but for a specific market sector.
Viable system	A term used by Stafford Beer to describe a system capable of surviving in a volatile environment.
Virtual community	A community consisting of a network of actors on a communication network.
Virtual organisation	An organisation built on an ICT infrastructure that enables collaborative eWorking amongst members. Also referred to as a network organisation. Characterised by a flat organisational hierarchy, formed around projects and linked by ICT.

Term	Definition
Virtual private network (VPN)	A form of network which employs tunnelling technology to secure data transmission over the Internet.
Vocabulary	A complete list of the terms of a language. See syntactics.
Volume testing	Testing the application with large amounts of data and use.
W	
WAP	See Wireless application protocol.
Web page	Generally used to refer to the presentational aspect of a web document.
Web portal	A web page designed to be an entry point for users into the WWW.
Website	A logical collection of HTML documents available on the WWW.
Wide area network (WAN)	A type of communication network in which the nodes of the network are geographically remote.
Wireless application protocol (WAP)	An open international standard for application layer network communications in a wireless communication environment.
Word	One or more bytes treated as a unit.
World Wide Web (WWW)	A set of standards for hypermedia documentation. It has now become synonymous with the Internet.
X	
XML	Extensible markup language, a metalanguage for the definition of document standards.

Index